Pregnancy and Birth
– A New Generation

By Joy Wisdom

© 2009, Allonus Ltd

Pregnancy and Birth – A New Generation © 2010 Joy Wisdom

Joy Wisdom is hereby identified as the author of this work in accordance with Section 77 of the Copyright, Designs and Patent Act 1988. She Asserts and gives notice of her moral right under this Act.

Published by Allonus Ltd.,
Ty Cwm, Pandy, Glyn Ceiriog, Llangollen LL20 7PD
Tel/ Fax: 01691 718927
Email: info@allonus.co.uk
Website: www.allonus.co.uk

All rights reserved. No part of this book may be reproduced, stored in a retrieval system or transmitted in any form by any means (electronic or mechanical, through reprography, digital transmission, recording or otherwise) without the prior written permission of the publisher.

Illustrations by
Cover insperation and logo Juljia Constable
Personal photographs of children reproduced by kind permission of their parents
Cover Illustration by Siobhan Harrison
Typesetting by Andrew Davis
Printed by MPG Biddles Ltd

Heartfelt thanks are given to all media publications and authors who have kindly given their permission for copyrighted material to be used. Every effort has been made to trace the ownership of all copyrighted material. If any omission has been made please bring this to the publisher's attention so that proper acknowledgement may be given in future editions.

ISBN
978-0-9566899-0-0

I dedicate this book to all women and children
The voices not heard

All profit from this book will go to the authors
'One Generation Project' a not for profit organisation
to support parents, mothers and children in a
new vision for humanity and generations to come.

ACKNOWLEDGEMENTS

A book this size takes time and effort, not only from the author but those who support her, especially close family who feel the brunt of the effort. So I give a huge thanks to my long suffering husband Graham and my son Michael for all their support, gentle suggestions, patience and understanding in the long journey of this book.

My special thanks, to all the mothers, who have shared their stories and experiences with me giving me the insight to write and bringing the book to life. I am grateful to Mandy Johnson and Stuart Flack, who shared their personal experience of Preterm birth. Suzanne Nugent for unwavering belief, encouragement and support for the concept of bringing the book to life.

Words cannot express my thanks to all my friends who have encouraged, cajoled and supported.   Especially to those special friends for reading the draft, asking questions and pointing out omissions helping to make the book so readable.

I am grateful to Andrew and Angela for their assistance and especially Andrews brilliance in helping to set the book for print.

To Julijia Constable for her dedication and brilliance for the concept of the book cover and logo.

To Siobhan Harrison for the amazing interpretation of the design and beautiful illustration, bring the idea to life.

Dr John and Mrs Lisa Upledger for their advice and use of reference content for the book.

My thanks to all the following publishers and authors for permission to use their references.

From The Decisive Moment
by Jonah Lehrer, 2009
first published in Great Britain by
Canongate Books Ltd, 14 High Street, Edinburgh, EH1 1TE

"The Oxytocin Factor"
by Dr. U Moberg
Da Capo Press Cambridge 2003

"Truth about vaccines"
Richard Halverson, 2007
Gibson Square Books
47 Lonsdale Square, London

Dr Michelle Odent
Scientification of Love, 2001
Free Association books Limited

Joe Macfarlane
© Daily mail & The Mail on Sunday, 2006

Jane Symons
© The Sun 2007
nisyndication.com

Michael Day
© Telegraph Media Group Limited 2003

The Independent
Jonathan Owen

© Express Newspapers & Northern & Shell
Lucy Johnson

What Doctors Dont Tell you, 2001

CONTENTS

FORWARD

Young children are malleable; their future undetermined. Right from the moment of conception their future lives are unknowingly predetermined by their parents and those assigned to look after them.

Influences exerted at a young age go on to affect them throughout the whole of their lives. With prudence and understanding, we can improve their lot in life and in society, giving them the confidence to be better people, both physically and psychologically.

Alternatively, we can saddle them with untold emotional anxiety, concerns and disadvantage, piling on our own hang-ups in the same way our parents did to us.

Which would you rather give your child?

INTRODUCTION

Giving birth is a million dollar business

Forty six per cent of USA births are carried out by Caesarean section and America also has the highest newborn death rate in the developed world. In the UK, on average 40% of hospital births are by C-section and it appears to be very much the norm these days. It is the wealthy countries in the western world which seem to have indicators of high intervention during birth, but is this a help or a hindrance to the infant and mother[1]? In this book we will explore all aspects of birth and pregnancy, providing new ideas and scientific facts to help new and existing mothers.

Medicine has improved a great deal over the last 50 years. Most medical disciplines now acknowledge that the mind and body are not separate; that the two work together. Emotionally however, I believe that health and welfare systems have a lot of learning to take on board. In hospitals today, we are, to a great extent, emotionally ignored. Scientifically, the premise that emotions are often the root of disorders and unhappiness is not fully understood.

Having a baby is a very emotional experience. The birth process can sometimes be easy and sometimes difficult, but the more the mother is in control, the easier it is for nature to help. With natural instincts taking over, the body already has the tools for birth in readiness for the event.

When the mother becomes stressed, so does the baby. You might consider that to be perfectly logical, but it is something which seems to be ignored in today's birthing process. Intervention and stress interferes on many levels, shutting off and overriding natural abilities and making the process more painful and emotionally destructive. It causes babies to be born in shock and to suffer post-traumatic stress (PTS). Just like being in a car crash, both mother and baby are left in shock and with the added burden of PTS. Is this how birth was meant to be?

Through my own practice, I have treated mothers and babies suffering unduly from the most natural process in the world – giving birth. I have been able to help women and children when the general medical profession has ignored them. As a result, I felt compelled to write about the many areas of unexplored health issues because, despite a lax approach from many establishments, there is help and assistance available. Children do not need to cry continuously; there is always an explanation. Babies don't cry for nothing and they won't grow out of it as health visitors and the medical profession often suggest. I have treated 70 year-olds still suffering the trauma experienced from their birth process and lack of bonding. I found the original problem created patterns that were carried on into adulthood.

Emotionally there is a price to pay if problems are not dealt with, but often these can be corrected very effectively at an early stage. The older we get, the more ingrained the pattern, so it makes sense to tackle it early on. I have proved this time and time again in my practice. Fortunately, I have been able to help on all levels through non-invasive clinical techniques and releasing emotional impacts, clearing a foundation for growth and life.

Not that long ago, it was still believed that when children are born they do not feel anything. Let me assure you that they do. While in the womb, they feel and sense, picking up on mum's emotions and taking on board her stress and anxieties. In general this is not an area spoken about or discussed. Why are some babies more distressed and anxious than others? Why is it that a mother can deliver one child naturally and have a baby which is calm and laid back, then have her next by C-section and the child needs constant attention, won't settle and is prone to allergies and chest problems?

In this book I explain the reasons why 'How', 'When' and 'Where' are all important in birth. How the baby arrives. When – if it is according to the baby's schedule or induced before the child wants to arrive. Where – at home or in hospital, where women are waiting for beds and are on a birth production line according to hospital convenience. All will have an impact on the baby and mother, with long-term consequences for some.

I am a mother of two. I had my children in the 1970s when we were more in touch with the mother's requirements and more in tune with her natural abilities, instead of being subject to a quick-fix delivery to clinical time-tables. We were given time to bring our children into the world in the time-honoured way, when the infant itself decided by instructing hormone activity, preparing mother and baby for the event.

I have seen so many women who were bruised and shocked emotionally from their experience. I have also seen infants who have suffered shock because of either a quick or a long and traumatic birth and are still suffering ongoing nightmares at five months old as a result. Parents have been at their wits end, with the whole family anxious, stressed and confused. 'It should not have been like this,' I hear over and over again. 'No one would listen to me. They just kept telling me they would grow out of it.'

The majority of my clients are referrals. They come via word of mouth, the recommendation passed on from one mum to another. Through my experience, I have been able to help them, giving practical advice and clinical treatment, offering a helping hand and a sympathetic ear to listen to their concerns. Together we have lightened the load and the children have stopped crying, sometimes overnight after their session, and begun to show almost immediate contentment. A happy child creates a happy and contented family.

I believe that we have lost the knowledge of the original village elders who passed their wisdom down from woman to woman. In recent times, clinical intervention has taken over, changing our thinking and handing our power over to the medical profession. Instead of using and connecting to an inbuilt intuition that has served women through the centuries, we now let others decide, often to our cost.

This is what I want to share with women in this book. Pregnancy is not an illness. Women should be revered when pregnant. They should be nurtured and cared for. It is a special time. It is the most natural thing in the world and is a magical time which involves the re-creation of life. Being pregnant should be a time of good health, happiness and joy, not full of fear, pain and stress as more and more women experience today.

We shall explore all aspects of pregnancy, infertility and miscarriage and see how you personally can help yourself. Through simple steps and information, you will discover how to make changes, which will improve egg and sperm quality, your general health and your emotions.

A healthy pregnancy and a healthy child are things that we all strive for and outcomes that we all want. I believe that preparation is the key, preparing a good foundation for your union to grow.

[1] 'Pain free birth – 46% of USA births are C-section' Human Givens Journal V15. No 4 2008 Pg 29

Chapter 1

INTRODUCTION TO PREGNANCY

Pregnancy is a wonderful thing. To have a child made from love produces a living being that is wanted and needed as it blossoms into form. It is said that when a woman is pregnant, she is at her best; she radiates energy around her and, as the child grows, she expresses that with her beauty.

It is the miracle of nature that a woman's body waits patiently for both parents to unite and sow the seed, allowing it to take over and play its part in the production and support of the mother and child during the nine months of pregnancy. For some, however, pregnancy is not this wonderful and beautifying experience. Some expectant mothers feel ill throughout the whole pregnancy. Not just for the first three months, some feel out of sorts and experience illness and distress during the course of the entire nine months.

These days, we are becoming more aware of the psychological effects on our children during pregnancy and the birth trauma. The traumas of birth, pregnancy, miscarriage and infertility are emotional roller-coasters for women. With the changing approach from natural birth to intervention, coupled with society's demands in relation to career and home, the pressures on women in the twenty first century are huge.

In the book, we will explore many different aspects of pregnancy, including:

- The traumas of miscarriage for women - the loss of an unborn child can take its toll for life. For some women, a part of them dies when they lose a child and they are left feeling filled with grief. Many cannot come to terms with the loss

- Infertility - on the other side of the coin, we have those women who cannot have children, but want and need them desperately. The traumas of the infertility path are long and hard for both parties and can involve IVF, adoption or just coming to terms emotionally with what will not happen for them

We will also explore:

- Key factors of nutritional benefits for women in pregnancy
- The impact of nutritional deficiency and the part it plays in infertility, miscarriage and pregnancy
- The stresses and emotional impacts of pregnancy
- Alternative ways of caring for yourself and your baby
- New visions on birth
- The emotional impacts of labour for you and your child
- How to cope when you go home from hospital
- Breast-feeding
- Old wives' tales
- Allergies, ADHD and eczema and some of the reasons why children suffer from these disorders

Many women are aware of their child's soul presence long before conception and, once pregnant, that feeling goes away. I have been aware of a soul waiting to be incarnated for several years around my son and his wife. They are now thinking about starting a family and my daughter-in-law confided recently that she has felt a presence around her very strongly over the last few months. We laughed when I said the soul was getting fed up waiting.

Nothing can express the way a woman feels when she realises she is pregnant. Especially in this day and age, many women are leaving it later in life to start their families, so when they do become pregnant the child is really wanted and needed. No matter what her age, however, there is a feeling of surprise, excitement, wonder and the joy of having a child. The changes she will feel are directly due to her body switching into automatic, to allow the best possible conditions for the child. She does not have to order it up and nor is there any need to organise the changes; through evolution, her body knows and is primed and prepared for the nine months to follow.

By the time the mother realises she is pregnant (probably six to eight weeks after conception) the embryo has gone through several changes and is already formed.

- At five weeks, it is about Tic-Tac size. The arms and legs are formed, with the brain flexures, spinal cord and column already in place

- At seven weeks, the embryo is slightly bigger than a jellybean. Bone formation is now visible, cartilage is being formed and muscular movement begins

- At eight weeks, the foetal foundation is laid, with the embryo having undergone many formations and changes during this early stage since conception

One of the first signs the mother will probably experience is morning sickness, or in some cases this can also happen in the early evening. I remember having both during one of my pregnancies and rushing off to be sick in the morning and evening.

Blood sugar levels will drop in the early stages of pregnancy, so it is important to eat little and often. Ginger is a favourite of mine to help combat these early stages, while the super-food 'millet' is also known to help ward off these unpleasant feelings.

In the early stages, some mothers feel movement like a fluttering in the abdominal area and know they are pregnant without taking a test.

When you first realise that you are pregnant, you will want to confirm it with a pregnancy kit before going to the doctor.

At the surgery, you will be assigned a time to see the midwife who will go through your options for birth. There will be lots of decisions to be made from now on and you will need to discuss with your partner what the best course of action is for you both. Do you choose a home birth, a hospital birth, a private independent midwife to attend or birth centre attendance? Through the medical route, it is normal for tests and scans to ensue to check that all is as it should be for you and your baby.

Hormones are kicking in and the body has automatically started to change with possible feelings of movement (fluttering), nausea and morning sickness from hormone imbalances. Dipping or low sugar levels can also cause a sickly or nauseous feeling during the day. A feeling of tiredness and fatigue is common. All of this is normal as the body adapts to pregnancy.

Once pregnant it is beneficial for you to connect to your baby on a regular basis with communication and feelings. Your baby feels what you feel and hears what you hear. It is therefore essential that reassurance be given to your baby while in the womb, and especially in the run-up to birth and during the third trimester.

Chapter 2

INDEX

Chapter 2

PREPARING FOR PREGNANCY

As with so many things in life, the amount of time and effort that you put into preparing for your pregnancy will have a direct impact on the experience and the final outcome. Spending a few months beforehand caring for your own physical well-being can not only boost your fertility rate, but also help your baby to thrive in the first few critical weeks of gestation.

CONTRACEPTION

Once you and your partner have decided that it's the right time to have a baby, the first thing that you will need to consider is your current method of contraception. If you are taking, or have been taking the contraceptive pill, you will need to allow the effects of this to wear off in your body. Full readjustment can take up to six months, and in some cases longer.

When they stop taking the contraceptive pill, some women experience amenorrhoea, a condition where menstrual bleeding does not occur regularly. Although it can be tempting to start celebrating straight away, having no period during these early months will not necessarily mean that you are pregnant.

If you have been using an IUD as your form of contraception, it is best to have this removed three months before you wish to start your family.

LIFESTYLE

In order to give yourself the very best chance of conceiving and of experiencing a healthy pregnancy, the next thing you might want to think about is your lifestyle. In some cases, this might mean replacing harmful habits with healthy ones, but in addition you also need to reconsider what were previously just everyday activities. Here are some suggestions for diet changes, as well as some helpful tips to bear in mind if you are hoping to become pregnant, and indeed during pregnancy itself.

- Avoid/stop smoking
- Avoid alcohol
- Cease taking all non-essential medicines and drugs
- Avoid X-rays, including dental X-rays
- Avoid soft, unpasteurised and blue cheeses
- Avoid uncooked eggs
- Avoid liver and products containing liver such as pâté
- Avoid peanuts
- Cut down on caffeine
- Take essential vitamins and minerals
- Start taking folic acid as this helps in forming the foetus

To come back to two of these issues in particular, alcohol and caffeine, it is worth bearing in mind that:

- Reducing or cutting out alcohol while you are trying to become pregnant and continuing this regime while pregnant reduces the symptoms of AFS for your baby

- Caffeine will severely reduce your chances of becoming pregnant - just 300mg per day can reduce fertility by 27%, and this also means your partner reducing his intake

As we have said, lifestyle and diet will play a huge part in you trying to become pregnant and in ensuring a healthy pregnancy. Spending a few months improving and caring for your physical health and well-being will boost your fertility and help get your baby off to a strong start.

NUTRITION

For women, the awaited baby will place new demands on both health and emotions so getting into shape is vital. Fine-tuning your diet and nutrition intake will give you the best chance of conceiving, and eating well three months before conception can make a difference to the baby by giving adequate nutrients for the right development. The womb has a rich endometrial lining which nurtures the fertilized egg (ova) after implantation. Your diet and nutritional levels will directly affect its quality.

The placenta is also built from this lush nutrient rich layer. A healthy placenta feeds a healthy baby, with maternal hormones and nutrients nourishing the embryo via the mother's blood stream. Inadequate hormonal stores from the mother will result in poor nourishment for the embryo[2] , while vitamin B and magnesium are just two of the key elements, which play a part in ensuring optimum health.

- Low intake of vitamin B will slow down the ripening of the egg before conception and affect fertility

- Magnesium is required to build healthy cell membranes. Vegetables are the most important contributor of magnesium, but dairy products are also essential

A diet which is rich in vitamins and minerals, proteins, complex carbohydrates and natural fatty acids is essential to maximise the chances of conception and pregnancy. Proteins, cold pressed oils from nut seeds and oily fish are precursors to hormone and enzyme production. It is essential, therefore, to eat protein and cold pressed olive oil daily, at least once a day, to aid fertility as a low protein diet causes fewer ova (eggs) to ripen or be released.

Eating organic or good fresh local produce for at least three months before conception, as well as during pregnancy, will provide the right environment for your baby. Think about how and what your great grandparents ate - good wholesome fresh food, the purer the better, untainted by chemicals and without additives. This included foods such as:

- Fresh fruits and vegetables
- Peas, beans and lentils
- Seeds and nuts
- Oily fish
- Organic dairy products
- Lean fresh meat

Remember too that steaming or lightly cooking your food is the ideal, as in this way much more of the goodness is retained.

Giving your baby the best chance of being strong and healthy means ensuring that the pituitary gland has all the B vitamins that it needs to work correctly and send the right hormonal signals to the ovaries[3]. The ovaries, however, also have other needs, such as for:

- Vitamins E and C
- Minerals
- Iodine
- Selenium
- Zinc
- Magnesium
- Essential fatty acids

As we have said, most of these nutrients can be found in a good organic diet which contains lean meat, fish, fruits, berries, vegetables, pulses and some dairy foods.

Incidentally, if you are uncertain of your nutritional levels, I would advise hair analysis. Hair analysis would identify low levels of nutrients in the system which could be balanced by adjusting your diet and/or supplementation to bring about a faster change.

MALE CONSIDERATIONS

Of course, not only can your physical health affect your chances of getting pregnant, but also that of your partner. In men, it takes about two and a quarter months for sperm to develop and reach maturity, so proactive and early measures can help to ensure that they too are in tip-top shape. Here are some of the things that expectant dads can do to make sure that they are in the peak of reproductive health:

- Avoid/stop smoking
- Cease taking all non-essential medications and drugs
- Increase zinc consumption
- Take folic acid

We already mentioned that folic acid is essential for women because of its role in the healthy formation of the foetus, but it is also beneficial for men in ensuring the production of good quality sperm.

Hygiene

A good personal hygiene routine is another thing which is important for both sexes to observe and particularly when:

- Handling cat litter
- Being in the garden or gardening
- Handling raw meat

Always take extra care to wash your hands thoroughly after any of these activities.

Keeping a lifestyle diary

Because your health and well-being directly affect your ability to conceive, as well as the health and well-being of your unborn child, it is advisable to start early by keeping a lifestyle diary. Write down the amount of exercise that you take each day and your dietary intake, and record your levels of smoking and alcohol consumption. In addition, make a note of anything, which increases your levels of stress or tension.

Keeping a diary will enable you to see unhealthy patterns that recur in your life, especially those that need to be changed, as well as your diet. In this way you can take better control of yours, and your baby's life.

[2] Dian Shepperson Mills: 'Making babies the nutrition recipe' Article BioCare: The Knowledge-issue 8: 2008

[3] Doyle W. Crawford MA. Wynn AHA & M. 'The association of maternal diet and birth dimensions' Jrnl Nutri Med. 1: 9-16 1990

Chapter 3

INDEX

Chapter 3

CONCEPTION

Conception comes from synergy and energy. Making a child from the love of two people is magical, but consciousness and preparation are the keys to conception.

SETTING THE SCENE

When planning a pregnancy, you need to set the scene and attend to the smallest detail if you want to get it right first time. Thought is needed as to where you want to conceive. Is that at home or on a romantic holiday or weekend away in a hotel? The choice is yours, but if it is at home you can make it more of a romantic and sensual event.

The bedroom needs to be relaxing with soft music, candles or dimmed lights, bed linen clean and smelling seductive and perhaps some rose petals sprinkled upon the bed cover.

Have a relaxing bath with oils and put on his favourite clothes. Have loving thoughts and create a relaxed and peaceful atmosphere in the home in general. Maybe a special meal of your favourite foods, candles on the table set for dinner or with dimmed lights to create the optimum sensual occasion.

In some cultures, the women send secret signs with flowers or rose petals on the bed or by dressing in a certain way so that the men know immediately the proposed intimacy. No words are exchanged, just the knowing between two people. It sets the scene and creates an excitement and anticipation between the couple.

CREATING A LIFE

A woman's body has been waiting for this moment of conception. It is what it was formed to do - recreate. It is the most beautiful and wondrous event in the world.

When creation is born of love and contentment, a beautiful and magical event takes place and a child is formed from that love, giving the child the foundation for life. It feels safe and secure, wanted and loved from the moment of conception.

If you think about it, we create every day in all manner of things. We create the way that we live and how we interact daily. Even making a meal is an act of creation and whether we do it with or without love is of great significance. Creation applies to everything in our lives whether we are aware of it or not.

If we cook a meal in a hurry and are tired from the day, the meal tends to get thrown together without much thought or feeling as to what we are eating and how it is going to taste. In this scenario, ask yourself:

- Did you enjoy the food?
- Did you think it was good or mediocre?
- Did the meal make you feel uncomfortable or did it give you indigestion?
- Did it lie heavy all evening?

Alternatively, when we spend time in a relaxed manner and enjoy the time in preparation, it makes a difference in the taste of the meal. Because love and feeling have gone into the making, we can taste and feel the difference. We feel nurtured and content and a glow emanates throughout the body. This is why we enjoy food prepared by others, such as our partner or friends. We feel nurtured by it, we feel relaxed and we receive good energy because love has gone into the meal.

The same applies to conception and creating a life. If we feel loved and happy during intercourse, the embryo conceived will respond and feel nurtured and loved. If, on the other hand, conception occurs as a result of a quickie (a one night stand), some part of the melding goes missing (LOVE) in the process and the experience is incomplete. In this instance discord begins from day one. When the foetus is in the womb it is, and should be, nurtured by the mother's body and emotions.

If, however, the mother is unhappy, resentful and feels guilty, the emotional imprint will be taken into the child's patterns, which will create further discord and be compounded in life. We will look at this in more detail in Chapter 5 when we turn our attention to the mother's emotions.

If the pregnancy turns out to be a difficult one, further discordant patterns come into play, so that by the time for birth arrives, it transpires that the child is unhappy and unsettled. This shows itself through physical distress, aggravation and anxiety. Digestion problems ensue and the child continually brings back milk, showing signs of distress and agitation. And we wonder why!

When you are feeling ready to start a family, preparation is the key. Be mindful of what you are creating. Be mindful of what you want to create and whether you want this to be a happy child or an unsettled one. It is an easy formula - create a beautiful event with love and you will create a happy and contented child.

The emotional state of the mother is very important at conception and during pregnancy. In my opinion, not enough care and attention is given to the outcome. The woman should be nurtured and feel loved all the way through her pregnancy. She should not be made to feel anxious or unloved, as this will undoubtedly reflect upon the child. Mother Nature understands this, and indeed many animals will abort their young if they believe they are not being nurtured and fed by their mate. Awareness can make all the difference to your magical event.

FEMALE FERTILITY

Once you have decided to try for a baby, it is important to understand that it can take up to six months for an average healthy couple to conceive. For others who have factors such as age, health disorders and a pressured lifestyle against them, it may take longer.

As we have already seen, you will need to check out your menstrual cycle to determine the optimum condition for becoming pregnant. For most women, the menstrual cycle is 28 days, which starts from the first day of your period. For others, it can fluctuate between 21 to 40 days. As you become more aware of the factors which affect your reproductive organs, you will know when is the best time for lovemaking to ensure that it coincides with peaks in fertility.

Women have two ovaries which store thousands of immature eggs. The number of eggs that are stored is predetermined and individual for every female. When we have our menstrual period, a single egg matures, triggering a release of oestrogen. The oestrogen stimulates the womb lining to thicken and produces protective mucus which helps sperm to survive for as long as possible inside you. If your body is too acidic, however, this mucus changes from being a protective environment to a hostile one which kills off the sperm too quickly and causes infertility.
(See Chapter 5 on pH balances)

Age

Women can only become pregnant around the time of ovulation, which is typically a window of 2-5 days. As they grow older, however, they normally become less fertile and eggs start to decline at the average age of thirty. At the age of around 37–38, the eggs will disappear from the ovaries even faster.

Of course, in recent years we have seen a general decline in fertility as couples wait longer before trying for a child, but age is not the only aspect which plays a part in reducing fertility. Stress, pressure, diet, lifestyle and the condition of the body all contribute too.

Oestrogen

Another factor, which many people believe to be relevant to declining fertility, is the presence of too much oestrogen in our water. Without doubt it is affecting plant life, while fish reproduction in coastal waters is also declining in numbers relative to the rising levels of oestrogen. When you consider that oestrogen from the pill and HRT does not filter out of our water systems, it seems quite logical that, by leaching into waterways and ultimately into our drinking water, it must also be having an adverse affect on human fertility.

Progesterone

Progesterone, it seems, is yet another factor to consider in terms of female fertility. Although progesterone normally depletes when we begin the menopause, there is evidence to suggest that one of the causes of infertility is the lack or imbalance of the hormone. Lack of progesterone also affects thyroid function and will influence the body to become less fertile, thus making it harder to become pregnant. We will come back to this issue in Chapter 7 which deals specifically with infertility.

Weight

Weight has long since been understood to adversely affect fertility levels, and essentially your chances of becoming pregnant are improved if you are close to the recommended weight for your age and height. Not only does excess weight in women make it more difficult to become pregnant in the first place, but it can also introduce a higher risk of blood pressure related problems, as well as putting extra strain on the joints during pregnancy.

MALE FERTILITY

Generally speaking, there is much stress and anxiety linked to failing fertility rates in men and it is therefore of vital importance that men also prepare for fertility. As it takes about seventy days for healthy sperm to develop and mature, it is just as important for men to prepare for conception as it is for their partner.

Fertility in men has been declining in recent years due to a range of different factors, all of which indicate the importance that they need to attach to looking after their own well-being. Stress has been strongly linked to failing fertility rates in men and of course this can increase with the pressure to conceive. It is important, therefore, for you and your partner to take time out to relax and enjoy one another's company.

Here are some of the other things that men can do to improve their fertility:

- Take zinc to help strengthen the sperm (also good for the prostate)
- Avoid hot baths, as the testes need to be kept cool for optimum sperm production
- Change to wearing loose cotton underpants and trousers
- Eat a balanced diet with lots of organic produce
- Manage stress and exercise
- Avoid smoking and alcohol

EXERCISE

Exercise is not only a good way to stay healthy, but also to help you relax and relieve stress, although doing too much exercise can actually reduce fertility.

The ideal amount of exercise for non-energetic people is approximately 30 minutes, three times a week, but it is also worth remembering that making love is a great form of exercise!

During pregnancy, low impact exercises such as walking, cycling, swimming and gentle yoga are recommended. Not only will these help you to stay at the peak of health throughout the pregnancy, but remaining active will also help you recover more quickly after the birth.

Chapter 4

INDEX

Chapter 4

OVULATION

Ovulation is a term used to describe that brief time during which the egg is mature, receptive and can be fertilised. Once the egg has matured in the ovaries, a hormone called Luteinising hormone (LH) is secreted by the anterior pituitary gland, stimulating ovulation. This hormone secretion causes ovulation, making the ova (egg) receptive to sperm.

The release of LH will normally happen 24 to 36 hours before ovulation and this happens in all cycles, however long or short they are. Ovulation will normally occur around 12 –16 days before the start of your next period.

If pregnancy is intended, it is desirable to have sex just before or during ovulation. Enjoy the time with your partner and make it fun, not a chore, and if possible have sex regularly during this time. For guaranteed fertilisation success, once or twice a day is preferred; any more than this and the sperm can become less concentrated.

Although we will discuss this in more depth in Chapter 7, it is worth noting here that having a thyroid imbalance can prevent the release of Luteinising Hormone and thus affect ovulation.

OVULATION TESTING

A good and reliable way to check ovulation in each monthly cycle is by taking your temperature with a basal thermometer, starting from the second day of your period bleed. The method works by indicating when ovulation has taken place by a small increase in body temperature, known as the basal temperature. You should do the test first thing in the morning when you wake, bearing in mind the following:

- It is important to do the test immediately upon waking and before you talk to anyone, go to the loo or brush your teeth
- Remember to shake the thermometer before use

- Put the thermometer under the tongue and leave for 1-2 minutes
- Record the level in a book and keep the record by your bedside
- Do this each morning up to the 21st day

By the 14th day you should see a slight day-by-day fluctuation.

When you ovulate there should be a rise and noticeable change in the recorded temperature level by one to one and a half degrees.

- Normal body temperature is 98.4° Fahrenheit or 36.9° Centigrade
- If there is no significant change then you have not ovulated

Basal body temperature kits contain a chart, fertility diary and thermometer and are very simple to use. Not only will they help you to see if you are ovulating, but also if you ovulate regularly. All you need to do is, over a period of weeks, continually use the test kit to take and record your temperature every day. By adhering to the same time each day, as soon as you wake, it helps to build up a picture of what your cycle is. Discovering your cycle will enable you to plan and predict the days in your next cycle where you will be at your most fertile (ovulating), thereby maximising your chances of pregnancy.

An alternative to this method is an ovulation test kit, which can be bought over the counter at most chemists or pharmacies and nowadays is also readily available in many supermarkets. There are lots of products on the market which can predict when you are about to ovulate, and these work in a similar way to pregnancy test kits. By detecting and measuring the level of Luteinising hormone (LH), which controls ovulation, they allow you to find out when you are at your most fertile.

Most ovulation kits provide a fertility monitor that indicates two peak fertility days. These are the best two days each month to conceive naturally and are found by detecting the LH surge in your urine. The days you notice the greatest surge are the days of peak fertility.

Some monitors, such as Clearblue, not only offer indications of the peak days, but also additional fertile days when you can conceive. By indicating rising oestrogen levels, the test pre-empts peak performance coming into action which gives an indication of the best time to make love.

With two options combined, digital ovulation kits and ovulation tests are thought to be around 99% accurate. Some kits offer an easy way to test, with no confusing lines to check. A simple smiley face displays if your LH is surging. Other ovulation kits contain test sticks, but if your cycle length varies by more than three days, you may need additional test sticks to detect the true LH surge.

Always read the manufacturer's instructions carefully before using ovulation test kits. Be aware that certain medical conditions and medications can adversely affect the results and accuracy of the tests.

PREGNANCY TEST KITS

Of course, once the time comes when you think you may have conceived, you are going to want some positive or negative confirmation. Pregnancy test kits are freely available over the pharmacy counter or in supermarkets and are considered fairly accurate if done correctly. By following the instructions to the letter, claims of 99% are reported on positive results from pregnancy test kits and indeed their accuracy is trusted by most GPs.

Pregnancy tests work by measuring a hormone called human chorionic gonadotrophoin (hCG), which is present in your urine. Do beware, however, as the test can be affected if you are taking fertility drugs already containing hCG. In fact, irrespective of whether you are using fertility drugs or not, you should always read the manufacturer's instructions carefully before using pregnancy test kits. Certain medical conditions, as well as other types of medications, can adversely affect the results and performance of the tests.

Most kits are digital and give an easy-to-read, plain language result within minutes. Although simple to use, it is advisable to test within four days of your due period as testing earlier can give an inaccurate reading. Some test sticks change colour at the tip to show the urine has been absorbed and that the test is working accurately, and a line in the window shows the result.

Although there are many on the market for you to choose from, it is important that you feel confident about doing a pregnancy test. Testing for successful pregnancy can be an emotional time and many emotions can be evoked.

Chapter 5

INDEX

Chapter 5

SELF-CARE IN PREGNANCY

The way that you treat yourself, and are treated by others, has the potential to affect your baby from the moment of conception. Taking every possible step to ensure your own well-being is vital. In this chapter, therefore, we are going to look at some of the key areas that you need to consider, beginning with one of the most crucial aspects, that of diet and nutrition.

SECOND TIME AROUND

When pregnant a second time around it can be a challenge. You may already have a toddler and he or she is probably quite a handful. The toddler has only known the full attention of you and your partner. If you are single parent, you are his or her entire world.

There will be little or no time to rest while pregnant a second or third time around. Your other child(ren) may be very demanding, so when baby arrives there will be no time to rest between feeding, putting baby down and changing, as there was when you just had one infant. Time will be short or taken up by your other children.

Without family support, it is not only challenging but stressful and overwhelming for everyone, including the unborn child. Sometimes the mum may not be as well, with the second child giving an added complication. Each pregnancy can be different and you may be more tired and need more rest. As a lone parent, there is little hope of much respite.

When we become pregnant with our first child, we usually take care of ourselves and prepare. For the second it is just as important to do the same. Very often it is a surprise when we discover that we are pregnant again. The additional baby may not necessarily be planned or prepared for. You may already be tired from looking after one child and may therefore be starting on the back foot. If you are unprepared health-wise, your immune system may be lower and lacking in iron or B vitamins. It is best to get these issues checked with a health professional or midwife.

Often diet goes astray and you find yourself only eating snacks or snatching food on the hoof. One of the first things you must do, therefore, is to rectify the diet. You need to eat little and often to help with nausea and morning sickness. Since your new infant will take what it needs from you, reserves are needed to help you through the pregnancy.

My Tips:

1. You must build up the body to support both of you, so eat regularly and don't miss meals.

2. Take a supplementation of iron, minerals and vitamins to give inner strength.

3. Use Bach flower remedies to assist on the emotional front.

4. See a homeopath to assist through the first stages of pregnancy.

5. Early nights will help – you must get your rest.

6. Ask for help from your partner or spouse if it is not offered.

7. Reflexology will help to put the hormones in balance, help you to relax and de-stress. The more relaxed you are, the better you can cope.

8. Do your shopping on-line and get help from others for the heavy work.

9. Start to think of ways to lighten the load and get others to assist in day-to-day chores. Some suggestions are - a childminder to give you space, a cleaner to lighten the chores, someone to take on the ironing.

All the above will help your pregnancy run smoothly.

Don't try to be a martyr or it will take its toll. Ask for help. Other mums can help out by taking your child for an extra hour or simply picking up from play school or nursery for you, (as you would probably do for them). Although you may not believe it, families do rally round when asked. Partners can take their roles too, so talk it through and give instructions and guidance as to what you need help with.

Make your life easier and your unborn will appreciate it.

DIET AND NUTRITION

A healthy diet is essential for a healthy body and, as whatever you eat will ultimately affect your baby, it is best to achieve a healthy start for both of you by eating a balanced diet with plenty of fresh fruit and vegetables, pulses, protein and carbohydrates.

If you are vegetarian, it is especially important to make sure that you get sufficient supplies of iron, calcium and B12 into your diet. Orange juice will help you to absorb iron, and both soya milk and tofu are good sources of calcium.

Caffeine

Another important aspect of diet, which is equally vital during the course of pregnancy as it is when trying for a baby, is caffeine consumption. As we indicated previously, more than 300 milligrams of caffeine per day may reduce fertility by as much as 27%, but for those who are serious about having a healthy baby, you need to look at your caffeine intake during pregnancy too. Along with foods like dried fruits, processed convenience meals, fried foods, fizzy drinks and confectionary, caffeine encourages bowel toxicity and therefore should be avoided altogether or at least cut back.

Coffee is a stimulant and it will depend on your genetics how long the buzz will last. It normally kicks in around 15-20 minutes after the drink and to the body it can give the same withdrawal effects as a drug. It is believed through trials that the more we expose ourselves to caffeine, the more the cravings and addiction. I have known people who have had a headache for several days after cutting out coffee. This is because the caffeine restricts the blood vessels in the brain and, as they swell again, the headache begins. Other symptoms may be stomach upsets, nausea, mood swings and fatigue. I advise to take it slowly and reduce daily to avoid severe withdrawal symptoms.

Smokers process caffeine quicker, sometimes up to 50% quicker, than those who do not smoke. Those taking the pill will take twice as long to get caffeine out of their systems as those not ingesting oral contraceptives. Patrick Holford believes that substances such as coffee are treated as toxins by the body, with inflammatory hormones being activated above normal levels and homocysteine levels raised.

A black coffee contains zero calories, as opposed to a coffee shop latte, which can contain as many as 341 calories. Caffeine is abundant not just in coffee, but in all sorts of foods and preparations from painkillers to tea, chocolate and alcohol[4].

Women are advised to lower their caffeine intake while pregnant and should consider changing to non-caffeine drinks such as herbal teas, green tea or fruit juices, or switch instead to decaffeinated tea and coffee.

The Food Standards Agency, however, does say that up to 300mg of coffee a day is acceptable for pregnant women.

Wheat and Gluten Free

The lack of sunlight during dark winter days often plays havoc with the psyche and encourages the cravings for stodgy, clogging foods and carbohydrates, many of which contain wheat. Wheat can, however, have a bloating effect, so try to reduce or cut out wheat-based bread, cakes, biscuits, pasta, pastries and pies. Instead, look out for products in the supermarkets which are wheat and gluten-free to replace your normal products. Such products will be marked accordingly, so all you need to do is check the labels.

Here are some more dietary considerations to take into account too:

- Go easy on dairy products such as cheese, milk and yogurt, as these can encourage mucus in the upper respiratory tract and cause/encourage sinus problems. Change instead to soya products, rice or oat milk

- Include plenty of fish in your diet, particularly mackerel and herrings which are rich in essential fatty acids (EFA's) for all round well being

- Eat chicken, eggs, nuts, seeds (rich in zinc), whole grains, rice, millet, Quinoa, buckwheat, oats and rye

- Eat fruits and vegetables which are grown locally and go organic where possible

- Antioxidants known for immunity and possible anti-ageing properties are prevalent in grapes, broccoli, bilberries, watercress, garlic, beetroot and carrots

- Increase your intake of dark green leafy vegetables such as watercress, kale, and cabbage

- Fruits which are blue, red or purple are normally rich in antioxidant vitamin C

As we have said, it is vital for the mother to have a good healthy diet during pregnancy to give the foetus the nourishment it needs. Even if she has a good diet, however, supplements can also be required to help build up reserves and building blocks for the foetus.

During pregnancy, the body can feel the effects of the drain of nutrients needed to feed the growing infant. That is why, during the first few months when everything is changing, the mother experiences morning sickness and nausea as an indication of hormonal and nutritional change.

When the mother is not eating as she should, the effects of a poor nutritional diet can take its toll both physically and psychologically. This is especially true in cases of malnourishment, famine and anorexia.

RESEARCH

At Columbia University, USA, a study of the records of women and their sons from the 1944 Netherlands famine found that many of the male group became severely overweight later on in life. The degree of obesity was influenced by the stage of pregnancy that the mother was at when she became malnourished, with the greatest effect occurring during the first 4-5 months of gestation. This altered the setting of the hypothalamic clock for later life while in utero, causing the body to be over-economical with its use of nutrients and predisposing the child to gain weight when fed a 'normal diet' after birth, thereby creating a 'hunger for life' that is never completely satisfied[5].

The study concluded that starvation in utero set the hypothalamus and metabolic rate for life. The hypothalamus is part of the survival structure of the brain stem and regulates the autonomic nervous system maintaining homeostasis, influencing the body's physiological responses to the environment. It is also involved in regulating:

- Blood pressure
- Heart rate
- Breathing
- Body temperature (involved in the menopause)
- Appetite
- Thirst
- Sexual desire

The hypothalamus also plays a major role in emotional reactions, stimulating the release of hormones from the pituitary to promote the fight or flight response.

FOLIC ACID

Folic acid is vital for the healthy development of a baby's neural tubes, which eventually form to become the brain and spinal cord. It helps to prevent birth defects of the spine and brain and a daily supplement will ensure that you get the right amount in your body.

Trying not to get too technical, folic acid is part of a water-soluble vitamin B complex and functions in the body as a co-enzyme. It also contains vitamins B12 and C. It is active in cell division and performs the basic role of a carbon carrier in the formation of haem, the iron-containing protein found in haemoglobin, which is necessary for the formation of red blood cells. Folic acid is also needed in the formation of nucleic acid, which is essential for the processes of growth and the reproduction of all body cells. It works hand in hand with iron to do its job, and indeed folic acid and iron are found in the same foods. If there is iron deficiency, therefore, there will be folate depletion too.

Absorbed in the gastrointestinal tract by active transport and diffusion through the vascular system, folic acid is stored primarily in the liver. Any disease which has symptoms of vomiting and/or diarrhoea can result in a deficiency of folic acid. In addition, alcohol interferes with the absorption of folate, as well as increasing its excretion. Experts believe that smoking too depletes the body's levels of folic acid. Research has also found that oral contraceptives interfere with the absorption of folic acid.

In general, greater amounts of folic acid are needed to maintain the correct balance and combat losses caused by regularly consuming alcohol, taking drugs and stress and disease, which increase the body's need for folic acid. Higher levels of folic acid, however, also assist during preconception, pregnancy and lactation. Therefore it is best to start taking a folic acid supplement straight away from the moment you decide to start a family, paving the way for better health for your child.

The recommended daily allowance (RDA) guideline for folic acid is 200ug. However the government recommends that all women of childbearing age take 400ug daily to prevent neural tube defects in foetuses. In addition, folic acid supplementation is associated with increased birth weights in developed countries[6]. It is usually taken in tablet form and can also be found in fortified cereals.

The name folate is derived from the term 'foliage', giving an obvious indication of where the vitamin is most commonly found. Folic acid is prevalent in green leafy vegetables such as:

- Spinach
- Broccoli
- Brussels sprouts
- Leafy greens

It is also found in:

- Oranges
- Beans
- Rice
- Yeast extract
- Liver
- Fortified breakfast cereals
- Nuts
- Pasta
- Wholemeal bread

Another thing to consider with regard to folate is that vitamin B12 is essential for its uptake. Vegans are known to have poor intakes of vitamin B12 and may need extra supplementation. If taken in foods, B12 is protein bound and requires intrinsic factor R proteins and trypsin for absorption, whereas the manufactured pure form is easily absorbed via diffusion. Infants are more vulnerable than mothers to vitamin B12 deficiency.

Folate deficiency during pregnancy causes 'magaloblastic anaemia' which, although uncommon in the UK, is linked to:

- Spontaneous abortion
- Toxaemia
- Intra-uterine growth retardation
- Premature delivery
- Foetal malformations

It is recommended that folate supplements be taken early, before conception. As we have already mentioned, it has been known for some time that supplementing with folic acid can reduce risks of birth defects of the brain and spinal cord if taken before conception and during early pregnancy.

You can find out more in the section on anaemia in Chapter 6.

ESSENTIAL FATTY ACIDS (EFA's)

Since the 1970s, fish oils have been known to help prevent heart disease, as well as being good for the brain. Trials took place in the 70s after Greenland Eskimos were found to have exceptionally low incidences of heart disease and arthritis, despite the fact they had a high fat diet.

Several studies have also established a clear association between low levels of Omega 3 fatty acids and depression. Countries with a population having high levels of fish consumption have shown far fewer cases of depression.

Essential fatty acids also help with pain and arthritis symptoms and research indicates that a high blood level of Omega 3, combined with a low level of Omega 6 acids, reduces the risk of developing breast cancer. Daily supplementation of as little as 2.5 grams of Omega 3 has been found to be effective.

It is estimated that 85% or more of people in the Western world are deficient in Omega 3 fatty acids. Apparently the Western world gets too much Omega 6 fatty acid in their diet these days, with vegetarian diets in particular tending to be very high in Omega 6.

Trials have shown that, during pregnancy, daily supplementation of EFA's are beneficial for both mother and baby. Fish oils and cold pressed oils from nuts and seeds are precursors to hormone and enzyme production within the body[7] and EFA's are also known to assist those with behaviour and learning disorders. The recommended daily intake is 1–10g daily during pregnancy and lactation.

One thing to bear in mind is that you need to check out the quality of your fish oils. Not all are pure. Low quality oils may be unstable and contain significant amounts of mercury, pesticides and undesirable oxidation products from water-borne pollution. High quality oils are usually guaranteed to be clean and packaged in an area that precludes the sensitive delicate fatty acids from light.

Another thing worth knowing is that cod liver oil and fish oils are not the same. Cod liver oil is extracted from cod liver and is excellent as a source of vitamins A and D. Fish oils, on the other hand, are extracted from the flesh and tissues of fatty fish like salmon and herring. Both are excellent sources of EPA (Eicosapentaenoic acid) and DHA (Docosahexaenoic acid) but, in the main, fish oils contain little vitamin A and D, whereas cod liver oil contains high levels of each. Supplementing with fish oils on a daily basis has been found to be highly beneficial, with trials showing no significant adverse effects reported.

Omega 3 acids can be found in flaxseed oil, walnut oil, hemp, pumpkin, soybean and marine plankton, as well as in fatty fish. The main component of flaxseed and walnut oil is alpha linolenic acid.

Omega 6 fatty acids come mainly from vegetable oils such as corn and soy and contain a high proportion of linolenic acid. Safflower, sunflower and sesame are all excellent sources of Omega 6.

So, how do you know whether your body is deficient in either of these essential fatty acids? Ask yourself the following questions:

- Do you have dry skin?
- Do you have inflammatory health problems?
- Do you suffer from water retention?
- Do you get tingling in the arms or legs?
- Do you have high blood pressure or high triglycerides (the name for fat in the blood)?
- Are you prone to infections?
- Are you finding it harder to lose weight?
- Have your memory and learning ability declined?
- Do you suffer from a lack of co-ordination or impaired vision?
- If you are a child, are you small for your age or growing slowly?

If you have answered 'yes' to five or more of the above questions, you may be deficient in Omega 3 fats.

- Do you have high blood pressure?
- Do you suffer from PMS or breast pain?
- Do you suffer from eczema or dry skin?
- Do you suffer from dry eyes?
- Do you have inflammatory health problems such as arthritis?
- Do you have a blood sugar problem or diabetes?
- Do you have difficulty losing weight?
- Do you have MS?
- Do you drink alcohol every day?
- Do you have mental health problems?
- Do you suffer from excessive thirst?

Again, five or more 'yes' answers indicate that you may be deficient in Omega 6 fats.

The supply of EFA's and their derivatives to the foetus is essential for normal development, particularly of the neural and vascular systems. Arachidonic acid (AA) and Docosahexaenoic acid (DHA) are the most abundant fatty acids in the brain cell membranes. Their levels increase steadily in the foetal brain during the last trimester when the brain weight will increase four to five fold.

For most women, the placenta may be able to produce the AA form of linolenic acid, but increased levels of the longer molecule DHA are unlikely to occur from foetal or placental metabolism of its precursor alpha linolenic acid. This makes dietary supplementation of DHA advisable for all mothers.

VITAMIN AND MINERAL SUPPLEMENTATION

It is often during pregnancy that we start to look at all sorts of lifestyle changes and diet to ensure that we stay healthy and active. Logically of course we want to give the best start to our unborn child. As most of us do not eat a good balanced diet every day, taking supplements may be another option alongside general dietary improvements. With the depletion of nutrients in our soils and other factors like genetically modified foods, spraying and environmental influences upon the food chain, adverse effects are being felt by everyone.

Supplementing with a good multi-vitamin and mineral combination such as a liquid solution like Neways Maximol Solutions can give a good foundation. Being liquid, it gets into your system much faster than capsules and I recommend this solution to my clients because from personal experience I know that it works.

The aim of the supplement is to maintain and boost trace minerals, vitamins and foundation minerals. It also helps to support with diet and body changes. In addition, taking a good multi-vitamin and mineral foundation during pregnancy can help support low blood sugar levels. Neways have an excellent reputation and are recommended by Cancer Care Prevention, CANCERactive and other top health researchers.

Many pregnant mums feel tired during pregnancy and often symptoms like lethargy, palpitations and dizziness (especially when standing up quickly) can be indicative of deficiencies in essential vitamins and minerals. Simply taking supplementation can create dramatic improvements in just a few days. After all, the body is changing so much over the nine months that in many cases pregnant mums need all the help they can get.

Not only do supplements help during pregnancy, but we also need to get the body in good shape beforehand. Unbeknown to us, we can be lacking in essential vitamins and minerals, thus affecting our performance in becoming pregnant in the first place. Once balanced, it is best to carry on with your good work by keeping the body in shape during your whole pregnancy. As we have mentioned before, hair analysis can help you quantify what your true mineral levels are.

By supplementing from the start, you may be able to avoid deficiency and low levels of iron. Correcting levels of magnesium can also help to avoid pre-eclampsia. Taking probiotics and Noni juice supports the immune system for both you and your baby, helping the build-up and retention of friendly bacteria colonised in the bowel. Aloe Vera juice helps the skin and digestion, whilst essential fatty acids are beneficial to the quality of milk when breast-feeding. Of course, the wonderful thing about all of these supplements is that both you and your baby will feel the benefits.

Zinc

The efficient placental pump is not thought to be effective with minerals, yet it is recognised that there are complex adaptive hormonal mechanisms which alter the rates of absorption from the gut and retention in the body. One of the best correlations of positive birth weight is a high zinc to copper ratio.

We have mentioned already that zinc is an important component of a well-balanced diet and this is especially true because it is known to play a critical role in all nucleic and acid metabolism, as well as gene expression and immune functions. Low zinc and magnesium levels have also shown to be a cause of depression.

Animal studies have shown that adequate maternal zinc status is essential for normal embryonic and foetal development and human studies are now concluding that zinc is also an important requirement for optimal birth weight in infants, especially if the mother is in an 'at risk' group.

When considering the amount of zinc required, it is important to bear in mind that low folate and iron levels can interfere long-term with the absorption of zinc.

Calcium

The body's requirement for calcium increases during pregnancy. Supplementation may boost maternal stores ready for transfer, rather than relying on the mutual scavenging of stores from the maternal skeleton for the foetus. Young pregnant women are at particular risk of calcium deficiency as they are still growing themselves and need their own body's existing supply.

Iron

Iron deficiency, some of the symptoms of which include a constant feeling of tiredness and looking pale, is the most common pregnancy problem worldwide. Anaemia is a condition where there are too few red blood cells or lowered ability of the red blood cell to carry oxygen or iron. Tissue enzymes are dependent upon iron and a lack of iron will affect the cell function in nerves and muscles[8] (see the section on Anaemia in Chapter 6).

During pregnancy, there is a steady increase in both plasma and blood volume, while red cell mass expansion rises proportionally less. The World Health Organisation (WHO) minimum value for haemoglobin is 11.0% g/di (at sea level). Any woman who has levels below this will be classed as anaemic. Haemoglobin contractions and haematocrit values fall in parallel with red cell volume during pregnancy. The lowest value of iron occurs in the second trimester of pregnancy with a rise in the third.

One in three women have been shown to have low iron ferritin levels[9] and supplementation would be vital for this risk group entering pregnancy.

During routine blood tests at 28 to 36 weeks, Hb levels are tested. Any iron deficiency anaemia will be detected showing low serum iron levels with a hypochromic microcytic blood film and low serum ferritin.

Increased iron needs suggested during pregnancy amount to:

- 1mg per day in the first trimester
- 4mg in the second
- 6mg in the third trimester

Deficiency arises from a combination of:

- Low iron stores
- Inadequate dietary iron intakes
- High demands from the foetus

Low levels of iron have been linked with low birth weight[10]. Impaired haemoglobin production seems to occur at 24 weeks gestation and has been associated with increased rates of prematurity, low birth weight and perinatal mortality. Research in 1991 showed that if a mother is severely iron deficient during pregnancy, the baby is born with low iron stores and is therefore at greater risk of death or learning disabilities[11].

Enhanced intestinal absorption is an important physiological adjustment that assists pregnant women in meeting their needs. If there is a gut imbalance, iron may not be absorbed from the diet as it should be. Tea and milk inhibit the absorption of iron and so it would be best to avoid either for one hour either side of taking supplements or eating food containing iron, such as spinach. Vitamin C, however, increases iron absorption and you should therefore eat foods rich in vitamin C when taking iron supplements.

I suggest to my clients a liquid iron called Spatone, which can be used from the age of just two. It is natural spa water, which contains iron already in solution and which is easier for the body to ingest, so being particularly useful for those who are intolerant to tablets. The high iron content is already there as the water pours forth from the rock. Spatone can be taken pre-natally to prepare the body for pregnancy, during pregnancy to help with additional demands that diet alone cannot supply, and post-natally to combat fatigue and blood loss.

In some cases additional iron is known to cause nausea in early pregnancy, so if you are taking iron consult your doctor.

Iodine

Thyroid hormones are critical for normal brain development and maturation. Correction of any iodine deficiency must occur preconceptualy or before the end of the first trimester, as maternal iodine deficiency can lead to foetal hypothyroidism. The severity of retardation together with short stature will depend on the stage of pregnancy when hypothyroidism develops.

HEAVY METALS

Evidence is overwhelming concerning the toxicity of lead and cadmium on the health of the sperm and ova. Hair analysis can show accurate toxic levels in the body and you can find out more about heavy metals in Chapter 7 on the subject of infertility.

KICK-START THE METABOLISM

Exercise is good for the cardiovascular and musculoskeletal system, the digestive process and the psyche. Exercising for at least 20 minutes, three times a week or more has been shown to lower cholesterol levels along with blood pressure. In addition, exercise also releases endorphins (hormones) which give the 'feel good factor' and can help temper anxiety, uplift the mood and sharpen the mind.

Ph Balance

Again, pH balance is something that we will return to shortly, in Chapter 7 under the heading 'Body Acid Levels'. For the moment, however, suffice to say that our blood tissue and brain function best when they are slightly alkaline and you will therefore benefit from alkaline-forming foods such as vegetables and fruit, salads, vegetable soups, pure fruit juices and smoothies. You can check the alkaline/acid balance in your body using pH balancing strips.

SMOKING AND ALCOHOL

Smoking

Smoking is addictive and, for the smoker, often provides comfort and relaxation. However, smoking by the prospective father reduces fertility through lower testosterone levels and a lower sperm count, as well as through increasing the incidence of abnormal sperm. If mothers smoke during pregnancy, it will affect the development of the foetus, as is often evidenced by low birth weights and premature births.

- Nicotine depresses the appetite at a time when pregnant mums should be gaining weight to support the growing foetus (the hormone vasopressin is also believed to play a part in burning off calories)

- Smoking is known to reduce the amount of oxygen to the placenta. The foetus therefore becomes deprived of nourishment and oxygen, growth slows and the foetus does not develop as it should

- Smokers process caffeine up to 50% faster than non-smokers[12]

Whether smoking yourself or simply breathing in another's smoke, the amount of oxygen in the blood stream reduces. In pregnant women this deprives your growing baby of oxygen. Boys born to mothers who smoke during pregnancy (particularly in the early stages) are more likely to have small testicles and a low sperm count as an adult. Men who smoke, as we have seen, are also believed to have poor quality sperm[13].

Of course, smoking whilst pregnant is not the only issue here though. In nursing mothers, it decreases oxytocin and the production of breast milk[14] is affected by producing less milk . Also, it is believed that smoking doubles the chances of your baby developing colic[15].

It is suggested that a smoker inhales only 15% of the total smoke from a cigarette, while the rest goes into the air for others to breathe. We have come to know more about the effects of smoking over the years and it is now established that second-hand smoking in bystanders can be just as dangerous to health as the effects endured by those who take the personal decision to smoke. Logically then, for children it is second-hand smoking that will do the damage.
Second-hand smoke reputedly contains over 4,000 toxic chemicals and 69 of these are believed to be cancer causing[16]. When we breathe in air laden with second-hand smoke, we are not only passively smoking, but also risking the same diseases and infections as those who actually smoke.

When planning a pregnancy, it is advisable for both the mother and prospective father to stop smoking beforehand. To do so promotes better health for the child and mother, not only during pregnancy, but also beyond.

One Imperial College study published in the British Medical Journal indicated that when parents exposed their children to passive smoking, those same children were three times more likely to suffer lung cancer in later life. In addition, children born of smokers are more likely to develop mouth or throat cancer and respiratory diseases.

Asthma and passive smoking

We now know, that children living in households where there is regular smoking, can also be affected by the reduced oxygen in the air that they breathe daily. Because children are more vulnerable to infections, living in this environment makes them more prone to chest, ear, nose and throat infections. It is believed that over 3,000 new cases of asthma are diagnosed every year as a consequence of parental smoking[17].

Remember, cigarette smoking during pregnancy appears to raise the risk of miscarriage or preterm births.

Alcohol

We mentioned in Chapter 2 about the desirability of stopping or cutting back on alcohol consumption when trying for a baby, but this is equally important during the course of pregnancy too. Alcohol has been linked to complications in pregnancy as well as to miscarriage. Additionally, it has been linked to learning disorders such as attention deficit and hyperactivity disorder (ADHD) in children. You can read more about the problems caused by alcohol in Chapter 6.

HOME AND BEAUTY PRODUCTS

Although most of us would like to think of our homes as being relatively safe places, the everyday household products that most of us use are actually full of chemicals, poisons and toxins. Here we will look at some of the most common ones and give an indication of the risks that they can represent.

Bathroom and household products can adversely affect us by inhalation and through the skin. Any of the products that we put on our skin, such as cleanser, body lotion, shower gel, hair shampoo and conditioner can contain harmful additives such as formaldehyde.

I have treated both children and adults who have suffered allergic reactions to the everyday products used for washing their clothes. When washing our clothes, soap powders and lotions are not as pure as we think. The moment we put clothes next to our skin, absorbed chemicals in the product can cause irritation, especially in people with overly sensitive skin.

Toothpaste

Did you know that despite the constant drive to eliminate causes of child hyperactivity, a lot of toothpastes contain artificial colourings and flavours known to cause hyperactivity and worse?

In the US, it is common to see a warning on the box, which states, 'Do not allow children to swallow toothpaste' and yet swallowing is unnecessary since the sensitive lining in the mouth is the quickest way for chemical ingress into the blood stream (apart from injection).

Antiperspirants

Antiperspirants often contain aluminium, a substance proven to be linked to Alzheimer's disease and cancer. Aluminium is also used as a carrier in many vaccines.

Hair dyes

Some hair dyes contain Hydroxyanisol, which is believed to adversely affect the female reproductive system and Teratrogen, which is known to adversely affect the carried embryo.

Talc

Talc is used frequently as an ingredient in our make-up, even though it is known to block the pores of the skin and is also associated with the increase of ovarian cancer[18].

Baby products

Unfortunately, even baby products are not as safe as marketing would lead us to believe. I suggest that mums go back to basics and use ordinary sunflower oil for their baby as a natural baby lotion. Sunflower oil is non-toxic and is easily absorbed into the skin without causing harm. It strengthens skin and promotes elasticity while reducing dryness at the same time.

Household products

Have you ever used a spray to clean furniture, only to find that the fumes immediately hit the back of your throat, making you cough or catch your breath? Again, this is another example of ingesting toxins and poisons and, being so fine, aerosol sprays can penetrate the lungs and get into the bloodstream[19].

Before buying any chemical product, you should look at the label to see what it contains. If you are unhappy with any of the components, my advice is to use non-aerosol products where possible (see the following list).

Nowadays, we have far more awareness than ever before, with most supermarkets offering safe alternative products to use instead. If we keep buying the toxic products, manufacturers won't willingly change the composition. Although it may seem obvious to say it, to stay healthy we need to reduce the poisons and toxins we ingest and deliberately put on our skin. Just because a product is claimed to be good on a TV advert doesn't mean it is right for you.

For our own well-being, we need to be more aware of what we are using in our homes and the consequences of what each product will do to our bodies, our family and the environment. Take a look at the key list of products and the harmful effects linked to disorders below if you need any further convincing.

I openly support companies who make and supply chemical-free products by using them in my own home. I hand out bathroom and personal care information to my clients to help them when buying future products.

In addition, I use lymph drainage and detoxing to help cleanse the body of poisons and toxins for clients and myself. Hair analysis shows in detail the amount of toxicity the body is holding onto in the cells.

Many personal care products contain any number of ingredients that are either toxic, or their addition is considered by experts to be highly questionable. The substances listed below are alleged to be some of the most common ones which are believed to be harmful.

Always look at the label before you buy

Key List numbers:

1. Some products are linked to cancer in animals and humans
2. Some products can be an irritant to the skin and cause allergic reaction
3. Some products will accumulate in the organs
4. Some products such as Toluene are linked with causing asthma
5. Some products are neurotoxins, causing damage to the central nervous system

See key list above for number reference:

Hair sprays and styling:
- DEA (Diethanolamine)   1,2,3,5
- BHA (Butylated Hydroxytolune)   1,2,3,4
- TEA (Triethanolamine)   1 & 2
- Alcohols   1 & 2
- Methylene   1,2,5
- Toluene   1,2,4,5
- Fluorocarbons - Can penetrate the lungs and get into the blood stream

Hair Dyes:
- Phenylenediamine - Can cause serious eye problems if in contact with the eye 1,2,4,5
- Coal tars - Linked to cancer   1 & 2
- Hydroxyanisole - Linked with affecting the female reproductive system   1 & 2

Skin care and cosmetics:

• Propylene Glycol	1,2,3,5
• DEA - Diethanolamine	1,2,3,5
• TEA - Triethanolamine	1 & 2
• Formaldehyde	1,2,4
• SLS /SLES - Sodium Lauryl/ Laureth Sulphate	1,2,3

Some nail treatments include:

• Acetone	1,2,5
• Formaldehyde	1,2,4
• Toluene	1,2,4,5
• Isopropanol	1,2,5
• Acetonitrile - forms cyanide if swallowed	

Hair care: Some shampoo and conditioners can contain - Formaldehyde, SLS, SLES, Cocamiopropyl, Betaine, Glycerine, Quaternium, DEA, TEA, alcohol Propylene glycol.

PROBIOTICS AND PREGNANCY

Pregnancy, birth and infancy are vital times for the development of an appropriate balance of microbiota and flora in the gut, but in fact more and more people are finding it necessary to take a daily supplement of probiotics to counteract a variety of lifestyle-induced problems.

Probiotics support the production of B vitamins, especially folic acid, biotin and vitamin K. If you are not metabolising very well, it would be worth taking a probiotic supplement for a few months, especially in the preparation period before pregnancy and in the run-up to birth, ensuring a good colonisation for baby to pick up. Those with candida and other disorders would need to take the supplement for longer.

Probiotics essentially support protein and carbohydrate digestion via probiotic enzymes. They help to remove toxins and support the immune system, as well as producing lactic acid for the digestive process and to ensure colon pH balance. (See the section in Chapter 15 on lactose intolerance) Probiotics can be used for children as well as adults but you would be well advised to speak to a professional nutritionist or therapist who specialises in digestive GI tract disorders as there are different strains to counteract a variety of complaints.

Before birth, the gut is devoid of microorganisms, but colonisation takes place during birth, when the newborn is exposed to the mother's vaginal and faecal microflora together with organisms from the environment[20]. Depending upon whether the birth is natural or C-section, the resultant microflora has been shown to differ. C-section babies have profoundly different microflora in the first months of life, with abnormalities found to remain up to 7 years. In some cases, this abnormality continues into adulthood giving lifelong problems. It has also been shown that from C-section there is an increased risk of allergy compared to a natural vaginal birth.

Developing appropriate colonies of probiotics organisms in the baby is critical to the long-term immune function and oral tolerance of food.

Problems begin if the child starts life with a deficiency of bacterial flora from the birth process, especially if the mother's own gut flora is weak from reduced gut protection through suffering candida, thrush and so on.

Add antibiotics to the mix and the child's minimal gut defence system can become wiped out and open to eventual invasion by further infection and inflammation. This process can be passed down from one generation to another, with the mother passing on less protection to her child and subsequently becoming weaker at each birth. The mother needs to address her own imbalances to give natural protection to her child.

BREAST VS BOTTLE

Breast-fed and bottle fed children also have differences in micro flora. In breast-fed infants, good bacteria (Bifidobacteria) tend to dominate.

'Bifidobacteria provide unfavourable conditions for the growth of pathogens. For instance, studies on Shigella sp infections and enteropathogenic Esherichia coli in Guatemalan breast fed infants have shown low incidences of both infections due to the predominance of Bifidobacteria in the intestinal area. The species Bifidobacterium in infants showed the greatest protective effect.'[21]

A recent trial showed that gut flora of breast versus formula-fed babies was still significantly different at 6 months[22]. Results showed that formula-feeding led to a persistent reduction of good bacteria compared to breast-feeding, even after the breast-feeding period was completed. It was found that it could be rebalanced and adjusted through taking probiotics or probiotic supplementation.

Trials have shown that probiotics prevent multiplication of candida ablicans[23]. Obviously, before birth and while breast-feeding, the mother can increase the good bacteria for herself and her child with a supplementation of probiotics. If there has been a history of gut imbalances, vaginal infection, thrush or candida, it would be worth taking supplementation during pregnancy to minimise incorrect flora.

For those who are bottle-fed, a correction by supplementation of probiotics can increase the good bacteria for the infant (discuss this with a nutritionist beforehand). Homeopathy is another option to correct the condition for both mother and child.

Taking antibiotics while pregnant will also curb the good bacteria in the mother's system. If there is no alternative, it would be advisable to take a course of probiotics afterwards to rebalance.

Hospital
Because of the wide range of infection found in hospitals, it is worth taking a probiotics supplement to counteract any infection picked up there, and after returning home as a precaution against gut infection[24].

Stress and trauma
Trauma and stress will also affect the balance of the microbial flora in the body. It can result in reduced gastric and intestinal

secretions, thereby changing the desired pH and creating conditions for favourable growth of pathogens such as E.coli, yeasts, etc.

Administration of a range of antibiotics such as Penicillin, Clindamycin, Vancomycin and Tetracycline can encourage candida ablicans and trigger an inflammation response in the gut. Trials also showed an increased risk during pregnancy or when taking the contraceptive pill[25].

A natural alternative is chlorophyll found in parsley, which is anti-bacterial and has anti-fungal activity. It can be purchased in liquid form and has a minty taste.

- Relieves mucus congestion, sinusitis and other damp conditions

- Can be used in cases of cystitis as it has the ability to flush out waste

The importance of water
Did you know that water makes up over 70% of the human body?

I see many people who are dehydrated because they do not drink enough water throughout the day. A dehydrated body will not eliminate toxins and puts undue stress on major organs such as the liver. This in turn creates further disorders.

The body cannot function properly without water. Just imagine running your car without putting water in the radiator. Your engine would begin to labour as it overheated, eventually creating malfunctions and seizure in the moving components. The same thing happens to the body and human joints wear more quickly when deprived of adequate water.

Dehydration is the root cause of many disorders. To help maintain a healthy body we need to drink at least eight tumbler glasses of water per day. Not drinking enough clear still water can be the cause of constipation, headaches, migraine, kidney stones, various skin conditions and digestive problems. Other symptoms of bodily dehydration include:

- Stomach disorders
- Lethargy and tiredness
- Lowered immune system

Water is used to cleanse the body. It clears the systems, especially if your body is running a bit slow. Many people say, 'I know I don't drink enough', while others jokingly quantify their liquid intake with 'I do drink water but it has tea or coffee in it.' It is clear still water that benefits the body most however. Tea and coffee may have water in them but they also have chemicals and caffeine (which is a stimulant to the body and needs to be avoided if stressed or anxious). In addition, if it has been left in damp conditions, tea can house mould and fungus which can get into your digestive system (the right environment for candida).

Water contains hydrogen and oxygen. The oxygen we breathe is used by the body,to burn hydrogen from the water we drink, producing energy in the body to keep us going. Harmony is reached by the correct pH (parts of hydrogen) and occurs when the body's pH level is 7.3. Our DNA uses hydrogen as the glue in the double stranded helix.
The amniotic fluid (water with a pH of 6.7) is necessary for the heartbeat to start in the developing foetus. Amniotic fluid provides a gentle energy to start developing the foetus.

The key is to drink at least eight glasses of water a day. Your body will soon recognise it does not need to store fluid if it is getting a regular supply daily. If you find it difficult to drink plain water, try adding a little apple juice just to cover the bottom of the glass. This tiny addition can make it more palatable until your taste buds adjust to drinking plain water (not fizzy).

Alternatively, add lemon juice. Lemon juice metabolises as an alkaline and helps to cleanse the body, while the combination of hot water and lemon juice each morning will cleanse the skin.

You could also start the day with ginger. Try pouring hot water over grated or chopped fresh ginger and letting it brew for approx

3-4 minutes. This is an old way of helping the digestion and was originally used by the Romans to help their soldiers in the field. It is also good for morning sickness, helping to settle the stomach and digestion process.

It is good practice to always start the day with hot water. Good for curing constipation, it will help with digestive problems and soften stools in the colon. (Be patient it may take a few weeks in chronic conditions). Herb teas and green tea are a healthy alternative to normal tea, coffee and fizzy drinks.

Alongside hydration, it is worth noting that liquid chlorophyll made from alfalfa helps to detoxify the body. Historically it is known to be a blood tonic and as a cleanser and deodoriser it provides a rejuvenative tonic to the body. It also helps to relieve inflammation and has a soothing effect upon the inner body. Eating alfalfa sprouts regularly in salads also helps as a good maintenance habit.

Make water your fluid for life.

STRESS

Our Aim is to change Powerlessness into POWERFULNESS

Powerlessness turns raindrops into cloudbursts.

Molehills into mountains

Puddles into oceans

Overlooks resources

Stress became the big threat of the 90s and has since evolved to the extent that people are now suffering even greater impacts in terms of disruption and disease to the body. We all work at breakneck speed these days and this has put more pressure on all of our body systems. With constant pressure, the mind cannot cope with the ever-flowing and increased speed of information. There is simply no break in transmission and no time to recoup and relax. No wonder we feel overwhelmed these days!

Stress is responsible for many disorders and diseases. In fact, scientific research has shown that at least 75% of all disorders start from emotional and stressful conditions or events and, in addition, stress increases recovery time.

When we are stressed, angry or emotionally upset, we secrete chemicals into the body, which put our internal systems on red alert (fight or flight mode). The adrenalin kicks in as an automatic response, with an explosion of hormones being released through the body to help you deal with the situation i.e. a life threatening emergency.

This response closes down some of the body's less important systems and diverts energy to more important areas. The digestive system is one of the first to close down. Meanwhile, blood pressure, heart pulse and breathing are enhanced and blood flow improved to the muscles for a quick getaway. This reaction is fine if it is in response to a genuine emergency, but harmful if it is ongoing due to pressure or worry.

The changes to the endocrine balance, which are triggered by emotions, tend to have a greater impact on women than men and act to impair blood supply and blood pressure, impede digestion, change body temperature and sustain a state of emotional stress. Together, this causes physiological changes, which can lead to disease. Some studies are showing that under stress cortisol is released and increases fat around the middle of the body therefore putting weight on the individual.

As stated earlier, more than three quarters of all illnesses are stress-related. Stress is such an insidious condition because it creeps up slowly, depleting the body systems over a period of time and making us feel unwell, tired, aggressive, and anxious. Continual stress can lead to a weakening of our body's defence system so that we become more vulnerable to illness and disease. Likewise, it makes us tense, and tense muscles restrict the circulation, reducing oxygen and nutrients to all the cells of the body.

Long-term stress also prevents the proper disposal of waste products so that the body becomes sluggish and is unable to function properly.

This may cause aches and pains, or it may develop into serious problems in underlying organs. The stress build-up explodes internally by blocking parts of our system and creating imbalance.

In our lifestyles today, we have many kinds of physical, emotional and mental stresses. We often repress feelings and bottle up harmful emotions. Each individual though reacts to stress in a unique way. Mentally, it might show through:

- An inability to make decisions
- Poor memory/concentration
- Panic
- Nervousness and a whole range of other symptoms

In a physical sense, our bodies can present us with a variety of sometimes frightening symptoms, including:

- Palpitations

- Headaches or migraines
- Shakiness
- Exhaustion
- Stomach problems
- Irritable Bowel Syndrome
- Lethargy
- Allergies
- Colds, flu, etc
- Tension
- The reduction of efficiency of immune and endocrine systems

Despite all of its negative effects, stress can be a life-saving reflex. It is the alarm call in our body when we need extra energy, such as in an emergency. When the emergency is over, we feel our heart pounding and experience a shortness of breath. We start to shake and may even feel sick. It is at this stage that the body starts to return to normal.

So, what triggers all this activity in a physiological sense?
Basically it is the chemical and nerve transmission response, which we know as 'fight or flight'. When the brain stem is activated, the hypothalamus sends out chemical messengers to alert the whole system. Chemicals are released into the blood stream and the sympathetic nervous system speeds up and powers our whole system as follows:

- Heart beats faster to pump more blood into tissues at speed
- Blood pressure rises to speed up circulation
- Blood clotting increases in case of accident
- Blood flow increases to the limbs, powered for movement
- Breathing rate increases from the top lobes of the lungs and breathing becomes shallow
- Oxygen and other nutrients speed to all muscles so that wastes are carried away faster
- Adrenalin and other hormones are released into the blood stream to speed up systems

- Steroids are released to give more power to the body's systems
- Stores of glycogen are released from the liver for energy
- Pupils dilate to let in more light
- All senses are heightened

Our body is now powered for rapid and all-out effort, but at the same time some of our functions are suspended. Our digestive systems, the muscles of the bladder and rectum, kidneys, sex impulses and immune system are all depressed. As you can imagine, if our digestion and immune system were stopped for long periods it would cause major problems to the running of our body, but all of this happens in a nanosecond and we don't need to think about it as it happens automatically.

Stress is broken down into 3 stages

1. Mobilising Energy- Primary stress
2. Consuming Energy - Emotional distress
3. Draining Energy - Burn out

1. Primary Stress

This is a fight or flight reaction that is automatic and easily switched on or off. During this first stage, adrenalin is pumped into your system to speed up your reactions so that you act more quickly and think faster, such as might be the case if you were crossing the road and a car were approaching fast - you quicken your step to get out of the way.

2. Emotional Distress

Emotional or cognitive distress is a more complex stress response which is activated in the frontal lobes of the thinking brain. Emotional centres of the brain activate emotional stress. If we continue to live at a demanding pace which requires extra energy, our body essentially sets itself to red alert and our system is unable to return to normal. We end up draining and consuming our energy stores.

Our energy will keep us going for a time depending upon how fit we are and how much rest and relaxation we have had, but if we take out more than we put in, this is when we start to feel the effects. This might happen, for example, in the case of a working mum who is trying to juggle work, home and family needs.

Additional pressures and problems then become very demanding through emotional stress, so the body responds with the big guns - the chemical defence system. Cortisols (steroids) act by breaking down stored fats and sugars to cope with distress calls, energy stores become low, parts of the system breakdown and we are open to infection and illness of all kinds.

The symptoms of this type of stress include:

- Feeling tense, overwhelmed by pressures and difficulty in sleeping
- The brain won't switch off, we feel inclined to over/under-eat and crave comfort foods
- Alcohol intake often increases
- Sex drive reduces
- Lack of concentration makes decision making difficult and the memory becomes unreliable and slow

In addition, we can suffer from a range of physical symptoms, including:

- Headaches, migraine and back pains caused by tension
- Muscles become tense which affects menstruation, etc
- Parts of the body are slowed down to compensate for other parts which are speeded up when the stress response is activated

3.Burn out

When faced with near exhaustion and with emotions dried up, the system feels clogged up. All motivation disappears and everything is an effort. We become irritable and anger flares up at the slightest thing. Insomnia conflicts with a tired mind and we become tearful, depressed and begin to feel wooden. In addition, we notice some, or even all of the following symptoms:

- Palpitations
- Chest pains
- Heartburn
- Stomach cramps
- Twitching limbs
- Light headed
- Recurrent headaches
- Head noises
- Ringing in the ears
- The immune system is completely suppressed.

The body is now open to disease, which can thrive through anxiety and emotional stress, and indeed the breakdown of the immune system is linked to long-term stress. Not only does it impair antibody production, but it also reduces 'B' blood cell activity and changes 'T' cell counts, which normally destroy invading viruses or bacteria.

Long-term stress is also linked with some cancers, which it is now acknowledged can start on average 6-9 months after an emotional or stressful event.
This is why it is essential to release pent up and buried emotions with professional qualified therapists trained in the innovative emotional release techniques such as (DARE) Dissolve and Resolve Emotions and Somoto emotional release (SER).

Suggestions for dealing with stress

To help put us back on track after mild attacks of stress, the body needs sleep, rest, exercise and good nutritional food.

- Check your diet - are you getting enough vitamins and minerals?
- Are you taking enough time for yourself to enjoy your leisure activities?
- A vitamin supplement may be advisable but take advice if you are unsure of which ones. Our bodies sometimes need a top-up - a vitamin B supplement also includes B6 and B12, vitamin C and zinc, which are good for the brain and body

Stress puts our nerves on edge and causes fatigue, which in turn affects the nervous system. This vicious circle makes us become irrational. What we need to calm the nerves is rest, quiet, relaxation to build up our reserves of energy and, of course, sleep to recharge the body.

In order to deal with stress, you need to look at those things in your life that make you anxious, if possible in a detached manner, and see what you can change to make life easier.

- Can you delegate some of your workload, shopping, etc? – as even simple tasks can become a burden
- Perhaps you need a complete change
- You could also look at whether there are particular things that you dislike but which you have fallen into doing, such as a job or a sport that you feel obliged to do
- You need to analyse situations, as often it is not immediately obvious what is upsetting you

Getting a good night's sleep is essential to help you cope throughout the day, so try and stick to a bedtime routine for at least a month. Going to bed two hours before midnight gives you a better quality of sleep. Also, go to bed when you feel tired. If you fight sleep, you will go past the time when your body tells you that it needs to rest, and fighting sleep invariably results in difficulty sleeping when you do eventually go to bed.

To help you relax, read a book or a magazine as opposed to watching television when you go to bed, as the latter activates and stimulates the brain, creating the wrong environment for sleep and relaxation. The same is true of working on the computer until late at night, which is also counter-productive for sleep.

Exercising, although generally extremely beneficial, is another thing which should not be left until bedtime as it overheats the body and delays sleep. To enjoy sound sleep, the best time to exercise is 5-6 hours before bedtime and certainly not within two hours of retiring.

Eating too late in the evening can also interfere with sleep patterns as it causes digestion activation during sleep time, raising both temperature and metabolic rate. It is best to eat at least two hours before bed but if you do become hungry later on, have a light snack such as a cracker, biscuit, cereal or a piece of toast half an hour before bedtime.

Caffeine and large quantities of alcohol should also be avoided for up to six hours before bedtime. Alcohol not only disrupts sleeping patterns and shortens REM sleep, but it also dehydrates the body and invariably we are woken during the night with an incredible thirst. Instead, take a herbal drink before bedtime. Valerian or chamomile tea helps to relax the body and the mind, although some prefer warm milk, which also seems to soothe and puts us in the right mood for sleep. (Valerian also comes in tablet form)

Developing a wind-down ritual such as a warm bath, meditation or listening to soft music is an ideal way to induce restful sleep. Research has confirmed that a temporary slight rise in body temperature will be followed by a drop, which helps to trigger sleep. Avoid taking a bath which is too hot, too long or too close to bedtime, as this will not give the desired effect for relaxed sleep and, if you are not pregnant, use a few drops of essential oils to enhance relaxation. i.e: Lavender

When you do go to bed, sleep in a dark room with a comfortable temperature, the cooler the better. Open the window during the day to change the air and keep the window open at night as fresh air while you sleep improves sleep patterns.

Far from being a home entertainments centre, the bedroom should be associated with two things only - sleep and intimacy. The décor of the bedroom should be relaxing so try to use neutral colours when choosing decorating themes.

Alternative help for stress
There are more alternative and complementary therapies available than ever before and many are looking to this non-invasive way to help cure their ills. They treat the cause but will, in some cases, not change symptoms overnight. Alternative therapies tend to take a little longer to work as they are working with and stimulating the body's own healing potential. The beauty of working with alternative therapies, however, is that they are non-invasive for the body. Below is

a list briefly explaining the different therapies on offer. See appendix for more detailed information.

Reflexology

Reflexology is a method of using pressure and massage to affect reflex points on the feet in a particular way that affects other areas of the body. As all the body systems are inter-related, anything affecting one part eventually affects others. Used throughout the past 5,000 years and originally known as 'zone therapy', it balances all the body systems by stimulating underactive areas and calming overactive ones, including the endocrine, lymphatic, blood circulation and nervous systems. Reflexology sessions are intended to improve the body's homeostasis and assist the body in speeding up the healing process.

Reflexology works particularly well for specific aspects of our well-being. In a physiological sense, it benefits by ensuring a relaxed and healthy body, whilst psychologically it affords a calm state of mind at the same time as promoting a positive outlook on life (homeostasis).

Acupuncture

Acupuncture is an ancient Chinese system of medicine which uses meridians or energy channels throughout the body. Using fine needles at external points along these meridians, it stimulates healing.

Shiatsu

Similar to acupuncture, shiatsu is a Japanese system which works on the meridians for a complete system of healing through touch. Pressure and contact is applied through the hands, thumbs, fingers, arms, knees and feet and this type of therapy involves stretching, holding and leaning the body weight into various positions to improve energy flow, blood circulation and flexibility.

Homeopathy

Homeopathy is a therapy which has been about for around 200 years. Using the theory 'like cures like', patients are treated with potions made from animal, mineral and vegetable sources.

Bach Flower Remedies

Based upon the belief that 'a healthy body equals a healthy mind', Bach flower remedies use wild plants, bushes and trees to treat emotional disorders.

Herbalism

Herbalism is the oldest form of treatment using natural medicines concocted from herbs and plants. Although it is effective, it does need longer timescales to see results compared to some other methods.

Hypnotherapy and Psychotherapy

Hypnotherapy and psychotherapy can both be used to relieve stress. Based on the principles of psychology, they aim to achieve mental and physical relaxation.

Emotional Release techniques

New methods are available in releasing stress, core behaviour and emotional issues. i.e: Dissolve and Resolve Emotions (DARE) and Somoto Emotional Release (SER)

FINDING THE CAUSE IS THE ANSWER

Dealing effectively with stress involves finding the cause of the problem and dealing with it. If change is not initiated, stress is sustained and manifests itself in disease.

With emotional stress and burnout, more drastic measures may have to be taken. Doctors may prescribe tranquillizers and/or anti-depressants as a short-term measure. While these can be helpful in buying some time in order to sort out problems, or for problems to sort themselves out, they will not, in themselves find the root cause of the problem, which still needs to be addressed. In some cases, if drugs are taken over a long period of time they can cause addiction. Like anything, the body gets used to the effects of the drug and craves its daily dose in just the same way that it does with caffeine and chocolate.

Although we have moved on in terms of mental health, modern medicine seems poorly equipped to handle complex problems like stress. Prevention, education and counselling must form a major part of treatment, but sadly GPs are neither trained enough in these areas, nor do they have enough time to spend with patients who need to explore the root cause or require specialist care. Patients go in with a condition such as chest pains or digestion problems, which although connected to stress, are not instantly recognised as such. More specialised centres and education are needed to recognise and identify the early stages.

I believe that it is essential to bring early prevention into healthcare, to help society to deal with its ever-increasing workload and fast lifestyles. Rather than dealing with prevention, however, Western medicine is often all too preoccupied with intervention. Only 10% of our GNP is spent on health and health education and many of our preventive programmes remain unfunded.

In addition, the workplace needs to change. Greed has taken over, and people do not matter any more. In modern industry, the policy of reducing the numbers of employees in order to provide greater profits to shareholders puts pressure on the remaining employees. They are pushed to the limit and expected to give over 100% on a daily basis to make up for shortages.

People are not machines. The body can only take so much before it eventually breaks down and, in many cases, stress management can be common sense. If we think of our bodies as vehicles, then we need to feed them, service them and take care of them just as we would with our cars. A battery does not run forever without recharging, and neither can we. We are only human after all!

Stress and Emotions

As we have seen, doing too much causes the body to become overwhelmed by the pressure that we put upon ourselves and stress is the result. Stress can materialise from our jobs, families, relationships and environments. Just one or all could be making an impression upon you, leaving you feeling as though you are always on a short fuse. As others infuriate or distress you for no apparent reason, life becomes one long drama and you can become prone to depression. You may have always been anxious. Perhaps it is all that you can remember and you have never known anything different.

Stress is another name for feelings and emotions, and emotions are the outward expression of what we are feeling inside. We can feel love, joy, sadness and hurt, either one after the other or as a cocktail of emotions. They can be triggered by something that we see on the television, a word, a song or a film, which reminds us of a time past. They can also stem from something that we have done or said or even from a place, a meal or just a conversation. Although the memory itself may be either positive or negative, it will evoke emotions and feelings. Interactions affect us on all levels of our being every day, and what we feel will influence our judgements and future decisions. Emotions can create challenges, emotional disharmony, crisis in our lives and even physical diseases, and they will affect how we perform physically and emotionally.

As humans, we bury feelings and emotions all the time. We have a tendency to tamp them down with mental concrete in the hope that they will never show again. Like time bombs waiting to go off, emotions smoulder and ferment!

Sometimes we try to bury things so deeply that even the mind will subconsciously assist the block by putting the trauma in a place, which is numb from feelings and emotions. This can come from childhood and even from within the womb, picking up on our mother's feelings and anxieties to create patterns that we will put into our foundation for life.
Emotions go deep into our bodies - into our cells as a memory and into our subconscious as trauma. Good or bad, everything is memorised and nothing is forgotten. All emotions are indelibly printed as events that happened and made an impression on us, to the point where our bodies cry out to be released from their turmoil of repressed feelings and denial (see Case Study 4 section 9)

Emotions are important messages and we can all too easily create harmful barriers to block them. When we do this, we lose energy and become temporarily underpowered, and being underpowered affects our bodily functions until eventually we become seriously fatigued. Just like a battery that needs recharging regularly, the bodily equipment that we rely on doesn't work as well and runs down very quickly. This is what holding emotional trauma does to the physical body, and it results in:

- Low energy levels
- Feeling fatigued and tired all the time
- Low immunity
- An inability to renew our energy so that we wake feeling tired before we even start the day. Having gone to bed exhausted, we wake the same way!

Reaching this point creates 'energy debt' in the cells of our body. Energy is stored in our cell tissue and, if we are in 'energy debt', we begin drawing from the cell structure itself, making it weaker and eventually causing physical illness. Waves of energy can become solidified or frozen into non-movement matter and this is where illness and depression sets in. (This is explained in more detail in my course entitled School of Life)

Exhaustion - running on empty

When the body is running on empty, it is at a low ebb. Physical systems become overloaded and one of the first to go down is the immune system, leaving the body unable to fight off disease. At this point we become more prone to catching colds, viruses, and so on, which in turn makes us feel tired. The lymph system, which looks after us in conjunction with the immune system, becomes under par. Glands and nodes, which clear poisons and toxins from the body, can't perform as they should, allowing toxicity to build up within the body. Obviously, this does not provide a good environment to develop an embryo.

Stress also affects the abdominal area, shutting down the fragile performance of the toxin elimination system. Another area where we hold emotions is in the solar plexus.

When we are stressed or anxious we have what is commonly known as the fight or flight syndrome that takes place automatically. It can happen to us at any time and often very quickly. For example, when we are driving, a car pulls out in front and we have an automatic response to swerve, break or stop to avoid an accident. At that moment adrenaline (a hormone) will be pounding around the body's systems, alerting all the muscles with new blood to allow immediate action. As the heartbeat increases, we can breathe more deeply and our mind becomes very alert in deciding whether to stand and fight or run away. Although we might not appreciate its origins, this reaction has evolved all the way from cave men days!

Because we no longer live as cave men and endure their hardships, we don't run or fight any more. In these comparatively frightening situations, we are more prone to have these chemicals going around our bodies for some hours before we calm down. The body diverts energy from other systems to give maximum energy performance for the situation on hand, even though we don't need it. One of the first areas to suffer energy loss is the abdominal area and digestive process.

When we are stressed or anxious all the time we can have this shutdown process going on continuously, with the digestive process switching on and off and adrenaline kicking in several times a day. Hormones and chemicals then circulate the body for weeks and even months at a time, leading to physical disorders such as:

- IBS (Irritable Bowel Syndrome)
- Bloating
- Flatulence
- Constipation
- Diarrhoea
- Acid reflux

Some of us live on adrenaline daily. In fact, some would say that they thrive on it. In the short term, adrenaline is a good thing. Used correctly it provides excitement and gives us a buzz. Just like driving fast cars or bungee jumping, it is the adrenaline kick that gives us that feeling of enjoyment. Being fit and well we are able to recharge our batteries and dispel adrenaline quickly.

However, if we are not able to deal with the adrenaline because of depletion in other areas of the body, it can be a way of depleting us even further. It saps us emotionally, physically and energetically, hence the continuing fatigue and tiredness. With nothing to give any more, we struggle to see the day through and since our energy battery is now flat, we cannot even recharge at this point. Logically, starting the day on empty does not provide the best scenario for the rest of the day and, as women, we tend to run on empty regularly. When this happens it can also affect our thyroid.

When we feel tense, our body is tense.

With organs, tissue and muscles all tense, we don't even notice the change as it grows, creeping up without us consciously knowing. Our posture changes, causing us to walk and stand stiffly, creating new inner patterns to cope with the anxiety and stress. This may have been happening for some time and we begin by getting aches and pains, fatigue and tiredness. Muscles become tight and can go into spasm with a tendency towards restless leg syndrome. Over long term this can result in declining health and living in a body on a constant 'alert' state.

The body tenses up automatically when we are stressed. Without us knowing, our shoulders tend to be lifted up toward the ears. Neck and shoulder pain soon follow as headaches and sleepless nights ensue. I often find that tense people cannot even sit quietly. Feeling restless, they have to be moving at least one part of their body. It could be hands, feet or legs, fidgeting in their seat or moving and adjusting their clothes. As a visible sign it is the body language for distress and feeling uncomfortable.

All too often we become unaware of the consequences of tightening up the digestive area. Put simply, it becomes more difficult to eliminate. Sometimes we are so unsettled inside that the body reacts in a completely opposite way by rejecting what we put into it, causing nausea, sickness or loose bowel (diarrhoea). The process of instantly rejecting food and drink can come without warning, inducing everything to pass straight through our system. Being unable to digest nourishment causes further unrest in the abdominal area, a disorder to which women are apparently more prone.

Our nervous system is involved in this failing process as it gives commands to the major organs of the body such as the abdominal area, heart and lungs. The central nervous system (CNS) is our communication between the brain and the body and vice versa. While tense and stressed, messages from the body via the CNS become less clear and normal communication eventually breaks down.

According to the Health and Safety Executive (HSE), stress is the single largest cause of occupational ill health in the public sector, accounting for around half of all days lost. Work-related stress leads to depression and/or anxiety and led to an average of 13.8 million working days being lost in 2006/07. Sickness and absence, in the UK alone costs approx twelve billion pounds a year.

Tackling stress can have a positive effect upon a person's commitment to work, something which can be achieved by managers and supervisors valuing staff and evaluating their concerns and complaints on a regular basis. As a result, productivity and personal performance improves and staff retention is much improved. After all, staff want to stay where they are happy and valued.

We spend most of our lives working, so it is logical that we want to feel appreciated and satisfied in what we do. Everyone has their down days, but it is most important that we feel happy and stress-free (the majority of the time) in our lives and our work place.

Stress management is the key and this involves knowing how to make the most of time and resources as well as learning new methods and techniques of relaxation. Stress management allows us to regain order in our lives and helps us to look at our lifestyles. It teaches us how to cope with day-to-day problems by using practical strategies, methods and applications for:

- Lifestyle,
- Workload
- Relaxation
- Attributes

THE GUT-BRAIN AXIS

The term 'gut-brain axis' refers to the bi-directional communication between gut and brain, mediated via neurohumeral signals

Stress plays an important role in the expression of gastrointestinal diseases and indeed many organic gastrointestinal diseases such as peptic ulcer and ulcerative colitis were once thought to be psychosomatic.
Stress has a dramatic effect on the mucosal barrier by increasing

the permeability of tight junctions, enhancing the uptake of macromolecular antigens and promoting the internalisation and translocation of bacteria. This in turn causes mild inflammation in the ileum and colon, giving implications for IBS and gastrointestinal disorders. Scientific tests have shown that stress, temporally distant from the event, can influence susceptibility to inflammatory signals. Studies have shown that chronic H. pylori infection produces changes in gastric motor sensory physiology and feeding behaviour. This indicates that chronic bacterial infection localized in the gut can produce direct changes in the function of the brain.

The stomach area in fact listens very carefully to the brain and the entire digestive system is closely tuned to a person's emotions and state of mind. People with IBS often suffer flare-ups during times of stress and anxiety. Their misery is very real but often the doctor cannot find the answer. Sufferers can worry their way to:

- Stomach pain
- Nausea
- Diarrhoea
- Constipation

Doctors and scientists have, in the past, treated the mind and body as separate entities and some doctors even declared that digestive distress with no sign of organic disease was all in the mind. In very recent years, however, most doctors have accepted the connection between the nervous and digestive systems, and in particular the relevance of the vagus nerve, which feeds the major organs and digestive system. The gut and the brain constantly exchange information by chemical and electrical messages, so that anything that affects one, will also affect the other. The connections are so tight that scientists often refer to them as one entity - the Gut-Brain Axis. They now acknowledge that reducing stress, depression and anxiety will go a long way toward calming the gut area.

Like the spinal cord, the gut contains many neurons (nerve cells) and acts like a local mini-brain in the gut, containing different patterns of gut behaviour. The brain is like a large mainframe computer with extended memory and processing circuits. It receives information and sends commands to the intestinal computer. The central nervous system releases chemicals (acetylcholine and adrenaline), which tell the stomach:

- When to produce acid
- When to churn
- When to rest

Similar signals help guide the movements of the intestines.

'Gut feeling' is no longer a figure of speech. The digestive system responds in kind by sending electrical messages to the brain and scientists have found that stimulating the nerves at different frequencies can cause a range of responses from anxiety to a strong sense of well–being. These responses create such sensations as:

- Hunger
- Fullness
- Pain
- Nausea
- Discomfort
- Sadness
- Joy

The Vagus nerve

The vagus nerve is also thought to shape our moods. Essentially this nerve is a large electrical cable, which runs between the brain and the digestive system. Doctors once believed that its main job was controlling acid production in the stomach, but better understanding of human physiology now shows that 95% of the nerve fibres carry messages in the other direction from the gut to the brain[26]. Just like a long telephone cable, the nerve group extends from the head to the gut.

When the brain senses a threat, either real or imagined, it sounds the alarm by flooding the body with adrenaline and CRF (Corticotrophin Releasing Factor), triggering the fight or flight response. Suffering from frequent emotional distress and the unrelenting flood of hormones such as adrenaline and CRF means that the body is in a constant state of alarm, something, which in turn takes its toll on the digestive system. Hormones can make the cells in the stomach and intestines extra-sensitive to pain, making normal contractions and movements excruciating. New signals can disrupt the normal motion of the intestines, which goes on to produce bouts of constipation or diarrhoea. A recent survey showed that 68% of normally healthy people complained of stomachaches when stressed.

In the 1980s, scientists and doctors came together to develop criteria for diagnosing more than 20 digestive disorders, known as Functional Gastrointestinal Disorders (FGIDAs). The criteria, which are unrelated to diagnosable physical disorders, include:

- Persistent constipation
- Diarrhoea
- Bloating
- Abdominal pain
- IBS

IBS (Irritable Bowel Syndrome) is very common, especially in nervous individuals, and is often characterized by painful cramps, bloating and constipation alternating with diarrhoea. Whilst it is believed that emotional distress alone cannot cause IBS, stress and over-sensitive emotions or a mood disorder can certainly worsen the symptoms. In fact, an Australian study found that chronic stress arising from traumas such as divorce, lawsuits, job troubles and serious illness were found to account for 97% of all changes in IBS symptoms.

The influence of the mind on the gut goes beyond functional disease. Two conditions with clearly physical origins are Crohn's disease and ulcerative colitis, but both lead to flare-ups during times of emotional stress.

Prozac and antidepressants are often used to help with gut disorders and work by blocking pain messages to and from the gut area, but breathing exercises also help. Breathing is not only a physiological function which can be consciously activated, but can also be governed in part by the nervous system via the vagus nerve, cranial and certain spinal nerves. The vagus nerve dictates the rhythm, frequency and intensity of breathing patterns and by deeper in–out breathing, you can oxygenate your systems and stimulate your blood flow.

The vagus nerve runs from the skull, down the neck, across the chest and into the abdomen, affecting the cardiovascular, respiratory and digestion systems. By relaxing the body, we affect the nervous system and this in turn helps inner organs and systems to relax and so puts us in a better place to be able to conceive. Deep breathing enables us to start to stimulate blood flow and improve overall health.

Exercise – Breathing method

Deep breathing into the gut area ten times, twice or three times a day, improves the gut-brain connection, increasing the pituitary and brain response. Simply feel the rise and fall of the gut and be aware of your breathing. Push the gut out as you breathe in and pull in as you breathe out. It has been observed that just doing this exercise three times a day will improve overall brain and gut performance and, of course, it is something which can be done by anyone of any age while waiting in a queue, doing the washing up, sitting on a train or bus or at any other time.

Alternative therapies such as reflexology are known to relieve stress and are very effective with rebalancing digestive disorders. I use reflexology all the time for digestive disorders and I find it very effective. People who suffer with constipation tell me that sometimes within less than 24 hours of their session they emptied their bowel. For others it is within a very short time. Professional Reflexologists are trained to go to the core of the problem and, by using finger and thumb movements, they can clear blockages within the digestive tract without the need for laxatives and enemas. In chronic conditions, reflexology sessions may need to be done on a regular basis to clear the backlog in the colon.

Reflexology is very useful for people of all ages, especially those who have had operations and do not want to strain. Even babies and children, who can also suffer constipation and disconnection from the vagus nerve as a result of the mother's bacteria, can benefit from this non-invasive technique. Regular sessions can, in addition, help those who are taking medications which are known to cause constipation.

SELF HELP TIPS FOR REDUCING STRESS

It may seem simple but we need to make time for ourselves. Very often we are so work-orientated that there is no time for anything else. We can become obsessed with work or the home and nothing can deter us from the routine or schedule that we have created for ourselves.

Nothing changes unless you do. This is the place to start looking at what you are doing in your life and what you would like to change. Very often people do not know what they want in their lives but they do know what they don't want. This is the starting point.

1. Write down what you don't want in your life as this will then give you ideas of what you would like. Imagine you have been given a wish list of what you would like to do with yourself and the rest of your life.

2. Start to make plans and schedules of what you would like to do and when. This might include, for example, that special holiday that you have always wanted to take or that place you have always wanted to visit.

3. Give yourself permission to leave the office at the appointed time each day. Staying on each evening for several hours mounts up and leaves little time for you and your leisure time. Over time, this can feel like being on a treadmill where, becoming ever more tired and lethargic, everything seems like an effort.

4. Don't be a martyr to the home or the office. It is far better to spend quality time with the family than stress about whether the ironing gets done.

5. Make time for yourself. Whether you choose to go to the gym, take a nice relaxing bath or spend time gardening is your choice.

6. Delegate at work and at home and ask yourself whether everything really needs to be done by you. I have found that the more you do the more will be expected of you. If you are doing more than your share, you either need some help or someone is not pulling their weight. Partners and children can help out at home. Picking up the shopping, putting away bags and helping with the hoovering are

all good places to start. The days of women being servants have gone and anyway, helping out around the home is a good exercise as children need to know how to do these things for themselves when they leave home.

7. Ensure you have some time out with your partner/spouse/friends and so on. It doesn't have to be an expensive night out and it could be once a week or just once a month. Go for a coffee and a chat, see a movie at the cinema, share a meal or a barbecue – whichever is your preference. It is far healthier to get into this routine because it brings everything into perspective when we are away from the problems making us stressed.

8. Talking about your stress to a friend, relative or practitioner is a bonus as a trouble shared is a trouble halved. Whoever you choose to talk to will not be on the emotional see-saw and can objectively give advice and suggestions that may be all you need.

9. Join an evening class or volunteer organisation. Be an uncle or aunt to a single parent family. The options are endless.

10. Meditation is a good relaxing way of quietening the mind. Yoga is a philosophy of life and incorporates both exercise and meditation.

The world is your oyster and you just need to look at what you want to do in it.

MIND AND EMOTIONS

We often talk about reducing the toxins in our bodies and sometimes take the important step of actually participating in a cleanse programme to detox the poisons which our bodies ingest and absorb daily. But what about your emotions? Isn't it time you had an emotional detox?

We experience emotions every second of every day. We feel sad, happy, bitter, angry, uneasy, anxious or depressed. Sometimes we cry or even feel overwhelmed and most people are unaware that our biochemistry actually changes when we make these emotional responses. Not only do peptides and neuropeptides, which are mainly produced by the brain, act as chemical messengers, but hormones and immune cells also influence communication and reaction to the physical state.

Emotions have a huge part to play on our physical well-being through what we think, say and do each moment of our life. Ask yourself the question - is it you, or are your emotions in control? Do you feel out of control and lose perspective on life?

Although changing emotions are part of daily life, it is only when we are overwhelmed by them that it starts to become both physically and mentally unhealthy. In many cases, our emotions arise from habit or a pattern that our mind recognises. In certain situations we get into ruts and, just like a record, the tune goes on and on, replaying over and over again. In other cases, someone may be pushing our buttons, creating a steady build-up which at first goes unnoticed, but which ultimately needs to act as a wake-up call for us to consider serious change by looking at our lives, our job and our relationships.

An emotional detox works not only to influence and protect you on the physical level, but also to make you feel happier and more peaceful, which will in turn help with your relationships and interactions on a daily basis. Also, it will make you more effective in your environment, such as in the workplace and other areas of your life where you need to communicate and co-operate on different levels.

By keeping a daily record of how you feel emotionally, together with the time or event which triggered emotions such as anger, irritation, fear of anxiety, you begin to take control. Look at the causes:

- You are happy, sad, listless, because?
- Why are you jealous, irritated or feeling insecure?
- Do you need to look at the root cause of your emotion?
- Why are you giving your power away?

Understanding patterns will help you to understand why you feel the way that you do, but emotional detox is a continual process which will only bring about gradual change. When you start to make changes, it could take at least 21 days before you begin to notice a difference. Nevertheless, even minor changes will begin to filter through and, although the effects may appear to be subtle, these small improvements will become more apparent as the days pass.

Adverse effects of our emotions

One of the things, which can have a huge adverse effect on our emotions is negative talk. Negative talk often comes from past interactions when we were told:

- 'You are stupid.' (We then think that we are not good enough)
- 'You will never be good at this.'
- 'You will fail this exam!'

Negative talk leads to depression. Our energy becomes weak, dense and heavy and we feel as though we are carrying the weight of the world on our shoulders. All of this happens because we believe what we were told. We repeat it and our unconscious mind takes it on board as fact so that we end up telling ourselves:

- 'I am hopeless at this.'
- 'This always happens to me in my relationships.'
- 'When I get to this point in my relationships something always goes wrong.'
- 'I can't do this.'

So, how do we get out of this negative mindset? Affirmations are known to assist.

Saying affirmations is a way of changing mind patterns, which have been there for some time and have become imprinted grooves in our mindset. Whilst saying affirmations might make you wince or feel embarrassed, and some might even make you say 'Yuk!', this is because they have struck a chord within you.

- 'I love myself.'
- 'I nurture myself.'
- 'I approve of myself.'
- 'I am a good person.'

- 'I will achieve....today.'
- 'Every day, in every way, my life improves.'

Be patient with yourself, as it takes time to change mind patterns. Once you have started, however, it will become a habit to think more positively about yourself and others.

If you want to understand more about mental and emotional patterns, my School of Life workshop provides unique skills and information, which will assist you to 'Get your Life Back'.

Emotions and the Subconscious Mind

Our mind is active all the time with random thoughts. We have fleeting memories, captivating fantasies, snatches of things seen, heard or otherwise perceived.

It is our perspective that creates problems. The Eastern world tends to see life from a different perspective to the West. Buddhists see the darkest and most upsetting moments in life as opportunities for uncovering natural wisdom. In the West we often see these as threats or problems.

How we perceive will affect how our mind stores information. The subconscious mind stores everything that we experience - what we see, hear, think and feel emotionally. It takes everything literally – whether we actually experience an event or fantasise about it, the subconscious mind registers it as fact. Therefore, if we continually watch negative and emotive programmes on TV, listen to negative media, watch aggressive violent films and play violent games, we can become hyperactive, angry and violent. It can also make us feel depressed and negative.

This is why it is so important to change negative, debilitating past events into positive memories. We need to be mindful of what actions we want our thoughts to initiate as mindfulness shifts the brain from disturbing to positive emotions.

Little changes can make a huge difference to people's lives. Watch comedy and turn off the TV from frightening and negative programmes.

Laughter makes us feel good as it lightens the mood. Change your children's habits and get them outside in nature so that they can learn to play again. Have family outings, do positive things together, talk to each other, go for walks and sit and eat together.

Expressing feelings

From a very early age, we are conditioned to the beliefs of our parents, siblings and schoolteachers, as well as to those promoted by our culture and religion. By limiting ourselves solely to these teachings, however, we create an artificially narrow world and by continuing to live in this narrow world we miss the opportunities to see our greater qualities within.

In our minds we carry this inner strife with us everywhere through repetitive cycles and story lines, which are like endless recordings playing over and over again, despite some small variation. In one sense, the memories create false barriers in our world, holding us back to a particular time or event. When around those who have doled out injustice or criticism, we are made to feel lethargic by the sheer weight of someone else's hang-ups.

Our emotional reactions to this impact often distract us from the present reality. With minds filled with relentless thoughts about another time and place, our bodies become overwhelmed with turbulent feelings.

Emotion is the outward expression or reaction of the inner feeling. It is the result of thought and feeling coming together. To release emotion is MOST IMPORANT. Emotion is held in our energy field not only by attitudes, belief systems, concepts and constructs of being, but most of all through attachment to an earlier event or trauma. Whether through pain or pleasure, we are involved and attached to that experience or event.

Memories are like photos. They are held in our physical, emotional and mental systems, being attached to the experience that is etched upon us in taste and feeling. These emotions represent us and how we see ourselves and the roles we play, our wealth, our health and our unhealed emotional pain. If we don't release trauma and emotional pain it can eventually cause physical disease and serious disorders.

When stored, emotions of anger, bitterness and hate incurred from our cultural or religious beliefs can be passed down through the ages from one generation to another. Often the original issue is not understood but accepted because it is the belief of the family or culture. Brainwashing from an early age promotes repetition as we are caught up in a loop of emotions from war and religion of a bygone age.

As children we learn not to express our true feelings. How often have we been instructed by our parents, teachers or others to:

- 'Don't cry!'
- 'Cheer up!'
- 'Take that smile off your face!'
- 'Be quiet!'
- 'Speak when you are spoken to!'
- 'Don't ask!'

When faced with verbal, physical or sexual abuse, we often deal with it by cutting off our emotions. If we are abused often enough, we mentally deny the experience, shutting down our emotional needs and, in extreme cases, becoming numb and frozen. Consequently, as adults, we then find it difficult to deal with our own and others' emotions and feelings.

As children all we want is to love and to be loved. We want to be accepted as we are with unconditional love. Unfortunately, however, many of us were not given that kind of love and tried to get attention in other ways. Although we might have tried everything, perhaps we still felt unloved and so learned to play mind games to get attention, becoming the pleaser, victim, bully or manipulator, habits and behaviour patterns which continued into adult life.

The first thing we do as children is to build mental barriers and walls around ourselves to protect our hurt feelings. As we progress into adulthood, those mental barriers and walls become thicker and stronger, leaving us wondering why our relationships don't turn out right!
Our true emotions have been buried and we are still conditioned to

those feelings and emotions held in our bodies and minds, even if it happened 30 years ago. In this situation we need to find a way to stop giving our energy to those emotions and feelings derived from trauma and unhappy events in the past. Clearly we need to find a way of understanding and releasing those patterns and this is where techniques such as emotional release therapy can help.

For too long, patterns and behaviours have grown with us on a subconscious level and in some cases the fear of letting go can be more daunting than holding on. Behaviours and patterns, which are comfortable, become so much a part of our make-up that we are unaware of the irrational havoc and chaos they cause in our lives.

When we first learn to do something new, such as driving, we are consciously aware of what we are doing and why. As we progress over time, however, we adapt so far into this pattern or skill that it becomes second nature. Filed in the mind, the new skill is now known to us unconsciously and this is exactly what happens to our buried emotional patterns and feelings.

We file away emotions in our solar plexus area (situated just above the belly button) where all the criticism we have ever received is stored. The solar plexus is an emotional storehouse and when combined with the sacral centre (the gut area) it allows emotions to affect our physical health. This is why disorders such as irritable bowel syndrome (IBS) are often associated with stress and anxiety. It is now widely recognised that there is a definite gut/brain connection and I often see clients with bowel and stomach disorders which relate to stress and anxiety. When we understand the emotional impact, it makes sense that the solar plexus and sacral centre can give a negative physical reaction.

The solar plexus also stores feelings of self-esteem and self-confidence, including logging insults and aggressiveness. In addition, it collects fear and rejection. Sensitivity to criticism always hits the gut area and feels like a punch in the stomach after an insult is received. Although it is an emotion, we can feel the physical effects instantly; effects which over time can cause real disorders such as ulcers, gallstones and stomach disorders. Mental and emotional triggers come in the form of:

- Feeling embittered, enraged and angry
- Feeling that the world is unjust, NOT fair, and disorderly
- Self-criticism – I don't deserve any better!
- Being afraid of other's opinions

The sacral centre is closely associated with our relationships, personal power, money, lack of self-esteem and self-confidence. It gives us feelings of lack of control and betrayal. These are destructive memories that go deep into the cells of the body and they provoke mental and emotional reactions such as:

- Excuses, frustration and anger
- Childhood blame
- Everyone/anyone else's fault but one's own
- Not living a dynamic life
- Not taking responsibility for oneself

Realistically, self-confirmation and self-respect can only come from within ourselves. When we continually seek respect from outside sources we lose energy, perpetuating a cycle of low self-esteem and self-worth.

Emotions are messages and they are the expression of how we feel. We can feel love, joy, sadness, pain and hurt within seconds of each other. As stated previously, it can be anything that triggers emotions, from a TV programme, a song, an excerpt from a film to a single word, and the emotion will be felt immediately from the memory.

Emotions affect our entire well-being and can cause anything from a heart attack to a cold sore! They create challenges, emotional disharmony, physical diseases and crisis in our lives. They affect how we perform physically and psychologically and indeed it is now acknowledged by the medical profession that a large percentage of our physical disorders have psychological roots.

In her book 'Molecules of Emotion', molecular biologist Candice Pert calls the mind 'some kind of enlivening energy in the information realm throughout the brain and body that enables the cells to talk to each other and the outside to talk to the whole organism.' From this, we deduce the mind to be located throughout the brain and body, not just above the neck. She sees the emotions as a connection between the mind and the body.

Likewise, scientists have demonstrated that the immune system has an intelligence of its own, yet they are still unsure why in some people the immune system chooses to fight a particular disease while another person gives in to it.

Emotional trauma

In the subconscious mind, there are often long-forgotten memories of emotional trauma buried within. Grief, the death of a loved one, even the loss of a pet or a favourite toy can cause impact upon our emotions. Emotions are registered in the vibrational field (aura) and in our electromagnetic body (the energy field that is close to physical body).

The mind can decide whether we heal or remain damaged, depending upon our emotional and physical state at that time.

If emotional trauma stems from an injury to the physical body, such as a broken arm, the memory of the shock and impact of the fall is held in the joint and the energy field (aura). Here, the memory is held in the body's cells. Although the joint heals and everything seems to be physically okay, the energy field may remain affected and the energy to that part of the body deteriorates over time. A holding or compensating pattern will ensue within the damaged muscles as the body tries to adapt, perhaps leading to a change in posture which creates weakness in the area and means that other joints and systems have to compensate for the imbalance.

Emotional shock is held in the physical body and as the mind and body have a connection (through the central energy system known as chakras), any shock will lodge itself in the physical, resulting in dis–ease and causing pain, discomfort and numbness. From my own clinical experience, we need to release energy blockages before physical healing can take place.

GENERAL ADVICE AND TREATMENTS

Rest

Rest is important while pregnant and as the pregnancy progresses it is a good idea to rest for an hour after lunch if possible. Listen to your body - it knows what is needed and what is best for you. Putting your feet up when you sit down helps with swelling in the legs and ankles.

Reflexology

Reflexology has been proved to help throughout pregnancy. A regular treatment during your pregnancy will be beneficial and will help to maintain homeostasis of the body (known as perfect balance).
Start with monthly treatments and increase the frequency in line with your midwife appointments to fortnightly and then weekly, relaxing and reducing stress for yourself and your baby. It is also helpful at the beginning of pregnancy with techniques to smooth the way when suffering morning sickness and nausea.

Reflexology also helps in preparing the body and activating the endocrine system for labour. Your Reflexologist, with the appropriate training, can prepare the body for labour if you are overdue and the baby is ready to arrive.

Cranio Sacral Therapy (CST)

CST is beneficial throughout pregnancy as it helps to keep the body aligned and to maintain good posture. It is a deep relaxing treatment that helps with stress and relaxation and is especially good for relieving Symphysis pubis discomfort.

Apart from preparing you for the arrival by opening up the pelvis, it is also useful to have a treatment after birth as it helps to realign the body. CST works with the nervous system and spine too, helping with the negative effects of epidurals and emotional blockages from the trauma of birth.

Baby will also benefit from a personal CST treatment after birth as it helps to relieve emotional trauma to the body such as is caused by the misalignment of bones, muscles, etc due to being in the cramped conditions in the womb and birth canal. It is especially recommended for children who experience births through Caesarean, forceps or vontau (suction or cap births). You can find out more about CST later on in Chapter 13.

Homeopathy

Homeopathy is recommended as a safe treatment for mother and baby. It is an ideal treatment as it is a gentle yet effective system of medicine.

Homeopathy uses 'remedies' which are given in the form of powders, small pills (about the size of rice grains) or liquids that are easy to take and more palatable than some conventional medicines. Remedies are made from plants, animal substances, minerals and salts which are diluted to such a high extent that few or no molecules remain in the medicine.

Homeopathy works on an energetic level stimulating the body's own natural healing, just like acupuncture, reflexology, Bowen and Cranio Sacral Therapy, Reiki and spiritual healing.

Remedy kits can be bought from a homeopath or direct from Helios Homeopathics. The latter are designed specifically for childbirth and include a booklet and 18 remedies. Basic kits and travelling kits are also available.

Please ensure that when you look for a therapist they are accredited and registered to a professional association such as:

- Association of Reflexologists
- The Society of Homeopaths
- Cranio Sacral Society or Cranio Sacral Association
- NHSTA - supports primary care groups/trusts

See appendix for contact details

BACH FLOWER REMEDIES

Bach Flower remedies are ideal to help adjust to life and are safe when pregnant. Use for pre and post-natal emotions.

- **Beech** is for intolerance
- **Crab apple** is a cleansing remedy which, during times when she is feeling bloated, helps a woman to feel whole again, to love and respect herself. It helps to remove feelings of self-loathing and disgust and is also useful for controlling nausea
- **Cherry plumb** is used when you feel out of control or imbalanced in life
- **Elm** is for apprehension, fear or foreboding
- **Gentian** helps you to think more positively and is used at times when you are suffering from feelings of disappointment, such as when you are coping with infertility issues or have experienced a miscarriage
- **Gorse** is used for lack of hope and is once again helpful for infertility and miscarriage
- **Impatiens** is for short temper, irritability or impatience and helps with dealing with infertility
- **Olive** is used for fatigue
- **Pine** helps with feelings of guilt or self-reproach and in dealing with back-lash and the unexpected. It is also useful for infertility and miscarriage
- **Mustard** is useful for depression or lowness in spirit and for infertility and miscarriage
- **Star of Bethlehem** can be used to buffer shock and trauma and is useful for infertility, miscarriage and post-natally for shock
- **White Chestnut** is helpful for worrying thoughts and agitation and is useful for infertility
- **Willow** helps with resentments and bitterness towards yourself or others
- **Walnut** is helpful for adjustment to change

[4] Helen Foster 'Health article 'Spilling the Beans' Sunday Express magazine - Article: 09.2007

[5] Sally Goddard Blythe, 'What Babies and Children Really Need' Hawthorn Press 2008 (ref:Ravell; GP and others 'Netherlands study' Obesity in young after famine exposure in utero and early infancy' New England journal of medicine 12/8/76:349-53)

[6] Cytoplan RDA 'folic acid' product information hand book; 2007

[7] Dian Shepperson Mills:'making babies the Nutritional recipe': Bio Care The Knowledge; issue 8: 2008

[8] Health library 'anemia definition- high risk pregnancy' – http://www.chkd.org/healthLibrary/Content.aspx?pageid=PO2428 (accessed May 2008)

[9] Health encyclopedia –NHS direct 'Anemia definition'
http://www.hhsdirect.nhs.uk/articles/article.aspx?Article ID=19 (cited-May 2008)

[10] Dr M Glenville: Biocare Infertility seminar; Nov 2008:'Low levels of Iron has been linked with low birth weight' SNSWGDP 1990 & Murphy 1986

[11] Ibid 'Iron deficiency anaemia' (Ref: Scimshaw 1991)

[12] Dr M Porter; 'Warding off infertility' Sainsbury magazine; Oct 2007

[13] Dr. M Porter; 'Health'; Sainsbury's magazine; Oct 2007

[14] Dr. U. Moberg 'Oxytocin Factor' p153; Da Capo Press, Cambridge: 2003

[15] NHS Direct 'Passive smoking' http://www.nhsdirect.nhs.uk/articles/article.aspx?articleId=1119 (cited 05/2008)

[16] NHS Direct 'Why I should not smoke around my children' http://www.nhsdirect.nhs.uk/articles/article.aspx?articleId=1119 (Cited 05/2008)

[17] NHS Direct 'Health questions' http://www.nhsdirect.nhs.uk/articles/article.aspx?articleId=1119 (cited 05/2008)

[18] Neways 'Product information leaflet' 2007

[19] Neways 'Bathroom product information' 2007

[20] BioCare:'Science of Probiotics' review (2008) p2 cl2/3 (ref 6/7/8)
(Ref: Drisko JA Giles C.K,Bischoff BJ. 'Probiotic in health maintenance and disease prevention' Alter Med Rev 2003 May:8 (2): 143-55 & Mackie Ri, Sghir A, Gaskins HR: Devel 'Microbial ecology of the neonatal gastrointestinal tract' AM J Clin Nutr. 1999; 69 (supp): 1035S-45S

[21] Ibid:'Science of Probiotics' review (2008) p2 cl2/3 (ref 9) (Ref; Rasic. J 'Bifidobacteria and diarrhoea controls in infants and young children') Intern Clin Nutr Review Jan 1992:

[22] Ibid 'Probiotic intervention in the first months of life' p2 cl2/3 (ref11) (Rinne M. Kalliomaki M, Salminen S and Isolari E (2006): 'Short term effects on gastrointestinal symptoms and long –term effects on gut microbiota' 2006 Journal of Paediatric Gastroenterology and Nutrition 43, 200 -205)

[23] Ibid 'Ecology of Candida albilcans gut colonisation' p2 cl2/3 (ref 14:Kennedy MJ. PA Volz 1985:'inhibition of Candida adhesion, colonisation and disseminating from the gastrointestinal tract by bacterial antagonism'. Infec. Immun. 49:654-663)

[24] Ibid 'Probiotics' p2 cl2/3 (Jennifer AJ. Madden, Susan F Plumer, James Tang, Iveta Garaiva and others. 'Effect of probiotics, on preventing disruption of the intestinal microflora, following antibiotic therapy'. A double blind study, placebo-controlled pilot study:2005)

[25] Ibid 'International Immuno-pharmacology' p2 cl2/3 (Ref15/16:   5 (2005) 1091-1097:

[26] The British Medical Association Family Health Encyclopaedia 'Vagus Nerve definition': British Library Cataloguing Data 1990:P1043:p2

Chapter 6

INDEX

Chapter 6

PROBLEMS IN PREGNANCY

In Chapter 6 we are going to explore the common problems that can be experienced during pregnancy and provide tips and information to help for a smooth pregnancy.

COMMON PROBLEMS IN PREGNANCY

Pregnancy is not an illness and should be a euphoric, happy time for all mums. The radiance (or glow), which accompanies pregnancy, is a feeling of deep emotional happiness and expectation. Women who are pregnant do, however, quite normally suffer some of the symptoms and disorders listed below, together with some general discomfort.

Some of the most common problems during pregnancy include:

- Morning sickness and nausea
- Inflammation of the Symphysis pubic
- Heartburn
- Cramp
- Heavy legs
- Round ligament tendonitis
- Constipation and gas
- Backache and/or sciatica
- Headaches
- Superficial Thrombophlebitis and varicose veins
- Carpal Tunnel syndrome
- Oedema
- Palpitations
- Recurrent cystitis and urinary tract infections
- IBS (Irritable bowel syndrome)

Other problems can occur during pregnancy, such as miscarriage, indigestion, circulatory leg pain and stretch marks, but in fact most of the issues that arise, are the result of hormonal changes within the mother's body. Nutritional deficiencies and weight distribution caused by sudden weight gain will also cause discomfort and strain on the body's systems.

Although many of the problems which are experienced by pregnant women are relatively minor, there are certain symptoms which are sometimes indicative of more serious issues and which need prompt attention, including:

- Vaginal bleeding
- Severe abdominal pain
- High fever of 37.8°C/100°F or above
- Absence of foetal movement for 24 hours from the 30th week of gestation
- Sudden swelling of the feet, ankles, face or hands/fingers
- Severe headache that won't go away

Should you experience any of these symptoms, you should take immediate action by resting in bed and contacting your doctor or calling an ambulance. If you do have to go to hospital, contact your clinic and inform them that this is happening.

ALCOHOL-RELATED ISSUES

Alcohol is recognised as the greatest single cause of birth defects worldwide. Drinking heavily throughout pregnancy (more than 80g or ten units of alcohol daily is equal to one bottle of wine) is firmly linked with Foetal Alcohol Syndrome (FAS), although not all women who drink heavily during pregnancy will automatically have a child suffering from FAS.

It was once believed that the placenta was a safe place, protected from the outside world and impervious to modern everyday poisons and toxins. Unfortunately, however, this is not the case and it is now understood that alcohol crosses the placenta barrier to the unborn child. Researchers have proved that as nutrients and oxygen flow across the placenta between mother and foetus, so too can harmful chemicals, such as ethanol, as well as infections. Essentially, whatever the mother ingests, the foetus will also receive and be affected by. This is why women need to look after themselves more carefully when they are pregnant. Perhaps it might seem obvious to say, but a good diet is essential and, because of recent findings and adverse effects on the growing child, drinking and smoking during pregnancy are not advised.

Alcohol is now seen as a dangerous drug, as it breaks down chemically to a cell-damaging compound, which is readily absorbed by the foetus. Whilst a small amount of alcohol will probably not cause any major ill effects, no safe level is as yet defined and the safest level would be to avoid alcohol altogether while pregnant. This is paramount in the first stage of pregnancy when the foetus is most vulnerable to alcohol's damaging effects.

In 1999, it was estimated by the Royal College of Obstetricians and Gynaecologists that FAS occurs in 3-5 of every 1,000 live births, but this figure may well be a gross underestimation today as drinking habits have increased in certain age groups[27]

FAS is a worldwide problem. In 2003 it was estimated that FAS affected 0.097% of live babies born each year. The UN estimates births for 2003 to be 128.6 million, which gives us the figure of 127,742 affected. This is comparable and, on occasion, greater than worldwide rates of Down Syndrome[28]

In addition, certain ethnic groups are seen to be biologically more susceptible. The common characteristics of FAS, which are found in babies include:

- Poor growth and low birth weight
- Small head – (known as microcephaly)
- Undeveloped brain, leading to persistent mental retardation
- Abnormal facial features
- Heart defects
- Cognitive impairment – from basic learning and attention to severe mental retardation

FOETAL ALCHOHOL SYNDROME (FAS) RESEARCH

A study, which was carried out in Italy in 2006, showed definite correlations between alcohol consumption and FAS and confirmed that these physical growth problems are indeed indicative. The study also found that women drinking just once a week produced children with a lower IQ. From their research they indicate that FAS is more prevalent than expected and that numbers in Western Europe and the USA are underestimated[29].

Through the unusual method of active research, which involved going out to look for signs in children at school and in the mainstream population, they picked up as many as three times more incidences than expected. In their opinion, the results from previous passive trials, which involved waiting for the results to show themselves later in life, underestimate those who really do suffer from the FAS disorder.

Their research also highlighted that many women thought drinking alcohol with a meal was considered to be all right. With alcoholic drinks now commonplace at meal times, the research considered the amounts drunk by Italian women while pregnant to be at binge levels, despite ingesting food at the same time. Their results show a population of damaged children because of this myth.

During a radio programme on Radio 4 which highlighted an FAS lecture due to take place in London in April 2009, one of the lecturers made the announcement that alcohol foetal syndrome is now linked with low-level crime and anti-social behaviour. Research carried out in the USA and Canada since the 1970s also found associations between 60% of low-level crime and FAS, linked to the fact that children born with this syndrome tend to behave impulsively and don't plan well.

Although not always recorded, many children are found to have milder forms of FAS, showing learning problems but no actual physical signs, but live births are not the only indicator of the damage that alcohol can cause. Evidence from research conducted in 1998 indicates that women drinking 5 units or less a week are seen to be twice as likely to conceive within 6 months as those who consume 10 units or more.

So, how much is safe? The jury is still out on this one, although research is now proving that heavy and binge drinking does have a detrimental effect upon the development of the foetus. The National Institute for Health and Clinical Excellence (NICE) 2008 guidelines in the UK however suggest[30] that:

- Pregnant women and women planning pregnancy should avoid drinking alcohol in the first three months of pregnancy if possible because it may be associated with an increased risk of miscarriage

- If women do choose to drink, they are advised to limit their intake to 1-2 UK units once or twice per week

Something that is well worth bearing in mind of course is that modern wine glasses are far larger than those in use 30 years ago. One modern wine glass is equal to 3 to 4 normal glasses of wine consumed in the 1960s. Think of the tiny sherry your Gran used to have! A UK 'unit' actually equals:

- One shot or 25ml spirits
- One half a pint of ordinary strength lager or beer
- One small (125ml) glass of wine is equal to 1.5 (UK units)

NICE suggest that at this low level there is currently no evidence of harm to the unborn baby, although there is uncertainty regarding an actual safe level of alcohol in pregnancy. 'No evidence', however, does not necessarily mean 'no risk'. In the USA, recommendations suggest NO alcohol consumption at all for women who are planning a pregnancy or during pregnancy. I personally believe that FAS is preventable with support and education.

A joint study of Russian and US researchers has announced that probiotics have been seen to reduce liver dysfunction from alcohol intake within a very short space of time[31]. Within literally just five days, by taking probiotics, we can allow the body to heal itself from the onslaughts of alcohol. This represents an excellent approach, which would reduce the effects upon the unborn infant without any harmful impacts.

Anaemia

Anaemia is a condition where there are too few red blood cells in the body or where the ability of the red blood cell to carry oxygen or iron is lowered. Tissue enzymes are dependent upon iron, and lack of iron will affect the cell function in nerves and muscles[32].

There are several types of anaemia and each one has a different cause. The most common cause is iron deficiency anaemia, where your body lacks enough iron to keep the red blood cells functioning properly[33]. Iron is the key component in haemoglobin, which carries and stores oxygen in the red blood cells. Other causes of anaemia are related to the lack of B12 or folic acid.

In pregnancy, a woman's blood volume increases by as much as 50% and of course the foetus uses the mother's blood cells for development and growth. Whether she is prone to anaemia or not is entirely down to the mother's reserves of red blood cells stored in her bone marrow. If she has good supplies, the body will be able to cope with the needs of the foetus. This drain on reserves is especially heightened during the third trimester.

Iron deficiency anaemia during pregnancy is quite common and can cause poor foetal growth, low birth weight and premature birth. While pregnant, your body needs extra iron to supply sufficient blood to the baby so that it receives all the oxygen and nutrients it needs while in the womb. It is essential, therefore, to ensure good nutrition before pregnancy to build up reserves, as well as during pregnancy.

A deficiency in vitamin B12 interferes with the body's ability to form red blood cells and enable protein synthesis. A diet which includes milk, eggs, poultry and meat can help to keep B12 supplies heightened. However, vegans (because they eat no animal foods), can become B12 deficient and are recommended to take B12 supplementation.

Blood loss experienced during and after labour and delivery can also cause anaemia. A vaginal delivery blood loss is normally about 500 millilitres, whilst a Caesarean delivery blood loss will be approximately 1,000 millilitres.

While some symptoms of anaemia may not be obvious, the most common ones to look out for are:

- Pale skin or lips
- Ringing in the ears
- Sore tongue and/or ulcers on the corners of the mouth
- Pale underside of eyelids
- Tiredness and fatigue
- Dizziness
- Headache
- Laboured breathing
- Increased heartbeat or palpations

Some symptoms of anaemia may resemble those attributable to other conditions so if in doubt it is always best to consult your doctor or midwife. Deficiency is tested with routine blood tests at 28, 32 and 36 weeks. These and other evaluation procedures are used to diagnose types of anaemia, such as haemoglobin levels and haematocrit, which is the measurement of red blood cells. Although the first routine blood test may not be carried out until 28 weeks into the pregnancy, some women may require iron supplementation earlier in pregnancy, from approximately 20 weeks.

In cases where anaemia is diagnosed, treatment will depend on the severity of the condition. The treatment is normally effective and rarely causes complications. However, iron deficiency anaemia will require supplementation. I recommend a liquid iron supplementation as this is absorbed into the body much quicker and tends to have fewer contra indications. Taking iron with citrus juice also helps with absorption but you do need to be careful when taking with antacids as these decrease absorption. It is also worth noting that some prescribed iron supplements can cause nausea and constipation, stools may become dark in colour (black or dark green in some cases).

Good nutrition is the key to helping prevent anaemia, both before and during pregnancy. For an iron-rich diet, see the suggestions below:

- Beef, pork, lamb and liver
- Black pudding
- Poultry
- Fish
- Greens - cabbage, kale, spinach, watercress
- Some cereals and bread have added iron, B vitamins and folic acid
- Bananas – high in iron and can stimulate the production of haemoglobin in the blood
- Dried apricots
- Beetroot
- Avocado

Bananas are also high in iron and they can stimulate the production of haemoglobin in the blood, which helps greatly in cases of anaemia. Make sure that you incorporate a banana a day into your diet. It is also believed that drinking port wine or eating grapefruit three times a week helps to reduce the symptoms of anaemia.

You can find more information on iron later in this chapter when we talk about minerals and EFA's.

Amniotic fluid

Amniotic fluid is the fluid that surrounds the baby in the womb. It is formed mainly with water from the time of formation and fertilization at around two weeks. The fluid contains proteins, urea, electrolytes and carbohydrates, which support foetal growth.

The fluid volume increases with foetus growth and, although continually replaced, it is being constantly swallowed, inhaled and urinated in by the foetus. 'Breathing' the fluid in the womb helps formation of the lungs and the fluid also protects the baby within the mother, cushioning it from any blows or bumps that the mother may encounter.

The amniotic fluid is what drains from the mother's body when labour begins and her 'water breaks'. This is also referred to as spontaneous rupture of the membranes (SROM). Although most babies are born healthy in the majority of cases, too little amniotic fluid can result in underdeveloped lungs, clubbed feet or hands.

Using ultrasound, medics will detect the amount of amniotic fluid and foetal growth. Amniotic fluid is also used to detect the health of the foetus, often taken from the mother's abdomen to check genetic health irregularities early in pregnancy. The fluid contains foetal cells and is used in modern science to detect genetic disorders.

Backache and Sciatica

Poor posture is very common during pregnancy. The lack of the hormone progesterone causes the muscles to relax and in turn tends to shift the mother's centre of gravity, making the pelvic sacro-iliac joint unstable.

Cranio Sacral Therapy and reflexology treatments benefit the mother by helping to rebalance the endocrine (hormonal) system and realign sacrum and iliac. Both treatments will help stimulate new blood and tonicity to back muscles and with Cranio Sacral Therapy, the head and the sacrum energy would be rebalanced and restored via the energy link through the spine.

Cramps

Cramps are caused by electrolyte imbalances and nutritional deficiencies, together with the extra strain on the legs caused by weight gain during pregnancy. Elevation of the legs above the head will help the lymphatic system to drain more easily (lie on the bed with your feet on the head-board for a few minutes daily) and taking extra calcium and potassium to improve nutrition will also benefit. Bananas, almonds, salmon and sesame seeds are all excellent sources.

Supplements such as biochemical tissue salts, often known as Schussler salts, taken regularly will also help. Three grams taken twice a day for one week will produce a noticeable reduction of cramp. Tissue salts are not mineral salts in the usual sense. Working in a biochemical sense, they are potentiated through dilution and directly nourish the cells in the organism giving the mineral greater effectiveness by combining acid and alkaline elements.

Cystitis

Cystitis is known as an inflammation of the urinary tract and is more commonly found in females. It can occur in adults and children alike and even babies have been known to suffer from it.

The symptoms of cystitis include a burning sensation when passing urine and discomfort in the groin and abdominal area. In severe cases, kidney pain and even bleeding may occur when urinating. Urine is dark and an odour may be present.

One common cause of cystitis is heavy protein consumption from eating a lot of meat. This creates an acidic environment, which causes more crystallised particles in the bladder. Infections can also be picked up through your partner during sexual intercourse. Structural abnormalities in the kidneys or bladder can be another cause as these allow bacteria to migrate through the urinary system, so causing repeated infections. Women who are low in iron have also been found to be susceptible to recurrent bacterial infection. Additionally, pregnancy and childbirth can weaken the bladder valve, which makes it easier for the urethra to become infected. In this latter case, thrush is also a symptom.

There are certain things that you can do to help prevent cystitis, and here are some useful tips:

- Urinate after sexual intercourse, as this helps to prevent recurrent cystitis
- Use a bidet frequently to wash the crotch area. Use a cotton face cloth to bathe the area
- Avoid bubble bath and concentrated products. Avoid soap in the crotch area
- Make sure that the tampons or towels that you use are of natural ingredients, as some products have been known to contain formaldehyde

Tights have been linked to cystitis, especially if worn with tight-fitting jeans or trousers, and wearing stockings is often a better alternative. Also, only wear garments which are made from natural products such as cotton or wool and stick to loose-fitting clothes to improve ventilation around the crotch. Nylon especially should be avoided next to the vaginal area and any underwear, which is made from synthetic materials should have a cotton gusset.

If you do find yourself suffering from the discomfort of cystitis, here are some suggestions to try:

- Drinking cranberry juice is known to help reduce symptoms as it acts as an anti-adhesive, which stops the bacteria sticking to the bladder surface and other membranes. Drinking 80-100ml per day, twice a day, will help to prevent recurrent disorders
- Milk will also dilute the acid. I took this myself as a drink when I suffered cystitis in my early wedding days. A glass of warm milk and a hot water bottle or a hot wheat bag does the trick in soothing the area and relaxing the muscles
- Drinking barley water is also good for soothing symptoms
- Consider probiotics after repeated antibiotic use. You will need to take longer courses if recurrent attacks occur frequently and you can also use probiotics for bouts of thrush

Making the urine less concentrated and diluting the acid within the bladder is the key to controlling the symptoms of cystitis, so the more you clear and dilute the better. The golden rule is to drink plenty of plain water rather than soft drinks and tea, but how long the symptoms last will of course depend upon the concentration of proteins. As in many things, prevention of cystitis is better than cure, so try to limit your animal protein intake to prevent recurring disorders. A short cut is to take alkalising supplements such as Alfalfa and liquid Chlorophyll for a week to help dilute any build up of acid.

Diet changes

If you are prone to cystitis, there are other diet changes that you might want to consider too, such as avoiding alcohol and sugar as well as high levels of meat. Get your protein instead from vegetable sources such as soya, pulses, beans and Quinoa. Having a good immune system helps to fight infection, and by eating more alkaline foods such as vegetables and fruit, you can reduce the acid within your body and achieve the right pH balance.

Although doctors will normally prescribe antibiotics to treat cystitis, there is also a range of homeopathic remedies available to treat those of all ages who are suffering from cystitis and thrush. Cantharis 6c, for example, can be taken 2 hourly to begin with and then 3 times a day.

In addition, reflexology helps to activate, clear and soothe the kidney, bladder and lower back, to relax muscle areas and rebalance the metabolic equilibrium. Firm massage around the lower back is also beneficial.

A 'Sitz' bath is something else that you could try to help alleviate the symptoms of cystitis, and in this case it is used to stimulate the nerves which supply the bladder. The Sitz bath should be cold and deep enough to immerse the bottom completely and the water used to wash over the groin area. Drop into it seconds after urinating (30-60 seconds) or during a morning wash. Initially you will feel shock as the cold water hits the area, followed by numbness and then tingling and the effects should last for up to two hours. Although beneficial, it is not a quick fix, with improvements only being felt over several weeks. It can, however, be repeated up to four times a day.

Diabetes

Women who have insulin dependent diabetes tend to be more at risk during all stages of pregnancy. In addition to this, they also have a higher risk of miscarriage or of giving birth to children with birth defects.

Ectopic pregnancy

Ectopic pregnancy can be common in some women, especially in their first pregnancy. An ectopic pregnancy means that the embryo develops outside the womb and usually in the fallopian tubes. When this happens, it will cause stretching of the fallopian tubes as the embryo develops, the woman can feel abdominal pain and bleeding can occur in the abdomen.

The women who are most at risk of an ectopic pregnancy are those:

- With a history of pelvic infection
- Who use a contraceptive coil
- Who have experienced a previous ectopic pregnancy

To correct an ectopic pregnancy may, in some cases, require surgery, or sometimes drugs are used to end the pregnancy. Surgery may result in the loss of an affected tube which can of course affect fertility and further pregnancies.

Fallopian tube dysfunctions are often caused by blockages from chronic inflammation in the tubes. Damage to the tubes can cause infertility as the egg and sperm have no contact.

Heartburn

Heartburn can be a frequent occurrence during pregnancy and it happens because the expanded size of the uterus affects the stomach flow of fluids into the oesophagus. To help avoid heartburn, you are advised to eliminate the following from your diet:

- Soda
- Antacids
- Alcohol
- Spicy foods
- Greasy foods

Regular treatment of reflexology will help to reduce heartburn, clear blockages and relax the digestive organs. In addition, the homeopathic remedy 'Nat phos' is a godsend after a meal. Peppermint and fennel tea are also effective in reducing heartburn.

Insomnia

Insomnia is common during the last weeks of pregnancy and often results from deficiencies of vitamin B, magnesium or calcium absorption in the latter stages. It is also acknowledged that emotional changes in pregnancy contribute to insomnia and disturbed sleep.

Taking the homeopathic treatment, Mag phos, will assist relaxation and encourage sleep. Cranio Sacral Therapy meanwhile will work on the emotional, mental and physical areas and Bach flower remedies on emotional and mental issues.

Morning sickness

Morning sickness is often the first sign of pregnancy and it can occur even before the woman suspects that she is pregnant. Fifty per cent of women experience it at between six and twelve weeks of pregnancy. In some cases it happens regularly in the morning, whilst in others it occurs at any time of the day. For some women, the feelings of queasiness or nausea can remain throughout the course of the entire day.

The symptoms of morning sickness usually improve as the pregnancy progresses and become less evident in the third or fourth month. It is quite usual for the mother to be affected during the first few weeks, but for some the effects can last throughout the duration of the pregnancy. It is worth remembering, however, that this somewhat unstable time can also be due to:

- Drugs
- Toxicity
- Pancreatitis
- Bowel disorders
- B6 deficiency

Multiple pregnancies carry a higher risk of sickness. High levels of chronic Gonadotrophoin (a hormone imbalance) can occur due to the presence of cysts in the uterus or multiple pregnancies.

It is thought that morning sickness is a defence mechanism to protect the mother from potential toxins in food, which might damage the baby, especially those that tend to have a strong or bitter taste. In support of this, it is believed that women who have morning sickness are much less likely to suffer a miscarriage. Some of the foods, which typically provoke sickness, are alcohol, caffeine and spicy foods.

The effects of morning sickness can become severe when the condition lasts throughout the pregnancy and can lead to dehydration, acidosis, malnutrition and weight loss. Since the Thalidomide tragedy in the 1960s, medication against sickness in pregnancy is not recommended, but there are certain home remedies which can offer some relief.

My recommendations include:
- Peppermint or raspberry leaf tea - since peppermint is known to calm feelings of nausea
- Eating regularly - every few hours to keep blood sugar levels up
- Fresh ginger infused as a tea to calm digestion, or alternatively there are capsule forms of ginger
- Snacking on bananas between meals keeps blood sugar levels up and helps to avoid the feelings of nausea and morning sickness

Eating bland foods such as crackers and dry toast can also help and it is handy to keep these at the side of the bed to eat before you get up. A few grapes first thing also helps as it raises the blood sugar level and you can also try:

- Pasta
- Rice
- Potatoes (without butter)
- Vegetables
- Soups – non-spicy are best

Iron is also known to cause nausea in some cases, so if you are taking iron supplements consult your doctor.

In addition to the drinks and foodstuffs that we have already mentioned, there are also certain supplements and treatments which can help with morning sickness. The following can be taken daily to help reduce symptoms:

- Vitamin B6 - 50mg every 4 hours
- Magnesium - 400mg upon rising
- L Methionine - 1000 mg daily

Reflexology, a safe, non-invasive treatment which helps to calm and relax the body, is known to help with pregnancy and infertility and is especially helpful with morning sickness. In addition, it:

- Regulates bowel and bladder movement
- Alleviates headaches and balances the hormones
- Reduces stress and anxiety

If you do decide to use reflexology, be sure to choose a professional accredited therapist who has been trained in pregnancy techniques.

Digestion and hormones are the key areas to treat in reducing pregnancy sickness symptoms. I have treated many women with reflexology during their first months of pregnancy, helping the body to settle during the initial hormonal adjustment for pregnancy.

As we mentioned previously, being sick, especially if this happens three or four times a day, can dehydrate the body, so it is important to drink plenty of fluids. Sometimes, when we lose more fluid than we can put back, we start to lose weight and begin to experience the symptoms of dehydration, including:

- Light headedness
- Dizziness on standing up
- Passing very little urine - often the urine is cloudy or darker in colour

Aim to have eight to ten glasses of water a day. Juice is also good as it helps with blood sugar levels, and herbal teas such as fennel or ginger can be soothing too.

Oedema - swelling of hands, legs and feet

In pregnancy, there is a tendency to retain fluid. Whilst this can be caused by dehydration, the most common cause is increased fluid as a result of increased oestrogen in the body. Oedema can be the first sign of toxaemia and serious complications, which lead to eclampsia.

Pre-eclampsia is a hypertensive disorder and is a major cause of both foetal and maternal mortality. A number of studies have shown an inverse association between calcium intake and the incidence of hypertension. In other words, low calcium uptake can cause hypertension. (See section below)

I have found that treatment by reflexology and lymph drainage will help to reduce the swelling, and lymphatic drainage alone can give rapid results. Drinking at least eight glasses of still water per day is necessary to prevent dehydration that can be common in many individuals.

PRE-ECLAMPSIA

Pre-eclampsia is the most common of the dangerous disorders during pregnancy and is a hypertensive disorder. Only one out of every one hundred pre-eclampsia cases goes on to develop serious complications called eclampsia, a major cause of both foetal and maternal mortality.

Pre-eclampsia is usually diagnosed when a pregnant women develops high blood pressure of 140/90 or more, although some women will suffer high blood pressure alone, without symptoms of pre-eclampsia. This is known as pregnancy-induced hypertension (PIH) or gestational hypertension. Both cases are seen as serious conditions in pregnancy and it is believed that one in five women will go on to have pre-eclampsia if they suffer high blood pressure[34].

It is normally diagnosed when two of the symptoms of the condition occur together, such as high blood pressure and pains in the abdomen and, if this is detected, you may be admitted to hospital where more tests will be carried out. These include:

- Continual blood pressure checks every 4-6 hours
- Urine samples taken daily to check protein levels
- Ultrasound scan to check blood flow through the placenta
- Foetal heart monitoring using a CTG (cardiotocograph)

Pre–eclampsia can develop at any stage of pregnancy, although early onset from just twenty weeks is seen as rare. Symptoms usually occur in the second or third trimester, or after week 32 into pregnancy, and can continue for up to six weeks after the birth (known as postpartum pre-eclampsia). It is most common in the last three months of pregnancy and the first 48 hours after birth.
Women are pre-disposed to, or more likely to suffer from pre-eclampsia if:

- It is a first pregnancy
- There is a genetic link – family history of the condition
- Pre-eclampsia occurred in previous pregnancies - approximately 20% of affected women will have pre-eclampsia in subsequent pregnancies

- The mother is a teenager or over the age of 35
- It is a multiple birth, such as twins or triplets
- The mother is obese or overweight

In addition, it is more likely to occur if you already have a medical disorder pre-pregnancy, such as:

- Kidney disease
- Diabetes
- Migraines
- High blood pressure

Mild forms of pre–eclampsia affect 1 in 14 women and do not always need treatment. Some women will just need more regular checkups, while others are controlled with drugs to lower blood pressure, although this does not actually cure the condition[35].

Pre-eclampsia can be confused with other diseases:
- Chronic hypertension
- Renal disease
- Primary seizure
- Swelling of limbs and ankles (common in pregnant women and may be due to a less worrying cause)

The cause of pre-eclampsia is not fully understood and there is no known cure for the disorder other than birth, although the condition can be managed with hospital treatment. Although it is a disorder associated with significant amounts of protein in the urine (called proteinuria), researchers have found high levels of the hormone activin A in the blood stream of women suffering from pre-eclampsia.
Some researchers believe there may be a link to substances in the placenta which may cause endothelial dysfunction in the maternal blood vessels of some women i.e: inadequate blood supply to the placenta allowing chemicals and hormones to be released and leading to endothelium damage. It is also thought that the placenta could become underdeveloped due to a problem within the blood vessels of the placenta itself[36]. Links have, in addition, shown to be from

a shallowly implanted placenta, which becomes hypoxic, or oxygen deficient[37].

It is possible that women with higher baselines of inflammation, stemming from chronic conditions such as high blood pressure or an autoimmune disease, may have less tolerance for the inflammatory burden of pregnancy. This is thought to stem from the maternal immune system's response to the placenta, i.e. the mother's immune system lacks tolerance to the placenta and foetus[38]. Low levels of selenium have also been associated with higher incidence of pre-eclampsia[39].

The main sign of pre-eclampsia is slower growth of the foetus compared to the normal rate and this will often be due to poor blood supply from the placenta to the baby. Called intra-uterine growth restriction, there will also be lower levels of nutrients and oxygen received by the baby via the placenta.

The symptoms of Pre-eclampsia

Pre-eclampsia symptoms will be more instantly recognisable by the mother, and are:

- Oedema - swelling or sudden swelling in hands, face and feet
- Pitting oedema, which leaves an indentation when pressed and should be reported immediately
- Circulation problems which show up as high blood pressure
- Protein in the urine
- Fluid retention
- Nausea and vomiting
- Severe headaches
- Excessive weight gain
- Vision problems such as seeing flashing lights and blurring

Should you develop any of the above, you should seek medical advice immediately.

Figures for the UK estimate that pre-eclampsia is responsible for 7-10 maternal deaths and the loss of as many as 1,000 babies every year[40].

Eclampsia, as we have mentioned, is a rare complication, which is considered serious and usually occurs late in pregnancy or post partum (just after the birth of the baby). It will normally include convulsions, seizures and even coma, and symptoms such as high blood pressure and oedema (pre-eclampsia) may occur before the onset of eclampsia.

Further complications can also develop in the form of HELLP syndrome, a combined liver and blood clotting disorder, which is estimated to affect 1 in 5 women who suffer from pre-eclampsia. The condition is characterised by:

- The breakdown of blood cells (known as (H) haemolytic anaemia)
- Elevated liver enzymes (EL)
- Low platelet count (LP) which can lead to kidney or lung problems

Management of the symptoms of pre-eclampsia is paramount during pregnancy and all attempts will be made to lower blood pressure until after 36 weeks. In addition:

- Rest is necessary
- Medication to lower blood pressure, such as calcium, channel blockers and/or anticonvulsant drugs will be prescribed
- Hospital admission will be recommended to monitor medication, rest and so on

These measures do not cure pre-eclampsia, but they do help to hold the symptoms in check.

Research and Pre-eclampsia

Whilst the research into pre-eclampsia is ongoing, some recent studies have shown that certain vitamins and minerals do make a difference.

The Medical Research Council (MRC) has revealed, for example, that giving women with pre-eclampsia injections of magnesium sulphate (the same chemical as in Epsom salts) has halved their risk of developing eclampsia.

As we mentioned previously, a number of studies have also shown an inverse association between calcium intake and the incidence of hypertension. Pregnant women with pre-eclampsia were given 2g of calcium daily which resulted in a fall in blood pressure and has been demonstrated to work effectively[41]. New research suggests that antioxidants contained in vitamins C and E, together with Selenium and Lycopene, can reduce the chance of pregnant women developing pre-eclampsia.

Treatment by manual lymph drainage (MLD) has proved to be successful in the later stages of pregnancy. The treatment was able to reduce oedema considerably, allowing the mother to feel more comfortable and able to cope at home instead of having to be admitted to hospital. Body brushing helps with the earlier stages to avoid the build up of oedema and correcting levels of magnesium can also help to avoid pre-eclampsia. Also check with your homeopathic practitioner for pre-eclampsia remedies.

As the only medical cure for the condition is to deliver the baby and placenta as soon as possible, in serious cases it may be necessary to deliver the baby early. In fact, pre-eclampsia is the cause of approximately 15% of premature births[42]. The preferred birth delivery is by Caesarean or C-section, which is done by an incision in the mother's abdomen.

I for one, however, have treated women with MLD for the condition, helping them to avoid hospital stays, reducing blood pressure and symptoms overall.

Placenta disorders

Sometimes, the placenta can move from the uterine wall, something which is known as placenta praevia. This means that the placenta has moved partially or fully over the cervix. It is classed as being dangerous for the foetus when labour takes place, because the placenta effectively blocks the entrance to the cervix and prevents a normal birth.

In this position it can also cause bleeding, known as abruptio placentae. If the placenta detaches from the uterine wall it will bleed, and blood will build up until it escapes through the cervix. When this occurs, bed rest is the only option, although severe abruption is classed as a medical emergency and the mother may need a blood transfusion.

Ultrasound is used to detect the position of the placenta and monitoring will take place on a regular basis during pregnancy, if and when this disorder occurs. An elective C-section or induction is the normal delivery option.

Stretch marks

Stretch marks appear as wavy stripes on the abdomen, buttocks, breasts and thighs and are caused by rapid weight gain. Basically, the skin overstretches and fibres in the deep layers tear. Once they appear, they are permanent but will become less noticeable over time.

Vitamin E and vitamin A cream, or base oil such as sunflower oil (consult an Aromatherapist to determine which is right for you) used on the skin daily during the whole of your pregnancy will help to reduce stretch marks. One person I know used Aloe Vera gel and it worked well for her, reducing the stretch marks considerably.

Regular supplementation of zinc also helps skin formation, as does a balanced diet rich in omega oils. Regular exercise will enable better circulation as well as reducing varicose veins in legs, which may appear later in life.

Thrush

Many women suffer from thrush (Candidiasis) while pregnant. It often occurs at this time due to less acidic flora caused by the hormones produced during pregnancy. This encourages candida ablicans, normally present in the gut and vagina in small numbers, and taking antibiotics knocks out good bacteria allowing the candida ablicans to flourish. For full information on candida, please refer to Infertility section.

Good personal hygiene is essential when suffering from thrush. Ensure that you wipe your region from front to back when passing a stool, as this helps to reduce infection. Bathe regularly and keep your vulva clean and dry. Although today many of us seem to prefer to shower rather than use a bath, I believe that having regular baths two or three times a week helps to clear infection as well as to maintain a healthy vulva area.

Scented soaps and bubble baths should be avoided when suffering from thrush. Instead, a few drops of vinegar or a weak solution of cider vinegar should be added to the bath water to relieve symptoms. I like to use salt in the bath to help clear any troubling symptoms and I also use tea tree oil, although the latter should not be used while pregnant*.

Yoghurt can also be used to balance the body's bacteria and a supplement of probiotics will help rebalance from within. Some diet changes are also advisable. Yeast products should be avoided and you should cut down on sugar, alcohol and fizzy drinks as these will cause aggravation. Again, you can find out more about this in the section on candida in Chapter 7.

As when dealing with cystitis, avoid wearing tights and choose cotton underwear and loose-fitting clothes as opposed to tight trousers or jeans, as these allow more air around the area.

*Oils are restricted while pregnant, and it is now suggested that they be avoided in pregnancy.

TAKING MEDICATION WHILE PREGNANT

Many prescribed and over-the-counter medications have side effects, some of which may be harmful during pregnancy, with their short-term benefits masking the long-term risks to the unborn foetus.
Some of the medications, which have been highlighted in previous research are:

- Anticonvulsants (used for seizures) – linked to heart defects
- Migraine drugs - linked to risk of premature birth
- Pain killers – have been found to interfere with blood clotting*
- Anti-inflammatory drugs – linked to blood clotting dysfunctions*
- Even Paracetamol has been known to cause problems, with natural elimination being slow

*Some drugs such as Aspirin, ibuprofen and NSAIDs (anti-inflammatory drugs) have also been found to hinder the production of hormones towards the end of pregnancy. By obstructing and hindering the important hormones, which help and stimulate labour, these medications can therefore extend delivery time[43].

Using Recreational drugs while pregnant

While pregnant, it is vital that the mother leads a healthy lifestyle. After all, even pregnancy follows the old adage that 'what you put in is what you get out'.

Most of the foetus' systems are formed within the first ten weeks of conception. During this period of development, some drugs and alcohol in particular can cause malformations of organs such as the heart, limbs and facial features. After the tenth week, the foetus grows rapidly in size and at this stage taking drugs could affect the development of the nervous system and eyes, with continued drug use potentially causing miscarriage or premature birth.

For a pregnant woman, drug abuse is doubly dangerous. Not only does it harm the mother's own health, but it also interferes with the development of the foetus. Recreational drugs such as cocaine, smoking and even excess alcohol can have severe effects upon the growing foetus.

Children exposed to recreational drugs can, in addition, be affected by many other potentially harmful influences. Heavy drinking, smoking, poor maternal nutrition, serious mental health problems in mothers and no parental care can all have serious, if not fatal, consequences.

Cocaine, including crack and methamphetamine (speed or ice), albeit that they are known as recreational drugs, are powerful stimulants of the central nervous system. Although research on cocaine has produced mixed results, it has revealed effects on the foetus similar to those caused by smoking, which include:

- Low birth weight
- Dangerous birth complications in which the placenta separates from the uterus prematurely (known as placental abruption)
- Damage to internal organs of the foetus

It has, in addition, been linked with causing severe malformations of the foetus and also causes damage to the baby's brain[44]. Researchers have in fact been almost unanimous in their findings that children exposed to cocaine in the womb have:

- Lower IQ scores
- More learning, emotional and behaviour problems

Another effect of cocaine is that it suppresses the mother's appetite and exerts drastic forces on her body, causing:

- Blood vessels to constrict
- The heart to beat faster
- The potential for blood pressure to soar
- Miscarriage
- Premature labour
- Abruptio placentae – the partial separation of the placenta from the uterus wall which causes bleeding

If drugs are taken late in pregnancy, then the baby becomes drug dependent and when born will suffer withdrawal symptoms such as:

- Tremors
- Sleeplessness
- Muscle spasms
- Suckling difficulties

Some experts also believe that learning difficulties will develop later.

Cigarettes can have the same biological effects as cocaine since nicotine and cocaine have similar effects upon the brain and circulatory system, although the effects of nicotine are weaker.

Marijuana is often used with other drugs such as tobacco and alcohol and is associated with low birth weight and pre-term delivery. Although many women do not see the harm in continuing to smoke while pregnant, the total harm caused is, in effect, parallel to the more harmful substances such as cocaine and marijuana. Clearly the message is to avoid both cigarettes and recreational drugs per se.

More powerful substances such as heroin give a higher risk of premature birth and can lead to birth problems such as[45]:

- Breathing difficulties
- Hypoglycaemia – low blood sugar
- Inter-cranial haemorrhage - bleeding from the head

PCP (phencyclidine), also known as angel dust, has been found to cause alternating lethargy and tremors in children born to mothers who take this substance.

By injecting herself with narcotics, the mother runs a high risk of contracting HIV virus from dirty needles. Apart from developing AIDS, she will also pass on the virus to her unborn baby.

Babies born to mothers who take narcotics will also suffer withdrawal symptoms having become just as dependent on drugs as the mother. The physical effects on the baby are:

- Diarrhoea
- Vomiting
- Joint stiffness
- Irritability

Organic solvents used as inhalants may also cause birth defects. Links have been found between at least one inhaled substance, Toluene, and birth defects. Toluene is widely used in paints and glues and has been found to cause malformations similar to those produced by alcohol[46].

As well as avoiding recreational drugs and narcotics during pregnancy, therefore, it is also best to avoid inhaling paint fumes and other chemical substances.

SCREENING AND TESTING

Modern day technological equipment often begins with military applications. Its use for humanitarian purposes invariably comes as a later by-product.

Ultrasonography machines (USG) were used in the Second World War to detect submarines. In the mid 1950s, a Scottish doctor by the name of Dr Ian Donald pioneered the same technology for medical use. Ultrasound was first used to detect tumours and later used for scanning babies in utero, thereby revolutionising obstetrics.

Nowadays ultrasound is often used for two purposes:

1. A routine scan at 18-20 weeks of pregnancy checks both size and integrity to discover the expected due date

2. To investigate any problems in pregnancy

The machine sends sound waves through the body and reads the reflected echoes as 'pictures' and some mothers notice that the foetus shows increased movement for a considerable time following the scan.

Mothers 'at risk' will tend to have more than the normal number of scans and ultrasound examinations. Although considered safe, some are questioning (in some cases) the excessive use of the ultrasound machine. Long-term studies have yet to be researched as it will need generations of children to decide.

In 2002, a report on the safety of ultrasound did express concern. 'Until long-term effects can be evaluated across generations, caution should be exercised when using this modality during pregnancy.'[47] Our children are becoming more and more sensitive to electromagnetic screening and testing. Mothers are telling me that they know it is affecting their children when screening is being done and these children don't like it. In most cases, mums know better than anyone else what their children need. Is this the baby's way of letting mum know that they want it to be more natural?

This also begs the question, 'Are we doing the right thing by giving our mothers drugs during pregnancy and labour?' Some drugs are known to pass through the placenta to the baby! What long-term effects do they have on the newborn child? After all, fifty years ago smoking was considered a healthy practice!

[27] Royal college of Obstetricians and Gynaecologists: 'FAS stats' Bio Med publications Ltd 1999

[28] Foetal Alcohol Syndrome: Diagnosis, Epidemiology, Prevention, and Treatment, NYU 19/07/2004 (http://www.bbc.co.uk/dna/h2g2/A2788563-1996 (cited 04.2010.)

[29] Robert J Sokol MD: 'Alcoholism clinical & experimental research' Italian study 27.08.2006: hhtp://wwweurekalert.org/pub_rleases/2006-08/ace-fis082106.php (cited 07.2008)

[30] NICE 'Drinking in pregnancy guidelines' 03.2008 http://www.nhs/news/2008/03March/Pages/pregnancydrinkinglimits.aspx (cited 07.2008)

[31] Dr.M. Grenville PhD: BioCare seminar 11.2008: "Women warned to avoid alcohol when trying to conceive" Jenson TK et al 1998 (BMJ 1998:317,7157,505-10)

[32] Health Library Article 'High risk pregnancy – common types of anemia' http://www.chkd.org/HealthLibrary /content.aspx?pageid-PO2428 (cited 05.2008)

[33] NHS direct 'Health encyclopedia Anemia' http://www.nhsdiect.nhs.uk/articles/article.aspx?ArticleID=19 (cited 05.2008)

[34] NHS Direct 'Health encyclopedia Preeclampsia' http://www.nhsdirect.nhs.uk/articles/article.aspx?articleIdID=431&sectionID=1 0 (cited 05.2008)

[35] NHS direct – 'pre-eclampsia' http://www.nhsdirect.nhs.uk/articles/article.aspx?ArticleID=431 (cited May 2008)

[36] NHS Direct 'complications of pre-eclampsia' http://www.nhsdirect.nhs.uk/articles/article.aspx?ArticleID=431&sectionId=10 (cited 05.2008)

[37] 'Pre-eclampsia Epidemiology- http://en.wikipedia.org/wiki/Pre-eclampsia 'postpartum pre-eclampsia late onset' BMJ 2005:331:1070-1071(5th Nov) doi:10.1136/bmj.331.7524.1070 (Cited 05.2008)

[38] Free encyclopedia Wikipedia 'Pre-eclampsia causes' :http://en.wikipedia.org.wiki/Pre-eclampsia p2 (cited 05.2008)

[39] Dr.M Glenville PhD. BioCare seminar Nov 2008 (Ref: Rayman MO, Bode P. Redman CW 2003 'Low selenium status is associated with the occurrence of pregnancy disease pre-eclampsia in women form the UK'. AMJ Obsete. Gynecol 189(5):1343-9 doi.:10.1067/S000-9378 (03) 000723-3PMID 1463-4566.)

[40] Health encyclopaedia NHS Direct 'Pre-eclampsia' http://www.nhsdirect.nhs.uk/articles/article.aspx?articleIdID=431 (Cited 05.2008)

[41] Bio Med 'Pre-eclampsia' newsletter issue 18 Sept.1998: (Ref:Viller et al1987 & Belizan 1991)

[42] NHS Direct 'Pre-eclampsia treatment' http://www.nhsdirect.nhs.uk/articles/article.aspx?articleIdID=431&sectionId=11 (cited 05.2008)

[43] 'Drugs and pregnancy' American council for drug education 1999: http:// www.acde.org/parent/Pregnant.htm (cited 09.2007)

[44] American council for drug educators 'taking drugs while pregnant' 1999 cited at http://www.acde.org (cited 09.2007)

[45] Ibid 'Drugs and pregnancy' 1999–p3 http://www.acde.org/parent/Pregnant.htm (cited 09.2007)

[46] Ibid 'Drugs and pregnancy' 1999–p3 http://www.acde.org/parent/Pregnant.htm (cited 09.2007)

[47] Sally Goddard Blythe, 'What Babies and Children Really Need' Hawthorn Press 2008, Stroud, Glos.UK. 2008, (p37/38 Early development)

Chapter 7

INDEX

Chapter 7

PSYCHOLOGICAL ISSUES DURING PREGNANCY

I have treated many individuals with birth trauma issues, and in fact some people can become stuck in life as a result of birth trauma, the problem often following them into adulthood.

Although many people are not of aware of this fact, birth trauma can lead to both physical and emotional difficulties. Dyslexia, Dyspraxia, skeletal pain, low thyroid function, headaches and migraines can all be indicative of birth trauma. Together with emotional conditions like anxiety and fear, claustrophobia, anorexia, aversion to being touched or even discomfort from clothing around the neck can also be associated with the birth process.

There is also a link with drug addicts and birth trauma, where the individual wants to dull the senses. Birth trauma can often be traced back to drugs prescribed to the mother during childbirth.

Strong emotions

As the baby moves through the birth canal, the umbilical cord is squeezed, temporarily shutting off the supply of oxygen and nutrients. When the cord is cut too soon, there can be a period when the infant receives no oxygen, giving a feeling of suffocation to the newborn. If the first breath is hampered or delayed and the right to life impaired, it is logged in the emotional memory and may be triggered in future events when breathing or shortness of breath is an issue, such as in the case of panic or anxiety attacks.

Emotional consciousness is recorded from within the womb, with all the mother's experiences being received. Every sound and feeling is logged, the information unfiltered and accepted as if they were the child's own thoughts and feelings.

Every mum has a psychological effect on her growing foetus. How a mother feels when she is pregnant, as well as the birth experience itself, can cause good, happy, positive vibrations or lasting problems for the child. The attitude of the mother, position in birth, a sound, odour and even the absence of the mother's consciousness because of drugs or medication are taken in by the child. In later life, any of these things can act as triggers and prompt the recall of strong emotions, such as those which might have been experienced by the parents or attending staff during delivery.

Often a woman will incorporate her mother's fears during her own prenatal period, with memories being activated from her own womb development and birthing experience. This can be the case particularly if mum is:

- Feeling guilt
- Experiencing anxiety
- Feeling that she does not want the child
- Taking drugs
- Drinking alcohol and smoking
- Indulging other addictions
- Having problems with diet and nutrition, such as comfort eating or starving

Recent trials have proved that unborn children often take on their parent's troubling issues. Children born from addicts are more likely to follow suit and take drugs or smoke like their parents. Anxiety and guilt is easily passed on, leaving children wondering why it's always been with them!

Birth can be traumatic for many reasons, but not least because of medical thoughtlessness. We are now, however, becoming more aware of the long-term physical and psychological effects of pre and perinatal events, which have often been ignored by attending medical staff in the past.

ANXIETY AND DEPRESSION

Through my own experience working with those who suffer from anxiety and depression, I have found that a lot of their issues go back to the womb. When asked how long they have suffered these feelings, they tell me they have not known anything else and 'have always felt anxious'.

'I've always felt unhappy.'
'Feeling sad has always been part of my life.'
'I've never felt wanted or loved.'
'I have no feelings for my Mum and feel closer to Dad.'
'I can't make a decision.'
'I have relationship difficulties.'
'I am constantly looking for love.'

'I don't feel this anxiety is mine,' they tell me. 'Why should I feel like this when I have nothing in my life to feel anxious about'?

These are just some of the comments made by clients whom I have treated for emotional issues in their lives. I have successfully been able to help them to move on and draw a line under the situation by:

- Resolving issues which have plagued them since birth, setting them free to get on with their lives
- Lifting the weight which has allowed them to feel lighter and have an explanation as to why they have constantly felt like this
- Allowing them to understand that they are not going mad When we understand the root cause we can move on in our journey through life.

It is sad to realise that, in many cases, these people have suffered throughout their whole lives. Not until now have they been able to find someone who could help them deal with these issues, and it works with any age.

This is why it is so important to have children treated with emotional release treatments. When they are young, an emotional release session can free them from the start, leaving a clean slate from which they can grow without mum's emotional issues plaguing them for the rest of their lives. After all, we pick up enough of our own, don't we?

The realisation that these emotions could have been released sooner is apparent. Quite often, after their treatment sessions have ended, I hear clients say 'Why did I wait so long? I could have been free much sooner.'

I have heard these comments from many of the people that I have treated. Some have been in their late sixties and seventies and have suffered throughout their lives, but when investigated through emotional release techniques such as Somoto Emotional Release (SER), the root cause of their distress has revealed itself to stem right from the womb. In addition, some of the psychological causes from the womb that I have uncovered have actually come from how the sufferer's mum felt during pregnancy!

Many causes were found (as detailed below), some of them stemming from the mother being overwhelmed by becoming pregnant again. She might have felt:

- Not ready emotionally for another child
- Unable to cope with another mouth to feed
- Tired of being tied to the family
- Worn out with caring and family pressures
- Not maternal, believing herself not to be cut out to be a mother

Relationship issues with the father
- Home life was not good
- Relationship was strained
- Father was too strict and abusive to mother

Felt ill during the pregnancy
- Mum felt unwell throughout and did not carry well
- Did not enjoy her pregnancy and was disappointed with the whole event

Became pregnant because of a mishap (one night stand)
- Ashamed and not accepted within the family
- Having to marry someone she didn't love
- Feeling guilt
- Unhappy with her life and situation
- Indecision - What will she do now? How will she manage?
- Should she go it alone?

Rape

- Ashamed
- Feeling dirty and unclean
- Invaded
- Fear and anxiety
- Can she go it alone? What will she do? How will she do it?
- Indecision and pressure to have a termination
- Family pressure and exclusion stemming from the shame she has put upon them
- Life changed beyond measure – it will never be the same again – she has lost her freedom

If she decides to keep the child it may be with regrets, making it difficult to bond with the baby as a mother should. She will have subconscious resentments, feeling stuck with the child, knowing it goes on for life. The child is also a constant reminder of the rape experience, bringing back emotional feelings of the whole event. The woman may also find it difficult to have another relationship.

Grieving

- Not recovered from a previous miscarriage and still grieving for the lost child
- Death in the family – naturally leaving mum grieving and unhappy

Through this particular emotion, (grief) I have found correlations to those suffering from skin disorders and asthma with patterns forming in the child when born.

Depression

Depression or feeling low while pregnant can continue into postnatal depression. Even before it is born, the child will be affected by its mother's emotional signals and can close down to emotion, becoming numb and frozen. This then creates emotional and relationship problems later in life.

As a baby, my brother cried for three months and nothing would appease him. My mother walked the streets with him in the pram, trying to calm him. He was her third child and she didn't know what to do. His birth was induced and he became an anxious child who turned into a worrier as a teen and as an adult, forming anxiety right from the beginning with behaviour patterns to match. I was seven at the time and I remember my mother was unwell throughout her third pregnancy and it took her a long time to recover. When my brother was approximately a year old, she was diagnosed as having arthritis.

Having treated many individuals with birth trauma issues, I know that some people can become stuck in life as a result of birth trauma, the problem often following them into adulthood. The following case studies give further insights.

CASE STUDY 1 –
PRE-TERM BIRTH IN THE SECOND WORLD WAR

During the treatment session of one lady who was in her late 60s, she could see herself being left on the slab to die.

A World War II baby, born in the lift as mum was on her way to the hospital, she arrived pre-term and was not expected to survive. During the war, they did not have the technology and knowledge that we have today, so children were often left to die without resuscitation.

She did survive, however, although unbeknown to her she received a stroke down one side of her body when she was only weeks old. The cause of the stroke turned out to be acute shock.

It was revealed to me that she had been a twin and the shock of realisation and loss was the paralysing effect down the side of her body. This left her body weak on one side and she had suffered pain and discomfort from it all through her life. The twin had not grown and had been reabsorbed into the womb. Mum had not known she was carrying twins and consciously neither did my client.
By clearing out the emotional trauma from her body, we were able to work on the physical pain and discomfort, giving her relief for the first time in her life.

When we have emotional trauma absorbed into the bones (as stated previously it can be absorbed into the skeletal), we are only touching the surface of the pain if emotions too are not removed.

Emotions create barriers, and while those barriers remain we cannot get to the core of the problem. By removing the emotions, we then have a clear foundation to work with.

CASE STUDY 2 – VICTORIAN ATTITUDES

A man in his seventies came to see me. He was very concerned that he could not express love and wanted to find out why. He was an only child and a late arrival in his parents' life, born into a family of some wealth. A helper to mum had looked after him from birth. He had been sent off to boarding school at the age of seven, where he found it difficult to integrate. When he returned home during school holidays, his parents were too busy to interact and spend time with him, wishing only to shake his hand formally upon his return. No hugs or love had been expressed to him by his parents; in fact he could not remember having hugs at any time.

As a consequence of his background and early life, this man had grown up not showing his feelings. At school he had been instructed that 'big boys don't cry', that it was weak to show your feelings or emotions, and he was ridiculed if he cried.

This grown man had tears rolling down his face while he told me his story. He did not know how to greet his own children and continued to shake their hands when they came to stay, even into their adult years. Just like in his own upbringing, he had never given them a hug and didn't know how to!

The tamping down of emotions had been huge and he struck me as a gentle soul who had been scared beyond measure during this life. All he had ever wanted was to feel and share his love in a way that was reciprocated. His wife was emotionally cold and, although they had produced children, there was no blazing love between them.

They slept in separate rooms. He had even thought of seeking solace elsewhere but didn't have the courage to do that either.

The Victorian age in which his parents had been brought up meant that they valued not showing emotions, because they had not experienced love themselves. Most didn't know how to show love and therefore didn't know how to pass it on to their children. His parents' lives had been as companions or the equivalent of sisterly love. They did not know how to express the true deep love a mother has for her child; something he desperately needed to feel.

I discovered that his mum, who was in her forties when she was pregnant with him, endured a difficult birth and he had been taken away immediately after delivery. Mum had taken some time to recover so the bonding process had never taken place for either of them. Having money, they followed materialistic values and did not understand that the child needed love and affection.

This man was a sensitive soul and needed love, as we all do. His heart had been broken with the starvation of love. Despite having all the materialistic items money could buy, he was not happy. Something was missing from his life, a basic ingredient called LOVE. Because the bonding process had been missing from his early life, he'd always felt bereft and unloved.

Love was not on his parents' agenda and they probably didn't even realise it was needed. Apparently this was how they grew up themselves, with a lack of love, and so the process just goes on and on...

When this happens, the child's heart does not grow energetically with the rest of the body. Emotionally it becomes frozen in time.
In two sessions I was able to help him release the trauma from his life events going back to the womb, opening his heart to emotions which had been numb and frozen all his life. I talked to him about his relationship with his own children and offered suggestions to help him get closer to them.

He now realised he was continuing his parents mind-set about how to treat children and knew that just because it was done to him did not make it right! We normally change things for our children to make their lives better; this includes love as well as materialistic items. You cannot buy love; it must be given freely.

I sensed that he was here to change those patterns by not allowing it to continue into his children's lives. Unfortunately, he was so frightened by his earlier years that he couldn't see what had happened in the first place. It hurt too much!

From treating others, my experience leads me to believe that many are here to change thinking on bringing up children today. With consciousness, we have learned the importance of removing physical and sexual abuse. But have we come far enough?

The old ways of excluding love are still practiced in many quarters. In my opinion the nanny way of bringing up children with little parent interaction has caused many emotional disturbances in adults and children alike. This has been proved many times with the people I have treated and continue to treat. Most of the emotional issues we suffer arise out of the LACK of LOVE!

We need LOVE.
We need to express LOVE.
We need to feel LOVE, with a hug, by holding a hand and by giving cuddles.
Love makes us feel safe.
It makes us feel whole.
It also makes us feel wanted.

These are the memories we carry with us into adult life. This is what gives us our foundation for life.

Make sure your child carries real memories of love.

MATERNAL STRESS

A baby communicates and listens to its mother's rhythms and emotions through the chemical changes taking place in her body and her environment. The infant hears the tone and rate of her speech, together with experiencing physiological changes such as those which affect the mother's heartbeat. This is a communication, which takes place between the unborn child and the mother on a 24/7 basis.

In 1956, Hans Selye proposed in his book The Stress of Life:

'No one can live without experiencing some degree of stress all the time. Stress is not necessarily bad for you; it is also the spice of life, for any emotion, any activity causes stress. But, your system must be prepared to take it. The same stress that makes one person sick can be an invigorating experience for another.'[48]

As mentioned previously, the condition of the mum while pregnant will affect the condition of the child within. Old wives' tales say that a mother who is stressed, anxious and fearful will produce a fretful baby. One might say that this is an obvious conclusion.

Not all mothers experience the rush of excitement at being pregnant. For some, the pressures of home, together with stressful pressures of lifestyle, a career and a growing family and perhaps even the feelings associated with sexual abuse or rape, create a scenario where one more child can be just too much. How can she cope physically and mentally, let alone endure the anxieties of monetary worry over another mouth to feed and clothe.

Scientific studies carried out on rats have shown that high levels of stress in the mother, lowers testosterone (male hormone) in the womb[49]. Why is this significant? Because testosterone is key at certain stages of embryonic development and can influence how the brain develops.

Stress results in a change of biochemistry within the body, heightening the secretion of hormones such as adrenalin and dopamine, which in turn affects the emotional centre activity within the brain (the amygdala). The amygdala is involved in the making of memories, particularly those of an emotional nature. Increased activity in the amygdala has been associated with decreased activity in the frontal lobes of the brain where attention-focusing, organising and planning activity take place.

In her book Why Love Matters, Sue Gerhardt shows how a young child's earliest relationships actually shape the child's nervous system. Love and contact from parents is essential and fundamental to a child's development. Babies arrive with an intense need for attachment and studies have shown the impact upon us all, with social and health implications on all levels, when we don't receive the emotional nurturing we expect or feel we deserve. Unfortunately, these impacts will have an effect on us throughout life, with further traumas and emotional knocks and shocks taking the levels of emotional detriment further into the abyss.

PREGNANCY AND THE LONG-TERM EFFECTS OF EMOTION

The emotional state of the mother while she is pregnant is not always taken into account. It is only recently that we have started to realise that emotions are responsible for our behaviour from a young age.

A Finnish study which was carried out in 1978[50] showed that the mother's emotional state has far reaching effects upon her child much longer than the first year of life.

Research found that children whose fathers died during pregnancy (while the children were still in the womb) were at increased risk of mental disease, alcoholism and criminality. Thirty-five years of medical records were researched in this study, which spanned from childhood to adulthood.

Through my own research and treatment sessions with adults, I have seen over and over again the effects from the womb and the surmountable damage it has caused, not only in youth but also on into adulthood. This is evidenced by the case studies are included in this book.

Grief

Although we have previously spoken about the mother's grief, I have also discovered through treatment sessions with children that they have taken on their mother's grief while in the womb; deep grief from the loss of a loved one or family member which has shown itself through disorders of the skin (eczema) and lungs (asthma) and when treated with emotional release techniques they have improved considerably.

Unwanted children

Research conducted in the 1950s on unwanted pregnancies showed that mothers who applied for an abortion were refused because, at that time, it was very much frowned upon, and so the pregnancies were continued to full-term. A Swedish study followed the development of the children until the age of 21[51] and concluded that the sociability of this group of children who were effectively unwanted by their mothers, was much lower than those who were in the control group and were wanted.

Schizophrenia

An extensive follow-up study in 1966 asked mothers who were in the 6th month of pregnancy and who had also had an abortion application refused:

- If the mother wanted the baby?
- Even if the pregnancy mistimed, was it wanted or unwanted?

Significant risk of schizophrenia was noted in the babies who were not wanted compared to the other group studied.

Schizophrenia creates an impaired capacity to love. Sufferers feel detached from their environment and feel as though they do not belong. They also find it difficult to fit into daily life.

Anorexia Nervosa

In his book Scientification of Love, Dr M Odent includes a Swedish study, which indicates a link between anorexia and birth, and notes a significant risk factor with cephalhaematoma at birth. Cephalhaematoma is a collection of blood between two layers of skull bones and is an indication of trauma from a mechanical process such as forceps or ventouse deliveries. (See chapter on CST for more information)

[48] Sally Goddard Blythe 'What Babies and Children Really Need' Hawthorn press Stroud, Glos.UK. 2008
(Ref: Hans Selye 1956 'Stress of Life' Mc Gaw-Hill New York)

[49] Ibid p (Ref:Moir A Jessel D Brain Sex 'study on rats showing high level of stress in the mother'. Manderin London 1991)

[50] Ibid 'Finnish study' p12 (Ref: M Huttunmen P. Niskanen 'parental loss of father and psychiatric disorders' Arch Gen Psychiatry 1978:35:429-31)

[51] Odent M book 'Scientification of Love' Free Association Books Ltd: 2001 (Ref: Swedish study H. Fossman Thuew:Acta Psychiatry. Scand 1981:64:142-9)

Chapter 8

INDEX

Chapter 8

INFERTILITY

Today we have a whole host of fertility problems with unexplained core reasons and in many cases nothing is medically wrong. Science certainly does not have all the answers and in the majority of cases the simple fact is that the body is not in optimum health to create reproduction.

Whilst IVF and drugs are the medical answers to infertility, they do not work for everyone. I feel that a simpler and a more efficient way is to help the body to regenerate with easy steps which work nutritionally and naturally to give the reproductive process the right ingredients to work with. If we want to sow our seed, we need the garden to be fertile and healthy and the same applies to the physical body. When the body is below par, stressed and toxic because of lifestyle choices and lack of education, commonsense that tells us it will be hit and miss to become pregnant. I believe, therefore, that preparation is the key.

Infertility can happen for many reasons. In addition to physical causes, it can be emotion or stress-related, with the body becoming so tense that it locks down internally. Here are just some of the main causes of infertility:

- An ovary disorder such as Polycystic Ovarian Syndrome (PCOS)
- A pH problem where there is too much acid in the body creating a hostile environment for the sperm to survive
- Blockages within the fallopian tubes – a twisted tube or infection can also cause blockages
- Failure to ovulate or an ovulation imbalance
- Poor egg quality
- Irregular periods
- Hormone imbalances
- Weight issues - over or underweight

- History of anorexia
- Menstrual problems
- Poor sperm quality
- Endometriosis
- Fibroids
- Ovulation dysfunction

I'm ready

When a woman becomes broody or, my preferred term, 'ready to become a mother', there is not a lot that will dissuade her. The feelings of needing and wanting a child take over. Everywhere she looks she will see and notice more babies, pictures of babies, babies in the street, in shops or on the TV. Often she will become obsessed with babies. Feeling maternal, her hormones and internal chemical production will support and nurture this feeling within her.

It is at this time that those husbands and partners who are not yet ready to have a child may decide to distract by getting a pet in the forlorn hope that it will take the edge off their partner's maternal instinct. Sometimes it will succeed for a while, but the feelings will persist and are quite likely to come back again. Giving in, they will then discuss and usually agree that the time is right to start a baby.

The mother's wellbeing is paramount during the formation of the embryo. Quite simply, she must be in tiptop condition.

For many years I have treated women for both infertility and pregnancy. These are some of the symptoms I find when I first treat for infertility and miscarriage:

- High levels of stress
- Exhaustion - running on empty
- Inner body is tense
- Body too acidic
- PH balance needs correcting
- Thyroid imbalance
- Fluid blockages

- Emotional barriers and grief
- Incorrect weight & Anorexia
- Overwhelmed emotionally
- Frustrated
- Age - overly aware of the ticking clock
- Diet and nutrition need correcting/ balancing

When we plant in the garden we want the seed to germinate and flourish.
If the soil is not in the right condition, the seed may still germinate but be in a sickly condition and fail later. If the soil is fertile and the ambient conditions correct, the seed will grow strong and flourish to maturity, giving the best fruit.

The human birth process is no different. It is exactly the same with our bodies. If the body is not in good condition, it will not be able to support the maturity of the embryo and will reject it prematurely, intending to start again when the body is healthier and more able to do its amazing job naturally. Nature is wonderful. It knows when things are not right and, as with all life, it struggles to support anything that is not in the condition it should be.

Age

Age is a risk factor. As she ages, the quality of a woman's eggs deteriorates and she is therefore more at risk of miscarriage. Although controversial, some believe that the use of the contraceptive pill slightly reduces egg deterioration and ultimately the risk of miscarriage.

It has become common practice in recent years for women to start a family in their thirties, instead of their twenties as it was in my day.

Many women who are looking to start their families later in life tend to have had a busy career that has taken up the earlier years. I have found that the majority of these women are under pressure in their chosen profession, unknowingly building up long-lasting stresses in their bodies. Unfortunately, wanting to start a family in later life brings its own challenges.

Our bodies are actually in their prime to conceive during our late teens and twenties. The female body is normally ready to start a family from the time our periods start, usually in our teens or, in some cases even earlier. In our early teens, however, we are often not ready emotionally to start a family as we are still growing up ourselves. Fortunately, these days we have a choice.

Although every woman is different and this may vary from person to person, at the age of approximately thirty we start to become gradually less fertile. After that, ideal conditions begin to decline until a general cut-off age at about 37-38 when the body changes dramatically. This is when egg cells begin to disappear from the ovaries at a higher rate.

It is possible for women of twenty-five to have a body more like a thirty-five year-old, depending upon her lifestyle, her diet and how much trauma she has had in her life. A great deal also depends upon how much she has taken care of herself up to this point. Smoking, drugs and drink all have their part to play in the physical decline.

With a suitable health programme, it is also possible for the process to work the opposite way around. A woman of thirty-five can be super-fit and have a body which is not dissimilar to when she was in her late twenties.

Stress

As women, we juggle many things during our lives. Life today is accelerated and we often do too much, trying to fit so much into our lives. For many, their schedules include going to the gym during the evening or playing a game of squash before meeting a friend for a drink after work. Some women shop daily for their food, adding further delay before they get home.

In other cases, women feel impelled to stay on after the normal finishing time to complete the day's heavy workload. Beginning with an hour or two per day, this builds up week after week until they become workaholics. Without realising it, the day slips away with no time to rest or simply to be.

Research has indicated that stress may play a role in pregnancy loss. Even working through lunch without stopping for a break, the body becomes overwhelmed. Over time this puts extra stress on our bodies, on our muscles and eventually on our inner organs. 'I am relaxed,' some say as they tap their foot continuously and can't sit still!

Sometimes, when a stressed individual lies on my treatment table for a reflexology session, they will have one leg and foot in the air! When I suggest that they relax the leg, they appear surprised, having failed to realise they were doing it. Treatment shows that their body is on red alert, clearly tense; in some cases it is like an explosion waiting to go off, yet they think it will be easy to become pregnant!

For a woman in the above state, the body is not in the right mode for conception, as it is not relaxed.

After you have decided that it is time to start a family, you expect to conceive within a few months. When nothing happens after six months of trying, testing is the usual next step. The testing starts with calculating the ovulation period, which indicates when the prospective mum is in the best condition to conceive.

The process of making love to order can be very exhausting and put more pressure on both partners to perform on cue. This can become a time when frustration and disappointment start to kick in.

Hormone stimulation

When a woman appears to be having difficulty in conceiving, she will often start to question why. The respective mothers on both sides of the family were all right and other siblings had no problem, so why not them? A trip to the doctors usually follows, where all manner of tests are taken by the GP and, if nothing is found, a consultant appointment is commonly arranged to help find the missing link. Blood tests and scans can also follow and, if nothing is conclusive from the tests, the doctor's next step is usually to suggest taking a medication such as Clomid, the UK's NHS preferred option, which is designed to stimulate the natural hormones, allowing the body to respond in a more favourable condition for fertility.

Clomid

Clomid, also known as Clomiphene, is a fertility medication which is prescribed for couples facing female infertility. It has been used for over thirty years and is used to induce and regulate ovulation by stimulating the women's ovaries to mature an increased number of follicles each month. It is thought that this increases the likelihood of pregnancy and indeed the success rate can be good, with 70% of those taking Clomid becoming pregnant within three cycles.

Taken orally and normally over the course of a few cycles, Clomid is prescribed in different strengths (50mg-200mg), 50mg being the normal level to start although this may be increased if no results are seen. Taking the drug carries a 5-10% risk of multiple pregnancy (i.e: twins)[52].

How does Clomid work?

Clomid, targets three hormones involved in ovulation and tricks the body into believing it has lowered levels of oestrogen. As a result, the brain stimulates the release of FSH (follicle-stimulating hormone), LH (luteinizing hormone) and GnRH (Gonadotrophoin releasing hormone).

Side effects of Clomid

The side effects of Clomid are considered to be mild on the lower dose. Higher doses, however, have been seen to create the following symptoms:

- Mood swings
- Nausea and vomiting
- Breast tenderness
- Headaches
- Fatigue
- Changes to cervical mucus – making the mucus hostile (more acidic) to sperm

Some women who take Clomid become pregnant straight away but then miscarry within a few weeks. If this happens several times, they are referred to a consultant who may suggest tests to find out if there is a mechanical reason for the problem. If that all turns out to be fine, the usual suggestion by most consultants would be to start IVF treatment, which can become a postcode lottery for most people in the UK, many of whom cannot afford private care.

For women who have been on the pill for some time or for older woman wanting to start a family, preparation is the key. I find that women are turning to alternative therapies first to help eliminate some of the obvious issues such as pressure and stress from their lives.

Using a combination of reflexology, Cranio Sacral Therapy (CST) and emotional release techniques, I have treated women taking Clomid and helped to support them through the early stages of their pregnancy with success. I have also treated women during and before IVF treatment.

Everyone needs a different type of help, as we are all unique. Sometimes I have been able to help women achieve more favourable egg production, with huge success. One woman in particular went from producing poor grade eggs, to grade one egg production.

Some women have told me after experiencing miscarriage as part of their attempts to conceive that they could not go through it again - that the emotional experience is just too much to bear. Fear and uncertainty takes over and, although they feel compelled to try for a baby, the miscarriage process becomes far too daunting. (You can find more information on miscarriage in Chapter 9). For others, however, the determination to conceive is all consuming and dominates their lives to the detriment of their partners and their home lives. This is where they start putting up mental and emotional barriers to help them through the trauma and crash even further when it is not successful!

IVF

Research indicates that one in six couples has problems conceiving and the number of couples who are opting for IVF treatment is growing.

From my experience of treating couples on IVF programmes, being on IVF has its own challenges for both men and women. The pressures, however, are not just associated with the treatment itself. IVF in the UK is apparently a lottery, the outcome of which is based on geographical location. Where you live, which council you come under and what the health authority's strategy is will determine the availability of fertility treatment. No matter what our government says, the overwhelming evidence suggests that it is not a level playing field.

Even those who are childless can be on waiting lists for years and often, prospective mothers are vetted for financial status and how many children they already have to determine whether they get the thumbs up or down. Some couples who have had previous relationships and families are being told in some parts of the UK that if they have a child from a previous marriage they will not be eligible for IVF. This is because their particular authority only has funds for childless couples.

Authorities fail to take into account the fact that brand new relationships begin after marriage and relationship break-ups, and that often these new couples have a burning desire to start a family. The over-simplistic set of financial and status rules (which many authorities operate) restrict couples which in their own opinion, should be eligible. It must be very frustrating for genuine couples that want to have a family to enter a fertility programme only to be declined, simply because of monetary decisions. Clearly the system is causing untold grief and depression for some couples using the facilities set in place by the NHS.

Not surprisingly, it would appear that those who are prepared to pay privately for fertility treatment are more successful. Private treatment is big business and private clinics are there to fill the gaps in the NHS. Unfortunately, not all couples can afford the high cost involved in undergoing just one private IVF treatment.

The strain of IVF

When couples go through the fertility journey, they are assessed, tested and finally judged. Although the process is intended to be kindly done, those involved are still judged in the final outcome and put into a box or field of expectation.

As individuals, when we don't come up to scratch we feel disappointed. There is the tendency to feel criticized, with the full blame or absolution being heaped on to one partner or the other. In some cases, one half of the couple is totally responsible for the lack of fertility and feels guilty, whereas in others the couple simply wants to know why they cannot conceive. Being provided with a genuine medical reason can help some, but for others this is not enough. Either way, the whole scenario induces a lot of pressure, stress and anxiety all around.

The IVF process and the testing alone can cause women to feel overwhelmed and distressed. Not only can having their eggs graded into good specimens and bad cause them to feel under pressure, but so too can the period when they are injecting hormones and undergoing the fertilisation procedure.

Men suffer too as they are graded according to the fertility of their sperm, and additionally many can also feel out of the loop. Rather than producing the sperm to fertilize the eggs, some feel as though it is all happening to the female partner without them being involved. Although in some cases male partners are very compassionate and supportive during the process of fertility treatment, for others it can be too much, pushing the relationship to the limit and eventually causing it to break up.

Even freezing sperm and eggs for use at a later date can have its problems, as was seen with the now famous case of a woman having to go to the extreme lengths of appealing to the EU Court of Human Rights to claim her own fertilised eggs for use in a new relationship. Her old partner did not want them to be used and, after several years of trying through the courts, his views were upheld. The lady in question had had the eggs taken as a precaution prior to treatment for cancer, a practice which is recommended and is quite common. The eggs and sperm are frozen and kept indefinitely but, unfortunately, in this particular case the eggs were fertilised before freezing, giving her ex-partner (the sperm donor) equal rights over their final usage.

Research into the effects of IVF

These days, many women wait until later in life to have children. Because they choose to follow a career and, in many cases, are pressured to work in order to keep their home and pay the rent or mortgage, the desire to start a family takes second place. Unfortunately, delaying starting a family until later in life can mean a greater likelihood of disappointment, not only because of the decrease in fertility, but also because the risk of problems such as miscarriage, ectopic pregnancies and premature birth increases with age.

Women over the age of 35 are also at greater risk of diabetes and high blood pressure during pregnancy and, although many pregnancies in older mothers are plain sailing, for first time mothers aged 35 and over there can be challenges and hiccups. They are, for instance, seen to have more problems during birth, including foetal distress in the second stage of labour, which increases the probability of intervention via C-section, forceps or ventouse.

Another issue, which affects fertility and pregnancy is the fact that women these days are more sexually active, and indeed some have many partners. These lifestyle and behavioural choices not only increase the risk of problems in conceiving, but also affect the overall good health of mothers during pregnancy.

Some gynaecologists are concerned about the increased percentage of late pregnancies, together with raised infertility issues and the fact that women are more frequently looking for intervention to defy their biological clocks. Indeed, it is estimated that 'late' pregnancies (those which take place when women are in their 30s and 40s) has doubled in the last 20 years.
In her book 'What Babies and Children Really Need', Sally Goddard Blythe states that 1.4% of children born in the UK during 2004 were produced as a result of IVF treatment, the long-term effects of which are still not clear.

In June 2006, meanwhile, the International Committee for Monitoring Assisted Reproductive Technologies (ICMART) reported at their annual meeting of the European Society of Human Reproduction and Embryology in Prague that 3 million children had so far been born through IVF[53]. Apparently, nearly 56% of all IVF treatments are in

Europe and almost half of the techniques are performed in just four countries - the United States, Germany, France and Britain.

The growing number of IVF treatments is not the only issue to be raised however, but also the associated problems for mothers and babies alike. A Finnish study, for example, showed that 14% of women who had undergone IVF treatment had serious complications, including miscarriage, ectopic pregnancy and the side effects of drug treatments[54].

IVF and infertility in men

The use of IVF has also highlighted the question of growing infertility in men. One Danish study, which compared the fertility of males born from mothers needing help to conceive versus those who conceived naturally, found that 50% of males conceived through fertility treatment were more likely to be infertile themselves compared to men conceived naturally[55] and that men born from hormone-based fertility drugs had the poorest quality sperm of all.

The increased risks brought about through the use of IVF are becoming more apparent as the years and the research go on. In some cases, treatment is simply ineffective because the mother's immune system treats the embryo as an unwanted invader and so rejects the implantation. This is especially the case with mothers who have ultrasensitive immune systems. In others, results highlight gut problems such as defects in the abdominal wall or organs not being in the right place, problems which are nine times more likely to affect IVF children[56].

Even with IVF intervention, nature still needs a good quality, healthy egg together with quality sperm to produce a healthy child. The quality that we put in determines the outcome, so it is essential for both partners to prepare for pregnancy and to be in good health in order to produce a strong and healthy child.

At the end of the day, nothing is guaranteed with fertility processes. For some couples, IVF just doesn't work and invariably there is no explanation as to why this is the case. Sometimes they are forced into the realisation that nothing can be done, a fact which induces them to relax and move on. Assuming that nothing is going to happen, and with the stress of the infertility treatment behind them, they get on with their lives, only to find some time later that they are pregnant. Isn't nature wonderful!

IVF and nutrition changes

Research conducted as far back as 1993 indicated that more men are showing increasing numbers of sperm abnormalities and that sperm counts are dropping, so it is small wonder that sub-fertility is a growing concern. Thirty per cent of fertility problems originate from the male partner, although in some cases nothing can be found to be medically wrong.

As we have said, even in cases where IVF treatment is necessary, the preparation that both partners make when trying to conceive is vital and nutrition changes have been shown to help the quality of egg and sperm. Research has shown, for example, that:

- 500mg of vitamin C a day given to women undergoing IVF treatment significantly increases the pregnancy rate from 23.7% to 34.2%[57]
- Genetic materials (DNA and RNA) both need folic acid and vitamin B12[58]
- High levels of Homocysteine, (found in follicular fluid) have been found in women who have miscarried. Oocytes (eggs) exposed to low homocysteine concentrations have better quality and higher degree of maturity[59]
- 200g of caffeine a day is associated with a 25% increased risk of miscarriage compared to 12% for women who avoided all caffeine[60]
- Zinc is an essential component of genetic material and plays a vital role in cell division. Zinc deficiency causes a decrease in sperm count seminal volume and testosterone levels[61]
- A group of men who took zinc and folic acid for 26 weeks were found to have sperm counts increased by 74% [62]
- The fertility rates of men with low fertilisation rates in IVF cycles were improved significantly from 19.3% to 29.1% after one month of taking 200mg of vitamin E daily[63]
- Vitamin E can help to increase the number and quality of eggs in older women on IVF cycles[64]

- In cases where women were normally resistant to Clomid on its own, the combination of Clomid and vitamin C resulted in ovulation[65]

Lymph drainage

Lymph Drainage is used to clear blockages in fertility issues.

The lymph system is a vast complex and network of capillaries, vessels, ducts, valves, nodes and organs. It helps to protect and maintain the internal fluid environment of the body and one of its main functions is to filter out the poisons and toxins that we receive daily from our lifestyle and environment. Ingested chemicals and medication steadily build up a level of toxicity from the environment and day-to-day products such as cleaning products, body and other sprays and bathroom products. The lymph drainage system therefore has a very important role to play.

Lymph fluid is normally moved by body dynamics and it filters bacteria and virus particles as well as producing and circulating lymphocytes, T cells, killer cells, phagocytes and so on. It also transports fats, proteins and other substances to the blood system and restores fluid (60% lymph fluid).

All massage is wonderfully relaxing, but little is known of a variation called manual lymph drainage (MDL), which is successfully used for:

- Easing swelling caused by fluid retention
- Oedema from pregnancy
- Various injuries
- Breast cancer or general puffiness

IVF clinics and infertility groups recommend lymph drainage. It is a recognised fertility treatment, which helps to clear sluggish areas and blockages. Lymph drainage, together with reflexology, is recommended and accepted as a combined therapy approach for those who are on a fertility programme.

Sometimes blockages and fluid retention in certain parts of the body can become stagnant in the lymph channels. Lymph drainage has been found to help women who are trying to become pregnant, by moving stagnant fluid in such areas as the groin, adrenals and abdominal areas. It also helps with lymph disturbance following surgeries such as mastectomy.

How does it work?

Manual lymph drainage works by stimulating the effect of nature's own internal cleanser, the lymphatic network of channels carrying lymph fluid.

This fluid clears the tissues of bacteria and waste and the collected waste is passed into the lymph nodes in the neck, groin and (axilla) under the arms.

MLD is a gentle, almost feathery massage which unblocks nodes and prevents them from becoming congested. It is a relaxing, calming and gentle treatment which is suitable for people of all ages and helps to reduce the symptoms of:

- Chronic unrelenting stress
- Reduction of white blood cells
- Acute virus/flu - depleted immune symptoms
- Glandular fever
- Tissue damage
- Fluid blockages after mastectomy
- Lymphoedema
- PMS - sore breasts and underarm discomfort

Used for the face, arms, legs and other parts of the body, it:
Improves elimination by increasing bowel/bladder movements, reduces mucus in adults and children suffering with congestion of ears, nose, sinus and head, and also assists to relieve the symptoms of asthma and hay fever.

I have used lymph drainage with great success on pregnant women who have struggled with high blood pressure and borderline eclampsia. By reducing the swelling and blood pressure using MLD techniques, I have enabled satisfactory home stay instead of hospitalisation before labour kicked in.

The natural lymph function can become sluggish because of serious illness such as a virus or a glandular disorder, (especially the condition known as glandular fever), impeding and depleting the efficiency of the lymph system. Lymph disorders creep up slowly, so slowly that often we don't recognise that we are depleted. Sometimes we just know that we feel under par and unwell most of the time. Unfortunately, we often don't get symptoms which are clear enough for the doctor to diagnose and may be prescribed wrongly in the process. In some cases we are born with inadequate nodes in our lymph system to help clear the body efficiently.

A full lymph drainage treatment can take approx 1 to 1 ½ hours, or alternatively treatment can be broken down into segments of the body such as the head and neck for sinus problems, the legs for cellulite and so on.

Manual lymph drainage reduces body fluid, working wonders in reducing puffy areas of the body. As a spectacular skin treatment, it tightens up the saggy bits and reduces puffiness. Some say it is 'likened to having a face-lift without surgery' (See appendix for more information).

FAILURE TO OVULATE

Many women are failing to ovulate regularly after the age of thirty-five and are thus faced with infertility later in life. The cause, however, is not necessarily directly related to the chronological age of the women concerned, but the ageing of their bodies, with recent testing showing that some women may be ageing much faster than their years. One example of this might be a 28 year-old woman whose lifestyle involves drinking alcohol, taking drugs, poor diet and so on. Whilst her chronological age is 28, the ageing process brought about by her lifestyle choices means that the condition of her body is actually on a par with somebody who is 33 – a whole five years older. Such a woman might think that she has plenty of time to have children, but her body is actually on the decline towards menopause much sooner than she is consciously aware of.

Although it might be tempting to think that if a woman is bleeding every month that ovulation is also taking place, it has actually been found that she may be neither ovulating nor producing progesterone. For women who are having difficulty conceiving therefore, it is a good idea to check this out first of all. Infertility can be a process of elimination and I like to tick the box on this one first in order to avoid wasting precious time. As we mentioned previously, when you ovulate, there should be a rise and noticeable change in the body temperature by one to one and half degrees. If there is no significant change, then you have not ovulated.

Fallopian tube disorders

Balance in the fallopian tubes is another problem, which can affect fertility, but it is also one which can be difficult to recognise. The normal function of the tubes can be affected by infection, which causes the tubes to become blocked. In quite a number of cases, sexually transmitted disease is the cause of the infection and often it is not until a woman tries for a baby that she becomes aware of the disorder.

Chlamydia is one of the most common causes of damage to the fallopian tubes and is a silent disease transmitted by sex. Although it can remain undetected for a long time and cause no obvious symptoms, it is estimated that approximately 70% of cases involving fallopian tube disorders result from this condition, leading to the tubes becoming infected and blocked.

Weight issues

Diet and weight are another two issues to look at in connection with infertility and pregnancy, as the body needs protein to build and support the extra load. Being overweight may be creating an overload to the systems of the body, resulting in it no longer being able to cope with the additional services needed in pregnancy.

Those who have suffered with anorexia, on the other hand, will have either had irregular periods or none at all at times in their lives. These menstrual irregularities can cause other imbalances with respect to fertility that will, in most cases, take time to correct. Regular periods, even if they are on a 30–35 day cycle, need to be corrected for ovulation patterns to be identified. I find that reflexology is excellent at helping to rebalance hormones and de-stress the body, bringing it back to homeostasis and well-being once more to provide the basis for conception.

Natural helpers

The addition of Agnus Castus and vitamin E also helps towards a more harmonious and balanced body to create the optimum fertile environment. Agnus Castus can be taken to help with menstrual problems too, such as irregular and painful periods.

Animal studies have shown that adequate maternal zinc status is essential for normal embryonic and foetal development. Low zinc and magnesium levels have also shown to be a cause of depression.

When considering any changes to diet or nutrition, always speak to a registered practitioner who specialises in pregnancy for assistance.

Adrenal stress and fertility

Adrenal dysfunction is linked with a combination of stress and low adrenal function or low adrenal reserve. Adrenal glands hold reserve energy just like a battery - your battery of life.

Low adrenal reserve describes the state where the adrenal output is adequate for normal usage but there is no reserve to cope with stress or upward changes in activity levels, producing adrenal stress. A rise in Adrenocorticotropic Hormone (ATCH), which is regulated via the pituitary, causes high levels of cortisol which can lead to adrenal burnout or exhaustion.

The risk factors which contribute to adrenal stress include lifestyle, diet, environmental influences and simply being female, while the symptoms manifest themselves through:

- Anxiety, nervousness and mood swings
- Low blood pressure

- Headaches
- Dizziness upon standing
- Dark rings around the eyes
- Hot flushes
- Pre Menstrual Syndrome (PMS)
- Loss of libido
- Grinding teeth
- IBS (irritable bowel syndrome)

Lifestyle

Our modern lifestyle has seen an upsurge in burnout for many people, with a possible cause of chronic fatigue. The 'over-achievers' are often people who push themselves too far, tending to be very ambitious or conscientious or wanting things done in a particular way. It could be due to a pre-existing low adrenal function, often preceded by an early symptom of over-activity. In women, this could be connected to their menstrual cycle, with over-activity present in the run up to her period.

Today, women in general tend to juggle so many things in their lives and are put under greater pressure with today's modern way of living. Apart from the normal female role, women need to go out to work to help pay for the mortgage etc. Unfortunately, the days of staying at home to bring up a family like their mothers did are a misty memory.

Sometimes women need to make a deliberate choice to look after themselves more and often it is essential to hand duties over to spouses and partners. By getting them more involved in the day-to-day running of the home, you can spend quality time relaxing and being with the children, especially bonding together at weekends.

Diet

To put it crudely, the western diet is not what we were originally designed to eat. We have evolved over millions of years based on a complex carbohydrate and low sugar diet. Basically, our bodies see sugar as poison. Eating high sugar foods such as fizzy drinks or chocolate causes a rapid increase in blood sugar. The body then needs to produce a large amount of insulin to lower the blood sugar levels, often resulting in the sugar level going too low through overcompensation. When we have low blood sugar (hypoglycaemia) we need adrenal hormones.

A high sugar diet greatly increases the demand on the adrenal system. Low thyroid function is associated with the over-production of insulin, causing mild hypoglycaemia, which in turn increases the demand on the adrenal system.

All adrenal hormones are made from cholesterol so a low cholesterol diet may well affect adrenal output. In addition, vitamin C has its greatest concentration in the adrenals and B6 is also important for good adrenal function. A diet which is low in carbohydrate and fat, however, will not help as it forces the body to compensate by craving carbohydrates, fat and cholesterol to create rebalance and so leads to other problems.

A change in diet and fine-tuning will be all it takes for some. Others may need more help through treatments such as reflexology, together with nutritional and vitamin short-term support which is especially formulated to help balance and support adrenal and thyroid dysfunctions. To reduce pressure on the adrenals we need to keep the intake of all stimulants to a minimum, especially tea, coffee, fizzy drinks such as soda pops, Cola drinks and alcohol. Underactive adrenals and thyroid caused by hypoglycaemia or malfunctioning as a result of autoimmune disease may be lacking in vitamin B12. As a result, what little vitamin B12 there is may not be absorbed very well in the body.

Being Female

In human females, the adrenal system produces some of the reproductive hormones. This puts the female adrenal system under greater demand, especially when you consider that women have naturally lower DHEA levels than men. Dehydroepiandrosterone (DHEA) is a natural steroid hormone precursor (medically known as a prohormone) produced from cholesterol by the adrenal glands, gonads, adipose tissue, brain and in the skin and it builds up bone and muscle. In women, the normal DHEA levels are approximately half that of men.

Environmental influences

Chemicals and medications can upset the balance between the adrenals and thyroid. As we have mentioned previously, excesses of environmental oestrogen have been upsetting the balance between oestrogen and progesterone for some time and this can also upset the thyroid utilisation in women. Oestrogen from the contraceptive pill and HRT cannot be filtered out of sewage, eventually getting into our fresh water system and making us more oestrogen dominant without our knowing. In addition, problems stem from the use of steroids in livestock, which subsequently get into the human food chain.

Perhaps this is the reason why we are seeing more men lose their hair so early in life and infertility becoming a problem for men too. Passage of Power by Lesley Kenton is worth a read and gives more information.

BODY ACID LEVELS AND FERTILITY

The issue of body acidity is something, which many people are not aware of. When I am treating a client for infertility or miscarriage, one of the first things I will advise is to check whether the body is too acidic. Indeed, even if you are just beginning to try to become pregnant, it is advisable to test your pH balance to check if your bodily fluids are too acidic. Logically, we have to provide the right environment for the sperm to swim in. Too much acid can affect how we are able to accept sperm in the uterus and, more to the point, how long the sperm will be able to survive in that environment.

When the body is generally too acidic it makes the mucus acidic too, which means that the mucus used as a lubricant for the vaginal area will also be affected. In this area, if the lubricant mucus is too acidic it will kill off the sperm before it has a chance to get to the egg and fertilise it.

Testing

As I have mentioned, when I see a client who is suffering from infertility problems or preparing for pregnancy, I normally suggest that the client's pH level is checked to establish whether her body is too acidic.

The term pH stands for 'parts of hydrogen' and is the measure of acidity or alkalinity of a solution. It is measured on a scale of 1-14, with pure water giving a mid-point value of 7. The lower the pH number, the more acidic the solution and the higher the pH number, the more alkaline the solution. When measuring fluids in the body, we either test urine or saliva.

Saliva testing indicates the activity of digestive enzymes in the body, these being primarily manufactured by the stomach, liver and pancreas. Without these enzymes, the body cannot maintain a balanced pH, resulting in a saliva pH reading which is too low. A reading of below 6.5 indicates that the body may be producing, and becoming overwhelmed by, too many acids, because it has lost its ability to adequately remove them through the excretory process. When the saliva reading is too high (over 6.8), the body is likely to be suffering from excess gas, constipation and the production of yeast, mould and fungus. Ideally, the saliva test should show a reading of between 6.5 and 6.8.

Urine testing can indicate how well a body is excreting acids and assimilating minerals, especially calcium, magnesium, sodium and potassium. Calcium and magnesium are two of the most important minerals to help maintain a balanced pH level. This is where the alkalinity and acidity can become extreme, in some cases overburdening and overwhelming the body because it has to work harder to excrete the excess. The ideal urine pH will fluctuate between 6.3 and 7.0.

The correct pH balance

Harmony is reached when we have the correct pH balance. Water contains both hydrogen and oxygen, as previously mentioned. The oxygen we breathe is used by the body to burn hydrogen from the water we drink, and in turn produces energy in the body to keep us going. In a healthy adult, water accounts for approximately 70% of total body weight. An ideal pH range is balanced through our cells, regulating the cell fluid both inside and outside.

Many bodily functions including digestion, enzyme activity and hormone balance are completely dependent upon the inner workings of the body itself to maintain this ideal balance.

Body harmony is reached by the correct pH balance and if the pH is properly balanced, the saliva or urine will clearly demonstrate this fact when testing using pH test strips.

In pregnancy, the amniotic fluid (water with a pH of 6.7) is necessary for the heartbeat to start in the developing foetus and it provides a gentle energy to start development, so it is essential to get it right.

Maintaining a perfect pH can be difficult and the body has three primary systems for maintaining the ideal balance – the respiratory system, the urinary system and the gastrointestinal system, including the liver and pancreas. Despite these inbuilt protective systems, today's pressured lifestyles and fast-food diets often overwhelm and fluids become imbalanced within. This can happen as a result of:

- Poor diet
- Stress
- Dehydration
- Chemicals
- Lack of exercise
- Thyroid imbalance

Since each of us is different and unique in our own right, the above are just some of the causes of pH imbalance, which is why it is best to consult a professional therapist or nutritionist who deals with pH testing. These practitioners will be able to look at all the possible causes for the imbalance within a particular individual.

When our body becomes pH imbalanced it may lead to serious health concerns such as:

- Hormone imbalance
- Cardiovascular weakness
- Weight gain/loss
- Bladder and kidney imbalances
- Immune deficiency
- Acceleration of free radical damage and production
- Structural system weakness
- Low energy

- Slow digestion and elimination
- Yeast and/or fungal growth and disorders
- Liver dysfunction
- Disturbance of the oxygen affinity of haemoglobin in the blood

A balanced pH allows and maintains a proper metabolic function, permitting the body to function optimally, resulting in increased energy levels, better digestion, a stronger body and weight loss.
Where an imbalance exists, we can use food and drink to change pH levels, although nutritional help may also be needed in the short term to help accelerate the process. It can take only a few weeks to change the pH in some women. In others, however, it can take a little longer depending upon the extent of the imbalance.

If your diet is full of protein and dairy products, it will metabolise as acid in the body. The whole process is all down to how different foodstuffs and drink metabolise within the body when ingested. When the body becomes too acidic, it indicates an imbalance of pH, a condition which forces the body to borrow minerals such as calcium, sodium, potassium and magnesium from vital organs and bones. It will do this to buffer the excess acid and safely remove it from the body but, over time, the process of borrowing minerals can weaken organs and bones.

High alkalinity in the body also causes a pH imbalance
Though less common than high acidity, high alkalinity causes many of the same kinds of problems, but this condition often takes more support and time to adjust than an acidic imbalance because the body has become less capable of excreting acids through the kidneys. In this situation the liver and bowel compensate by producing ammonia.

Diet

Diet has a huge impact on how our bodies perform and our ultimate wellbeing. We need to give the body all that it needs to sustain us in the right way, to be strong, balanced and healthy. When preparing for pregnancy, prospective mothers will benefit from a healthy balanced diet and good quality nutrition. A lack of good nutrition will result in health issues for both mother and child.

They say that we are what we eat and, if this is the case, then our lifestyles today certainly do not help. We often eat on the run with a sandwich in hand as we work through our lunch hour or walk around eating. This is not the best way to do things for the digestive process. When we sit down to eat in a relaxed atmosphere, we are giving the body, and especially the digestive system, the right state to receive and digest the food that we are eating.

As stated previously, when our diet contains too much fast food and sugar-loaded fizzy drinks, we force our bodies to accept unstable foods. This causes imbalance and creates disorders in the digestive system, leading eventually to high or low blood sugar and increases in blood pressure and cholesterol.

Poor diets also leave our bodies depleted of nutrients and vitamins, since enzymes and vitamins are responsible for converting food into energy, stimulating the metabolic process and accelerating biological functions. If we eat food which is not right for us, it can make us feel physically ill or just generally under par and leave us short of energy. Eating and drinking the wrong foods can easily overburden the liver, which is not only involved in converting and storing the energy from the food we eat, but is also involved in hormone regulation. As each system in the body relies on every other one, it is essential to get the balance right.

A run-down state of the body is the cause of the problem and disease is the effect. Whilst poor diet, stress, a lack of exercise and poor lifestyle can all deplete nutrition and energy, disease can further reduce the amount of nutrition taken into our body.

Our modern day processing and manufacturing systems being such as they are, food can be harvested too soon so that enzymes are not formed correctly and, as a result, we do not receive the goodness that we expect. In addition, when produce is stored for too long it depletes in nutrients and vitamins. Trials have shown, for example, whole batches of oranges containing literally no vitamin C. Vitamin C is water-soluble. It does not remain in the body for long and is constantly secreted, needing to be topped up and taken daily. If depleted by even one of the foundation minerals, your body will not open the gates to allow absorption of other nutrients and vitamins.

We therefore need good quality food which contains all the necessary nutrients and vitamins for our bodies to respond and grow in a healthy manner.

With the lack of animal manure and an increasing use of artificial and synthetic fertilisers, the soil in which our food grows is also becoming depleted over time. As a result, we are often not receiving all the nutrients that we should. Agricultural sprays and chemicals are also getting into the food chain, making it vital that we wash all fruit and vegetables before eating in order to minimise the contamination. Over the course of many years, I have seen a huge number of people who are allergic to wheat, dairy produce and even potatoes. These foods have been recognised as a cause of allergies for some time.

Steroids are also getting into the food chain and GM production is believed to be having an adverse impact upon us. Our bodies are not able to fully process these foods and, over time, natural rejection increases, allowing more susceptible individuals to become allergic and to suffer from skin problems, asthma, eczema and digestive disorders. Never before in the history of mankind have we suffered to this extent from such problems and skin complaints. Does it not make you wonder why?

By improving our diets and correcting our nutrition levels, we can not only improve our health and create wellbeing for life, but also address a number of disorders, such as:

- Hyperglycaemia
- Hypoglycaemia
- Gall bladder problems
- IBS
- Constipation
- PMT
- Thyroid problems

- Menopause
- Candida
- High blood pressure
- High blood pressure
- Diabetes
- Stress
- Anxiety

ACID AND ALKALINE FOODS

Certain foods are more acidic to the body, and these include:

Sugars:
- White and brown sugar
- Nutra sweet
- Equal Sweet'N Low

Meats:
- Pork
- Beef
- Turkey
- Lamb
- Chicken

Drinks:
- Beer
- Soft drinks
- Coffee

Dairy:
- Homogenised milk
- Cheese
- Ice cream

Grains:
- Wheat
- White flour
- White rice

ALKALINE-FORMING FOODS INCLUDE:
- Vegetables and fruit
- Salads
- Vegetable soups
- Pure fruit juices and smoothies

I always suggest that clients who come to see me keep a food diary to get a feel for what needs changing, or even just to fine-tune the individual's diet. Their daily intake of water, tea, coffee, alcohol, smoking and drugs will also be evaluated.

CANDIDA AND WHEAT IMBALANCES

I see people of all ages who are suffering from candida disorders. It is a very common complaint but unfortunately one that is not generally recognised by the medical profession. Despite findings and evidence to support it, many medical practitioners refuse to accept that candida even exists. This is a tragedy, as those who suffer the serious symptoms are often directed to a psychiatrist for their 'mental disorder'.

I first came across the symptoms of candida in the early 90s and realised immediately that I also had the disorder. There are many levels from slight to chronic and it can run in families being passed on through the mother. Severe infection can result in quite neurotic and even schizophrenic behaviour. Chronic candida symptoms are very dangerous as the ablicans (fungi) can spread from the colon and get into organs in the body such as the lungs.

Candida Symptoms

Candida can give many symptoms across emotional, mental and physical areas such as:

- Yeast infection
- Recurrent thrush and/or cystitis
- Chronic tiredness, poor energy and fatigue
- Inability to lose weight

- Depression, anxiety and uncontrollable mood swings
- Allergies - also linked to chronic skin problems such as acne and dermatitis
- Fluid retention and premenstrual syndrome
- Diarrhoea or constipation

Sufferers can experience any one or a number of these symptoms. All can have symptoms of hypoglycaemia, which results in sugar cravings, and diabetics are also susceptible to candida because of the high blood sugar.

Symptoms can be slow to show themselves and, in the meantime, the candida can take a serious hold. Bloating and constipation may show themselves quite early on, together with not being able to lose weight despite dieting. Sugar and chocolate cravings continue and we find these difficult to ignore. Mood swings and headaches may follow but can also be symptoms in their own right.

Skin disorders and allergies can also occur as the body only has three excretory systems to get rid of waste - the bowel, the skin and the kidneys. The skin will often be affected first, becoming weak. Malabsorption will occur, so good food with vitamins and minerals needed to make the body strong will not be absorbed. Over time, the body becomes even weaker.

The intestinal tract is there to balance the colon and acid in the body. Too much intake of acidic foods such as dairy, meat and wheat can therefore cause an imbalance in the digestion process as they metabolise as acid in the body. Like in a pond where the water becomes overgrown with algae, it becomes murky and smells. This means that the pH of the water is imbalanced. Likewise, the same imbalance can also happen to our stomach.

I love the TV advert where a woman is putting food into her handbag, (the advertisement is for a laxative). She just keeps putting it in and taking nothing out until it is bulging, smelling and fermenting. It is a good way to show just what is happening when we suffer constipation and don't clear waste products from our bodies daily.

When we are not clearing out the bowel and colon it creates an imbalance with the stomach, fermenting and bloating. It feels as though it is about to burst. When this happens on an ongoing basis, it creates the right conditions for the yeast to get a hold in the colon, creating the disorder of candida and interfering with the natural process of the colon. It then interferes with other processes in the body by allowing toxins to build up, affecting the immune system, the liver and causing the sufferer to feel generally under-par. In fact, research has found that most of those who have suffered from cancer have also had an imbalanced colon disorder such as constipation.

What causes the proliferation of Candida?
Anything that unbalances the 'friendly bacteria' in the colon will allow yeast to proliferate. A depleted or compromised immune system will allow bacteria like yeast to flourish and endocrine imbalances from stress and blood sugar imbalances, which manifest themselves in the form of low thyroid or depleted adrenal function, can also support the growth of candida.

Antibiotics can wipe out our entire colony of friendly bacteria and leave the yeast intact, while the frequent use of steroids can also deplete good bacteria. Yeasts feeds on sugar and their growth is promoted by the yeast added to food and drink, such as bread, vegemite, alcohol and other fermented products. Diets, which are high in sugar, additionally provide the yeast with more to feed on.

Environmental moulds such as fungi and mould found in damp bathrooms or house foundations can promote the problem and it is usually the case that women suffer more than men. A root structure develops and burrows through the walls of the intestinal mucosa in search of nutrients. Proteins then enter the blood stream and can cause symptoms of leaky gut.

Yeast produces 80 different toxins, ten of which are proven neurotoxins.
Debilitating symptoms develop causing chronic tiredness and vaginal thrush or cystitis. Progesterone also favours the growth of yeast. This can be found in the birth pill or hormonal treatment cortisone (HRT), making the condition worse. Susceptible people have a low

resistance, especially those who have a poor diet and high antibiotic use. Poor resistance will often result in a degree of food and chemical intolerance.

We have a natural gut system which controls the balance of yeasts and bacteria by producing its own antibiotics, thereby avoiding dominance of one organism and maintaining a healthy environment for the body as a whole. Candida is a yeast which is seen as normal to the body (in the skin, digestive tract and vagina) but when it becomes dominant, yeast becomes a problem and overgrowth occurs. When this happens, harmless round cells change into filament shapes, allowing them to develop the ability to attach to intestinal walls, making them strong and persistent.

Diet and candida

I know from experience that a programme to kill and eliminate yeast is the only way to rid the body of this condition. A programme of elimination from diet, together with supplements to kill off candida ablicans and support body systems, will be required.

When food sources are removed from the diet, candida will return to a cyst form and use its ability to remain dormant, waiting to strike again when alcohol, antibiotics, carbohydrates or sugar are reintroduced. That is why it is best to kill off the ablicans with an anti-candida programme, destroying the spores and ultimately reducing the toxins in the body.

Die-off reaction while on the programme can result temporarily in headaches and in feeling generally unwell. Nausea may be felt as the breakdown of products and toxins from the body are released into the blood stream and digestion for elimination.

While on the anti-candida programme, support products will be suggested to help the liver and other organs during the die-off period and after. It is wise to see a nutritionist or a candida specialist who can help and support the programme.

A strong gut immune system is essential for a healthy body, so treating candida is essential. Getting rid of it, however, can take up to 3 months for a mild dose and, depending upon the severity of the condition, it could take up to 12 months to clear completely.

Naturopaths regard the use of wheat in diets as suppressive to the constitution and contributing to the acidity of the tissues. It creates an imbalanced pH in the stomach acidity. Where inflammatory symptoms occur together with mineral imbalances, it is recommended that dairy items be excluded from the diet, since dairy products (from cow's milk) are also acidic to the body's natural balance. Lactobacteria (good bacteria) from yoghurt etc., keeps yeast in check and, without it, yeasts can take hold.

Diagnosis and Treatment

The difficulty with candida is that these are all innocent symptoms which could be from anything. That is why it is sometimes mistaken for a depression disorder.

The lymph and immune system can soon become overloaded with toxins and we may find ourselves susceptible to picking up any virus or cold that is going around. If given antibiotics to help clear it up, this will knock out the friendly bacteria and allow the yeast to flourish even more, resulting in a strengthened candida within the body.

I use hair analysis to check the levels of minerals and toxins in the body. Stool testing can also be used to ascertain the level of candida ablicans (low, moderate or high), with both giving very accurate results for the client.

Find a professional therapist who does this type of testing if you suspect or identify with any of the descriptions or symptoms listed. If nothing else, it is a programme of elimination.
See appendix for anti-candida diet recommendations

POLYCYSTIC OVARIAN SYNDROME

Polycystic Ovarian Syndrome (PCOS) is the most common hormonal reproductive problem in women of childbearing age and estimates suggest that up to 10% of women suffer from this condition.

Despite many theories, the medical profession does not seem to know the exact cause of PCOS, although frequently women with the complaint have a mother or sister who has also suffered. To date, however, evidence to suggest that it is a genetic disorder or condition has not yet been proved sufficiently by researchers.

What is Polycystic Ovarian Syndrome?

Polycystic Ovarian Syndrome (PCOS) is a health condition, which can not only affect a woman's menstrual cycle but also affects:

- Fertility
- Hormones
- Insulin production
- The heart
- Blood vessels

It is notable that many women with PCOS also have a weight problem and so research is currently ongoing to look at the connection with weight and the relationship between PCOS and the body's ability to make insulin.

Some women with PCOS make too much insulin. When this happens, the body reacts by telling the ovaries to produce an excess of male hormones (androgens). These high levels of male hormones circulating in the body lead to:

- Skin problems such as acne
- Excessive hair growth
- Weight gain
- Ovulation problems
- Irregularities in the menstrual cycle and sometimes no menstrual cycle will occur at all
- Cysts in the ovaries (cysts are fluid filled sacs)

It is believed that many cysts in the polycystic ovary are follicles which have matured, but due to abnormal hormone levels, were never released[66].

Symptoms

Infertility, or the inability to become pregnant, is one of the main indicators that PCOS may be an issue. Because the egg matures in the ovary but is not released into the fallopian tube for fertilization, conception cannot take place. Other signs of the condition include:

- The ovaries produce high amounts of the male hormone testosterone
- Ovulation dysfunctions
- Infrequent and irregular periods
- Acne
- Oily skin
- Male pattern baldness
- Type 2 diabetes
- High cholesterol levels
- High blood pressure
- Pelvic pain
- Weight gain or obesity leading to excessive weight around the waist
- Thickened patches of black/brown skin on the neck, arms or thighs
- Increased hair growth on the body, including the face, back, chest, toes, thumbs and stomach.

Weight Loss and PCOS

Trials have shown that menstrual cycles can be normalised and fertility re-established through weight loss[67]. Studies have also indicated that long-term calorie restriction and weight reduction could restore regular ovulation, while regular exercise is also linked to a lasting effect upon insulin production and responsiveness. Simple changes can have a huge impact on this condition and one study showed that symptoms of acne, dysmenorrhoea and menstrual irregularities significantly decreased in those taking more than eight hours of sporting activity a week[68].

Obviously, eating disorders should be evaluated as a matter of course, especially in adolescents.

Medication for PCOS

Some medication used for treating PCOS has been found to have side effects. Effects like abnormal uterine bleeding, weight gain and liver disorders have all been discovered using conventional approaches.

Other treatments for PCOS

Aside from traditional medication, there are other things that sufferers of PCOS can try. These include:

- Improving the diet and consuming more fibre
- Exercising at least four times a week
- Rebalancing hormones and adrenal functions. Balancing the adrenal function also helps the body to cope with physical and mental stress
- Detoxing the liver - the liver needs to be detoxed to help it function normally and this will also help with hormone metabolism and enhance hepatic insulin clearance. Be sure to take advice on this from a registered practitioner.

Diet assists reduction of PCOS symptoms

PCOS sufferers should take in more nutrients, herbs and super foods to support the body, such as:

Agnus Castus

Agnus Castus is a herb which is more commonly known as Chastetree berry. It does not contain hormones and yet is thought to exert hormonal activity by its action on the pituitary gland, thereby helping with Lutein hormone (LH) release. LH stimulates corpus luteal secretions after ovulation to produce progesterone, which ultimately regulates a woman's cycle.

Alfalfa

Alfalfa is a wonderful super food for women and a great tonic. It:

- Neutralises acids and toxins in the body and nourishes the blood, kidneys and guts

- Tonifies intestines, regulates digestion, digestive disorders and malabsorption and reduces heartburn, gas and bloating
- Contains all the vitamins and minerals necessary for life
- Is high in natural digestive enzymes and contains more than 40 different bioflavonoids
- Contains amino acids, most vitamins and minerals
- Has four times more vitamin C than most citrus fruits
- Breaks down fat, cellulose and starch in the body
- Reduces inflammation in the lungs and is therefore useful for those with asthma, pneumonia and bronchitis
- Is a natural deodoriser and infection fighter because it has a high content of chlorophyll and vitamin A
- Helps carry intestinal waste from the body, softens stools and improves the contracting action of the colon. Through the same action it also relieves water retention and excess fluid

Aloe Vera

In the Sanskrit language, aloe translates as 'goddess' and of course it is well known as being one of nature's healers and strengtheners.

Ayurvedic medicine considers aloe to be oestrogenic - vitalising and tonifying for women. Aloe Vera is commonly used by women who are going through the menopause and adjusting to the changing state of their bodies, as at this time they tend to be low in fluids that nurture the liver.

Both aloe whole leaf and organic liquid are widely used for their immune regulatory properties and are known for their anti-inflammatory properties. The inner leaf is used more as a gel to treat sunburn, wounds, cuts, grazes and blemishes, as it is higher in salicylates and tends to be kinder for skin use. The benefits that it provides include:

- It is rich in plant sterols, amino acids and polysaccharides
- It is good for the liver
- It strengthens and repairs all organs and damaged cell tissue

- It reduces inflammation
- It assists digestion
- It promotes free flow of energy through meridians
- It is good for counteracting candida or yeast-related problems, as it is active against bacteria such as fungi. Aloe Vera is known to contain Caprylic acid, which kills fungi ablicans.

Chromium

Chromium is used in the treatment of glucose and insulin-related irregularities. It is an important ingredient which:

- Helps with carbohydrate metabolism
- Stimulates the activity of enzymes involved in the metabolism of glucose for energy and the synthesis of fatty acids and cholesterol. When the glucose tolerance factor is too low, the activity of insulin is blocked and blood glucose levels are elevated

Whole grains, eggs and meat are the best natural sources of chromium, however, most fruit and vegetables contain only low levels, except for broccoli, which has a naturally high level. A chromium supplement taken daily, has been proven to reduce glucose tolerance and improve insulin circulation.

Fibre

Fibre reduces insulin secretion by slowing the rise of nutrient absorption following a meal. Studies have shown that insulin sensitivity increases and body weight decreases in people on high fibre diets. It also helps give a bulking effect to increase faecal volume, limit caloric intake and slow the stomach emptying.

Increasing your fibre intake also acts as an anti-candida diet, helping to clear any yeast ablicans from the body. Reducing caffeine, eliminating all sugar from your diet and cutting out alcohol is also advised for this purpose.

Fish oils

Fish oils are an important part of the treatment for PCOS and your body will need a balance of Omega 3 and 6 oils. Regularly take a good quality fish oil or eat oily fish. Some fish are harvested from polluted waters where heavy metals can accumulate in their livers, so it is always best to get fish oil from a good source.

Fish oils have been shown to:

- Increase thermo-genesis
- Decrease body fat
- Improve glucose clearance
- Help with brain function
- Improve skin and eye health
- Maintain cell membrane integrity
- Increase joint mobility and liver function

Flax seed

Flax seed is classed as a super food and is proven to have numerous chemo-protective effects. I suggest powdered sprouted flax seed as it is easy to take and has additional benefits from the sprouting. Seed and capsule forms are also available. Flax seed:

- Is known to help reduce mammary tumour growth and formation
- Helps regulate weight and bowel functions
- Lowers cholesterol and blood pressure
- Enhances skin
- Improves and strengthens immunity and reproduction
- Helps to prevent colon and breast cancer – as it combats tumour growth
- Elevates moods
- Helps to alleviate allergies
- Cleanses arteries
- Is rich in essential fatty acids Omega 3 and 6

Nettle

The roots of the stinging nettle have a complex mix of water and alcohol-soluble compounds, including Lectins, phenol, sterols and Lignans and it is the Lignans which are thought to provide the positive effects of taking nettle. Nettle is also a diuretic and can be taken as a tea, but as it is an acquired taste it is better to start weak and then increase the strength as your taste buds adapt.

Available in teabags from the supermarket or you can pick the leaves and make your own brew, alternatively you can take nettle in capsule form.

Parsley

Parsley is a warming food which can either be taken fresh or in multivitamin form. It is immune enhancing, a multivitamin and a mineral complex which supports kidney, liver and adrenal glands, helping to purify blood and body fluids. Its main characteristics and benefits include:

- Multi vitamin and nutrient powerhouse
- Contains B12, chlorophyll, calcium and high levels of beta-carotene
- Contains all other known nutrients such as iron, calcium, phosphorus and manganese, sulphur, vitamin K and Flavonoids.
- Good for digestion.
- Chokes negative bacteria
- Helps the body's defensive mechanisms
- An immune booster
- Balances and stimulates the energy of the organs, helping them to utilise and assimilate nutrients

The chlorophyll in parsley is anti-bacterial and promotes anti-fungal activity. It relieves mucus congestion, sinusitis and other damp conditions, suppresses viruses and helps the lungs to discharge residues from environmental pollution. Used in cases of cystitis, it has the ability to flush out waste.

Body detoxification is another important consideration that we mentioned in relation to PCOS and indeed this is something which is used to prepare the body for pregnancy – although it should NOT be done during pregnancy.

Saw palmetto

This herb, also known as 'Serenoa Repens', is one of the most widely-used botanicals in the treatment of PCOS. It has been found to be comparable to the pharmaceutical agent Finasteride[69].

THE LIVER AND DETOXIFICATION

In preparing for pregnancy or if you are having difficulty in becoming pregnant detoxing can help prepare and clear the body. Detoxification of the liver is especially important because the liver is one of the most important organs in the body and it is essential that we keep it healthy. It is involved in the elimination of poisons and chemicals from the body but can sometimes become overloaded by alcohol, medication, diet and fatty substances.

Liver flush and milk thistle can be used to detox the liver if you are preparing for pregnancy or post-natally. Milk thistle (also known as Silymarin) is part of the sunflower family and in its natural state it has prickly leaves. Its ingestion is extremely effective in detoxing the liver and keeping it in better condition, and combined with a liver flush to detox when we have over-indulged in rich foods. As we have said, however, it should not be used when you are pregnant or if you are breastfeeding.

Be sure to see a good nutritionist to help with diet and give support during any kind of detox process and as a basic diet improvement.

A 7-day liver spring clean detox suggestion list is shown in the appendix.

THYROID IMBALANCE

Sometimes we give too much in all that we do. As women, we juggle so many things at once and wear so many hats. Caring for family, acting as nurse, holding down a full-time job and looking after house and garden leaves no time for ourselves. When we are continuously depleted of energy, the thyroid (a small gland) will be affected.

The thyroid gland is part of the endocrine system and the main part of the endocrine or hormonal system comprises the pituitary, thyroid, adrenals, pancreas and gonads. The pituitary also produces thyroid-stimulating hormone (TSH), which regulates the thyroid. If the thyroid is not producing enough hormones, the TSH pushes the thyroid into making more, therefore balancing the thyroid to the proper levels. However, if the thyroid is making too much hormone, the TSH levels will fall and the thyroid will not make as much. Consequently, the pituitary can be involved in dysfunctional thyroid disorders.

Essentially, hyperthyroidism (overactive thyroid) is a condition where the thyroid produces an excess of hormones, which speed up metabolism, anxiety and weight loss. Hypothyroidism (underactive thyroid), on the other hand, is the result of hormone production failure and failure of processing and tissue uptake[70]. In this case, the thyroid gland does not make enough hormones which leads to the metabolism slowing down, causing tiredness and weight increase.

Among several others, the thyroid gland makes two hormones, T4 (thyroxin) and T3 (tri-iodothyronine). More T4 is produced than T3 and as much as 50 times more T4 than T3 is normally found in the blood stream.
Most of these hormones are then carried around the bloodstream bound to two proteins, although some manage to float around on their own. On arrival at their allotted destination, the hormones are then released from the protein. T4 hormone is then converted to T3. Only T3 is active on the cells, making this the most important hormone used by the body.

Some doctors believe it is possible that even though blood tests are normal and the conversion of T4 to T3 within the organs is taken into account, some form of brain or body hypothyroidism due to the lack of T3 can still exist. Having a normal TSH level does not necessarily mean that your brain and organs are receiving the exact amount[71]. Research has shown that a lack of T3 may be linked to the cause of residual symptoms such as depression and mental alertness, lack of libido and being overweight[72].

Under active Thyroid

Thyroid under-activity is more common than we think and its most common cause is destruction of the gland or interference with its activity by abnormal action of the body's immune mechanism. Factors, however, are poorly understood. Sometimes it is inherited and runs in families, while in other cases stress and anxiety over a long period of time can affect thyroid gland production.

It is already well known that if you have an under-active or under-par thyroid it can be more difficult to become pregnant and a lot of the women that I have seen, and continue to see, have underactive thyroid symptoms, which might have been caused by any of the following:

- Pituitary or hypothalamic failure, causing secondary thyroid insufficiency and adrenal dysfunctions
- Major emotional or physical trauma
- Glandular fever - very common and insufficiently recognised
- Genetic dysfunction - can be from birth
- Traumatic or multiple pregnancy - a major cause of massive weight gain
- Tonsillectomy - often damages the thyroid blood supply
- Environmental challenges or deficiencies - chemical or dental amalgam can interfere with thyroid production
- Surgery - especially gall bladder and more commonly, hysterectomy
- Auto immune conditions and dysfunctions

Symptoms

The symptoms of the condition which are most commonly seen include:

- Tiredness and fatigue
- Lack of concentration
- Poor memory
- Brittle nails
- Muscle cramps
- Light head and dizzy spells
- Muscle aches
- Constipation
- Dryness of skin
- Weight gain and difficulty losing weight
- Heavy menstrual periods
- Puffiness around the eyes, face and ankles
- Blurring of eyes or poor focusing
- Hair loss
- Headaches
- Tendency for candida and thrush
- Adrenal problems

An underactive thyroid can also cause an increase in prolactin, the hormone produced by the pituitary gland, which induces and maintains the production of breast milk in a post-partum woman.

Known as sub-clinical hypothyroidism, a large percentage of the population can have a slightly underactive thyroid with no apparent illness, although this is more common in women than men. Even celebrities are known to suffer thyroid imbalance with stress and overwork being the cause.

Oprah Winfrey recently suffered from thyroid imbalance due to overwork and needed to rest and take time out for herself. It took her some time, going from doctor to doctor, to find out why she felt so ill. Even after a month's rest, she could still feel the effects of the condition. Indeed it can take time for the thyroid to recover on its own, although a diet, which includes more foods containing iodine does help. Of course, rest is the key factor in recovery.

Testing

For women who are being treated for infertility and miscarriage, I suggest a Barnes test to find the basal body temperature. The test acts as a guide to whether thyroid problems exist and should be used together with consultation because care must be taken as virus or infection could affect the results.

It was Broda Barnes MD who pioneered the body temperature test, which needs to be done first thing in the morning when your body is at rest. To ensure a valid reading, you should avoid alcohol the night before. Menstruating women take their temperatures on the 2nd, 3rd and 4th days of their periods only and those who are non-menstruating can take the test at any time of the month.

The test is taken using a mercury thermometer, which is placed under the arm and left for ten minutes. By taking readings five days in a row, it does provide fairly accurate results and was a system used regularly before blood tests were introduced. If your temperature falls below 97.8°F (36.6°C) you should consult your doctor.

Blood testing took over as the best means of detecting thyroid imbalance and is the preferred method used by the medical profession today. However, blood tests are also known for not picking up hypothyroidism accurately, although they do show acute cases of thyroid imbalance, especially where the symptoms are severe.

Unfortunately even in a mild imbalance of thyroid or hypothyroidism, symptoms can make you feel very unwell. Although it does not show in the band that determines whether you have imbalance or dysfunction, the symptoms you feel are very real and you need to take action to alleviate them before they become severe. This is especially true if you want to increase your chances of becoming fertile and eliminating further miscarriages.

Thyroid and the affects of ovulation

Thyroid imbalance is associated with anovulation, a term used to describe the lack of ovulation or release of an egg. With no egg to fertilise, conception becomes impossible. It is also associated with other menstrual irregularities. Some women also experience a short luteal phase. The luteal phase needs to be of sufficient duration (normally 13-15 days) to nurture a fertilized egg. Too short a phase can cause what appears to be infertility. Actually though, it is the failure to sustain a fertilized egg which is the problem, with the loss of the very early pregnancy occurring at around the same time as the next menstruation would typically begin.

If you are having fertility problems and yet your blood tests have come back 'normal', you may be mildly 'hypothyroidal', which in turn could be causing your infertility. Have yourself checked by a thyroid specialist for symptoms of hypothyroidism.

In terms of treatment, the drug Thyroxin has proved to be effective to rebalance thyroid hormones, although in chronic cases radiotherapy or surgery may also be recommended. Alternative remedies and supplements can help for those who choose not to use the drug.

If you are already on a thyroid hormone during pregnancy, do not stop taking it. Until the foetus is thirteen weeks old it has no thyroid of its own and takes all its thyroid hormone from you. Thyroid hormones are critical for normal brain development and maturation. Correction of any iodine deficiency must occur before conception or certainly before the first trimester if it is to be of value, as maternal iodine deficiency can lead to foetal hypothyroidism. You therefore need to have your thyroid hormone levels checked early in your first trimester as well as later on in your pregnancy.

It is also worth noting that, according to the August 1999 edition of the New England Journal of Medicine, children born of women who suffered from untreated underactive thyroids during pregnancy are nearly four times more likely to have lower IQ scores.

Sometimes when the blood prick test is done on newborn children, it may show a false positive because of the mother's own thyroid condition. Hence it is important to let your doctor know if you (the mother) are prescribed regular replacement treatment for a thyroid dysfunction.

Doctors who specialise in the condition can do testing for thyroid privately. See appendix for details

TOXIC OVERLOAD

A toxin is defined as any substance that has a detrimental effect on cell function or structure. Toxic overload in the body can come from a variety of sources. Anything from cigarette tar residue to a mouthful of mercury fillings can trigger serious disorders in susceptible people. The overload condition may be endogenous (from the body) or exogenous (environmental) and exposure may be acute or chronic.

The body always has a certain amount of free radicals (damaged cells). A toxic build-up increases the free radical level, which can accumulate with age. Free radicals are implicated in a wide range of disorders from Crohn's to ulcerative colitis. Exposure can come from chemical toxins in the environment or from products that we use every day in the bathroom and for household cleaning. Overload typically results in immune dysfunction and/or disorders of the nervous system, respiratory illness and increased incidence of cancer.

Heavy metals such as lead and cadmium within the body can undermine the function of the brain, kidneys and immune systems. The primary organs normally responsible for clearing the body, such as the colon, liver, kidneys and skin, are also affected. If the organs are put under too much pressure then the problem will show on the skin. This can result in disorders such as skin rashes, spots, eczema and even psoriasis.

The toxic problem has grown in so-called 'modern times'. We now pollute the environment more and more with the way that we live, what we eat, what we buy for our personal use and the things that we use in the home.

The holistic approach

A holistic approach to counteracting toxicity build-up is the use of optimum nutrition, regular exercise and hydration. Six to eight glasses of water a day is recommended, as water is a wonderful cleanser. Another effective way is to use nutritional supplements, which help to maintain the body's detoxification process based upon nutritional support.

We need to support and look after our livers. Using antioxidants such as vitamins C and E and beta-carotene, either in single or combined supplement form, helps the liver to do its job more effectively. Minerals are also essential. Calcium, magnesium and zinc are fundamental in our body's balance.

Copper and magnesium are also important in the neutralisation of some toxic chemicals. We need substances which promote bile flow and fat mobilisation within the liver. If our liver is not effective in its function, then eventually all our body systems become overloaded. Clay has also been used successfully to remove toxins such as aluminium and mercury from the body.

Modern-day living, stress and the environment all leave our bodies vulnerable to toxins. We only need to fill the car with fuel and we have breathed in fumes. Most of our food contains additives and has been sprayed several times with chemicals before harvesting. We even breathe in car fumes when we walk down the street and our deodorant, soaps, toothpaste and cleaning materials can all contain toxic chemicals.

Although we may be exposed to these substances in very small doses, over time our bodies can accumulate a wide range of toxins that they are unable to excrete. If we do not look after our body and the elimination process is further hampered by constipation or the lack of acids to break down the contents of the gut, we can suffer a build-up of unwanted microbes and parasites. Bacteria begin to grow within the gut and can affect other systems and organs if the condition becomes critical. When the colon becomes sluggish or blocked, additional demands are placed upon the other organs, leaving our entire body sluggish and fatigued.

Regular detoxing allows the body to work more efficiently. If we fail to put our car in for a service and have the dirty gummed-up oil changed by the garage mechanic, the engine doesn't work well, and yet we expect our body to work efficiently on that premise. We constantly fill up on detrimental foods that don't suit us, but fail to clear out often enough.

WEIGHT & ANOREXIA

Anorexia can have a dramatic impact upon a woman's menstrual process and the natural fertility of her body. Recent studies have found that anorexia has links with emotional impacts from the womb and birth.

I have treated women who were anorexic in their earlier years and who, despite a return to near normal body weight, found that when they later wanted to start a family, had problems conceiving. In these cases it is often necessary to change their diets because, in most instances, they still do not eat enough and are not getting the right oils and minerals into their systems. For their bodies to function normally and for them to become fertile again, certain nutrients need to be replenished.

The key to overcoming infertility issues in anorexic or formerly anorexic women lies in improving basic menstruation. Correct menstruation is essential in these cases, as often they are not having regular periods. Addressing this issue provides a starting point in balancing the hormonal system using treatments such as reflexology and lymph drainage to clear fluid blockages.

Additional approaches to infertility :

- Taking a hair sample for laboratory analysis to check for imbalances in the tissues and cells of the body. Based on the results of this analysis, we can improve the basic health with vitamins and minerals to rebalance hormone levels and ultimately rebuild and support the body structure. It is important to improve the diet and levels of essential oils ingested to ensure they are getting sufficient Omega 3 and 6 into the body, as well as to improve the body's energy levels so that it is in the right physical condition

- Sometimes emotional blockages can get in the way, especially since anorexia usually stems from an emotional disorder. For this, we need to find the key using emotional release techniques

- Deep relaxation techniques can be used to de-stress the body and improve normal sleep patterns

- Like a gardener creating good soil conditions a women's body needs to be physically ready for growth. I suggest pH testing to check the body for excess acid in vaginal mucus and tissue so that work can begin on improving and balancing the conditions and general health. Like a pond, when the pH levels are incorrect we see lots of unwanted growth and fermentation and the same thing happens in the human body

In my experience it can take a little time to put things right after a woman has suffered from anorexia. Although of course everyone is different, it may take up to a year to put things in the right balanced condition for natural fertility to kick in again but, it can be done so don't lose heart.

I have achieved great success in helping women who have been anorexic and wanted to start a family. Following the announcement of conception, I have also helped subsequently to support these women through their full pregnancy, with alternative therapy techniques.

HORMONAL IMBALANCE

Oestrogen and progesterone are both hormones made naturally within the body and, essentially, progesterone works to counteract the effects of too much oestrogen in the body. Whilst the body makes three types of oestrogen (oestradiol, oestrone and oestriol), it only makes one type of progesterone.

Progesterone

As far back as the 1940s progesterone was found to be beneficial to women. It is found in the nerve sheaths, cells in the bones and in the brain cells and is a vital component, not only in relation to female fertility, but also in terms of supporting a growing embryo. It can only be made in the ovaries while the woman is ovulating and it is the hormone secreted by the ovary in the second half of the menstrual ovulation, made by the empty follicle or egg sac after it has released an egg by the process of ovulation. It goes into production at the time of ovulation and, if no conception occurs, then progesterone levels fall and menstruation is triggered. If conception does take place, however, levels of the hormone rise and remain high throughout the course of the pregnancy in support of the embryo.

The lack of progesterone has been linked to infertility, something which has been highlighted through testing thyroid dysfunction. Many women fail to ovulate regularly after the age of thirty-five and hence suffer infertility later in life. Although these women bleed every month, they do not ovulate or produce progesterone. Use of the birth pill, diet and the environment can all play their part in hormone imbalances and can lead to women becoming oestrogen dominant. Where this is found to be a factor in infertility, natural progesterone can be used to redress the balance of progesterone.

A US doctor called Dr John Lee conducted a series of hormonal trials and successfully treated women suffering from infertility imbalance with progesterone cream. When treated with natural progesterone (over time) they became fertile once again. For women who come to me for fertility imbalances, I normally suggest that they use an ovulation kit to check if and when they are ovulating, as well as the use of progesterone cream where appropriate.

Natural progesterone is produced from a plant called the Mexican yam. Used in a cream, it is absorbed into the skin and blood, affecting the hormone balance directly. It is identical in every way to the hormone produced in the ovaries and is called 'natural progesterone'

Ray Peat PhD, professor of Blake College Oregon, studied female hormones for some years and came up with the idea of using progesterone in vitamin E. He found that it could be absorbed through the skin much more efficiently than taking it orally[73].

Synthetic progesterone - is known as progestagens (progestins in the US). This synthetic hormone is similar, but not identical, to natural progesterone. As progesterone is a natural substance, it cannot be patented and is therefore not profitable for pharmaceutical companies to obtain a licence to produce it. However, if the natural substance is changed even slightly, it can then be licensed as a medicine. Confusingly, doctors and researchers have used the name progesterone to mean both natural progesterone and the synthetic progestagens. When prescribed, the synthetic or natural origin is unclear to the user.

Synthetic progesterone, which is usually taken orally, was originally prescribed by doctors who believed that it was also metabolised naturally in the body. Unfortunately, it was later found that synthetic progesterone could be highly toxic and has different effects from the naturally produced progesterone in the body. Being taken orally, it was ingested into the liver instead of directly into the bloodstream where the hormones can be more effective.

Synthetic Progesterone does not mix well with alcohol. Professor Peat discovered that using solvents that do mix with progesterone only makes the combination highly toxic to the body[74].

Oestrogen

Oestrogen continues to be produced in the body indefinitely, held in the fat cells and muscles, adrenal glands, liver and brain, although it is known to decline at the time of the menopause. Progesterone production can also decline to very small amounts and even reach zero levels in some women at the time of the menopause.
Oestrogen has a stimulating effect within the body and when produced

to excess can be toxic. We now know through various research, including that undertaken by Dr Lee between the 1960s and 2002, that too much oestrogen can cause fibrocystic breasts, increased heart and cardiovascular disease and is also linked to an increased risk of breast cancer[75].

Oestrogen also stimulates the lining of the womb (the endometrium) and is linked with an increased risk of fibroids and endometrial cancer. Fibroids are a very common and painful disorder that many women suffer from and which can often lead to hysterectomy.

When we reach puberty, oestrogen hormones come into play. Sexual organs mature and girls start to grow breasts, curves and pubic hair. Oestrogen builds up in the first half of each month, stimulating and thickening the womb lining in anticipation of a fertilised egg.

Synthetic oestrogen is used in the contraceptive pill, with some varieties of pills also containing progesterone in small amounts. It is also used during the menopause in HRT formulations and patches.

Imbalance occurs when there is an excess difference between levels of progesterone and oestrogen in the body. This condition is manifested as oestrogen dominance. Because of our over-use of oestrogen with the contraceptive pill and HRT, we are seeing oestrogen dominance in many women.

Oestrogen balance is essential for a healthy body. However, many women are receiving too much oestrogen by ingesting extra synthetic oestrogen hormones via the birth pill, steroids through their diets and the food chain, in medication and even remnants of oestrogen in drinking water (oestrogen cannot be filtered out). Over time, their bodies become out of balance with high oestrogen and low progesterone levels.

Not only is oestrogen itself an issue

Many of the chemicals in our food and environment act like oestrogen in the body. Unknowingly, we ingest oestrogen look-a-likes from the use of pesticides, toxic substances used in plastics, hair dyes, cosmetics, spermicdes and even drinking water. Sometimes called Xenoestrogens (foreign oestrogens), they mirror the oestrogenic effect and are capable of doubling or trebling the influence of oestrogen in the body.

Xenoestrogens are very potent and Dr Lee believed that one of the consequences of being exposed to such chemicals was that some women used up the eggs in their ovaries far too quickly and often reached 'burn out' in their mid thirties. Clearly this is far younger than we expect. According to Dr Lee's reasoning, long-term exposure to modern toxins in the environment eventually leads to inadequate ovulation and less production of progesterone. In addition, oestrogen dominance creates infertility with an increased risk of breast and endometrial disorders, including cancer. Judging by the rising incidence, this certainly seems to be the case today.

Symptoms of oestrogen dominance

Sometimes the symptoms of oestrogen dominance have been put down to age or diet dysfunctions, but it is important not to assume that these are the cause. If you find yourself suffering from any of the following and are in any doubt as to the cause, check with your doctor or health practitioner.

- Allergy
- Breast tenderness and swelling
- Bloating
- Cravings for sweet things
- Depression and anxiety
- Dizziness and foggy mind
- Hair loss
- Heavy or irregular periods
- Facial hair growth
- Fatigue
- Fibroids
- Loss of sex drive
- Mood swings
- PMS
- Water retention (oedema)
- Weight gain - especially around the hips and thighs

As pointed out previously, progesterone is there to counteract oestrogen. However, if not enough progesterone is being produced in the body there will likely be a dominance of oestrogen. We know that progesterone can be diminished by not ovulating or going through the menopause but, depending upon our diet or even just drinking water, we are probably getting more oestrogen than we know of on a daily basis.

Are we creating a world of infertility?

Daily we are seeing signs of the effects of oestrogen in the water with our fish stocks diminishing, men losing their hair earlier in life and more women becoming less fertile. All this is happening because we cannot filter out the effects of oestrogen from our drinking water and urine.

Dr Lee carried out hormone tests, which proved oestrogen dominance in women. Even in younger women he found much lower progesterone levels than normal and, from this, he discovered that progesterone was the missing hormone in most women, being responsible for disorders such as:

- Menopausal problems
- Some cases of infertility
- Low libido
- Breast disease and disorders
- Uterine fibroids
- Cervical hyperplasia
- Endometriosis
- Ovarian cysts
- Osteoporosis

Natural progesterone is prescribed for many imbalances and disorders and indeed Dr Lee used progesterone cream in his practice for over 20 years with huge success. He made the case for prescribing body-identical progesterone for women's hormonal health, including during the menopause and in cases of infertility, along with publicising the benefits of using a natural progesterone cream, which is ingested into the blood for best effect. He held that progesterone in tablet form mainly goes into the liver, whereas the cream, is more easily absorbed by the hormones through the blood.

Progesterone cream

Progesterone cream is used on any soft tissue of the body once or twice daily, beginning twelve days after the first day of your period. Cream is applied daily for fourteen days and then discontinued. After the first day of the next cycle, the application is repeated again for twelve days. Over his many years as a GP, having pieced together the information that many women were progesterone deficient, Dr Lee helped a large number of women using natural progesterone with the following results being achieved:

- Premenstrual tension vanished
- Fibrocystic breasts began clearing up
- Water retention which had built up over the years reduced without the need for diuretics
- Women suffering from depression were starting to feel good about themselves
- Low thyroid function reverted to normal
- Fibroids were reduced in size to avoid surgery or shrank completely

Dr Lee also linked infertility with thyroid dysfunction and in his practice used progesterone cream to help women clear and rebalance these dysfunctions to a normal state. The women he treated with this imbalance became fertile once again. Used as a preventative for menstrual bleeding, progesterone can help to reduce the pain of endometriosis, although the lack of it is not the cause.

Using progesterone from day 10 to day 26 of the menstrual cycle, Dr Lee found that pelvic pain and bleeding were reduced. When used over time, he found that the body had a chance to recover and, in his book Natural Progesterone, he stated that none of the patients who followed his regime needed surgery, but does advise that this must be carried out under the supervision of a doctor or health practitioner.

It is believed that osteoporosis also starts silently in our thirties.

Dr Lee believed that although oestrogen can help slow down bone density loss in a limited way, it is primarily a progesterone deficient disease, as progesterone stimulates the osteoblasts cells responsible for laying down new bone. Natural progesterone is also shown to protect from endometrial cancer. In research, however, synthetic progestogens have been shown to give the opposite effect in the body and can cause cancer.

In an Oxford University study, Dr Lee proved without doubt halfway through the trials that synthetic HRT hormones increased the risk of heart disease and strokes for those on the drug. This data was published in the Lancet under the title of The Million Women Study (MWS). Dr Lee spent his life pioneering information about oestrogen dominance in the UK, Europe and the USA before dying in 2003, shortly after the positive results were made aware to the public. He wrote several books and papers and made videos on women's health and progesterone, enabling women and doctors to decide if natural progesterone usage was right for them. He also founded a natural progesterone information service

Outside the UK, natural progesterone cream has been used to rebalance progesterone and oestrogen levels for many years, although there are some doctors who are only now coming around to the evidence supplied by Dr Lee. Unfortunately, at present it is not available on the NHS in the UK but can be imported privately from areas such as Ireland, Jersey and the Channel Islands. See appendix for details.

PHYSIOLOGICAL EFFECTS OF OESTROGEN AND PROGESTERONE

Physiological effects of oestrogen

Stimulates body
Stimulates endometrium
Breast stimulation

Impairments to the body
Interferes with thyroid hormone
Impairs blood sugar control

Increases in the body
Increase body fat
Salt and water retention
Increase blood clotting

Increased risk of cancer
Breast cancer
Endometrial cancer

Emotional reactions
Depression
Depletes libido
Can cause headaches

Reduces
Reduces oxygen levels in the
cells of the body

Mineral affects on the body
Loss of Zinc
Retention of copper

Skeletal effects
Slightly restrains bone loss
Reduces vascular tone

PHYSIOLOGICAL EFFECTS OF PROGESTERONE

Protection
Maintains endometrium
Protects against fibrotic cysts in breasts

Normalises body
Normalises thyroid function
Normalises blood sugar control
Normalises blood clotting

Reduces in the body
Burns fat
Natural diuretic reduces
water retention

Preventive for Cancer
Prevents endometrial cancer
Helps to prevent breast cancer

Restores
Oxygen cell levels restored
to proper levels.

Emotions balanced
Restores libido
Natural anti-depressant

**Restores mineral effects
on the body**
Normalises zinc
Rebalances copper levels

Stimulating Skeletal
Bone building

To check whether you are progesterone deficient, have a saliva test
done on day 21 of your cycle, which is when progesterone levels
should be at their peak.

It is also worth pointing out that males too make progesterone,
although they do not appear to suffer the same deficiency as women.
Additional progesterone is, however, reported to help restore male
libido and has helped with cases of osteoporosis.

MALE INFERTILITY

Male infertility can be common and some statistics suggest that as many as 25% of males are infertile. Studies show that one in six couples have fertility problems and that male infertility is responsible for around 15% of cases in which couples are unable to conceive.

It takes three months for men to develop a new batch of sperm and men, like their female partners, are being affected by age. Research has found that male fertility is going down with age and apparently, for some, this factor alone has accounted for drops in sperm counts of 50%[76].

Sperm disorders are of course responsible for a good many cases in which conception proves to be difficult or impossible. Investigations into men's infertility often show low serum and semen levels and it is stated that in the case of approximately 5% of infertile couples the problem is due to sex, failure to ejaculate or ejaculating too soon. Common issues include:

Sperm

1. The number of sperm produced - toxicity in the environment and lifestyle can lead to reduced sperm counts
2. The quality of the sperm - conditions such as diabetes can affect quality
3. The shape of the sperm

Low semen volume - too small a volume is estimated as under one millilitre, which is not enough to carry the sperm to the woman's cervix. Obstruction or infection, which reduces semen volume, can be treated with antibiotics

Excessive seminal fluid – a high volume of fluid means that sperm can be diluted and if the sperm count is low this clearly affects fertility potential

- Incompatibility of sperm and partner's cervical mucus
- Erections and/or ejaculation dysfunctions – for example, the sperm may be squirting back into the bladder instead of ejaculating
- Persistent coagulation - sperm clump together, either tail-to-

tail or head-to-head, instead of swimming in a straight line. It is thought that approximately 40% of men suffer from this condition

Sperm abnormalities caused by the use of either street drugs or certain medications – marijuana is known to impair fertility in both males and females and some medications can impair semen production. Research has shown that smoking and alcohol also play a part alongside solvents and toxins in the production of abnormal sperm, although reducing contact with these substances will lead to improved sperm production

Testicular stress -this is thought to be associated with infection and illness, causing immature sperm and underdeveloped semen. The problem can be exacerbated by the fact that infections can be passed backwards and forwards from male to female on a regular basis, although infections such as the sexually transmitted diseases gonorrhoea and unesplasema do respond well to drugs, albeit that they can take several months to clear

Scrotal heat - men who are exposed to intense heat as part of their occupation have been found to have reduced sperm counts and higher levels of abnormal sperm. Such as: welders, bakers and firemen are groups particularly at risk[77], and even professional drivers suffer similar problems[78] because hot seats in trucks and cars can affect their genitals.

In addition, the sperm of males who wear tight Lycra shorts, underwear and other types of close-fitting clothing can also be affected. For efficient sperm production, keeping the testicles at the right temperature is vital. Testes are normally cooler than the rest of the body, a state which occurs naturally in loose clothing. Therefore, an environment, which is too warm and constricted by tight garments, is counter-productive.

General abnormalities and medical conditions which impact upon fertility

The presence of heavy metals in the body - there is overwhelming evidence of the effects on the health of both sperm and ova due to toxic metals such as lead and cadmium. Hair analysis is a very effective and accurate method of detecting levels of these and other toxins in the body.

Caffeine consumption

The problems experienced by men in terms of sperm count, mobility and abnormalities have been found to be related to the number of cups of coffee they drink per day[79]. For women, even just one cup of coffee per day is associated with an increased risk of a delay in conception of one year or more[80]

Stress

IVF can be traumatic for males, resulting in raised stress levels and impaired fertility. Not only does stress have an impact on sperm count motility and increase the levels of abnormal sperm[81], but it also lowers the levels of testosterone in the mother. This fact is particularly relevant when you consider that testosterone[82] has an impact on the growth of the foetus, with mothers' stress levels influencing and decreasing the efficiency of the hormone.

Sperm quality

It is thought that all men actually produce abnormal sperm, although the reason why this happens is unknown. In some cases where conception is proving difficult, semen analysis may be required to quantify the quality and quantity of sperm.

Of course, sperm disorders do not account for all male fertility problems and blockages in the tubes that carry sperm are another potential cause. These can be caused by:

- Injury to the groin area
- Groin surgery
- Sexually transmitted infections and diseases

Genetics also has its part to play and conditions such as chromosome abnormalities can sometimes be the key to infertility, as can male hormonal deficiency, the signs of which are thinning hair or beard, scant pubic hair and small testicles. In addition, some research has shown a link between varicose veins and infertility in men, although when the varicose vein was repaired fertility has returned.

Male mumps is, of course, well known as an illness which can deplete male fertility. Although children experience only a mild version of the illness, adult males can suffer a rare complication of mumps in the testicles called orchitis or testicular inflammation, which has been known to make adults sterile. Some information suggests that the performance of ejaculation is reduced in that the pump no longer works as effectively as it should and sperm only travels half as far as it should.

All factors found in infertility will be medically investigated thoroughly to find the root cause and I usually request as a matter of course that the partner or spouse comes for a consultation. Diet is one area that I like to concentrate on, especially in view of the fact that a 1994 study reported that men who ate organically grown food might be twice as fertile as those who do not. With strong links between body toxicity and fertility in males, I also suggest a hair analysis as an elimination procedure to check toxic levels and possibly a treatment or two to make sure that everything is flowing as it should. Reflexology is also very helpful in this area as sometimes the spouse is as stressed as his wife.

Sperm counts

A statement in a magazine recently reported that sperm counts across Europe have dropped by 50% since the Second World War and, according to experts, male fertility levels have dropped considerably over the last thirty years.

At the present time, the reasons for this drop in male fertility remain uncertain. While some believe that it stems from lifestyle, others point to the long-term effects of rising oestrogen levels in both food and water. Throw pollution and stress into the equation and we have any number of different things affecting different people. Logically, the decline may well stem from a combination of many factors, but what we do know is that men in general are losing their hair earlier in life and women are also becoming less fertile.

We are already seeing clear signs of the effects of excessive oestrogen in the water through diminishing fish stocks and deformed spry. Because we cannot filter out the effects of oestrogen from urine, ultimately it returns to pollute our drinking water and unfortunately this is having a detrimental effect upon our natural fertility.

Researchers are now saying that boys born to mother's who smoke during pregnancy, particularly in the early stages, are more likely to have small testicles and low sperm counts as adults. This indicates that what we are now producing are children who are deficient in the things that they should be born with. Perhaps it is simply rapid evolution, but whichever way you look at it, falling infertility is definitely an issue for those who want to start a family and are having difficulties.

Under normal conditions, the vagina is a hostile environment for sperm, although sperm is nourished and protected by the carrier fluid known as semen. Following ejaculation, sperm normally only live for an average of 3-5 days inside the female body, although they can survive for up to seven days if they are in good condition. In order that enough sperm survive the acidity of the vagina, it is logical therefore that they need to be of good quality, strong, energetic and shaped well to penetrate the egg.

Men who smoke are believed to have poor quality sperm and prospective fathers who smoke suffer the risk of reduced fertility due to lower testosterone levels, a lower sperm count and the greater incidence of abnormal sperm. It is also now known that drinking alcohol, and more especially, binge drinking, also plays a part in sperm deterioration.

Fish oil supplements or eating oily fish has been shown to improve fertility and sperm count. Finnish men have the highest sperm counts in Western Europe and it has been attributed directly to the high amount of oily fish that they consume. Evidence suggests that sperm count can also be increased with vitamin and mineral supplementation such as:

- Vitamin C
- Selenium
- Zinc
- Folic acid

The supplementation of zinc and folate can increase sperm counts by as much as 70%.

FEMALE INFERTILITY

It is thought that 15-20% of infertility cases are unexplained, with doctors unable to find the root cause of the anomaly. Whilst some women tend to turn immediately to the more 'traditional' forms of infertility treatment, therapies such as Reflexology have been used very successfully with fertility imbalances and, through my own experience I have found that a combination of treatments works well with women.

Of course, every couple is different and these differences need to be taken into account when designing their course of treatment. I use a unique programme for each client, which is designed to help correct the imbalances in the body and make it a fertile area for the seed to grow.

ALTERNATIVE PROGRAMMES TO BEAT INFERTILITY

The treatments that I use to help women with infertility issues may include any or all of the following:

- Reflexology – to rebalance and de-stress
- Lymph drainage – to remove blockages in the body (recommended by infertility clinics)
- Hair analysis – to check the levels of toxins, poisons, lack of nutrients and so on in the body
- Diet and nutrition – to adjust and fine-tune the diet and make any necessary additions
- Bio detox – to clear out any poisons or toxins from the body

- Detoxification programme
- pH testing – to check the levels of acidity in the body and correct them
- Check ovulation
- Check progesterone levels
- Emotional release – to remove barriers and overwhelmed emotions from previous experiences of miscarriage, disappointments and so on.

Any of the above can also be used to help male fertility disorders.

[52] Women's Health information "How does Clomid work" http://www.womens-health.co.uk/clom id.asp (Cited 08 2007)

[53] Daily Mail '3 million IVF babies' July 2006: Innovative Media Inc. ZE06070103 2006.07.01 www.zenit.org/article-16464?1=english (cited 03.2009)

[54] Sally Goddard Blythe, 'What Babies and Children really Need' Hawthorn Press 2008. Glos.UK 2008 – A Finnish study -cited

[55] Ibid 'A Danish study' p13

[56] Dr.M Glenville PhD, BioCare seminar 'Infertility': 11.2008: (Ref: El-Chaar, D. 2007 Feb 9 - Fertility treatment raises birth defects risk – Society for Maternal-fetal medicine San Francisco)

[57] Ibid (Ref: Crha I et al, IVF and Vit C, 2003 Cent European Jrn. Public Health. 11.2.63-7)

[58] Ibid 'Folic Acid' BioCare seminar 11.2008

[59] Ibid 'low homocysteine' BioCare seminar 11.2008 (Ref: Symanski W et al -'low homocysteine', 2003 Ginekol Pol 4, 10,1392-6)

[60] Ibid 'Caffine' (Ref: Weng X et al, caffeine and miscarriage' - Am J Obset Gynecol Jan 21 2008)

[61] Ibid 'Zinc and cell division' BioCare seminar 11.2008 (Schwabe, JWB and Rhodes D, 'trends in biochemical science 1991 61,29-96)

[62] Ibid' Zinc Deficiency causes a decrease in sperm count seminal volume and testosterone levels' BioCare seminar 11.2008 (Hunt, CD et al 1992; American Journal of Clinical Nutrition 56,1. 148-57) '.

[63] Ibid 'Men with low fertilisation rates in IVF cycles Vit E' BioCare seminar 11.2008 (Geva E et al. 1996; Fertility and Sterility, 66, 3. 430-4)

[64] Ibid 'Vitamin E can help with egg quality' BioCare seminar 11.2008 (Ref: Tairn Et al, 1998 Reproduction, Nutrition Development 38, 5, 499-508 –)

[65] Ibid 'Clomid and Vitamin C' BioCare seminar 11.2008 (Ref: Igarashi M 1977 International Journal of Fertility 22, 3 168-73)

[66] Keri Marshall 'Health article -Polycystic Ovaarian Syndrome' The Alternative magazine by Cited P6 2007

[67] NHS 'Frequent questions PCOS' http://www4woman.gov/pcos.htm (Cited 2008)

[68] Keri Marshall 'Observational study The Alternative medicine review p6c2 2007 and NHS 'frequent asked questions PCOS 'www.4woman.gov.faq/pcos.htm 2008 (cited 2008)

[69] Ibid The Alternative medicine –Women's Health review PCOS – (Cited 2008)P7

[70] Thyroid Action Group 'Hypothyroidism' Thyroid UK action group magazine (1997) - p14

[71] Ibid 'T3 conversion' Thyroid UK action group magazine (1997) - p15

[72] Ibid 'Failure to produce' Thyroid UK Action Group magazine (1997) p15

[73] John Lee MD 'Research progesterone cream' Well women's information service handbook (2004) - p13

[74] Ibid 'Synthetic Progesterone' Natural progesterone handbook (2004) - p13

[75] Ibid 'Oestrogen'' Natural progesterone handbook (2004) - p.12

[76] Dr. M. Glenville Phd 'Male fertility' BioCare seminar (11.2008) Ref: Swan SH et al. 'male fertility is going down with age Sperm counts have dropped by 50%' Env Health Persp, 108,10,961-6)

[77] Ibid 'Scrotal heat' BioCare seminar (11.2008)(Ref: Bonde JP, Int Jnl Andrology, (1993) 16.1)

[78] Ibid 'Scrotal heat' BioCare seminar (11.2008)(Ref: Sas M ad Szollosis J. Arch Andrology, (1979)3,57)

[79] Ibid 'Sperm count' (11.2008)(Ref: Parazzini F. et al. 'sperm count, mobility and abnormalities' Archives of Andrology (1993)31,2,105-13 –

[80] Ibid 'Conception' BioCare seminar (11.2008) (Ref: Bolumar F. et al 'Risk of a delay of conception of 1 year or more' American Journal of Epidemiology (1997), 145.4.324-34)

[81] Ibid 'Fertility' BioCare seminar (11.2008) (Ref: Giblin, PT et al 'Stress has an impact upon sperm count motility and increases levels of abnormal sperm' Fertility and Sterility, (1998)49,127-32)

[82] Ibid 'Stress and Testosterone' BioCare seminar (11.2008)(Ref: Negro-Vilar A, 'Stress lowers levels of Testosterone' Environ Health Persp Supplement, (1993)101,2 59-64)

Chapter 9

INDEX

Chapter 9

MISCARRIAGE

The word 'miscarriage' is defined as a spontaneous loss of pregnancy before 24 weeks. There is no common reason why some women miscarry and in most cases prevention cannot be helped medically[83]. Each year, however, hundreds of thousands of women in the UK are affected by miscarriage and in fact it occurs in 10%-20% of all confirmed pregnancies, normally during the first twelve weeks of pregnancy.

A study, which was carried out at Erasmus MC University Medical Centre in the Netherlands[84] looked at common problems in the first 3 months of pregnancy. This research showed that a history of miscarriage was linked to future pre-term births and, in addition, that:

- Vaginal bleeding in the early weeks of pregnancy was associated with an increased risk of pre-eclampsia or premature delivery. There were also links to risks of low birth weight
- Extreme early morning sickness was associated with a higher risk of premature delivery and low birth weight
- Events and complications in early pregnancy are the most common complications in women during their pregnancy and can be extremely distressing

Some factors contribute to an even greater risk of miscarriage. A history of one or more miscarriages, for example, is seen to double the risk of premature birth or premature rupture of the membrane surrounding the baby. Termination is also indicated as a high risk for premature birth and underlying health problems such as diabetes and hypertension, together with lifestyle choices such as poor diet and nutrition, smoking and alcohol were also factors in women who were at greater risk.

MISCARRIAGE AND FERTILITY

As we have said, there doesn't seem to be any rhyme or reason for some women to miscarry, although it is believed that one in four women do so, and predictions are that by 2010 it will be one in three.

It is essential for the egg (ova) and sperm to be of the right quality to produce a strong, healthy child. By using preparation as the key, we can eliminate a lot of the heartache from the fertility process. It is within the first two to three months that miscarriage normally occurs and as this is the time when the formation of the embryo is most critical, the mother's wellbeing is paramount.

I have treated women for both infertility and pregnancy for many years and these are some of the symptoms that I have found when I have first treated for infertility and miscarriage:

- High levels of stress
- Exhaustion - running on empty
- Inner body is tense
- Body too acidic
- PH balance needs correcting
- Thyroid imbalance
- Fluid blockages
- Emotional barriers and grief
- Incorrect weight and anorexia
- Overwhelmed emotionally
- Frustrated
- Age - overly aware of the ticking clock
- Diet and nutrition need correcting and re-balancing

The symptoms of miscarriage

The most common symptom is vaginal bleeding, ranging from light spotting to a heavier bleed just like a period. Blood clots and brown discharge may also be seen, with cramping and pelvic or back pain often associated.

When we become pregnant, the first signs are breast tenderness, feeling sick and nausea, together with having to urinate more frequently. For some, the only indication of loss may be that these early pregnancy symptoms stop unexpectedly. For others, however, they can miscarry without knowing. With no signs of either pregnancy or miscarriage, their symptoms continue and it is only through a scan that the occurrence of a miscarriage is confirmed. The medical base line for testing is after three miscarriages have taken place.

The cause of miscarriage

One theory as to why miscarriage occurs is the genetic combination of the sperm and egg creating self-problems in the way they fertilise. Other known causes are:

- Pregnancy hormone imbalances
- Immune system problems
- Age – miscarriage increases with age
- Infections
- Multiple births
- Egg quality
- Lifestyle – alcohol and smoking

In most cases it is difficult to find out exactly why it happened. From my own experience, it seems to be a cocktail of factors and very rarely due to only one. Of course, it can be genetic, but it could also be due to diet and the lack of the basic minerals and vitamins needed to allow pregnancy to take place. Infection is also recognised as a cause of early miscarriage.

As discussed in the infertility section, sometimes the body is simply not in the right condition at the start of the pregnancy. Maybe there have been body imbalances for some time that the mother was unaware of. Many factors are catalogued as reasons but, at the end of the day, we are all individuals and as we all react differently, individual care is needed to help discover the root cause.

NUTRITION AND MISCARRIAGE

Ovarian stem cells are regulated by the nutritional status of the woman. Poor nutrition affects stem cell condition, which in turn affects ovulation. The nutritional status of the woman may therefore either stimulate the stem cells to promote ovulation or interfere with it. Poor nutrition, along with poor lifestyle choices, can also affect the quality of the egg, which means that a cocktail of factors can contribute to sustaining a healthy pregnancy.

If the body is not in good condition, it will not be able to support the maturity of the embryo and will reject it prematurely, intending to start again when the body is healthier and more able to do its amazing job naturally. Our bodies are wonderful things. They know when things are not right and will not support anything that is not in the condition that it should be in.

I believe that nutrition has a huge part to play in ensuring that our bodies are ready to do their jobs in terms of reproduction. Indeed, nutrition has been shown to help with infertility and miscarriage, and of course it offers a simple, safe and natural way to ensure that we are in optimum condition and that any detrimental factors are reversed.

Nutritionally there is a need to prepare the ground before male or female can set seed to grow successfully. I would suggest a three to six month preparation time with changes to diet, nutrition and lifestyle. It is worth taking time to see a professional therapist who is trained in pregnancy needs and can explore with tests such as hair analysis, pH balancing and so on, to eliminate previous causes of miscarriage and suggest a programme of treatment to fine tune the body.

Research has proved that nutrition has helped in some cases of miscarriage, and certainly folic acid and vitamins B6 and B12 are three of the key ingredients that are crucial. Not only do the genetic materials DNA and RNA both need folic acid and B12, but follicular fluid, which contains homocysteine and bathes ovaries and eggs, also requires balanced levels of B6 and B12. High levels of homocysteine have been found in women who have miscarried[85] and oocytes (eggs) exposed to low homocysteine concentrations have better quality and higher degree of maturity[86].

Zinc deficiency, meanwhile, causes a decrease in sperm count, seminal volume and testosterone levels and women who have partners with a low sperm count are also known to have a higher risk of miscarriage. Organic farmers, however, have been found to have double the sperm count compared to engineers and electricians[87].

Exposure to solvents while pregnant has been linked to learning difficulties in the child[88] and those more at risk are those who work as:

- Beauticians/manicurists (with nail solvents)
- Dry cleaners
- Hairdressers

RECURRENT MISCARRIAGES

Some women will suffer miscarriage in their first pregnancy and then go on to have subsequent successful pregnancies. Others, however, can experience two or more miscarriages purely by chance and with no known reason, yet go on to successful future pregnancies. With any miscarriage there will be anxiety, despite subsequent pregnancies being normal.

When suffering recurrent miscarriages, after three it is advisable to undergo some tests to find out the specific cause, which could be down to:

- Genetic problems
- Hormonal disturbance
- Abnormalities to the uterus
- Immune system (known as 'Antiphospholipid syndrome') where the body's own defence causes blood clots in the placenta

As stated previously, most miscarriages happen in the first trimester, (the first twelve weeks). Pregnancy loss later in the developing stages of second trimester is far less common and usually arises as a result of different causes than those listed above.

Research conducted in the USA in 2007 showed that a third of all embryos failed[89]. The studies suggested that eggs ,which took a long time to implant may have been defective in some way and were therefore unlikely to last full term. They also highlighted that the uterus may only have a limited time window and shuts out defective embryos arriving too late.

Eggs are normally fertilised in the fallopian tubes and then travel to the uterus. There they are embedded for the foetus to develop. The US study found that eggs implanted nine days after fertilisation had a 13% chance of miscarriage, with the risk increasing to 25% on the tenth day. By the eleventh day it rose to 52% and for the twelfth day and later, miscarriage rose to 82%. The research could not explain why eggs which attach later should have this risk of miscarriage, however it was suggested that transit time for abnormal embryos might be much slower.

Immune system and Cells

Scientists have demonstrated that the immune system has an intelligence of its own. They don't know why some people's immune systems choose to fight disease while other people's give in to it but the immune system does rebalance itself as internal and external environments change. Internally there is a constant adjustment of metabolic activities as the energy demands on our bodies change, such as might be the case when:

- Digesting different foods and liquids
- Reacting emotionally to different circumstances
- Being affected by both subtle and radical changes in the environment
- Being affected by changes to humidity or pressure

Even the air that we breathe can be pure or laden with toxins as we move from inside to outside and it may also contain pollen or bacteria.

All of these things require bodily adjustments, which in turn make demands on your immune system. If our immune system is unable to adapt quickly and meet the constant array of changing challenges, we will probably start creating pressure on the systems of the body, which can lead to disorders and illness. The immune system maintains equilibrium between extreme reactivity and consequence, working at all times to release molecules and alert the appropriate immune cells to neutralize or destroy any foreign or toxic substances and organisms.

The immune system is kept in balance by killer T lymphocytes. Overloaded and out of control cells can create a severe allergic reaction such as anaphylactic shock, which can be deadly and could also evolve into an autoimmune disease or inflammatory response such as inflammation.

The bodily defence and healing activity is overseen by a variety of specific immune cells and molecules. When we become ill, it can be due to toxicity in the body. Cells begin to change and die and our army of immune and stem cells are put on full alert to deal with the intruders within the body.

Body Cells and feelings

Our feeling centres improve or deplete our energy sources and are affected by our emotions, thoughts and actions. Poor management results in energy leakage and overloading our systems drains the cells of vital life force, leading to illness, low self-esteem and unbalanced relationships.

Depending on how we invest our energy, we can either increase or deplete our reserves. Negativity, (through negative thoughts and actions) causes energy debt (loss) and body depletion. Thought equals form and so every thought, word and action creates a vibration which will attract like for like. They mirror you, what you say, do or hear.

Energy is stored in our cell tissue. If you are in 'energy debt', you keep drawing from cells, making them weaker and eventually becoming physically ill. Energy resources held in the cell tissue and every cell in the body must have a new supply of energy each day in order to thrive. Just as you require fresh water every day, your daily allowance is needed for everyday maintenance of the body, emotional life systems and to feed your creativity, relationships and optimism. The greater the debt, the weaker the cell tissue grows and if this is not reversed by recharging (resting), you will become more vulnerable to dis-ease and broken cells.

I run School of Life courses to help people understand the effects of energy debt and the power of our emotions, which are felt in all systems of the body.

MISCARRIAGE RISKS

Bacterial infection

Bacterial vaginosis, a form of inflammation of the vagina and the most common cause of abnormal discharge among women of childbearing age, poses a risk to a successful pregnancy. Reports indicate that pregnant women who contract a common bacterial infection of the vagina are more likely to miscarry in the early stages of pregnancy[90] and indeed bacterial vaginosis can affect up to 30% of pregnant women.

Although the cause of bacterial vaginosis is unclear, some believe it is passed on through sexual activity. Others believe that many women normally carry this bacteria, but at such a low level it does not pose a risk to normal health. The same bacteria has also been found in women who are not sexually active.

Research, which was conducted in Leeds, involved carrying out trials on 850 women who were undergoing IVF treatment and concluded that 24.6% of those tested had bacterial vaginosis, although the bacteria did not affect conception. The study showed that women conceived at the same rate, irrespective of the presence of vaginal bacteria.

Leeds General Infirmary found that infections can double the risk of miscarriage in the first three months of pregnancy. According to their study, 36% of those with the infection subsequently miscarried, compared to only 18% of women who were free from infection. One of the doctors who specialises in genito-urinary medicine, believes that there is a link between this infection and the causes of endometriosis and inflammation of the uterus[91] and states that:

'This could spread up into the womb causing inflammation of the lining of the womb and releasing various chemicals which would make a hostile environment for a fertilised egg that was trying to grow.'

One of the chemicals, 'tumour necrosis factor alpha', causes the blood vessels to constrict, effectively starving the fertilised egg of vital nutrients.

Research suggests that women who wish to start a family should seek medical advice about infection beforehand. Apparently, infection via bacterial vaginosis can be treated safely with antibiotics before conception. If you have experienced miscarriage before, this is one avenue that you might wish to explore.

Endometriosis

Endometriosis is a condition where the tissue of the uterine lining migrates out of the uterus and implants in other abdominal tissues. This cannot be released and results in cysts. The condition is believed to affect some 2 million women in the UK alone, with many diagnosed between the ages of 25-40 years[92].

It is thought that 30-40% of women with endometriosis are infertile and endometriosis is thought to be the cause of infertility for approximately 30% of women. Little is understood why endometriosis causes infertility. However, damage to ovaries and fallopian tubes by disease with additions of adhesions and scar tissue from surgery can also be causes.

If you have endometriosis, one of the symptoms may be painful intercourse, which is obvious by the lack of relationship contact. Reduction of times making love will only add to the delay in outcome.

Some other key factors[93]

- Antibodies can cause a hostile environment in the womb and can be present in women who suffer endometriosis.
- An increase in peritoneal fluid affects the transportation of egg and sperm and can affect implantation.
- An increase in prostaglandin levels can also affect the

transportation of egg and sperm allowing the egg to reach the womb when it is still immature.

- An increase of white blood cells (scavenger cells) can reduce the motility (free movement) of the sperm.

Although many women have no symptoms at all, others experience varying levels of pain and discomfort depending on where the endometriosis lies in the body. It can cause pelvic pain, particularly during the monthly cycle, heavy or irregular periods, pain during or after intercourse, fatigue and many may experience difficulty opening bowel functions. Another symptom is problems in conceiving.

Endometrial cells are normally found in the womb. However, they can travel elsewhere in the body and can be found in the fallopian tubes, ovaries, bladder, bowel and vagina. With hormonal change, the cells go through the same process as in the womb (i.e. discharging), which can result in inflammation, pain and sometimes formation of adhesions. In the ovary area, they can form cysts and indeed, infertility can be caused by endometriosis.

Most women who suffer endometriosis will have an event-free birth. Some research has indicated that the miscarriage rate may be higher in women with endometriosis and there seems to be a higher risk of ectopic pregnancy.

True cause of Endometriosis is unknown

The true cause of the condition is unknown, although research into both cause and treatment is ongoing. Some causes are suspected to be genetic, with the gene being passed on to other generations. Immune dysfunctions are also highlighted, as it is believed that the immune system is weak and cannot fight off the imbalances of endometriosis. Dioxin is also seen as a having a negative effect upon the body, causing toxins to build up over time. Endometriosis has additionally been linked to having too much oestrogen in the body, caused by the birth pill and HRT.

Diagnosis is normally carried out using a laparoscopy treatment via anaesthetic, which enables the medics to ascertain the degree of endometriosis and additional issues such as fibroids. Sometimes surgery will take place at the same time, although the endometrial tissue can return. Hysterectomy may be advised in some cases.

Research carried out during 2004-2005, found immune dysfunction with Th2 (T helper/killer cells in immune function) unable to remove viral and bacterial pathogens and therefore unable to clear inflammatory conditions naturally[94]. Anti-inflammatory treatment has been found beneficial in these cases. Improving diet and nutrition[95] also helps as, if these are poor, it assists to elevate the condition as seen with Polycystic Ovary Syndrome (section 7).

Some suggestions include supplementation of:

- Vitamin C, B1, B6 and B12 – NHS sources suggest that these will help with anti inflammatory incidence and pain relief
- Magnesium – to relax the uterine muscles to reduce pain
- Iron, fish oil, evening primrose oil and/or borage oil – are seen to help and are a healthy option for pro-inflammatory conditions. Fish oil, borage and blackcurrant oil are now recognised as reducing inflammation within the body.

Dysmenorrhoea

For relief of symptoms from Dysmenorrhoea, (heavy, painful periods), use vitamin E, zinc and bromelain to aid anti-inflammatory disorders and as a muscle relaxant. Several studies conducted during 2001 -2005 have found that vitamins C and E have given symptomatic pain relief from dysmenorrhoea disorders.

Anti-oxidants also play an important role with defence against oxidation. Some research is showing links to anti-oxidant stress and endometriosis, influencing the entire reproductive lifespan of a woman[96]. Some of the essential vitamins, minerals and nutrients to help clear oxidative stress in the body are:

- Vitamins A, C, E and B
- Minerals – selenium, zinc, manganese, copper and iron
- Flavonoids, Carotenoids and CoQ10

Research found that vitamins C and E, selenium and zinc had significant impacts upon women with endometriosis compared to a study group. They concluded that a lesser intake of anti-oxidants was present with endometriosis[97].

Fibroids

Fibroids are known to be tumours of muscle tissue, which imbed in the wall of the uterus. They cause symptoms of heavy bleeding, bleeding between cycles and can also cause anaemia. Oestrogen can stimulate their growth.

Endometrial Polyps

Endometrial polyps are tube-like growths, which develop from the mucous membrane in any part of the body, including the uterus. They may be a reason for infertility and a cause for heavy menstruation.

Body effects of miscarriage

The physical effects of miscarriage often clear up fairly quickly. Bleeding tends to stop after seven to ten days and a normal period usually follows in four to six weeks. Infection will make the bleeding last longer and discharge may also occur. It is advisable to see your GP or homeopath to help clear the infection quickly.

EMOTIONAL BARRIERS AND GRIEF FROM MISCARRIAGE

The emotional impact of a miscarriage can be much greater than the physical effects and when a woman loses a child, she understandably goes through a grief process.

Grief is a natural reaction and some women describe a feeling of emptiness and numbness, which in my experience, is caused by shock. Inconsolable, sometimes the event will cause women to push their partners or spouses away and, with this type of trauma, they can become very introverted.

Only those who have lost a child themselves can know what a woman is going through. Sometimes the grief is so strong they never get over the event and carry their grief to the grave. Some cope by closing down while others need to talk about their experience. It is dependant upon the individual.

Other emotions like depression can kick in too, with feelings of loneliness and isolation also being common. When these emotions start to interfere with daily activities it can be a sign of major depression taking hold.

Some women also blame themselves for the miscarriage. Like having a 'what if' tape playing over and over in their minds, they become convinced that the miscarriage would not have occurred if they had done things differently. Thoughts like these can go on for some time, making it harder to come to terms with the loss. Anger and jealousy towards other pregnant women are also all too common after miscarriage.

Men and miscarriage

Women are not the only ones to feel the effects of miscarriage of course – their partners feel it too. Men can become nervous and are often reluctant to talk to their partners about the event.

Quite naturally, they are upset about the loss and also go through a grieving process but at the same time they are worried about their partner and what she has experienced. This is when misunderstanding kicks in, as he may be fearful to broach the subject, erroneously believing he may upset her if he talks about the event.

In my experience it is better to be open and discuss the loss with your partner if you can. If you are not ready to discuss the matter with him, say so and let him know when you do want to talk.

CASE STUDY 3 –
INTERMITTENT BLEEDING PROBLEMS

A client I treated during her pregnancy phoned me afterward because she was having heavy periods and the bleeding was continuing in between. Could I help, she wanted to know. Margaret (name changed to protect anonymity) was feeling fatigued and the intermittent bleeding had been happening for some months, together with some dull pain, discharge and mucus which seemed to continue for up to five days at a time in between periods.

After a consultation, I suggested that I treated her with reflexology to start with and it did seem to help. When she returned some weeks later, the intermittent discharge had, for a while, reduced and her hormones were rebalanced but she still felt fatigued. Her adrenals were depleted and she informed me that she had moved house recently and reluctantly returned to work some six months previously after maternity leave. It was no surprise that her adrenals were not up to par.

However, something did not seem right. The response to treatment was not as expected and, although it was having some impact, it was not getting to the core of the complaint. Upon further discussion, she informed me that there seemed to be a pattern emerging and that she thought that the discharge happened when she was ovulating.

We discussed how she was after her last child's birth, which turned out to have been long and traumatic. She had suffered nerve damage (her leg felt numb) and distress from the epidural and the many subsequent boosts that she needed during labour. Margaret suffered infection and mastitis for several days after her return home and her uterus took much longer to go back than from her previous pregnancy.

I suggested that I treat her differently that day. When I intuitively tuned into her uterus, I found that there was still shock and trauma in the area. Margaret told me that she could feel a sensation like a ball in her abdomen and when she showed me where it was placed, it was the shock and trauma I had already detected.

I asked her how many pregnancies she had had and Margaret replied that there had been two. In fact her body told me that there had been three. She could not believe it. Three? It turned out that the body was correct and Margaret then remembered doing a pregnancy test at the age of 30 which showed negative. The test had been correct, but unbeknownst to her she had miscarried. Unfortunately the residue did not clear and for some reason it appeared to be draining away now.

She told me that the day she did the pregnancy test was her son's first birthday party and she was on the bouncy castle and thinking to herself, '*If I was pregnant I should not be doing this*'. She knew, however, that she did not want another child at that time - it was too soon for her partner and herself.

I continued with the session and removed the trauma and emotion from her body, allowing the uterus to release the remainder of the residue. Margaret told me that she felt so much better; the ball had gone in the abdomen and the area felt softer. She felt calmer and more relaxed in herself and had not realised that her body had previously felt so tense. I explained that the body sometimes needs to complete a process and that her body had felt incomplete. Memories do linger in the body and it comes out at different times and during different events.

Maybe it had been the shock from the previous birth that had delayed the completion. The body is a complex machine, which does not always give the answers we would like to know.

It made me wonder

Does this happen to other women without them knowing about it?

Throughout this session, it did occur to me that perhaps other women suffer this kind of miscarriage residue. Many have natural miscarriages without them knowing; they just have their next period and don't even think about it. When a woman is leaking between periods and has mucus on a regular basis as Margaret did, it can be put down to endometriosis, cysts or the start of fibroids as had been assumed with Margaret.

This is why we need to listen to our bodies. All the information is there and we just need to tap into it. From my own experience of treating women, they carry a lot of emotion and trauma in their reproductive areas and memories can linger in the cells to create physical disorders. Gives us food for thought, doesn't it?

HOSPITAL TESTS AND INVESTIGATIONS

When it is suspected that a miscarriage has occurred, the following tests and examinations will usually take place to confirm that this is, in fact, the case:

- Medical examination
- Ultrasound scan
- Blood tests to detect pregnancy hormones

An ultrasound scan is normally used to show the uterus and developing embryo and is even able to show the foetal heartbeat. If the pregnancy is in the early stages, ie 6–7 weeks, it may not be able to confirm pregnancy and, in these cases, it is suggested that the scan be done again in another week to ten days.

In pregnancy, hormone levels rise over time and so act as a clear indication of pregnancy. A blood test for beta hCG is taken to identify levels of pregnancy hormones and when the levels are found to be decreasing, it is usually an indication of pregnancy loss. The test may be retaken within 48 hours.

Treatment options

Most miscarriages happen spontaneously and women often deal with the effects on their own. If miscarriage has happened completely there would be no need for further medical treatment. For an incomplete miscarriage or when there is significant bleeding, however, surgery or medication may be recommended to remove the remaining pregnancy tissue.

The stage of pregnancy and the amount of bleeding will determine the treatment choice made by you and the medical team. The procedure and options available should be thoroughly explained to you by your doctor and time given for you to make your choice. Some women prefer to complete the process naturally (known as expectant management) and doctors can prescribe drugs to soften the cervix and make the uterus contract so that the remainder of the pregnancy is expelled without surgery. This type of treatment is, however, linked with an increased risk of bleeding.

Generally, surgery is used to clear the uterus. Known as a D&C (dilation and curettage), it is carried out under general anaesthetic by inserting a tube into the cervix and applying suction to remove the pregnancy material. With surgery comes an increased risk of infection.

Hospital and miscarriage

During my time as a therapist, I have heard alarming tales through my work treating women. For some, the medical insensitivities that they have had to bear have only made their loss even harder to endure. Sometimes nurses and medical staff have their own personal beliefs, which affect the care that these women receive. In addition, overburdened NHS staff and those who are not normally involved with these events can add to the trauma through inadequate training and lack of compassion.

Some women may end up in A&E where staff may not have the expertise in dealing with pregnancy problems and miscarriage. Those who have not been specifically trained to deal with pregnancy can be insensitive without realising. It is not that they mean to be, but some can be very off-hand and can often be heard to come out with comments such as 'Never mind love. You can always have another.' Medical staff can, in fact, be just as insensitive in the case of miscarriage as they are when a woman has had an abortion. Stamping their own personal beliefs and ignorance onto the distraught mother's feelings is, I believe, never justified.

There have been many instances of insensitivity quoted to me and all could have been avoided. Here are just a few examples:

- A post-miscarriage appointment at the doctor's surgery where the receptionist has made the appointment to see the doctor during a pregnancy clinic

- Going in for a D&C after a miscarriage and being put into a labour ward
- Knowing your pregnancy has failed and having to carry for up to six weeks before it is surgically removed, with the likely event of infection for the mother because of the delay

Unfortunately these occurrences are common, although they do not need to happen. With a little thought from the medical staff and more compassion for what the mother has been through, it would help with a gentler and smoother transition during what is a time of grieving.

If you have been unfortunate enough to suffer a miscarriage, you will know that after the event you cannot bear to hear a child cry; it is just too traumatic. Even to see a baby on TV brings emotional heartbreak and this can go on for many months and even years. In my experience, some women never get over the trauma and emotional experience.

Generally we are not aware what these women are feeling. If we have not experienced motherhood or pregnancy it is not always obvious that such emotional trauma and grief can happen. For those of us who have been through pregnancy, our experience does give us some basic understanding and insight into how the mother must be feeling. Our knowledge of the emotions involved gives us a glimmer of her trauma and despair without actually being in her shoes, although we have no idea of the full impact and effect of what she has gone through, nor how it can affect her for the rest of her life.

We all have different experiences and some seem able to deal with miscarriage better than others. One woman on her first pregnancy told me she knew she was losing her child. She could feel it energetically and emotionally leave her body, before the physical miscarriage happened.

I have treated women whose grief has been so overwhelming that they could not consider having another child. Through the emotional release work that I do, however, I have been able to help them release their grief and move on to their next pregnancy within months of treatment.

Coping emotionally

In many cases we underestimate the loss through miscarriage or infertility. We are not told about how we will feel when we lose a precious and sometimes long-awaited addition to the family. Whilst in hospital our emotions seem to be ignored and some staff even adopt an indifferent approach. Others are angels and give kind words and advice just when we need it.

Inevitably, grief will occur when parents go through the loss of an infant, even if it is only a few weeks into the pregnancy. A closure time is needed for them to come to terms with the loss.

When a woman loses a child through miscarriage, the distress can be overwhelming and she suffers a cocktail of emotions, which can include frustration. Not only is her physical body overwhelmed, but she becomes overwhelmed emotionally too. This can take its toll in all areas of her day-to-day influences, in her relationships, her work and her lifestyle.

Through grief, we can easily lose interest in our relationships and partners will find it hard to understand why we do not want to have intercourse. We can lose interest in our work and, for some, it will take much courage just to return to work, especially if work colleagues knew of the pregnancy. Often though well-intentioned, it can be those compassionate, caring words from friends that seem to hurt the most. The result of all this is that we have no interest in our day-to-day living and our world loses its sparkle. (This can apply to both genders)

To be around other people's children can be a major challenge. I often find this additional trauma induces most women to avoid family functions and seeing small children. While some don't seem to be particularly affected and take it all in their stride, others simply find it too upsetting.

Some women may not want to go out with their friends any more and some shut themselves away completely. Depression can kick in, along with feelings of very low esteem. Nothing interests them and there doesn't seem to be any point to life. Clearly the grief process has kicked in!

CASE STUDY 4 -
RUNNING ON EMPTY

One woman I treated had endured eight pregnancies and none of them had been successful. Ectopic pregnancies and several miscarriages were interspersed with a few that had been absorbed back into the body. This all happened over the course of several years and I met her eight years after the last pregnancy.

When we first met, this woman was grey. As she walked in through the door I could see the emotional trauma in every line on her face. With dull eyes, her walk carried all the burden of intense grief. Her relationship with her partner (the father of the pregnancies) had long since dissolved. All that grief and emotion had split them apart. So badly wanted by both partners, this was one child that would never be.

Barbara, as we will call her, was told after the eighth attempt that her womb would not support a child and that it was impossible for her to bear children after all, so now she also had guilt and failure to add to the list of emotions. Blaming herself for the loss and break-up of her relationship, she had been taking antidepressants. For Barbara, even counselling and well-meaning advice only seemed to put a plaster on what she was feeling.

After an initial consultation, I did a two-hour treatment session using Dissolve and resolve emotions (DARE), emotional release techniques. Clearly her body was hanging on to the grief and the incomplete body process. With each trauma the wounds had gone deeper and were emotionally festering. Unable to move on, she was stuck in the past with no future in sight, reliving every moment and nuance of each trauma in the past.

Without doubt the body holds memories of past events and emotions. They go deep into the cells where they are stored for future reference. As the cells replicate, the harmful memories are also replicated, creating dis-ease in the physical body. This has been proved scientifically, by many including Candice Pert, a scientist working on the Aids programme. Her book, Molecules of Emotion is widely available in paperback.

At the end of her first emotional release treatment, Barbara looked like a different person. Her eyes were bright and she confessed that she felt lighter - as if a burden had been lifted from her shoulders. There was now a spring in her step and she looked ten years younger.

The next day she phoned to thank me and described the scene when she walked into the office. Her colleagues could see the transformation and wanted to know where she had been and what she had been doing the night before. Because she looked so great, they wanted whatever it was she was taking - this new elixir of life.

Emotions are messages and we can all too easily create harmful barriers to block them. When we do this, we lose energy and become temporarily underpowered. Being underpowered affects our bodily functions until eventually we become seriously underpowered and fatigued. Just like a battery that needs recharging regularly, the bodily equipment we rely on won't work as well and will run down very quickly. This is what holding emotional trauma does to the physical body, resulting in:

- Low energy levels
- Feeling fatigued and tired all the time
- Low immunity
- The inability to renew our energy - we wake feeling tired before we even start the day. Having gone to bed exhausted, we wake the same way

RELATIONSHIPS AND MISCARRIAGE

Relationships after miscarriage can become extremely strained. Dealing with grief and loss can cause many couples to withdraw and move away from each other. Communication becomes difficult and sharing your feelings may seem out of the question.

Some prefer to ignore the event, believing that if it is not acknowledged, it has not happened. Although simplistic, that is how some people cope with loss and traumatic events. This is often when a woman becomes angry and hurt, failing to understand the lack of response she is getting, although it may simply be a case of crossed wires, with the woman's partner not wanting to hurt her and treading on eggshells in his attempt to avoid a scene. Yet more than ever, this is the time when a couple need one another for support and care. Both parties have suffered disappointment and are feeling bereft.

Friends and family are the ones we usually turn to in times of crisis in our lives and they can help to provide support. Remember though that you hold the key to when you do and don't want to talk. Please keep them informed of your feelings and let them know of your decision when you feel it is time to communicate.

Sometimes women find it easier to talk to someone like me in a one-to-one therapy situation, especially since the therapist is not part of the family and therefore not so close to the situation. I find that they feel confident to talk frankly about their experience and how it has affected them. This, of course, is the first step in coming to terms with their loss.

Talking to other women and couples in support groups is also very helpful. To hear of other women's experiences and how they coped can be a lifeline for some, breaking down the isolation and loneliness. At the end of the day, talking and communication with those who love you is the key.

Trying again

When is it time to start trying again? There is no 'right or wrong' answer to this question and you just have to go with your gut feelings as to when you both feel ready. From a medical perspective, it is recommended to wait one normal period before trying again, although having sex is believed to be safe once bleeding has settled.

Some couples decide to try again for a pregnancy straight away. Others feel the need to wait. They see it as being too soon after the event and are still going through the grief process.

Trying to become pregnant is not all it seems to be. When pregnancy does not happen on cue, the pressure of failure takes its toll on both parties. Rifts start to come between them. He stays out late because she has changed. Suddenly life isn't fun any more and she mopes around the house dejectedly. It is easy to become frustrated with herself as well as with her partner for not being around when she wants him. In addition, it can be extremely frustrating if he is not there when she is ovulating and needs to make love at a specific time.

In this situation, if couples don't communicate, they tend to drift further apart, no longer having anything in common. Sometimes it can be difficult to talk about what has happened as it rakes over the trauma, causing more pain for both partners. You do need to talk about it though, especially about how you both feel. At this point it is vital that you get it out in the open. It is far better for your long-term health to do so.

If you don't share what you are both going through, you will not be able to understand where your partner is coming from and how wounded you both are. You feel frustration from the situation you find yourselves in. It can be distressing for all concerned parties and even grandparents feel the wave of disappointment.

Some women deal with it by becoming jealous of their friends and siblings for having the child that they cannot, but this approach is soul-destroying as the yearning goes on indefinitely. Coming to terms with the jealousy is difficult on all levels of our being.

CASE STUDY 5 -
MISCARRIAGE

One client had been so overwhelmed after the miscarriage of her first child, she could not bring herself to move house because the baby's ashes were in the garden. She felt that if she moved away she would break the bond she still felt with the lost child. Although her husband was very supportive, he was also confused as to why she was shutting him out of the event.
He too had been emotionally distraught, but his partner still felt unable to share with him what she felt. He wanted to try again for another child, but she could not do that either.

Sinking deeper into a vicious circle, he heard about the work I did and asked me to try and help her. At first she was not keen to come, but eventually he persuaded her. We had just one session, where I was able to bring her to resolution and understanding, thereby releasing her trauma and deep emotion.

Sometimes the body feels that it has not completed the task it began and is unfinished in the process. With the training and experience I have, I can help the mother and her body to complete that process and enable her body to respond to and accept further pregnancies.

Within two months, this particular woman was pregnant and ready to move house. Indeed, the couple did move just three months before the second child was born. The second pregnancy was completely normal, with mother feeling healthy and joyous throughout. They now have a beautiful son, who I treated with Cranio Sacral Therapy after his birth. CST treatment for newborns is advised for all children, to rebalance and align them after birth. (Section 15)

STILLBIRTHS

In the UK, stillbirth numbers are currently as high as ten times more than the level of cot deaths. When a child is lost, it is devastating for the parents and family alike. However, I believe that stillbirth is even more of a trauma for all concerned as it is usually a shock and unexpected.

Who is at risk?

Women in the most deprived areas are most at risk, being twice as likely to have stillbirths.[98]

- Infants of poorer women are twice as likely to suffer a fatality by a month old
- Asian and black ethnic women are high-risk groups for having stillbirth babies
- The incidence is higher in multiple births
- It is more common in women who smoke
- Older women in pregnancy are more at risk, especially over the age of 35
- The risk is also higher if there is a pre-existing medical condition
- Lower birth weight is a risk
- Congenital abnormalities can also cause stillbirths

Other causes include:

- The stress of the birth can be too much for the infant
- The placenta can fail in late pregnancy or during labour
- Complications can arise during labour

Stillbirth is a term used for a baby who dies before birth and after twenty-four weeks of gestation, whereas sudden infant death (SID) is a neonatal death within four weeks of birth. Most neonatal fatalities happen within one week of delivery and in the UK this represents one in one hundred births[99].

In 2007, new research highlighted the high number of stillbirths as being due to what was called 'sub-optimal care'. This seems to be the key factor linking foetal growth restriction and stillbirths. This is not the 'cause' of death but a prior warning sign that can be positively dealt with by the medical profession[100].

Britain is not the only country in Europe to suffer high stillbirth numbers. Ireland, Andorra, Portugal and Luxembourg have higher stillbirth rates than the UK.

In 2006 almost 4,000 babies were stillborn in Britain and, according to government figures, over the last decade numbers have remained fairly constant apart from a slight rise from 5.3% in 2001 to 5.7% in 2003. In most other European countries the rate is 3%.

There is no national strategy to reduce the figures. Stillbirth is still not completely understood and most of the time it is unexplained. It is estimated that ten babies die every day in the UK from stillbirth and further fatalities happen within the first four weeks of life. Government figures do, however, show regional variations. London at 6.3% and the East Midlands at 5.7% show the highest rates in the UK.

In 1960, stillbirth rates fell dramatically when 30 out of every thousand were stillborn or died after delivery. These falling numbers have been credited to the advances in maternity care at the time, with new technology and care reformed beyond measure over the previous fifty years. However, research in this area has been neglected of late and it is the lack of information on the cause of death that is now hampering a reduction in stillbirth numbers.

Stillbirth prevention

Lack of growth in the womb seems to be the key as to why so many children are, even today, stillborn. Foetal growth restriction affects 10-20% of all pregnancies, giving a 5-10% increase of stillbirth, and research shows that as many as 40% of stillbirths are associated with this problem. It is, however, believed that many of these deaths could be avoided if different structures were put in place for carrying out check-ups and if adequate resources were made available in terms of midwives and hospital ultrasound examinations.

Only around one third of cases of foetal growth restriction are recognised at present in the UK, this being due to high midwife caseload and the lack of ultrasound examinations being offered in high-risk cases. The same report, which identified these problems also highlighted an issue with quality of care and a growing concern surrounding overstretched maternity systems resulting in unnecessary foetal deaths.

The problem of foetal growth restriction has been underestimated in the past, as the same charts were used for all types of pregnancy. With customised growth charts now available for hospitals and midwives, however, it is hoped that a more accurate idea of the baby's growth will help to highlight any risk for the foetus and that numbers of stillbirths will, in turn, begin to fall.

Surviving stillbirth

Undoubtedly the shock and grief for the parents of a stillborn child can be overwhelming. Although most will ask, 'Why? What did I do wrong?', in the majority of cases the outcome was probably unavoidable and it is always best to discuss all the details with your midwife and doctor. In most cases a post-mortem will be carried out to ascertain the cause of the stillbirth and, although very upsetting, this will not only help to answer your questions more accurately and help with any subsequent pregnancies, but will also contribute to the database of knowledge which will help to prevent other women from suffering the same tragedy.

Naturally it is a sad time for everyone and it is important that the grieving process is allowed to take place. It has been found that taking photos and connecting with your baby helps with this process. In addition, you may like to request that the hospital chaplain serves a blessing or carries out the christening of your baby.

Unfortunately, one of the things that make stillbirth even more difficult to cope with is the fact that the mother's body does not know the difference between birth and stillbirth, and automatically goes into the normal process and production to support the missing infant. Normal reactions such as tiredness and blood loss will occur, together with the production of breast milk, which can be very upsetting. Although the milk will dry up naturally, there are drugs available to speed up the process and both your midwife and your doctor will be able to advise on these. An alternative natural way to achieve the same end is to use parsley, which can either be taken in tablet form, in the form of parsley tea or used fresh as part of your diet.

If you find yourself struggling to recover from the effects of a stillbirth, you can contact the Stillbirth and Neonatal Death Society (SANDS), a nationwide service which provides a network of self-help groups.

SELF-HELP TIPS FOR MISCARRIAGE

Women who have suffered a miscarriage sometimes need all the help that they can find and so here are some self-help tips which you might want to consider.

Writing

Writing helps with many different kinds of emotional distress, so try keeping a journal and be honest with yourself about what you are feeling. Studies have actually found that this helps to accelerate the recovery period during sad times.

Boundaries

Let family and friends know what is 'off limits' in terms of discussion. For instance, they will not know if it is comfortable for you to hear about other's pregnancies, births or losses.

Time Off

Don't be in a rush to go back to work if you are not ready to face the world; take extra time off. After all, you have been through a traumatic experience and most employers will be sympathetic to your needs. Try to arrange some time away for you and your partner to be together and/or spend some quality time in one another's company.

Solace

Try changing the event into a positive experience. Many find solace by having a special place in their garden in which to remember and let go of their grief. Plant a tree or a favourite shrub and have a seat nearby so you can sit and meditate, making it yours. You can get some lovely garden ornaments such as angels or animals or even a water fountain to enhance your chosen place. If you don't have a garden, you could buy a plant or tree for the local park or school.

Some women use their experience to write articles or books, while others prefer to help women by creating a web site. Nothing is set in stone and you should do whatever helps and feels right for you. Find a way of marking the experience in a way, which soothes the soul for both of you.

[83] Bupa's Health Information Team 'Bupa fact sheet - Miscarriage causes and symptoms' (11.2006) http://hed2.bupa.co.uk/fact_sheets/html/miscarriage.html (cited 08.2007)

[84] Sally Goddard Blythe, 'What Babies and Children Really Need' Hawthorn Press 2008 Stroud Glos.UK 1998 'Netherlands study' p39

[85] Dr. M Glenville PhD 'The nutritional approach to infertility' BioCare seminar (11. 2008)   (Ref: Russell RM, 'High levels of homocysteine in women who have miscarried' and B12' JAMA (1996) 275,1828-9)

[86] Ibid 'The nutritional approach to infertility' BioCare seminar (Ref: Symasnski W et al, 'low homocysteine' Ginekol Pol (2003) 4 10,1392-6)

[87] Ibid 'Zinc Deficiency' BioCare seminar (11.2008) (Ref: Abell A et al. Lancet (1994) 343 8911. 11490)

[88] Dr.M. Grenville PhD., 'The nutritional approach to infertility' BioCare seminar (11.2008) (Ref: Laslo Baker D.et al. 'Exposure to solvents' Arch Pedator Alolec Med. 158.10.956-61)

[89] BBC News: US National Instate of Health – 'Miscarriage risk of slow eggs' New England Journal of medicine -ref http://newsbbc.co.uk/1/hi/health/365648.stm. (Cited 02.2007)

[90]: BBC News Health: 'Health infection increase miscarriage risks' British medical journal (1999)- http://newsbbc.co.uk/1/hi/health/400989.stm. Dr. S Ralph and colleagues Leeds General Infirmary (cited 02.2007)

[90] Ibid 'Infection increase miscarriage risks' BJM report (1999/09)   http://newsbbc.co.uk/1/hi/health/400989.stm. (cited 02.2007)

[92] NHS 'patient guides to Dysmenorrhoea and Endometriosis'.http://www.basildonanthurrock.nhs.uk

[93] National Endometriosis Society information leaflet 'other key factors' (cited 02.2007)
National Endometrias society information leaflet 01.2001

[94] Cytoplan Article – 'Guide to Endometriosis' p12-13 (cited 06. 2009) / national Endometrias society fact sheet (cited 02.2007

[95] NHS 'patient guides to Dysmenorrhoea and Endometriosis' http://www.basildonanthurrock.nhs.uk (cited ref 02.2007)

[96] Dr M. Glenville PhD. 'Supplements and infertility' BioCare Seminar (11.2008) (Ref: Agarwal A. Gupta S Sharma RK, 'Antioxidents and female pathology' Reprod Fiol Endocrinol (2005)14:3-28

[97] Dr M. Glenville PhD. 'Antioxidants and Endometriosis' BioCare seminar (11.2008)

[98] Tommy's 'Still Birth stats' http://www.tommys.org/media/statistics/key-statistics/stillbrith-statistics.htm (cited 07.2008)

[99] Jonathan Owen 'Maternity Crisis' Independent on Sunday (cited 23/9/07)

[100] Tommy's 'Still Birth' http://www.tommys.org (cited 07.2008)

Chapter 10

INDEX

Chapter 10

TERMINATION OF PREGNANCY

No one likes to talk about termination. It is a controversial subject, which touches on religious and cultural views and personal beliefs in general. Writing this book has made me think about all aspects of pregnancy. It can be wanted but, realistically, it can also be unwanted for some women. A pregnancy, which has resulted from rape, for example, is one instance where a woman may wish to consider a termination.

Termination can be a hurtful and grieving experience for many women and can cause just as much grief as a miscarriage - after all, a miscarriage is nothing more than a natural termination. Having a termination can be very emotional for many reasons. I have treated women who have had terminations in their late teens or their early twenties and still carry psychological scars from the event. It continues to haunt them even though they bury it deep inside and it is now understood that it takes a high toll emotionally upon women in general. It is, in fact, believed that one in five women suffer from post-traumatic stress (PST) after a termination, with symptoms of flashbacks and nightmares being common.

I believe that no one should judge women for wanting a termination unless they stand in her shoes and understand her physical and emotional wellbeing. As this book is looking at all aspects of emotion and how it affects us, I felt that this chapter could not be left out. You, of course, will have your own views and are at liberty to draw your own conclusions.

Abortion law was brought in primarily to stop illegal back-street abortions which placed many women's lives at risk. Many, however, believe that it should not take place at all, albeit, for some it is a lifesaver. A lifesaver, either because they feel unable to cope with pregnancy/another child, or they may have found out that the infant has a severe foetal malformation (termination can be suggested if there are fears of defects in the foetus) or because the pregnancy occurred as a result of rape.

In the UK, regional numbers vary but abortion is more common in women within certain age groups. Statistics gathered in 2000 seem to show that the highest levels are seen in 20-24 year-olds. In 2000, London showed figures of legal abortions as follows[101]:

- 13,570 for 20-24 year-olds.
- 12,508 for 25-29 year-olds
- 9,058   for 30-34 year-olds
- 5.544   for 35-39 year-olds
- 1,607   for 40-44 year-olds

In 2000, the total number of legal abortions in England and Wales were 47,099, divided up as follows:

- 45,034 in England
- 2,065 in Wales

The figures quoted above represent only the number of legal abortions recorded.

The number of teenage pregnancies has increased since then, showing many deprived areas in the UK having more teenage pregnancies[102]. In the least deprived areas, 71% of pregnancies in under-18s end in abortion, compared with 39% in the most deprived.

The Office for National Statistics (ONS) also show that the overall conception rate in under-18s remained virtually stable, with 42,198 in 2004 and 42,187 in 2005. However, there has been a 4% rise in the number of under-16s falling pregnant, increasing from 7,615 pregnancies in 2004 to 7,917 in 2005.

No figures are shown for Ireland due to its illegality on religious grounds. Although Northern Ireland is part of the UK, women are seen as second-class citizens by not having the choice of abortion unless there are severe defects with the foetus. Owing to where they live, they come under laws, which are restricted, by the beliefs of MPs and the church.

Most Irish women in need of a termination tend to seek private help and pay the costs themselves, travelling outside Ireland to England or Wales to receive treatment. The numbers, consequently, are not recorded.

PREGNANCY FOR THE 21ST CENTURY WOMAN

The pressures on women to have children and reproduce can be enormous. With women in the western world wanting to have a career and a family, it can create its own pressures, especially with past health-abusive lifestyles.

Some religious beliefs see modern birth control as a sin. In the East, women are being overloaded by cultural beliefs, having one pregnancy after another, putting constant pressure on their bodies and minds to create the emotional distress of 'how can I cope this time' with yet another pregnancy?

For some, the pregnancy results from abuse or rape, with the child not wanted or needed at the outset. Psychologically, this can be a very difficult time for the mother who feels invaded and dirty. Having become overly anxious, a very unhappy nine months ensues. When the child is born, the mother then has to face the issues of caring for an unwanted child.

Some mothers cannot love their bundle of joy no matter what they try to do, because of what they themselves have been through. Consequently, the child becomes neglected and is put up with, sometimes being constantly criticised and verbally abused. This can progress quite easily to the physical side of abuse, with slapping or a 'clip around the head'. Understandably, each time the mother looks at the child it is a reminder of the trauma that she went through at the outset and this comes out as impatience, guilt and often continues into the child's adult life.

In this scenario, the child picks up on the lack of love, preventing true bonding of mother and child from taking place and making the child feel abandoned. In the womb, the child will already have picked up on the resentment and the feeling of not being wanted, producing anxiety and distress. Medically this is known as 'foetal origins' and it originates from growth programming within the womb.

From my own experience of treating people, I have recognised that emotions will put patterns in place for life. This was one of the reasons why I wanted to write this book, to create more awareness about the effects of emotions and share information to help women through this magical and sometimes daunting event.

METHODS OF TERMINATION

Surgical Procedure

A termination or abortion can be achieved either through a surgical procedure or by using pills if done early enough. In the case of the surgical procedure, I now know that a hollow tube is inserted to evacuate from the womb (no information was given concerning the technique in my day), however fragments may remain and bleeding may continue after the event. There is also a suction procedure which is quick and requires no painkiller. This technique is used at specialist termination centres.

In this 'more enlightened' age, some hospitals do not offer a termination service any more, because of staff objections based on personal or religious beliefs.

Medication

Pills containing progesterone are taken over a period of 48 hours and create a spontaneous abortion as the uterus contracts. This method can, however, cause cramps and bleeding as during a natural miscarriage. Sometimes a second pill is needed and it can take some time to completely evacuate.

Some have no choice other than termination but it can be a lottery with the facilities on offer, depending upon where you live in the UK. Previously the UK led the world in this field. However, at the moment, UK abortion legislation is lagging behind the rest of the world.

New thinking is to allow women to have a choice. If they want, they can take pills in their own home to evacuate and give the medical staff a ring if there are any problems or attend hospital or centres for assisted care. Their second choice is to have a termination in a nursing environment.

EDUCATION FOR BOTH SEXES

Some men think of the morning after pill or termination as a fall back for unprotected sex and the only option for an unwanted pregnancy conceived in this way. This is where more education and explanation is needed for both sexes, but especially for the males of the world.

Both sides of the partnership need to understand that termination is an emotional and fearful experience for a woman of any age and not a walk in the park or akin to going to try on a pair of shoes or drop off the dry cleaning. Indeed, many women do not themselves realise the consequences or the hormonal explosion which affects the female physically for some time after an abortion.

The medical profession is now realising that some women do take the termination experience very badly in an emotional sense. It is a hurtful emotional experience which takes a heavy toll for many. Perhaps if we educated all parties (including teens) from an emotional perspective, it would create a better understanding all round and prevent it from happening in the first place.

TEENAGE PREGNANCY

It is acknowledged in the UK that we have the highest rates of teenage pregnancy in Europe. Some would say that this is because of sexual promiscuity, whilst others believe it to be as a result of the availability of the contraceptive pill. Although there is much more education available in this area nowadays, the message is not, (in my opinion) affecting or enlightening youngsters as it should.

Although it might seem as though the availability of the contraceptive pill ought to alleviate the problem, it actually allows teens to try sex at an earlier age. We certainly see children having sex at the age of 12 and 13 as the norm these days. Some parents also allow teens to sleep together in the family home more readily than in my day and there is a lot more freedom of promiscuity extended to teenagers than ever before.

I personally feel that this kind of leniency and freedom sends the wrong message. Although they might be old enough physically to have sex, these youngsters are not emotionally mature or stable enough to be able to handle the result of a child, as they are still children themselves. In the majority of cases, it is the parents or grandparents who step in to help their children and grandchildren.

Media coverage is now bringing to our attention the new idea of implants (lasting for 3 years) as a means of contraception for teenage girls as young as 14 years old. Apparently, this decision has come about because girls are not good at remembering to take the pill daily for contraceptive protection. Because of the free sex policy that has been bred into society over the last 30 years, we have males and females taking risks by having sex without condoms, thinking that the pill is enough, but unfortunately not taking it regularly. During this time we have seen diseases such as Chlamydia and gonorrhoea rise dramatically.

Surely moves such as this will send the wrong message for teens to start sex experimentation even earlier. As a mother myself, I am surprised that thinking is moving in this direction. Surely there must be another way.

CASE STUDY 6 - TERMINATION

Because of suspected defects in the foetus, I myself had a termination in the 1970s. I had been undergoing treatment for some time to try and clear an infection in the fallopian tubes and ovaries, which involved connecting me to a deep heat machine for half an hour each session. The programme had been running for over eight weeks before I suspected I was pregnant. Naturally I was concerned about the treatment received and its damaging effect on the foetus.

When he found out about the length and type of treatment, my doctor asked immediately if I wanted a termination. It was a difficult decision to make and my husband and I discussed all the options before deciding that we could not knowingly bring a malformed child into the world. It didn't seem fair to the unborn child. We knew of others who had had no choice and their lives had been full of trauma. With severe strain on their relationship, they endured a 24/7 timetable with no thanks and no relief. Although much loved, they continued to care for a child that knew nothing of the world around it.

All was arranged for me to have the termination. Unfortunately, in those days termination was not as accepted as it is today. Many, including medical staff, did not agree with it and my own experience showed a bigoted and judgemental approach in hospital. This, in some cases, still goes on today, especially in NHS hospitals, where some staff mistakenly assume the decision to be a life-style choice.

When I awoke from the operation I experienced acute guilt, feeling very emotional and shameful for having decided to have a termination. Although I knew it was the only answer, that knowledge didn't make me feel any better.

When they came to see me, which was not often, the nursing staff made it very clear that they did not approve. Having already judged me, they were very curt and had no time for nursing me. Despite not knowing my case history, they rightly or wrongly had already formed an opinion about me and clearly showed it. Even to this day I don't know whether their views stemmed from a religious upbringing or simply their own disapproving view on abortion in general.

I had been admitted in the morning for the operation and when I awoke it was after 5.30pm. As a result of reacting badly to the anaesthetic, I vomited the moment I woke. At 7pm a nurse informed me that they needed the bed and I was to leave as soon as my husband could pick me up. I was shocked as I was told I would be staying in overnight. I felt so ill and emotionally drained.

When my husband came to see me at visiting time he was told that I would be leaving with him. Feeling so weak that I could hardly walk, I had to lean against my husband for support. He held on to me firmly, half carrying me out to the car in the parking area. At no time was a wheelchair offered to help me out of the hospital to the car.

I spent the next two days in bed, weak and emotionally lost. Crying for most of the time, I developed a headache, which turned out to be my first real migraine. It was my birthday; a birthday not to be forgotten.

Having endured the aggressive attitude of the hospital staff, I believed my ordeal was over. I was wrong, however, and another shock was on the way. My family felt it necessary to add their caustic comments into the mix. One brother thought I was terrible, asking, 'How could you do that?' He was not aware of the heart-wrenching medical reason behind my decision. Although not religious, straight away he disapproved and refused to listen to the medical reason. A second brother showed concern for my health and the third was disinterested. Parents were challenged; they didn't know what to say, although they seemed glad to pass on my brothers' comments as mothers do.

As a result of my termination, I suffered trauma that lasted for months and months with little understanding from anyone. I could not watch a programme on TV with a baby in it. To hear a baby cry was unbearable. It was like being electrocuted, going through to my very core and bringing tears to my eyes. I still had my two other children, who were two and four years old at the time, to care for on a daily basis and I found it difficult to cope.

My sister in-law had recently given birth to a baby boy and she wanted to return to work. Due to a prior promise, I had agreed to look after him for three months until Christmas and as this had been agreed well before the termination, I felt I could not go back on my word.

Unfortunately, I did not realise what it would do to me at the time. Each day I was faced with a five-month-old lovely baby boy who was brought at 7.30am in the morning and picked up at 5pm. The first week went surprisingly well until one day he cried and I found it difficult to cope. After that it went downhill, as I would wake each morning dreading him coming. It was like a daily torture. He was a constant reminder of my anguish and, although I didn't know at the time, I now realise that I was suffering from post-traumatic stress.

It was not my nephew's fault and I cared for him as I did my own, but I could never have guessed the emotional trauma that was to follow. Trying to will an end to my torment, I was counting down the weeks until half-term and then Christmas. My sister in-law then asked me to look after him for another three months until Easter but I could not do it and, despite my attempts to explain, she couldn't understand why. Words were exchanged and a row ensued which caused a family rift. As a consequence, she found it difficult to talk to my husband or myself for nearly a year afterwards.

The trauma from the event lived with me for thirty years until I was able to release it through a session of Somoto emotional release therapy. The wounds were very deep but I was finally able to reason that it would not have been fair to the child or myself and was ultimately able to forgive myself.

A painful process

No matter how we lose a child it is painful. Maybe it is a difficult decision which needs to be made solely by the mother. However, sometimes it is taken out of her hands with family and outside pressure making additional demands. Whatever the decision, even going ahead with a deliberate termination, to lose a child is painful.

Although it is a stressful and anxious time for all concerned, the memory trauma stays for longer with the mother. Few realise the long-term effects of these events and it can be a grieving process for many. Often nowadays, when women have terminations they are in and out of hospital like a production line. Little concern is given to the immediate after-effects, nor the long-term effects upon the mother and how it will affect her ability to cope with her future children when she has them, or upon the existing family.

Perhaps it is time we took a long look at the bigger picture and put more thought into how we can help with the emotional drama that goes on inside. As I have discovered, many women carry these feelings of trauma right through to the grave.

I believe this has been one of the reasons that I have chosen to specialise in women's health over the years, as I understand their plight through my own experiences. Although no help was available in my case, with my own experiences in life I have been given more insight and understanding to assist others with emotional disorders and needs. In my opinion, medication is not the answer to emotional events such as PTS, emotional discord and trauma. Those who experience them need specialist help which goes to the core of the emotion and eliminates the wounds of the past.

With therapy techniques such as emotional and trauma release, help is at hand. We don't need to carry these emotional burdens any longer.

[101] BBC News 'Termination'. (02.2007) http://news.bbc.co.uk/1/hi/health (cited 02.2008)

[102] BBC News 'Termination' (02.2007) http://news.bbc.co.uk/1/hi/health (cited 02.2008

Chapter 11

INDEX

Chapter 11

BIRTH

*'Our children are spiritual beings who come
through you, not for you'*

Dr. Wynne Dyer

Introduction to birth

We all experience being born, but for some people it is one of the most traumatic things that happens during their lives. The experience of the birth process, depending upon whether the delivery is a natural one, induced, forceps, or Vontau, can set the pattern for how we experience the rest of our life.

While still in the womb, our structure, confidence, abilities, likes and dislikes are all created. Our nervous system and how we will develop mentally and physically are also decided at this stage and this early period is what marks the start of our emotional development and anxieties. We take on these emotions and anxieties from our mothers according to whether she is happy, sad, anxious, or many other emotion's during the pregnancy. How she feels starts patterns, shaping our world for life, so as mums we need to get it right.

SENSITIVE CHILDREN

I have noticed that many babies born over the last decade are highly sensitive. To many, these children are known as Crystal and Rainbow children. I like to call them ' 'Sensitive's'.

Sensitive children have been coming into the world for some time and many are now adults and teens. The children I have come in contact with recently, however, are 'ultra sensitive'. They are ultra sensitive to their environment, drugs and certain foods such as dairy products, wheat and so on. They tune into and can become affected by emotional discord and negativity. They are affected physically and emotionally by the insecurity, unhappiness and anxiety of others.

These sensitive children have extra needs, more so than those who came before, and are demanding it right from the womb. As we know, chemicals and hormones are exchanged in the womb, providing a communication of needs from the foetus to the mother.

On several occasions I have experienced pregnant mums arranging an appointment to come and see me for a treatment, even though they are not sure why. In most cases it transpires that they have emotional issues or long-standing problems that their unborn baby wants them to deal with before he or she arrives. Because these children are so ultra sensitive, they need the right environment in their home and a balanced energy around them. They need understanding and support from their parents.

More importantly, however, they need their parents to have little or no emotional baggage; especially the mother. If the mother carries a lot of emotional negativity, it will upset the child's balance. This creates great emotional and energy discomfort for the child in the womb and when born.

Mum needs to listen to baby

I have known mums who come for treatment during pregnancy and post-natally as a direct result of the baby orchestrating the visit. By getting mum to deal with her own problems, the baby is tackling issues which are having a negative effect upon itself.

Emotionally, these issues can be from a previous labour trauma where fear continues to linger in the mum's body from buried stress and anxiety relative to the original experience. It could be that the mother herself did not have a particularly good birth or that her own mum had issues while pregnant. Now, in her own pregnancy, it is bringing up fears and memories of that early event.

It can be a cocktail of issues, often where the mother does not feel supported. There may, for example, be:

- Relationship issues
- Financial issues
- Health issues for the mother which are leaving her body

struggling and not strong enough to support the pregnancy

- Effects of the mother taking drugs, alcohol or smoking
- The mother may not want the child
- She may not be ready to have children and can feel invaded by the foetus
- She may be anxious because of previous infertility and miscarriage problems
- The last labour may have been medically invasive, causing her to still carry guilt and fearing a re-run of the previous experience

It is the child that is clearing the way for a better environment for birth.

NEW VISIONS BIRTH

Going into labour and the birth process itself can be an anxious time for the mother. Every birth is different and fear of the unknown is probably more worrying for some than actually taking part. The lack of knowing can be a blessing in disguise for many new mothers; ignorance is bliss as they say.

From my own experience, what most mothers want is to have a natural birth and they can easily become disenchanted when they don't get that opportunity. During many conversations that I have had with mums after their birth process, they have told me that they were disappointed as a result of not feeling in control. This stemmed from the medical process taking over without the mother being able to have a say in the matter.

Because of the modern trend towards elective inducements and caesareans, we have lost a lot of the important magic from the birth process. I would suggest that all mums do their own research when planning where to give birth. Find out what protocol is used in the hospital of your choice as there can be huge variations according to the beliefs and training of staff.

Check out what their procedures are and ask any questions that you might want clarifying. Don't just take their word for it and don't be put off. Look for another hospital or maternity unit if necessary. There will be a place where you will be satisfied and feel safe while giving birth, even if it is at home or through an independent birth specialist.

In times gone by, a woman would bask in the knowledge that she was in the womb of the feminine psyche. She felt cared for by her midwife, who was often an elder in the village, a nurturing woman who regularly helped out with childbirth. Viewed with high regard in her society as a wise and knowledgeable woman, she allowed the mother to be in complete control of the birth process. Unrushed, the labour took its natural course.

Unfortunately, today we are under a lot of pressure to fit in with the hospital schedule and when they have space available to perform a caesarean or to induce the mother. The mother is slotted into their timetable and not the baby's, despite the fact that in nature it is the baby who decides when it is time to come.

Nowadays the birth event has become a dispassionate process in hospitals overall, proving invasive to the mother's space. For the baby it can be a glaring and startling place to be born into. We can soften the experience through choices that are made by the parents beforehand.

Due dates

A formula for predicting 'pregnancy due date' was established in the 1850s by Franz Karl Naegele, a German obstetrician who used historical rather than observational data. We have used this process, which classes 42 weeks gestation as being overdue, ever since.

Although generally considered to be a more accurate method of determining the expected date of delivery, the early ultrasound scans that we also use nowadays to estimate the due date according to the weight of the unborn child, is not as accurate as we are led to believe. It can be under or over-estimated by several pounds[103].

Sometimes the given dates are not accurate and the correct due date can be up to ten days or two weeks after, but the modern process seems to follow a distinct pattern. When the mother has not gone into labour within a week of the given due date, she is automatically scheduled for inducement, something which creates undue anxiety for both mother and baby. Instead of being empowered, the mother feels powerless and fear and depression can set in.

I see many mums who come to me for reflexology treatment to start the labour process off because they are fearful of inducement. The benefits of a reflexology treatment are that it is completely safe for both mother and child. It can assist and accelerate the labour process, relaxing the mother and baby for the arrival.

From experience, I have a good idea if the baby is ready to come into the world and most of the time it isn't. I often tell mums they have another week or even ten days before the baby will be ready and I give them a first treatment to prepare the body for labour, making sure that the pituitary is primed and ready to release the natural hormones that can help with the birth process. After all, it is the baby who decides when to activate the pituitary for action and a reflexology inducement treatment will only start the process when the baby is ready to come into the world. Mums normally then come back for a second treatment nearer the baby's final date and most start labour the same day, while for a few it can take additional time.

I remember vividly when I was pregnant

Forty years ago the doctor's examinations took place with people walking in and out of the room while the mother's legs were in the air. The shame and humiliation were not encouraging to say the least. I felt as though I was being herded here and there and treated as a piece of meat to be pored over and discharged. I know it is just a job for many, but come on! We are human and we do have feelings.

Actually though, I was one of the lucky ones. For both of my children I was able to give birth in a maternity hospital, where I was supported by lovely midwives who had time to interact and took care of my babies and me. Midwives today are still lovely and caring, however they don't seem to have the time to interact the same.

Unfortunately for women today in the UK, government policy has meant many maternity hospitals being closed and integrated into the big hospital life where everything runs to a timetable. Despite

protests from mothers, grandmothers and other family members, their complaints go unheard by the big boys controlling the finances!
We had huge protests with petitions when they were closing my local maternity hospital. It didn't make any difference though and the protests fell on deaf ears. Like many, we lost a facility where whole generations of families were born and mums had confidence going there to give birth because it had such a good reputation to support mothers and babies.

Like many things in life, big is not always better. Health fund managers need to understand that saving money is not always the correct priority and should look at the bigger picture for the needs of the mother and baby. Believe me when I say that it makes a huge difference to both the child and the mother if they have a quiet, safe and comfortable place to deliver.

Unfortunately, those who make the decisions about maternity hospitals are mostly men. They do not understand the mother's needs when pregnant, although I suspect that if they were the ones having children things would be very different!

I am finding through my own experience that new mothers are facing even greater levels of distress and anxiety during pregnancy because of the invasive and dispassionate way they are treated in hospitals. Some hospitals seem to be completely detached from the mother's needs, especially when it comes to invasive medical interventions and technological devices.

Intervention means that mothers are ending up with operations to forcibly remove their babies, something which affects both of them deeply. This often results in post op recovery and in many cases causes post -traumatic stress and postnatal depression. Many mums are coming out of hospital suffering the equivalent of shell shock, instead of being wonderfully transformed by motherhood.

When we give birth naturally we work with our intuition. It is part of our female instinct to reproduce and the process is a natural one which, if interfered with, can seriously affect a woman's dignity and empowerment. Don't get me wrong, I am not totally against caesarean and induced birth. Everything has its place and the need for life-saving equipment and procedure is sometimes necessary for a baby and mother in crisis. However, they do seem to be used to excess in some cases, a fact which is borne out by statistics published in the UK.

Commonly nowadays, babies are being born to a world of bright lights, noise and bustle. They are immediately taken from the mother to be cleaned and wrapped up. Some will even be hosed out with equipment designed to clear mucus and so on, to help activate breathing.

CAR CRASH BABIES

Babies are being born with so much trauma and anxiety from the modern birth approach, which in my experience causes large numbers of infants to suffer from post-traumatic stress. It is as if they have been in a car crash.

Birth is a natural process when it has the correct hormones to help. Hormones such as oxytocin, adrenaline and prolactin are all designed by nature to help orchestrate the physical processes of birth by enhancing efficiency and ease for both mother and baby. They make the mother ecstatic and fulfilled, making her want to give birth over and over again. All mammals, in fact, share virtually the same hormonal crescendo at birth and this is a necessary pre-requisite for good mothering in humans. Basically we switch to instinctive maternal behaviour.

Oxytocin is commonly known as the hormone of love. It is released when we make love and makes us feel passionate, excited and tender. It is also one of the hormones used when we give birth, building up during labour and reaching peak levels at the moment of birth, activating tender, altruistic feelings between mother and baby. In short, it creates bonding.

Adrenaline and noradrenalin (the fight or flight hormones) are also involved for both mother and baby. These hormones protect the baby from lack of oxygen in the final stages of birth and ensure that the mother and baby are both wide eyed and excited when they first see one another. It is through this initial eye contact that the baby and mother form a powerful bond.

Prolactin, meanwhile, is known as the mothering hormone and helps the mum to surrender to her baby, allowing her to activate and release tender maternal feelings towards the child.

Natural power and grace

Women's bodies are full of natural power and grace to give birth. It is an innate knowing and instinct derived from the heritage of our foremothers, passing on the inherent knowledge of how to give birth and a physical body built to do just that.

Pregnancy puts pressure on the mother emotionally and physically, making big demands on the body to support the process. Everyone is different and as mothers we all have unique experiences; each pregnancy is different, as is the labour. Giving birth can be a painful experience that is huge for some, while others take it in their stride. In my first pregnancy, I found the labour process to be just like a period pain but more severe and which dissipated quickly after the birth. Believe me, you do forget the pain once you have seen your wonderful baby. The appropriate hormones kick in and everything is seen through rose-coloured glasses (for a little while at least). All the painful memories seem to disappear and the excitement and love take over.

Dr. Sara Buckley says in her book, Gentle Birth, Gentle Mothering[104]
'Being pregnant is equivalent to running the marathon, but when a woman feels confident in her body, is well supported and able to express herself without inhibition, the pain that she may feel can become easily bearable, and is just one part of the process.'

As mothers, we need to reclaim our power during pregnancy and birth and it is important for you to choose your birth setting, your midwife, Doulas and attendants before labour takes place. When we take control, we are allowing space for an easier passage for our baby. We are then more relaxed with the whole situation instead of handing our power over to someone else who does not necessarily know what we need or want. The transition will be more straightforward and there will be less intervention, allowing the mother to stand in her new role with confidence and grace.

Are we allowing tests, scans and the opinions of others to sway our own inner knowing? Are we putting more faith in technology than in ourselves? By allowing these things to disempower us, we are automatically handing over our power to others.

Often during labour, a mother's protests are not listened to, producing a huge trauma from the birth process and unnecessary medical intervention. One mother described to me the awful scenario as she protested and was not listened to. She said 'No' over and over again when staff wanted to break her waters and she said emphatically that she did not want to be induced. Staff though went ahead and broke the waters and induced her and she endured a prolonged and difficult birth. Feeling out of control and resentful of the whole process, she asked, 'Where in the conversation did the midwife not understand the word NO?'

Many mothers have told me they felt as though they had been raped when similar experiences happened to them. The whole situation left them depressed, with post-traumatic stress symptoms, post op symptoms and postnatal depression and of course on top of this they needed to look after their new bundles of joy. This is where the challenge comes for many, trying to recapture the mutual bonding that should have taken place at the time of delivery. Without this, it can take many months to bond with the new baby and some, unfortunately, don't make that original connection ever again with their child.

Is this the way birth should be?

We live in a culture, which rewards and puts faith in technology. We believe that our doctors and nurses know better than we do what our bodies need. But do they?

Did you know that, during labour, a mother's natural production of oxytocin is reduced drastically by the use of epidural pain relief? This is the hormone which helps produce the powerful final contractions to help the baby birth quickly. It also creates bonding and reaches peak levels at the precise moment of birth, activating in the mother tender, altruistic feelings between her and her child. Even when an epidural has nearly worn off, it continues to lessen and weaken the effects of oxytocin in the body, meaning that the mother is more likely to require further intervention via forceps or C-section.

The synthetic oxytocin drug Syntocinon is used for induction and augmentation (acceleration in labour) and is known to be used in large doses during labour in some developed countries. When mothers are given the drug by drip for induction, her body's natural oxytocin levels weaken and receptors can lose their sensitivity and ultimately their ability to respond to this hormone. It is thought that this is one of the causes of haemorrhage after birth and requires greater doses of Syntocinon to counter that risk.

The medical profession does not know what the long-term genetic effects and consequences are for mothers and babies of interfering with natural oxytocin production, especially with regard to parental bonding and their ongoing relationship. Is this why some children do not feel loved?

LISTENING TO BABY

In quiet moments, during yoga or meditation, the pregnant mother can feel a deep mindfulness and connection to her child, which is satisfying spiritually, emotionally and physically. During pregnancy, you will be given messages from your baby. Being in constant communication with your body via the placenta, the baby's needs initiate changes such as transference of blood and nutrients together with hormones. Mothers can have cravings, yearnings, inclinations and even dreams, which are orchestrated by the baby as it communicates with mum to organise both bodies and psyches for the specific mothering that is required by the child.

Baby talk

While pregnant, we can say affirmations and connect to our baby in the womb and right from the start it is important to talk to your unborn baby and communicate on a daily basis. Prepare your baby for the birth process by explaining what will happen and reassure him or her that there is no need to be afraid. Your body is there to guide and help you, with hormones and natural chemicals to alleviate pain and discomfort for both you and your baby.

Saying affirmations is a way of changing mind patterns which have been there for some time and of changing an outcome for the future.

Improve the way you feel during your pregnancy.

- 'I am happy and healthy during my pregnancy.'
- 'I will have a perfect birth process.'
- 'I am excited about the birth.'
- 'I am in control.'
- 'I decide what is best for me and my baby.'
- 'I am confident and trust my instincts during pregnancy and birth.'
- Your baby has been long awaited, so let him or her know that you are excited and happy about your pregnancy

Prepare for birth with affirmations

- 'The birth of my baby will be graceful and as painless as possible.'
- 'My midwife will guide me through the birth process in a loving and compassionate way.'
- 'My body will alleviate pain with surges of oxytocin during the labour process, giving me and my baby a graceful and natural birth.'
- Tell your baby how much it is loved by you and others
- Tell your baby how much you are looking forward to their arrival

Be patient. Believing in your affirmations may take longer than expected. For some it can be a long-term process, especially those who have been entrenched in mindsets that no longer serve their best interests in life. Even though you have made the first step, remember that the body needs to catch up with the mind. Give it time and you'll be pleasantly surprised.

Use visualisation methods to help you. Feel the infant within your womb, feel the connection and the bond within. Envisage the birth and holding your newborn, perfectly healthy, safe and well. Imagine the baby in your arms and feel the warmth of its body lying on yours, imagine the elation, the joy, relief and happiness that you and your partner will feel as proud parents. With these methods, you will connect more closely to your baby, feel more relaxed and in control.

A diary or journal helps in keeping track of your emotions and what is happening in your life. It is also acts as a good reminder on which you can look back and see the changes that have happened in such a short period of time.

Keep a check on your emotions. It is worth taking stock every few months as to what you are feeling. This can become an automatic and helpful process over time. Take Bach flower remedies too, to help with the transition.

The above are self-help ideas but for more traumatic experiences contact a practitioner specialising in emotional disorders who is registered in programmes such as Dissolve and Resolve Emotions (DARE) or Somoto Emotional Release (SER). My own School of Life courses inform and explore ways to resolve and remove mental patterns, emotion and de-stress to 'Get your life back'. (See appendix for details)

Disconnection

All sorts of issues, problems and disconnections can come together during pregnancy to affect the child on all levels. The mother's disconnection from her baby is something I have experienced in my practice. Although it doesn't happen often, it occurs when the mother puts up barriers to protect herself completely from the baby. This could be for many reasons, including lack of natural hormones from an induction process. For whatever reason (it may be a combination or something completely different), the child feels nothing from the mother and is left isolated and alone. Unfortunately some mothers don't feel pregnant at all.

In this situation I treat mothers with techniques for emotional release to find out why she is feeling like this. Once we have found the core of the problem and cleared it to a resolution for the mother, the next step is to reconnect the mother and child again, so that she feels more in touch with her baby. Sometimes it can take several treatments to achieve this.

Within the womb, the child needs to feel love and to feel secure, otherwise, after it is born it will continue to feel isolated, unloved and even abandoned, feelings, which will manifest into patterns for life. Clearing these issues while the mother is pregnant releases the baby from the negative emotions and feelings, thereby giving the child a better balanced foundation to grow from, and making it easier for the child to bond with the mother, both before and after the birth.

On occasion, I have needed to do similar treatments to adults who have experienced emotional issues since the womb, where they have taken on their mother's problems, anxieties and depression. While still in the womb some knew that they were not wanted, while others erroneously believed that this was the case. As a result, they failed to bond with their mother and, feeling anxious from their first day of life, they could not release this feeling no matter what they did.

SELF HELP

Yoga or meditation during pregnancy can help pregnant mothers to feel a deep mindfulness and connection to her child, which is satisfying spiritually, emotionally and physically.

In addition, certain of the Bach flower remedies that we looked at can be particularly helpful in times of emotion including:-

- Beech is for intolerance

- Crab apple a cleansing remedy when feeling bloated, it helps a woman to feel whole again, to love and respect oneself. Helps remove feelings of self-loathing and disgust.

- Cherry plumb – use when feeling out of control or imbalanced in life

- Elm – use for apprehension, fear or foreboding

- Gentian – use for disappointment - Gives a feeling of more positive thoughts

- Mustard – use for depression or low in spirit

- Olive - use for fatigue

- Pine - use for feelings of guilt or let others down helps with back - lash and the unexpected.

- Sweet Chestnut – use for feeling trapped or despair – useful after pregnancy

- Rockrose can be used during those times when you may feel slightly shocked or panicky and sweet chestnut when you feel trapped or despairing. The former can prove very helpful during the final days of pregnancy and both are useful after the birth.

  (See appendix for more details)

CASE STUDY 7
THE MOTHER WHO COULD NOT STAND
TO HEAR HER CHILDREN CRY

One mother came to see me because she could not stand to hear her children cry. Although she didn't know why, the sound of her baby crying went right through her. It made her feel anxious, even though she understood that children do cry and that it is a natural way for them to draw attention to the fact that something is wrong. Norma (name changed for anonymity) had two children, but her uneasiness kicked in far more after the birth of her second child. Since this child (another girl) suffered a long and traumatic birth, being unsettled she cried even more, therefore creating a vicious circle.

During an emotional release treatment, Norma told me that she had had this feeling of uneasiness for as long as she could remember. It transpired (unbeknown to her) that Norma's mother could not stand her crying either when she was a baby, as her mum had lost a previous child through miscarriage. This caused a deep traumatic side-effect that her mum had not yet come to terms with.

Once Norma knew it was not her issue but that of her mother, we were able to release the trauma from her patterning and behaviour. It took only one treatment to achieve full release. A few weeks afterwards, I received a phone call from Norma, who told me that her children's crying no longer upset her. She told me she could handle it from a different perspective and even laugh at her daughter's tantrums.

To complete the process, I suggested the need to treat her crying daughter and release the child from her own birth trauma. One session could have brought calm again in the household. However, sadly, Norma's husband was not keen for his daughter to be treated. He did not understand that his child would hold the birth trauma just like his wife. And so the cycle goes on and on....

HYPNOBIRTHING

Hypnobirthing is becoming more and more popular as switched-on women look for alternative ways of helping the birth process. Hypnotherapy is synonymous with stage performances by the likes of Paul McKenna who has spent many years pioneering its virtues.

Hypnobirthing:

- Uses methods to achieve deep relaxation
- Helps to calm fears and anxiety patterns
- Uses breathing techniques
- Helps to connect to instincts and trust
- Instils confidence and trust in the self
- Connects you to your inner power and strength
- Offers pain management techniques
- Includes positive thinking techniques

It has been seen as a success for new mothers and women who have had a previous unfortunate experience of inducement. They use the same breathing techniques that I used with my own birth process. In those days it was not called anything other than breathing exercises to help us relax and we practised them in anti-natal classes back in the 1970s. It is a rhythm breathing technique as taught in yoga. I have used this type of breathing for relaxation and spiritual classes before.

Hypnobirthing works by lowering stress levels through the introduction of controlled breathing. Using breathing techniques helps to open the cervix gently. Undue pushing only creates tension in the body and muscles, working against the cervix and causing greater restriction. The breathing technique works well and I would advise pregnant mothers to explore Hypnobirthing as an aid in labour.

The technique simply consists of breathing in to a count of say 4, and breathing out to a count of 8 (doubling the figure). Alternatively there are also 7/11 and countless other numerical techniques which help to regulate breathing and bring the heart rate down to lower levels. There are specific techniques for labour, using quicker and shorter breaths.

Breathing techniques have, of course, been around for some time and we know that these help to relax muscles, to slow heart rate and to reduce the adrenalin hormone in our system. I have treated mums who have used Hypnobirthing and they say it made a huge difference the second time around. With the first experience being so traumatic, they decided it was not going to be repeated a second time. Consequently mum was in control and, when baby arrived, it was calm and slept well. What a difference to the previous birth, where the child was anxious and unsettled for months because of the birth intervention, an experience which proved to be difficult and more to the point painful to both mother and child.

Check out yoga and Hypnobirthing courses. They are run in many places around the country and you have nothing to lose and everything to gain.

CASE STUDY 8 –
HYPNOBIRTHING

A friend of mine is a Hypnobirthing practitioner and has kindly offered a case study of his own to share the insights of events and outcomes from the technique.

Vicky - experiences of her first child.
'Others people's birth experiences had instilled a deep-seated fear in me of both labour and giving birth. I had convinced myself that I too would not be able to cope with the pain.

I desperately wanted a natural water birth with no drugs if at all possible. I therefore sought help through hypnotherapy. Over a series of sessions we focussed on positive thinking, pain management techniques and visualisation of labour and birth.

As a result, Charlotte Ellen was born after an 18 hour induced labour with no drugs whatsoever. I didn't even need the birthing pool! I can honestly say it was the most positive and rewarding experience of my life.'
Vicky

DOULA SERVICES

'One of the greatest privileges of a human life is to become a midwife to the birth of the soul in another.' - Plato

Doula is a Greek word meaning 'woman servant or care giver'.
Doulas are usually people who care very passionately about women and birth and they normally work with the philosophy of 'mothering the mother'. Although mostly women, there are some men now in the Doula profession and their services have been born from a need to fill the gap created by the loss of the old-time wise woman or elder of the community who helped out at birth.

Experienced in childbirth, Doulas need a good knowledge and understanding of the physiology of birth and the impact of this life-changing event. Often women who have had a difficult experience want to help other women get the best out of the birth process. From my own experience there is certainly a need.

Doulas help and assist midwives during birthing and are involved in the run-up to the event, providing flexible, individualised care to suit the pregnant woman's needs. I believe that having a Doula is essential for the busy and pressured lifestyles we follow today. They can help to take the pressure off already over-stretched midwives by giving breast-feeding advice, general information and explaining care structures.

It is proven that having a Doula present can make a big difference to the birth process with:

- 60% reduction in epidurals
- 40% reduction in forceps deliveries
- Higher success rates of breast-feeding
- Increased satisfaction of childbirth
- Fewer complications
- Fewer interventions
- Lower caesarean section rates

Some Doulas class themselves as birthing advisors, bringing their extensive personal and professional experience to help during maternity. Others include exercises and meetings with fathers, giving advice for support during and after birth. Look for Doulas in your area. Although a privately-run service at present, it is often associated with birth centres and independent midwives.

MATERNITY CARE IN THE UK

In 2007, Unicef published a report putting the UK at the bottom of a list of twenty-one rich countries in terms of the wellbeing of children. They cited that, in the UK, new mothers were not supported after the birth, something which is in total contrast to other areas, including parts of Europe where new mothers are nurtured and cared for to a much higher standard. The report highlights how far down the NHS has gone over the past twenty years. There was a time when we were leading the world and proud of our hospitals and the services they provided.

With a reported UK birth rate of 670,000 in 2006, it is commonsense that mothers and babies need support of the highest standard. In treating mothers and babies regularly this report has highlighted and substantiated my own findings and prompted me to write about my experiences.

David Cameron, the present leader of the Conservative party, announced proposals to correct the imbalance in 2008 and called for dedicated maternity nurses to help all new mothers during the first week at home. A nanny or Doula (maternity assistant) was suggested to help out with the child's progress and, where the child is not the first, such assistance means that the mother has help with the simple tasks of washing and caring for siblings in the home. This solution is deliberately intended to offer general help so that the new mum can rest and be with her family in a calm and nurturing environment as she eases back into the family life. Essentially, what David Cameron is looking for are ways to correct the problem of support for parents in general, especially in view of the fact that when a new arrival is brought home it can be a frustrating and anxious time for all.

The scheme that he has proposed is a copy of the system used in Holland. The Dutch programme has agencies which provide support for mothers in this way and is financed partly by the state system, insurance and partly by the parents.

Authors note: David Cameron became prime minister in May 2010 and we look forward to him putting his suggestions in to practice - time will tell.

Private birth centres are becoming more popular and are springing up in different parts of the UK, giving couples the option of structured support including Doula services, Cranio Sacral Therapy, complementary therapies and homeopathy support during pregnancy and the first weeks at home. I am involved with a birth centre in Northwich, Cheshire, which supports women in all sorts of ways including through counselling and emotional support.

In the course of opening the centre, the organisers were under severe scrutiny (far more than an NHS programme), with much negativity from the powers that be who could not understand why independent midwives would want to support women in this way. This speaks for itself and goes a long way to explaining why there is no conception of what has gone wrong over the years. It is indicative of a head-in-the-sand attitude and hoping that it will all go away. In many respects, however, these holistic birth centres are leading the way, pioneering what women need and want and creating interest within other maternity units. Those who have visited have taken note of the improvements that they are making to society.

Unfortunately, the Unicef report highlights the demise of the original high standards of care in the UK, proving that women's needs are not being met by the NHS however they wrap it up. I believe the UK needs more centres like this and hopefully, with enough support, they will come with time.

So far, the existing centres are private and it is only those who can afford the cost who are reaping the benefits. What David Cameron is suggesting is that these structures should be a right for every new mother, avoiding a situation where proper care is a lottery according to how much we earn. His scheme (part of the childhood report) would require thousands of maternity nurses or nannies to be trained in specialized maternity care for the child and mother and it is suggested that each one would only be able to look after two mothers per week.

Maternity care is already under-funded and struggling to meet the demand in all areas of the UK. With our services being under such huge pressure, the numbers of maternity nurses declining and the government closing maternity cottage hospitals all over the country, maternity care in the UK is in crisis.

National survey 2007

A national survey of maternity care in 2007 has already revealed complaints about post-natal care. Hospital cleanliness again came up as an issue, particularly in relation to the rooms and bathrooms used during labour and during postnatal care. In addition:

- 26% of mothers reported that they were alarmed at being left alone during labour and after the birth
- As many as 43% complained that they were not being offered home births
- 36% complained that they had not been offered anti natal classes
- 18% reported that they had not been treated with kindness and understanding during their labour

Of course, these reports come only from the few who have spoken out, and unfortunately I feel that this could just be the tip of the iceberg. With not enough beds or room to accommodate the demand in maternity wards, women are having shorter stays in hospital after the birth of their baby, with some mothers leaving within twenty-four hours.

The Royal College of Midwives has repeatedly raised concerns about the shortage of midwives and in 2007declared that at least 5,000 were needed to fill the gap. It is freely acknowledged that part of the problem is due to the shortage of midwives, together with increasing pressure and stress put upon them to meet the needs of the NHS. Until the shortages are addressed, the problems for new mothers worsen daily. Mothers are becoming increasingly unhappy with their care and the NHS is struggling to correct the situation because of the lack of available midwives. Independent midwives are having to be brought in to cover the shortfall, which is costing the NHS even more of their dwindling resources.

Resources for community midwives have been steadily declining and again there is a critical shortage of maternity nurses and midwives to help with the care of mothers after birth. With more mums choosing to have their birth at home, this will only put more pressure on the role of the community midwife. Obviously, if we had kept the numbers and resources there for the community midwives, we would not have slipped to the level we seem to be at right now in caring for our new mothers. Calculations indicate that the UK would need an injection of £150 million to start to copy the Dutch programme.

Midwives have been leaving the NHS for some time as they become more and more dissatisfied with the conditions and the pressure they are put under. Some are leaving the profession altogether and others are going it alone, working independently in conditions where they feel better able to care and support the new mum. This is, of course, what they were originally trained to do and why they went into the profession in the first place.

The Dutch system

The Netherlands and Sweden have quite a different approach to childcare and childbirth - I believe they lead the way in compassionate welfare care in the West practices we could learn by and should introduce in the UK.

The proposed Dutch system (known as Kraamorg) provides a package of care for both mother and baby. Mothers report that the Dutch approach to childbirth is both relaxed and liberating, with most mothers choosing home births during which they are cared for by a midwife and a maternity nurse. The mothers feel in control and are able to structure the environment in which they give birth, giving them the nurturing and relaxed caring environment they need and want at this momentous time.

The Dutch system provides basic care which should be standard everywhere, including:

- Teaching mothers how to breast-fed
- Teaching mothers how to bathe their babies
- Feeding and caring for other children

- Household cleaning and laundry
- Visitor monitoring and ensuring rest for the mother

This system is a must for new mothers because we no longer have the family support or structure in the twenty first century. The government relies much on family support nowadays as they have eroded structures of care. Gone are the days where mum, granny and aunty were around to help out and show new mums the ropes. These people are all out at work themselves.

This was the care structure that the UK had in the 1950s before mothers needed to go out to work to support the family. Nowadays, however, most women are forced to work in order to meet the additional burdens of higher taxes and larger monthly mortgage payments. Because these days it is common to have families which are scattered around the country, and even around the world, the family unit structure has gone in the West. Whilst this is considered to be a mark of progress, today it means that we have to look to the maternity hospitals and nurses to fill the gap. Unfortunately however, with government cutbacks such as they are, the gap is getting bigger week by week.

Health care commission report

The Health Care Commission report was published in 2004 and highlighted huge weaknesses in maternity care in the UK and noted that 'much more needs to be done'. In 2008, a subsequent report was issued and the news was that not much had improved during the intervening four years.
In 2004, they highlighted poor communication between staff and pregnant women and indeed 26,000 mothers reported that they felt there was NO CARE during labour.

The 2008 report was the most detailed report ever on maternity, giving a scary picture of treatment to pregnant women and confirming all that I have been saying over recent years and highlighted in this book.

On the subject of bathing facilities on maternity wards, the report stated that these were woefully insufficient. Relatively few units had one bath per delivery room and, despite the fact that hygiene concerns should mean that all delivery rooms have a shower room en-suite, only 38% of units actually did. The report highlighted that, because of the lack of facilities, it would be a long time before this level is reached.

Beds in delivery rooms, meanwhile, were in such demand that, in some cases, several women were giving birth in the same bed each day. As each woman gave birth, she was moved and another took her place with some reporting that they felt as though they were in an airport being herded here and there. In addition, women were often turned away from their maternity unit while they were in labour because the unit could not offer them a bed through being over-subscribed. Some units actually close for more than 55 days a year, which seems madness when there is so much demand.

Although our UK Government has stated that it has key aims to give every woman a choice over where she gives birth (i.e. by midwife at home or in hospital), one has to ask whether this is rhetoric or fact. The 2008 Health Care Commission report pointed out that, in practice, pregnant women have very little choice about anything.

Another thing that the report concerned itself with was the numbers of C-sections carried out and how there seem to be huge differences between trusts. In addition, some hospitals have higher rates than others, though these are always higher than recommended. The levels indicate rates of between 14% and as much as 39%, with the average being 24%, although my own research has found some inner city hospitals have a rate which is in excess of 40%, way beyond the World Health Authority (WHO) safety recommendations.

Big is best?
Surely this cannot go on. The government policy of 'big is best' is not working in practice, as anyone with common sense could have told them.

Business strategy does not always work in health and welfare care because it only looks at profit and takes care and compassion out of the equation.

Unfortunately Hospitals in the UK today seem to be more concerned with turnover and statistics and we seem to have lost the human care and attention in the changeover. This leanness has done nothing more than drive us to the point where we just don't have enough staff or materials to do the job properly.

The Royal College of Midwives is calling trusts to take maternity care more seriously.

'Real choice is needed for women in maternity care. Funds and staffing levels need to be greatly improved. The government have targets of 4,000 more midwives before 2012 and in reality we are nowhere near hitting that target.' RC Midwives

Again, the 2008 Health Care Commission report reiterates areas of concern which had been previously raised, stating:
'Women and babies deserve high quality care and support throughout their pregnancy, labour, birth and postnatal care.'

Some areas, which have not improved since the 2004 report, include:

- Antenatal and postnatal services were not up to the level of care required
- Team working and staffing levels
- Neonatal units are set to shut over the next few years
- Maternity units are set to be downgraded in the next few years

The facts are that, in reality, women have less choice and midwives are being put under increasing pressure to cope with demand and are lacking the necessary facilities. I personally know a number of midwives and the pressure that some of them are being expected to endure is simply unbearable. Many are becoming ill because of the amount of stress that they are under and, of course, this helps no one.

The NHS has issued a statement since the publication of the 2008 Health Care Commission report to say that maternity care is to be prioritised in every region and that they will be developing plans to help frontline care with midwives. Unfortunately, however, we have heard all this before but have seen little change on the front line. Some trusts are doing all that they can but the reduction of funds is the key to the demise in hospitals.

A pregnancy care planner is being launched by the NHS in 2009 to help solve the current problems, its aim being to provide a resource where women can find out about:

- Antenatal care
- Different options of pain relief during birth
- Where to give birth

The planner also compares the performance of maternity services across England.

I believe that this proposed planner will be of little help to women in the light of the report. The horse has already bolted and the planner will be of little use when more hospital beds are a more immediate concern!

Midwives

We are all very aware of the shortages in the maternity sector and for years there have been calls for more investment in staff and training. Sadly the pleas for common sense are falling on deaf ears as our government's words and actions fail to match.

In 1997 we had 18,053 midwives in the UK[105]. Nine years later, in 2006, there were only an additional 800, giving 18,862 to deliver all our babies in the UK. This is an increase in midwife numbers of 4.3%, while births have risen by 12.5% - the birth rate in 2001 was 564,871 rising to 635,679 in 2006. In the UK in 2007 there were an estimated 1,835 live births every day.

Even though falling numbers have been acknowledged, instead of encouraging more student midwives to train and put more money into the maternity system, the UK government has instigated further cuts by removing bursaries for trainee midwives and limiting job opportunities to an even greater extent when they qualify. How mad is this when we have chronic shortages around the country and are being faced with media headlines such as, 'It is a crying shame' and 'We need more midwives to save lives.'

Urgent attention is needed now to end this plight for mothers. The increased birth rate is putting more of a burden upon our existing maternity services and midwife numbers and, in addition, it has been reported that almost half of all current midwives are due to retire in the next decade. Clearly we need them to pass on their wisdom and knowledge before all is lost.

As we have mentioned, it is estimated by the Royal College of Midwives that we will need 5,000 more midwives by 2012. The time for talking is over and it is now time for action.

The mere fact that you are reading this book suggests that you probably have an interest in maternity issues. If you are pregnant, want to become pregnant or are already a mum or a grandmother, therefore, then please help to raise awareness. Our women and children need safe and effective treatment by highly trained and caring staff. We also need support for our midwives who do a tremendous job under great pressure, despite shortages in the system. It is their dedication to the profession that does them credit.

Write and lobby your MP for action, not words. The sooner we do this, the quicker we can influence improvement and change.

The Department of Health have put together a list of 'What women want'?

- To have confidence in staff providing care during the birth process
- To be treated with kindness, support and respect
- One-to-One care from a named midwife throughout pregnancy, labour and birth.
- A pleasant and safe birth environment

- Receive adequate information and explanations about their choices for childbirth, pain relief and hospital practices
- Access to medical help if complications arise

At the time of writing and listening to women who have gone through the birth process, we have a way to go to have the above list fulfilled.

[103] Wikipedia 'Article Franz Karl Naegele' www.wikipedia.com (Cited 02.2009)

[104] S G Blythe "What babies and children really need' Hawthorn Press Stroud. Glos.UK 2008 (Ref: quote S Buckley 'Gentle Birth, Gentle mothering' One Moon press)

[105] Jonathan Owen 'Britain's maternity crisis' Independent on Sunday article (09.2007)

Chapter 12

INDEX

Chapter 12

....

NATURAL BIRTH

Monday's child is fair of face

Tuesday's child is full of grace

Wednesday's child is full of woe

Thursday's child has far to go

Friday's child is loving and giving

Saturday's child works hard for their living

But the child that is born on the Sabbath day is good and kind, bold and gay

Today, birth is much like a series of medical events, with check-ups, antenatal visits, scans and so on. We are told that it is necessary for us to have these medical checks in order to have a healthy child and mother. Pregnancy, however, is not an illness but a natural way to reproduce. Unfortunately, the whole process is governed nowadays by the people who work within our health industry.

There is no doubt that technology has proved to be very beneficial to helping us live longer. Scans, for example, provide an understanding of what is happening within the body, giving the healthcare professional a physiological road map to highlight deficiencies and obstructions which can slow down recovery.

In the past, however, birth was a sacred time for the mother and involved the input of the wise women of the village (what we would call a midwife today) to care and oversee the pregnancy and delivery. By the time the baby was born, there was a bond and confidence between them, with the birth taking place in quiet and familiar surroundings. In this scenario, the mother was more relaxed and comfortable and the birth was dealt with according to nature's timetable. The mother was in control and happy during the course of the birth event, which has evolved since time began in all reproducing species.

With hospital deliveries, women come into an environment, which is clinical, unfamiliar and tended by unfamiliar staff (midwives), depending upon which shift she catches when she is there. It is not a private time at all.

There are people coming and going and the birth process normally takes place in front of strangers, often in noisy and brightly lit conditions. Vaginal examinations are frequent during pregnancy and delivery, often carried out by different people, none of whom are known by the mother-to-be. In this environment, the mother is more tense and anxious than she would otherwise be and even a natural, vaginal birth in the twenty first-century requires the expectant mother to make intellectual decisions and give consent for procedures in the least conducive of circumstances.

Natural birth has served women for centuries

Unfortunately, because of all the interference during the natural birth process, a lot of women look upon their deliveries negatively. Natural birth has served women for centuries, although it is not the process it used to be.

Although it is true that vaginal birth can be painful, normal labour pain is just like a strong period pain which can be either all in the back or all in the front of the body. I had two children and with the first the pain was all in the front. The second was completely different and the pain was in the lower back and thighs.

Natural birth can also seem messy, what with fluids and afterbirth, not to mention all the hard work of pushing. Having said this, however, it is also very invigorating and, as unlikely as it may sound, the pain is very soon forgotten after the delivery. Naturally secreted hormones kick in which make everything rosy when you see your baby and indeed a mother's natural hormonal state supports the birth process rather than fighting against it.

During the course of the birth itself, the hormone oxytocin acts on the uterine muscles and helps them work in harmony. Its presence causes the ligaments to soften and loosen, allowing the baby through. It also allows the horizontal muscles to loosen their hold and open to let the baby arrive. Whatever the size of the baby, a woman should be able to give birth naturally because the baby's head moulds to the shape of the cervix. Some babies are born with a cone shaped head that should bounce back into shape within minutes when born naturally.

It is well known that women who have a natural birth usually recover quicker. They are normally able to drive within days of giving birth and they have no problem integrating back into family life. I know of women who returned home hours after giving birth naturally, where they immediately felt at ease and in the womb of their family and children. Achieving this causes less disruption to family, toddlers and other children.

Babies too benefit from a vaginal birth as the birth process activates many processes within the baby while going through the birth canal. Essentially it gives an all-over massage to the child and wakes up various systems in the baby's body, including cranial activation, which is needed by the body to be able to function quickly and naturally. Hormonal surges and activity with physical compression also initiate body systems, preparing lung activity and releasing fluid for incoming oxygen.

According to statistics, babies that are born vaginally are able to breathe better and have a lower risk of respiratory problems. It is those which are born by C-section who are more likely to suffer from asthma in later life (as discussed later). It is believed that vaginal births help babies to adapt better to the outside world by going through the birth canal.

In some cases the birth canal is too small to allow a baby's head through comfortably, squeezing the skull sections over each other to allow passage (this is a normal function of birth). In some cases the skull sections can stick or jam and the result can be pain and/or pressure in the head. In this case, the child should be treated after birth with Cranio Sacral Therapy to release any residual pressure.

Women were giving birth long before modern technology came into being and they managed perfectly well. Given the chance they probably would again. Because of the measured treatments devised for a small minority of women who need assisted birth treatment, we regularly find that these methods are now being applied to the vast majority of women whether they need it or not.

Having your child in a straightforward manner is the most practical way for your baby to be born. Intervention-free, it is a healthy and natural way devised by nature and evolution to be a process which happens automatically.

Birth contact

The contact between mother and child should not be interrupted immediately after birth. Those few moments (30 minutes to an hour) are very important and the first 15 minutes, when oxytocin is apparent and the love hormone is being released, are critical for bonding and recognition. Many trials have shown the benefits of a baby being left with mum to bond after birth. However because of the high levels of clinical intervention nowadays, this no longer happens in many cases. It has been shown that for mothers who received pethadine during the birth process, the baby showed signs of sedation after birth and did not suckle at all[106].

A small Canadian study found that increased parental carrying in the first 3 months of life was associated with a substantial reduction in crying and fussing behaviour in firstborns. This is true especially at crucial times, such as at around 6 weeks old, when fretfulness late in the afternoon and evening revealed distress creeping in. This research found that increased physical contact created contentment in the infant.

An infant's crying can become excessive at times and this in itself can produce negative emotions in the mother, leading her to question her ability to cope. When this happens, not only does the baby become more demanding (picking up on mum's distress), but it also takes longer to calm and soothe, causing a vicious circle for both mum and baby.

Where a secure foundation and consistent and positive care has been provided by parents in the early days, infants have been found to be more confident and better able to regulate their emotions. While young, an infant is unable to distinguish between temporary and long-term separation from mum and is more likely to experience distress and anxiety. All the child has known is mum and dad; it knows their smell and touch instantly and recognises their voices. Without this safety net of recognition they can become fretful, something which is, of course, only natural.

When we are born, we have an etheric cord attached to us from our mother and this is our energy connection to her for the rest of our lives. It is something that we cannot see with our eyes but can feel instinctively. If we could see the etheric cord, it would look like a spiders strand, very fine but strong and made up of millions of energy particles. By this connection, some know instinctively when their parents are hurt, injured or have died.

It is the same for the mother and she knows when there is something wrong with her child. This connection from giving birth creates an inbuilt intuition and, just like a fax machine, she knows 'energetically'. The information is fed back to her, making her aware of the occurrence.

OXYTOCIN

Oxytocin is known as the birthing and nursing hormone. It creates a chain of events when labour and birth occurs, affecting:

- Maternal instincts
- The production of breast milk
- Bonding and social contact
- The sense of calmness in mother and child
- The activation of senses
- Digestion
- The lowering of blood pressure and pulse
- The balancing effect upon our physiology by keeping the blood stream from being flooded with stress hormones

Oxytocin is also one of the few hormones which create a positive feedback loop. A uterine contraction stimulates the release of oxytocin, which in turn increases contractions until the baby is born. The more stress in the mother, however, the more cortisol is released, with cortisol acting to inhibit the release of the oxytocin hormone.

How does Oxytocin work?

Oxytocin is found in all species of mammals. It is a hormone that works through the blood and is known as a peptide (a signalling substance in the nervous system). Peptides are made up of small proteins and amino acids and research has found that an oxytocin molecule is composed of nine amino acids. Peptides influence the cell by activating receptors on the outside of the cell membrane, therefore affecting the cell and emotional response via the pituitary and hypothalamus. The large cells send oxytocin to the pituitary, one of the master glands in the brain, whilst smaller cells send oxytocin to other parts of the brain.

When powerfully stimulated, such as in a nursing mother, oxytocin tends to go out on clusters of nerve impulses rather than individual impulses. This stimulates the brain stem, which controls blood flow, feelings and alertness. The nerve impulses connect to the spinal cord influencing the autonomic nerve process and sensation of pain. Using oxytocin as a hormonal messenger, the hypothalamus (known as the computer of the brain) communicates through the nerve fibres to coordinate many physiological functions and activities at the same time. Oxytocin is also found in the blood as well as in the nerves in the body. Used by special receptors, it can plug in to several functions at one time and it is believed that there are several receptors, although some have not yet been identified through research.

Although found in both sexes, oxytocin is believed to have more of an effect upon females than males, and of course we know that one of its functions is contracting the uterus. Chemical messengers carry information to the hypothalamus which can increase oxytocin activity or slow down and inhibit flow. New research, however, has also found that oxytocin is locally produced in the ovaries and testes and has been found in the walls of blood vessels and the heart[107].

The main characteristics of oxytocin are:

- It can stimulate its own production release via oxytocin-producing cells and receptors
- Oestrogen can influence the production of oxytocin by increasing the amount of receptors
- Serotonin also stimulates the release of oxytocin
- Dopamine plays a role in controlling movement and concentration and can raise oxytocin levels
- Noradrenalin from the brain activates both alertness and aggression, and when released can have a stimulating affect upon oxytocin

Some drugs, such as Prozac, can include serotonin and have a passive oxytocin effect upon the body.

The Effects of Oxytocin

As we have said, oxytocin has been described as the love hormone and its effects are first experienced at the time of birth, when it helps to contract the uterus and move baby from the womb.

Touch feels pleasurable as a result of oxytocin. When we have pleasurable contact, oxytocin is released and produces a feeling of love. During intimate moments, for example, oxytocin allows us to feel pleasure and is responsible for creating ecstasy and orgasm when we make love.

The oxytocin hormone affects both genders, and some research has found a positive link between this and the transport of egg and sperm. Due to their physiology and the fact that the oestrogen in their bodies enhances oxytocin, women are believed to find it easier than men to become calm and relaxed and indeed this is one of the reasons why women tend to be calmer in general. Men, on the other hand, have testerone to enhance the effects of the hormone vasopressin (known as oxytocin sister), which is known to stimulate defence, aggression and physical activity. They are more active on the fight and flight syndrome and on red alert. Both sexes, however, have all of these hormones to some degree and it depends upon your anxiety, stress levels, lifestyle and activities as to which hormone is more dominant at the time.

The same oxytocin release happens when we are calm and relaxed. It also occurs when we are experiencing other pleasurable activities such as having a massage or simply eating good food. Oxytocin is released when we receive a massage, as a result of the touch factor, but even during exercise and meditation it is also released. It makes us feel friendly and caring, as though there is less to be afraid of. We feel more in control. Oxytocin also gives us feelings and sensations of calmness within.

MATERNAL BEHAVIOUR

As we have described, bonding is accelerated with oxytocin release. It is released during labour and suckling, stimulating the muscles around the milk ducts to contract and expel breast milk. It also allows bonding to take place between the mother and child instantly after birth. A mother recognises her own child through the connection of oxytocin. When both love and oxytocin are present, a memory pattern of recognition is instilled in the brain.

During the birth process itself, the hormone also relieves the effects of pain. High oxytocin levels have been associated with forgetting, such as is the case with the fading memory of labour pain. The mother seemingly forgets after seeing her new baby.

Oxytocin also plays a part in regulating blood pressure and pulse. It controls body temperature, for example, so allowing mothers who are breast-feeding to help keep the baby warm, giving warm chests and rosy cheeks. In addition, it regulates digestion by influencing the vagus nerve, stimulates growth and development, rejuvenates mucous membranes and produces anti-inflammatory reactions.

It even works with vasopressin to control and regulate fluid levels within the body. When we experience stress, the available levels of vasopressin and corticotrophin hormones (CRF) are increased within the body and these in turn heighten our desire for an intake of salt. The raised levels of vasopressin decrease urine production, as well as contracting blood vessels, so causing high blood pressure. Oxytocin works to reduce the enthusiasm for the intake of salt and to stimulate the release of urine and sodium from the kidneys. This makes it an important factor in promoting a reduction of sodium and water retention in the body.

The Pros and Cons of Oxytocin

Mothers who give birth via Caesarean section have been found, on average, to have lower oxytocin levels. Pulses created by synthetic oxytocin have been seen to be much less compared to those who have had a vaginal birth, as the hormone is known to help us relax mentally and physically.

C-section mothers tend to be less calm.
Anaesthesia and analgesics such as epidurals are seen to be part of the problem. Whatever is given during delivery will affect the oxytocin levels and their natural effects during birth and afterwards. The child can also be affected, feeling drowsy from pethadine and other drugs.

It is also known that bonding between mothers and C-section children is more problematic and that women who have C-sections have more trouble breast-feeding. The development of breast-feeding patterns and behaviours are often delayed in these women and it is not known as yet what long-term effects there are in the relationships and bonding between such mothers and infants.

BREAST-FEEDING AND SOCIAL CONTACT

Although suckling is believed solely to provide the newborn with food, the action is also connected to social contact. Through research with animals, it was found that those who are naturally fed by the mother have higher oxytocin levels than those fed by bottle. It has also been shown that pre-term babies respond well to being breast-fed, becoming calmer and gaining weight rapidly if allowed to suck as much as possible on the nipple[108]. Even when given a nipple substitute such as its own thumb, a dummy or pacifier, a baby receives comfort and strength.

Having oxytocin released during labour and breast-feeding gives the mother more maternal instincts. She is more relaxed, has caring instincts when bathing, feeding and cleaning and tends to be more interested and protective of her child. As a result of oxytocin deep lasting bonds form between mother and baby and these mothers tend to feel very close to their children.

Is the lack of oxytocin the reason we have such bad social behaviour in the 21st century? It is clear that oxytocin plays a huge role in the bonding and social aspects of mother and child, but are we now seeing the long-term effects of too many C-Sections and too much medical intervention at birth over the decades? Is nature no longer able to provide in a natural way through maternal instincts, breast-feeding and bonding at birth?

ANTISOCIAL BEHAVIOUR AND OXYTOCIN

Our children are becoming increasingly anti-social and often they have NO bonding with their parents and siblings. Many are frustrated, anxious and on edge. These are all indications of being low or non-existent oxytocin levels in our children. Are C-Sections the reason?

I believe that we are seeing the lack of oxytocin at birth become clearer each day with social behaviour headlines daily and calls for a stricter regime from parents. How can this work though when there is no bonding or respect for parents? Children have been born feeling isolated since birth. There is no contact or bonding on which to build a relationship because of the lack of the hormone oxytocin from the mother setting a foundation for children to grow from. The children of today have lost the balancing effect of oxytocin upon their physiology, an important issue when you consider that it plays a huge part in keeping the blood stream free from stress hormones.

Have we created this behaviour within our children? Are we responsible?

It certainly begs the question. Have the medical profession, combined with social needs, unknowingly created this scenario for our children?

We have been seeing more and more C-sections over the last 30 years. At one time they were very rare, even as recently as when I was having my own children in the 1970s. Now, however, we are seeing up to 40% of all births involving C-section and intervention, with such deliveries taking place every day in some hospitals. This is not just the case within the UK, but all over the western world, with some European countries showing even higher levels of C-section deliveries. Despite its intended positive aspect, intervention is making a huge detrimental difference to society. I believe the points made above are highlighting areas which have not been taken into consideration before.

Does this information indicate that we generally have less oxytocin in our bodies? Are lower levels of the hormone from birth having their effect upon our daily physical wellbeing? Indeed, oxytocin has many known effects on both our physical and mental health. Although constantly released in the body, lower levels can create dependencies, such as those on alcohol, drugs and smoking. In addition, as this hormone acts to inhibit the stress hormones in the blood, again lower levels create more stress and anxiety.

We now have a generation of C-section deliveries who are adults and having their own families. If they hold less oxytocin, does it mean that they are reproducing a generation who are even more deficient in oxytocin, a condition being passed on through their genes? I believe it answers many questions raised about our children's behaviour and that it has a huge part to play. It certainly makes you think, doesn't it?

AUTISM AND OXYTOCIN

Through trials, it has been found that autistic children have lower levels of oxytocin. Autistic children do not seem to demonstrate love easily and perhaps this is one of the reasons why. They find it difficult to look you in the eye and have difficulty sustaining relationships. These are all factors of the love hormone oxytocin.

Digestion and Oxytocin

From the time we are born we receive a connection to food, bonding and emotional closeness that lasts for life. Whatever level of understanding and patterns are formed in our early days will be with us as a foundation for future growth, such as how we were fed as an infant.

- Was milk easily available?
- Were we nourished enough?
- Were we frustrated with not enough milk?
- Did we need to work hard to receive the breast milk?
- Did we guzzle and gasp for air?
- Were we fractious?
- Were we content?

Despite C-section intervention, the Vagus nerve, which is influenced by oxytocin, can still be affected during the infant's time in the birth canal, causing digestion difficulties in later life if not corrected.

When we swallow food, oxytocin is released in the brain, giving feelings of enjoyment. This triggers the response of being full and contented. The suckling process and Vagus nerve activation during digestion and eating also play a part in this process. Less healthy ways can still lead to the release oxytocin, with the hormone being artificially induced through alcohol, drugs and fatty foods.

When we feel full (by the release of oxytocin), we feel more comfortable, calm and happy with a full tummy. We want to lie down and rest, which helps with digestion and the storing of nutrients. Logically, when we are calm we are more sociable and have a positive attitude. If we are hungry, on the other hand, we feel agitated, fretful and suffer discomfort. This can cause anxiety and inhibit digestion, causing dysfunction and even constipation. Anxiety and stress associated with eating and food ultimately forms adaptive patterns around food and feeding times.

As a culture, we see eating as a social activity which involves getting together and meeting people. We often use eating as a way of creating the right atmosphere for discussion, such as is the case with business meetings or a wedding proposal over dinner. This time can be used to thrash things out or smooth the way forward. Over a simple meal we get to know one another and share information. Indeed, food and eating have gone beyond the basic need for sustenance and become a cultural aspect of our lives all around the world.

EATING DISORDERS

Many people have complex thoughts on eating, creating excessive eating patterns which can have a negative effect upon us emotionally and physically. Conversely, if we do not feel comfortable when eating, it can cause eating disorders and maladaptive digestion responses.

Eating is connected with emotional problems and depression – we either stop eating or comfort eat to deaden pain and trauma. Comfort eating, for example, acts for some as a substitute for love and care, but the metabolism is affected and excessive weight becomes harder to lose, resulting in the physical body having more strain put upon it. Not eating, meanwhile, disrupts the body's nutritional storage and has ongoing effects upon the physical.

Research is continuing with the connection between oxytocin and eating disorders such as anorexia and bulimia, but we already know that it is seen as essential to our physical and mental relaxation and plays an important role with food by creating a feeling of fullness when we eat.

CASE STUDY 9 – EATING

One chap I treated was in his sixties and had skin and digestive disorders, including flatulence, which over the years had become increasingly embarrassing. Upon investigation, I found he had malabsorption through a lack of digestive acid, preventing good digestion. He had a good diet and his wife was always thinking of new ways to get him to eat beneficial foods.

Emotionally, there was an underlying core from his childhood. He did not enjoy his food and from what he told me, he thought of food as 'something that was done before the washing up'. He ate in a hurry and did not think of food as nourishing.

He had little emotional nourishment during his younger years. His parents had him late in life and consequently he was an only child. Apparently his parents had been strict and he needed to live up to their high expectations. Looking back, he realised that he did not get the love he deserved.

Emotionally, I don't think he had been nurtured and nor did he nurture himself or think of his own needs. The extent of his silent suffering caused burn-out on several occasions. He took his duty to his work seriously and provided for his family, but had lost the honour to himself somewhere in his early life, believing that he did not count. Nothing gave him the 'wow factor' and life was not exciting and new. This had been the norm throughout his life and even when he had a grandchild, he was pleased but not over the moon like his wife.

Certainly the food he ate did not nourish him emotionally. When I asked him what he loved in the way of food, the only thing he could think of was his breakfast. He loved his porridge.

We explored ways to help him think about his food while eating. By enjoying the taste and thinking about the nourishment within, he began to appreciate its true purpose and not as something that went straight through his system. It was a huge change for him as the symptoms had been with him all his life, even from childhood, and were still causing disorders sixty years on.

With physical and emotional release sessions plus vitamin and mineral supplementation he was helped on the road to recovery. His skin and digestion improved and he started to live life in a better and more fulfilling way.

He did not know if he was breast-fed, nor if he bonded with his mum from birth. From discussion with other clients, I have found that even though some were breast-fed, they did not feel nurtured. Their mothers did not have the love and affection to go with the milk. What they got instead was resentment, impatience and reluctance while being breast fed, which put another connotation entirely to the concept of nurturing and being fed.

This then sets the foundation of how we feel about, or receive food, and whether we are satisfied both emotionally and physically.

Smoking and Alcohol with Oxytocin

Smoking and Oxytocin

Nicotine suppresses appetite and increases the burning of calories. Because of this, people usually gain weight after they stop smoking. Despite the warnings and risks, women continue to smoke simply because of the weight reductions. It is believed the hormone vasopressin (oxytocin's sister) is responsible for the increased concentration and burning of calories.

For many, smoking generates the same emotional response as a baby sucking a thumb or nipple. Consequently, oxytocin is released in the same way as when suckling, thereby giving a feeling of comfort and creating the effects of well-being.

Despite the known dangers, smokers also seem to have a mental bond with their cigarettes, often refusing to go anywhere without them! Smoking creates an additional social aspect, especially the intimacy of sharing cigarettes and offering someone a light for their cigarette, cigar or pipe. Basically, smokers share a common ground psychologically.

Unfortunately, however, smoking decreases oxytocin in nursing mothers, therefore affecting the production of breast milk and producing less milk.

Alcohol and Oxytocin

Experiments with both rats and humans have shown that small amounts of alcohol increased concentration of the hormone oxytocin in the blood. However, higher amounts of alcohol had precisely the opposite effect.

Drugs and Oxytocin

Research is still ongoing in the area of drugs and oxytocin but recent reports have indicated that low levels of oxytocin in the bloodstream could be involved in the physiological process of drug dependency and alcohol addiction. Drugs like cocaine are connected with higher activity of the neurotransmitter dopamine, which is influenced by oxytocin.

In her book 'Oxytocin Factor' Dr.K.U.Moberg also highlighted in this research similar effects of combining marijuana and oxytocin. It is believed that oxytocin is artificially stimulated with the use of this drug, creating calmness and social ease.

We are only now coming to realise the effects and the physiological functions of the body and our stress-orientated imbalances from birth, with its detrimental effect upon society.

We need to make informed choices if we want a different society.

HIGH EXPECTATIONS

Our age, health and general fitness all play a part in the delivery process and how well a pregnancy goes, and the time in between pregnancies also seems to have an impact. In reality some pregnancies are better than others. Even if you have four or five pregnancies they can and will all be different.

My mother had six children but only four of us survived. Twins died in the second trimester of her second pregnancy. Her final pregnancy at home was long and arduous and, being in her late thirties at the time, the whole process proved difficult. The midwife was inexperienced and as my mum relates, 'stuck by the book'. My mum knew that she wanted to push and that the baby was ready, and yet the midwife deterred her, believing that this was not the case. Fortunately, at 11.30pm, a new midwife came on shift and my youngest brother was born an hour later in the early morning. He had been in the birth canal far too long and had swallowed mucus. I remember him needing to be propped up in the cot to help him discharge it.

I had two children of my own. I carried them differently and each labour was a different experience. On my first I was twenty-one. I felt very well and healthy throughout and worked until eight months. The labour pain was all in the front and, although not a big baby at 7lb 13ozs, I was ripped and needed stitches. I started labour on the Friday evening and she was born at 4am the next day, a contented and very happy baby. My recovery time was normal.

With the second pregnancy, I was twenty-four and a full-time mum. For most of the pregnancy I felt sick, nauseous and unwell. Labour pain was all in the back and started about 10.30pm until he was born at 4.15am. At 10lb 2oz he was a big baby and clearly fractious and unhappy. He screamed from the moment he arrived. I now realise it was a quick birth and he was suffering from shock.

It took me a while to get over the second pregnancy. Feeling so ill for nine months did pull me down physically and emotionally. With having my two year-old daughter to care for, there was no respite - at least with the first I could have a rest while the baby slept.

Despite this, both my pregnancies went fairly smoothly. I had natural vaginal births and the pain was like severe period pains. I had no drugs and was given gas and air just like my mother - epidurals and other inducement aids were not available in those days. I have what some would call 'childbearing hips' and I guess that makes a difference.

My niece recently gave birth to her second child within 13months of her first. Although the first delivery went well, the second baby's shoulders got stuck and both mum and baby had a rough time.

Labour is not text book

Clearly not all labours are textbook deliveries. Not all go smoothly and we should expect some pain and discomfort. Media headlines even recently called for 'women to be warned over pain of childbirth.' The article claimed a big gulf between what is expected and what happens in reality, stressing that women should be prepared for the worst. With my own experience and from my practice I can agree with this.

Some claim this is fear mongering, but I don't think so. Many women now suffer because of a lack of education and informed choice during maternity and labour. In my opinion, far too many are opting for C-sections instead of natural childbirth because of the sensationalist stories of pain during labour. This option only brings its own complications, with modern studies showing that C-section is causing emotional and behaviour patterns in our children, which have not been seen previously with natural birth (read the full debate later).

Labour pain can vary from one birth to another but it makes sense and is logical to believe that there will be some pain; to think differently is foolish. As females, we have period pain from an early age and that can be worse for some than for others. So it is with labour. My own experience of labour pain was bearable and felt like severe period pains in both cases. As we all have different levels of pain threshold, some can tolerate pain better than others, depending upon their experience and personal tolerance.

Research

Research calls for more education for the birth process. Reported in the BMC Medicine journal, a study from Newcastle University shows four areas of concern for women regarding childbirth:

1. Level and type of pain
2. Access to pain relief
3. Control over decision-making
4. The level of control during childbirth

The study concludes that many women underestimate the intensity of pain involved and have unrealistic expectations for a drug-free birth. They showed that although half of the women questioned beforehand didn't want drugs while in labour, they went on to use them because of the intensity of the pain.

The research showed evidence, however, to prove that the more informed a woman is about her labour, the better. With awareness she is prepared and if allowed a familiar environment, such as being at home with those she knows around her, less pain is felt.

I believe that antenatal education needs to be more factual, giving realistic information and awareness for women during labour. If the true facts are known, realistic expectations can be empowering. Having awareness allows women to be prepared for all eventualities and able to make realistic decisions, thereby receiving a better experience. This means that the woman is in control of the situation instead of being disappointed, in shock and suffering an unexpected outcome.

Have we softened up?

It begs the question 'have we softened with our easier lifestyle?' Over the last fifty years we have had a less physical lifestyle. Women before the 1960s endured a physically tougher lifestyle than we have today. Perhaps all that manual work helped with childbirth, because women then were more toned and physically stronger than we are today and hence able to tolerate more pain. Most women today, however, have a 'dread' of giving birth because of its association with pain.

THE CRAFT OF MATERNITY

In the Middle Ages, the church denied women in childbirth the help of other women, as atonement for their perceived sins as seducers of men. Over the ages generally, however, women have been helped and cared for during maternity and labour by their own gender. Often mothers helped their daughters through labour, giving instruction and sharing wisdom, and as a result they felt nurtured, loved and private in their birth process. Herbs and aromatic oils were used to soothe, relax and create the best relevant atmosphere for birth. Maternity assistants were usually the healers, herbalists and wise women (who were ultimately burnt at the stake as witches). Nowadays they could be compared to the Reflexologists, homeopaths, healers and therapists.

Men, supposedly trained as surgeons took, over the maternity process, pushing midwives to one side and leaving them as the assistants instead of first-line maternity health care. These medical surgeons were taught the 'craft' of maternity. In those days only males were considered to be bright enough to engage in such work while the woman's place was considered to be only in the home.

During this time, a lot of women died in hospital because of a simple lack of hygiene. Surgeons would often come from operations or dissecting corpses to consult and examine women. Moving from one bed to the next, they would spread their germs. Huge numbers died from 'childbed fever' as it was known. This created a lot of fear among women regarding childbirth and the fear-tension-pain syndrome was born. Sadly, the previous joy and magic had been forgotten.

As late as the 1800s, infection was rife and women and children died because of it. In the 18th and 19th centuries it affected 6-9 women in every 1000 deliveries with 2-3 deaths. It was the single most common cause of maternal mortality.

It was Florence Nightingale who taught about hygiene and influenced better practices[109]. Some would say we have improved upon those times, although hygiene is still in question even today in some hospitals.

Today 'Childbed fever' is known as Puerperal fever and is a form of septicaemia contracted by a woman during or shortly after childbirth, miscarriage or abortion. C-section is know to be a risk factor. If untreated it can be life threatening. It was reported by a confidential enquiry into maternal and child health (UK) that between 2003-2005 genital tract sepsis accounted for 14% of direct cause of maternal death, making puerperal fever a significant factor even today.

Safe delivery

In this day and age we expect our health care staff to bring about a safe delivery and a smooth labour. Unfortunately, we have been lulled into a false sense of security and in fact shortages in staff and services are the reality for most, in the UK at least. Our hospitals are often short-staffed and many maternity services are inadequate. An NHS report in October 2007 showed that more than half of women had been left alone during labour, with neither midwife nor doctor attending them for long periods of time. Not surprisingly, new mothers were very frightened as a result of this experience and, unfortunately, at the time of writing not much has changed.

It is logical that women can't relax in an environment filled with bright lights and people they don't know, and indeed some women see hospitals as being totally alien environments. I know the décor has improved in some, but it is still not the safe environment of 'home' where a woman can walk around and relax. This is why birth has historically been at home, attended by the wise women and elders who were trusted and accepted by the woman giving birth. She knew she was comfortable, secure and in safe hands. This is not the case in hospitals, since these are reactive environments and not calming for anyone. Noisy, bright and uninviting surroundings, with stressed and under-resourced staff do not lend themselves to calmness by any stretch of the imagination.

The body is a machine, cleverly designed and evolved to re-produce. It is a unit which can smoothly give birth if we allow it to, but women need to be in an environment where they can focus totally on what they are doing, for the sake of themselves and their unborn.

The sensual experience

Giving birth can, in fact, be a very sensual experience, given the right conditions. Oxytocin is there to smooth the way for us, acting as a natural pain relief and producing the joy and love which is essential for bonding. When we are relaxed, this love hormone can flow, but for that to happen we need privacy and intimacy with our loved ones during this magical time. Believe it or not, belly dancing was invented to help women to relax during labour and is still used in many parts of the world. To practice belly dancing during labour would, however, require freedom of movement and not being tied to a hospital bed with cables attached to machines.

Today our expectations are high when we give birth. Most women are fearful of the labour process as, through the media, we have been bombarded with images of screaming women giving birth and told that we need pain relief when in labour. This creates a false negativity in the mind and we believe it. It is unnecessary, however, to create stress and anxiety to the mother and child. With a little forethought and care, it can be avoided. Fearful thoughts create stress, which subsequently equals pain in labour and lower levels of Oxytocin.

Aristotle's words 'The mind of a pregnant woman needs to be cared for' come to be all the more relevant.

Eighty per cent of women say that childbirth was more painful than they imagined and for many the experience is full of fear instead of love. Mothers frequently feel guilt and condemnation because they believe they have let themselves and their babies down. It is true, labour can be painful, but unrealistic delivery expectations can also be disappointing for parents.

Terminology

Even the terminology used during interactions with midwives, health visitors or parents can be important in the run-up towards giving birth. These people can, with one word, create worry and stress which could be avoided with a little mindfulness. Instead of explaining using negative terms such as 'pain' and 'suffering', why not use positive descriptions and encouragement such as 'sensations of baby moving through the birth canal' or 'muscles work by forming contractions for the body to move baby down the birth canal?' By expressing things in this way, pregnant mothers would be better able to stay calm and relaxed, to work with their bodies and to allow them to dictate the rhythm and tone.

Pregnancy and childbirth are potentially filled with opportunities for mothers to become stressed and even just going for a medical appointment can be the cause. Many women arrive at this conclusion during the long wait at hospital. Even sitting in a doctor's surgery waiting room can be quite an anxious time. Scans and tests can be another area that becomes daunting. Nine times out of ten it is just another check-up and everything is normal but it does get the adrenaline going, doesn't it?

Neither does it help when we have superficial relationships with our midwives and doctors. Even twenty years ago our doctors and midwives knew us personally but unfortunately that is not the case today. With micro management come feelings of isolation and lack of trust.

Adrenaline and Birth

By adding levels of stress from external sources during labour, it restricts the natural hormones, which are designed to help with pain relief. When we realise that we are not going to have the delivery as planned, emotional impacts and fear can kick in, making muscles contract and adrenalin levels rise before the process even starts. Adrenalin inhibits labour contractions and the more stressed we become, the more it does so.

When we suffer from fight or flight syndrome, oxygenated blood is diverted to the arms and legs so that we can run away. However it also diverts blood away from the uterus and the baby. In late labour, a woman may be told that her baby is in distress and needs intervention for a quick birth. This produces more stress for mum and baby alike and, unfortunately, stress does the opposite of what is needed, leaving even less oxygen for the baby.

Women who are relaxed during the birth process will more frequently have smoother births and suffer less tearing and bruising. Fear restricts and makes it harder for the mother and the baby, whereas when we are relaxed we get feel-good hormones such as oxytocin released into the body.

The memories remain

Our subconscious stores information, not only on a day-to-day basis but in relation to everything that we have heard and experienced. At a gathering of middle-aged women, the question was asked 'did you feel fear at your child's birth?' I was amazed by the response. Out of the eleven women, nine said they had felt fear in pregnancy, one had never been pregnant and only one had not felt fear, but in control during her pregnancy. They all agreed that external influences had seeded their fear.

Some of the reasons that came out were:

- Fear that the child was not right inside her – an instinctual feeling (even though the child was in fact perfectly all right)
- Realisation of being responsible for another human being was daunting
- Anxiety concerning being on her own, with her partner working away and no one to support her
- Gravity of leaving other children at home - a feeling of abandoning when taken into hospital in labour
- Fear of doing something wrong while pregnant – fear of the unknown
- Not feeling part of the process while giving birth in hospital

What was brought home to me was that some of these women still felt emotional about their experiences even in their forties and fifties, despite now having grandchildren of their own. Their maternity experiences still had an emotional hold and the memories were of fear and anxiety.

We need to help women to bring their thinking to a more positive maternity experience before, during and after birth. Old wives' tales and fear mongering are common when pregnant. I would suggest that you do your own research and investigations. Here are some suggestions of where to look and what to look for:

- The Internet is wonderful for gathering information and looking at things in balance

- Read and ask questions about hospital protocol
- Get to know your midwife
- Find out what choices you have in reality
- Look for alternatives if you don't like what is being offered
- Talk to people you trust about their experiences
- Talk to other mums, especially those who have had more than one child
- Go with your own discernment and instincts. People embellish tales and the horrors can get bigger with each telling.

Remember, it is down to you to choose your own experience.

FREE BIRTHING

The term 'free birthing' describes the desire by some women to move away from a traditional hospital birth because of the fear and anxiety it has caused them previously. The traumatic experience they received has produced a post-traumatic reflex of not wanting to repeat the experience, no matter what.

Free birthing means unassisted birth and there has been a lot of exposure recently regarding free birthing, where a woman gives birth on her own in her home, without midwife or hospital attendance. It is becoming more popular with some groups of women in both the USA and in the UK, although exact numbers are not known as most of this happens underground, quietly away from society and is not recorded.

Channel 5 ran a programme in July 2008 called *'outlaw births'* where they followed three mothers who chose to use this methodology. The reasons why were explained as:

- Modern maternity is increasingly 'over-medicalised'
- They don't want to be 'scrutinized'
- During the previous birth process they felt as though they had been 'raped'.
- They were previously shown 'no respect' for what is a women's natural experience
- Medical profession 'over-managed' them
- The midwife was 'more interested in machines' than mum and baby
- They were threatened with C-section which created much fear and trauma
- ' This is my body and I need to give birth in a manner that is comfortable for me'

I had already heard most of these comments during my experience treating women and babies so, although it was not news to me, it was received as a shock programme to many.

I have already explained the emotional consequences suffered by new mothers and babies. Unfortunately, few realise that this is happening every day. Most of society is unaware of the reality of giving birth today but as they become more so, women are looking for alternatives to the modern production-line birth strategy in many hospitals today.

The television programme pointed out that these women experienced birth as nature intended, the way in which women have given birth through the ages. The women reported that the birth was sensual and erotic and indeed the televised birth scenes were very moving and both my husband and I watched teary-eyed when the moment of arrival took place. Just like the parents, I expect thousands of others who watched were also moved to tears. It portrayed a very emotional and moving experience that is as natural as nature intended.

Some experts thought that this method was 'far-fetched' and that the mothers had 'skewed vision'. I do not advocate free births per se but I think in the context of the book it had to be included. Every child should, however, come into the world in a relaxed and comfortable environment. When a mother is in control, instead of pain she receives pleasure. From an emotional point of view it is a win-win situation for both mother and baby.

For those already undecided, the obvious choice is to have your natural birth at home with a midwife standing by. This can be arranged and I know of birthing centres that do just that.

DRUG-FREE AND PAIN-FREE BIRTHS

Drug-free and pain-free births are available. You don't have to opt for the Caesarean or epidural route if you choose not to. Independent midwives and birth centres are offering alternatives, with a choice of water births and other options transforming standard birthing options with intimate surroundings at home[110].

Women who take this option are reporting birth as a *'pleasurable'* and *'ecstatic'* experience. Some independent midwives are encouraging *'sensual birth'* which builds to a crescendo at birth. These techniques are not isolated or rare. They are readily available but most women are not offered the choice. The result of sex is pleasure and pregnancy, so why should it not be associated with the birth event. It seems pretty obvious when we think about it.

The Unassisted childbirth organisation

This US website confirms erotic childbirth giving graphic details and cosmic orgasms at the point of birth. Having an orgasm during pregnancy is estimated to be 22 times more relaxing than the average tranquilliser. Sexual arousal also widens the vagina significantly, naturally helping with the birth process.

One US midwife (Ina May Gaskin) has been pioneering the 'climax birth method' and has written a book entitled 'Ina May's Guide To Childbirth'. Not exactly the type of information normally provided to pregnant women through the usual health care channels!

HOSPITAL BIRTHS

These days, new mums are in and out of hospital very quickly and, in my opinion, some mothers are not getting the help or the foundation they should, especially if it is your first child. Reading baby books does not always give the advice and confidence you need that a person (such as a midwife) can put things right very quickly if anything does happen to go wrong.

With the incidence of bacteria such as MRSA in hospitals I can, of course, see the reasoning not to linger in hospital, but by the same token I feel that we have lost the nurturing side of pregnancy. New mums frequently tell me that they do not feel confident when they leave hospital. After all, in some cases they have been through a trauma too and are generally feeling tired, sore and overwhelmed.

When I had my children in the 70s, I went to a maternity home. For my first child I stayed in for a week, I was shown how to bath my baby, breast feed and express milk, change (using towelling nappies then) and, for better or worse for the duration in the home, the baby was taken away at night so that mums could sleep. We had our babies next to the bed during the day but often we woke during the night by tuning into our babies' cries and would go and feed or cuddle them. The staff did not encourage this, however, as this was their job!

Being at the nursing home gave mothers the feeling of being cared for and nurtured. The result was when I left the home, I felt confident in every way looking after my baby. Prenatal classes with a doll is not the same.

The story today is, of course, quite different. We rely on our mums to help out, to show us what needs to be done and pass on their skills learnt from having children of their own. If we don't have our siblings, mums or mum-in-law around, it can be a tougher time, having to rely on health visitors or visiting midwives in the main to give support. In this case it can often be a day or two before the system kicks in and the first home visit takes place. In the meantime, mums can become overwhelmed with the responsibility of their baby, which relies on its parents for everything.

Mums who have their child at home have a better start as midwives are a wonderful support. They cover huge areas and travel long distances to do their work, dedicated and always at hand. When you choose to have your baby at home, you have the opportunity to get to know your midwife during your pregnancy and he or she becomes a friend. Because of this friendship, you are confident and relaxed with them when you begin your labour.

Having your baby at home means that you are more relaxed in your own environment with your family and the father of the unborn with you and close by. Not only can you dictate the pace and say what you want and when, but you can walk around and rest when you want to. Remember you are the one in charge!

HOME BIRTHS

A recent announcement in the media suggested that home births are as safe as hospital births.

The Netherlands has the highest rate in Europe of babies dying during or just after birth. From the largest study of its kind covering 530,000 births, they found no difference in death rates between home or hospital preference. One third of Dutch women choose home births and home birth is encouraged with low-risk women in the Netherlands. (Published in the Journal BJOG 2009)

In Britain, home births dipped to an all time low in 1988.
By 2006, only 2.7% of all registered births took place at home in England and Wales, with slight regional variations. While the Government has pledged to give all women the option of home birth by 2009/10, the Royal College of Midwives has raised concerns, stating there would need to be a 'seismic shift' in the way maternity services are organised in order for this to be possible.

Today, women are funnelled into the maternity hospital care structure where the majority of births take place, because the NHS is not ready to outsource to midwives. Midwife numbers would need to increase considerably to make the option of home birth credible. Wales, however, has a policy of reintroducing home births and has targeted 5% of all births to be home delivered.

TERMINOLOGY EXPLAINED

Intervention

Normal gestation is anything from 37 to 42 weeks and at 42 weeks hospitals normally suggest inducement. At this point, however, the baby may still not be ready, especially if the calculated dates are inaccurate. In some cases, for example, the mother's dates and the hospital dates might differ.

Inducement

It was back in 1991 that the decision was made to introduce induction at 42 weeks as it was thought that the placenta could go past its 'sell by date' – i.e. that it would start to deteriorate and cause risk to the child. With today's technology, however, we can continually monitor the child's heartbeat and vital signs via scans and so on, thereby negating the original logic.

Although the number of inducements in 2008 is not clear, approximately 20% of all births were expected to be induced in hospitals with only 2% induced by independent midwives[111].

If you are offered inducement, please be clear on the procedure before it begins. I have had some new mothers explain to me that they did not understand the inducement programme and implications. They admitted to being unaware of the consequences of intervention and the subsequent levels of pain, shock and so on.

Inducement means taking artificial hormone stimulants to induce contractions or forcibly breaking your waters (the amniotic fluid which surrounds the baby) for you. It then becomes a medical birth, with synthetic oxytocin being used to increase contractions. When birth is induced, the process is more painful than in natural childbirth as natural hormones such as oxytocin are suppressed. Very often the mother will need pain relief drugs and/or an epidural, the contra indicators of which are outlined in the sections of this book concerning oxytocin and C-sections. It is best, therefore, to check with your midwife beforehand to be absolutely clear of all the options.

INTERVENTION

Forceps delivery

Forceps can be used if the baby's head is engaged and descended but the contractions have stopped. They are used for:

- Rotation of the baby's head if in the wrong position
- Foetal distress
- Maternal fatigue
- When prolonged pushing is contra–indicated
- Where the mother is unable to push due to epidural or analgesics

Because the mother will have been anesthetised beforehand, the baby may be born suffering from the effects of the analgesia and be slower to breathe and feed - in other words it may be knocked out and feeling the effects of the mother's drugs.

The procedure can be distressing for both mother and baby. Forceps may leave temporary marks or bruising to the baby where they have been applied. Depending upon the amount of force used, there can be damage to the baby's head, spine and neck.

When forceps or firm fingers are used in a birth delivery they can interfere with the finely tuned meridian channels such as the small intestine running in the head section where forceps or pressure would be used. (Ear problems are also associated with a dysfunctional small intestine meridian)

The small intestine meridian will affect the digestion process and can be associated with colic symptoms. In this case nutritional quality of food should be looked at with quality of formula or mothers diet to increase nutritional value to baby's milk. As discussed in the breast-feeding section, some baby foods are too high in sugar giving a child a tendency to crave high sugar content in development. This can then lead to blood sugar imbalances that can lead to diabetes.
In these cases I would strongly suggest a Cranio Sacral Therapy session for the baby as soon as possible to release the pressure and bruising to the head and to realign neck, spine and head. This can be

done within days of the birth, avoiding problems with sleep, suckling, posture and even avoid possible learning difficulties later on.

Vacuum or Ventouse delivery

This process involves the use of a vacuum extractor, which is applied to the baby's head, to pull the baby from the vaginal tract. A cone-shaped cup attached to a pump creates the vacuum with which to extract the baby.

When the baby arrives, he/she could have a cone-shaped head and most have a cephalhaematoma or blood blister, which forms on the top of the head, although I have also seen them on the side of the head too. In addition, the baby probably has a huge headache to go with it.

Some believe that the blood blister clears within a few days, but I have seen children still showing a very prominent blister at 5 and 6 months old. In these cases it can cause a certain degree of cerebral trauma, together with internal shock and distress. I have treated many children who have experienced forceps and ventouse deliveries and have found their shock and trauma to be very real even many months after the birth.

In both cases I would strongly suggest an immediate CST session to deal with the shock and physical affects from the birth process, relieving the distress for all the family and especially for the child.

Epidural

While in labour, you may be offered an epidural. Epidural is a local anaesthetic, which is injected into the spine, giving a numb feeling and pain relief. The nerves are deadened around the lower back area, thereby preventing messages in the nervous system from travelling to the brain. The result is the woman loses all feeling in the lower part of her body and is unable to use her legs. With her movement being restricted, she is only able to lie on a bed or be propped up.

A 'low dose' upgrade of the epidural drug is now available in the form of an opiate mixed with local anaesthetic. This alternative allows some use of the legs, although mobility is still restricted for the mother.

Because of the restricted mobility and numbness, women who opt for the use of an epidural clearly cannot be upright when giving birth and therefore have a higher instance of intervention and assisted delivery by C-section, using forceps or ventouse.

The Cochran Review showed women opting for epidural were likely have a longer second stage of labour and have a need for drugs to stimulate contractions. They also found a risk of low blood pressure with a greater risk of the mother unable to move for a short period after birth.

Experts have found that women who have epidural pain relief are more likely to need medical help to have their baby with 40% more likely to have a need of assistance with instrumental delivery such as forceps or ventouse, indicating that instrumental delivery is more common after epidurals.[112]

Pethadine

Pethadine is a drug similar to morphine and is often given to a woman while in labour to help her relax if she is tense during the birth process. It does, however, have certain contra indicators such as:

- Making the mother feel drowsy
- Causing feelings of nausea or sickness
- Affecting the baby with drowsiness when born
- Affecting the baby in the womb and during birth process, especially if given close to birth
- Affecting the baby's breathing

Although not proven scientifically, anecdotal evidence shows slowing up of the bonding process with mother and baby both affected by the drugs.

Drugs, which are used as an alternative to pethadine, include Diamorphine (heroin) and Meptid. Diamorphine is seen to work better as a painkiller than pethadine, but also affects the baby's breathing. Meptid is seen to have fewer side-effects (contra indicators) for the baby, but it does have more of an effect upon the mother than pethadine, causing increased nausea and vomiting.

A study carried out in Australia in 2006 indicated that mothers who receive pain relieving drugs such as epidurals and pethadine at childbirth are twice as likely to give up trying to breast feed. They also linked baby's suckling impairments at the breast to babies born with the effects of drugs given to the mother[113].

[106] Sally Goddard Blythe, 'What Babies and Children really need' Hawthorn Press Stroud. Glos.UK. 2008 (cited ref - Richard L and Aldade MO 'Effects of delivery room routine on success of first breast feed' Lancet 3/336 (8723) (1990):1105-7)

[107] Dr.Kerstin Uvanas Moberg 'The Oxytocin factor' De Capo Press, Cambridge 2003:p56

[108] Dr.Kerstin Uvanas Moberg 'The Oxytocin factor' De Capo Press, Cambridge 2003:p100

[109] Free encyclopaedia 'Puerperal fever information' http://www.wikipedia.com (02.2008)
Dr Dick Read 'Childbirth without fear' Pg 24 p3

[110] Article Independent (07.2008) http://www.Independent.co.uk (id=441049) (Cited 07.2008)

[111] Birth Choice UK 'Interventions explained' (ref: Induction)(10.2007) http://www.birthchoiceuk.com/interventions.htm (cited 10.2007)

[112] BBC News (10.2005.) http://www.bbcnews/health/epidurals increase birth aid need' /1/hi/health 4371552 The Cochran review 'Epidurals increase birth aid need' (cited 06.2009)

[113] BBC Woman's Hour article 'Australian study' http://www.bbc.co.uk/radio 4/womanshour/03/2006_50_tue.shtml (cited 12.2006)

Chapter 13

INDEX

Chapter 13

CAESAREAN

Queen Victoria is reported to be the one who started the *'too posh to push'* syndrome because she insisted on chloroform when she gave birth. Women who followed Queen Victoria's pattern and used chloroform took days to come around from the effects of the gas, whilst the effect on the babies must have been horrendous. They too would have been affected by what the mother took. There would have been no natural bonding either, as oxytocin levels must have been non-existent. Victorians were not noted for showing their love or emotions to one another in general. No wonder we have the Victorians to thank for so many emotionally confused, not to mention the physiological defects in our parents and grandparents.

Today we continue to look up to celebrities and follow their lead by taking alternative drugs while giving birth. Although we have dispensed with chloroform, we have replacements, which still have an effect upon the infant.

The Caesarean procedure, or C-section, is used to allow the baby to be born without going through the birth canal. Put simply, the baby is born by surgical operation and children delivered in this way are sometimes known as *'sunroof babies'*. The decision to use a Caesarean procedure normally comes about in two ways – it either happens as a matter of choice (an elective Caesarean) or in an emergency situation. Either way, having a Caesarean will mean a major operation which will involve cutting through the abdominal wall, the cut being made just in line with or above the pubic hair line.

Elective C- section - In the case of an elective Caesarean, the operation is planned with the permission of the mother and obstetrician before labour begins, which means that the date and time for the delivery of the child is agreed beforehand.

Emergency Caesareans, meanwhile, happen when the mother is already in labour and complications or unexpected problems arise which require the baby to be born quickly. Sometimes the mother will have been in full labour for some time before a C-section is considered necessary.

Recovering from a Caesarean can take weeks, or even months. During this time the mother has to observe certain restrictions in terms of lifting and so on while the abdominal area and stitches heal. The recovery from a C-section is, in fact, treated the same as the recovery from a hysterectomy.

Just because a mother has a Caesarean delivery for one pregnancy, does not necessarily mean that she will need to do so again with her next child.

COMPLICATIONS ARISING FROM CAESAREAN SECTIONS

Because a C-section is a surgical operation, there are certain complications which can arise as a result. These include:

- Haemorrhage
- Transfusion (donated blood quality and the risk of Aids or hepatitis)
- Infection
- Scar tissue infection
- Ileus – abdominal discomfort caused by disruption to the gastrointestinal motor activity
- Pulmonary embolism – blockage to the pulmonary artery
- Mendelsons syndrome – a chemical pneumonia caused by aspiration during anaesthetic

Bleeding lasts longer after a C-section than after a natural birth. It is reported that, on average, twice the amount of blood is lost as a result of the uterus taking longer to return to its normal size. Other problems which can arise are:

- Infection occurs from opening up the abdomen and exposing the uterus and other organs to air contamination
- can take longer, with four to five days in hospital considered normal

- A large abdominal scar and cut tissues don't heal as well as the original tissue and nerves. Muscles which have been cut will not normally grow back as well as before
- The need for a hysterectomy due to haemorrhage after Caesarean section is reported to be ten times more than after vaginal delivery
- A recent London study found that women who had previously undergone C-sections were 27 times more likely to need obstetric hysterectomy after subsequent births[114]
- They also found that the risk of maternal death was increased 16 fold with a C-section

Many of the long-term problems associated with Caesarean births are not monitored or recorded. Most women tend to want to keep away from further medical intervention after their delivery trauma and so tend to suffer in silence. Some of the issues which have been reported, however, include:

- Formation of adhesions
- Intestinal obstruction
- Bladder injury and uterine rupture
- Stress incontinence is frequently reported some years later

Postnatal depression is another problem which can follow C-section deliveries and can result from feelings of guilt and inadequacy after birth intervention. Mothers are often left with the feeling that they failed to complete a natural process and feel the bonding between themselves and their infant is affected. They also frequently suffer as a result of not being in control and out of the equation, especially if they have had a general anaesthetic for the operation.

CONTRA INDICATIONS FOR BABY FROM C-SECTION

Mothers, of course, are not the only ones to experience the effects of C-section deliveries and there are a number of contra indications for the newborn too:

- Increased mortality rates

- Increased incidence of respiratory problems
- Laceration and cuts to the baby if the incision is too deep
- Impaired brain function a result of obstetric intervention
- Digestive disorders
- Greater risk of allergic disorders
- Emotional trauma and stress
- Hypertension
- Higher activity of the hormone dopamine leading to risk of schizophrenia
- Oxygen deprivation

Mortality rates have consistently been found to be about 1.5 times greater with Caesarean deliveries than vaginal births[115]. One American study, for example, found a higher level of death rates from C-section deliveries, and indeed the lacerations or cuts to the baby do contribute to the increased death rate[116].

Research conducted in 1996 highlighted risks such as laceration to the child from C-section delivery. Foetal laceration injury during Caesarean delivery is not rare[117], especially when it is performed for nonvertex presentations. Although documentation is usually kept of such laceration, it is not always recognised by obstetricians as a complication in the birth process.

Contra indications in breathing

Respiratory symptoms seem to be worse for a child born as a result of the C-section process. Lack of oxygen (intra-uterine hypoxia) can be both a reason for performing a C-section and the cause of death. The vaginal process produces physical compression of the baby during labour, which is also useful in removing fluid from the lungs and helping the baby to prepare to breathe air. In addition, hormones are released during the vaginal delivery process which activate and promote healthy lung function. With a C-section delivery, this natural process is bypassed, leaving the lungs in a more delicate position with excess lung fluid needing physical compression to help the fluid removal after birth[118]. Babies are often thought to have pneumonia in these cases, but can be suffering from 'wet lung' due to a non-vaginal delivery.

Allergies

Research has also shown that Caesarean babies have an increased risk of allergic disease. This is thought to be because they are not exposed to their mother's natural bacteria at birth.

Elective caesarean can increase the risk to the foetus[119]. Respiratory distress syndrome is seen in 'term' infants, with a considerable source of morbidity and mortality in this group. Mechanical ventilation is usually needed to treat presumed surfactant (respiratory) deficiency and is 120 times more likely to be needed after elective delivery at 37-38 weeks than after delivery at 39 -41 weeks. With each completed week of gestation from 37 - 41 weeks, the risk of respiratory morbidity is halved. This data suggests that there is no clear benefit to having an elective C-section before 39 weeks gestation if there is no medical reason for doing so.

Digestion

German research carried out in 2006 found that a natural birth could help a baby's digestion by squeezing through the birth canal and swallowing bacterial molecules, which help their gut to grow healthy bacteria[120]. C-section deliveries miss out on this process and, in theory, this could mean that the intestines of the children born from C-section are not exposed to normal bacteria in the birth canal; hence the possible cause for subsequent digestion problems with long-term effects for the baby's health. A study in 2004 substantiates these findings, with indicators showing that children born by C-section were more prone to diarrhoea during their first year of life than those who had a natural birth. One Canadian study also raises the question of the neonatal state affecting intestinal cells in adulthood and calls for further research to examine the connection between inflammatory bowel disease and the birth process.

A database study in the US revealed that persistent pulmonary hypertension in newborns delivered by C section is nearly five times higher than that observed among babies delivered vaginally[121]. During the natural birth process, the infant is physically compressed in the birth canal enabling pulmonary vascular activity.
Normal hormonal activity is constantly sending messages to and from the mother and child via the placenta. When the mother is allowed to

start labour in a natural way, it gives the child time to begin priming its stress hormone system, but because of the nature of C-sections this time is not available and often results in the infant experiencing stress problems.

Behaviour

The question also needs to be asked as to whether C-section babies are more susceptible to schizophrenia. Canadian research into the pattern of behavioural changes observed in animals has shown some significant similarities to the responses that we are finding in humans. Increases of dopamine in the central nervous system have been found from uncomplicated C-section birth procedures in animals, with long-term alterations in the steady state levels of dopamine. Dopamine is released in response to repeated stress. Increased levels of dopamine have not been noticed, however, in animals which have been born through vaginal birth controls.

Findings from research carried out in 1998 suggested that C-section human babies are indeed more vulnerable to schizophrenia[122]. This disorder has been linked to birth complications before, because of an overactive dopamine (hormone) system. The absence of the hormonal surges, which occur naturally during vaginal birth, may increase the risk of schizophrenia and several other studies have substantiated these findings.

Epidemiological evidence (in animals) indicates a higher incidence of pregnancy and birth complications among individuals who later develop schizophrenia, a disorder linked to alterations in the mesolimbic dopamine (DA) function[123].
Genetic predisposition and environmental factors such as perinatal complications are believed to contribute to the etiology of schizophrenia – a disorder involving enhanced central nervous system (CNS) and dopaminergic activity.

Diabetes risk for C-section children

A new Irish report in 2008 showed a consistent 20% increase in the risk of type 1Diabetes in children. This type of diabetes is on the increase in Europe and the report suggests that environmental factors are to blame[124].

It also highlights, however, that the way the baby is delivered could affect how it develops later in life and cited Caesarean deliveries as part of the risk.

Although children born by C-section carry a 20% higher risk of developing type 1 diabetes than those born by virginal birth[125], the report concluded that contact via exposure to hospital bacteria was part of the cause. In their view, it is possible that C-sections are responsible rather than by maternal bacteria. This was, however, a small study and further research is needed.

Type 1 Diabetes is controlled by insulin and would need a lifetime of injections and blood tests to be properly controlled. It is estimated that there are 250,000 cases of this type of diabetes in the UK. Type 2 Diabetes, on the other hand, is controlled by diet and normally ensues later in life with age.

Are we creating a diabetes time bomb with C-section deliveries on the increase and in some UK hospitals showing an average in excess of 25% of total births? Indeed, research is certainly suggesting that some doctors are too quick to recommend the caesarean option and perhaps there is a case for mothers who do have a choice to be informed of all the risk factors. Personally, I would recommend that all risk factors be taken into consideration before opting for a C-section birth.

NEW TECHNOLOGY

Lack of oxygen during any type of birth can cause brain damage or, in extreme cases, death. In such cases as these, however, technology can help. A machine called a 'foetal pulse oximetry' continuously measures, via a tube placed into the uterus during labour, the level of oxygen in a baby as it is being born. It works by shining a light onto the baby, the reflection from which shows the level of oxygen in the infant's blood. This method was previously used externally, on both adults and babies and as a non-invasive measure it is reassuring for parents.

More widely used in Europe, you may find that this equipment is only used in larger hospitals in the UK where C-section levels are high. Medical professionals believe that this machine could lower the number of C-section, vacuum and forceps deliveries because of fears of the risks associated with lack of oxygen for the baby.

It would be interesting if more research could be used to show correlations between birth and other disorders later in life, although this is not a new concept. Many trials were carried in the 1970s to look at birth and disorders later in life and the outcomes were astounding. Clearly we need better records of birth defects and obstetric intervention right across the world.

Why has Caesarean delivery become more popular?

In this section we will look at the beliefs, myths and contra-indicators of C-section.

The National Sentinel Caesarean Section Audit report indicates that maternal requests for elective C-section ranges from 1.5% to 48% according to area. The higher figures are possibly due to the facts that:

- An elective C-section can be scheduled
- The baby's birthday can be chosen
- A C-section is quick compared to most labours
- C-sections are perceived as pain free, with the operation carried out under anaesthetic and no labour pains endured
- Sometimes nicknamed as 'too posh to push', there is little interaction by the mother-to-be – 'Just let me know when it is all over'
- Some women mistakenly think that the baby will be squashed and damaged in the birth canal during a natural birth
- Some women mistakenly think it is easier for the baby to be born through a C-section birth
- C-sections are perceived as clean because of the antiseptic environment. Being clinical, most believe it to be safe for both mother and baby
- The mother thinks she is in control of her birth process without actually taking part and believes she can get on with her life quickly and cleanly

The cut, which is made during a C-section delivery is normally about 5-6 inches (12-15cm) and is made just below the pubic hairline. The stitches used after C- section can pull together as the body heals, with itching being experienced around the area during healing. Although many believe that return to normal life is quicker after a Caesarean delivery, the fact is that full healing can take up to three months as it involves waiting for layers of muscles to regenerate back to their full function. Though some women do recover sooner, this is not always the case.

Despite being a clinical operation, the recovery period can be long and painful. Far from being easy, C-sections impose post-op restrictions and their effects on the body can make recovery both slow and difficult. Just going to the toilet, moving around or handling the baby must be tackled slowly and carefully.

Many women suffer infection after their C-section operation, which could include bladder and kidney infection. However, UK figures suggest that only 20% of women who have a natural birth, suffer from infection afterwards, with those experiencing C-Section deliveries being at greater risk.

Post-op and C- section contra indicators

As we have mentioned, the post-op rules are the same for a C-section as they are for women who have a hysterectomy. 'Don't lift', however, is a daft thing to say after you have just given birth to a 10lb bundle of joy. While the severed muscles heal, normal activities will prove difficult and lifting your baby will be a challenge. Even changing baby's nappies may cause pain, and it may prove completely impossible to lift heavy objects such as laundry baskets and shopping. Other children may feel left out, as it may be difficult to pick them up and cuddle them during your recovery period.

Women who undergo Caesarean sections experience a longer stay in hospital, with the suggested time being up to 5 to 7 days depending upon complications. For most, driving will also be out of the question during the six to eight week recovery time, six weeks being the average.

Aside from the practical aspects of life, women also have to cope with the discomfort and embarrassment of flatulence after a C-section. Flatulence can be a problem after any operation and, in addition, pockets of wind trapped in the shoulder area can cause discomfort, together with the effects of anaesthetics wearing off and leaving the patient feeling spaced out or nauseous.

The numbers of elective C-sections are increasing dramatically all over the western world. A major concern from most medical professionals is that these are being chosen for the wrong reasons, such as because the time of birth can be more accurately planned. An elective C-section may not be the answer after all however, especially when you take into consideration the contra-indications listed for the baby too.

Despite this, in certain circumstances a C-section may be necessary, but remember that it does constitute major surgery and carries alternative risks for both mother and child. Some mothers suffer increased bleeding and even infertility risks as a result, and the child encounters greater likelihood of breathing difficulties, digestive disorders and other risks as detailed previously.

Most women that I have spoken to would not volunteer to have a C-section again and have found the experience to be far from what they expected. I believe that there are mystical beliefs regarding C-section, which cloud the real facts. We often have the famous and wealthy opting for elective C-sections to fit in with their lifestyles, believing that is the best way to go. Unfortunately this can greatly influence others into thinking 'if it's good enough for them, it's good enough for me.'

C- sections do, of course, have their place and there may be good medical reasons to have an elective caesarean when complications or health issues occur. I would advise that you talk to your consultant and midwife to get the full facts and, if you do need to go ahead with a Caesarean delivery, that you arrange support and back-up for when you come home.

While some women believe that it is better to avoid a possibly prolonged labour and the ongoing discomfort of any damage which may be caused by the natural birthing process, opting for an operation, which is perceived as being easier, can have detrimental long-term effects on the baby. Women today have a choice, and the choice is yours.

INCREASED GROWTH OF C-SECTION

The World Health Organisation (WHO) recommends that the C-section procedure should only be used in 10 -15% of births[126]. While a UK national study showed that back in 1980 only 9% of births involved Caesarean sections, doctors are now warning that 'the rate of C-section is running far too high.'[127] Levels are also on the increase in the USA, with birth data showing the number of Caesarean deliveries rising each year from 20.7% in 1996 to 29.1% in 2004.

As a result, more and more women are being taken back into hospital after C-section delivery suffering from:

- Uterine infections
- Surgical wound complications
- Appendicitis
- Cardio pulmonary conditions
- Gall bladder problems

Even assisted vaginal delivery is showing complications for women according to one US study, with assisted birth complications (where forceps were used) such as:

- Haemorrhage after birth
- Surgical wound complications
- Pelvic injury

Cleaning strategies are blamed for an alarming amount of disease and infection in our hospitals and, in the UK, it is the responsibility of the NHS trusts to have prevention and control strategies in place to avoid this.

My own research of UK statistics showed the results to be either misleading, several years out of date or completely unavailable. One of the main problems with accurate audit systems is an inability to show the reasons why elective C-sections were done in the first place. Ireland, for example, does not even break down figures into elective or emergency C-sections.

Although national average figures seem low, when I looked at individual hospitals, some revealed a much bigger percentage of women receiving C-sections. The Royal College of Midwives reported in 1999 that some hospitals were having 48% of births by C-section, with the numbers varying from region to region.

Because of the Government's new funnel system (which involves using only large hospitals), we are seeing cottage and maternity hospitals being phased out, despite coming up to the mark in terms of what pregnant women want, giving a more compassionate service. Now, we find women being shuttled to large, indifferent regimes where the C-section option is preferred as a means of fitting in with a consultant's diary and hospital bed availability.

The Boon

In my view, some of the statistics I saw for C-section usage were appalling, with rates of over 40% in some areas very common, year after year. It is interesting to note that, in the 1950s, less than 3% were C-section deliveries, whereas in 1995-96 UK C-sections accounted for up to 20% of hospital deliveries, with figures rising to 25% in 1999. 2006, however, showed a rise approaching 40% in some hospitals.

The Royal College of Midwives reported in 1999 that in parts of the UK only 52% were traditional births. Figures show that one in ten births north of the border (England Scottish divide) involves an elective Caesarean[128].

As we have mentioned, the World Health Authority set a target in 1985 of 15% as the ideal level of C-section rate. In 2001, C–section births around the world actually accounted for[129]:-

- 8% of all births in Japan
- 22% in the USA
- 25% in Argentina
- 40% in Chile
- 38% in Mexico

Today the figures have escalated even higher. In more wealthy areas of the world, the percentage goes even higher with[130]:

- Nuevo Leon showing a level of 50%
- Italy demonstrating one of the highest rates, running at close to 60%
- Private hospitals in Monterrey showing 73% of all deliveries

Figures grew during the 1990s as some women wanted convenient 'diary' births without the effort of labour, and it was particularly professional women and their partners who wanted to take advantage of the convenience of C-section. Some women have even been so organised as to put an announcement in the press, quoting the due date well before the event.

Many doctors also saw the C-section process as a boon since it meant they could utilise their schedules and diaries, giving them huge benefits. Suddenly, there were no middle-of-the-night callouts and their appointments could all be fitted in between 9am and 5pm.

Research has shown that there are down sides for the child and mother when elective C-section is agreed for convenience, with researchers and some doctors calling for more advice and detail to be provided to mothers before their decisions are made.

A C-section delivery takes about twenty minutes to perform and in the year 2000 it was believed to cost on average £1000 more than a traditional natural birth in hospital, with a reported annual cost of £80million[131]. In 2008, natural births cost £3000 per delivery and C-sections nearly double this figure. Maybe this immense revenue-earning capacity is one of the reasons why the numbers of C-section is going up? To my mind, wouldn't it make sense to have more natural births, giving women what they want and saving the NHS and welfare millions?

The national childbirth trust

The National Childbirth Trust (a charity for parents) believes that women are undergoing the procedure far too much, with the level of C-sections now double the level recommended for developed countries by WHO. They advise, 'Women are recommended to avoid Caesarean section unless medically necessary' – i.e. they should only undergo the procedure when it is necessary to save both the baby's and mother's lives[132].

The UK national average takes into account all hospitals, but because of obstetric departments being transferred to large hospital trusts, only a few are kitted out to do this kind of operation or intervention. At the present time, funding is only available to provide specialist care in these hospitals, which is fine for those who live in the city, but not so good for those who live in more rural areas.

From the rural location where I live, if I was pregnant I would need to travel some twenty-five miles to attend an appropriate hospital, as all the local cottage hospitals have either been closed or the maternity capability removed to larger central hospitals. If I wanted specialist attention, I would need to travel even further, some fifty or seventy-five miles away.

Big is not always best and, for some, the new approach is actually discriminatory. Specialist care can involve even longer journeys, with one case recently reported to me of more than a 150 mile round trip. For those who don't drive or are too ill to go by public transport, the extreme cost of private transport and an inability to pay can put lives at risk. As I understand it, this is also contrary to the government's own green mile policy. How long will it take for the government to apply public policies to itself?

[114] UK Midwifery Archives 'General risks of Caesareans' http://www.radmid.deamon.co.uk/csrisks.htm
(Ref: Gould D et al 'Emergency obstetric hysterectomy, an increasing incidence' Journal of Obset. Gynaecol (1999) vol 19 p580-583 (cited at 04.2007)

[115] Ibid 'Risks of Caesarean Section' (09.2006) http://www.radmid.demon.co.uk/esbaby.hm (Ref: Nicholas Bakalar 'Neonatal Mortality' New York Times (Cited 04.2007)

[116] Ibid 'Voluntary C-sections Result in more baby deaths' http://www.radmid.demon.co.uk/esbaby.hm (Cited 04.2007)

[117] Ibid 'Risks of Caesarean Section' http://www.radmid.demon.co.uk/csrisks.htm (Cited 04.2007)

[118] Ibid 'Lung mechanics' http://www.radmid.demon.co.uk/csrisks.htm (Ref: Milner AD, Saunders RA, Hopkin IE. Arch Dis Child "Effects of delivery by caesarean section on lung mechanics and lung volume in the human neonate' (1978) Jul;53(7):545-8 2006 Neonatal mortality) (Cited 04.2007)

[119] Ibid 'Elective Caesarean':http://www.radmid.demon.co.uk/esbaby.htm. (ref: Laubereau B. et.al)'Elective caesarean can increase the risk to the foetus' Arch Dis.child., BMJ 89.993-997 (2004) (cited 04.2007)

[120] Ibid Canadian Study (ref:7/8/9) http://www.radmid.demon.co.uk/esbaby.hm
(Ref: Canadian Study - Immune system and 'friendly bacteria" article Helen Pearson News @ nature.com Hornef 2006 – ref: Lotz M et al. Journal of Experimental Medicine 203.973-984 (2006) (Cited 04.2007)

[121] Ibid US 'Database study' http://www.radmid.demon.co.uk/esbaby.htm (Ref: Dr. Elliot M and associates (2001.03) Obstetrics & Gynaecology. 97:439-442 (cited 04.2007)

[122] UK Midwifery Archives 'Risks in Caesarean Sections' http://www.radmid.demon.co.uk/esbaby.htm (New Scientist 1998.11. schizopjrenia') (Cited 04.2007)

[123] Ibid 'C-section compared to vaginal birth' http://www.radmid.demon.co.uk/esbaby.hm (Ref: El-Khodor BF, Boksa P 'Long term reciprocal changes in dopamine levels – rats born by C-section compared to vaginal' Dept of Psychiatry McGill University Douglas Hospital Res Centre, Canada.' Exp Neirp; 1997 May;145(1):118-29. (Cited 04.2007)

[124] BBC News 'Queens University Belfast – (small study Diabetes) http://news.bbc.co.uk/1/hi/health/7576829.stm (cited 08.2008)

[125] Ibid – "Queens University Belfast - small study Diabetes' http://news.bbc.co.uk/1/hi/health/7576829.stm (cited 08.2008)

[126] BBC News 'Big rise in caesarean births (08.2000) (Ref: World Health Organisation) http://news.bbc.co.uk/2/hi/health/872386 (cited 02.2007)

[127] BBC News 'Big rise in Caesarean births' (08.2000) (Ref: Study by Royal College of Obstetricians and Gynaecologists   http://news.bbc.co.uk/2/hi/health/872386.stm (Cited 02. 2007.)

[128] BBC News 'Caesarian section 'too common' (11.1999) (Ref: Royal college of midwives) http://news.bbc.co.uk/1/hi/health/532018.stm (cited 02.2007)

[129] http://www.alternative-healthzine.com/html/0104_2.html

[130] BBC News 'Big rise in caesarean births (Ref; stats around the world) (08.2000) http://news.bbc.co.uk/2/hi/health/872386.stm (cited 02.2007)

[131] Ibid 'Big rise in caesarean births' (C-section costs)

[132] BBC News 'National childbirth trust' – http://news.bbc.co.uk/1/hi/health/742156.stm (2000.05) (cited 05.2008)

Chapter 14

INDEX

Chapter 14

PREMATURE BIRTHS

In 2001/02 it is estimated there were over 650,000 babies born in the UK and, of these, 50,000 were born prematurely. In 2008 the figures have risen to 80,000 preterm births and it is estimated that 17,000 will need intensive care[133]. Premature birth or pre-term delivery is when a baby is born too early. A normal pregnancy is considered to be full term at 37 weeks, although it can go up to 42 weeks naturally. The charity Tommy's estimate over 200 babies are born prematurely each day in the UK[134] and the UK has the highest rate of premature births in Europe, with figures showing no decrease since the 1960s.

Premature labour is not fully understood and identification of risks to both mother and child are difficult to assess in most cases. A third of premature births happen for no apparent reason, with the majority of women having no known risk factors yet still having premature births.

It is thought that although a woman may have one premature birth, it is not always the case for future pregnancies. The risk of the same scenario in the next pregnancy is approx 15%, or only one in six[135].

Research
Research has identified several reasons why a baby might arrive early.

They are:
- Multiple pregnancy
- Pre-eclampsia
- Mother's age under twenty or over thirty five
- Pregnancy-specific maternal disease and vaginal infection
- Stressful event such as flying long distance
- Lifestyle factors such as smoking

The over-stretching of the womb in multiple births (such as twins or triplets) can also increase the risk of going into labour prematurely.

Pre-eclampsia is responsible for approx 15% of premature births in the UK and in these cases the development of the child can be impaired due to the placental blood supply. Doctors will initiate early delivery if there is an antepartum bleed and risk to mother's and baby's health.

Age, although not a major factor, does put women into the higher risk bracket. Teenage mothers and those below fifteen years old are at greater risk and women who have children later in life and are over thirty-five are also in the high-risk bracket.

The same recent report that stated women have more premature births in the UK than any other European country, also blamed the early births on stress, poor diet and nutrition (lack of vitamins and minerals), drugs and smoking. Without doubt, a mother's lifestyle can have a huge impact upon her baby and increase the risk of premature birth through:

- Smoking and alcohol
- Taking recreational and other drugs
- High caffeine intake
- Diet and poor nutrition
- Weight – being underweight
- Over-strenuous physical activity such as sport and exercise during pregnancy.
- Stress and domestic violence

Research has indicated that stress may play a major role in pregnancy loss.

SMOKING & ALCOHOL

Smoking

Women who smoke during pregnancy have been found to have a higher risk of pre-term birth. Being a smoker yourself or even breathing in other's smoke reduces the amount of available oxygen in your bloodstream. During pregnancy, this deprives your baby of oxygen. When planning a pregnancy it is advisable for both the mother and father to stop smoking before attempting conception.

Passive smoking after birth is also an issue and we now know that children living in a household where there is regular smoking can also be affected by the reduction in the oxygen they breathe. Living in this type of environment can make them more prone to chest, ear, nose and throat infections.

Alcohol

Alcohol is now seen as a dangerous drug as it breaks down chemically to a cell-damaging compound which is readily absorbed by the foetus. A small amount of alcohol will probably not cause any major ill effects, however, no safe level is yet defined and the safest practice would be to avoid alcohol altogether while pregnant. In fact, this is paramount in the first stage of pregnancy when the foetus is most vulnerable to alcohol's damaging effects.

Lifestyle changes can help

High caffeine intake and recreational drug use should be avoided while pregnant. Cut down on coffee and other caffeine drinks including, alcohol, tea and the various varieties of fizzy drinks.

The FSA has now released new guidelines based upon UK research[136] and these highlight the following:

- Caffeine is an artificial stimulant that the body treats as a toxin
- 15 -20 minutes after you drink caffeine the effects kick in and can last for up to 4 – 5 hours
- The average latte contains 180mg of caffeine, while decaf has only 0.3mg

- Look out for caffeine-free drinks. Change to herbal teas, dandelion coffee (caffeine free) or decaffeinated tea and coffee
- Research from the Universities of Leeds and Leicester report that caffeine intake during pregnancy is associated with increased risk of foetal growth restriction. They also reported that high caffeine intake is associated with spontaneous miscarriage[137]

Perhaps it is best to give up caffeine altogether while pregnant and so avoid symptoms for both yourself and your baby.

Over-strenuous physical activity

Over-strenuous physical activity such as sport and exercise during pregnancy does, as we have mentioned, carry a risk of pre-term birth. It is therefore advisable to move to a more gentle exercise regime such as yoga and walking instead of the full extreme workout.

It is also important to make time to rest during the day. Get out into the fresh air at lunchtime instead of having a working lunch or eating at your desk and also try to avoid stressful and tiring situations.

Discuss work issues with your employer and ask if working conditions can be adjusted to suit your needs while pregnant. Some employers are more than willing to accommodate.

Pregnancy-specific maternal conditions

As we have said, certain pregnancy-specific maternal diseases and conditions can mean a greater risk of premature birth, including

- Pregnancy-induced or gestational diabetes
- Pre-eclampsia
- Obstetric cholestasis - liver disease
- Infection
- Maternal medical conditions

Infection

Infection can cause problems and so it is important to report any signs to your midwife or GP. Urine will be checked for issues such as vaginal infection or infection of the vaginal tract. Vaginal infections often lead to symptoms such as itching and possibly a discharge with odour. They can even trigger contractions in some cases. Bladder infections too can be painful, with frequent trips to the loo and/or odour from urine.

Maternal medical conditions such as:

Systemic lupus or renal disease, which existed prior to pregnancy, will also be a risk factor, as will cervical incompetence. This latter may be caused by previous gynaecological history such as damage from surgery on the cervix and it may cause the cervix (opening of the womb) to open too quickly. In some women, the cervix can also shorten, producing the same symptoms of opening too soon and leading to spontaneous labour.

Recent research has also found another important symptom - chronic gum disease in the second trimester. Studies have highlighted this as a risk factor and potential cause of premature births, with women who suffered from this disease being seven times more likely to have a pre-term birth[138]. It is advisable, therefore, to have regular checkups with your dentist while pregnant to avoid gum disease.

Hormonal protection

In 2007, research carried out by The Lancet suggested that 'women who give birth prematurely develop less long-term protection against breast cancer than women who go full term.'[139] Links with breast cancer and hormonal protection were highlighted with slightly lowered protection within five years of delivery compared with full term births. The reason for this is that preterm birth is not accompanied by the surge of oestrogen hormone production in late pregnancy.

Treatment for pre-term labour

Pre-term labour can be controlled by what are known as tocolytic drugs and, once the situation is suspected, they will be administered to slow down and delay the contractions. Steroids may also be used to help improve the baby's lung development through the mother. Regular checkups with your midwife and GP can help to detect early risk signs for premature birth. The baby's weight and size are monitored regularly, checking that the child is thriving and growing as normal. When a baby is not responding to normal growth patterns, it is known as intrauterine growth restriction and will normally be flagged up and monitored more closely.

A stitch may be inserted in the neck of the womb for those who have a history of pre-term births. This method is used to help reduce the cervix opening and will normally be inserted at 14 weeks of pregnancy and removed at 35 weeks. This method has helped many women to see their pregnancy through to a normal term, thus avoiding the trauma associated with premature birth which affects not just the mother and baby, but the whole family.

Survival rates

The organisation Bliss has estimated that 1 in 8 babies born in the UK are born premature or sick. In the UK alone 17,000 babies every year need intensive care and the figure is rising. Neonatal care, however, has improved enormously and advances in this field occur all the time.

Preterm babies have less time to mature and develop and are therefore more at risk of medical and developmental disorders. Those who are born before 30 weeks are small and very skinny, with the head looking large compared to the body. Blood vessels may be protruding through the skin and the skin will probably be covered by down (a fine hair called lanugo).

Whilst those born nearer to their birth date and those with good birth weight have a greater chance of survival than those who are very small, we often hear stories of premature babies who survive against all odds. Many are fighters, fighting for life from the moment they arrive and determined to stay in the world. This is when the parents' contact and love is needed most.

THE HUMAN TOUCH

Research and trials have proved that baby massage helps pre-term babies and in fact one trial showed that babies who were massaged improved on the normal weight gain by 50% daily. In addition, other trials have shown that children born to mothers who were drug addictive have had 28% better weight gain through the simple treatment of baby massage.

It has been proven that those children who are given physical touch, even from just stroking a hand or arm, improve much quicker than those who are not. One well-known trial split a whole nursery in half. One group were given regular touch, including picking up and being held by nurses, and at every opportunity they were talked to while being changed and fed. The other group were dealt with in the normal way, being changed and fed without any conscious contact or voiced communication. The result was that those who were talked to and given physical touch improved much quicker than those of the second group.

Physical touch does make a difference, as does being acknowledged. Importantly, however, it was realised during the trials that connection to the child was very important, as the baby can easily feel abandoned without the touch of the mother. The bonding process, however small, is paramount to the child to give security, confidence and feelings of belonging instead of those of abandonment. After all, the baby has known nothing else other than the mother for nine months. To be separated from her is very scary and emotionally traumatising. Simply holding mum's hand or a finger is reassuring and comforting to the baby.

It makes sense too that if a child is not given touch or shown affection, it will begin to relate touch with pain, especially from mechanical tools and medication, even though these are used for their own benefit during premature birth and intervention in hospital.

BABY MASSAGE

Baby massage has many benefits to both infant and parents. We use our feelings to express and with baby massage we use touch to connect and sooth the infant. It gives the baby a feeling of being secure, loved and wanted and, in addition:

- Helps to relax the baby and improve sleep patterns and quality of sleep
- Stimulates health systems by enhancing circulation and the nervous system
- Helps to regulate and strengthen the digestive, respiratory and immune system
- Improves skin condition
- Helps to develop co-ordination and awareness of their body

Baby massage, in fact, has benefits for all. It allows the critical bonding action to take place between parents and infant and gives parents a connection so that they better understand the baby's needs through non-verbal communication. The baby's body language is learnt and observed, eye-to-eye contact is promoted, facial expressions are readily learnt and the child receives soothing sounds which promote interaction, allowing them to feel part of the family instead of in isolation. It also:

- Allows the infant to become more aware of its environment using touch and smell
- Stimulates lactation in breast feeding
- Promotes a nurturing instinct in parent, grandparents and other family members
- Gives quality time to parent and infant
- Allows connection to your growing child and can be used for all ages

Baby massage needs to be part of your daily routine. Set a time that is acceptable for you and your child as it needs to be done in a quiet environment and at a time when you are not rushed. If not, it will be remembered as a stressful time for you and your baby, creating aversion therapy instead of a relaxing and beneficial time for both.

If your baby is tired and needs feeding, it is a good idea to postpone until another time when both are in a more receptive mood. The memory needs to be of a pleasing and happy interaction for both, so it is important to feel calm when giving baby massage. It should be relaxing for the giver and the receiver with smooth movements and gentle interaction promoting relaxation with nothing being forced, just given.

(See appendix for baby massage method instruction)

CASE STUDY 10 – PREMATURE BIRTH

A friend of mine told me of her experience of premature birth when she knew that I was writing this book. Even six years on and now with a healthy and happy son, she cried and was very emotional as she told me her story and was also surprised by the feelings that she still held. It was as if it had only happened yesterday, as though this traumatic time was imprinted upon her body and mind. I suggested that she might want to write down her personal experience to share with others and this is her story, which was kindly written for other women.

M's story

We had been on an extended holiday in the USA lasting 12 weeks. It had been planned prior to falling pregnant, but I still decided to go anyway as it was a once in a lifetime decision. I had taken medical advice and decided to fly at 16 weeks and return at 28 weeks. That was according to British Airlines guidelines at the time.

All went according to plan until we were on our way home from the airport, after being picked up by my in-laws. I felt uncomfortable as I had not slept on the overnight flight and I was tired. My back was also sensitive due to the travelling, baggage handling and so on. On our drive back, I fell asleep, but just a few minutes from home our driver took a country lane a bit sharply and I was hit in the right side of my stomach by some hand luggage that had worked itself loose. I awoke with a scream and a severe jolt, as it was very painful.

Earlier than expected

Feeling tired and uncomfortable, I went to lie down once in the house. I could not settle. I felt my pelvis aching and opening up. I went to the toilet and rapidly realised that I could feel the hair on my baby's head. He was already engaged. I did not panic, but got into the shower to freshen up and for pain relief. I had my first few contractions there and then.

Luckily, the ambulance was only 10 minutes away. By the time they arrived, I was on the bed open- legged and I knew the baby was coming. I tried to answer the questions of 'What is your name?', 'How old are you?', 'How many weeks pregnant are you?' and 'What is your mid-wife's' name?' as best as I could in between gasps, but inside I was thinking, 'I know this baby is coming now.'

As no-one had checked me out, I was wondering if anyone was actually taking me seriously. Only my husband was tending to me, saying, 'He is coming. I can see his head!' The ambulance men stood open-mouthed alongside my mother-in-law. I knew he was coming, whether anyone was ready for him or not.

Our son then shot out like a bullet and landed safely on the bed. I was so relieved, as he was wriggling and moving about and looked perfectly healthy, albeit small. He had a little cough and a cry and, as I looked down at him, he looked straight back at me and I saw his beautiful bright blue eyes shining out at me like little lights. It was as though a light bulb had gone off in his head. I knew it was his spiritual energy and I was so at ease then, as I knew he was strong, a fighter and would be okay. I was also comforted by the fact that I too had been a premature baby and I was still here, wasn't I? I also knew that I was going to do everything I could for him. We were connected.

The ambulance men soon sprang into action. They scooped up my son and checked his airways, wrapped him in a towel and took him to the ambulance whilst phoning ahead to the hospital to prep the NICU for our arrival. I was left to put on a dressing gown and hobble downstairs. I must have looked a spectacle as I tried to hoist myself into the ambulance and strap myself in on the bed. I was being tended to on the right side and the baby was on the left. We sped off towards the hospital 25 miles or so away and I ejected the placenta in the ambulance with as much force as the baby!

We arrived at the hospital and were instantly separated

My husband stayed with me, but the baby was taken straight from the ambulance and put into an incubator. I was a bit perplexed at this, wondering 'well where am I going to?' I was taken to a single room for examination and was very surprised when I had to get out of my wheelchair and hoist myself onto a bed that was very high because it had been elevated. As I am only 5ft tall, it was a bit of an effort!

Unfortunately during this process I lost a lot of body fluids, which started to send me into shock. I got into the bed but could not answer any of the usual questions, as I was starting to be sick. I began drifting in and out of consciousness and only then did the nurse look up from her clipboard and move into action to put me on a drip. I suddenly felt very drained, which was the only time I remember that my poor husband actually looked worried.

In-laws and husband were allowed to see the new arrival but not mum. This really upset me because they could see the baby before I could, due to me not feeling 100 per cent. However they did come back with some Polaroid's, which was a lovely gesture but made me feel even worse! When I started to feel better, I asked a nurse if I could go and see my son. I was told 'no'; I had to wait a bit longer.

I was allowed to see my son at about 11pm, which was about 6 hours after he was born. It was still a shock to see him so small and frail looking, made worse by the number of tubes and things attached to him in the incubator. I just stood with my husband and stared. I was upset at how small and vulnerable he looked. Also, all of the tubes stuck into his hands, feet and other areas dismayed me. He was almost translucent, like a little bird fallen from the nest before he had any feathers on. The incubator was a translucent barrier. I noticed all the machines bleeping and humming and thought how noisy it was for him, when he was sleeping so peacefully.

We seemed to be standing around him for ages, looking at him from every angle. We were told not to open or touch anything, especially him. We were told that premature babies did not like to be touched or messed about with, as they were early (before their time). We went to bed in a state of shock at 1am. I was exhausted, we both were...

I was woken at 6am by a nurse, to ask 'could they give our son a dummy' as he was screaming the place down! I was in a state of shock after such a short sleep. Why was he screaming? Did I really want him to have a dummy? I was upset that he was distressed. I did not get much sleep after that. I realise now that he was probably hungry (he was not fed for the first 48 hrs).
However the ambulance men, Martin and Matthew, popped in to say hello and brought a pink pig from the front of the ambulance for the baby and that cheered me up a lot. They were in shock when he was born and it turned out that one of them was expecting his first child any day too so that explained a lot to me. Bless them.

We stayed in that room for a few days and were both fed. Staff were very kind to us. We were mistaken for some sort of hippy travellers, as we had been away. Some people even asked, 'Did you know you were pregnant?'

Did I know I was pregnant?
I had two scans done at 12 and 22 weeks, but no one seemed interested. I also told them that I had been diagnosed with group B strep, even though I did not have any blood taken whilst there. I had been pressured into taking antibiotics, because I was told I might have a brain-damaged child if I did not. I took the tablets reluctantly. I had not taken any medication for 8 years up to that point. This greatly distressed me.

As it turned out, my GP in Essex had mixed me up with another pregnant girl who lived in the same apartment block as me. I never had group B strep at all. I gave the hospital all my notes, which were subsequently lost.

Luckily, I still had my scan copies. Paediatricians came round to see me like I was some sort of spectacle. I found myself repeating, 'Yes, I did know I was pregnant'. People came to various conclusions about why I had my baby early. It was thought that because I was also a premature baby, it was an inherited defect. Most people assumed

I was reckless travelling and that was why he arrived early. I was criticised for that.

I knew my placenta had ruptured and that was why I had gone into an emergency labour after the bump. Staff told me about the placenta being jagged. No-one really checked me out to see whether any remained inside me. Fortunately, a week later whilst on the phone laughing about something, the rest came out.

It was like being on a treadmill

We had stayed in the hospital for almost three weeks, giving him as much time and attention as possible. We were in the fortunate situation that we were able to do that. Travelling to the hospital from Diss each day, we would get up, eat breakfast and go, returning 12-14 hours later, just to sleep. We ate at the hospital canteen.

I think I did it all like a zombie and purely by instinct. Some staff appreciated that we were trying to do as much as possible and that we were there more frequently than other parents. They considered that he was our baby and we were trying to make life easier for them. However, some were more 'old school' and made us feel like we were ageing hippies who had been a bit wild and had this baby not knowing what to do with it. That may have been partly true as I had not read a score of books, or even been to an antenatal class, but I actually did not have the chance to go before he was born. He had been conceived on 24 November and born 1 June, so he was approximately 28 weeks. Everything I had done had been by instinct. I knew my baby was going to be a boy. I knew he was going to be okay.

These old school nurses made me feel like I was just a spare part and that the baby was not mine. He belonged to them. He was in their care, not mine or my husband's. Breast-feeding was not encouraged but I sat defiantly in front of them and breast-fed anyway. My son suckled and was noisy - so much for him not being capable of doing that. He had done that from our first attempt when he was 5 days old. I could not believe it when the consultant came around and announced, 'How unusual it is to see a premature baby being breast fed!' He was obviously surprised or being sarcastic. I never bothered to find out which.

At the hospital, they considered the babies to be too small and not capable of breast-feeding. Formula was encouraged over breast milk, but not where I was concerned. I wanted to change opinion! If my baby could do it, surely others could too?

Unfortunately, whilst away from the hospital, staff gave him formula milk instead of my supplies. When I did get there, he was too full to suckle despite my best efforts and I was upset, as I had made huge efforts to get there and keep him supplied, together with ensuring supplies of expressed milk in the fridge. On one occasion, staff had changed his feeding times and we only found out when we phoned to say we were coming in. A week later we phoned ahead to say we were on our way, but the nurse fed our son and did his cares because we were 5 minutes late! I was very upset; we did not just live 5 minutes away.

Hospital Diary

Our son was born on the 1st of June at 28 weeks weighing 2lb 13oz and left the hospital on 19th July. By 17th June he gained weight and had advanced to the well baby room (aka room 3). He had regained his initial weight loss and was back to his birth weight of 2.13lb. By June 19th he had snuffles and his eyes were infected. On June 20th, unfortunately he was put on antibiotics and reverted back to room 2 again. By 23rd June he was off the antibiotics and up to 3.1lb in weight. On June 24th he was in a thermo-bed for the first time and we were very pleased and on June 27th his oxygen saturation monitor was removed, which made us even happier. He now weighed 3.7lb and was breast-feeding at every opportunity. I was determined to fatten him up and get him home as soon as possible. By 29th June he was 3.8lb!

On July 2nd we were told that our son was to have the eye examination that all the parents dreaded. Parents were not allowed to be in the room when any child was being examined. Apparently, the eyes were anaesthetised slightly and examined in depth and it was not pleasant. We were not given any choice over the matter, it was routine for all premature babies. I did not like the idea at all and I was not entirely sure that it was necessary. Afterwards, our son looked uncomfortable and slightly distressed. We did some healing on him and stayed with him until 11pm to comfort him.

Come July 3rd we spent the day running around trying to get a Maternity Certificate and eventually the hospital agreed to sort one out for us. We needed to prove that we were capable. On 7th July we kept him in the room with us all that day and fed and cared for him, eventually going to bed at 12.30am. We were trying to prove a point. At last it felt like we were a proper family!

July 8th saw a breakthrough, as we actually managed to see a doctor and we discussed the breast-feeding. A nurse who had been observing backed us up. She said he did brilliantly well and was the best she had ever seen. We were very grateful for that! The day was topped off, by seeing him have his first ever bath. That was great, as his little face showed he loved it. We stayed at the hospital again that night, elated that at last someone was listening to us. We had him all to ourselves overnight. We were exhausted, but excited. We could feed and care for our son all night, without any interference. We could see a light at the end of the tunnel – finally.

On July 9th we gave him his first bath ourselves. Things were definitely looking up. He now weighed 4.6lb. July 15th we had to prove that he could accept a bottle rather than the breast in order to get him home. This baffled me immensely as I had no intention of stopping breast-feeding. I did not want to bottle feed or use formula. I felt as though I had to toe the line.

The hospital were prepared to discuss letting him come home in the near future, even though he did not yet weigh 5lb. I did not want to jeopardise that in any way so we bottle-fed and luckily he guzzled down the milk I had expressed! His feeding tube was finally removed.

On July 18th we received the best news ever! The doctor had checked our baby out and decided to let him go - the next day. We were so excited, we could hardly contain ourselves. After a final run of bath, feed and clean, we completed all the paperwork and gave the unit a present of two lamps that they needed for the night duties. We thanked everyone, although some more so than others.

I will never forget a nurse saying to me, 'I bet he doesn't feel like your baby. You must feel like he is hospital property'. Now we were taking back our property, our baby, and taking him home for the first time.

Our little boy is now 6 and although petite, is perfectly formed and very bright. We have looked after him to the best of our abilities using homeopathy, healing and crystals. He is very intuitive. My only regret is the time he spent in hospital and the vaccinations we were pressurised into letting him have prior to him being released. We were told that he could not go home unless we consented. This is something that greatly concerned us at the time and continues to do so. I believe that this should be a personal, not enforced choice.

I would advise any parent to obtain as much information about vaccinations beforehand, especially with regard to their content and side effects. There are alternatives out there. You have a choice. A child is precious and pure. We should not be interfering with that. Homeopathy does provide other options that should be explored.

I would also advise any new parent to be positive, strong and assertive. Stand up for yourselves and your child. I would like to add that I am grateful to all the lovely caring people I have met along the way.

I have found writing and sharing my experience to be cathartic and I hope it will be helpful to other women.

M. 2008

The need to know syndrome

Although this story has a good outcome, the unnecessary stress and dogma has been highlighted by hospital protocol. This is common because of the lack of understanding that people need to be treated as human beings. They have emotions and sadly this fact is not taught or considered in many hospitals today.

Customer care seems to be lacking. The 'need to know' and 'we know better' superiority is not kindly or appreciated in these sensitive situations. Why not explain? At least the parents would be informed and consulted. They would know what was going on. Do they not understand that being kept in the dark with no communication is worse? Unfortunately though, this happens across the board in hospitals, not only in neonatal care.

Isn't it time we started training people in hospitals with emotional understanding and sensitivity skills. It would go a long way to help reduce undue stress which only adds to problems. Surely the coming together of the expertise of hospital staff and the love of the parents would be a super force for the health and well being of each of these babies.

I have heard of stories of excessive stress being put upon patients because of lack of understanding and hospital protocol, which could have been avoided with a little thought by hospital staff. Unfortunately, making the patient worse with stress consequently adds to the underlying problem.

I know hospitals are understaffed and underfunded in the UK, but human kindness costs nothing. In my opinion, we are not pieces of meat or superficial, but human beings with feelings and sensitivities.

PREMATURE BIRTH STATISTICS

In the UK we have the highest rate of premature birth in all of Western Europe. Is that something to be proud of? I don't think so. In my opinion it highlights that there is not enough care for our women overall. My research has shown gross gaps in the system catering for pregnancy and during labour and I believe that we should look after and revere our women while pregnant. With help and support we can reduce their stress very simply and quickly. With the right help from partners and family, we can also reduce their tiredness. As a culture, we are not fully aware of the emotional burden that can be put upon mothers and our precious children during pregnancy.

The UK is not the only country to see increases in numbers pre-term births. The USA has seen numbers climbing since the mid 1990s and the increase has been linked to Caesarean deliveries. In 1970, the percentage of C-section births stood at 5%. By 2004 this figure had risen to 31%. Once again, calls have been made to look at the need for such numbers of C-section births and especially to question how many are really medically necessary.

When statistics were closely checked, they found an increase in pre-term births of 60,000, with 92% of these by C-section[140]. US premature births rose from 354,997 in 1996 to 414,054 in 2004[141].

Calls are now being made for doctors to take into consideration the additional burden of premature birth, the findings of which are staggering, especially with behavioural and learning disorders highlighted. Surely we must take a positive step back where we can.

In some countries they have already seen the light

In Canada, for example, they also had high pre-term birth rates a few years ago. Canada improved their system for pregnant women, simply by giving them free vitamins and minerals. They also:

- Subsidised the cost of fresh fruit and vegetables
- Gave them access to alternative therapies with free treatments of reflexology, (which is known to be successful in reducing stress and helping to rebalance systems within the body) good for the mother and developing baby

It is not rocket science

We could do this very easily in the UK and it would be an easy way of reducing hospital involvement and costs at birth. It would certainly be a start in the right direction, wouldn't it? What are we waiting for?

In Britain there is currently a shortage of specially trained nurses dedicated to the premature baby field. Recent calls in the UK for more one-to-one care has highlighted the growing need for day-in and day-out neonatal care. With their job being intensive and emotionally draining, these nurses are under considerable pressure. To make their job easier they need good support and networks in place.

Unfortunately we are in a post-code lottery for proper funded hospitals in the UK, with the right equipment and staff being dependant very much on where you live. Intensive pre-term wards are not available in every hospital and certainly not across the board as we might expect. Although the government has acknowledged the gap in services, there is no positive action currently being taken to properly address the situation. Because the training and education of nurses has suffered negative changes, trainees no longer rotate through neonatal nursing as was the practice previously. As a result, nurses are qualifying with no experience or training in this field. Without experience in neonatal care, they subsequently discount this field when choosing a line to specialise in.

These days, funds are not forthcoming for neonatal training and we urgently need more money to support the demand for this specialist care, especially in view of the increasing demand. Currently there are just not enough experienced staff to go around and the shortage is putting undue pressure upon both staff and hospitals, affecting parents and neonatal care equally. It is a vicious circle that goes on and on. Experienced staff should be given specialist training as we need front line staff to be trained and supported in all aspects of neonatal care. Many hospitals are finding it difficult to cope with demand and often lack even simple and essential equipment like cots.

The costs of pre-term care are rising and we need positive action from government departments to address this issue. Talk does not save lives; action and funds do.

Both Bliss and Tommy's premature birth associations have leaflets and fact sheets available and you can log on to their websites at www.bliss.org.uk and www.tommys.org for further information - see appendix.

CASE STUDY 11 –
DAD'S EXPERIENCE OF PREMATURE BIRTH

The ambulance arrived very quickly and the paramedics were reassuring. Overall I think we were just very relieved that they had arrived. They worked very quickly and efficiently on our baby but seemed to ignore my wife, even to the point of whisking our son off to the ambulance and leaving my wife to make her own way down the stairs and into the ambulance.

The only other aspect of this part of the events which stood out is that the paramedics were not very positive in their language and explanation of the situation. We were confident and positive that our baby was going to be okay, but what we kept being given were negative statements, which seemed to be a back-covering exercise in case anything went wrong.

Positive thinking

Positive thinking is very powerful and a more positive atmosphere in the ambulance would have been much more productive. Comments like 'he is very early and very tiny', 'they don't always make it when they are this small' and 'he may have difficulty breathing' may well be true, but in such an emotional situation it is not what you want to hear as it only adds to the stress.

A general observation about the NHS dogma is that they seem to tell the truth when news is bad and withhold the truth when news is good, seemingly in a bid to be over cautious and not build up one's hopes or get sued if it goes wrong. Personally, I think it would be a much better and more powerful strategy if they reversed this principal. Being positive and convincing patients to be positive is a much more powerful healing tool than anything medical science has to offer.

Hospital

Once the three of us had arrived safely at the hospital, everything seemed to happen very quickly, very secretively and all out of our control. The feeling you get is that the baby is hospital property, a feeling that we soon learned would last throughout our entire stay in hospital.

Our son was quickly placed in an incubator and whisked off to the baby unit. At first we were full of relief at having arrived safely at the hospital, but that soon passed when we realised that the baby had suddenly disappeared and we had no idea where he was or what was happening.

My wife was taken to a bedroom on the maternity unit and was given a quick check over. We were told that we could both stay in the room together, which was a great relief after 3 months together 24/7 and then the trauma of what had just happened. We were given tea and toast but then just left for hours without anyone checking up and no chance to see our baby. This was a very worrying time, as we knew nothing about what was happening and my wife was not very well and not being looked after.

The first time we got to see our son in the incubator in the special care baby unit was a very difficult and emotional time. He was very strong and doing very well but we were not allowed to take him out to cuddle and we were concerned about both mum and baby missing out on the vital bonding which is so important.
It was very evident from day one that the baby is treated as hospital property, absorbed into the system, and we felt very much like outsiders looking in. Most of the treatment he received was given automatically, without explanation and without asking for our consent. Various tests and injections were carried out over the first few weeks and it was all very secretive.

It actually took 3 days and the intervention of a very kind and supportive nurse before we got to take our baby out of the incubator and cuddle him. What was also very difficult to take, more so without a proper explanation, was that special care babies are not fed for the first 48 hours. This means that a very small baby gets even smaller and weaker, rather than bigger and stronger.

Another very difficult aspect, which seemed to add to the secrecy, was that parents are asked to leave the room when the consultant is doing his rounds. This makes you highly suspicious and you feel even more like an outsider. The treatment of your child is clearly none of your business. Several times we noticed needle marks on our son's feet with no explanation as to what they were there for. We had to make a special arrangement to meet the consultant one day to discuss our son's progress and find out what was going on.

Grateful

We have to be very grateful to all the staff at the hospital and the paramedics because the simple fact is that our son came out 100% healthy. The feeling of your baby being hospital property was the worst part of the experience and was not pleasant. We always wanted a natural birth in relaxing surroundings, doing things our way, with natural remedies and no drugs. Unfortunately, that is not an option once you enter an NHS hospital. A natural birthing centre would always be our first choice and our recommendation to all parents-to-be.

Perhaps the most important aspect for others to consider is that we were fortunate enough to be in a very new hospital with an advanced special care baby unit. We are grateful for that as things could have been much worse, but whilst our son received the best care that science could offer, we were never allowed to use complementary treatment alongside the traditional. It should always be the parent's right to decide what kind of treatment their child receives. It should always be the parent's right to be in control of their baby's care.

S 2008

PREMATURE BIRTH RESEARCH

Research has shown that long-term disability is related to the gestational age of the baby and, according to studies made as far back as 1967, in babies born between 22-27 weeks, mortality rates up to the age of 6 years were five times higher in boys and almost ten times higher in girls. In addition, it was found that their lives were still affected in adulthood. Taken as a whole they were less likely to complete secondary school and less likely to go on to have children themselves. Of course, as things have improved overall in terms of hospital care and nutrition since then, the picture may look somewhat different today.

One recent long-term study carried out in Norway, however, suggests that premature babies may well suffer health consequences that can be seen in adulthood. They also found a poorer educational record with pre-term children[142]. What it does highlight, therefore, is that premature births could have more of an impact than we think and further long-term trials are needed for researchers to fully understand and identify the risks to mother and child. If this can be done successfully, it will allow babies to be born with the best chance of good health.

In 1999 a further study in the UK (started in 1979) also came to the conclusion that babies born more than five weeks prematurely could be more likely to suffer brain damage, affecting the white matter of the brain and possibly leading to behavioural and educational issues in adolescence. The white matter of the brain is involved in carrying signals between different areas of the brain and the spinal cord and the conclusions reached by the researchers were as a result of observations using MRI brain scans[143].

Not only have mortality rates and learning difficulties been directly linked to pre-term births, but researchers have also highlighted fertility issues in pre-termers. For example, pre-term children are less likely to have children of their own and some research shows that only14% of men and 25% of women had their own children. Mothers who were preterm are also more likely to give birth early.

In terms of mortality rates, however, this is logical through evolution. Current birthing methods undermine the survival of the fittest. Are we generating a society of less healthy beings?

The suggestions, which come out of the research include:

- Because of the lifetime risk of poor health, doctors should be reminded more often of an individual's pre-term history so that further information can be logged and assessed
- More focus and heightened awareness is needed for children as they grow up and the subsequent medical conditions which might occur in adolescence
- Pre-term babies require special treatment and monitoring for much longer

Jaundice

Jaundice is very common in newborn babies and can affect up too 60% of all newborns. Jaundice is seen as a temporary problem in the majority of cases

Some babies when newborn develop jaundice within days. Symptoms start on the face and head with a yellowing of the skin and sometimes the eyes will have a yellow tinge in the whites.

It is caused by an abundance of red blood cells breaking down. When this happens they release a pigment called bilirubin, which the liver eventually removes. As the liver is still immature the excess load can take time to clear.

Treatment

In some cases the baby will be put under a lamp (phototherapy) until yellowing starts to show signs of clearing. The blue light breaks down the bilirubin accumulated in the blood and the yellowing tinge should dissipate within a few days.

Side effects are seen as minor and harmless from the light treatment, however the baby may be affected by a rash and/or diarrhoea.
In some (rare) cases a blood transfusion may be necessary to alleviate symptoms.

[133] Bliss 'Premature births' http://www.bliss.org.uk/pagebuild.ph?texttype=howbliss_info_causesprem (cited 05.2008)

[134] Tommy's - cited at www.tommys.org/pregnancy-information/problems-in-pregnancy/premature.htm (Cited 05.2008)

[135] BBC News 'Long term risk of premature births' http://news.bbc.co.uk/hi/health news 7314117stm
(Ref: 'Norwegian study': Journal of the American Medical association) (cited 05.2008)

[136] BioCare seminar 2008.11 (FSA guidelines)

[137] Helen Foster 'Health article 'Spilling the Beans' Sunday Express: 09.2007

[138] Tommy's - cited at www.tommys.org/pregnancy-information/problems-in-pregnancy/premature.htm (cited 05.2008)

[139] BBC News ' Premature birth 'offers less cancer protection' (1999.08) http://news.bbc.co.uk/1/hi/health.314637.stm (Ref: Lancet medical journal.1973-1989 International team of scientists study - of 807,874. 'Swedish women gestation period of at least 28 weeks'.) (cited 02.2007)

[140] BBC News 'Long term risk premature birth' http:// news.bbc.co.uk/1/health/7314117stm (Ref: March of Dimes advocacy group and infant health) (cited 05.2008)

[141] William Dunham 'Premature births of USA' (Journal clinics in perinatology and March of Dimes research) http://uk.reuters.com/article/healthNews.Molt/idUKN28439837.(cited 05.2008)

[142] BBC News 'Long tem risk to premature birth' http://news.bbc.co.uk/1/hi/helath/ 7314117stm (Ref; Norwegian study: Journal of the American Medical association) (cited at 0.52008)

[143] BBC News Premature babies may face teen troubles' http://news.bbc.co.uk/hi/health/343231 1999.05 (Ref: Lancet medical journal. 1999 University College London 'babies born more than five weeks prematurely could be more likely to suffer brain damage') (cited 02.2007)

Chapter 15

INDEX

Chapter 15

CRANIO SACRAL THERAPY

Trials have proved that a lot of problems can come from birth. Surprisingly, being born will be the most traumatic thing we will ever do in our lives. The birth process, depending upon whether it is natural, induced, forceps, or Vontau, can set the pattern on how we will be for the rest of our lives.

While in the womb, our experiences create our structure, confidence, abilities, likes and dislikes, as well as our nervous system and how we are both mentally and physically. It is the start of our emotional development and anxieties, and we take on these emotions and anxieties from our mothers, depending upon how they are during the pregnancy, such as whether they are happy, sad, anxious and so on. This will affect us throughout our lives and starts patterns that shape our world for life.

Cranio Sacral Therapy (CST), a non-invasive therapy, which works by gently balancing the Cranio Sacral system, brain and spinal cord, can help with difficult birth dysfunctions, skeletal disorders and emotional trauma. Trials have shown that CST has helped with ADHD (hyperactive) dysfunctions, autism, dyslexia, Dysphraxia and much more. It is not only useful on newborns but works with all ages, helping to put right what went awry at birth, through accidents etc.,

The key factor in many of these cases is a problem birth, resulting in a dysfunction to the Cranio Sacral system. Research has shown that hyperactive behaviour can often be linked to emotional problems, where food and chemical intolerance contribute to ADD or ADHD. From my experience, emotional problems can come from the birth process. A long induced labour, for example, can cause anxieties and distress for the baby, instilling emotional anxieties for life and creating foetal origins. Going on into adulthood, children born with such anxieties become worriers, their behaviour anxious from the start with behaviour patterns to match. We will also discuss the physical imbalances below.

A traumatic birth process or an accident at a young age can change the position of the head and neck, the areas surrounding the brain stem and occipital bone. As previously discussed, emotional trauma from birth can also cause various physiological disorders and behaviour patterns.

Being non-drug related, CST can help with behavioural and emotional problems as well as improving overall health and wellbeing. It can be used to treat all systems of the body and can help to realign bones and tissue from any birth, including those, which are traumatic. It helps with the nervous system and can connect through to tissue and cellular level. Although CST can treat any age and I regularly treat children of all ages, what has been remarkable is how beneficial and easily applied it is to newborns.

DIFFICULT AND TRAUMATIC BIRTH

'I believe that taking a few minutes to conduct a Cranio Sacral system evaluation in the delivery room or shortly after birth is a worthwhile investment in any child's future health and well-being.'
Dr John Upledger DO, OMM[144]

Dr Upledger believes that the vaginal delivery represents the child's first Cranio Sacral treatment and spinal mobilisation, with sensory stimulation and myoneural system treatment. During labour, and as the uterine contractions take place, the child is twisted and turned in the birth canal, creating mobilisation of each joint of the spine and pelvis, together with activating the torso and stretching the child's muscles and soft tissue around every area. Nature has provided the birth canal for this very process and purpose, relying on pushing from uterine contractions and enhancing the birth event for both mother and infant.

Forceps

Children who have forceps or vacuum deliveries are often born with misshapen heads, sometimes beyond the child's own healing abilities. When vacuum delivery takes place, for instance, it creates a negative force in the head, which creates a suction and accumulation of abnormal amounts of intra-cranial fluids in the top of the skull.

The resulting 'oedema' can cause a lasting dysfunction of the cranio sacral system, causing fibrous changes in tissues and losing flexibility of the meningeal membranes, which should be pliable.

Induction

The medical preference for induction, to bring about the birth of baby before it is ready, invariably causes long labour, which results in exhaustion for the mother and often necessitates the use of suction or forceps. Although emergency intervention and care is sometimes unavoidable, less unnecessary intervention, (giving more time and allowing natural birth) would avoid the risk of damage to the delicate foetal head. As such damage caused by intervention can take some time to correct, even if treatment is started in the early days of life, if possible wouldn't it be better to take another option? After all would you like to have your head pulled about in a tight space?

CRANIO SACRAL DYSFUNCTIONS AND C-SECTION

In his long experience, Dr Upledger has found that C-sections also cause significant CranioSacral dysfunctions. He suggests that the experience results in a loss in pressure comparable to the bends of a scuba diver coming up too fast. He recounts an occasion where he remembers seeing amniotic fluid spout up into the air as he cut into the uterus during the course of carrying out a C-section. In his work with CST, he later deduced that a C-section caused a sudden reduction in pressure inside the uterus, something which could challenge the physiology of the foetus. This could then create a rapid expansion in the head, giving membranous inter-cranial strain and causing micro-tears in the meningeal membranes and capillary bleeds[145].

The damage can cause bio chemical changes that will turn into bile salts, causing brain tissue irritation and fibrous change, loss of compliance together with possible small amounts of intramembranous adhesions.

Bile Salts occur from the breakdown of capillary bleeds (blood cells), when the red blood cells leave the vascular system and break down within the tissues instead of the blood system. The product of blood cell breakdown is bile salts (Bilirubin and Biliverdin) which is quite irritating to the surrounding tissues. The brain and meninges are particularly sensitive to bile salts. The salts can cause inflammation and fibrosis within the layers of the meningeal membranes, restricting the mobility of the membranes causing adhesion and therefore compromising the craniosacral system.

These problems, however, can be helped and corrected with Cranio Sacral therapy, as CST can assist in reducing the fibrosis with gentle movements which help to stretch fibrosis, the Dural membrane and accommodate growth.

When we have fibrosis within the skull it compromises dural expansion and forces the brain and skull to grow against resistance, therefore compromising brain function and development. Bile salt degradation tightens tissue compromising blood flow, which can also affect neuronal function. In this instance neurons 'die off' spreading the damage as the severity of the condition increases. CST can help to enhance fluid motion, thereby reducing neuron 'die off'

Dr Upledger's observations showed that problems such as maternal injury, emotional upset or foetal mal-position in the pelvis over a prolonged period (all things which can lead to difficult and traumatic births) were also more likely to produce specific clinical symptoms related to Cranio Sacral system dysfunctions that were discovered quite easily with the application of CST. He stated that, 'For proper application of CST, the earlier, the better.' CST was found to be more effective if applied early.

Delivery

During birth delivery, when there is excessive traction of the child's head due to the use of forceps or vacuum extraction, it puts excessive strain on the muscles, ligaments, fasciae and joints. As a result, the body responds with tissue contracture and small amounts of blood may also be extravastated, which may later show as induced fibrotic changes in any soft tissues. This can take place in the cranio sacral system and the para-spinal (cervical, thoracic) and pelvic tissues, interfering with the proper functioning of these systems.

Dr Upledger found through his observations that CST treatment released strained and contracted tissues, therefore relaxing and allowing tissue fluid exchanges to take place, encouraging extravasted blood dispersal. Joint mobilisation is also encouraged with CST. He believes that if these issues are not corrected as a child, they can cause a whole variety of Cranio Sacral problems later in life, including skeletal disorders such as Scoliosis of the spine, cervical, thoracic and pelvic imbalances[146]. These imbalances can interfere with the organs and the proper functioning of the body.

Hard and soft palate

Other problems can also occur in the Cranio Sacral system, especially in relation to the hard and soft palate and in connection with the disruption of the nasal passages because of the tubes or suction bulbs used on the child after delivery. This process can sometimes be done rather roughly, yet we know these areas are very delicate. The use of tubes causes the tissue to contract, which in turn compromises the function and mobility of these areas.

Hard plate dysfunction (suckling) is usually related to the sphenoid and/or temporal bone dysfunction and distension to the pallet and can manifest in severe irritability, together with eye-motor system dysfunction. The Zygomata (cheek bones) can also be affected by misalignment, putting pressure on the Temporo Mandibular joint (jaw joint). In these cases, the child cannot tell you what is wrong and simply cries to show it is suffering pain and great discomfort, with disorders such as ear ache, grinding jaw joint and headaches.

Space in the womb and restriction

A child only has a small space available in the womb. As it grows into this space, it contorts into different positions as it grows too big to be accommodated, something which is even more of an issue now that we are reportedly delivering bigger babies.

What happens is that the baby's facia, muscles and ligaments start to grow in an abnormal way, due to pressures within the womb which, if not corrected, will continue to grow in the same way and cause problems later in life. The whole posture of the body can become misaligned in such a way that, when walking, more pressure is put on one side of the body, causing hip, spine and pelvic disorders. This, in turn, compounds misalignments and causes more problems with inner organs and their functioning.

The process can be likened to a plant growing in an undersized pot. Being confined to a small space, it can only grow so much without its roots and trunk becoming distorted. Eventually it grows in a misshapen way and if it is not corrected early on will continue to do so.

In the human body, it only takes a short amount of time to correct these misalignments with a CST treatment (given by a competent CST therapist) in the first stages of the baby's life, providing a clean foundation to grow with. Why are we not providing such treatment as a matter of course at birth, as they do in other countries?

During the process of birth the newborn skull has ample room for movement as the bones override and change the shape of the head, allowing it to pass through the birth canal. Dr Upledger believes that this passage represents a 'manipulation' of the skull bones by the wall of the birth canal; this then ensures their proper mobility, so that after delivery the bones are able to comply with the hypoglossal canals, located beside and beneath the joint surfaces of the Occiput as it articulates with the atlas[147].

Authors Note: The hypoglossal canal is located in the opening in the occipital bone, transmitting the hypoglossal nerve and a branch of the posterior meningeal. The Hypoglossal canal transmits the nerve that supplies the muscles of the tongue.

SUCKLING DIFFICULTIES

Jamming of the bones can cause suckling difficulties. If the birth process does not happen correctly, there can be a jamming of the bones, which can result in tongue control problems and hence suckling difficulties. Dysfunction can come from spasm of the sternocleidomastoideus and/or trapezius muscle in the neck (very painful and uncomfortable at any age) and it can also result in compression or irritation of the tenth and eleventh cranial nerves as they exit the jugular foramen, which may then produce a torticollis (spasm).

Torticollis

Dr. Upledger calls this 'an occipital base compression' and I have seen a lot of children with these problems. If both sides of the occipital base are severely compressed, it is common to see the child suffering from any of the following symptoms:

- Colic and/or food regurgitation
- Oesophageal reflux
- Respiratory difficulties
- Rapid heart rate
- Compromised bowel function (constipation or diarrhoea)
- Spasm of the neck muscles

Any combination of these symptoms may be seen as a less severe disorder such as jamming of the occipital base (may be only on one side or the other, right or left occipital bones) and backpressure, if this is not corrected it could result in ADD (attention deficit disorder) and/or hyperactive behaviour (ADHD).

During CST trials they found that temporal bone dysfunction occurs if neck muscles go into spasm. If this is allowed to persist, it indicates a strong contributing factor in children with Dyslexia and other reading problems. Trials carried out on school age children suffering from Dyslexia, however, found that when they were treated with CST it allowed them to catch up to normal reading levels in a matter of weeks, unless psychological and/or emotional scars were in the way. Emotional and psycho-emotional therapeutic modalities can be incorporated into the CST treatment programme to help[148].
From my own experience of dealing with both newborns and children, I have found that a child can respond quickly to treatment. As Dr Upledger found during his trials in 1977 and a result of the substantial number of treatments that he has carried out since, the younger they are, the less treatment is needed.

In 2003, Dr Upledger and his team were involved with conjoined twins who were famously separated. The twins were treated with CST on several occasions to prepare them for the long 34-hour operation.

Dr John Upledger is a man before his time. He founded the Upledger Institute in 1987 in Florida USA and has taught and shared his experiences and findings with other therapists (of which I am one). The UK headquarters for his work is located in Perth, Scotland and

Ennis in Southern Ireland. The Upledger Institute is dedicated to the natural enhancement of health and is recognised worldwide for its groundbreaking continuing clinical research, education programs and therapeutic services. You can view the website for the Institute at www.upledger.com. (See appendix for further information)

LONG AND SHORT BIRTH EFFECTS

Having the experience of being a mother for the first time can be daunting and if the child has a long traumatic birth (or even, from my experience, a quick birth) it can be damaging both emotionally and physically.

The child comes into the world with bright lights, lots of noise and being held upside down. What a shock it must be to the system when all the child has known for the last nine months is being in the womb, safe and sound, surrounded by mum's warmth and protection. As if that weren't enough, in some cases the baby will be taken away from mum (although done with the best of intentions on the hospital's side) when in fact mum is all that the child wants and nobody or nothing else will do.

When I had my children, they were both born in what was, at that time, a nursing home especially for pregnancy and birth. Being classed as a nursing home, mothers were lucky as they were also allowed to rest – a rare thing now! Because of the thinking in those days, this created a conflict of interests, since the child was taken away to the nursery at night so that mums could rest. My second child cried all the time and I was not allowed to see or go to him. Being a sensitive Indigo child, he was traumatised and felt bereft at not being with his mum. At the time, as a young mum who thought that the nursing and medical professions knew better than me, I accepted what I was told, although I now realise that they were wrong.

Long birth

A long birth understandably leaves mum exhausted. If she has had stitches, she is also sore and suffering pain from the birth event. She is trying to get to grips with looking after this little bundle of joy who will not stop crying. Being inexperienced, mum starts to think that she is doing something wrong and, of course, bringing a newborn home adds further complications with the rest of the family. Everyone feels the effects of the newborn's discomfort. It is like throwing a pebble into a pond, watching the ripples of stress and frustration all round. For a first-time mum and dad it can be horrendous. Perhaps it isn't the first but the other births have gone well and the parents have not experienced a crying infant before.

Quick births

This is what happened to me with my second child. Following a fairly short labour of 4 hours, I gave birth to a big baby who cried from the time he came into the world. Nothing would pacify him, especially when he woke just before 4am every morning (the time just before he was born), although the significance of this did not occur to me at the time as it was well before my training with Upledger CST. We were all distraught. If only I had known then what I know now.

With hindsight, I now know that he had an occipital base dysfunction and bowel irregularities, problems which followed him into his adult years, but which I have subsequently been able to reverse with CST. He also had bad bouts of colic and, most of all, emotional trauma. For about 6 months, he was a very unhappy and distraught baby. Health visitors were no help; they did not know what was wrong with him and only advised giving him more food. This was no help to me when I was walking the floor day and night. 'He will grow out of it,' they told me. 'It will pass.' Clearly, this wasn't enough.

Most emotional problems come from birth and my own mother's experience is another example which bears this out. As a baby, my brother cried for three months and nothing would appease him. My mother walked the streets with him in the pram, trying to calm him. It was her third child and even with a wealth of her experience, she didn't know what to do to help him. One of the differences was that his birth was induced, whilst all the rest of her children were born naturally. He became an anxious child who turned into a worrier as an adult, forming anxiety right from the beginning. With behaviour patterns to match, this went on into his adult years.

Application of CST in Newborns and Infants

Cranio Sacral Therapy has proven to be effective in identifying a number of disorders affecting children and adults, such as dyslexia, hyperkinetic behaviour and motor-control problems. It is also good at alleviating such conditions when they are caused by restrictions in the Dura matter membranes of the cranio sacral system.

For 30 years, Dr J Upledger has pioneered work with children and says, 'Some cases of ADD/ADHD can be considered as a symptom of an underlying misalignment or malfunction of some kind.'

Dr Upledger, an osteopathic physician and surgeon, arranged for trials 30 years ago in 1977. They were carried out on 203 children with an independent statistician and psychologist who correlated the results with data from the children's academic and behavioural performances, together with the medical/obstetrical history of each mother and child. The results of statistical data analysis revealed that the process of Cranio Sacral Therapy was capable of identifying children suffering from dyslexia, hyperkinetic behaviour, seizures and motor control problems. He also identified babies delivered by Caesarean section or forceps and those who had suffered oxygen deprivation at the time of delivery.

Based on those results, Dr Upledger received funding and opened a clinic for brain dysfunctional children to research relationships between autism and Cranio Sacral system dysfunction. This research was carried out over a period of three years from September 1978 to June 1981. The results highlighted some interesting correlations between maternal viral infection during the last six months of pregnancy and the dysfunctions related to delivery process.

MATERNAL VIRAL INFECTION

Dr Upledger states that maternal illness or toxicity during pregnancy usually results in a generalized tightness of the foetal Dura matter, making the membrane less able to comply with the rhythmic volume changes of cerebrospinal fluid flowing within the Cranio Sacral system[149]. He found that it was frequently a consequence of a maternal viral infection during the last six months of pregnancy and dismissed maternal bacterial infection as a less likely cause, as proposed by other studies. This has since been substantiated via other research as discussed in the book

During trials, he also concluded that tight membranes seemed to relate to the mother's respiratory difficulties, such as asthma, or to toxin problems whether from a single experience or ongoing exposure. The toxins could be taken into the mother's system in many ways, such as via:

- Medication
- The use of street drugs
- Air pollutants
- Airborne allergies
- Food and drink

All of these can have an effect on the mother and foetus.

Generalised tight membrane syndrome shows itself as a gross dysfunction of the child's central nervous system, manifesting in sensory and motor deficits. Trials found that if this was allowed to persist and not corrected by CST, the noncompliant membrane syndrome may be severe enough to become a strong contributory factor to the development of autism, although Dr Upledger concluded that Cranio Sacral Therapy in some cases, greatly improved or completely corrected these problems and was particularly effective when applied during the early stages of a baby's life.

The Vagus nerve

The Vagus nerve connection can be a problem for all ages. Situated in the neck, it is the single most important nerve in the body and can be adversely affected from birth. When the baby's head is at a particular angle in the birth canal, it can affect the efficiency of the connection to the Vagus nerve. In later life, the Vagus nerve can also become dysfunctional or cause problems as a result of injuries such as whiplash.

The word 'Vagus' is a Latin word which means 'wandering' (the words vagrant, vagabond and vague come from the same root) and the vagus nerve, sometimes referred to as the Cranial nerve X or the pneumogastric nerve, is a paired cranial nerve, the tenth of twelve such paired nerves.

It is the only nerve to start in the brainstem, within the Medulla Oblongata and it extends below the head through the jugular foramen to the abdomen, connecting both the lungs and stomach to the main nerve system. In other words, its sphere of influence extends all the way from the brainstem to the splinic flexure of the colon. When required, it will slow our heart rate and stimulate digestion, and it is even connected to our taste buds.

Doctors once believed that the nerve's main job was controlling acid production in the stomach, but better understanding of human physiology shows that 95% of the nerve fibres carry messages in the other direction, from the gut to the brain[150].

Why is the vagus nerve so important?

The Vagus nerve supplies sensory parasympathetic fibres to all the organs (except the suprarenal glands) from the neck down to the second segment of the transverse colon. This nerve also controls some skeletal muscles including the muscles of the larynx (speech).

The Vagus nerve is responsible for:

- Heart rate - nerve stimulation is linked by the vagus nerve
- Muscle movements of the mouth
- Speech (via recurrent laryngeal nerve)
- Keeping the larynx open for breathing

- Gastrointestinal peristalsis i.e. the wavelike movement of the colon
- Receiving sensations from the outer ear

Branches of the Vagus nerve go to:

- The lungs for broncho constriction
- The oesophagus for peristalsis (muscle movement)
- The heart to slow down heart rate

Additional abdomen branches go to the stomach, pancreas, large and small intestine and the colon for secretion and constriction of smooth muscle activity. The sensory part of the Vagus nerve comes from receptors in the abdominal viscera, oesophagus, lungs, bronchia, trachea, heart and aortic arch.

The Vagus nerve has distinct functions[151]:

- Bronchial motor - involved with the functioning of the muscles of the pharynx, larynx and extrinsic muscle of the tongue
- Visceral motor muscles - parasympathetic nerve supply to the smooth muscles and glands of pharynx and larynx. It is also involved with the viscera of the abdomen and thorax
- Visceral sensory muscles – gives sensory information from the larynx, oesophagus, trachea, abdominal and thoracic viscera, plus chemical receptors from the aortic bodies and stretch receptors of the aortic arch
- General sensory – gives general sensory information from the skin at the back of the ear and the external auditory channels
- Special sensory – gives taste sensation from the epiglottic region

Emotional and Physical effects of a dysfunctional Vagus Nerve
A dysfunctional Vagus nerve can show itself in many ways. Nervousness, inability or impairment to speak, increased heart rate and palpitations are all indications of this condition, as well as excessive perspiration, stomach disorders and/or irritations.

During emotional stress, an over-activation of the Vagus nerve can take place. The parasympathetic nervous system then acts as an over-stimulation to compensate for a strong sympathetic nervous system, commonly associated with times of stress. Mood swings can also be affected and, in times of fear, loss of bladder control can also be experienced, something which is far more prominent in women and children.

As you can see, it is essential to have a good working connection from the Vagus nerve from day one of a child's life.

ASSOCIATION OF BIRTH AND DYSFUNCTIONS IN CHILDREN IN LATER LIFE

The connection to criminality by birth intervention, separation and rejection by the mother is not a new idea. Adolescence dysfunctional behaviour, addiction and suicide, are also considered to be connected to the type of birth and mother bonding issues.

In his book Secret Life of the Unborn Child, Dr Thomas Verney suggests that whatever the mum goes through, so too does the unborn child, a concept which is also believed by other notable paediatricians such as Dr M Odent.

Trials between health and behaviour patterns later in life

There have been many studies dating from the late 1970s, which have concentrated on health and behaviour patterns later in life and which show the connection between birth, childhood and teens. Retrospective trials, which had common factors, have looked at the links between the 'primal period' (which includes foetal life, birth and the year following birth) and health and behaviour patterns later in life, highlighting birth risk factors over and over again.

Incapacity to love

Dr Michel Odent and his Primal Health Research Centre have established a data bank of hundreds of references and studies from scientific and medical journals. From this data, he has concluded that those who have an impaired capacity to love (themselves or others) show links to risk factors in the period surrounding birth[152].

Autism associated with hospital protocol

A observational trial conducted in 1983 by Niko Tinbergen linked the risk of Autism to the birth process and type of hospital[153] as a result of:

- Deep forceps delivery
- Birth under anaesthesia
- Resuscitation at birth
- Induction of labour

In 1991, a Japanese psychiatrist associated autism risks with the place of birth, concluding that children born at certain hospitals were significantly more at risk as the hospital policy was to induce a week before the expected due date[154]. It was also hospital routine to use a combination of sedatives, anaesthesia agents and analgesics during labour. His observations lead him to believe there was a link between birth and Autism.

Criminality

In 1994, a Californian research team evaluated over four thousand males born in the same period and at the same hospital. They found that 18 year-olds with violent criminal risk factors had a common association of birth complications, together with separation from or rejection by the mother[155], although early maternal separation or rejection was found not to be a risk factor by itself.

It is believed by some sources that anger is already patterned and instilled by the age of three.

Teenage Suicide

In the late 1980s and 90s, trials took place which looked at any links between teenage suicide and birth, and the results were astonishing. One US study[156] found that 52 late teens committed suicide before their 20th birthday, a common risk factor being that they were all resuscitated at birth.

A Swedish study[157] of suicide by asphyxiation, meanwhile, found a link with asphyxiation at birth and suicides by violent mechanical means were linked with mechanical birth trauma. Jacobson also concluded that men who had traumatic births were five times more at risk of committing suicide by violent means than others[158].

Drug Addiction

A Swedish study, which looked at addicts born between 1945 and 1966[159] found that mothers who had been given certain pain killing drugs during labour gave birth to children who were at greater risk of becoming drug addicts in adolescence. These trials have since been repeated in the US and confirmed the original findings[160]. Trials found that if three doses of opiates or barbiturates were given to the mother during labour, the child was five times more at risk of becoming addicted.

Anorexia

Research has also made correlations between birth and another form of destructive behaviour, anorexia. It was discovered from a Swedish trial done on 781 individuals admitted to hospital for treatment (the girls had been born between 1973 and 1984) that the common factor was cephalhaematoma at birth[161]. In layman's terms, this means that blood had collected between skull bones and is an indication of a highly traumatic birth during which mechanical intervention was probably used. Forceps or ventouse deliveries are also risk factors in these cases.

Despite their findings, it seems that these types of trials have not been taken seriously enough and, unfortunately, the medical profession, midwives and health visitors have their own sets of beliefs. I have given talks at seminars for midwives and when I have explained about the emotional impacts, I have been told that they were unaware of this aspect of birth. Perhaps it is time they were trained.

Millions of pounds are spent every year on trying to eradicate the types of destructive behaviours that these studies have taken into account, and yet few seem to look at the core reasons.

I run courses and give talks to help professionals understand the core emotional consequences of trauma and so on. Maybe it is too simple an answer that we are creating these scenarios from the way we are medically treating women during labour. Are we too impatient to allow the child to come of its own accord, in its own time without intervention?

Ultimately, the question has to be asked...when will we start to listen? When will it sink in? How many more need to suffer!

[144] Dr J.E. Upledger. Article 'New Born and Infants' – Upledger Institute 2003

[145] Dr J.E. Upledger. Article 'New Born and Infants' – Upledger Institute 2003

[146] Dr J.E. Upledger. Article 'New Born and Infants' – Upledger Institute 2003

[147] Dr J.E. Upledger. Article 'New Born and Infants' – Upledger Institute 2003

[148] Ibid 'New Born and Infants'

[149] Dr J.E. Upledger. Article 'New Born and Infants' – Upledger Institute 2003

[150] British Med Assoc Family Health encyclopaedia: Dorling Kindersley London: 1994.p1043

[151] Yale University School of Medicine: "Cranial nerve X Vagus' http://www.med.edu/caim/cnerves/cn10/cn10_1html (cited 08.2006)

[152] Michel Odent 'The Scientificatation of Love' Free Association Books, London 2001

[153] Ibid (ref: N.& A.Tinbergen 'Autistic children ' Allen and Unwin London 1983)

[154] Ibid P18; (Ref: Hattori R 'Autistic and developing disorders after general antithetic delivery' - Lancet 1.6.1991; 337;1357-8 letter)

[155] Ibid 'Violent crime' (Ref: A. Raine, P. Brennan, and SA Medink. 'Birth complications combined with early maternal rejection at age 1 year predispose to violent crime'. Arch Gen Psychiatry 1994.51:984-8)

[156] Ibid 'suicide' (Ref: L Salk, LP Lipsitt, et al. 'Relationship of maternal and perinatal conditions to eventual adolescent suicide' Lancet 16th March 1985 624 – 7)

[157] Michel Odent 'The Scientificatation of Love' Free Association Books, London 2001 (Ref; A Swedish study of 'suicide by asphyxiation found a link with asphyxiation at birth and suicides by violent mechanical means were linked with mechanical birth trauma'. B. Jacobson, K Nyberg et al. 'Perinatal origin of adult self destructive behaviour' Acta. Psychiatr. Scan 1987; 76: 364-71)

[158] Ibid 'offspring suicide' (Ref: B. Jacobson, M. Bygdemany 'Obstetric care and proneness of offspring to suicide as adults case control study' BMJ 1998 317:1346 -9)

[159] Ibid 'addiction' (Ref: B. Jacobson, K Nyberg ' Opiate addiction in adult offspring through possible imprinting after obstetric treatment': BMJ 1990; 301:1067-70)

[160] Ibid 'Drug abuse' (Ref: K. Nyberg SL Buka and LP Lipsitt – 'Parental medication as a potential factor for adult drug abuse in North American cohort' Epemiology 2000; 11(6): 715-16)

[161] Ibid perspective Pg 17 (Ref: S. Cnattingius CM Hultman. M Dahl, P Sparen – 'Very preterm birth, birth trauma and the risk of anorexia among girls'. Arch Gen Psychiatry 1999; 56: 634-5)

Chapter 16

INDEX

Chapter 16

BONDING

The bonding process takes time for some mothers and their newborn babies. We are led to believe that 'mother love' is an instant rosy glow of bonding with her child, which happens the minute she receives him/her into her arms. As we know, this is an automatic process from the natural hormone oxytocin, which is activated during a vaginal birth.

In reality, however, things can be very different. Many women can be so distraught after the birth event and are so traumatised, exhausted and numb that it may take from 24 to 48 hours before any feelings for the baby are felt to any degree. I know of some mums who have told me that it has taken several months before they could feel love for their child.

There is nothing wrong with a woman if she feels like this after her delivery. The love hormone, oxytocin, can be at a lower level in some women and this could be the case for you. Lowered levels can be due to having had an induced labour or because of intervention and drug intake, all of which will lower natural sensitive abilities and will take time to wear off for mother and baby.

For some women, the feelings of caring, protectiveness and love cannot be pre-arranged and it needs to develop naturally in its own time through hormone activity. Allow yourself time to get to know your baby. After all, the experience of childbirth can be a bit overwhelming!

What nature intended

The bonding process between mother and child is what nature intended. It is an essential natural process, which takes place automatically during the birth process because of the intervention of oxytocin in both mother and child. Through my own experience of treating young and old, however, I find that children are not receiving the bonding with their mothers because of the experience of intervention in birth:

- Through Caesarean birth

- Due to synthetic oxytocin being given in inducement
- Because of the mother's emotional state - in fear, grief, etc
- Due to rejection/abandonment by the mother when the child is not wanted

Emotionally the mother needs to be supported by her mate, otherwise she can go into survival mode and will be compromised herself due to the fact that feeling unsupported creates a psychosomatic response and an invasive action emotionally. As in nature, if the animal does not feel secure and supported by its mate, it will most often abort.

The actions and interventions noted above can reflect in all sorts of emotional ways on the child in the womb and upon arrival. The infant can be left feeling shock, for example, either from the trauma received from within the womb due to the mother's emotional state during pregnancy, or from the birth process or the sense of being abandoned after birth.

BIRTH THROUGH THE AGES

Over the last sixty years we have changed our thinking many times on parenting and childcare. In the 1950s, those who could afford it had a nanny brought in to look after the baby and act as a substitute for the child's mother. Although only those in middle and upper class society could afford to do this, the status that hiring a nanny held for the family created a formula for other mothers to follow.

Brought in at birth in most cases and working to a strict regime, nanny bathed, fed and changed the child and also took the infant out in the pram every day. After being fed and changed, the child would be put down in a cot or pram to sleep, with no time being given for cuddles. Nannies in those days were like strict teachers and wore a uniform to show their status.

Although the children were well cared for physically, it has since been realised that no nourishment was given to them emotionally. They were left to cry and not picked up between feeds as it was thought that it would only interfere with their development. The 'nanny' way of thinking was that if you picked up a child when it cried, it would only teach them to cry more for attention.

Some of those who had nannies as children are now in their fifties and sixties. Many, if not most, say that being with the nanny gave them structure and security as they were with them day in and day out and the nanny was the person the child bonded with, not the mother. Of course mum and dad would visit the nursery at certain times of the day, but it was the nanny who made all the decisions for her wards. Nanny knew best and mum was deterred from interfering in the timetable and day care.

The Age of Dr. Spock

Moving into the 1960s, we had the revolution of Dr Spock. Benjamin McLane Spock was an American paediatrician who lived from 1903 until 1998. He first published a book in 1946 called Baby and Child Care which is reputed to be one of the best sellers of all time. It contained a revolutionary way of thinking, giving the clear message to new mothers that 'you know more than you think.'

Although seen as radical in his thinking at the time (his fame seemed to hit a peak in the 1960s and early 70s), Spock's books brought about major changes in childcare. He advocated that childcare was not the one-size-fits-all approach that had long been the thinking of experts. Children were individuals and he urged parents to look at their child's needs individually.

Previously, experts had advocated regular sleep patterns with a very strict regime for babies. There was to be no picking up or holding when the baby cried, no emotional contact, no kissing and no hugging. It was believed that this regime would make them strong and independent in the world. Sadly though, this thinking had come from the Victorian age of principles and was not always appropriate. Dr Spock's views, however, saw him being blamed for the new permissive society, and indeed Vice President Spiro Agnew called him 'The father of permissiveness'[162]. As he advocated that children should not be smacked or punished, some experts believe that Dr Spock was responsible for the move towards more permissive parenting in general, and blame him for the long-term negative results that we saw in the 60s.

In their eyes, lawlessness caused by young people has followed on through to today. Spock's supporters, however, believe that his books have been misinterpreted. In 1994 he wrote a follow-up book entitled Rebuilding American Family Values: A better World for our Children.

Tribe Values of the 1970s

In the 1970s we had tribe values, which became very fashionable after Dr. Spock's era in the previous decade had opened up women to new thinking in terms of parenting and childcare. In complete contrast, old values from the tribe came in, with mothers carrying their babies with them in slings at all times. Tribe values brought feeding on demand.

The main theme was of close contact at all times, of having your baby sleep with you in the same bed or next to you in a cot, so that the child could hear you breath. Basically, the child could be near mum and dad, day in and day out. It became a time of hugging and kissing the child and listening to their needs. By being held on the back or carried in a sling next to the heart, the child was part of the mother again and always in close proximity. The child was happy and content in this environment, with its emotional nourishment fulfilled.

In the 80s – let your baby cry

We had the swing back to control and strict regimes for our children. The thinking changed back to the nanny rules of 'let your baby cry and don't give in.' More women were working and needed structure to their lives but the tribe way of living took time and effort. As a result, mums were under pressure both at home and at work. The result was no more time for cuddles and hugs. Bath, feed, change and put down became the fashion in childcare. Let your child cry and no matter what the consequence, don't give in to him/her. It was a simple case of, show them who is in charge. As a result, some children were left to cry and cry until they fell asleep, exhausted. The nanny state had returned in parenting.

Control parenting

The 90s brought the nanny state to another level of control in parenting. The thinking changed to the bizarre belief that, 'Although I have a child, it will not rule my life. I will continue to go out to work and arrange for others to look after it. My life will be the same as it was before.'

As the need for women to go out to work increased, having a child to look after became a quandary. Women tried to juggle each day between work, home and family. The demand for nurseries and day-care increased and children would be dropped off as early as 7.30am and collected in the evening as late as 6pm.

Au pairs too became fashionable during the 90s. These were normally young women who were paid to come and help in the home, living as part of the family. They took on the nanny/childcare role but also did housework and nightshifts with the child/children. Au pairs started off from foreign nationalities because they were young and cheap to pay. They worked long hours and were taken into the womb of the family. Many professional women could not manage without them.

For many, this situation proved ideal since the parents ruled, not the children. However, the children often became distant from their parents, as they were no longer cared for in a nurturing way. Finding time for the children had to be fitted in around the parent's schedules and basically it was back to the 50s ideas of the child's physical wellbeing taken care of but no time allowed for emotional nurturing.

Mismatch

In the 2000s we have a mismatch of all of the above. We have more interference in birth and parenting than ever before. More Caesareans are performed for the convenience of the professional working mother and the hospital schedule and, in my opinion, children are suffering from shell shock when they arrive because of our present day birthing structures.

Emotional nurturing is still being ignored to a great extent, leaving children's needs unmet. Mothers are confused and often pressured into adopting many odd ways and systems without choice. They are not encouraged to think for themselves, nor to look at what is best for them or their children.

Childbirth is a natural process. When a baby goes through the birth canal normally, it actually triggers certain processes within the child. This does not happen when they arrive via C-section. Have we become too technical in the twenty-first century? It seems that technology has taken over completely in western society, pushing aside the very concept of natural childbirth to fit in to the lifestyle demands of the parent.

In a very small way, perhaps the tide is finally turning once more. In some European countries, such as Holland, they now have a progressive approach of only interfering in childbirth in an emergency. They prefer to restrict the number of scans and the amount of interference to the mother and child. Logically the body has natural resources and systems to deal with childbirth and it begs the question why interference is necessary when nothing appears to be wrong?

Unfortunately, even late in the first decade of the 21st century, the nanny structure is still dominant in society, with (in my opinion) misguided authors leading the way. However, the TV nanny Jo Frost has a softer approach and one that I welcome. Isn't it time we had a happy medium?

EMOTIONAL NURTURING

It appears that we have not learnt the value of emotional nourishment being the key for the development of a confident and happy child. We need balance and yet I continually see people (of all ages, some in their 50s and 60s) who are still suffering from the effects of the disjointed nanny process of childcare that we have had over time. They come to me, and others like myself, still suffering and coming to terms with not receiving the emotional nurturing which was missing throughout their childhoods. Isn't it time for change and enlightenment?

I agree with Dr Spock that new mothers know more than they think. Women have natural instincts and if these are allowed to work via natural hormones and less interference, mums can tune into their baby's needs from day one. They can develop an awareness of their infant's emotional and physical expectations, creating a balance that is needed in the 21st century.

I believe that this type of parenting structure is essential for a happy child, providing a good family foundation and building a strong base for home and society.

nderstanding and education, we can bring new enlightenment into the parenting structure and awareness for generations to come. This is one of the aims of the 'One Generation Project', a non-profit organisation of which I am the founder. I have identified key areas that would help struggling parents and children, and set it up to help educate parents and families with new structures for health and information, giving support for all ages. (See appendix for details)

The need for attachment and memory learning

Babies come in to the world with an intense need for attachment. For infants who experience a lack of bonding, a state of dependency and memory learning is created at cell level. This causes memory patterns to develop which go into life and adulthood, affecting how they interact with others and continuing as a state of stress at a cellular level as the child grows. Such children lack biological nurturing at a foundation level because the natural enhancement through maternity and childbirth has been by-passed.

Our sympathetic system is reliant upon love and care, to reproduce a compassionate and loving nature. The brain responds to experience in order to develop the appropriate nerve and moral response. Maturing moral and emotional response is the key to a positive foundation from parents and carers.

Emotionally, the brain develops and responds. When a child is abused physically, verbally or sexually, the experience leaves an imprint of damage upon the developing brain. This is especially true when the child is unloved, molested or neglected in its early years, leading the brain to become skewed or warped to others' feelings and needs. Sometimes they can be numb or frozen and seen as non-functioning. They feel nothing.

We only know what we are shown

The old adage, 'we only know what we are shown', comes into another scale. Abuse creates more abuse and cruelty will make us cruel. A loop of non-emotion becomes established, creating tragic repercussions for the sufferer of the cruelty and others.
In the 1950s, USA research carried out by Harry Harlow on monkeys gave him some insight into emotional behaviour. By isolating the infants from their mothers at birth, he bred a colony of strong but

lonely monkeys who did not know how to socialize or interact with their peers. Although nutritionally well-fed, they were not emotionally nurtured and this made a huge difference to their social skills. Harlow found that the youngsters felt threatened by others and would lash out violently and shriek with fear when they came into contact with other monkeys. Harlow found that nutrition was not enough.

The second batch of monkeys to be born were again isolated, but given cloth nappies. The monkeys became obsessed with the cloth and the cloth became their comforter. Harlow improved upon this experiment with both a cloth mother and a wire mother, each holding food for the infants. The juvenile monkeys soon learned the difference and would spend time nuzzling and cuddling the soft fabric, feeling and replacing the warmth and tenderness of their real mother, whilst interaction with the wired substitute was kept short, just enough to take food[163]. Harlow concluded that, 'If monkeys have taught us anything, it's that you have got to learn how to love before you learn how to live' (as written in his biography Love at Goon Park by Deborah Blum).

He also found those who had nothing in their cages became psychopaths. They became sad and lonely, numb to all emotions, starting fights without provocation if they came into contact with another. They even attacked their offspring with vicious outcomes. If the offspring tried to cuddle they would be pushed away, perpetuating the cruelty. It seemed as though the mother felt nothing for them and, unfortunately, this pattern can also be formed in humans with no bonding at birth.

Romania's legacy

With contraception banned in Romania in 1966, the country saw a glut of unwanted children that parents couldn't feed. Orphanages were overwhelmed and, to this day, they are not supported much better. We have all heard the stories of babies left in cribs and toddlers tied to their cots. In most cases these children were not even touched and nobody spent time with them. These children were unloved and many who survived the orphanages (many died before they were five years old) became psychologically scarred. They were socially incapable of interaction and were often hostile to strangers. Many suffered severe emotional trauma and impairments, which led them to behave abusively towards one another, while others suffered physical disorders which ranged from untreated infections to stunted growth.

Couples who adopted Romanian children reported that the children suffered an array of behavioural disorders. Some cried if they were touched, while others would look into space for hours and suddenly fly into a rage, attacking anything within reach[164].

Effects on mental ability and social interaction

Research showed that these orphans had less brain activity in the regions which show emotion and which are essential for social interaction (the orbitofrontal cortex and the amygdala) and that they could not perceive emotions in others or feel sympathy. Like autistic children, they could not interpret facial expressions. They also showed significantly reduced levels of the hormones oxytocin and vasopressin, both of which are essential for the development of social attachments[165]. (as discussed in section 12)

I have treated adults in their 60s and70s who were still being affected by the birth process, the lack of bonding that took place at birth and the emotional effects received in the womb. The patterns instilled left them with emotional weaknesses which endured throughout their lives and which affected their interactions in relationships with others, leading to low self-esteem and self-confidence. Feeling as though they did not belong, they felt lost and experienced unexplained anxiousness and nervousness.

SENSITIVE CHILDREN

I have noticed that many babies born over the last decade are highly sensitive. To many, these children are known as Crystal and Rainbow children, although I like to call them 'Sensitive's'.

Sensitive children have been coming into the world for some time now and many are already adults and teens. The children that I have come into contact with recently, however, are 'ultra sensitive'.

The sensitive children have extra needs emotionally, more so than those that came before, and they are demanding it right from the womb. As we know, chemicals and hormones are exchanged in the womb, providing a communication of needs from the foetus to the mother. I have known mothers suffering longer periods of morning sickness carrying these children. (I was abnormally sick throughout one of my pregnancies) I now believe (as I didn't know then) that it is because we are adapting and blending their higher energy with ours.

Children known as crystals

Crystal babies are usually big babies whose heads initially seem bigger than normal (proportionally too big for their bodies.) They tend to have large piercing eyes and will often stare at people intensely for long periods of time, something that can be disturbing for adults who are not used to being energetically read by an infant.

Crystals are very loving and caring children who have an intense bonding with their mothers. Crystals are so sensitive that it can be traumatic to their system if they are away from mum (more so than their parents known as Indigos and elder Crystals who came before them).

Even the temporary absence of the mother can be disruptive and can create emotional trauma for the child, such as when taken to nursery in order to allow mum to return to work. In fact, I know of one child who started to have asthma attacks the day he began attending nursery. So severe were the attacks that he went through a tough time and ended up using inhalers at a very young age, as well as being officially labelled as asthmatic.

Another effect of the strong bond that Crystals have with their mothers is they may feel overcome by mum's pain and suffering. They have the ability to feel what mum feels, which in situations like this will overload their own energy system. They can even be traumatized to the extent of having seizures and I knew one little boy who had anaphylactic shock when mum went into hospital.

Because Crystal children are so sensitive to energy and emotions, they readily pick up on other's issues, anxiety and distress, especially those of the parents. Sensing and homing in on other's unresolved issues can be negative and toxic to the child, which will ultimately affect them physically, energetically and emotionally. This can be felt, by both adults and children (in fact all ages – as over time we have learnt where and whom to avoid).

The sensitive's, will also be affected by visitors and environmental energies. Many parents now screen who they allow in the home and are mindful of where they go as they know it will affect their child(ren). This has become common practice for some parents.

Baby crystals and rainbow crystals

Crystals are usually very calm and good babies. They bond well, but always intensely with their mothers, a bond which is so intense that it has been known to last up to the age of 4-5 years old.

Rainbow Crystal babies, however, may be seen as having clingy behaviour. From my own observations they are extremely sensitive to food and drink and some do not fare well on allopathic medicine (prescribed drugs). Sensitive children seem to be better suited to homeopathic medicine and alternative therapies such as Cranio Sacral Therapy, Baby massage, Healing and Bowen Technique.

Known as Rainbow children, they seem to be fearless and see everything as new and exciting. They want to try everything and even trying to (jump) fly from an upper window has been known. Unfortunately, being fearless, they have no knowledge of the dangers of doing such things.

Rainbows are hugely sensitive to their environment and parents of Rainbow children need to be willing to deal with and work through their issues in order to provide a stable home for their children. Rainbow children can become very frustrated and angry when they find their world restrictive. Tending to have a steady focus on what they want to do and achieve, they are determined children and parents need to have lots of patients when dealing with them.

Sometimes they appear unsure how to handle their body and I sense they are exasperated by the physical limitations of the human body in general. I have seen this in my own practice when treating Rainbow Crystal children. They can be seen to be in a paddy or tantrum as they reach toddler age, especially if they cannot get their own way.
It is an exasperation more associated with himself or herself, than with anyone else however. Being very determined, they know what they want and take little notice of warnings from parents or carers as they are fixed upon their intent. Some may see these children as angry and aggressive. (See case study 18, section 24)

SENSITIVE'S' FOOD & ALLERGIES

As with sensitive Indigo adults and teens, Crystals have sensitive digestive systems.

Giving them cola drinks and chocolate is like giving them a drug - they will over-react and become hyperactive or aggressive by throwing a tantrum. This is normally followed by a crash in blood sugar level when the effect wears off and to the child it will feel like the awful withdrawal symptoms that follow a sudden cessation of sugar or caffeine, just like an adult addicted to drink or drugs.
Crystal children struggle to tolerate our normal diet, finding it too dense for their refined high-energy systems. Many will only eat vegetarian food and sometimes fish. Usually they don't like meat. They have a tendency to allergies resulting from dairy and wheat intolerance, sometimes from birth.

Mums would need a careful diet while breast-feeding and might wish to consider useful alternatives such as soya, rice, oat or goat's milk. Obvious allergies or disorders from what most people consider a normal diet would include eczema, digestive problems, sinus, ear, nose and throat disorders.

Right-brain orientated children and adults (see below for details) need a balanced diet of:

- Protein,
- Vegetables
- Cooked food
- Good fresh air and exercise

Left-brain orientated children and adults prefer a lighter diet of:

- Juices - vegetable and/or fruit juices
- Raw food
- Good fresh air and exercise

Regular detoxing and fasting are needed to balance the diet in left-brain adults and teenagers, although these methods should not to be used for babies and children.

This is a general observation and tendencies will also be active through previous conditioning from parents etc.,

See appendix for details on organic and free-from products

Natural abilities

We are hearing more and more reports of children not talking or interacting as young as they used to and health care programmes being put in place to help with speech therapists etc., interacting with young children. I have observed that Crystals and Rainbow Crystals are children with natural abilities and special gifts. Some have no need for speech and receive input in other ways. Through telepathic communication they make contact with other crystals, siblings and parents, and are apt to read energy fields constantly.

They are very lovable, caring and compassionate. Born with full consciousness of the heart, their heart chakra is open from birth, meaning that they have been born with unconditional love already integrated.

Being telepathic in some respects, they may be late in showing verbal communication and also late developers in terms of crawling and walking. In some cases they only realise the importance of direct speech when they begin to socialise outside of the home, forcing a need to communicate with those who are not telepathic.

Crystal Rainbows have another unique way with communication. Not only do they communicate with telepathy, but when they meet you they will look above your head to read your energy field and soul connection. They seem to look right through you and only once they have observed who you are through your energy system, will they then look into your eyes. This is particularly common with Rainbow children.

Through their own unique way they can look at your soul-being to read and perceive who you truly are. From this, they also know what is in your heart. They will sense if you live your life with love and can see if your heart chakra is open. What the child is doing is reading who you are via your soul records. At the same time, they will also read your aura and energy fields (chakras), giving them an overview of you. Your energy field will tell them about your consciousness, of how open you are or to what level of consciousness you aspire and even down to the condition of your health.

Our energy field holds an enormous amount of information about our past, present and future. For those with the eyes to see, this can be most informative, as they know everything about you in an instant.

Rainbow Crystals are highly evolved consciously. They come with a natural inbuilt ability to translate obscure energy fields, often reading information and understanding in a heartbeat. This is a giant leap beyond reading simple body language.

I run regular workshops on the 'New Kids on the Block' in which I explain in detail the needs of our sensitive children and adults. (See appendix for more information)

[162] Wikipedia the free encyclopaedia 'Benjamin Spock' http://www.com/article,O,15104298+agemo.200 and http//en.wikipeadia. org/wiki/Benjamin_spock (cited 07.2008)

[163] Jonah Lehrer 'The Decisive Moment' Cannon Gate 2009 (Ref: Harlow p184)

[164] Ibid (Ref: 'The scars of abuse' p185)

[165] Ibid (Ref: 'Fellow Feeling' p179)

Chapter 17

INDEX

Chapter 17

BREAST FEEDING

Breast milk is produced and stimulated by the baby suckling. When born and placed on the mother's chest, a baby will climb up to the breast if allowed to do so. It will automatically root for the nipple and massage the breast with its hands. Oxytocin will be released at this time to activate and stimulate milk production as blood vessels dilate to create warmth. Nerve impulses from the hypothalamus release oxytocin into the blood stream, affecting the muscles and milk ducts.

The contraction of the muscles and cells produce and squeeze milk out through the nipple. Oxytocin stimulates prolactin, a hormone which increases milk production, as well as stimulating glucagon (an insulin hormone) which encourages the release of nutrients from the mother's body storage area to provide baby with enough resources.

Remember, when the child sucks it stimulates the milk. It is a reflex action that is remembered and when the mother sees or hears her baby cry she may experience a tightening of her breasts from the pressure of milk. The front of the mother's body will become warmer to nurture and give warmth while feeding. Skin to skin, baby will not cry and the warmer the mum, the warmer the baby. The child also feels safe next to the mother's (or father) chest, with a feeling of security and protection within their energy field being instilled into the child. Breast-feeding also increases other senses between mother and child, including hearing, smell, sight and eye contact.

Breast-feeding is the age-old way to feed and nourish your newborn baby. It is not a fad but a basic survival process adapted over millennia by many animal species, including humans. Basically, mankind evolved to our present day greatness through breast-feeding. With the advent of bottle-feeding, the whole concept of breast-feeding became secondary, depriving newborns of essential immunities normally passed on from the mother to child.

Although breast-feeding is now the new preference, it is still an old and proven way of caring for your child when it is born. However, there are a lot of pressures and conflicting advice on the subject given to mothers, which can be a minefield if it is your first child. Modern mums need to negotiate their way through books and the words of councillors and health visitors. Even parents and in-laws want to have their say, often repeating 'in my day we did…'. Of course, you want to do the right thing as a mother, but it can put more pressure and anxiety on a new mum to make the right decision before the baby arrives.

Breast feeding does not suit all

Some mothers find the breast-feeding process so difficult they begin to despair. They are hurting and the baby is crying, upset and unsettled. No one can give a straight answer as to what is best for mum or what she should do. My advice, since it is your choice at the end of the day, is to do what feels right for you.

Sometimes it just takes a different feeding pattern for baby and, after adjustment, everything calms down for both mother and child.

Suckling

Occasionally it is the baby that cannot suckle as well as it should do. Baby becomes just as frustrated as the mother, who is trying her best. I have found that a Cranio Sacral treatment can help correct suckling disorders very easily, with immediate improvement in the baby-suckling reflex. Having successfully treated children with this disorder in recent years, the response can be instant, giving overwhelming relief for both mother and child. I wish I had known about this for my first child.

Previously new mothers have thought it was their fault that they could not breast-feed. However through trials and investigations we are now seeing other links to poor breast-feeding including hormonal imbalances and drugs taken in childbirth.

Drugs have also been linked to poor breast-feeding

A 2006 Australian study indicated that mothers who receive pain-relieving drugs, such as epidurals and pethadine, at childbirth are twice as likely to give up trying to breast-feed. They also linked baby's suckling impairments at the breast to baby's born with the effects of drugs given to the mother. [166]

New research shows that Hormones affect breast-feeding abilities

A recent Norwegian study[167] has indicated that some women have higher levels of Testosterone (male sex hormone) while pregnant, with the impact of negative implications in the development of glandular tissue in the breast having the knock on effect of a reduced ability of being able to breast-feed.

They have concluded that the hormone balance in the womb dictates the direction of the ability to breast-feed rather than the breast milk itself.

Not all mothers succeed with breast-feeding. It can make some feel utterly miserable, which in turn has an adverse effect on the child, who also picks up mum's feelings and reacts accordingly. A vicious circle ensues.

My own personal experience

After my first pregnancy, I tried to breast-feed. It turned out to be unsuccessful and I was only able to breast-feed for ten days. I found that my daughter was not suckling enough and I needed to express, which was painful. I then developed mastitis, which was very sore and my breasts became hard like footballs. I had no option but to change to bottle-feeding in the end, as we were both getting frustrated and upset with the situation.

When we find difficulty in breast-feeding, we can feel that we have let ourselves and the baby down, but even giving breast milk for the vital first ten days will give your child what is needed, so it is not a waste of time. Remember, baby needs the immunity you pass on through your own milk.

Getting to know your baby's cries will tell you when he or she is hungry. Sometimes, however, it can take a little time to identify what baby is crying for. Is it wind? Is it frustration? Is it that the child's nappy needs changing and that he or she is uncomfortable? Is the baby tired and in need of sleep? Does he or she just want a cuddle to feel safe? To start with this can be a hit and miss process but eventually instinct takes over.

Theories about breast –feeding

At an anti-natal class, mums may be told to use 'the walnut theory' where the stomach of the child is compared to a walnut because a baby's stomach is small and only holds about an ounce of milk. It needs to be fed often, sometimes up to 12 to 15 times a day according to some wise folk, the theory being that as the stomach expands, so the child can take more feed. However, if your child is bottle-fed it will take 2–3 ounces from day one and some professionals will suggest that a baby be fed only six to eight times a day.

It is normal for most babies to feed approximately every two to four hours during the first six weeks of life, which works out as six to nine feeds a day. If they start to sleep through the night, this will reduce to five feeds.

In the first six weeks the baby will sleep between feeds, providing that it does not have too much wind or colic to unsettle it. Having wind is very painful, as you know yourself. Wind can get trapped in the shoulder area. and nooks and crannies of the colon causing pain.

The vagus nerve can cause problems because, as we have already described, vagus nerve dysfunction from being at an awkward angle in the birth canal can cause digestion problems. Cranio Sacral Therapy can help to alleviate digestion problems in babies and re-establish the correct nervous system function. Baby massage also helps with colic and trapped wind. (See the sections on baby massage (12) and (13) for vagus nerve and CST)

DIET AND BREAST FEEDING

Diet is important when breast feeding, as a mother who breast-feeds can inadvertently cause stomach disruption for the baby. Care is needed when eating, as certain foods can adversely affect the baby's health with stomachaches and wind being the result of the mother's diet. Beware, therefore, of eating too many dairy products, as well as pulses, cauliflower, cabbage and spicy foods, which can also contribute to baby's colic problems. Steer clear too of too much caffeine in drinks such as coffee, alcohol and fizzy drinks like cola, as well as avoiding smoking.

Diet has a strong influence on mothers during breast-feeding, and even more so on the choice of foods for baby when weaning. Various foods have an influence on the respiratory system, especially where there are breathing problems such as those caused by phlegm, colds and bronchitis. Dairy foods, chocolate, fried foods, red meat, oranges, bananas and peanuts all increase mucus in the body and are better avoided by mother and baby while suffering these disorders.

Immunity

Before birth, the gastrointestinal tract (GI) is sterile. Colonisation starts from the birth canal as bacteria is collected from the mother, unless of course the child is born via C-section. Additional 'good' bacteria come from breast milk, which builds a sound foundation for the infant's immune system, increasing its health and survival as a result of receiving its mother's immune-enhancing protection.

Whether a child continues to receive the mother's protection through breast milk will depend upon the time that she can give to the child. Opting to move to formula will not give the same lasting protection and it will depend entirely upon how healthy the mother's immune protection and bacteria are during the time it is available. Unhealthy bacteria from the mother, equals unhealthy immunity for her child. (As discussed in section 7 'Candida')

Although not often realised, we spend the rest of our lives trashing the immunity we were given in the first instances of life, through inappropriate eating and poor diet. Lifestyle choices in adulthood cause the wrong kind of bacteria to breed within the GI tract. A healthy GI tract is crucial for a good immune system overall for you and your baby.

Good bacteria aids digestion and nutrient absorption, helping prevent the growth of bad or undesirable flora. Previous generations have been exposed to a variety of bacteria and have built up a natural resistance with time and through our mothers, but today we seem to be less exposed to all types of bacteria, including 'good' sources. Antibacterial products and hand sanitizers have made our environment a lot cleaner, but are we healthier?

We have shifted our focus to the extent that it has become necessary to add good bacteria to our food for daily ingestion. However, due to strict food safety regulations, the pasteurisation and sterilisation processes, which are intended to kill off all forms of bacteria also see less of the added good bacteria actually surviving.

More and more people find it necessary to take a daily supplement of probiotics to counteract a variety of lifestyle-induced problems. If you find that your child is suffering from conditions such as colic, taking a probiotic may help while breast-feeding, as the child will receive the benefits of good bacteria through the milk received.

Differences in micro flora

Breast-fed and bottle fed children also have differences in micro flora. In breast-fed infants, good bacteria (Bifidobacteria) tend to dominate. A recent trial showed that gut flora of breast versus formula-fed babies was still significantly different at 6 months of age[168]. Results showed that formula feeding led to a persistent reduction of good bacteria compared to breast-feeding, even after the breast-feeding period was completed. It was found that the imbalance could be corrected and adjusted through taking probiotics or prebiotic supplementation.

Human breast milk, in addition, contains a higher ratio of omega 3:6 EFA, a level beyond that which is found in formula milk. Breast-feeding, therefore, is associated with possible enhanced brain development. Omega 3 fats are necessary for the development of the human brain during pregnancy and during the first two years of life.

Flow of breast milk

For some mothers the supply of milk can take time to come into full flow during the first few days. Nipples can be sore and excruciatingly painful, although this can subside fairly quickly. For others it can continue to be a painful and unhappy experience. Sometimes this is the case because the child is not latching on correctly and an expert (midwife) can show techniques that will correct the problem quickly for you. The National Childbirth Trust can also give advice on breast-feeding.

Once latched on correctly, you will notice that the baby will pat or knock the breast with his or her hand, this being an instinctive way to stimulate the flow of breast milk.

Smoking and breast-feeding

Unfortunately, smoking decreases oxytocin in nursing mothers. The production of breast milk is therefore affected by producing less milk[169] as discussed in section 11. NHS information suggests that smoking doubles the chances of your baby developing colic.

OBESITY AND EARLY FEEDING

A Bristol University study in 2006 found that babies fed on formula milk and weaned on to solid food too early were heavier than expected at 5 years old, therefore having a greater risk of developing obesity[170].

They also found that formula-fed babies were less likely to eat fruit and vegetables, with a liking for more commercial infant drinks, suggesting a basic desire for higher calorific food and drink.

Another issue with bottle-fed children is that they are given an allotted quota of formula, whereas breast-fed children will self-regulate their intake. Subsequently, when solid foods are introduced, breast-fed children will reduce and regulate milk intake accordingly, whereas bottle-fed children are often given the same fixed quantity and in most cases accept it, taking in more calories and forming patterns for overeating. As a result, some experts conclude that breast-fed babies are better able to regulate their food and energy intake than formula-fed children.

ALLERGIES LINKED TO BOTTLE-FEEDING

Allergies are now being linked to bottle-fed babies, as breast-fed children do not seem to have the same reactions. Allergies are seen as a major factor in ear infections and it is now understood that cow's milk is richer in proteins and will produce more mucus within the body. I would say that nature knows best.

Feeding bottles

In 2007 we had headlines of scientists calling a ban on chemicals used in plastic containers, baby feeding and sports water bottles. The chemical called 'bisphenol A' (known as BPA) was used in baby bottles sold in the UK. At a scientists meeting in the USA research was highlighted where animal studies showed an adverse effect of BPA as it mimics Oestrogen causing abnormal development of reproductive organs in females. It is also linked to ADHD, obesity, type 2 Diabetes, Autism, low sperm counts and an increase in breast and prostate cancer.

Scientists also highlighted that the chemical was used in products such as microwave dishes, liners in canned food and water cooler containers.[171] Since this revelation we have had other calls for care with chemical release into food and drink from plastic containers, and especially those heated in the Microwave. We are still learning about adverse affects from plastics and time will tell who was right.

In the meantime, concerns are with the effects of BPA and its interference on organ development with the developing child.

 Whether you are expressing breast milk or using formula, I suggest using a glass feeding bottle. Plastic contains dioxin chemicals, which cause cancer and are highly poisonous to the cells of our bodies. John Hopkins Hospital suggests the following measures to ensure optimum health benefits:

- No Plastic containers in the microwave
- No water bottles in the freezer
- No plastic film wrap in the microwave

For the good health of your baby please do not, under any circumstances, put baby bottles in the microwave.

Discomfort during breast feeding

Some women suffer from pain and discomfort during breast-feeding other than for the reasons already mentioned, such as due to:

.

- Uterine cramping
- Engorgement
- Blocked ducts
- Mastitis

Uterine cramping

For some women, the same hormone that stimulates milk production (oxytocin) can also cause uterine contractions while breast-feeding. These are usually felt in the first few days after giving birth. Medication, can be prescribed by your doctor to alleviate the pain and discomfort.

Engorgement

This is a feeling of fullness in the breasts. It comes from both milk production and increased blood flow to the breasts for the muscles to release milk more easily. For some women, breasts feel only a moderate increase, while others feel engorged. Here are some tips that could help:

- Buy a good bra to help support while breast feeding
- Breast-feeding every two hours will help to relieve the pressure build-up
- Express milk between feeds
- Use a warm compress on the breasts
- Ice packs can help
- Kneading gently on particular areas of pain can offer some relief (try doing this in the shower with warm water)

Please note - over-expressing or pumping large amounts can send the wrong message to the body, producing more milk and exacerbating the situation.

Old wives tales recommend raw cabbage leaves over the breast for relief of engorgement and hardness. I have not tried this myself but others tell me that it has given them some relief.

Blocked ducts

Blocked ducts should be treated promptly to avoid infection. Pain is usually local to one particular area and is often apparent with a reddened area of the breast. Blocked ducts occur when the flow of milk is obstructed. Again, here are a few suggestions that you can try:

- A warm compress before feeding can help reduce the incidence
- Have your baby feed on the sore breast first to allow most suction to occur
- Change feeding from one side to the other more frequently to allow for more even feeding
- If the problem persists, you will need to seek professional advice
- Always consult your doctor if a fever or pain increases and the lump is not going down

Alternatively contact your health care professional for homeopathic remedies to help with the disorder.

Mastitis

This can be a local infection involving part of the breast or even the entire breast. It is very painful and can occur without warning, with the symptoms being similar to those for flu. You may experience headache, flu-like symptoms, fever, redness on the breasts and feeling tender, although breast symptoms may not show immediately and can often occur a few days later.

If you think you might be suffering from mastitis, you must seek medical advice. Antibiotics are often prescribed and can clear the disorder within 36-48 hours. Do not stop breast-feeding suddenly as this can lead to a breast abscess, but instead try and feed if you can with the sore breast first. It can taste a little more salty than normal and baby may not like the taste, although it is not believed to be harmful to the child. Alternatively, you can pump and express instead. Don't use ice packs, but warm compresses used frequently may help to ease the discomfort.

Homeopathic remedies

There is a range of homeopathic remedies, which can help with breast-feeding related pain or discomfort.

- Bryonia 6c is useful for abscess brewing with hardening of the breast tissue and pain
- Belladonna 6c for symptoms as above with red streaks on the affected breast
- Hepar sulph 6c for pain, irritability and extreme tenderness
- Phytolacca 6c for when the armpit glands are swollen, for when you are looking generally pale and feeling shivery
- Silicea 6c for nipples which are cracked and discharging pus and general exhaustion

For more information, a good book to consult is The Family Guide to Homeopathy by Dr. Andrew Lockie. (see appendix for details)

USEFUL TIPS

If you have stitches from the birth process, you need to keep the area clean. Use Rescue remedy and Crab Apple in the water when you bathe or wash. Apply Rescue remedy cream and take arnica for a quicker recovery rate.

You can also use Rescue Remedy cream for sore nipples, as this is soothing and healing or, alternatively, arnica cream. For a cracked nipple, use calendula ointment.

- Old wives tales suggest geranium or small cabbage leaves inside the bra for relief of sore nipples.

Bach Flower Remedy suggestions - useful post-natally

Gentian – use for disappointment. Gentian gives a feeling of more positive thoughts
Mustard – depression or low in spirit
Olive – use for fatigue
Pine – use for feelings of guilt or let others down
Pine – use with feelings of back-lash and the unexpected.

Rock Rose – use for those times we may feel stunned or slightly shocked/panic – useful during last days of pregnancy and post natally
Sweet Chestnut – use for feeling trapped or despair
Star of Bethlehem – use to buffer shock and trauma - generally useful post-natally

ESSENTIAL FATTY ACIDS AND LACTATION

Since the 1970s, fish oils have been known to help prevent heart disease as well as being good for the brain. Trials took place in the 70s after Greenland Eskimos were found to have exceptionally low incidences of heart disease and arthritis, despite the fact they had a high fat diet.

Essential fatty acids have also proven to be beneficial during pregnancy and lactation[172]. Trials have shown that during pregnancy, daily supplementation of EFA is beneficial for both the mother and the baby. The recommended daily intake is 1g–10g daily during pregnancy and lactation.

Several studies have also established a clear association between low levels of Omega 3 fatty acids and depression. Countries with a population having high levels of fish consumption have shown far fewer cases of depression.

Essential Fatty Acids also help with pain and arthritis symptoms. Research indicates in addition that a high blood level of Omega 3, combined with a low level of Omega 6 acids, reduces the risk of developing breast cancer. Daily supplementation of 2.5grams of Omega 3, have been found to be effective.

Deficient in Omega 3

It is estimated that 85% or more of people in the Western world are deficient in Omega 3 fatty acids, which can be found in flaxseed oil, walnut oil, marine plankton and fatty fish. Apparently the western world gets too much omega 6 fatty acids in their diet these days, with vegetarian diets especially tending to be very high in Omega 6. Omega 6 fatty acids are mainly from vegetable oils such as corn and soy containing a high proportion of linolenic acid.

As we have mentioned previously, when buying fish oils, be sure to check out the quality as not all fish oils are pure. Low quality oils may be unstable and contain significant amounts of mercury, pesticides and undesirable oxidation products from water-borne pollution. High quality oils, however, are usually guaranteed to be clean and packaged in an area that precludes the sensitive delicate fatty acids from light.

WHEN YOU WANT TO STOP BREAST-FEEDING

Milk depletes naturally, usually within six months, at which point you will need to substitute breast milk with formula (powdered milk). Some mums, however, do continue to breast feed until the child is much older.

Children today are more sensitive to milk and dairy products overall and you may find that your child does not enjoy or like formula. They may react and have skin rashes, become chesty and/or be lactose intolerant. In these cases, you would be best to change over to an alternative non-dairy or lactose free option from your doctor. Older children can change to soya based or oat milk, or even goat's milk if your child is not lactose intolerant, although some health visitors may question this suggestion. (See section below on lactose intolerance for more information)

It is a good idea to introduce your child to drinking water between feeds. Warm or cool is ideal, but not cold water, as this is not good for the digestion. In the old days, sugar was put into warm water as a soother to settle in the night, but this can be counterproductive. We now know the pitfalls of bestowing the child with a sweet tooth, which can become an addiction to sugar in later life and lead to the onslaught of early diabetes and tooth decay.

When I was a baby my mother gave me Delrosa (sugary syrup) and I distinctly remember when small that she used to dip my brother's dummy in sugar to comfort him. We now know that these pacifying habits were not good for us and it certainly didn't help me.

FEEDING ROUTINE

Some mothers feed on demand, which is the native and Eastern way of caring for children. With on-demand feeding, the child has constant physical contact - the necessary expectation of a newborn. In the east they use this as the normal way to care for their babies. During the day, the child is kept close to the mother via a sling. At night, the baby sleeps next to the parents and is fed on demand. For the child, this is the natural progression from pre-natal life.

Because of our hectic lifestyles today we seem to be pressured to just feed and change the child, with no contact in between. This was the way it was done by the nannies - a strict regime where the child was left to cry and cry. They were fed to a schedule and had absolutely no contact in between.

This approach has left a lot of children (and adults) feeling unloved. For a prime example, look at Prince Charles with the legacy of his mother only shaking his hand. After being away for months on end, he would stand like a lost soul to meet her on the station and then shake hands. His wife Diana showed a different way, by hugging and kissing her children when she saw them. Contact and love is what our babies need. It is what they strive for.

Some mums feel the need to put the baby in their own bed, whilst others find it easier to put the cot or crib next to their bed, so that the child can feel the presence of mum and dad nearby. This makes the child feel secure and safe. Putting your child in a separate room right from the start will make them feel unwanted and abandoned. How do I know this? I know this because I have treated many, many adults who have abandonment issues of feeling unloved (even in their sixties and seventies). Invariably it goes back to the lack of bonding and absence of love from their parents, especially their mother. The child's subconscious knows and registers everything. Nothing is forgotten.

From the moment of conception, all your baby has known is you (their mother). To be separated from you for whatever reason, whether at the hospital or in the home, can bring fear and trauma to the child. When you have your baby nearby, you continually bond with him or her. Your baby will feel loved, cared for and wanted. He or she will feel supported by the parents, having confidence and feeling safe as a result. This gives children the foundation for life.

Once this confidence is achieved, your baby will not be too affected by any temporary separation. For some children this can take between six to nine months, whilst for others it could take longer, depending upon the trauma and time of separation. Every child is individual and you should go by your own instinct (mother's intuition) to know when the time is right for you and your child to stop breast-feeding.

NAPPIES

Real nappies vs. Disposables

Apart from deciding how best to feed your baby either breast or bottle-fed, you will also need to decide which nappy to use.

Over the last few decades we have had the change-over to disposable nappies – believed to be a boon in their time and very convenient for mum, especially when out and about away from home.

When I was bringing up my children, I used terry towel nappies, cotton squares which I admit added to the washing. However, they were soft, kind to skin, appreciated by the infant and I always thought a line of white nappies blowing in the wind was a pleasure to see. I found them easy to use but bulky when travelling away from home.

The real benefit to buying cotton nappies, as in my day, was you bought them once and they lasted for the term of the child till potty training and beyond. Obviously some would need to be replaced over the term, although if in good condition they would be put away and used for the expected next child.

Today we have a reawakening to real nappies This time they are shaped like the disposable ones, with poppers that expand the nappy as the child grows. Because they are shaped and less bulky (they also come in different sizes) there may be several purchases of different sizes as your baby grows. However, the benefits are that they will save you money overall. No longer will you need to buy them weekly as with disposable nappies.

The other benefits to cotton nappies are that it is good for the environment. I remember when disposable nappies came in and we had a family close by who used them; the amount they went through astonished me. Logically, when you think about it, if a child is changed every couple of hours and several times a day for up to two years (in some cases) the amount purchased must be phenomenal. Of course you also have the trips to the supermarket to collect them and room to store them, I heard of a supermarket who put the beer next to the display of disposable nappies so that when dad was calling off on his way home to collect the next few purchases of nappies he would buy his beer - a good marketing ploy that paid off.

Now unfortunately, we are hearing that disposable nappies take a long time to decompose, so not as green as we thought for the environment. With the boon of disposable nappies comes the disposal at waste tips, which has been talked about by the media and councils as an addition to our ever-building waste problems.

Here are some facts from Waste Watch:

- It can take hundreds of years for a disposable nappy to biodegrade in our diminishing waste tips and land fill sites.
- Where I live in Wales, a staggering 240million are thrown away every year, almost 500 every minute. Figures suggest that a child would use a total of 5850 nappies in their lifetime and amazingly the weight of this would equal the same weight as an average family car! This does not take into account the cost of thousands of disposables purchased, which is staggering.
- Real nappies are made from natural fibres with no chemical gels or paper pulp
- No pins are needed as in my day. They come with poppers or Velcro fastenings.
- No need to boil or soak – nappies can be washed in the washing machine at 60 degrees, and biodegradable liners can be flushed down the toilet.

I believe that mums have the best of both worlds today, with cotton nappies that do not leak like the disposable ones; they are more comfortable for the infant and cost less. They are also easy to use and can be put in the washing machine. The benefits are both environmental and pocket friendly.

Use disposable ones when out and about away from home, although I know the new shaped cotton ones are smaller and take up the same room.
Investigate the benefits of cotton nappies. I know mums who have used disposable ones in the past and find the cotton ones even better.

I would say it is a win-win situation for all, comfort for the child, reduced costs, good for the environment and convenient to change to real nappies.
(See appendix for details and suppliers)

GROWING WITH LOVE AND CONTACT

Research has shown that premature babies grow faster with touch and contact. In one trial, an entire group was only fed and changed whilst the other group was also cuddled, talked to and touched in a loving way. The group, which had full contact, responded with increased bodyweight daily, while the ignored (nanny) group were slow to put on weight.

Obviously schedules are needed, but don't force your baby into a harsh routine. Routines are primarily for mums and do not necessarily suit young children. I knew a mother who used to splash water on her very young baby's face to wake her when she wanted to feed her. She used a strict feeding schedule so that the baby would fit in with their family life! There were no lapses, nor reprieves; baby had to feed to mum's schedule. Since she was not ready to feed at that time the child would sometimes posit (vomit) and bring it all back.

Your child will let you know when he or she is hungry. Give your baby a chance to settle and let them find their own routine. Every child is different and no two babies are exactly the same. When you have had more than one child you will know that this is true. Listen to their emotional and physical needs, as what suits one will not necessarily suit another. Your child may, for example, have had a traumatic birth and need reassurance, although all babies need to feel safe. Contact gives them that security. Don't forget that mum is the only person the child has known for nine months. They know her smell, her breathing pattern and her voice.

Over time, you and your baby will get to know which routine suits you both and indeed babies and mum both need a compatible routine. It helps you get through the day and sometimes you can and will break that routine to suit the events of the day. Introduce your routine gradually so that you both get used to it and don't be afraid to adjust and fine-tune it for both your needs. Babies are not dolls to be brought out to play with and then put away. Remember, a healthy baby thrives far better on a happy routine rather than chaos.

Dad's role

You need to be realistic about your baby's needs and contact, and not only does the child needs both parents, but Dad needs to feel part of the event too. Lots of new mums forget this by pushing partners and husbands away. They feel that it is their duty alone to look after the new arrival.

Breast-feeding is a wonderful bonding experience for the mother and child, but we need to balance the Dad's role too. Include Dad as much as possible in your routine and don't be the martyr! You will soon realise that you need some rest between feeds, especially if you are breast-feeding, so get into the routine of expressing your milk so that Dad can do some of the evening and night feeds.

Baby massage is also a wonderful way to include Dads. This is a role where he can indulge himself and enjoy his new pride and joy while you do something else, or just to give you a break from the routine to have a rest. It creates a bonding that will be with them for life, as what you do at this stage is life forming. After all, it has been a partnership to produce the baby and the partnership goes on through all stages of development. Dad's involvement during pregnancy is as support for mum and, when the baby arrives, in caring for and looking after the baby together as a team, bringing baby up in a confident and loving manner and sharing all aspects of care.

Bonding with the father is so important and can influence from the start how a child's behaviour is founded, so affecting them later in life. I treat teenagers with behavioural issues on a regular basis and find that the bonding process can still be a big issue, with anger and frustration kicking in at the adolescent stage in life.
Discussing adolescents' behaviour and the issues from birth with a senior school headmistress recently, she confided in me that she believed 'most boys who were struggling with anger and frustration were doing so due to a lack of bonding with their parents, especially the father.'

Alfalfa and Breast-feeding

Alfalfa is a natural product, which contains all the vitamins and minerals necessary for life and so offers a huge number of benefits to people of all ages. It is high in natural digestive enzymes, full of amino acids, vitamins and minerals and contains four times more vitamin C than most citrus fruit, as well as more than 40 different bioflavonoids. Not only is it useful for the mother to take while breast-feeding, but the baby receives the benefits too.

In nursing mothers, alfalfa works by enhancing the quality and quantity of the mother's milk. When taking alfalfa in your diet or in supplement form it will also help with:

- Combating fatigue and anaemia
- Relieving water retention and excess fluid
- Acting as a tonic
- Nourishing blood and improving digestion

Alfalfa nourishes the blood and guts by tonifying the intestines and digestive energies and neutralising acids and toxins in the body. It nourishes kidneys and guts, carries intestinal waste from the body, helps to soften stools and improves the contracting action of the colon. As a result, it regulates digestive disorders and malabsorption, reduces heartburn, gas and bloating and breaks down fat, cellulose and starch in the body.

Alfalfa is also useful for those with asthma, pneumonia and bronchitis, as it reduces inflammation in the lungs. It is a natural deodoriser and infection fighter because it has a high content of chlorophyll and vitamin A.

Taken in tablet, powder, tea or tincture form, you can either:

- Drink 2 cups of alfalfa tea every other day
- Make your own or buy alfalfa sprouts and use in salads
- Take 2 x 2000–4000mg capsules 3 times daily
- Take it in liquid chlorophyll form on a daily basis

For optimum results, you need to take it for 3–6 months in whichever form you prefer.

Ionising Radiation

Working environment and ionising radiation

External radiation can get into the body through swallowing or breathing in minute radioactive particles, although it is believed that the amounts of natural radiation that we receive are very small. If you work with radioactive materials or equipment, which emits radiation, you will need to talk to your employer to avoid being in these areas while pregnant.

According to the 1999 Health and Safety Executive guidelines, even exposure while breast-feeding can be hazardous as it could contaminate your milk and affect your baby.

If you work as a member of a team of air-crew, travel by air or are employed as an X-ray diagnostic technician in a hospital, you are also at risk of being affected.

The general belief is that single X-rays do not cause a lasting effect on the body. However, the same cannot be said for multiple X-rays. If you receive a lot over a short period of time, it could affect your baby so, if in doubt, it is best to consult your medical practitioner.

If you work with diagnostic X-ray machines, it is advisable to stay away from the patient and X-ray tube while working. Stand behind a protective screen during X-ray exposure and make sure that a lead apron is used and is securely fastened to completely protect the abdominal area.

Even if you are only working next door to the X-ray department in a hospital or in administration at a nuclear power plant, you could still be affected. Working conditions would need to change to accommodate less exposure during your pregnancy and time of breast-feeding.

Who is at risk?

Of particular relevance to air crews and frequent flyers, cosmic radiation from outer space is one of the sources of natural radiation. It is also present as a result of radon gas coming up through the ground and is found in trace amounts in our food[173]. Air travel for frequent flyers should be reduced and it is advisable to cease flying altogether while pregnant in order to reduce the levels of additional exposure to cosmic radiation of your baby.

Employers have responsibilities under the Ionising Radiations Regulations (IRR) 1999. These include:

- Undertaking a risk assessment and identifying additional actions if necessary
- Altering hours of work with radiation
- Providing additional protection
- Offering alternative work
- Consulting and informing safety representatives about general arrangements for employees who are pregnant or breast-feeding

BREAST–FEEDING - AN OBSERVATION STORY

Recently, I treated a lady who found the pressure of breast-feeding overwhelming. She had breast-fed for eight weeks but, because of milk over-production and her little one not receiving as much as mum would like, she reverted to expressing in between feeds, with the excess going into the freezer. This took up even more of her time.

She became so tired that she did not have time for anything else and found the whole experience of coming home one of isolation and loneliness with no time to visit friends or other mums for some respite.

She felt guilty when her partner suggested that she put their daughter on formula. She wanted to be a good mum but found it challenging to fit everything in. Lost in the melee of child-care, she realised that there was no time for herself and her partner became more worried about her than their daughter.

She was also disappointed with herself as the birth did not go as she had planned. Full of sadness, she seemed to have lost part of herself, buried in her chest and abdomen. (I believe she fragmented emotionally and energetically during the birth process). She had deep tissue misalignment in her neck and back from the position she had been on the floor during the birth and suffered sciatica and shoulder pain. It was a surprise to her that she felt pain, having taken hypnotherapy as a precaution, but as the labour progressed in time, she felt more pain.

This proved to her she was not as proficient as she wanted to be and had found it tough those first few months. 'No one tells you. It is not in the books.' 'It was not as I had expected.' 'It was not easy.'

This lady had no family around to assist or help out and her partner needed to return to work after his paternity leave. Unfortunately, he worked away and returned home only at weekends, so there was no respite. She had organised herself well with a Doula maternity helper for the first eight weeks, but even so it was not as expected.

It is tough being a lone parent with a new baby and no immediate family to help out. Unfortunately, we rely on that help more and more these days, especially when it is a new mum with no one to help, pass on knowledge or take responsibility and nobody to offer relief or respite 24/7.

I talked to her about using and connecting to her own intuition and suggested some Bach flower remedies for emotional support at home. Using clinical and emotional techniques, we had two sessions that released her trauma, together with realigning her back and shoulders. I had already treated her daughter with CST and she was now calm and laid back. Mum needed some TLC and had a further session of reflexology to rebalance her hormones and de-stress.

In thanking me, she declared she felt whole again and more confident after our chat. She thought she had done something wrong. I explained that what she felt was normal.

This case provided one more reason to write this book and let women know that they are human and not super-human. Sometimes emotions can reflect and overwhelm us.

Giving birth is a changing time, emotionally, physically and spiritually.

We take on responsibility we have not encountered before. Hormones are rife and need rebalancing after the explosion caused by pregnancy and labour. This can take time and we need patience. It is also where the wonders of reflexology come in. Treat yourself and have a helping hand to rebalance and bring harmony back to your body. My advice would be to arrange a reflexology session early after the birth.

COLIC

The cause of colic, (also known as infantile colic, baby colic and gas and acid reflux) is officially unknown, although it does affect approximately 20% of all infants. Some researchers have suggested that it is simply indigestion, while others believe it is the gut maturing. Others again have indicated lactose intolerance as the source and, without doubt, children certainly are more sensitive these days to milk products and lactose intolerance. As discussed previously, dairy products eaten by the mother can affect breast milk and irritate any intolerance in the infant.

The NHS states that if your baby has repeated episodes of crying or screaming for no obvious reason, having been well-fed and being clean and warm, then they probably have colic. NHS sources also believe, however, that there is little scientific evidence to support the above theories. They do consider that smoking while pregnant plays a part though and, in fact, it is believed that smoking doubles the chances of a baby developing colic[174].

As a guide, the medical profession says that if a child cries intensely more than three days a week, for more than three hours or for more than three weeks in a month, they could be suffering from colic. For some children, it is a common disorder which can last from when they are a few days old and continue for several months. It generally starts when the infant is between 2–4 weeks old and seems to discontinue at about four to five months old as the child goes on to solids.

Symptoms and causes of colic

The symptoms of colic are:

- Body posture - the baby may clench its fists, be stiff in the body and arch its back
- Intense crying during which the face becomes red and flushed
- Difficulty sleeping
- Restlessness

The above are noticeable at certain times of the day and can show more in the evening. The discomfort, which is experienced by the child and the associated crying, can, of course, mean that feeding may take longer.

Although colic is regarded as harmless and the NHS has no evidence that it has any long-term effects, it is, however, very distressing for the infant and the parents, creating sleepless nights and periods of time when some children are inconsolable. Parents feel helpless and sometimes angry, and depression during this time is not uncommon. When dealing with a distressed child demanding attention for someone to help stop the pain, the continual crying can bring parents' nerves to breaking point.

Colic is thought to be triggered by:

- Bottle feeding
- Swallowing air while feeding (causing trapped air)
- Constipation
- Mum's diet
- Birth and vagus nerve dysfunctions

Some researchers are now showing evidence from different sources that colic could be due to a gut flora imbalance. The gut flora pattern is different for each baby, with breast-fed babies getting their gut flora (probiotics) and protection from the mother's breast milk, automatically benefitting from the mother's good bacteria during the vaginal birth process. Researchers have acknowledged that there is a big difference in gut flora between babies who are bottle-fed and those who are breast-fed. (See breast-feeding section above for details)

I believe that colic can stem from several individual reasons and sometimes from a combination of more than one. One of these, I believe, is wind or trapped gas and indeed I have seen and treated many children with the disorder. Having also had personal experience with a child of my own suffering from colic many years ago, I wish I'd known then what I know now. We all appreciate how painful wind is, even for an adult, so imagine the distress of an infant who cannot communicate to us where and how it is affected. My son suffered with colic but my daughter did not. However my son did have a quick birth, but more on that later.

Some children suffer milder symptoms than others and the condition affects both sexes. Bottle-fed children do indeed seem to suffer more than those who are breast-fed and when a breast-fed child shows symptoms of colic it may have more to do with lactose intolerance and/or the mother's diet. A useful tip, which is worth remembering, is that children with lactose intolerance or reflux disorder seem to cry harder when left to lie on their backs.

Treatment for colic

Medical treatment is not normally recommended for colic. However, the reduction of trapped gas and wind often helps. Try self-help techniques such as:

- Changing the baby's formula - if the feed is not agreeing with baby
- Checking if the infant is lactose intolerant
- Burping every two–three ounces
- Massaging the baby's stomach in a clockwise movement (see section on baby massage)
- If breast feeding, taking care of your own diet

Demand feeding is also thought to help. A study was used to assess and compare the two main approaches to feeding - the 'traditional' one, where the infant had a fixed eating and sleeping regime and 'infant demand feeding'. The results showed that those on whom the traditional approach was used cried more over a 24-hour period but slept better during the night. Demand feeders, on the other hand, cried less over a 24-hour period but woke more during the night.

Weakness in digestion

From my own experience, when I have investigated the histories of parents, it has more often than not come to light that one or both have food intolerances of their own, although usually in a milder form. The child, therefore, has inherited the weakness passed on by the parent(s) and this pattern can go from generation to generation, with the weakness becoming more severe as it is inherited. This happened in my own son's case.

I had candida (little did I know at the time) as did my mother before me. My son ended up with a combination of complaints, including weakness of bacteria and vagus nerve complications, and he had a quick birth as well. Poor child. No wonder he had colic! I just wish I had known then what I know now. Hindsight is wonderful! It could have stopped the discomfort for my son and sleepless nights for us, his parents.

Mum to be can make a difference

I find the best way to change and prevent colic for the forthcoming newborn is for the mother to identify her own disorder or weakness and take probiotics during and after pregnancy to correct the imbalances for herself and, more importantly, for her infant. This way, the patterns will have a chance to change and improve for the next generation. For more severe conditions such as candida, a programme of elimination and diet changes would be advised, although not during pregnancy or while breast-feeding.

Research carried out at Brown University Colic Clinic[175] has identified that children who suffer from colic have common symptoms such as mild gastro-oesophageal reflux, the symptoms of which are suckling disorders and being sick. This is believed to come from lactose intolerance or lactose overload and some children showed these signs with green stools!

Babies who suffer from colic have been noted to have weak gut patterns and to lack good bacteria (lactobacillus acidophilus). This can be as a result of deficiencies from the mother (suffering gut imbalances such as candida) and by not passing the natural collection of bacteria through the birth canal (i.e. birth via C-section).

MOTHERS DIET

Careful diet is essential for the mother who is breast-feeding as the mother's food intake is also linked to symptoms of colic, with dairy products being top of the list of things to avoid. The proteins from cow's milk pass from the mother to the child and unfortunately, if the child is sensitive to digesting milk proteins (milk allergy), it will cause a reaction and show either as colic, a skin rash or breathing difficulties.

For best results, therefore, the mother will need to eliminate dairy, wheat, spicy and acid products from her diet while breast-feeding as, logically, the baby will get either the benefits or the adverse effects of anything that the mother ingests. It has been shown that once these products have been eliminated for just one week, the symptoms start to alleviate for the infant.

Finding the cause of colic while breast-feeding can be a process of elimination and so, having left out a variety of possible foodstuffs from her own diet, the mother can experiment slowly to determine the true case. Try taking small amounts of the offending food items one at a time, and note any changes in the baby. This is one way of recognising the primary cause of the child's condition.

Some babies, of course, may be completely intolerant, whilst others will only be intolerant to large concentrations of milk and cheese but be able to take small quantities without reaction. In addition, some children will grow out of it, while others continue to be intolerant for much longer. From my experience, some will even take it into adulthood but the whole process is very much dependent upon the individual and on the infant's gut flora, digestion and nervous system.

It can take a week to ten days for the lactose or acid to eliminate properly from the body, so do be patient. The breast-feeding mother can, however, ingest probiotics or acidophilus at the same time as eliminating certain products from her diet, so that the baby gets the benefit of the good bacteria.

Natural remedies

Homeopathic colic remedies are also available for baby and mother and I recommend the use of herbal teas, which are safe natural remedies for the breast-feeding mother.

- Fennel, dill, peppermint, ginger and chamomile teas are known for their digestive health benefits. Use independently or mix (depending upon individual taste) for relief.
- Fennel, dill and chamomile are ingredients used in gripe water to relieve symptom of gas, teething and colic
- Fennel is an old remedy which is very successful for colic

Again the mother can ingest and the child will get the secondary benefits.

Researchers are looking at other indicators for the cause of colic, including:

- Circadian rhythms
- Smoking and stress of the mother in the third trimester
- Melatonin production by the pineal gland - melatonin production does not begin until twelve weeks of age, approximately the time of the reduction of colic symptoms

Some see colic or excessive crying as a sign of stress-release necessitated by the effects of maternal or parental stress or even the birth trauma, requiring support and facilitation rather than suppression or cure[176]. From my own experience, helping a child to recover from the birth trauma (which is often caused by quick or long births) makes a huge difference to the general digestion of the child, as stress and emotion release will effectively reduce the crying, allowing the child to relax outwardly and internally.

The Gut Brain axis

Stress plays an important role in the expression of gastrointestinal diseases. Many organic gastrointestinal diseases such as peptic ulcers and ulcerative colitis were once thought to be psychosomatic. Today however, the medical profession has firmly established the brain and gut link.

During periods of emotional stress, an excessive activation of the vagus nerve can take place via the gut-brain axis. The term 'gut-brain axis' refers to the two-way communication between gut and brain through neurohumeral signals. When we are stressed, the first thing we do is to tighten up and the abdominal area is where it hurts the most. Ask anyone who has IBS. Since there is a gut/brain connection, by relaxing the gut we improve breathing and digestion overall.

Scientific tests have shown that stress, although temporarily distant from the event, can influence susceptibility to inflammatory signals. Stress has a dramatic effect on the mucosal barrier (gut) by increasing the permeability of tight junctions. This increases the uptake of macromolecular antigens and promotes internalisation and translocation of bacteria. This in turn causes mild inflammation in the ileum and colon, giving symptoms of IBS and other gastrointestinal disorders. Gastro-ensophageal reflux can be helped with Cranio Sacral Therapy, reflexology and baby massage. Each of the methods work equally well with adults as with children.

The vagus nerve, meanwhile, controls the cycles of digestion. Abdomen branches go to the stomach, pancreas, large and small intestine and the colon for secretion and constriction of smooth muscle activity. The sensory parts of the vagus nerve come from receptors in the abdominal viscera, oesophagus, lungs, bronchia, trachea, heart and aortic arch.

A dysfunctional vagus nerve can show itself as nervousness, inability to speak or impairment of speech, increased heart rate and palpitations. Other signs are excessive perspiration, stomach disorders and/or irritations.

As we have explained previously, the vagus nerve is the single most important nerve in the body and is situated in the neck. It is a nerve that controls digestion and can be adversely affected during the birth process. When the head is at a particular angle in the birth canal, it can affect the efficiency of the connection to the vagus nerve. Vagus nerve disorders can be adjusted with Cranio Sacral Therapy.

Another reason for Colic is the intervention process by forceps, which can interfere with the small intestine meridian and can disrupt the finely tuned meridian channels affecting the digestion process and colic symptoms.

Ear problems can also be an outcome and associated with a dysfunctional small intestine meridian. (Some CST therapists are trained in Meridian correction techniques)

BABY MASSAGE

Baby massage is excellent as a soothing aid for colic, as well as allowing bonding with your child. The techniques for colic have been proved to help all babies and are very effective for this disorder.

Lifting the baby's knees up towards their stomach will help to relieve pressure in the stomach and you can also try doing this while holding your baby against your chest. (See section 14 and appendix for methods of baby massage)

Another technique that you can try is an old one, known as the *'cuddle cure'*. Wrap the baby in a blanket or shawl and place the baby on their side or stomach. Swing or rock the baby gently from side to side in your arms and use a soft 'Shhh' sound.

LACTOSE INTOLERANCE

It wasn't until the 1960's that lactose intolerance was finally recognised as a genuine disorder. Before then it was seen as faddy not to drink milk, and in countries such as China it was often regarded as part of natural cultural differences. At least one in twenty people in the UK are thought to suffer with lactose intolerance and it is estimated that 4.5 million suffer worldwide, although many people do not, in fact, know that they have the condition. It is a common complaint in adults, but over recent years has become more common in children too.

A sugar compound known as lactose is found in all animal and human milk (cow's, goat's and sheep's milk all contain lactose). Lactose is normally broken down into glucose by 'lactase' in the small intestine, but lactose intolerance develops if unprocessed lactose reaches the colon in large quantities. Lactose makes up less than 8% of milk solids and is an enzyme which breaks down eventually into glucose if sufficient intestinal 'lactase' is present.

Yoghurt, however, is one of the few products that some people can still tolerate, as it is seen to empty from the stomach more slowly than an equivalent amount of milk. This gives the natural intestine lactase more time to split the lactose content, resulting in less lactose reaching the colon.

People who suffer with lactose intolerance either cannot properly digest lactose (milk sugars) from food sources or don't digest it at all. Some people suffer because they have a missing enzyme or have low levels of 'lactase' within their small intestine. Digestive diseases or injuries to the small intestine can sometimes also cause lactose intolerance, as the damage to the lining of the small intestine reduces the amount of lactase produced.

It seems that in our multi-cultural society, two thirds of the world's population lose the ability to split lactose not long after weaning. After weaning, the body stops producing lactase, the enzyme that the body needs to digest sugar lactose. Without lactase, the lactose passes through the stomach undigested and enters the large intestine where bugs feast and multiply on the lactose. The sufferer is forced to belch out the gaseous by-products, giving feelings of gas, nausea, discomfort and bloating which, for a baby, can be especially distressing.

Lactose is considered important for general nutrition with the uptake of calcium in milk and babies' early development. It is an important source of energy, especially in the first twelve months of a child's life, and it creates the development of physiological gut flora for the child. Indeed, it represents the most important carbohydrate in the milk of all mammals and the respective concentration depends entirely on the species.

The symptoms of lactose intolerance vary from person to person, depending upon the consumption of lactose and the levels of missing enzyme (lactase) produced by the small intestine, which can be absorbed into the blood stream. It becomes a double-edged sword; people who are lactose intolerant are unable to process and cannot produce enough lactase.

Some scientists agree that there is currently a genetic link. That we have not all evolved with this enzyme and have not therefore all adapted to the consumption of milk production and dairy produce[177] . Some think that we were all lactose intolerant at one time during our evolution and that lactase persistence evolved after people domesticated animals and began drinking their milk[178].

The levels and degree of the disorder are widespread

95% of people of Asian origin and 75% of Afro Caribbean origin are prone to this disorder[179]. Whilst mal-digestion of lactose is a worldwide problem, however, there does seem to be a distinct North/South gradient.

- In the Mediterranean, lactose intolerance is approximately 70%
- In Africa and close to the equator it is 98%
- In Austria, only about 20% of the population is lactose intolerant
- In Germany it is even less, at 13-14%
- Scandinavia is the lowest at only 3-8% of the population

Lactase persistence seems to be most common with North European people who have had a long tradition of dairy farming, whereas in countries where milk has not traditionally been part of the diet, incidence of lactose intolerance seems to be a much bigger problem. This is especially true for South America, Africa and Asia where more than 50% of the population are intolerant to lactose, rising in some parts of Asia to one hundred percent[180].

Over millennia, we have mutated from mammals which lost the ability to digest lactose in later years and have retained approximately 10% of the capacity to produce lactase. However, some babies are born without this retention at all, so cannot comfortably process any milk products throughout their life.

Where is lactose found?

Lactose is not only found in milk and milk products such as yoghurt and chocolate, but also in bread or any other product where milk is used in the preparation of the food. In addition, since it is a tasteless substance, it is used in the food industry as filler, in products such as:

- Bread
- Cereals and breakfast cereals
- Cottage cheese
- Margarine
- Ice cream
- Salad dressings
- Pancakes
- Biscuits.
- Cakes and icings.

It is also commonly used in canned and frozen vegetables to prevent discoloration and is frequently used in the production of industrial food products where it works as a binder and carrier for aroma substances and is used for giving higher volume and additional firmness. The type of preparations where is it is commonly found include:

- Sweets
- Meat preparations such as pâté
- Low-fat foods

- Convenience foods
- Spice mixtures
- Artificial sweeteners
- Baked products

Powdered ready meals are another type of product where lactose is commonly hidden and these include:

- Dehydrated potatoes
- Soups
- Meal replacement supplements

Beware of foods which are labelled non–dairy as these can still contain lactose from ingredients such as dry milk solids, non-fat dry milk powder, curds and whey. Lactose is also usually found in coffee creamers and whipped toppings.

In Western countries, commercial lactose is usually derived from cow's milk, whereas Middle Eastern and African counties normally use by-products from camel or goat's milk.

How do I know if I am lactose intolerant?

If any of the symptoms below occur up to two hours after drinking milk, you may be lactose intolerant. Keeping a diary of diet consumption and resulting symptoms can also help to highlight changes.

The direct symptoms of lactose intolerance are:

- Diarrhoea or diarrhoea-like problems
- Mushy stool
- Bloating
- Constipation
- Feeling sick after food
- Belching
- Colic-like pain
- Tummy rumbling or tummy ache
- Wind

- Vomiting

The non-specific symptoms include:

- Chronic Tiredness
- Depressive moods
- Fatigue
- Restlessness
- Exhaustion

There are also more subjective symptoms, such as:

- Headache
- Nervousness
- Feeling Tense
- Skin impurities
- Deficiency symptoms
- Nausea
- Lack of concentration
- Sleep problems
- Feeling low

Diagnostic Testing For Lactose Intolerance

Scientists have diagnosed a better way to show if we are lactose intolerant in the form of a gene test showing quantity and quality of lactose[181]. The original lactose tolerance test had been used for some time and basically measured blood glucose levels but this was replaced with an H2 concentration test. Both methods have not been fully proved and have still led to severe symptoms in lactose intolerant patients who fail to register as sufferers.

A new detection method has now been discovered, which is a gene test to determine the quantity of lactase produced. It is performed from a simple swab of the mouth mucosa from inside the cheek and can be used for all ages[182].

I find this method more accurate, as well as more convenient, and I use it in my practice to help clients define their level of intolerance and enzyme deficiency. Other tests are:

- Blood glucose test
- Stool acidity test
- Intestinal biopsy
- Breath test

Alternative choices are kinesiology testing to detect presence of allergies. Allergy testing can also be done through a health practitioner.

Treatment

There is no medical treatment for lactose intolerance, but symptoms can be avoided by controlling the amount of lactose in the diet. Contrary to popular belief, acidophilus bacteria do not split lactose, and products containing acidophilus are not beneficial since they contain as much lactose as regular milk[183].

The only effective long-term solution is to take lactose out of the diet. The less lactose consumed, the less severe the disorder, and symptoms should steadily improve during this time. If you do not notice any improvement, go to your GP who can recommend tests to find out the cause or find a therapist who is capable of offering the new genetic lactose testing which we have just outlined.

Those who are intolerant to even small amounts of lactose will need to adhere to a severe regime in terms of diet. All products containing lactose must be avoided and foods containing prepared milk products should be completely eliminated. This can make eating out quite a challenge, as sufferers would need to check ingredients, including all sauces and dressings.

Good home cooking is the way forward with a diet of plain, organic and non-processed food. Reducing the amount of milk products in the diet normally gives relief and, for most sufferers, the elimination of all major milk-containing products seems to be enough to obtain sufficient relief from the disorder.

This includes the elimination of:

- Yoghurt (although in some cases, as we have indicated, yoghurt may be tolerated)
- Cottage cheese
- Milk
- Ice cream

Studies have shown that full fat milk is better than skimmed milk for those who are lactose intolerant. It appears that the absorption of lactose from skimmed or semi skimmed non-fat milk is greater than from whole milk (containing fat). Meals containing fat reduce the rate at which the stomach empties into the small intestine. This reduces the overwhelming full load of lactose to be dealt with at any one time by the intestine[184].

The problem of lactose intolerance is so huge that you can now buy lactose-free milk in the supermarkets. In addition, you can try alternatives such as soya, rice or oaten milk, the latter of which is made from oats.

When considering diet, it is well worthwhile bearing in mind that scientists believe long-term avoidance of milk and milk products can lead to a deficiency of calcium and vitamin D, which could lead to bone disease in later life. However, supplements can be taken to rebalance the calcium and vitamin D deficiency.

Lactose in Medication

Lactose is not only used in food products, but also in medications, many of which contain lactose as a filler for taste correction. It is used in hundreds of over-the-counter chemist products and prescription drugs as a coating or filler, including children's and baby products. Indeed, it is thought that lactose is used as a base for more than 20% of all prescription drugs and about 6% of over-the-counter drugs[185].

Surprisingly, it is also included in chewable products like throat lozenges and is even found in a range of products which include:

- Birth control pills,
- Stomach acid tablets
- Medication for the reduction of gas

Some may argue that the amount in these products is minimal, but if you are lactose intolerant, the overall amount consumed adds up each day, each week and each year. Small amounts, however, will only adversely affect people who have a severe intolerance.

Diabetics should also limit their uptake, as lactose is a sugar substance and the body will use it that way. Sufferers are therefore advised to talk to their doctors when prescribed new medication to check the lactose content of the drug or product.

Lactose Intolerance - What Does This Mean To Society?

As you can see, lactose is used in many, many products and is, in fact, in almost everything that we consume. Since 2005, EEC labelling rules have required pre-packed foods to state the milk content or to state if one of its ingredients contains it. Reading the labels on products can mean the difference between having a good day or not if you are lacking the lactase enzyme. Look out for the hidden ingredients and remember to check all medications, as it is also in children's drugs and related products.

A lot of the sensitive people (including Indigos, Crystals, etc) are highly affected by the additives in food and drugs. From my own experience, I have found that this group are mostly lactose intolerant, with reactions ranging from the severe to the mild. Most suffer from some or all of the symptoms which you will find listed below, with many additional unpleasant reactions.

Thankfully, some children grow out of the disorder by three to four years old. Many more, however, continue to suffer from lactose intolerance well into adulthood. We are finding that many children cannot process powdered milk and are sickly and vomit (posit) most of it when fed. Naturally, mothers are looking for alternatives.

Soya is a common and a well-tried alternative, which seems to be more readily available as another option for babies. At the time of writing, however, a lactose-free formula is available on prescription only.

There is also a lactose enzyme prepared in drops or tablet form to help the gut break down lactose in the body. This helps by altering the gut bacteria and with the way that bacteria handle the lactose, therefore reducing symptoms of gas and secretion of water and giving less diarrhoea. It is advisable to check with your doctor before giving them to children.

A homeopathic remedy, Okuabka (ocubaca) is also used to counteract food intolerance symptoms.

The shelves in the supermarkets are now filling up with alternatives to dairy and gluten. We now have lactose free milk, soft cheese and yoghurts. As a recognised national problem, it is big business and shows how many people are buying and looking for new products that are intolerance free. Check out products which are lacto free (see appendix) such as www.lactofree.co.uk. It also shows that the intolerance figures are rising as our bodies find ever more disagreeable substances, producing intolerances directly related to the twenty-first century.

The true figure of lactose intolerance is not known in the UK. Since we have a large ethnic community who are far more likely to suffer unless diagnosed and logged (which most are not), the real figure could be as much as half of the population. Sadly, most people just get on with it, live with it and accept it as their lot in life.

IBS vs lactose intolerance

Some people do not understand the difference between food intolerance and food allergy and, as a consequence, this can impact upon their general health. In my own practice, I see a lot of people who say they have Irritable Bowel Syndrome (IBS), but the symptoms of lactose intolerance and IBS are very similar.

IBS, however, tends to have its root causes in diet, stress, anxiety and other outside influences, whereas lactose intolerance is seen as the genetic inability to digest lactose. When we have the flight or fight reaction (which can be turned on and off like a switch many times a day when we are under pressure), the first thing the body will do is recruit energy from other parts of the body. This allows us to run away or fight. One of the first systems the body closes down or puts on hold is the digestive system. This can be out of action for several hours at a time, so you can see how over long periods of stress, the digestive system can become dysfunctional.

The lactose intolerance disorder is sometimes misunderstood in the UK and, as we have mentioned, is often misdiagnosed as IBS. Unfortunately, many IBS treatments contain lactose, which only makes the intolerance condition and symptoms worse.

Dairy Intolerance

Another area of lactase deficiency occurs in those who suffer from Coeliac disease. As an autoimmune disorder triggered by gluten intolerance found in wheat, barley and rye, sufferers can also have dairy intolerance and problems digesting all milk products. Like genetic intolerance, the Coeliac disorder also prevents the gut from producing lactase and the key is a gluten-free diet which is shown to help repair the gut lining and relieve lactose intolerance.

A German report in the Lancet 1997 stated that some children with atopic (allergic) dermatitis were allergic to cow's milk and got better when it was removed from their diet[186]. The symptoms were severe dermatitis and breathlessness.

Investigations found that a 10-month old child was allergic to cow dander, the scales of the skin and bits of hair that all animals shed, as well as being allergic to cow's milk. Cow dander is also known to be the cause of asthma in farm workers but has not been directly linked to atopic dermatitis. The study found that other children, some of whom came from dairy farms, had the same problems and one in particular whose parent was a veterinary surgeon. The child was receiving dander from Dad!

[166] Radio 4 'Australian study' http://www.bbc.co.uk/radio 4/womanshour/03/2006_50_tue

[167] BBC news 'Hormones govern ability to breast-feed' http://newsvote.bbc.ci.uk/mpapps/agetools/print/news.bbc.co.uk/1/hi/health/8443904.stm?ad=1 (Ref : Professor S.Carlsen, Norwegian University of Science and technology:' A study- relationship between breast-feeding and health' published in Acta Obsetricia and Gynocologica Scandinavica 2009) (cited 01.2010)

[168] BioCare 'Science of Probiotics' 'Gut formula of the breast vs formula fed babies' 2008 (Ref 11: Rinne M. Kalliomaki M, Salminen S and Isolari E (2006) 'Probiotic intervention in the first months of life: short term effects on gastrointestinal symptoms and long –term effects on gut microbiota'. 2006 Journal of Paediatric Gastroenterology and Nutrition 43, 200 -205)

[169] Dr. K.U Moberg 'The Oxytocin Factor' Da Capo Press Cambridge UK. 2003. p153 (Ref: 'smoking and breast-feeding')

[170] Sally Goddard Blythe, 'What Babies and Children really need' Hawthorn Press 2008.Stroud Glocester. UK 2008; (Ref: Bristol University study: By Nobele S & Emmett P.'Differences in weaning practice food and nutrition intake between breast and formula fed infants' Journal of Human Nutrition and Dietrics 2006 19/4.303)

[171] Sunday express 'Call to ban danger chemical in bottles' Lucy Johnston and Martyn Halle 09.2007

[172] Dian Shepperson Mills: BioCare 'Making Babies - The Knowledge' Article (pregnancy and lactation) issue 8 2008

[173] Health and Safety Executive, 'Working safely with ionising radiation' (guidelines for expectant or breast-feeding mothers') INDG334 03/01 C400 -1999.

[174] NHS Direct 'Colic' http://www.nhsdirect.nhs.uk/articles/artice.aspx?articleID=106 (cited 05.2008)

[175] Bupa factsheet: http;/Bupa.co.uk/fact_sheets/mosby_factssheets/infant_colic.html (cited 05.2008)

[176] Wikipedia 'Baby colic' http://en.wikipedia.org.wiki/Baby_colic (Ref:Solter AJ. 'What to do when babies and children cry' Shining star press1998) (cited 05.2008)

[177] Foods Standards Agency 2007/7 http://www.eatwell.gov.uk.healthissues/foodintolerance/foodintolerancetypes/lactoseintol/?view (cited 06.2009)

[178] New Scientist article 01.2002 (Genetic basis for lactose intolerance revealed) 2002.01 http://www.newscientist.com/article.ns?id=dn1787 (cited 07.2007)

[179] Christiane Pies MSc; BTS 'Lactose Intolerance widespread cause of digestive problems' (article) 2004.p1&2

[180] FSA 'Lactose intolerance' 2009 http://www.eatwell.gov.uk/healthissues/food (cited 06.2009)

[181] Christiane Pies MSc; BTS 'Lactose Intolerance widespread cause of digestive problems' (article) 2004.p1&2

[182] Ibid' Gene Testing ' (article 2004.p1&2)

[183] Medicine Net.com. 'Lactase enzyme' http://www.medicinenet.com/lactose_intoloerance/page7.htm (Cited 07.2007)

[184] Medicine Net.com. 'Lactase enzyme' http://www.medicinenet.com/lactose_intoloerance/page7.htm (Cited 07.2007)

[185] Wise Greek 'What is lactose?': (ref: over the counter meds): http://www.wisegreek.com/what-is-lactose 2007 (cited 07.2007)

[186] Doctors guide 'Kids with dermatitis may be allergic to cows' Letter to the Lancet http://www.docguide.com (cited 07.2007)

Chapter 18

INDEX

Chapter 18

SETTLING IN

Unexpected as it may be, for some, motherhood can take time to adjust to. The rosy vision of mum and baby sleeping contently can be a fallacy when you return home with your bundle of joy. Some mothers have said to me, 'I did not expect this' or 'No-one told me it would be like this.'

Having a child can be a shock to the system. Not only is mum exhausted, perpetually tired and sometimes prickly to others around her, but being a new mum she wants to do everything right. The pressure is on her and everyone is watching to see how she performs.

When baby becomes fractious and only wants mum, things don't seem too bleak and mum can cope. However, when he/she becomes discontent and feeding turns into a nightmare (as Dad looks on bewildered and helpless), realisation kicks in. The realisation that you are responsible for this very precious and, in some cases, long-awaited child can be daunting.

Having children can change you and how you see your world. When you return home, everyone wants to come and visit. Grandmothers can be well-meaning but cause problems and conflict for new mums who have ideas of their own on how to care for their child. When mum is traumatised from the birth process, this conflict can come to a head. Tired and with patience strained, mums clash with their elders and harsh words can be spoken which often lead to tears. Some new mums just need peace and quiet with their baby, while others cope well and enjoy all the fuss. It just depends on the individual.

Offering lots of advice beginning with, 'In my day....' grandmothers often relate stories of how they brought you up. Believing 'they know better', some fuss too much, wanting to do their best however, forgetting the real feelings surrounding coming home and preventing mum and baby from resting and bonding.

Perhaps the new mum wants to do things differently, especially if she felt she missed out as a child herself. Having your own child certainly highlights holes in your own care and parenting.

Despite the personal idiosyncrasies, it is a process of adjustment for all. We need to allow time for the immediate family (mum, dad and siblings) to get to know one another under the new regime. Give them time to adjust to the new addition.

Grandmothers beware. It is most important that you allow your children time to bond with their new baby and adjust their lifestyle accordingly so please remember to give them space. Of course it is nice to have help, but don't overwhelm them; they can contact you if they need you.

BIRTH AND EMOTIONAL DEVELOPMENT

During the first years of life, the child is dependent upon parents and others for support and development. Michel Odent calls this the primal period; a crucial time affecting the course of stages of development and future regulation[188]. 'The only time the human being is completely dependent upon its mother.'

Daniel Siegal explains the first years of life as follows:

'Caregivers are the architects of the way in which experience influences the unfolding of genetically pre-programmed but experience-dependent development. The release of stress hormones (at key stages in early development) leads to excessive death of neurons in the crucial pathways involving the neocortex and limbic system – area responsible for emotional regulation'

The roots of emotional development begin with attachment. Babies will use adults to teach them how to survive (a basic instinct) and supplement their basic functioning until the knowledge is fully learnt and they can do it for themselves.

Children need protection, nurturing and love to feel safe and secure. It is how they receive this basic need and the attachment or feeling that goes with it that determines the expectations of the individual, or how the child expects to be treated by others.

Research – human interaction

In the 1980s, American psychologists studied twenty, two year-old toddlers from 'families in stress'. Half the children had suffered physical abuse, whilst the other half were from broken homes and were living with foster parents. When they were confronted with a crying child, the second group (non-abused) showed concern and they were upset to see another upset. The abused toddlers, however, did not know how to deal with a crying child. They were seen to try and be sympathetic and then would shift to aggressive threats if the distressed child didn't stop. Some would shout at them to stop and a few started to pat the child on the back, only for the patting to turn into slapping and then beating despite the child's screams189.

It was concluded that the abused children did not understand human interaction. Having been denied the sympathetic and tender approach, they did not have the education to teach themselves how to behave. Unfortunately, they came to expect punishment instead of love and the brain was wired to that approach. The children reproduced what they knew from their own parents, exactly as they had reacted to their own distressed state. Other research has also cited historical evidence that behaviour patterns have been passed down (from generation to generation) with abusive parents having been themselves deprived of physical affection during their own childhood.

Sympathy is a basic instinct. When a child is loved and does not suffer any detrimental development disorders (such as abuse) the brain will naturally reject violence as offensive and uncaring.

In their article (the hand that rocks the cradle) worldwide alternative to violence (UK) suggest that humans develop the patterns for violence between birth and three years old. A scary thought however, the human interaction information above seems to substantiate this thinking.[190]

Other research has cited the association between maternal state and the unsettled infant behaviour. This is logical when you think about it as described previously. Children can pick up and sympathise with parent's emotional behaviour, as they too become overwhelmed with the knock-on effects.

Relationship with your mum

As a new mother, the one thing you will probably notice most is the discrepancy with your own childhood. I believe that pregnancy encourages new parents to think about how they were brought up and what they would like to change as a parent bringing up their own children. How, and if, you bonded well with your mum and dad will now become apparent. This is especially true for the relationship with your mum and how close or otherwise you are to her.

How were you treated as a child and would you want that as a role model for your family? What memories will come to the fore? And the bigger question is how does it sit with you?

External influences create fear and anxiety
I expect you have already received a barrage of advice when you were pregnant, including what to expect during labour and how to look after your new baby. What grandmothers often do not recognise, however, is that practices used in 'their day' have moved on to new ways, although some ideas do still stand.

Hygiene, for example, is more relevant today, as we have better insights than they did twenty years ago, and this is most definitely the case compared to thirty or forty years ago. Unfortunately, the well-meaning 'old wives' tales that many grandmothers come out with can have the opposite effect than they intend. They can create fear and anxiety during pregnancy and cause-troubled minds for the parents when all arrive home, often causing worry about things that may not happen.

When we come home with our new baby, all the family will be keen to see you. Grandmothers from both sides will come with words of wisdom and you will need to make up your mind whether to accept them or not. This will, of course, depend upon patterns you and your partner have already developed. Are either of you pleasers? Can either of you say 'no thanks' when you want to do things your way?

Are you a Pleaser?

Throughout our lives we are conditioned by outside influences, other's beliefs, actions, rules, and expectations from family, siblings and peers. Almost everyone has an expectation of us and how we should behave.

For some this expectation has affected them since childhood. A past experience has made an imprint and the pattern created has become their standard behaviour. By continuing to please and constantly striving to get the right attention from others, they have changed and adapted to the point where they are unable to think and do for themselves. They have taken on other people's beliefs, their conditioning and their needs before their own.

In fact, their lives have turned into a drama to please others. Suddenly it is all that counts in their lives; it is what drives them. The pattern can become so powerful that in some cases they end up not knowing who they are any more or what they want in life!

Being pulled back and forth trying to please others, they come to realise over time that no matter what they do, it is not enough. Realisation hits them and they understand that they have not followed their own goals and have effectively sabotaged or victimised themselves. They feel lost, not knowing where their paths now lie, where they should be or where they want to go. Is any of this sounding familiar?

Even as a young child we soon learn to enjoy praise and dislike criticism

Very often, pleasing behaviour begins in childhood, when you want to get Mum or Dad's attention. You may have wanted, for example, to come first in the class because it afforded preferential treatment at home. Seeing how proud Mum and Dad were and how they praised you, the habit of pleasing others became a pattern.

You needed to constantly please your parents because failure meant they weren't happy with you and being displeased meant that they didn't pay as much attention as when you were top of the class. Everything you did was to get their attention. Even being third was not enough and you would dread hearing – '*you can do better than that*'. Criticism became a perpetual area of concern. When you came first or won the trophy you received praise. When you didn't win, you were criticised.

The pattern goes on beyond school and university, into the work place, where the stakes get higher. Winning in sport becomes a habit that needs to be filled. So great is the goal of achievement that even a friendly game of golf has to be won. Coming second is simply not good enough.

Unfortunately, what happens is that you become your own worst enemy. In order to please, you have to achieve at whatever cost and this is when the habit becomes toxic to the body. You push and punish yourself beyond normal limits to achieve and become a pleaser. Because the inner pressure and stress is unavoidable, you burn out emotionally, mentally and physically.

Becoming the pleaser also has another downside, one in which people take advantage of your good nature. They recognise your desire to please and put additional pressure upon you. They set higher goals for you to reach, knowing it will wipe you out emotionally and physically, then sit back and wait. For some, you become a source of entertainment.

The realisation that your happiness does not depend on what others say or think can come slowly. It can take some time for us to learn this. However well-meaning friends and family try to be, they cannot know what you really want or need. You are the only one to know that.

The relationship of your emotional vibration (feeling good, happy or sad) and what you want to be (your goals of who or how you want to be) will determine the outcome of your life. We are mirrors - most of the time, what we give out is what we attract in return. You need to make up your mind. Do you wish to change your life?

By changing your thoughts you can change your life

To continue with the same thoughts and actions will only continue to bring you what you have now. It will need focus and dedication to do this but over time, change can happen. Think differently and change to good and positive thoughts. See the change happening in your future.

- 'I can achieve.'
- 'I will do this.'
- 'I will have .....in my life.'

By continually listening to your emotions and paying attention to how you are feeling, you take the first step on the ladder. Does it make your heart sing or sink when you think of doing something? You need to be in touch with who you are instead of ignoring or burying your own feelings to please others.

Start asking yourself:

- 'Why would I want to do that?'
- 'Is it really what I want or am I doing this to please others?'
- 'Does it make my heart sing or sink?'
- 'When I think of this does it make me happy or sad?'

Unwanted things cannot jump into your experience uninvited. You create your present reality by your previous actions. By starting to change your thinking, you can then start to change emotionally, connecting to your self–esteem and self-worth. Have a stronger resolve to say NO more often when something doesn't ring true in your heart! It is your life. Try pleasing yourself from now on. (See appendix for info)

GOING HOME

It might have only been twenty-four hours away from home, but what a difference when you return. The new mum is different and she has another to care for; one that she may have waited a long time to produce.

When you come to hold your baby for the first time, you will have the overwhelming feeling of being responsible for this beautiful child you have produced. On leaving hospital, however, reality kicks in with day-to-day routines that both of you are still learning about.

Along with the new arrival at home come all the family and friends who can't wait to see you and to hold the baby. Although well intentioned, it can be a little overwhelming for you and your baby, as you will probably both be tired and still recovering from the birth process. Dad will be very proud and a little out of his depth, normally it will be you that everyone turns to for routine structure and arrangement.

The more organised you are before you go into hospital the better things will be on your return. Create and arrange everything so that it is close to hand in the nursery. Be well-prepared to delegate to others in the first few weeks.

Communication is the key

Family members and grandmothers will want to help and if you have a good relationship with them that will be fine. As a new mum you will be able to say 'No, I want it this way' without the alteration causing offence. If you want things done in a certain way then say so. It is the lack of communication that causes most discord between close family and friends. Be positive, assertive and keep saying what you want and they will eventually get the message.

Preparation is the key. It would be good to have a chat beforehand with those who will be with you when you come out of hospital, so that they will know what to expect and what you require.

When you return home, it is a logical practice to sleep while the baby sleeps. If you want to do this, then say so. Don't be polite by staying and chatting. Your health is important now and your baby needs you. Sleep is important and you may well be exhausted from the birth process and may not have slept well prior to the event. When we are tired things can get out of proportion. You will be sensitive and have a huge surge of hormones circulating around your body so it is not unusual to feel emotional and tearful after the event. This is normal.

You need to put yourself and your baby first. Rest and delegation are the keys to a smooth transition.

- Housework will slip over the next few weeks – this is normal. Don't worry about the housework - do the best you can and if you can, allow others to help out.
- Take the time to rest, especially if it is your first child, and enjoy the luxury of the cosseting. When you have a second child it is a little more challenging to find the time to rest because as one sleeps, the other demands attention
- If you are breast-feeding, you need to make sure that you are eating the correct diet (See section 15 on breast-feeding)
- Dad can play his role so allow him to get involved and don't be a martyr - after all, it is his child too!
- Don't be a pleaser. Do what is right for you and your new family. No-one else knows what is right and only you really know what suits your family

We all have instincts and this is especially true of women giving birth. Our maternal instincts tell us what our baby wants. This gives mum confidence and helps her to bond more deeply with the child. The deeper the bond, the more the instinct grows, so go with your instincts and allow them to help you. If you feel that your baby needs a cuddle, then go with that. Maybe your baby is feeling a little insecure with all the visitors and being passed around all the time. Perhaps he/she needs mum's touch and security to feel safe.

When your baby cries, it is to draw your attention to the fact that something is not right. There are cries for feeling hungry or needing a nappy changed, but there are also other cries for attention. You will use your natural instinct to tell you, so don't allow anyone else to say otherwise. You know your own child so trust yourself and have confidence in your instincts.

When we first arrive home it is natural to be fearful and worry that we are not doing the right thing for our baby. Everything is new and it takes a little time to develop a routine that suits both mother and baby. Each baby has its own needs and even though you may have already had four children you will notice they each have their own personality, feeding and sleeping in a different way. This is part of their makeup. Give yourself time and take it slowly. If one way doesn't suit you, you can change it. It is not set in stone.

Some new mums will gladly accept help and advice from their mothers while others will not. It depends very much upon the relationship and how much trust there is between you. There may be another person in whom you will feel more confident. It might be another woman who has had great experience in maternity and bringing up children. Midwives and health visitors are helpful and some have good experience to pass on. However, do not be bullied into doing anything that you do not want to do. Resist bottle-feeding if you want to breast-feed. The same principle applies if, as parents, you do not want to have your child vaccinated.

Please use your discernment and natural instinct as to what it is right for you and your child and remember to listen to your inner feelings. When you think of changing a routine, does it make your heart sing or sink? Does it feel right for you both? Remember - as parents you decide. You are in charge.

CASE STUDY 12 -
BONDING

I received a phone call from an ex client. She was in tears and asked if she could come and see me for herself and her two-week-old baby.

Mum had had a long and arduous labour. She was disappointed because she had planned to have a natural birth and instead ended up having drugs, including an epidural for pain, a pethadine injection and a drip to speed up labour.

Complications had occurred as her daughter had been presented face down (known as pubis frontal). This type of delivery is very painful for both the mother and child and in an attempt to get through the birth canal, the baby had kept pushing and knocking her head against the pubis bone for a long time during labour. Consequently, while doing this the baby was receiving bruising to the head.

Because of this complication, the hospital she attended was not geared up to help her. Still in labour, she was transported 35 miles by ambulance to a larger hospital. This journey only increased the trauma for both herself and the baby.

When Nia (name changed for confidentiality) arrived to see me, she was pale, tearful and looked exhausted. While chatting to her, I was told that she had been very tired during her pregnancy and often stressed about the delivery process ahead. She had attended counselling during her pregnancy to help with this.

Her baby was six days late and weighed 7lb 6oz at birth. Baby had a very bruised head upon delivery and had not settled since coming home. Her daughter cried constantly and needed to be held all the time for Nia to achieve even minimal relief. When baby finally fell asleep from exhaustion she was fretful and jumping. Being very unsettled, her arms would jerk and she was moving constantly. Throughout this time the baby was also positing (bringing back her milk).

Life had changed dramatically

Mum did not know what to do any more and felt as though the situation was her fault. She would get anxious and stressed when her daughter cried so much. Nia felt that her life had changed dramatically since the birth and felt so overwhelmed, not only with the birth process, but also with the responsibility since arriving back home. Everything was so different and it had all happened within two weeks!

Nia was confused, as some books advised not continuing to hold her baby as it would 'make a rod for her own back'. According to them, too much cosseting would not do. Nia told me that she wanted to do the 'right thing' for her baby, but was confused. Tears ran down her face as she talked. She was overwhelmed and finding the whole thing traumatic.

Both the birth and coming home was not like 'it said in the books'. Her book's advice was to feed and change the infant and then put baby down in the crib or Moses basket. In reality, her little one would not even go into the crib, even after having been left to cry (as the book advised) for one and a half hours. Nia told me 'the baby cried constantly during that time'. Mum had avoided picking her baby up even though it hurt her to listen to her crying. Eventually, however, she gave in as she could not stand the cries any more.

Nia now felt as though she had let her daughter down by letting her cry for so long. She felt guilty because she could not do anything right for her. Nia also felt that she had broken a trust between herself and her daughter. Since this episode happened, her daughter did not look at her anymore. Even her husband had noticed the difference. The baby had been all right in hospital and did not cry much for seven days, but when she brought her home it all went wrong. Nia asked me 'What have I done wrong?'

She told me that she found the 'nanny advice book' dis-empowering as a mother. She had stopped breast-feeding and put her baby on a bottle regime but this made no difference to the distressed child. Nia had planned to breast-feed and, in hindsight, this was what she had wanted to do after all. It had taken until day seven for breast milk to flow properly and during the intervening period, mum and baby both found this frustrating.

How was dad doing in all of this?

Nia explained that her partner had been trying to help out and was not as affected by the crying as she was. Although he was doing his best, their relationship was not as good since the baby had arrived and he found the whole situation at home frustrating. I had come across this home situation previously with other families. Mum felt out of control and in her despair shut out her partner.

I had experience of this mum and baby situation described, many, many times before with other newborns. From experience, I determined that immediately after the birth the child had been in shock. That is why she did not cry very much in hospital. She had suffered just as much trauma as her mum and the poor little mite had been numb and frozen in time. Afterwards, the baby did not want to go to sleep because she was reliving the birth trauma through nightmares; hence the jerking and fretfulness.

She probably had a huge headache from the long bout of head-butting she incurred trying to get out of the birth canal. Undoubtedly the head bruising would be tender, painful and uncomfortable for her.

Firstly, I explained to Nia that it was not her fault. She had done nothing wrong. Her daughter was suffering from post-traumatic stress from the birth process and in my opinion, so too was Nia.

At the time of her visit, there was a seesaw effect going on between mother and child. Mum was getting more and more upset, more stressed and emotionally her daughter was tuning into the stress, making her baby even more anxious.

Treatment

I suggested that I give mum a treatment first before treating the baby. In this way, it would stop the vicious circle between them. We settled the baby on the sofa with a pillow next to her so she felt safe and secure, as she had already shown a dislike of her baby chair. Using a combination of techniques including Cranio Sacral Therapy, I de-stressed and calmed Nia and realigned her hips and pelvis. Then I released the emotional trauma from her labour experience.

I explained that she needed to give herself some space and that she could stop blaming herself. The difficult labour was unfortunate and did not go to plan but sometimes this happens. Blaming herself and feeling guilty was not going to change anything except by making her ill. Relieved, Nia saw the sense in that and decided it was time that she dedicated more time to herself and her baby.

An hour later, Nia was looking more herself and smiled for the first time since she arrived. She told me that it felt as though I had removed a weight off her shoulders. She was less emotional and more in control.

Nia's baby was fretful during her treatment session of Cranio Sacral Therapy, despite it helping to reduce the bruising and swelling around the head. Emotional release techniques were used to release the shock and trauma from her little body. I showed Nia some simple techniques to help calm her baby and taught her basic baby massage techniques. I also suggested that she show the same techniques to her partner so that he could get involved more.

Baby massage is good for baby and parent, giving quality time for both. It is always a win-win situation when you use baby massage. As I have mentioned before, it not only allows time for bonding and is calming and relaxing for baby and parent, but it also helps baby become aware of their environment and allows mum to tune into the baby's body and get to know their needs.

Nia realised during our chat that in trying to do everything right for their baby she had pushed her partner out. She realised that she had not been very kind to him and decided she was going to make more of an effort. I explained that it was all right to ask for help and delegate more, as she couldn't possibly do everything.

I explained that the most important thing for Nia to do was to get to know her baby. If she wanted to cuddle her baby then she should. Her baby was very sensitive and needed to be loved and to feel love. Nia said, 'that is what I wanted to do but the books put me off!' Commonsense and mother instinct told her it felt wrong to leave her baby crying.

Connect to instincts

I explained that for a baby, crying is the only way it can communicate. It is their voice without words. Each cry is different and Nia would eventually get to know those different cries. A mother learns to differentiate between the cries when baby wants feeding, feels uncomfortable with a filled nappy or simply when she is bored. She would learn just by being close and bonding with her child. Soon she would know.

I told Nia that she needed to decide which schedule she wanted for her baby. I asked her to listen to herself and to get to know her own and her baby's needs. In doing so, she would get a gut feeling as to what felt right. By reading and listening to so many others she had become confused and her own instincts were being pushed out. Only a mum knows what is best for her child and it comes about during the bonding that occurs after the birth. Mums know instinctively when something is wrong.

These were Nia's instincts and she only needed to allow them to connect and listen to them. If she relaxed more, they would be able to kick in and all would flow smoothly for her. She was the only person who knew instinctively what was needed for her baby.

Having no mother living close by meant that her partner's family would need to be more involved with helping out. Obviously if Nia wanted to include them, it was a choice she needed to make. Nia needed to decide a strategy for what was best for them both.

Two and a half hours after coming to see me, Nia and her baby left looking a lot calmer. We decided that Nia would bring her daughter back to me the following week, however two days later she phoned to say that her baby was a different child. 'I don't know what you did, but she has been marvellous and there is no more crying except when she is hungry. She is calmer and much happier. We both are.' Nia didn't feel it was necessary to bring her baby back. She felt so much better and more able to cope with her baby. She was back in control.

From a professional point of view, I would have liked to see Nia's daughter again, as with that much trauma from the birth there is usually residue that just needs clearing and tweaking. I call it the mop-up session and two sessions are normally better from my professional experience. But mum knows best.

Dads can help too

Becoming a new dad is a wonderful experience and I remember being told by a friend that when our first baby arrived, my husband thought he was the only dad in the world. He was so proud. No-one had a daughter like his and it is true; they don't. All children are unique.

Despite the humour behind my own husband's experience, it is important to get dad involved from the pregnancy stage so that he knows and understands what is going on for you. He needs to know, for example, what decisions he may need to make, what your birth plan is and what you expect to happen during labour.

Men are more involved today than they were when I had my children. Then, it was frowned upon for the partner to be present during labour, which doesn't really make sense. After all, it is a joint effort to produce a child, so why should it not be a joint effort for the rest of the event?

Start by inviting him to hospital appointments and midwife consultations. Partners can help with decision-making since they are not as emotionally affected (by hormonal increases during pregnancy and after the birth). They can see things from a more pragmatic perspective and can smooth the way for you with family and friends. When you come home it can be a testing time for relationships, as your partner may feel out of his depth. You are tired after the birth process and maybe a little shell-shocked, and indeed he may be too after watching the whole event from the reality side. So many new mothers push their husbands or partners out of the picture because of the bonding process and the reality of responsibility at the homecoming. This is a time when you both need to support each other, so don't push him away; invite him in.

Overwhelming for parents

Men need to have enormous patience when you come home. The whole experience can be overwhelming for the new mum, but it can also be daunting for the dad. Remember, his life has been turned upside down too. With peace and quiet gone from the home, everything is now revolving around baby. It is a busy time of visitors and the phone constantly ringing, offering little quiet time for you all to bond as a family. Sometimes it can all get a bit much and that's when you need to be working together. He might spend his time in the kitchen making endless cups of tea, for example, and can hold the fort while you catch up on some sleep. Even fending off well-wishers is a help.

There are usually sleepless nights all round until you get into a routine and everything settles down. For some, the first two weeks can seem like a nightmare and, although very proud of their new baby, most men are more than happy to return to work after paternity leave.

Here are a few tips for including Dad in the process:

- It is imperative that he goes with you to anti-natal classes, hospital appointments for scans etc.,
- Your partner can help during labour with some relaxing massage techniques
- During labour he can help to remind you of the breathing techniques. He should learn them too
- Get him involved with the structure you want when you come home
- Let him help out with feeding and changing
- Alternate the night shift with him, using expressed milk if breast-feeding
- Encourage him to learn baby massage before the birth – it is wonderful for bonding and soothing, even for helping with baby wind and cramp (see section 12 and appendix on baby massage methods)
- He can do the shopping and help out generally in the home

A Woman's role ?

Some men have been brought up in a culture that believes giving birth is a woman's job. Nobody disputes the fact that only women can give birth, but it doesn't mean that the man cannot be with you during the whole process and get more involved before and after the birth event.

In the past, we have all been guilty of creating a mystery around birth and, as a result, men have not felt that they could interfere. This misconception is now changing and more men than ever before are involved with bringing up their children, right from the start. Some are house-husbands and full-time dads bringing up their children while their career wives go back to work. Indeed, more single parents are men these days and collectively have a huge input on the care and decision-making for their children's futures.

One of the reasons for this change has simply been the fact that fathers are more often present during the birth of their child, something which has hugely increased the natural bonding with the baby's father, increasing the hormonal affects of oxytocin to create feelings of love and ecstasy when they see their child. Both males and females are affected by oxytocin and it allows the bonding process to take place right from the beginning, with more love and care being felt for the child. When they are there at the birth, fathers feel more involved and part of the process and they actively want to be involved with their child's care and upbringing when at home. In addition, they have more compassion and understanding for the mother. Most people who were born before the concept of dads being present at the birth process have not bonded parentally as well as those since.

Forty-five years ago, I remember my father lying on the couch sleeping during my mother's difficult and long labour at home with her fourth child. I was fourteen at the time and could hear her distress in the next room while he slept through most of it totally unconcerned, or at least so it appeared to me.

I was furious with him. 'How could you lie there when mum is going through so much' I asked. 'She'll be fine. My mum is with her.' he told me. But it was his cavalier attitude that bothered me more. Why was he not in there with her? Clearly, in his mind this was a time when it was all down to the women. Men were not allowed in at this juncture in time, not even in their own homes!

When I was born in the 1950s, dads were not that close to their children and I firmly believe it was because of this absence of contact right from the beginning. Indeed my own experience was that I did not get close to my father until shortly before he died. I know that my brothers also had difficulty, and especially one, who never felt as though he could talk to dad. What a waste.

Thank goodness male bonding has changed

I am so glad we are changing the whole bonding aspect daily with our children. As a result of my own experience, I deliberately changed the way I brought up my own children. My husband was also keen to have close contact with our children from the beginning. Cuddles and hugs were always available, with time for them in play and reading especially in their early years.

They say memories are made of this and there is no doubt that this type of behaviour from parents gives children a good foundation to build from. Dad's input is essential for a child's balanced view of life and it is important for the infant to be aware of both parents' love and care.

To develop and grow in balance, children need both parents
Mothers are known to be the nurturers, being attentive to their child's needs and emotions. Dads, on the other hand, are more practical, helping their children to overcome 'negative or childish' emotions.

Dads want a rough and tumble relationship, often seen to be outgoing and ready to play. They extend the scope of security, opening doors for exploration and discovery and, although it can appear frightening, they are more likely to allow the child greater freedom than mum - especially at those times when the element of risk seems high to her. Dads tend to stretch the boundaries on safety and involve the child in self-reliant skills, creating self-confidence and self-worth.

I remember when we were building our home in the 1980s. I suddenly realised that my son, who was four at the time, had climbed to the top of a long ladder and was perched on scaffolding watching his Dad capping the chimney top. Naturally I was alarmed and, with my heart in my mouth, I started to panic. My husband signalled me to keep quiet and, after a few moments, he suggested that my son climb back down to see me, which he did quite safely on his own. Despite shaking, I let out a huge sigh of relief. I would not have considered letting him go up there in the first place, but he had climbed up on his own without either of us noticing. The first my husband knew was when he said 'Hello Daddy, what are you doing?'

A child that is never allowed to take risks will grow up fearful and be afraid to try anything new. Dads seem to be less tolerant to childish behaviour, whereas mums make allowances. We humans are naturally curious. Allowing your child to explore will create a free spirit approach to life.

Boys, especially, need Dad to teach them how to be a man and to be competent in male behaviour. Although children of all ages tend to want to be accepted by their peers, I think boys are more challenged here.

COT DEATHS

The tenuous link between bacteria and cot death had been around for decades but evidence was scarce. Recent research by Great Ormond Street Hospital published in the Lancet in 2008, however, proved that common bacteria such as Staphylococcus aureus and Escherighia coli are more prevalent in Sudden Infant Death Syndrome (SIDS) babies.

Although not considered the whole cause, it does have a huge part to play. The immune response to bacteria and toxins may help to explain how several known environmental and genetic risk factors for SIDS become fatal[191]. Some genetic differences in SIDS babies relate to immune response and it is known that smoking while pregnant alters the foetal immune response. In addition, when a baby sleeps face down, it increases bacteria absorption in the infant's upper windpipe.

Since 1991, numbers of cot deaths have fallen by 75%. Much of the reduction is attributed to the launch of information and awareness on cot deaths by the 'Reduce Risk campaign'. Cot death is the largest cause of baby fatality over one month old, with 2005 figures in the UK showing 300 babies dying suddenly. Some, it would seem, are definitely more at risk than others:

- Very few babies over a year old suffer fatality
- SIDS is uncommon in those less than a month old
- Premature babies are more at risk of cot death
- Children with parents who smoke and have smoked during pregnancy are at risk
- 90% of fatalities happen within six months of age

In his book printed in 1958, Dr Spock suggested that babies should be placed on their stomachs while sleeping, as this would allow the infant to vomit without choking. This practice was popular in the 1960s and 70s and I myself used the technique with my own children. The practice influenced health care providers and continued with unanimous support through into the 1990s[192].

SUDDEN INFANT DEATH SYNDROME (SIDS)

It wasn't until empirical studies took place during the late 90s that the thinking reversed. The research found a significantly increased risk of Sudden Infant Death Syndrome associated with babies sleeping on their stomachs[193]. This statistically based information changed the medical approach completely and it is now recommended that young children sleep on their backs.

However, research since then has revealed that bacteria and toxins in cot and crib mattresses are also to blame for many cot deaths. As children sleep on their stomachs, they are ingesting these chemicals directly into the lungs[194]. This, of course, highlights the need to be careful of the substances used in cot and crib mattresses, especially old ones, and when in doubt it is better to buy new, as there are now effective safety regulations in place. It also highlights the necessity for good hygiene to clear out bacteria.

Flat head syndrome

Since the advent of 'on-the-back sleeping', we are now seeing many more children with flat head syndrome. It is believed that this is because children are not developing muscles in the back, neck and head because they are lying on their backs too much. So, have we gone too far?

I believe that a balance is necessary. It is not natural to lie in the same position all of the time. My belief is that children need to lie on their stomachs for part of each day to allow development of all muscles and systems, so give baby more 'tummy-time' when awake. Also, change the position in the cot regularly. Babies are nosey and like to see what is going on. If you switch their orientation in the crib or cot with every nap so that they are lying on the left for one nap and on the right for another, it can even out any compression. There is an alternative medical option to counter flat head syndrome - a helmet, which reshapes the skull while it is still soft. Helmets are adjusted and changed as the child develops and grows.

Research

In Europe, research has shown that incorrect serotonin could also be a factor in cot deaths. Low serotonin levels have been found to create chemical imbalances in the brain. Signals to the brainstem from defective serotonin could play a critical role in SIDS, triggering changes to heart rate and body temperature[195]. The brainstem sits at the base of the brain and is joined by the spinal cord, coordinating vital functions in the body such as respiratory and cardiovascular functions.

How can you reduce the risk of cot death? There are a number of key steps:

- Smoking is known to affect babies, so it is important for both you and your partner to stop during pregnancy. Also, don't smoke in the same room as your baby
- The conditions during sleep are also vital so:
  - Place your baby on his or her back to sleep
  - Place your baby with his or her feet to the foot of the cot to prevent any wriggling down under the covers
  - Do not let your baby get too hot and keep the baby's head uncovered

The conclusions reached by researchers suggest that the safest place for your baby to sleep is in a crib or cot in a room with you for the first six months. A soother or dummy can reduce the risk of cot death even if the dummy falls out while your baby is asleep.

It is especially dangerous for your baby to sleep in your bed if you or your partner is a smoker, has been drinking alcohol, feels very tired or is taking medication or drugs that make you feel drowsy. Don't forget - accidents can happen and caution is required when you put the baby in your bed. Although most parents put their baby in bed with them (as I did myself), some researchers see it as a problem to the infant. At the end of the day, however, you are the parent and the choice is yours as long as you are aware that you can take appropriate steps to reduce any risk to your child.

[187] Michel Odent 'Primal Health' Clairview Books East Sussex 2002

[188] Sally Goddard Blythe; 'What babies and children really need' Hawthorn Press, Stroud Gloucestershire 2008 (Ref: Siegal D.J. 'The developing mind' the Guildford Press New York 1999 (Ref: 'Toward a neurobiology of interpersonal experiences'),

[189] Jonah Lehrer 'The Decisive Moment' Cannon Gate Books Ltd, Edinburgh 2009 ('The scars of abuse' p185)

[190] Cherry Bond, Positive Touch programme 'In the neonatal unit' article (Ref: Worldwide alternative to violence (WAVE UK) 'the hand that rocks the cradle' http://www.cherrybond.com (cited 07.2008 p5)

[191] New Scientist 'Do-bacteria-cause-cot-death?: Ref: Great Ormond St., report - 04.06.2008 newscientist.com/channel/health/mg19826593.300.html (cited 07.2008)

[192] Wikipedia 'Genetic Factors - Sleeping position and sudden infant death syndrome' (Ref: Dr. Spock) http://www.wikipedia.org/wik/Benjamin_Spock (cited 07.2008)

[193] New Scientist 'Do-bacteria-cause-cot-death?: Ref: Great Ormond St., report - 04.06.2008 http://newscientist.com/channel/health/mg19826593.300-do-bacteria-cause-cot-death.html (cited 07.2008)

[194] New Scientist 'Do-bacteria-cause-cot-death?: Ref: Great Ormond St., report - 04.06.2008 newscientist.com/channel/health/mg19826593.300.html (cited 07.2008)

[195] BBC News: Brain imbalance 'cot death key' http://news.bbc.co.uk/1/hi/health/7489300stm – (Ref: European Molecular Biology – Italy 04.07.2008) (cited 07.2008)

Chapter 19

INDEX

Chapter 19

POST TRAUMATIC STRESS

Birth Trauma for mum

Birth Trauma is now becoming recognised in some circles as a type of Post Traumatic Stress disorder (PTSD), which occurs after childbirth. There are also milder forms for those women who do not show all the clinical symptoms but clearly demonstrate some of the criteria listed for the disorder.

PTSD is the known term for a set of reactions following a bad experience, especially relating to a scary event or traumatic memory. It is related to experiences in life, which are deemed threatening to oneself, or of witnessing an event in which the PTSD disorder will be the outcome.

A traumatic event can be any experience involving the threat of death or serious injury to a person or someone close to them, such as their baby. Some areas of the medical profession now understand that PTSD can also be the consequence of a traumatic birth process.

The symptoms are beyond the control of the sufferer, who experiences flashbacks accompanied by genuine fear, terror and anxiety. The horrors are real as the individual relives the experience over and over again, and the symptoms include:

- A response of intense fear from the labour process
- Helplessness or horror of the birth experience
- Persistent re-experiencing of the event by way of recurrent intrusive memories or flashbacks and feeling panicky
- Some may feel angry, irritable and be hyper-vigilant (on their guard all the time and feeling jumpy)
- Being obsessive by talking about the event all the time
- Avoidance of anything that reminds them of the trauma
- Find it a challenge to bond with their baby
- Feeling anxious and distressed when they come into contact

with anything that reminds them of the experience. Even the baby is a daily reminder of the event, causing bad memories for the mother who will not want to bond with her baby

- Withdrawing internally and refusing to talk about the experience
- Reminders of the trauma will result in difficulty sleeping and concentrating

Those who suffer from birth trauma should understand one very important fact - it is the mind's way of trying to make sense of the scary experiences and is not a sign of an individual's 'weakness' or any inability to cope.

Birth trauma and PTSD are normal human responses to a traumatic experience. Sadly, because it is not often diagnosed and frequently unrecognised by the sufferer or those around them, medical advice is not sought. Indeed, PTSD in the form of birth trauma is often confused with Post Natal Depression (PND).

Research in this field remains limited and to date has focused largely on the importance of the type of delivery and not the risk factors for Post Traumatic Stress (PTSD), which include a very complicated mix of the objective (the type of delivery) and the subjective (feelings of being out of control).[196]

The statistics in terms of PTSD are astounding. It was estimated in 2007 that in the UK alone, birth trauma may result in 10,000 women a year developing Post Traumatic Stress Disorder and as many as 200,000 more women feeling traumatised by childbirth and developing some of the symptoms of PTSD[197]. This is a huge problem, which is not sufficiently recognised and apparently not dealt with in a compassionate way by the medical profession in general.

From my own research, I have found that most of the problems that ultimately cause birth trauma and birth-related PTSD usually stem from the medical process itself. With cattle-herding ways and inappropriate handling of the situation in terms of the mother's needs, some staff choose not to see, hear or understand the mother's views or wishes.

With limited resources and hospital staff, women are often left on their own to cope following the birth, whereas especially if it is their first child, what they need is guidance and patience from midwives and medical staff to help teach them how to look after their new baby. They should not have to rely on family and friends to do that. Contrary to pre-natal teachings, dealing with a real baby is far different to practicing on a doll.

Nowadays, our hospitals seem to be run like factories, with the process of baby delivery having to fit in to their bed schedule, using inducement and Caesarean deliveries when baby doesn't come to order.

As I have said before, I think of these as 'car crash deliveries'. The in/out schedule of having less than 24 hours in hospital often leaves both the mother and child overwhelmed and suffering from birth trauma/PTSD. Without the care and attention they need following the birth, mothers are being left for hours at a time with no contact or help.

To some it may not seem obvious, but treatment like this can only leave the mother and child suffering. Just like being in a car crash, these newborn children are experiencing PTSD like their mothers, and I have seen this in so many of those who have come to me suffering from distress. Clearly the children are also in shock, not only from the treatment they have received during the birth process but also from the drug affects.

More and more I have to question the apparent move away from genuine care in some hospitals. Some establishments have become so clinical. The staff appear to show no feelings, with the majority being almost totally detached. As so many have said 'treatment has become more about paperwork than compassion and care'.

Am I the only one who thinks that we have lost the care and nurturing in our hospitals? Understaffed and over-pressured, medical staff are often so stressed out themselves that they have to become detached in order to function on a daily basis. Occasionally, amidst the turmoil, shining examples of wonderful caring staff do remind us of how it should be all the time, but despite these few exceptions, financial considerations are generally taking precedence over treatment and appearing to focus on profit rather than care.

Metaphorically speaking, are we throwing the baby out with the bath water? More and more feedback suggests that there is no feeling of security and safety going into hospital any more. Many mothers are dreading going into labour because of the harsh treatment they may receive in hospital. Some women see it more as a torture session instead of being cared for in a loving and caring way.

From going into hospital feeling a little apprehensive about the birth but able to cope, they come out shell-shocked, overwhelmed and often suffering Post Traumatic Stress Disorder.

Clinical trials

According to Molecules of Emotion by Candice Pert, 75% of all disorders start from emotional events, and indeed clinical trials bear this out. In addition, trials on war veterans carried out by Dr John Upledger and his team using Somoto Emotional Release techniques have proved to be very helpful in understanding and treating post-traumatic stress.

Stress causes us to secrete chemicals in the body. Known as peptides, these chemicals coat the cells and the coating determines how our body is going to react in the future. In effect, this means that our cells hang on to the memory that created the action, so that physical and emotional disorders show themselves in the form of addiction, eating disorders, smoking, drinking, obsessive compulsive disorders (OCD) and so on.

Sometimes when we are anxious or stressed, angry, emotionally upset or just under pressure, it puts us on red alert (the fight or flight mode). The adrenal system kicks in, producing an explosion of hormones as an automatic response from the body to help us deal with the situation, such as is the case in an emergency.

Fragmented energy

The trauma of birth can fragment a baby's energy. This needs to be rebalanced, otherwise the child can be prone to falls and seen as clumsy as a direct result of the left side of the body being out of balance with the right and vice versa. This not only happens at birth but can occur at any time and any age, i.e. car crash or falls. Basically when we suffer severe shock to our systems our energy can fragment, exploding out proportionally to the severity of the event.

Trauma equals fear and it comes in many different levels or spheres of fear, from mild to extreme. When we have trauma in our lives, no matter what the cause, it can create an imbalance in our energy. The experience of birth can be mild for some but extreme for others, depending upon the delivery process.

The fragmentation of energy causes extreme trauma to the body, pushing the emotions out of control, and at this point all systems operate at an extreme level. It is the same with chakra energies. I have found that some children disconnect from their energy fields quite easily, and this can happen following other events. Apart from birth, the jolt from simple car accidents can put our energy fields out of kilter, such as in the case of whiplash injuries.

Fragmentation or disconnection from an individual's energy fields causes the essence of that child or adult to disappear and we often see this in depression.
Notably seen in the eyes. The eyes are dead and it is as though there is no-one home any more. The physical body is present but the essence or spirit of the person leaves and they become 'ungrounded'. Initially you notice that they are not the person they once were, the person you knew. Instead of the normal human interaction they are just the shell of a body. This nearly always happens when individuals are in trauma, and can result in depression.

Explained simply, the shock has become too much for the body to cope with, forcing the individual's spirit to shut down. They become numb emotionally and physically. If it can be recognised, however, all is not lost. I use advanced techniques to correct and rebalance energy shut-downs from shock.

Stress and shock is commonly seen amongst those who are traumatised from atrocities in war zones. Soldiers, seamen and resistance fighters suffer frequently. Those who endure such times have experienced this awful state over and over again. Now recognized as a legitimate illness, it has been labelled as Post Traumatic Stress (PTS).

PTS and Car accidents

I have seen and lived with the effects of my husband's PTS after he suffered a car accident on the motorway twenty years ago. The shock of having someone drive into the back of his stationary car, of seeing the approaching vehicle and knowing that it was going to hit him left a deep impression on his subconscious.

Fully aware that there was nothing he could do about it as he was blocked in with cars on either side, he sat in horror and waited for the impact. Despite the car being a write-off, after climbing from the wreckage he suffered no major physical injuries at the time and was considered fit to return to work after a few days.

What the medical assessment did not take into consideration, however, was the emotional injury. The nightmares, the insecurity, the withdrawal and numbness, all changed his personality. You could see the fear every time he got into a car, looking terrified in the rear view mirror each time he applied the brakes, waiting for and reliving that awful impact again. His emotional trauma went on for months.

Clearly you don't have to be in a war zone to suffer post-traumatic stress and PTS does not only affect adults. It often affects children more than we recognize. In some cases it is easily recognised, but not in others.

Babies also suffer PTS despite the lack of formal recognition amongst many professional bodies. The birth process can be sometimes too much for them to deal with and I have seen this over and over again in my own work with treating newborns and infants.

The symptoms are self-evident:

- Shock
- Trauma
- Depression
- Feeling emotionally numb

Children suffering PTS become fearful of sleeping, because closing their eyes forces them to relive the drama of birth. Nightmares and flashbacks make them fretful and cause them to jerk and jump during sleep. Distressed and anxious, the baby is inconsolable and cries. I have seen and treated five month-olds still suffering from this trauma but it is never too late to seek help.

Research has also shown that children who are born prematurely can cut off and withdraw emotionally, being more likely to have behaviour issues such as hyperactivity, leading to problems at school.

POST-TRAUMATIC STRESS DISORDER (PTSD)

PTSD is a specific form of anxiety that comes on after a stressful or frightening event. It can begin from a car accident, from being the victim of an assault or even just seeing an accident happen to someone else. Those prone to seeing horrifying experiences, such as soldiers, police officers, firemen or ambulance workers are more likely to have such experiences, especially those in the forces seeing friends being blown up, killed or injured.

Common causes of PTSD include:

- Natural disasters such as earthquakes
- Violence or personal assault (sexual, physical attack or abuse)
- Rape
- Torture
- Being diagnosed with a life-threatening illness
- Terrorist incidents and attacks
- Serious road and other accidents
- Physical injury, mugging or robbery
- Traumatic stress from employment or heavy workloads
- Abuse - child abuse, sexual abuse etc.,
- Birth trauma

In military combat, PTSD is already well known and in past times it was often referred to as battle fatigue or shell shock.
PTSD can start after any kind of shock to the body, from accidents, observed violence, violent personal assaults such as rape or even

surgical operations. Attacks of any sort, including having your home burgled, can leave the occupant feeling frightened, raped or invaded.

Symptoms may begin immediately after the trauma or may develop many months later. They are often made worse by any reminder of the original traumatic experience, no matter how small. The symptoms include:

- Recurring memories or dreams of the event
- A sense of personal isolation
- Disturbed sleep and concentration
- A deadening of feelings – numbness or a sense of feeling nothing
- Irritability
- Painful feelings
- Feelings of guilt

Over time, most people recover from PTSD or learn to live with the trauma in other ways. While suffering, they need emotional support and especially treatment such as emotional release and/or counselling. Sometimes, however, emotions can build up to form a true depressive illness.
Alternatives such as Bach flower remedies and Reflexology can help in some cases. (See appendix for details)

Prolonged physical deprivation and severe trauma resulting from war or concentration camps can scar people psychologically for life. In addition, physical manifestations follow as a result of emotional dysfunction, such as:- headaches, aches and pains, stomach malfunction, eating disorders and IBS being just a few examples.

THREE MAIN GROUPS OF SYMPTOMS FOR PTS

What does Post Traumatic Stress disorder (PTSD) feel like?
Symptoms can kick in within minutes of the trauma or lie dormant for weeks, even months. Usually they appear no later than six months after the event. Many people feel grief-stricken, depressed, anxious and sometimes guilty. Anger can also be very prevalent

after a traumatic experience. There are, however, three main groups of symptoms produced by traumatic experience, which cover most sufferers.

1. Flashbacks and nightmares
2. Avoidance and numbing
3. Being 'on guard'

Flashbacks & Nightmares

Sufferers will find themselves re-living the event again and again. This will happen as 'flashbacks' during the day and nightmares during sleep. Flashbacks invariably feel as though the individual is in the event again, re-experiencing everything. Like a video that won't shut off, some relive the experience repeatedly and replay the scenario over and over again. Despite reliving it in the mind, many actually feel the emotions and physical sensations as experienced during the original event, including the fear, sweating, smells, touch, sound and pain.

Avoidance & Numbing

Reliving the experience is horrifying and makes sufferers feel distraught, so others find ways of distracting themselves from the memories. They often start by avoiding places and people who remind them of the trauma and even refuse to talk about it. It becomes necessary to keep their mind busy and exclude everything else in the attempt by working very hard or spending time engrossed in a hobby. Some even start a course previously unconsidered; anything to distract themselves.

When trauma is so deep, the body will also avoid the memories by feeling nothing. To deliberately feel numb, emotionally numb, they withdraw into themselves, shutting themselves off. Communication becomes difficult as they talk less and less and the people around them find it a challenge just to live and work with them.

Being "On Guard"

Being on guard or 'red alert' means always looking out, fearful of repeating the original situation. If the trauma stems from a serious car accident, sufferers will be continuously looking around and in their mirror to check for drivers coming too close. They can't relax, always looking out for danger or the threat of attack. Irritable and jumpy, they keep themselves highly sensitive to any noise or unexpected disturbance. This state is called 'hyper-vigilance'.

The basic symptoms of PTSD are a mental reaction to narrowly-avoided death which can be so profound as to affect sufferers very deeply. They no longer have any sense that life is fair, safe or reasonable and they no longer feel secure. The experience or event makes them realize that they are vulnerable. Having seen that they can die at any time, the realisation will make them overly conscious of how tenuous and fragile life can be.

By being permanently on guard, they intend to react quickly if another similar event happens and this is often a symptom that earthquake survivors experience. Keeping this practice up, however, expends a lot of energy.

The more disturbing the experience, the more likely you are to develop a prolonged or long-term Post Traumatic Stress Disorder. It is thought that one in three will find their symptoms persist, as they fail to come to terms with what has happened. It is as though the process has become stuck, perpetuating the disorder for far too long. Often the symptoms seem to be worse when the events have:

- Been unexpected or sudden
- Involved being trapped and unable to get away
- Resulted in the death of others
- Involved harming children

Although distressing to recall, after being frightened we often remember things very clearly. Flashbacks force us to remember, whether we want to or not, and analysing the event makes us think about what we would do if it happened again. Over time (which can be different for each individual), we can think about these things without becoming upset. We slowly regain management of our thoughts and decide whether we want to think about these experiences again or not.

Family and friends are vital in keeping you going when you have PTSD, but with expert support, sufferers can come to terms with and understand the frightening event or experience in which they have been involved. Depending upon the depth of the trauma, it can take some months for this process to complete.

The part of the brain that processes memories is called the hippocampus, and high levels of adrenaline (which come into play as part of the fight or flight process) stop it from working properly. Just like blowing a fuse or a chip in your computer, the hippocampus begins malfunctioning. As a result, the flashbacks and nightmares continue because the memory of the trauma can't be processed as it should. If the overall stress is reduced, the adrenaline levels go back to normal and the brain is then able to repair the damage itself. It files and processes the memories properly and the flashbacks and nightmares slowly reduce.

Sometimes we don't share our experiences, failing to explain ourselves properly when we visit the doctor. We discuss the physical symptoms at length and yet say nothing of the emotional trauma. Not wanting to talk in detail about our traumatic experiences or upsetting events, we worry that such discussion will be considered a weakness or a sign of mental instability. People with PTSD therefore often find it easier to discuss side effects such as sleep problems, irritability, tension, family or work-related problems, rather than the real issues.

Emotional reactions to stress are, however, often accompanied by physical symptoms such as:

- Muscle aches and pains
- Diarrhoea
- Irregular heartbeats
- Headaches
- Feelings of panic and fear
- Depression
- Drinking too much alcohol
- Using drugs (including painkillers)
- Feeling out of control

- Relationship problems - finding it difficult to get on with people
- Needing to keep busy and to cope
- Feeling exhausted

Under normal circumstances, these symptoms should start to reduce at around six weeks after the event. If it is more than six weeks and these experiences don't seem to be getting better, it is worth talking it over with your GP.

PRESSURE ON NEW MUMS

Some women find that they suffer guilt and depression as a direct result of pressure put on them by their peers and family, as well as through breast-feeding and trying to juggle job, home and family.

It is fashionable and more accepted to breast-feed these days and there is a lot of pressure on women to feed their baby in this way. This can create a conflict if the mother is also busy with job, family and home. Simply feeling overwhelmed can be misconstrued as postnatal depression.

New mothers want to do the right thing and they will listen to the professionals who they believe must know better. However, it has to be what you want as a mum and what fits into your schedule. Don't feel guilty because it is too restricting to breast-feed; it does not suit all mothers. You have to find a feeding routine and daily schedule that suits you and your child. (as discussed in section 15 breast-feeding)

Hold and cuddle your baby and take the opportunity to get to know one another. That way you will know what your baby needs and what you are comfortable with. Don't let others bully you into something that you do not want to do and always remember that it is your child, your body and your choice!

Your partner may be feeling euphoric about the birth and displaying all the emotions of a proud dad, but he is not the one who has had the baby, who is feeling overwhelmed and maybe battle sore from the delivery. Which one is feeling fatigued and exhausted from childbirth? Your partner is not having his day restricted with breast-feeding - you are, so make the right choices for you.

Analyse how you feel and ask yourself 'Do I feel depressed or just overwhelmed with all the events that have happened since the birth?' The two are vastly different and require different solutions.

- Don't be pressured into taking anti-depressants if you don't want them
- Look for alternative help from family and friends, especially support with the extra workload
- Remember to ask. Others don't know if you don't tell them you need help!
- Get the new dad involved. Most men love bonding with their new arrival, so let them get used to the other side of being supportive by changing nappies, bottle feeding and helping to settle baby to sleep
- Some men enjoy doing the shopping, the washing etc
- If grandparents are keen to help, let them!

WHAT IS POST NATAL POST TRAUMATIC STRESS DISORDER? (PTSD)

Giving birth is a natural process, but because of interference and timing schedules in our hospitals, many women can suffer extreme psychological distress as a consequence of their child's birth.

For a variety of reasons, which are frequently related to the treatment and processes that they have been subjected to during labour, many women suffer unnecessarily. This is the outcome from the vast differences between their previous perception of childbirth assistance and their actual hospital experience. It leaves many women suffering from Post Natal PTSD as they find themselves isolated and detached from other mothers.

No voice

Often new mothers find that they do not have a voice in a society which increasingly focuses on the practicalities and fails to understand the deep psychology of childbirth. Brushing aside complaints with an expectation of 'getting on with it' or 'you will get over the effects soon', well-meaning staff dismiss the real problem out of hand.

Since support for women with Post Natal PTSD is not always understood, sufferers can be left for some time without the expert help that they need, as others find it difficult to understand their trauma, confusion and guilt. Most women will be misdiagnosed as having the 'baby blues' or Post Natal Depression, with those who could make a difference not understanding that the trauma is at a much deeper level.

Differences between PND and PTSD

There are, however, subtle differences between Post Natal Depression and Post Traumatic Stress Disorder and while some symptoms may overlap, the two illnesses are distinct and need to be treated individually.

PTSD is a profound disability, which affects any sufferer deeply, but for new mothers who have the combination of the birth experience and the new infant to deal with, it gives a double whammy effect that is overwhelming. For many women, it is not the birth process itself which is the sensational or dramatic event that triggers childbirth trauma, but other factors such as:

- Loss of control
- Loss of dignity
- The hostile or difficult attitudes of the people around them
- A feeling of not being heard
- Absence of informed choice and consent to medical procedures

For some women, the traumas experienced in birth are horrendous, as the process does not go as they had planned. They experience events during pregnancy, delivery and after childbirth, which would traumatise any normal human being. The factors, which lead to 'subjective' feelings of loss of control include:

- Lengthy labour or short and very painful labour
- Induction
- Poor pain relief
- High levels of medical intervention

- Traumatic or emergency deliveries such as Caesarean section
- Impersonal treatment or problems with staff attitudes
- Not being listened to
- Lack of information or explanation
- Lack of privacy and dignity
- Fear for their baby's safety
- Baby's stay in SCBU/NICU
- Poor post natal care

Previous trauma also has a place, as the memories of past anxieties will resurface when another event is being experienced, such as:

- Trauma in childhood
- Trauma from a previous birth
- Domestic violence

Many women suffer from some of the symptoms of Post Traumatic Stress Disorder after a difficult birth experience and this can cause them long-lasting distress and genuine difficulty. As we have said, often they will be classed as having the 'baby blues' instead of PTSD.

Women are not the only ones to suffer however. For the partner or husband, the trauma of watching and being involved during the birth process can also be severe; they can feel traumatised after the event and have a feeling of being out of their depth. Some feel a sense of failure, due to being unable to help their partner or spouse.

Because awareness of this issue is generally poor, many women are wrongly diagnosed with Post Natal Depression and are prescribed medication that may do little or nothing to help their situation[198]. My own research has shown that women are often told by healthcare professionals, family and friends to move on and get on with their lives' or that they should be grateful that they have a healthy baby. This type of misunderstanding only fuels their distress and exacerbates their feelings of guilt and isolation. Many women are prescribed anti-depressants because their local GP is not up to speed with Post Natal Post Traumatic Stress disorder.

Depression is, however, known to go hand in hand with PTSD. It is one of the symptoms, so not all are misdiagnosed. Medication may be appropriate for some, but if you are concerned about the course of action offered for you, please research further. Talk to your GP and Health Visitor and don't be afraid to ask to be referred for expert help. Leaflets are also available from some organisations such as the BTA and One Generation Project.

If you are suffering from PTSD, others may not understand your trauma completely and may even be hostile towards you because, in their minds, you should be getting better. They could be angry due to misunderstanding that you need a lot of time and space to return to your old self again. In some, compassion may be short-lived.

Family and friends finding that your traumatic energy is not helping them may decide that they don't want to be around you much of the time. When seen to avoid you because they don't want to listen to you reliving your trauma, as they too find it distressing, it appears as though they are leaving the sinking ship. They may simply see you as being weak and advise you to 'pull yourself together'. Some may even blame you for what happened while others might not allow you to talk about it because they harbour some personal guilt too, or in some cases, memories may come to mind from their own traumatic experiences.

SELF-HELP FOR POST NATAL
POST TRAUMATIC STRESS DISORDER

Don't beat yourself up because you did not have the perfect birth as planned. Don't feel guilty if you cannot breast feed because it is too painful for you. You have done your best and there are alternatives that will probably make your life easier.

No matter how painful it is, talking about what happened can help to relieve the symptoms. Like the old adage, a trouble shared is a trouble halved and it will also help your partner or spouse to understand what you are going through. In addition:

- Eat and exercise regularly - don't miss meals as you need to build up your energy
- Magnesium and zinc help to reduce and balance mood swings and depression
- Take time out with friends and family in a relaxing environment
- Don't take holidays on your own
- Try to get yourself back into as normal a routine as soon as possible
- Talk to your doctor and/or therapist
- Drive with care, as your concentration may be impaired
- When you are ready, return to work
- Expect to get better – it will happen eventually
- Watch funny or comic films (or something that you like) and programmes to lighten your mood

It is quite normal to feel overwhelmed when you arrive home with your baby. You have been through a dramatic event and can feel battle scarred.

- Allow yourself to see your beautiful child as a gift instead of a problem
- Allow yourself to delegate - don't be the martyr
- Don't be ashamed to ask for help when you need it
- Give yourself time

- Take one day at a time
- Don't worry if the washing does not get done - it can be looked at tomorrow
- Get your spouse or family more involved in mundane tasks; it will be easy enough for them to do it instead of you
- Grandparents and family love to help out when there is a new arrival, so allow them to help you
- If possible, rest when your baby sleeps

Trauma takes energy away from you and you need to recharge your batteries and allow your body to regenerate itself. Express breast milk beforehand and allow your partner to do the night shift feeding and changing so you can get some proper sleep. Remember - giving birth is exhausting - this is normal!

Don't punish yourself for feeling the way that you do. Whatever happened to you was a unique experience and the symptoms you are feeling are not a sign of weakness. PTSD is a normal reaction in people who have had a fearful experience so don't expect too much from yourself in the early days.

Following a bad experience, shock and fear can be very wearing on the body and you will need time to adjust. Don't avoid talking to others about your experience – talking helps. Don't bottle up how you feel either but instead express your feelings and talk or even write them down in a journal. Don't expect the memories to go immediately but know they will reduce with time.

If you find yourself still struggling despite using self-help techniques, you might also choose to seek out alternative help for your distress in the form of:

- Homeopathy
- Reflexology
- Emotional release techniques such as Somoto Emotional Release (SER) or Dissolve and Resolve Emotions (DARE)

TREATMENT FOR POST NATAL POST TRAUMATIC STRESS

As there are both physical and psychological aspects to PTSD, so there needs to be both physical and psychological expert treatment to counteract it. Ideally, treatments should be done through specialists and experts in PTSD. Sessions should be weekly and would normally continue for 8-12 weeks. Treatments may last between an hour and 90 minutes.

The types of treatment available include:

- Psychotherapy
- Counselling
- Cognitive Behaviour therapy (CBT) - which helps you to think differently
- Emotional Release - releases core problems
- Eye Movement De-sensitisation and Reprocessing (EMDR) - helps the brain to process flashbacks

Initially you may be in a trance-like state, almost like waking from a bad dream. Your situation may seem unreal or bewildering, especially if you can't remember exactly what happened. Confused, you may find that you can't put your feelings or experience into words or even make sense of it all, as happens in some cases. Eventually, however, you will start to feel safe again and once more in control of your feelings. When this happens, you won't need to avoid the memories as they gradually become less traumatic and distressful.

Physical bodywork such as massage, reflexology, Cranio Sacral Therapy and acupuncture can help to control the distress of PTSD, reducing hyper-arousal and the feeling of being 'on guard' all the time. By helping to develop relaxation and manage the stress, it often helps reduce the continuous loop systems of distress and anxiety. Other therapies that you might like to try include yoga, meditation and healing.

The National Institute for Clinical Excellence (NICE) guidelines suggest that trauma-focussed psychological therapies such as Cognitive Behaviour Therapy (CBT) and Eye Movement De-sensitisation and Reprocessing should be offered before medication wherever possible.

You can read more about the NICE guidelines on their website, which can be found at www.nice.org.uk, and you may also like to visit www.traumatic-stress.freeserve.co.uk , the website for Assist (Assistance Support and Self Help in Surviving Trauma).

Post Natal depression - Depression in women after birth

PND can be a common disorder for women who have just given birth and stems from a combination of sudden hormonal changes and a variety of psychological and environmental factors. PND ranges from an extremely common and short-lived attack of mild depression often known as 'the baby blues', to the most serious psychosis in which the woman is very severely depressed. In the latter case she will need expert help and the worst cases often require admission to hospital to prevent harm to the mother and her baby.

It is thought that approximately 10% of women experience psychological distress with significant depressive symptoms during pregnancy. Those with histories of major depression appear to be at a higher risk of depression recurring again during pregnancy.

PND is normally diagnosed or recognised by the health visitor or primary care team at about eight weeks after childbirth. In most cases, women seem to recover within approximately 4-6 months of the birth. The disruption to the rest of family during this time, however, can be considerable and of course it can affect the quality of the early bonding between mother and child. It will also hinder the physical and emotional development of the child.

Baby Blues

It is estimated that, after giving birth, more than two thirds of mothers will suffer from the 'baby blues', which often kick in four to five days after delivery. The symptoms include feelings of:

- Being overwhelmed as a result of the birth process
- Being overwhelmed with the sudden realisation of the responsibility associated with caring for the child
- Misery
- Mental confusion
- Discouragement

- Tearfulness and crying easily and often
- Having no bond with the child
- Having no interest in the child

Hormonal and psychological changes kick in following the feelings of anticlimax after the delivery and these can give an overwhelming sense of responsibility for the baby's care. With reassurance from spouse, family, friends and additional outside support, the depression can pass in a few days as the mother becomes more confident and feels calmer about her new role.

Are Shorter stays in hospital contributing?

The new trend towards shorter hospital stays does not help women who are feeling fragile and vulnerable at this time. They often feel as though they have no support and have not had time to adjust to their new role and responsibility. When a new mum can stay in hospital for a few days after the birth, it allows time for adjustment, as well as allowing the opportunity for her to be shown how to handle the baby and giving time for the mother and child to get to know one another in a supported environment.

In many cases this is not the practice nowadays and I feel that more women are suffering because of a system where financial consideration, statistics and protocols, takes precedence over the new mother's health. It also prevents expert experience being passed on in a valued way.

Severe depression

This type of postnatal depression occurs in about 10 to 15% of women after childbirth and is more noticeable. Sometimes with severe PND no risk factors are obvious and the condition strikes unexpectedly, although women who were depressive and anxious during pregnancy are more at risk of severe postnatal depression.

The symptoms which are likely to be experienced are a constant feeling of tiredness, difficulty in sleeping, loss of appetite and restlessness. This type of PND is more likely to occur if the mother:

- Has a strained relationship with partner/spouse

- Has no family support
- Is experiencing financial or other worries
- Has already experienced episodes of depression or anxiety, either unrelated to or during pregnancy
- Is a first time mother
- Suffered from a personality disorder

Anti-depressants are usually prescribed in the UK, to help clear up severe PND. With Fluoxetine being the most commonly prescribed drug.   Although in other European countries such as France they were the least preferred treatment for PND. [199]

I have successfully treated women with PND and have found that it is sometimes an old memory pattern, which has kicked in from fear or emotional trauma from a previous time or even a previous pregnancy. It can also come from a feeling of helplessness. Once the core of the issue is found and relieved with Emotional Release Therapy, the symptoms can disappear very quickly as can be seen from the testimonial and case study, which follow.

Research has shown that toddlers and infants of depressed mothers have a higher percentage of insecure attachments and more behavioural difficulties compared to children of non-disorder mothers. It also highlighted the association between maternal mood state and unsettled infant behaviour.[200]

Depressive Psychosis

This severe form of postnatal depression follows about one in 1,000 pregnancies and usually starts two to three weeks after childbirth. Depressive psychosis is marked by:

- Severe mental confusion
- Worthlessness
- Threats of suicide
- Threats of harm to the baby
- Delusions
- Rapid mood changes

- Having no bond with the child
- Having no interest in the child

Normal treatment requires admission to hospital, sensitive counselling and possibly family therapy. Sufferers are also often treated with anti-depressant drugs.

BABY MASSAGE

Baby massage (sometimes known as positive touch) is seen to help. In severe and depressive psychosis, trials have found that baby massage can help the mother and child to bond with touch and gentle stroking. Studies on depressive mothers and premature babies have found a huge improvement in mood change and baby growth with the mother's corresponding retreat from anxiety and depression over a very short period of time.

In 2001 a small trial at Queen Charlotte Hospital, London, proved that mums who had post-natal depression improved with baby massage. While this form of treatment gave them hope and improved their thought patterns overall, only mixed results came from taking drugs.

A testimonial after treatment of Post Natal Depression with DARE

I was diagnosed with PND and felt desperate for things to get better so in my frustration I organised an appointment with Joy. My main symptoms were:

- Insomnia
- Feeling constantly tired
- Feeling very emotional and out of control

From the first session my symptoms rapidly improved. I slept deeper and longer and this had a knock-on effect on every other symptom felt. I could not believe how quickly things improved even after one session.

I found the emotional release treatment quite bizarre as it was nothing like I had experienced before, but a strange sense of relief was felt on all levels. I felt more optimistic, stronger within myself, back to being more in control. I received a further treatment two weeks later.

I feel reassured that there is a treatment that is quick and effective and which can help women who need extra care in times of stress.

Thank you so much.
Jane 2007

START TO GET YOUR LIFE BACK

- Have some time for you; even a relaxing bath with some essential oils and Bach flower remedies will help you to feel better.
- Put on some lipstick, have your hair done differently; it is the simple things that make a difference.
- Try on some of your normal clothes instead of the loose fitting ones you wore during pregnancy.
- Do some simple exercises at home
- Go out for a walk. Being in the house too long will cause SAD; you need at least one hour of sunlight per day to help lighten your mood.
- Take vitamins and minerals such as zinc and magnesium daily for up to three months to help reduce the mood swings. (Take advice from a professional)
- Treat yourself to a massage, reflexology or emotional release session.
- See a good professional homeopath to help with mood swings and baby blues.
- Be sure to eat properly and don't skip meals - your body needs sustenance to regain that energy.
- Eat healthy food with plenty of fruit and vegetables. Don't snack on sugary foods as they will give you a brief sugar rush and then fall off again, adding to your low feelings and blues.

- Stay off caffeine - alcohol, coffee and tea. Substitute with green tea, herbal teas or Roobosh tea.
- Drink plenty of water.
- Stay positive when you're feeling low. We all have our off days.
- Diet is especially important when you are breast-feeding. Take alfalfa to increase quality and milk production. (See section 15 breast-feeding)

Some women often find it better to return to work after maternity leave and of course there is no right or wrong answer here; it is what you decide to do. Many women don't have an option but need to return to work because of financial commitments, whereas others need to return to work for themselves.

Floral helpers such as Bach Flower Remedies

We have mentioned Bach flower remedies to help with a number of problems and conditions, and the following ones can also help in the short term with mild cases of 'baby blues' and PND. The information is for self-help, which was how the remedies were designed. However, if in doubt please take advice from a professional therapist who is trained in remedies.

There are lots of books available on the subject of Bach flower remedies and you can also find further information from the Bach centre.

Beech	Intolerance, having to be right
Crab Apple	Self- disgust or self-loathing
Gorse	Hopelessness and pessimism
Holly	Envy, jealousy, hatred
Larch	Lack of confidence and self-esteem
Mustard	Depression
Oak	Grounding

Pine   Guilt and self-blame

Red Chestnut Over-anxiety and fear for others

Vine   Domineering

Willow   Resentment

White chestnut Persistent worries

Method: Put a few drops of your chosen remedy into a stock bottle, add spring water and shake. To use, add a few drops to water and sip throughout the day.
(See appendix for full details)

CASE STUDY 13 -
POST NATAL DEPRESSION (PND)

Nearly all of my clients are referrals and in 2007 a lady was referred to me via a previous client. The lady was thought to be suffering from PND and complained of sleep problems. She had a four month-old baby and a two year-old toddler. For privacy reasons we will call her Amanda.

Her symptoms were:

- Not sleeping - only falling asleep through exhaustion as the mind would not stop
- Anxiety about her family and going back to work
- Feeling as though her life was over - 'I want to die'
- Constantly tired
- Feeling physically weak and unable to get off the sofa
- Crying most of the time
- Suicidal - dark thoughts of 'Is this ever going to end?' and wanting to take her own life; even thinking of ways of doing just that

- Overwhelmed by the strain and burden of
  a family to look after
- Difficulty bonding at first with her baby
- Guilty about having to return to work
- Panic attacks – heart beating very fast
- Frustration and loneliness

Amanda was a professional woman in her 30s who was clearly intelligent. Looking worn out, pale and exhausted, her eyes were dull. Her whole body was depleted and her poor posture spoke volumes. When I asked her if there had been any significant changes in her life, she replied simply, 'having children.'

Her doctor had prescribed medication. Sleeping tablets were aimed at knocking her out at night and helping her to sleep generally, while beta-blockers and anti-depressants were prescribed for her anxiety. Her husband had given much support and took the 10pm feed so that she could go to bed early. Unfortunately, however, he was getting fed up with there being no end in sight, and had started to get angry with her for lying on the sofa so much. Fortunately, this new mum had wonderful home support from family and in particular from her mum and sister who called in daily to help out with the children.

This pregnancy (her second) was quite different from the first. The pregnancy was not planned and, although she was comfortable with her first pregnancy, this one did not start off well. Having felt so well with the first pregnancy, this was not what Amanda had anticipated. Consequently it did not enter her thoughts that a second pregnancy would not be a mirror image of the first.

Her second was, however, entirely different. Amanda felt unwell almost throughout, with persistent vomiting from early until late in the pregnancy. Amanda told me 'she only felt normal with the bit in the middle', either side had been miserable both physically and mentally. Amanda did not enjoy this pregnancy at all although she continued to work throughout and look after her husband and baby.

Her labour had gone smoothly enough but Amanda reacted badly to the pethadine given at the time, suffering more vomiting. All seemed well when she came home but she struggled when her husband returned to work. Having crashed completely, she told me she had forgotten how to relax again. Her mind couldn't switch off.

During Amanda's first pregnancy she had worked up to 36 weeks and enjoyed the whole experience. Labour proved a different story, being both difficult and long. Through the birth process the child was born with a misshapen head, suffered from colic and was most unsettled. After the birth, Amanda felt low emotionally and experienced 'baby blues' (as it was thought of at the time).

Amanda now realises that she had suffered before from Post Natal Depression and seemed to remember it kicking in one month after having her first child, although not as severely on that occasion. After the first pregnancy she adjusted fairly quickly, especially when her baby learned to sleep through the night at about twelve weeks old. Mum then learned to enjoy her baby and they bonded well from this point.

This time around however, Amanda was experiencing more severe symptoms and could not shake them off. Not only was she not bonding with her baby, she was also losing the previous strong connection to her two year-old from the effects of her post-natal depression.

Looking back, Amanda now realised she had worked too late into her pregnancy and remembered how she had struggled with trying to do everything as normal. Putting on her super woman mask, she inadvertently put her health in jeopardy in the process. With continuous feelings of exhaustion and tiredness, she could not be bothered to go out of the house and thought about it less and less. She found looking after her new baby a heavy chore and trying to do so made her feel so tired. The burden was too much to bear.

Another difference that Amanda noticed with her second child was to do with feeling lonely. None of her friends had come to see her as they did for her first child. Visitors were fewer and not as much fuss was made over her second child. She felt as though she had lost out and wondered whether the excitement had kept her going previously with her first baby. Feeling out of the circle of friends this time, she felt further restricted by now having two children to cope with.

Returning to work

As mothers, when we decide to return to work after maternity leave, guilt can be a normal emotion, however this lady felt guilty for several reasons. She felt guilt about leaving her children to be looked after by others, although she had no pangs on returning to work after her first child because her mum was taking care of things, which proved ideal. She felt guilt for not choosing to become a full time mum as her friend had. Some of Amanda's friends were choosing to stay at home after the birth and become full time mothers. However, Amanda had no option but to return to work. Apart from the loss in salary, she needed to go back to work for herself, her own self-esteem and future development. In addition, she felt guilty about the strain she was putting upon her husband. Since he was feeling the strain of the situation and not sleeping well, she became very worried about his health.

The anxiety that Amanda suffered was overwhelming and gave her heart palpitations that felt like panic attacks. Some of them had been all consuming. Her mum was going to take care of her children again on the days that Amanda worked (she was proposing to go back for three days a week) and, even though she knew they were safe, being separated from them still made her anxious. Although the mind was rational in knowing how much she needed to go back to work and her reasons for doing so were valid ones, the thought of separating from her children made her panic.

Constantly crying, feeling unhappy with life and her inner-self, together with sleep deprivation, she felt overwhelmed by guilt. The burden and anxiety had pushed her too far with thoughts of wanting to take her own life. 'When will it all end?' and 'I want to die' were her cries and depression had clearly taken over. As an aside, there are some theories that insomnia can cause depression.

Amanda and I talked for some time about her situation. I explained that all mums have their own way of doing things when they have a new child to cope with. Not only do they create practices and schedules that suit them and their child, each individual mother makes personal choices about returning to work. There is no right or wrong answer to this issue; it is only what is best for them at that time.

Some mothers need to return to work for their own sanity and development. Finding the role of full-time mum at home too mundane, it would shrivel them up. Some lose their sparkle, needing stimulation each day and interaction with other adults. Others feel more comfortable at home and decide to become a full-time mum on a more permanent basis, with the option of returning to work later when their children go to school. Some mums feel pressure to return to work because of the need for extra funds to supplement a partner's income. Often, without mum working, the family cannot manage on one wage. In this circumstance, these women do not have a choice and know they have to return to work.

I also explained that as far as I could see from our consultation, Amanda had been most responsible in her care for her children. She had thought it through in advance and made decisions with the best options. Her mother had agreed to care for her children when she worked and the children already knew their grandmother as she visited the home daily to check on and support Amanda. Amanda felt comfortable with her choice of nanny and trusted her mother in caring for them. In short, Amanda knew her children were safe.

Apart from the money, the main reason for choosing to return to work was because she loved her job. It felt right for her to do that and it was the right choice for Amanda and her family.

I asked her to arrange to have some time for herself, to do something she really liked doing, like going to the hairdressers, to the gym, for a walk, taking a soak in the bath or even indulging in some retail therapy. Perhaps she could go to a friend's home for a cuppa and a chat alone. It was important that she have at least an hour or two during the day when mum could give a hand and allow Amanda to do something for herself. I advised her to either get out of the house or allow her mum to take the children out and allow Amanda some time at home alone. She believed she could achieve this with no problem and decided she would like to read and get some exercise. I stressed the point that 'This is time for you and must be kept for you. Do not start doing housework. Do not start putting on the washing.'

Mind patterns

After her first child, Amanda had gone back to work part-time. However, as she explained to me in detail, she had had to fight for that right. Apparently her boss was not family orientated and had wanted her to return to work on a full-time basis. Amanda could not cope with the full-time option and her union was called in to help mediate. Eventually, over several weeks of discussion, her boss was persuaded to allow her to work for three and a half days a week. Despite an eventual amicable arrangement, the trauma of argument and persuasion only added to her stress at the time.

When we have stress and trauma it can create a pattern. This is a memory that is stored for future reference by the mind and body. When we begin to repeat the stress situation, the body says, 'I know how to handle this. I have done it before' and goes into automatic mode. Confronted with the same objections a second time, Amanda was now facing a mirror image of her past. By returning to work after a second maternity leave and also feeling guilty about leaving her child (which is quite normal), in her case the memory of the battle she had endured previously was now very real again and she was reacting to the old trauma. Although she knew from experience that it was all right, in her mind the trauma and fear remained, making her feel sufficiently anxious to affect her sleep patterns.

Treatment

During her first session, I treated Amanda by de-stressing her. I used emotional release techniques and Cranio Sacral Therapy. In certain parts of her body she had no energy, with the main indication coming from the belly. I could feel a great denseness and knew instinctively that this had come from the emotions stored during her miserable pregnancy. Amanda told me that she felt as though she had a band around her head causing pressure and it took me approximately ten minutes to clear the banded sensation and the belly was rebalanced soon after. Using Cranio Sacral Therapy, I realigned the head and diaphragm and went on to de-stress the body and mind.

Feeling deeply relaxed and calm, it took Amanda some time to come round after her first session. Tiredness is a normal reaction after this type of session, however her eyes looked brighter and she smiled for the first time. It was nice to see the instant change.

A week later, Amanda arrived for her second session and a different person walked through the door. Now Amanda was confident with a strong posture. Her eyes were bright and she told me that she had felt better immediately after her first session. Tired upon her return home the previous week, she had slept all afternoon. When she woke she felt more positive and stayed relaxed.

Since our first session, Amanda had slept much better and experienced a better quality sleep for 8 hours every night. Now she felt:

- There was no guilt
- She felt back in control
- Her depression had lifted – 'Even on my down days I have felt more positive'
- Amanda told me that she was also better at dropping off to sleep. She could now see how everything had been irrational
- As a result of the treatment she was enjoying her children, bonding well and beginning to make it up with her two year-old by having quality time with him
- She had made a definite decision to return to work and had been given a date to return with a two week ease-in period
- Amanda had also booked a holiday
- She felt very positive
- Her mum was not around as much as before and came only when Amanda wanted her
- Amanda had also started exercising and running

Previously, both children were being affected by Amanda's PND. She told me that her baby was now more content and she was making an extra effort with her son to include quality play, even taking him for a swim.

She now admitted to feeling as though she was finally bonding with both children. Her two year-old son's behaviour had improved considerably over the last week, as a direct result of the change in Amanda. Because of her previous state, Amanda's husband had also felt the strain and developed sleeping issues. Feeling responsible, Amanda also worried about being the cause, yet was also sympathetic for him.

'I am thinking more about what works for us as a family,' she told me. She is no longer bothered about her friend deciding to be a full-time mum. Convinced she had made the right decision for all the family, Amanda appreciated her husband being supportive of her return to work.

We talked about Amanda having clear and direct communication of her needs when she returned to work. Not only was it necessary for her husband help out in the home, but Amanda must decide and make clear what was expected and required of him and the role she wanted him to take on, such as:

- Putting the children to bed
- Reading them a bedtime story
- Taking turns to bathe the children
- Making a meal in the evening
- Regularly picking up shopping, especially if he is going out for other reasons
- Taking care of the children one afternoon a week
- Allowing her time for herself and scheduling one evening a week or at least part of an evening if possible

The list could be long or short and would take into account whatever Amanda needed help with.
If these things are not communicated clearly, your partner doesn't know and this is where frustration and martyrdom comes in – spouses do want to help but sometimes they feel in the way. Communication is the key.

I explained to Amanda that quality time with the family was essential. 'Your children will grow quickly and before you know it, they will be at school. Take time to have quality time as a family at weekends.' If the washing and cleaning does not get done that day, don't worry. Life won't stop – simply reschedule it for tomorrow.

These early years are the foundation of our children's lives. Our time together creates their memories of the love and bonding that we share. This is what parenthood is all about. By creating a safe, supportive and loving environment for our children to grow in, we give them confidence and self-esteem. Despite what some believe, materialism does not give children confidence. It is time spent together as a family that builds confidence - quality time with mum, dad and extended family to give the child love and understanding. This provides their foundation for life and the tools to pass on when they have families of their own.

We talked about Amanda's return to work and how she should approach regular morning handover to her mother. What did Amanda want her mum to do? She needed to be very clear and ensure that her mum understood.

Q. 'Breakfast - feed, bath and dress children?'
A. Amanda decided she would see to the baby and mum could help with the dressing and feeding of her two year-old when she left for work. Mum would do light housework and put the washing on and so on.
Q. 'Do you eat breakfast and is it at home or at work?'
A. Yes, but on the hoof at home whilst getting ready.

Q. 'Will you phone home several times a day?'
A. Yes, to start with on her first few days at work. Once settled down, the regular check would reduce to just at lunchtime.

Q. 'Will you feel guilty?'
A. Amanda admitted that for the first few days she probably would. However, this is perfectly normal.

I suggested that in the run-up to her return to work, Amanda could arrange for her mum to look after the children one afternoon a week. As a practice, this gives Amanda a dry run before leaving her children on a more permanent basis.

Q. 'Your mother has previously looked after your children when you have had free time for yourself or to go shopping. When this happens, do you feel guilty leaving your children behind? What is the difference between that and going out to work?'
A. 'Now you put it like that there isn't a difference, apart from the longer time span. I do look forward to seeing my children after they have been away from me for any length of time, even if it is only an hour.'

After just two sessions, the PND was cleared and Amanda was able to get on with her life. Back in control, she became more positive and bonded with her little ones.

There is no need to suffer for months on end with PND when help is at hand, especially when that help is non-invasive and safe. When PND sets in, it not only affects the mother, but her children and partner as well. The ripple effect brings stress and trauma to everyone involved. The sooner it is cleared, therefore, the better for everyone.

It is not always recognised that PND can be mirrored in later pregnancies. We often continue to carry the trauma of the birth process and stress of being unwell during pregnancy. As this case study has clearly shown, unless cleared properly, the problem can return to affect us again. The point is that you don't need to be pregnant for it to be cleared out.

Some weeks later, I had a card from Amanda to thank me. She wrote:

'Thank you very much for all you have done for me. Now I am better, I'm determined to make the most of my life and enjoy the two little ones.'

Depression and bananas

According to a recent survey undertaken by MIND and tested upon those who were suffering from depression, subjects found that they felt slightly better after simply eating a banana.

It is well known that bananas contain potassium, but few are aware that they also contain typtophan. This is a type of protein that the body converts into serotonin, widely known to help us relax. Serotonin improves our mood and generally gives us a feeling of being happy.

Mineral and vitamin depletion is also a cause of depression and I normally request a hair analysis to reveal any imbalances. Low zinc and magnesium levels are regularly highlighted in the hair analysis reports and linked as one of the causes of depression symptoms.

You see, there are simple changes that help. Worth knowing isn't it?

[196] BTA 'What is Trauma' http://www.birthtraumaassociation.org.uk/what_is_trauma.htm (Cited 09.2007)

[197] Ibid 'Who gets birth trauma'

[198] BTA:http://www.birthtraumaassociation.org.uk (Cited 09.2007)

[199] Cherry Bond 'Positive Touch' http://www.cherrybond.com (cited article ref Murray; PND' p4:07.2008)

[200] Ibid (Ref 'Henry Chabol 'Research from France' p3) http:// www.cherrybond.com (cited article 07.2008)

Chapter 20

INDEX

Chapter 20

ALLERGIES

Both children and adults suffer from allergies and, unfortunately, the incidence for both seems to be on the increase. I often see children and adults who have digestive malabsorption, which can be the root cause behind allergic disorders. Often difficult to detect and pinpoint by tests, allergies are not a cut and dried situation when being diagnosed and there may be no real intolerances or allergy to a specific food apparent.

What is sometimes overlooked, however, is a general weakness of normal digestive absorption, something, which shows up when the body is emotionally or mentally stressed. I have treated many sufferers in this situation and sometimes the allergy comes out as a rash, eczema, dermatitis, hay fever or sinus disorders, whilst in other cases it might simply show as inflamed tissue with runny eyes and nose. This can all come about simply from malabsorption in the gut. Our gut is one of four excretory organs that eliminate waste from our body, the others being the skin, bowel and bladder. If any one of these organs is dysfunctional or working under par it will often affect the other systems as they will then become overloaded.

The skin is usually the first to be affected if the gut is not performing well. It can also be affected by the lymph system, which is part of the body's immune system. The skin becomes dry and weak due to a lack of essential fatty acids and more prone to reactions from diet and chemical products used on the skin.

Despite the harsh term, 'chemical' refers to any non-natural element in personal hygiene and bathroom products, cleaning products and washing powders and can affect the skin of susceptible individuals when using clothes and bed linen washed in the offending substance.

Skin is our first line of defence for the external body, and yet many of the products that we use on a daily basis work against its intended protection. Some bath and hygiene products, for example, contain

Sodium Laurel Sulphate (SLS). Even baby products may not be pure and some of the well-known products are not absorbent to the skin. Talc is a known carcinogen as it blocks the pores and some believe that even roll-on deodorants are thought to play a big part in breast cancer, as again they block the pores and prevent the natural excretory process of sweat glands. Some tampons have been found to contain formaldehyde (the chemical product leaked at Bhopal) and we are using these products in a very sensitive place!

STRESS AND ALLERGIES

When we worry and become highly strung, the body becomes stressed. Children can become anxious and distressed about many things that seem unimportant to adults, such as school exams. A friend of mine, for example, recently told me about her ten year-old becoming ill. He had just taken his exams and had become very anxious beforehand. Fortunately he recovered sufficiently to attend school and take the exams on the day but some of his friends suffered in the same way and were not so lucky. Being unable to attend because of stomach cramps and diarrhoea problems, they failed to make the grade!

When we get severely stressed, we activate the flight or fight process, which shuts down various functions within the body. One of the systems that closes down first and is normally affected the most is the stomach. When the original reason has gone it can take hours before the normal digestive process comes back on line again. No wonder so many people suffer from Irritable Bowel Syndrome! When this is happening continually it will take longer for body systems to activate and eventually dysfunction occurs.

Our bodies also produce a chemical called histamine as part of the reaction to stressful circumstances. Histamine works to dilate blood vessels so that immune cells can get to an area under attack much faster than normal, as might be the case when we experience a bee sting. On some occasions however, excess histamine can make the skin red and rash-ridden as if plagued by a nettle rash or prickly heat, a rash which occurs under the skin. Histamine can also constrict the bronchi, closing off the airways and causing wheeziness.

NATURAL PRODUCTS TO HELP ALLERGIES

Natural products can help with skin disorders and allergies, and here are some which you may find useful.

Arnica Gel

Arnica gel can be used for bruises and skin problems and is believed by some to be as effective as ibuprofen.

Antihistamines

Urtica (nettle) tincture calms symptoms that look like nettle rash or prickly heat, where the skin looks red and bumpy and is itchy. Nettle tea taken several times a day will also help, although the tincture is stronger. Arthritis sufferers may also find Urtica useful as it helps to remove the build-up of uric acid from the joints, thereby reducing pain.

Immune system/Anti-inflammatory

Devil's Claw tincture helps to rebalance the immune system so that it does not trigger quite so easily. As an anti-inflammatory, it helps with allergic-type symptoms which tend to involve inflammation in the body and, unlike some medications, Devil's Claw does not damage the stomach lining.

Echinacea tablet or tincture is also used with low immune system function but can only be taken for a short while as it loses its effectiveness with continual use. Echinacea should be taken at the first signs of colds or flu and it can also calm an over-active immune response.

Essential Fatty Acids (EFA's) are also a mild anti-inflammatory.

SKIN DISORDERS

Zinc works well for the immune system and also helps to heal skin, whilst the tincture, Viola Tricolour, which is produced from the viola flower, is known to reduce skin inflammation. As it improves transport to and from the skin, it helps to deliver nutrients and removes wastes.

Centaurium is another flower tincture, this time working to stimulate the body to provide more of its own digestive enzymes, thus assisting in the proper breakdown of food.

Aloe Vera taken from the plant and applied on the skin with gel is used to treat wounds and leg ulcers, burns and scalds, sunburn and fungal infections. Taken in liquid form, it will strengthen and repair organs and damaged cell tissue, reducing inflammation.

Bee Propolis extract is used as a crème or gel for skin rashes and disorders such as eczema, while calendula plant extract is an age old remedy used in crème form for skin disorders.

ECZEMA

In recent years there has been an increase in allergies in children, and especially in those suffering with asthma and eczema. Parents of children with eczema can find the condition very worrying and stressful.

I have seen and treated many children suffering with varying degrees of eczema, each with different causes. As well as resulting from physical causes, the disorder can also be brought on by emotional stress to the body causing anxiety. I have found that it is often a variety of conditions that brings out allergies such as eczema and asthma.

Causes can often be due to environmental reasons, such as food allergies and E numbers. Dust mites have occasionally been shown to cause some of the problems and clothes made from materials such as wool and silk also seem to aggravate the condition once it is established. I have found that some soap powders and liquids can also have a detrimental effect on the skin. Even the purest soaps (as declared on the label) are not always safe for susceptible children and adults, and there may be something in these products,which can cause an eruption or outbreak.

Since I began dealing with eczema sufferers, I have seen children who have been covered with bleeding sores. Some of them have suffered the condition within days and weeks of birth. The medical profession admits that it does not have a cure and only offers ways of managing the condition with steroids, emollients and thick greasy creams. Sometimes children grow out of eczema, (which can also affect the nails as well as the skin), but in other cases they continue to suffer from skin disorders throughout their whole lives. In adults, the condition is also known as dermatitis.

Reasons for allergies?

When the skin is weak it has no barrier to protect itself from external irritants and so becomes weak and vulnerable to outside forces. Internal irritants come from the malabsorption of vitamins and minerals, digestive disorders and immune dysfunctions. Within the body, excretory systems such as the kidneys, the immune system, lymph system and the skin all function collectively to eliminate the build-up of unwanted poisons and toxins. If any one of these systems is impaired, the others need to work harder, and if they fail or become overburdened, then they too will become affected. The digestive system and skin are usually the first to show signs of excretory failure and dis-ease in the body.

When problems occur, it is commonsense to investigate these areas and thereby help the skin to recover its proper balance. In addition to other treatments, the medical profession suggests massage for some skin disorders and they see no harm in trying homeopathy as an alternative. They do, however, have doubts about Chinese medicine and have linked it to increased liver toxicity, which does not help the condition.

Allergies are now being linked to bottle-fed babies, as breast-fed children do not seem to have the same reactions. Allergies are seen as a major factor in ear infections and it is estimated that 90% of children with allergies will have ear infections, with recurring middle ear infection.
Cow's milk is richer in proteins than mother's milk and is thought to be an influence in some allergies. Dairy products also produce mucus in the body and can be responsible for digestive and sinus disorders. It is now accepted that mothers who avoid sensitive foods such as nuts during pregnancy, give their child a better foundation against allergies.

The infant's digestive tract is sensitive to toxins during the first 3 months of life and it is therefore vital to control what your child eats to avoid allergic symptoms. As there is a large amount of immune defence in the digestive system, keeping the mother's immune system healthy is the key while pregnant and when breast feeding. Again, the better the mother's good bacteria, the better able the baby is to fight off weakness within.

Mineral deficiencies

A lack of zinc can also contribute to skin disorders. Sufficient quantities are required within the body to maintain normal skin integrity. Many types of dermatological problems such as eczema have been associated with zinc deficiency and have often responded well to zinc supplementation. Increased zinc-rich foods in the diet such as spinach, seaweed, pumpkin seeds, green peas, beef and liver can all be used to help re-balance the body. Again hair analysis can be used to indentify imbalances.

Ear infections

Acute ear infections are normally treated with antibiotics. When I have worked with children with ear discomfort, I have used CST and lymph drainage to clear fluid restrictions in the head and face. This does the trick of getting fluid moving and easing the infection and discomfort, helping to clear the residue.

The homeopathic remedy Aconite 30 is helpful if the child becomes restless with discomfort and Pulsattila 6 will help to ease pain. Older children can also take zinc and vitamin B supplements as a safeguard.

Jan de Vries (a well known naturopath) suggests that parents use plantago drops. Place a few drops on cotton wool and place the cotton wool on the ear before bed and leave overnight. If the ear becomes blocked, use one or two drops of St John's Wort in the ear. Almond oil can also be used in the ear to help clear any blockages. I remember my Gran used to warm the oil first before administering. Echinaforce is used too as a natural antibiotic for ear infections.

Holistic approach

In my opinion we need to find and treat the root cause of the disorder and treat the whole person instead of treating the symptoms, which is all that steroids, creams and emollients are aimed at. Treating the symptoms is like applying a plaster and hoping that underneath, the problem will go away of its own accord.

It is advisable to have susceptible children tested for allergies such as eczema. Although some of the tests cannot take place until your child is approximately two years old, do not be put off asking earlier than this.

Diet has a huge impact and bananas, cow's milk, goat's milk, cheese, citric fruits, juices, potatoes, wheat, grains and eggs will affect some in varying degrees. Others might be affected by all of these.

Dairy products and wheat are high on the list to avoid with eczema and some children may prove to be lactose intolerant. I have found that citric acid intake is another constant that comes up with children suffering from eczema, and this is something which appears in citrus drinks, vitamin C in all types of food and drink, medication and over-the-counter supplements. I also advise all soaps, bubble bath and shampoos should be removed.

Medical recommendations

In severe cases of eczema, hospital specialists suggest:

- Bathing in oil
- Covering the skin in steroid creams and emollient creams
- Mummy wrapping - wet bandage wraps covered with dry bandages

In this latter case, if the lower bandage dries out it can have an adverse effect on the skin so some parents need to redo the above if the child has a bad night, with bathing in the middle of the night or early morning!

Doctors report they have learnt how to use steroids more effectively to treat inflammation, which then breaks the itch/scratch cycle. Some steroid creams, however, have been found to stunt children's growth and they can also make them more hyperactive.

Ultraviolet light has been used to help with the weakness of the skin. Another tactic used is the 'behaviour modification method' which works on the itch/scratch syndrome. By using a clicker to show how many times scratching takes place, behaviour can be modified accordingly.

Children will scratch and have been known to go through the pain barrier by rubbing the skin on a rough wall or gate until they bleed. When the itching becomes so intense they will do anything to get relief from the constant irritation, including scratching in their sleep. In severe cases, the child and parents are at their wit's end as a result of sleep deprivation and frustration.
Patience is a virtue but this is under sufferance to all.

STEROIDS AND OBSERVATION STORY

Many specialists believe that topical steroids do not thin the skin, but moisturise instead. Quite by accident, however, I learned first-hand many years ago how wrong this assumption can be. I remember my husband having dermatitis severely in his thirties, which was put down to the oils he was using at work as an electrical engineer. He was given numerous creams to put on his face and hands which were the areas that showed mostly, although he also had patches on his arms and legs that came and went. The creams he used damaged all the layers of his skin and consequently it was as if his face and hands had suffered from burns. Even today the skin has not recovered on his face and if he goes out into the cold weather the patches show up as red scars on his cheeks - and this is after 30 years.

He became very clever at scratching and, despite wearing gloves in bed, I would awake to find him scratching his hands severely. I would gently wake him to stop but, having been caught, he soon learned to put his arms in the air and scratch - this way I was not alerted so soon!!
We worked it out ourselves that the steroid creams were not helping and instead used natural products to help. He would use water

minimally and kept the skin dry as much as possible. He stopped all creams and soaps. One skin specialist told him that if he could sustain calm skin with no severe eruptions for two years, the skin would heal itself, which was exactly what it did.

However no one at that time took into consideration emotion, anxiety and stress as part of the reason for the body's reaction. It was all put down to external and environmental events. My husband did not like his job at that time. He had been moved without his consent to a new department and told that this is where he would work from then on. A few months later he started getting skin problems, which were diagnosed as dermatitis (another form of eczema). He was moved within eighteen months and guess what – when the job changed the skin condition improved all on its own.

Parents in isolation

Parents can feel isolated and helpless when dealing with a child with eczema, especially at 3 in the morning! The daily lives of siblings are also affected as everything revolves around the eczema condition.

In some cases it is recommended to:

- Remove carpets and curtains if the cause is a build-up of dust and dust mites
- Eradicate external irritants such as pets, soaps, bubble bath, etc
- Minimize the products used in cleaning the home and in washing
- Use steam cleaning equipment to improve the home environment
- Provide special bedding and pillows which are allergy-free
- Use only cotton clothing next to the skin
- Fit air conditioning in the home to make the environment cool and provide a constant temperature to suit the child's needs
- Put toys in plastic bags in the freezer periodically to eliminate mites.

Even simple things become questionable:

- When shopping, does the shop have air-conditioning?
- Does my child need to wear gloves?
- Do I need to continually cover their legs and feet?
- Can my child go to other children's homes to play?
- Where to go on holiday?
- Can we visit family and friends?
- Is the school environment going to make the child's life even harder, with more allergies and eruptions?
- At school or nursery, are they going to feel different and be stared at?
- Will it affect their confidence and self esteem?

Even the type of water can affect a child with eczema. Do you have hard or soft water? Hard water can be an additional irritant to already troubled skin, with soft water found to be better for skin affected by eczema. Frequent bathing is not advised for eczema or dermatitis as even ordinary water can sometimes have the effect of stinging and burning problem skin.

EMOTIONS AND ECZEMA

From my own practice of treating adults and children, I have found that emotions play a large part in the cause of eczema and asthma. This is especially true of toddlers and newborns who have suffered severe trauma from long or difficult births. The anger and fear goes internally, causing skin problems created from emotional irritation under the skin. Releasing the anger helps the body to heal faster.

I have also found a correlation with mothers who were stressed and anxious while they were pregnant. I have seen several children with eczema brought to me for treatment where the core of the problem was that the mother suffered a severe shock or bereavement while carrying her child. The child then took on this traumatic emotion internally and displayed it as an allergy, usually showing either as asthma or a skin disorder.

It can also show itself as anxiety, formed in the foundation of foetal origins. In addition, there may also be allergies in the family history on one or both sides of the parents, which can create an inherent weakness in the child's body and a tendency to skin problems.

Upon further investigation, I have also found one or both parents to have suffered digestive problems or candida themselves. Once there is a weakness, the child's body starts life with imbalances and the basic foundation is impaired. Add birth issues and emotions into the mix and the child can have a lifelong problem.

In this situation, children need specialist help to rebalance and strengthen their defences. A baby's body is naturally built to sustain itself and if given the correct environment internally, it can do that.

Skin troubled with eczema has no defence and can become so weak that almost anything will make it erupt. Commonly the digestive system is also involved through malabsorption and, together with emotional problems, the body comes under tremendous stress physically and emotionally, as all the systems are put under pressure.

Asthma and eczema tend to go hand in hand, so it is important to get the correct levels of oxygen to the skin and internal organs. Read the following case studies confirming the link between emotions and eczema.

CASE STUDY 14 -
ECZEMA

A brother and sister aged four and two years old were brought to me for treatment. The sister was covered from head to foot with eczema in the form of bleeding sores that she had endured since birth. The brother's condition was not quite as severe but specific areas such as the wrists, ankles, legs, face and parts of the body were affected. The four year-old's skin cleared almost completely overnight after her first session and, over a period of 12 months, the two year-old improved until his skin was completely clear.

Mably (name changed for confidentiality) had eczema within days of birth and her brother developed it at the age of six months. Late in her first pregnancy, mum had suffered a bereavement. It was her father who had died.

Prior to seeing me, their mother had done everything possible to help her children. Both children had been screened and tested for allergies and mum had used steroid creams and a mummy-bandaging regime on Mably for some years without relief. Their diet had also been changed and both children saw a homeopath regularly. Although a small improvement had been seen in her son (Jason), he still had a severe rash on the face, hands, feet, ankles and most of his body.

Mably, in the meantime, had eczema from tip to toe and I believe it is the worst case I had seen. She had dark circles around her eyes and her face looked very pasty. Mum said she did not know how to cope some days and often awoke with the dread of what she would need to deal with that day!

From my examination, I determined that Mably was suffering with:

- Digestive malabsorption
- Vagus nerve impairment
- Frustration
- Anger from birth trauma
- Taking on her mum's grief (there was a great sadness around her and dullness to the eyes)

Jason too was found to be suffering with:

- Digestive malabsorption
- Vagus nerve impairment
- Frustration

I suggested a programme of supplements for them both, which included:

- Vitamin C – to help build the immune system
- Zinc to help build up the skin barrier
- Bio-acidophilus – to put good bacteria back in the gut
- Aloe Vera - organic inner leaf juice – to help with gut and skin disorders
- Sprouted flax seed powder – for Omega 3 and 6

Treatment

The first time I saw her I gave Mably an emotional release treatment and used techniques to adjust the cranium with Cranio Sacral therapy (CST) rebalancing the body.

She came back the following week completely clear of eczema except for two patches - one behind her knees and another at the wrists. Her face and body were completely clear! Neither her mum nor the homeopath could believe the change after only one treatment.

As a result of the damage, Mably's skin was very weak. Her body had known only irritation and the powerful steroid creams had left their mark. It would take time for the skin to regenerate successfully. After several immediate treatments, the schedule was reduced and I saw her on a six to eight weekly basis and then as often as mum thought necessary. She then came to me during school holidays and had a flare-up when she started a new class at school, which I guess was caused by anxiety. This episode abated with just one further treatment.

Her homeopath told me she could see such a difference in Mably immediately. The dark lines under the eyes disappeared virtually overnight and she was now a happy and confident child. In total, her skin took nine months to regain its full strength and she was able to mix more at school. After a year, she was able to swim in the sea for the first time and was also able to go to the swimming baths without any skin reaction. Holidays abroad were also enjoyed for the first time.

Mum was a star and she used her own knowledge from her first-born to introduce a different diet for her son and avoided the use of steroid creams. As a result, the depth of the skin's weakness was not as severe on the boy. However, Jason was picking up on his sister's distress and, to a certain extent, was reacting accordingly. His malabsorption was also more severe than his sister's, producing a different cocktail of events for his eczema reaction.

His eczema reduction was more gradual as the digestive system improved, and although the ferocity of the condition was taken out almost immediately, it took about four to six weeks to improve sufficiently to show definite skin development. He also reached the point where he could enjoy swimming and going to the seaside, things which his parents had tried before but had since had to avoid due to his bad reaction.

The body can be in distress

It was wonderful to see the changes made with a treatment which combined therapy with mineral and vitamin supplements, changes to diet to support the body while improvements were made to strengthen the internal systems. On an emotional level, this helped to reduce the stress and anxiety which the condition itself created. With the dramatic improvements, the whole family benefited. Mum is much happier and not as stressed as she has less work to care for her children and the pressure is off all of them.

After taking the children for the latest private allergy tests, mum informed me that these showed only moderate allergic reactions instead of the original high alerts they issued for years before I treated them.

After improvement, dietary changes still need to be assessed regularly and preferably every six months. As the body improves, sufferers will be able to eat some of the things they were allergic to previously since the body can now cope and will not be affected by such intolerances. I recommend slowly introducing small quantities of some food stuffs which could not previously be tolerated, but it is essential to keep a food diary to note any reactions.

With treatment, once the symptoms abate, the body can work towards regenerating and balancing the disorders. This is not a magic wand and treatment can only work at the body's own improvement rate. For some, this will be quicker than others and a great deal depends upon the severity, how long the condition has been there and the damage that has already taken place. The sooner we can begin correcting the disorder, the better. If I had been able to treat Mably earlier, perhaps straight after her birth, the emotional trauma could have been eradicated immediately, which would have given her body a more stable foundation to build on.

If your child starts to react to allergies, I advise you to find a therapist who has trained in Cranio Sacral Therapy and emotional release, as well as a nutritionist and homeopath. This will help to nip the condition in the bud and rebalance the body fast before a chronic condition kicks in. We now know this is one reason why, the better the mother's internal good bacteria when she gives birth, the better the digestion foundation for the child.

We need to find and treat the root cause of the disorder

I firmly believe it is the weak condition of the immune system that sets the scene for allergies to occur at any age. We have immune response known as Pyres patches in the small intestine that is part of the strategy of elimination of poisons and toxins from the body. However, as we have discussed, stress also interferes with the gut process, weakening the fine balance of precision and order. In my experience, if we improve the immune system and reduce or eliminate the stress, the body can help itself to heal on a different level.

Better still, prevention is the key. Ensure the mother's gut has no deficiencies, reduce stress and be sure your child has a Cranio Sacral treatment when born and your baby can start in the best possible way. As discussed, a dysfunction of conditions, including allergies, can begin very early on.

CASE STUDY 15 –
AN 18 MONTH-OLD BOY 'S ALLERGY

An18 month-old was brought to me for treatment when he was showing an allergic reaction to just about everything. The birthing history revealed:

- A long birth process
- Mum suffered a bereavement during the pregnancy
- Mother had suffered from post-natal depression after the birth

The child had been taken into hospital many times, on one occasion with anaphylactic shock after digesting something, which seriously disagreed with him. All the family were suffering sleep deprivation, especially mum, who had just had another child. Being a sensitive child, her son had reacted badly when she was taken into hospital to give birth.

His little body was so stressed. Frustrated and scared of the feelings he was experiencing, the condition hurt him all the time with little let up. In hot weather and heavy pollen he was very uncomfortable and constantly scratching. His rash would rise to the surface when it was particularly severe, but usually stayed under the skin. His face would go red and the poor boy would say 'no, no, no' when he could feel his skin erupting.

Dogs and cats affected him, forcing his parents to give their family dog away. His grandparents could not visit unless they changed their clothes before seeing him as they had pets and a single animal hair would set him off on an allergic reaction.

Anything airborne would affect him. They could not go outside as he was affected by grass cutting and harvesting in the fields. Family functions became a nightmare and other family members could not understand why this side of the family were not allowed to attend.

Baby E suffered with stomach cramps and swung constantly between constipation and diarrhoea. With malabsorption of the digestion, his immune system was on overload and he was also taking antibiotics with steroids and steroid creams (which had been prescribed for him from a very young age). Since he was not responding to treatment, the hospital wanted to put him on a stronger dose (although the parents did not want this)

I found that baby E had been affected by mum's emotional trauma during pregnancy and her postnatal depression that followed. His trauma was deeper because he is a sensitive child and reacted accordingly. I also found that he was lactose intolerant.

Treatment

I began with emotional release treatment to help release his fear, frustration and stress inside, coupled with a variety of supplements to help restore the boy's equilibrium from the inside. I used:

- Vitamin C and zinc for the immune system and malabsorption
- EFA's for the skin
- Sprouted flax seed for elimination and digestive rebalance
- Aloe Vera to help reduce the inflammation on the inside which would work outwards for the skin's recovery
- Propolis and Aloe Vera cream for his rash to soothe and soften the skin

Besides the supplements, I continued to treat him with emotional release and Cranio Sacral Therapy. Baby E had a misshapen head from birth as a result of the Vontau suction delivery. Although he could not express what was going on in his head, the pressure and torsion was apparent. His mum told me he would suddenly cry out in pain and discomfort for no apparent reason.

After three treatment sessions, his parents could see the difference in his behaviour, especially as it was influencing his anxiety and stress levels, and he showed signs of calming down. They found that he responded well to weekly treatments and when we left a gap of two weeks his condition started to go backwards.

It is normally a long road to recovery in such a severe case but within weeks his parents were impressed with the improvements. Happier in himself, he was laughing instead of crying and sleeping through the night, which meant the parents were also getting some relief and rest.

In addition, I recommended that his parents also see a friend who is a homeopath as he had flare-ups from being given the wrong foods by other family members, sometimes grandparents and other family members who did not realise that the odd biscuit, for instance, would harm him. Homeopathic remedies brought about an improvement within days from the flare-ups. Of course, avoiding the food in the first place was the key.

The environment and temperature would affect him too. He needed to be kept cool as he would over- heat when anxious and distressed. In the initial stages they found that at night they could give extra homeopathic remedies if he awoke with an eruption during warm weather and it would calm everything down. Often he was back to sleep within ten minutes, which had been unheard of before.

Baby E was intelligent enough to be telling mum he needed his remedies as he could feel an eruption coming on. Knowing it was doing him good, he would get excited as soon as she got the bottle out. Eventually he started to refuse his steroid creams and antibiotics, preferring to take the homeopathic remedies. Smart kid!

The combined treatment works well to give the best possible results for the child, working on all levels instead of putting a plaster over the cause. They work with the core issues of dis-ease.

I continued to see Baby E twice a month for three months and then as needed. Mum has now ceased using steroid creams and antibiotics altogether as the skin has recovered and the immune system is able to rebalance and work as it should. Subsequent NHS checkups resulted in their amazement of Baby E's recovery and, knowing that mum had stopped NHS prescribed drugs, it was decided that further NHS treatment was no longer needed.

Conclusion baby E

Every case is individual and although miracles do happen it can take some months before more permanent signs are seen. Clearly, if I had been able to see him sooner, I believe his condition would not have been so severe. I cannot emphasise enough the importance of CST treatment and emotional release for newborn children.

In hindsight it is easy to be wise, but Baby E's mum knew there was something wrong from the beginning and yet the medical staff she approached did not listen.

One doctor told her he was just hyperactive! They could not see how distraught this child was, nor how he was suffering and the knock on effect of how the whole family was worried and anxious. Early treatment can make a huge difference.

NATURAL CLEANERS

When children are allergic, using natural products helps to alleviate symptoms in the home environment. Basics include vinegar, lemons, ketchup and baking soda. Here are some suggestions.

White wine vinegar

Vinegar is a dilute solution of acetic acid. Used as a general cleaner, it cuts through grease, deodorises smells and can be used as a mild disinfectant.
Vinegar can be used in many ways and is good to have as an aid in the kitchen and bathroom.

It also makes a good de-scalar for showerheads and furred kettle elements that are slow to boil (don't boil the kettle with the vinegar in it!) It cleans greasy windows when added to soapy water and can be used in a made-up spray in the home for glass and mirrors. You can also use vinegar in washing to keep colours bright.

Ketchup

Because it contains citric acid, ketchup is an effective cleaner for copper pots and pans.

Olive Oil

Olive oil can be used instead of furniture polish. Mix half a cup of oil and lemon juice in equal parts and put in a hand-spray bottle. Use a dry cloth to polish off afterwards. The spray is especially useful for removing stubborn fingerprints on stainless steel.

Bicarbonate of Soda

Bicarbonate of soda makes a versatile household cleaner. When mixed with water, it dissolves dirt and grease and it can also be used dry as an abrasive.
It is particularly useful for deodorising your fridge and can be used to clean both kitchen sinks and baths.

Lemon Juice

Known as citric acid, lemon juice can be used in washing to brighten whites and colours. Simply soak garments overnight in a bowel of water with added lemon juice. You can also use it to deodorise the microwave.

Tea Tree oil

An extract from the tea tree, tea tree oil can be used on mould and mildew. Simply mix two teaspoons of oil in two cups of water. It can also be used effectively to deodorise fabrics and musty clothing. Soak items overnight in the solution then air for a few days for the tea tree odour to subside.

The above is only a small selection of alternatives. As we are becoming more aware, there are many books appearing on the shelves reproducing non-invasive ways from the past.

We are seeing more natural cleaning and bathroom products in our shops and on line, which range in price and benefits. Being green will also help the planet and so offers benefits all around.

Chapter 21

INDEX

Chapter 21

HYPERACTIVITY & ADD

ADHD AND ADD

In recent years we have had an alarming rise in problems of the central nervous system, together with behavioural and mood disorders in our children. ADD (Attention Deficit Disorder) and ADHD (Attention Deficit Hyperactivity Disorder) numbers are rising dramatically and affected children are now prescribed corrective drugs from an early age.

For both complaints, children as young as seven are often put on anti-depressants. Even from the age of three, Ritalin (known by some as the wonder drug) is used to treat ADD. Unfortunately however, Ritalin is known to have side effects. It is an amphetamine and a stimulant and amphetamines can cause withdrawal and become addictive if misused. Many people, including doctors, are questioning the use of this drug on children. At the time of writing it is believed that over 5% of school-aged children (approximately 500,000) are having symptoms of ADHD, symptoms which can and will go into adulthood[201] .

In hindsight, parents of ADHD children looked to the medical profession to help them. Confused and fraught, they could not cope with these hyperactive children and were prepared to try anything that would bring their child back to 'normal'. We have to ask the question though, 'What is normal?'

The corrective drugs, which are used to treat ADHD are often cocaine derivatives and children are subdued into submission, turning them into drugged robots. Some people are concerned at the numbers of children who are coming off these drugs at sixteen, only to become hard-line drug and cocaine addicts. After all, these children have known nothing else and need a fix from somewhere, don't they?

Just because they reach an age where the medical profession believes them to have outgrown the problem, their bodies are addicted and need time to re-adjust. During this period, they are vulnerable and look for alternatives.

Are we creating a society of robots?

It is scary to think of the numbers involved. Not only does the treatment cost millions, but these children will not be able to contribute to society later in life because of their addictions. Both politicians, and we as parents, have made and enforced these draconian laws (in some areas in the world) and are ultimately responsible for the later problems. We are to blame and it is not a happy thought.

Quiet often, science does not look at the long-term chaos, especially if a short-term financial gain is involved. It looks at the achievements and objectives as its priority. As yet, we don't know the long-term impact or consequences of giving corrective drugs to young children whose brain patterns are still forming. One day we may look back and say that it was the worst disaster in history and admit that we did it to our own children.

Society's label

Many in the educational field mistakenly see these children as non-conformists and troublemakers. They want the children to be put on drugs so that they can be brought into the norm, to conform and become an average child (It does beg the question what is normal? Surely this is a different perspective to each of us). At the same time, some doctors are saying that they are just children who are at the higher end of the scale energetically, and that this needs to be recognised.

Right Brain activity

Normally, before being put on drugs, children are assessed via their brain activity. From this it has been noticed that most of these children have prominent right brain activity and are prone to using intuition, psychic abilities and can be telepathic. Being right brain orientated, they are using developed insights and gifts already present from birth. It is well recognised that right-brain activity is usually more pronounced in women and children. I run a course called New Kids on the Block which explains and gives insights into this area and is especially aimed at those who are involved with children or adults (families and professionals).

Any child can suffer from ADD/ADHD and those affected often miss out on school activities and hobbies, with their lives becoming restricted.

This has a knock-on effect, which is felt throughout the family, with a wider impact upon siblings. The most stressful times can be in the morning, before the drugs have had the chance to kick in, and in the early evening when the effects are wearing off.

Drugs

NHS Direct specifies that medication should be used in conjunction with behaviour therapies. Medicines produce a short-lived improvement after each dose but are not a permanent cure[202]. Ritalin (also known as methylphenidate) is the preferred choice in the UK, but other prescribed drugs include Dextro (an amphetamine) and Atomoxethine, which is not a stimulant and was launched in 2007[203].

The adult equivalents of these drugs, which are used for depression and anxiety, include Strattera, which was approved in 2002, and Datamoniter, which was introduced in 2006[204].

The increase in the volume of prescriptions for ADHD is staggering. In Scotland in 1996 there were fewer than 4,000 prescriptions for ADHD. By 2006 however, 46,000 prescriptions were recorded in Scotland alone and it is estimated that the NHS spends millions each year (estimated at £1.89 million in 2006 - Scotland figures only) compared to just £33,000 in 1996[205].

Concerns have been raised concerning the influence of drugs such as Strattera and Atomoxetine on the liver, especially in those cases where children are being prescribed them for hyperactivity. In 2007, the Medicine and Healthcare Regulatory Agency asked for a review of these drugs as they believed there could be a health risk, causing liver poisoning in one out of every 50,000.

It was estimated that up to two million children could be on the drug in the USA in 2007 and the figures were rising. In the same year in the UK there were 67 reported reactions to the drug and three reports of liver failure. The symptoms of liver problems include itchy skin, dark urine, abdominal tenderness, jaundice and unexplained 'flu-like' symptoms[206].

Prescribed medication such as Ritalin is used to suppress and calm the child or adult. The NHS admits that the drugs do not cure and in my opinion they are used as a sticking plaster (a band-aid metaphorically speaking), desensitizing the person so they are able to fit into society. In some cases, the user is literally being knocked out or left in a fuzzy world where they cannot think or function properly for themselves.

I believe that it is far better to find the root cause or core of the matter, deal with it and clear it out. From my own experience, this can often be from an emotional or mechanical fault and with the right treatment it can be helped and dealt with at core level, allowing the child or adult to function in life, taking part in and making positive contributions to society again. By getting to the core of the problem, it also allows parents and siblings to live their lives without the stress and anxiety that go with the effects of a drug wearing off (which must be very disorientating for the child) together with the before and after stress felt by all.

SYMPTOMS OF ADHD

As most people are aware, one of the main symptoms of ADHD is overactive behaviour (hyperactivity), but in addition, sufferers are also apt to behave impulsively and have difficulty paying and maintaining attention.

In 2007, the NHS suggested that ADHD occurred in approximately 5% of school-aged children and 2-4% of adults. Research indicates that these children will continue with the disorder into their adult lives, enduring social and working-life interference.

Being hyperactive

Boys are more commonly affected than girls and whilst the former tend to be hyperactive, the latter show symptoms of inattention and are sometimes seen as being quiet, dreamy or half asleep. They find it difficult to fit in at school and can be seen as disruptive and out of step with other children. They are easily distracted, finding it difficult to sit still for any period of time. They may, in addition, have language and speech issues and delayed social skills, finding it hard to wait their turn in games and so on.

A child with ADHD struggles to process information. Concentration is fleeting, so having to sit for any length of time is a challenge. They fidget and want to move on to other things. Just as with feelings of boredom, they need new things to keep their attention. This is why TV and games interest them. Children with ADHD enjoy the stimulus of TV and video games, but parents can sometimes be guilty of using the media to keep them entertained, setting a foundation of unhealthy patterns when they watch too much. Often, children with ADHD like the type of games which involve fighting or display aggressive behaviour, or cartoons with quick action and changing pictures. The format is fast moving and repeatedly moves backward and forward. If you watch modern children's TV programmes, this is what they do, repeating the information back and forth.

This process started in the US. Over there, programme lengths are reduced with sections between adverts much shorter than the UK. They have long spaces between the story section and continually break for adverts. Unfortunately, these are ways of keeping concentration spans short.

This type of abnormal media can inhibit the social skills of children with ADHD and their interaction with others. They get into a pattern of preferring their own company to that of others and are often isolated in their bedrooms with little interaction in the home and with the rest of the family. This can lead to added health problems such as obesity, diabetes, eye development and emotional disorders such as social and relationship skills.

Not just a childhood problem, ADHD grows with sufferers into adulthood. The NHS revealed in 2007 that 70% of children with ADHD will still have problems in their teens and 70% of those will suffer symptoms as adults[207].

These symptoms often show signs of delayed social skills. Signs of disruption in play and aggressive behaviour in children go hand in hand with tantrums when they cannot get things their own way. When I have treated children and teens with ADHD, I have found that they are not unintelligent. It is just that they cannot concentrate for long enough to achieve more in life.

Parents often struggle to cope with an ADHD child and this creates family stress. Giving a child with ADHD too much sugar is like giving him, or her, a drug. It sends them wild and increases the tendency to hyperactivity. Too much stimulation, such as watching excessive TV or constantly playing computer games, will do the same thing. Sufferers just do not fit into the social box, often coming from a psychological place which cannot be understood.

CAUSES OF AND TREATMENT FOR ADHD AND ADD
Birth

Although ADHD and ADD can be a problem from birth, both can be adjusted with Cranio Sacral Therapy. CST trials have found that the condition can stem from a mechanical imbalance in the head, which may have come from the birth process, especially forceps or vontau delivery. (As discussed in CST section13)

From my own experience, I have found that births involving the extremes of both very quick and overly long difficult birth processes have also been indicated. Premature birth (low birth weight) and the mother smoking while pregnant are also highlighted as causes in learning and behaviour issues.

It has, in addition, been noted that some children born prematurely can cut off emotionally and withdraw. Research has shown these children to be more prone to hyperactivity and problems at school. (See section 12 on premature birth)

Obstetrical delivery can also cause ADD and Hyperkinesis, causing an excessive back-bending of the occipital base of the skull upon the atlas. The head may be severely angulated upon the neck, resulting in a threatening situation for the nervous system and causing splintering of the tissues with difficulty in relaxing when born. Muscles and tissue in the neck, shoulders and head can be affected.

Sometimes, the Occiput does not self-correct, creating increased tone to the head/neck junction. In turn, the situation causes fluid restriction around the brain, reducing cerebrospinal fluid, blood, lymph and intracellular fluid. Once fluid motion is restored, the symptoms of ADD and Hyperkinesis often disappear.

The frontal cortex of the brain can be restricted during labour and this is where impulsive behaviour comes from.

Imbalances in chemicals released in the brain and lack of dopamine are highlighted in the front part of the brain. Autistics and ADHD sufferers have both been seen to have imbalances of dopamine.

Sutures can become jammed through the birth process, restricting the growth and expansion of the brain and causing imbalances of behaviour and thought process. By using small movements, the Cranio Sacral therapist can ease and adjust the position of the sutures, thereby releasing the restrictions. From my own experience, the changes can be made within a few sessions. Obviously an older teenager or adult may take 6–8 sessions to achieve the same thing, mainly because of the acute condition and length of time that the patterns have been there.

Other physical symptoms felt from a misaligned obstetrical delivery could be headaches, earache, mucus, neck and shoulder discomfort. Chronic ear infection affects up to 40% of children under the age of six and accounts for a large percentage of visits to doctors and paediatricians[208].

Medically, the course of action is antibiotics or antihistamines. When I have worked with children with ear discomfort, however, I have used CST and lymph drainage to clear fluid restrictions in the head and face, which does the trick of getting fluid moving and the infection and discomfort helped to clear. Adults can also suffer earache and fluid restrictions in this area from accidents and injuries such as whiplash.

This is why I suggest a Cranio Sacral session after birth, falls, injury or accidents. Releasing emotional blockages is also the key to a happy child. (See section on CST for further information)

Hyperactive Behaviour

In my opinion it is far too easy to label children these days. Perhaps children need to run around a lot more during their leisure time instead of watching TV or playing on the computer. Sports and dance are not core subjects any more at school and children cannot let off steam like they did in my day, by being creative (a right brain dominant feature).

In the past, show-offs have become actors and comedians, while those who have fidgeted have become musicians and dancers. Maybe we are not looking at the broader picture. From a young age, the patterns are there for our future passion and we just need to look out and identify them.

Parents and teachers need to make sure children find the outlet for their creativity, whatever that may be. Groups such as Brownies, Guides, Cubs and Scouts help children to bond and work as a group as well as helping to develop personal skills. Sometimes it takes someone outside the family group to identify talents and skills. We often hear about stories from celebrities who say 'if it hadn't been for my teacher/father/grandparents/uncle/auntie, etc, who encouraged me and inspired me in..., I would not be where I am today.'

I have often heard sports personalities talking about how their parents sacrificed, encouraged and inspired them from an early age. They could see the potential. Sebastian Coe and David Beckham's fathers were very inspirational characters, and it was their dedication and time which helped their sons become the successes that they are today. We just need to see the children outside society's label and the box we put them in.

Research

In 2007, Californian research indicated that children with ADHD have abnormalities in areas of the brain, with structural changes within the frontal cortex, which controls impulsive behaviour, and the dorsal prefrontal cortices which influence attention. Owing to the new scanning technologies, which are now available, they were also able to determine that the children had more grey matter[209].

Also in 2007 there were calls for new methods of treatment for ADHD, as those currently used are not always effective. It is costing the NHS a lot of money each year just to keep children and adults socially acceptable. The time has come where we can look back on many years of mainly drug-reliant treatment and see that it clearly isn't working. It is now critical to find more appropriate approaches to suit the individual, instead of treating them carte-blanche with left-brain thinking methods.

Dr John Upledger believes that every child should be treated with a Cranio Sacral session. I also believe that this could make a huge difference to our society, as it would help to release any restrictions in the head from the birth process and help clear emotional debris carried from the womb and the delivery process. It allows mother and child to bond earlier, reducing stress and anxiety in the child from an early age, thereby allowing a good foundation for the child to grow from. I believe that early intervention is the key to ADHD.

ADHD AND PRETERM BIRTH

The normal human gestation period is 40 weeks and the average preterm birth is between 28 to 36 weeks. Danish research has found that babies born between 34 and 36 weeks are 70% more likely to develop Attention Deficit Disorder and that those born at less than 34 weeks are three times more likely to develop it.[210]
Previous studies have linked ADD, behavioural and learning difficulties and low birth weight before, but have only based their results on premature births of 28 weeks and less. These statistics show conclusively that birth does have a part to play in behavioural and learning difficulties in later life.

Having linked babies born at low weights of between 3lb 3oz and 5lb 5oz (1.5k–2.5k) but born at term, 90% are more likely to develop a hyperactivity disorder (ADHD) than those who are at normal weight (classed as 6lb 7oz upwards) according to the organisation Tommy's. Those born between 5lb 6oz and 6lb 6oz have a 50% risk of ADHD and boys are 90% more likely to suffer from a hyperkinetic disorder such as ADHD. This is of significance as the UK has the highest rate of preterm births in Europe[211]. Indeed it was estimated that in 2008 UK premature births stood at 45,000 per year, with a large proportion being born between 34 and 36 weeks.

The link with ADHD - Fever and Flu during pregnancy

Colds and fever can be common during pregnancy and were once thought to have no detrimental effects, but new research has shed a different light on this assumption. Research in 2003 found that offspring from mothers who suffered influenza or other fevers (as opposed to the common cold) in the last six months of pregnancy were more likely to suffer emotional and developmental problems, including ADHD.

In 2003, a London Professor of virology at Queen Mary's School of Medicine stated that 'the surge in immune chemicals (called inflammatory cytokines), which the body produces to counter fevers, might also directly harm the unborn child'.

Published in the American Journal under the heading 'Birth Defect Research', one doctor blamed the high maternal body temperature caused by influenza rather than the virus itself for damaging the unborn child. Other forms of fever can also harm the foetus, and this doctor suggests that vaccines should be used to combat the influenzas that seem the most common cause of the symptoms. The current British Department of Health guidance, however, does not advocate routine vaccination for flu in pregnancy. Homeopathy, however, would assist in cases of flu and fever.

'Real flu is a severe condition. It seems likely that it causes such an extreme immune reaction that there are effects felt by the baby, even though the virus itself is not thought to cross the placenta.'[212]

One large Finnish research programme, which took place over a twelve-year period, studied children from birth until the age of twelve. It concluded that mothers who suffered fever during pregnancy had children who tended to be more depressed and were likely to be below average academically. A member of the research team stated that children who were exposed to fever during pregnancy were 30% more likely to show signs of developing ADHD and this could be an explanation for their poorer school performance. The true extent of the psychological effects of fever during pregnancy might not become apparent until the team has completed more research when the children are older. [213]

Previous smaller studies have concluded that the exposure to maternity influenza increased a baby's risk of developing more serious conditions such as manic depression and schizophrenia, which tend to appear in late teens.

According to the US assistant general, medicine has much to learn about the causes of birth defects, particularly in the second and third trimesters, when the unborn child's brain begins to develop rapidly[214]. Dr Upledger also cites fever as a complication for the foetus.

GROUNDING

One thing that I have found continuously with those suffering from ADHD and autism is that they are not grounded. Most of the children and adults I have treated have been in what I call 'La La land'. Logically, you might well ask how they could they be present if they are suppressed by drugs! Under these conditions I agree that it is very difficult for the essence of a person to stay in their body. It is similar to those who suffer from Alzheimer's. They are vague, as if they are in a dream world where no-one is at home. The eyes are dull, taking time for conversation to penetrate and be understood.

You sometimes see it in shops. The assistant on the till has become bored and clearly does not want to be there. He or she is in a dream world and thinking of something else, their attention elsewhere and not on what they are doing. Certainly their attention is not in the room. This behaviour creates patterns, promoting less time in their bodies and more in their dream world. I have devised techniques to help people to be more grounded and present in reality. (New Kids on the block and School of Life programmes www.allonus.co.uk)

Being ungrounded is a huge problem for some and not understood or acknowledged in general. Once parents have been shown how to ground themselves and their children, they have described how different they feel. Suddenly they are able to interact better within society and have more meaningful relationships. It is something so simple and yet most are unaware of it.

There are other ways of treating ADHD than drugs. In my opinion it just needs awareness and to look outside the box at something other than drugs and medication. Indeed, I have been able to help all ages with different approaches. Take a leap of faith. Surely it doesn't matter how it works, as long as it achieves results and gets to the core of the problem, allowing people to get their lives back. I think sometimes we analyse too much in the name of science where everything has to be black and white and fit into a box. Perhaps science needs to look at new ways of health care, as I believe drugs are not always the answer. ADHD is a gray area and in my mind won't fit into a box scenario. We need to look for other broader answers.

NUTRITIONAL BENEFITS FOR ADHD AND SENSITIVE CHILDREN

There is much evidence that autism, Asperger's syndrome, ADHD and ADD disorders can all benefit greatly from a change in diet and nutritional supplementation. This is especially true with unsaturated fatty acids (UFA's).

Our bodies need a wide range of micronutrients for optimal eye and brain function and studies have shown that a lack of Omega 3 and Omega 6 may contribute to the development of autism and a number of other disabilities such as ADHD, Dyslexia and Dysphraxia, all of which are often associated with a lack of essential fatty acids (EFA's).

Certain fatty acids are necessary for the development of co-ordination, learning abilities, concentration and memory and 20% of the brain and 30% of the retina contain these important nutrients. It is therefore vital to have a diet which includes high volume EFA's to meet our bodies' needs.

Unfortunately, medical evidence that fish-oil supplements and multivitamin supplements may help to relieve the condition has not been scientifically proved. It begs the question, 'Do science and the pharmaceutical industry really want to prove this association?'

Yet other observers have found positive results, which prove that taking supplements does work. The National Autism Society website, for example, mentions using a number of vitamins and dietary interventions. They suggest:

- Vitamin B6/magnesium
- Vitamin C
- Dimethylglycine (DMG)
- A gluten and casein free diet
- A yeast free diet
- Vitamin A
- Serotonin

Previous studies have shown that children with ADHD do suffer from vitamin and mineral deficiencies.

Carnosine

Although the L-Carnosine amino acid mechanism is not well understood, it is believed that it acts to modulate neurotransmission and affect metal ion transfer of zinc and copper in the entorhinal cortex, enhancing neurological function or acting in a neuroprotective fashion.

* Carnosine has been shown to improve autistic behaviour as well as achieving increases in language comprehension. It is a combination of two amino acids which are the building blocks of proteins (alanine and histidine) and are naturally present in tissues like muscle and brain. It is thought that this amino acid dipeptide enhances frontal lobe function and it also has the ability to chelate harmful metals in the body, meaning that it can become a metal binder to eliminate them from the body.

* Magnetic clay baths are part of the chelation treatment and are a protocol for removing heavy metals. Green clay was used by the Native Americans and is also used to cleanse toxins from the body. It is, however, an acquired taste, which may be better suited to older children.

(* See appendix for details)

In terms of depressive illness, there is a correlation between depression and the ratio of low tissue sodium to potassium. A depletion of copper can also cause depression and high blood pressure is often seen when low sodium to potassium levels exist[215].

Artificial colours - The Scotsman stated in December 2006 that 'there are now indicators that children may benefit from a diet free of artificial colours, flavours and preservatives.' The EU has taken this information on board and is now arranging for certain E numbers and preservatives to be removed. However, how long this will take to influence suppliers and our food chain, no-one knows.

ZINC AND NUTRITIONAL SUPPLEMENTS

Although some specialists believe there is little evidence to support how safe or effective nutritional supplements such as zinc and polyunsaturated fatty acids are, other experts agree that there are proven benefits to long term nutritional supplements together with B complex and B12 vitamins, fish oils, and antioxidants.

Previous studies have shown that children with ADHD are often lacking in vitamins and minerals. Through my own experience, I have seen many children who suffer from ADHD and the majority have malabsorbtion, which means that their bodies cannot maintain the benefits of the vitamins and minerals present in normal foods. We are all different and can each absorb some minerals and vitamins better than others according to our diet and lifestyle.

In 2004, doctors found evidence to suggest that hyperactive children might benefit from taking zinc supplements[216/217] , and indeed, trials which have taken place in different parts of the world have shown improvement in children who took zinc.

A six-week study of 44 children with ADHD in Iran found that those who were taking 55mg of zinc per day fared much better that those who were not given supplements. In this particular case, all the children were additionally taking Ritalin, which is commonly prescribed for the condition[218].

The research suggested that zinc might play a role in regulating the production of dopamine in the brain. The chemical is associated with feelings of pleasure and has been linked to low levels in ADHD disorders by other scientists.
Peter Hill, a UK professor of the Royal College of Psychiatrists, states however, that more research is needed. He used to recommend zinc to parents but is now concerned that without supervision from a professional, children could be given too much. In this case it would be advisable to consult a nutritionalist in your area.

What is Zinc?

Zinc is an essential trace mineral with more biological roles than all other trace minerals put together. As it has a crucial role to play in many human biological systems, it is important for us to keep maximum levels of this mineral in the body.

Zinc helps with:

- Cell growth
- Stabilising our metabolic rate
- Balancing blood sugar
- Keeping the immune system strong - zinc deficiency will cause an increased risk of viral and bacterial infection

As we have mentioned, zinc plays an important role in regulating the production of dopamine in the brain. It has been proven to work beneficially for those who suffer from depression and anxiety and, in a new study, zinc supplements have been found to help children suffering with diarrhoea[219].

A lack of zinc can also contribute to skin disorders as it is necessary to have sufficient quantities within the body to maintain normal skin integrity. Many types of dermatological problems such as eczema have been associated with zinc deficiency and have often responded well to zinc supplementation.

Zinc-rich foods such as spinach, sea vegetables such as seaweed, pumpkin seeds, green peas, beef and liver can all be used to help re-balance the body, and those who suspect that they may be deficient can use hair analysis to check their levels of vitamins and minerals.

CASE STUDY 16 - ADD

It is never too late to treat ADD or ADHD and I have found that, at any age, the right treatment can make a difference.

One concerned mum phoned me after seeing my flyer offering treatments for babies who had suffered from a traumatic birth process. She asked if I could help her son who was 17 years old and had suffered a long and arduous birth process. Throughout his life he found it difficult to concentrate and, despite the time lapse, his mum wanted to find a way to help him with his college work.

We decided that it was his decision to make and, when he came to me for a consultation, I explained what the treatment entailed. He had several questions which we discussed at length and to his satisfaction. He explained that he found it difficult to concentrate for long periods. While he talked, his feet were tapping and his hands were constantly moving. He told me he liked music and played the drums as a way of letting off steam. Sleep was variable and he could regularly stay up till two o'clock in the morning. He felt tired most of the time. He was not on any medicated drugs at present. John (name changed for confidentiality) was a gentle soul with long hair who just wanted to live life to the full.

During his first 50-minute session, he lay on the treatment couch and tapped his fingers, moving his hands and continually fidgeting throughout. He had torsion between the Occiput and sphenoid (a common imbalance during the birth process) which was restricting the frontal cortex. It seemed to be so well ensconced that I concluded it must have come from the birth process.

During the second session, the fidgeting was less and he told me he felt calmer. By the third session I could feel his body relaxing and I do believe he even went to sleep for a few seconds. He told me he stayed up and played on his Game-boy for 5 hours (unheard of before as he did not have the concentration to do it). His sleep was improving and he was feeling less tired during the day.

By the sixth session he lay quietly throughout, not fidgeting at all. He went to sleep as I worked on his head, releasing the sutures and allowing balance and realignment of the skull. We then had a few weeks break before I saw him again.

After three weeks, John walked in with his hair cut shorter. He had a different stance and posture about him and seemed to have an air of quiet confidence. He told me he had sat his first exam and was able to complete the paper. He was surprised as he had not been able to do that before his treatment. His concentration had returned.
We had one more treatment session a month later which proved to be a relaxed session with John completely still on the treatment couch. What a difference from the first time I saw him. He had completed all his exams and was very pleased with himself (a first for him).

Mum's idea had worked.

[201] BBC News 'Doctors 'failing hyperactive kids' 10.2003 http://news.bbc.co.uk/1/hi/health/3225209 (Ref: NADDIS report) (cited 02. 2007)

[202] NHS ADHD 'behaviour' http://www.nhs.direct.nhs.uk/articles.aspx?artileId=40&secionId=27014 (cited 02/2007)

[203] : BBC News 'New ADHD drug launch in UK' 06.2004 http://news.bbc.co.uk/i/hi/health/3767313.stm (cited 04.2007

[204] : BBC News 'New ADHD drug launch in UK' 06.2004 http://news.bbc.co.uk/i/hi/health/3767313.stm (cited 04.2007)

[205] Lyndsay Moss New Scotsman; Concern over rising use of 'Chemical Cosh' on disturbed youngsters; 12.2006 http://news.scotsman.com/health.cfm?id=18867220066catorgory=23 (cited 02.2007)

[206] Celia Hall, 'Children's drug can cause Liver damage' Eclub http://credencegroup.co.uk/Eclub/Eclubsearchable2/240205/children's.htm (cited 07.2007)

[207] NHS health Encyclopaedia ADHD 01.2007 http://www.nhsdirect.nhs.uk/articles/article.aspx?articleId=40&section Id=27014. (Cited 02.2007)

[208] The Sunday post - Jan de Vries 'Family matters' (Article p50 07.2009)

[209] BBC News 'Brain clues to attention disorder':http://news.bbc.co.uk/1/hi/health/3284629 11.2003 (cited 02.2007)

[210] 'ADHD Linked to premature birth'– http://news.bbc.uk/1/hi/health/5042308.stm (Ref: Danish study) 05.2008

[211] BBC News 'ADHD linked to premature births' http://news.bbc.co.uk/i/hi/health/ 5042308.stm (Ref:Tommy's article) (cited 05.2008)

[212] Michael Day 'Flu in pregnant women can cause brain damage to unborn babies' Sunday Telegraph Article 12.2003

[213] Michael Day 'Flu in pregnant women can cause brain damage to unborn babies' Sunday Telegraph (Article 'Finish research' 12.2003)

[214] Michael Day 'Flu in pregnant women can cause brain damage to unborn babies' Sunday Telegraph Article 12.2003

[215] Trace Eliments (ref:copper)

[216] BBC News 'Zinc helps hyperactive children' http://news.bbc.co.uk/1/hi/health/3608439 04.2004 (cited 04.2007)

[217] BBC News 'Zinc helps hyperactive children'http://news.bbc.co.uk/1/hi/health/3608439 04.2004 (cited 04.2007)

[218] Dr. Mercola http://articles.mercola.com/sites/articles/archive/2008/3/15/zinc-can-cure-diarrhea.aspx (Ref: Medical college of Georgia Augusta Pediatrics) vol121;02.2008;No2:p326-336. (Cited at 04.2008)

[219] Dr. Mercola 'Zinc can cure Diarrhea':http://articles.mercola.com/sites/articles/archive2008/3/15/zinc-can-cure-diarrhea.aspx (cited 04.2008)

Chapter 22

INDEX

Chapter 22

AUTISM (ASD)

What is autism?

Autism is a spectrum of conditions from mild (Asperger's) to severe. As a complex developmental disorder, it can be noticeable from a few months old but is not normally diagnosed until 3-4 years old when behaviour is easier to identify. It is normally a psychiatric diagnosis rather than a medical one.

Autistics like routine and dislike change. They prefer the same things and, when changes are made, they may rebel or have a tantrum. Autistic children will not usually cuddle, nor interact favourably within the family environment. They don't tend to form attachments and from a young age avoid eye contact. The child may seem detached emotionally, not needing cuddles or affection and seemingly dislike physical contact. This can be very challenging for the family as it is a natural instinct to kiss and cuddle your baby.

Symptoms include:

- Rigidity in behaviour
- Communication restrictions (no eye contact)
- Child does not socialise
- Obsessive compulsive tendencies (OCD)
- Dyspraxia
- Unable to conceptualise the thoughts and feelings of others
- Seen as being in their own world

Doctors have developed the term 'atypical autism' for a child who is developing normally and then suddenly changes and develops autistic symptoms, unlike a child who is diagnosed with autism from birth[220].

According to the National Autistic Society, autism was relatively unheard of in 1940 before the introduction of vaccination. In the

USA, where children receive the MMR vaccine at 15 months, 5 years and 18 years or just before entering university, it was reported by US congress that autism increased in the year 1998/99 by more than 30%, with a total 40% increase from 1992-2002 (figures do not include children under the age of six)[221].

The true causes of autism are, however, unknown. Some experts believe that there are several factors to consider, including:

- Foetal alcohol syndrome
- Genetic factors
- Brain stem defects
- Lead and toxic poisoning
- Nervous system defects
- Infections
- Infant vaccination reactions
- Digestive system deficiencies
- Food and inhalant allergies
- Body chemistry of the infant
- Lack of oxygen at birth
- Abnormalities of the brain during foetal development

Other factors include the mother's health and condition while pregnant, such as:

- Rubella while pregnant
- Candida infection
- Herpes infection
- High alcohol consumption
- Virus and/or high temperature

These conditions in turn cause disruption to the child from:

- Digestive malfunction or disruption
- Fatty acid metabolism/disruption
- Red/white blood cell production/imbalance

- Vitamin and mineral imbalances
- Electrolyte imbalances

Alongside genetic factors

Some research is indicating that there are distinct family emotional behaviours and patterns into which autistic children are born. Relatives sometimes show repetitive behaviour patterns and have communication issues, and manic depression is often a factor. These symptoms are shown to be either indicators or simply more common within families with autistic children[222].

Another factor under research is the eye-to-eye contact, exploring the initial bonding with the mother and eye–to-eye contact between mother and child. The effects of deep forceps delivery, birth under anaesthesia, induction of labour and resuscitation at birth are all factors of the imbalances measured for autism and autistic spectrum disorders[223].

AUTISM AND GUT IMBALANCES

Digestive disturbance may be a contributory factor to both ASD and ADHD, and a common factor of autism is a failure to establish a healthy gut flora from an early age.

Antibiotics given at a young age (which is sometimes the case when children are literally only days or weeks old) can disturb the delicate gut balance. This results in imbalanced gut bacteria due to C-section birth and formula feeding. (See section on probiotics and pregnancy)

This condition is known as Dysbiosis and in the long term it can cause inflammation in the lining of the gut. Clinical trials have found mild to moderate inflammation in both the upper and lower tract together with decreased liver sulphation and pathologic intestinal permeability in many children.

Significant Dysbiosis was found to be a widespread problem[224]. A known toxin producer, (known as clostridium histolyticum) was found in one group. Interestingly they had siblings with similar levels of gut C.histolyticum but no autistic symptoms[225].

Constipation and diarrhoea are known to be common in children with ADHD. A small trial showed a high gastritis marked CD8+ cell dominance, whereas Crohn's shows CD4+cells[226].

Sub acute chronic tetanus infection can be another potent gut and neurotoxin. C.tetani releases neurotoxins, which can be transported from the intestinal tract to the brain via the vagus nerve[227].

Food intolerance and ASD/ADHD

Both ASD and ADHD children are seen to be sensitive to certain foods and additives. ASD children are considered to be more sensitive to gluten and casein food proteins and a removal of these proteins has proved beneficial.

In 1991, Kalle Riechelt MD found a possible relationship between gluten, casein and autism. Riechelt hypothesized that urinary peptide levels may have an opiate effect. Opioid peptides such as casomorphines (from casein), gluten exorphines and gliadorphn (from gluten) are possible suspects as they create a chemical similarity to opiates.

Psychological effects

Dr. Riechelt also suspected that opiate peptides had an effect on brain maturation and contributed to social awkwardness and isolation. His findings have been substantiated by a further report, although mixed evidence was found[228].

Diet changes, especially the exclusion of wheat and dairy could result in improvements in autism. Probiotics such as Lactobacillus acidophilus and Bifidobacterium biffidum strains may reduce urine levels of opioid peptides.

To restore a healthy gut, eliminate products known to cause offence and introduce probiotics combined with glutamine supplementation. Be patient as the changes may take a few weeks or even months to adjust fully before seeing clear differences in behaviour and social interaction.

AUTISM AND BIRTH

An observation trial carried out in 1983 by Niko Tinbergen linked autism and birth and in particular births which involved: [229]

- Deep forceps delivery
- Birth under anaesthesia
- Resuscitation at birth
- Induction of labour

Together with hospitals having a protocol of intervention.

Umbilical Cord

New research shows oxygen depravation in some children when the cord is clamped too soon after birth. In some cases the cord is cut quickly after delivery and may reduce supplies of oxygen and nutrient rich blood in the crucial moments before the infant starts to breath. Researchers are suggesting that in vulnerable children this could cause brain haemorrhage, iron deficiencies, breathing difficulties and mental impairments including Autism. Experts believe this to affect one in one hundred children. It is common practice in hospitals to clamp within 30 seconds as many doctors believe it helps to reduce the risk of mothers bleeding to death. [230]

During the moments after birth the blood and oxygen supplies are rapidly reducing. As the infant's body is adjusting to come into use, the increase in blood volume is used to fill the organs and lungs to activate systems.

Some experts believe cord cutting should be left for up to three minuets after birth to allow the mothers blood from the placenta to continue to support the infant until he starts breathing. One recent Canadian study supports this theory, (published in the Journal of the American Medical Association), finding by delaying cord clamping for up to two minutes, it reduced anaemia by half and iron levels in the blood by a third, creating benefits beyond the neonatal period.[231]

Cord cutting is the first disconnection and separation felt by the infant, which can have its own emotional effects and shock with disconnection from the mother.

CRANIO SACRAL DYSFUNCTION

Dr John Upledger's research between 1978 and 1981, meanwhile, found a relationship between autism and Cranio Sacral system dysfunction. The results highlighted some interesting correlations between maternal viral infection during the last six months of pregnancy and the dysfunctions related to the delivery process. John Upledger's observations of autism are from historical information gained from interviewing parents in the USA, UK, Canada and Belgium[232].

Dr Upledger observed that a fever/febrile episode previously evident in the child (by approximately 2 weeks) preceded the onset of behavioural changes. He noted that the fever could be from a virus, vaccine reaction, or any other cause.

He noted that children with Autism often bang their heads, bite their knuckles or chew their wrists and thumbs, often sucking their thumbs and pushing hard against the roof of the mouth. These symptoms are the result of pressure and compression in the head and, using Cranio Sacral Therapy (CST), he was able to release the compression and noted the cessation of head banging.

During the CST sessions he actually observed clients releasing emotion, often by sighing deeply, but even crying and tears can been observed. Indeed, I have treated teens with this problem and found the same results. Once the pressure release occurs, the person can stop the head banging behaviour, with obvious frustration and discomfort removed. The individual then becomes more loving and affectionate, and consequently, improved social interaction can take place.

After the release of pressure Dr Upledger noted that the client (child) had increased warming of the body and he undertook Thermographic monitoring to confirm his suspicions. Increased blood flow is related to relaxation of the sympathetic nervous system, reducing physiological and stress factors within.
He has several theories regarding the chewing and biting:

1. Self mutilating to control pain

2. Self-mutilation to activate natural pain relievers (endorphins) giving biochemical pain relief and numbness

3. Inflicting more pain to exceed the pain threshold, therefore removing pain

He noted that all the children he treated during his study had very tight intracranial membranes, and that the Dura mater was not expanding along with normal skull and brain growth. He concluded that this was a large contributor to autistic problems. The parts of the brain involved seem to affect language and information processes and resulting behaviour could include:

- Rhythmic rocking
- Rituals or obsessive behaviour
- Banging the head against a wall or door
- Screaming and crying without tears (which I believe is frustration)
- Arm flapping and twiddling with fingers

Dr Upledger suggests that children should receive CST regularly to help relieve restrictions in the Dura mater and brain. He suggests a weekly session to start with and thereafter sessions should be tailored to suit the child/adult's progress. It is a long-term approach which should continue until the child is fully-grown, as adjustments would be needed in line with growth spurts. Some techniques may be shown to parents for home treatment, however, re-evaluation would be required by a professional CST therapist on a diary (weekly or monthly) basis.

During his trials he used hair analysis to test toxicity and mineral imbalances for each client. John Upledger also believes in supporting the body nutritionally as the brain needs to be restored with vitamins and nutrients. He advocates the following:

- Vitamin B complex and B12
- Quality fish oils and a good vitamin and mineral supplement
- A daily supplement of antioxidant (alpha lipoic acid)

AUTISM AND OXYTOCIN

Through trials, it has been realised that autistic children do have lower levels of oxytocin. As autistic children do not seem to demonstrate love easily, perhaps this is one of the reasons why. (as discussed in section 11 oxytocin)

In his book The Scientification of Love, Dr Odent concludes that in some cases of autism and autistic spectrum they can be shown as an impaired expression of love. Autistics do not socialise very well. As teens, they do not date or form relationships and the majority do not reproduce or marry. However, I have personally seen differences in behaviour before and after CST sessions, ultimately leading to more loving behaviour.

ASPERGER'S SYNDROME

Mild Autism is called Asperger's Syndrome and in these cases communication and language can be good, although sufferers do tend to have impaired social skills. They also tend to indulge in obsessive rituals such as obsessive-compulsive disorder (OCD) or attach rituals to actions or objects. It can be different for each individual and may involve ensuring that day-to-day items like shoes or doors are, to their minds, positioned correctly. They will repeat these actions over and over to get it right.

Emotionally, those who suffer from Asperger's can be hard to understand and often they appear self-absorbed and seem to prefer their own company. They tend to be seen as lonely people, and again they may avoid eye contact and will usually look away when talking. They can also suffer from anxiety and many will use rhythmic movements whilst others bang their heads against walls or doors.

Asperger's sufferers can be very intelligent, seeing letters and numbers in shapes. They don't process in the same way as others; the brain gives such clarity and insight in all things geometrically. Some see all things geometrically, the process absorbing their attention completely while watching the shapes that scenes and objects make. They pick out obscure details such as joining all the dots or seeing patterns in sand. In some cases of Asperger's, the individual can add and multiply quicker than a computer.
Their world can be like Swiss cheese with holes in their memories and minds. When they want to speak, they will want to spill it all out at once and won't stop until they have said what they wanted to say. They can often repeat the same things.

Very often, those with Asperger's know that they are different and are aware that they don't fit into society. With this knowledge, they become very lonely and sad inside. Despite the drawbacks, Asperger's sufferers can live a normal life and have partners.

Asperger's condition was sensitively highlighted in the film 'Rain Man' with Dustin Hoffman playing the lead role.

CASE STUDY 17 –
ASPERGER'S

I once treated a middle-aged man suffering from a form of Asperger's. He needed to put his shoes in a certain way and had a routine, which dictated how he took them off and put them on. They had to be in alignment and he would fiddle with them for up to ten minutes to get them right. Nothing would distract him from his mission and he would not stop until he was perfectly satisfied. When I spoke to him, he repeated what I said over and over with sometimes a space of 5-10 minutes between speaking.

This man was brought to see me by his family because he was having stomach problems. I found he had malabsorbtion and was lacking in good bacteria to help the digestive process. Digestive disorders are common in autistics and ADHD sufferers. He was put on a supplementation programme to adjust the imbalances and his diet was changed to help.

He told me about his youth. Apparently he reacted adversely and spoke out against something, although he could not remember what. Consequently, people had seen him to be dysfunctional. His medical practitioner at that time prescribed a course of electric shock treatment, which was duly carried out. He could not remember why this had happened, but did remember being taken to hospital, with no understanding of what he had done at the time. He still lived with his family. His mother and sister looked after him and made all the decisions, although he could converse and understand. I guess it was the loving family trying to do their best for him.
A few Asperger's sufferers have written books describing their view of life which have helped others to understand the condition even better. A good read on life, as an Asperger's sufferer is a book written by Daniel Tammet entitled Born on a Blue day.

Some I have treated seemed to be very sensitive to their environment and the sounds around them. They describe sound as being excruciating for them (this can be the same for ADHD sufferers). For these people supermarkets and crowed places can be a nightmare. Understandably they feel safe at home and don't want to interact with society.

Others (such as the sensitive children discussed previously) are highly sensitive to another's energy and will react to their emotions of sadness, fear or anger. They also react to negativity that others carry, not wanting to be around them or interact with them.

I know parents who have learned to screen those that they invite into their homes and those with whom their children come into contact. They have learned that without this vetting process there will be adverse consequences for all and they are the ones who will be up all night trying to calm and soothe their child. Awareness can reduce this reaction.

[220] What Dr's Don't Tell You, 'What the government doesn't tell you about the MMR jab' article (Ref:'Atypical Autism' 2002: col 2 p6)

[221] Ibid – 'US stats' p6

[222] Native remedies, 'Asperger's syndrome not another diagnosis' http://www.nativeremedies.com/Asperger's-syndrome-asperger-disorder.shtml?.ovchn= (cited 04.2007)

[223] Dr. Michel Odent 'Scientification of Love' (revised addition) Free Association Books, London.2001 (P17. 'eye to eye contact')

[224] BioCare 'The science of ASD' – Article 'The importance of digestion - significant Dysbiosis a widespread problem' p1.cl2 (Ref: Finegold et al. Gastrointestinal microflora in late onset of autism. Clin. Infec Dis 2002.11:1;35 (suppl 1):S6-S16.) (Erickson et.al. 'Gastrointestinal factors in Autistic disorder': A clinical review. J Autism Dev Disorder 2005.11: 3;1-15)

[225] Ibid 'toxin producer' (Ref: Parracho e al. 'Difference between the gut microflora of children with autistic spectrum disorders ad that of healthy children'. J Med Microbiol 2005.10;54 (pt 10) 987-91)

[226] Ibid – 'Constipation and diarrhoea'(Ref: Martrosian G. 'Anaerobic intestinal microflora in pathogenesis of autism'. Poostepy Hig Md dosw 2004 Sept 20;58;349-51)

[227] What Dr's Don't Tell You, 'What the government doesn't tell you about the MMR jab'2002 p5.col1.prg2 (Ref:Brain Dys,1991;3:328: ADV Biochem Psychopharmacol, 1993;28:627-43)

[228] BioCare 'The science of Probiotics' pg 3 (Ref:'Autism and developmental conditions' Kalle Riechelt MD 1991)

[229] Dr M Odent 'The Scientification of Love' Free Association Books, London 2001 p18 (Ref: Hattori R 'Autistic and developing disorders after general anesthetic delivery' - Letter Lancet 1.6.1991; 337;1357-8)

[230] Insert Lucy Johnson 'Cord clamping danger to babies' Sunday Express 2007.12

[231] Insert Ibid (Ref: McMaster University, Hamilton, Canada)

[232] John E Upledger 'CST awareness month 'Autism Observations Experiences and Concepts', Upledger Institute Inc., 04.2000 p3

Chapter 23

INDEX

Chapter 23

IMMUNISATION

I am neither a doctor nor a scientist. My knowledge of vaccines is based on my own research, on what other parents have told me and on the evidence I have seen through my own practice. In writing about immunisation, I have looked at evidence from parents, along with published scientific and medical literature, to discuss how effective vaccines are and even whether they are necessary at all. I seek only to give parents a broader view so that they are able to make informed choices as to what is best for their own children.

As each of us is unique and has individual needs with preferred results for recovery, allopathic medicine (prescribed drugs) may not be your first choice or the answer for you or your child. I show that there are alternative approaches and that you don't have to go down the allopathic route if it is not suited to you.

Please remember, even if you are being pressured to use vaccines by medical professionals, at the moment in the UK it is not compulsory to vaccinate and the choice to have your child vaccinated is your ultimate choice. Unfortunately, in other parts of the world this is not an option, as is the case in the USA.

The following chapter is my own personal view based upon current information. As a parent, or a soon-to-be parent, you will need to study the information and make an informed choice as to what is best to suit your family.

The UK Immunisation schedule

Immunisation was brought in to combat and protect our children and adults from serious disease. It uses the body's natural defence mechanism, the immune response, and all forms of immunisation work in the same way. Some vaccines, such as the MMR vaccine, contain live forms of the virus and, in the case of this particular example, MMR contains strains of measles, mumps and rubella which are given in a cocktail form.

For children under the age of 16, there are something like twenty vaccinations recommended by western governments and more are being proposed. Parents are put under huge pressure by local GP practices to have their children vaccinated from day one, when they give vitamin K hours after birth.

In addition to the virus itself, vaccines also contain preservatives and antibiotics such as modified toxins produced by bacteria and aluminium salt, to preserve the vaccine. In the past, vaccines have contained Thimerosol (mercury), but its use has since been reduced (in MMR) because of the outcry concerning the fact that mercury is a toxic metal which stays in the body and that some believe is also linked with autism. Please note some other vaccines still carry mercury.
Source: *www.drmercola.com*

If babies are born naturally through the birth canal, they receive their mother's antibodies, therefore giving them some immunity when they arrive.[233] Our children, however, are immunised with vitamin K from the moment they are born because NHS guidelines state that, in the first few years, young children need immunisation because their own immune system is immature. No matter whether the receiver of the vaccine is young or old though, it does not mean that they will not catch the disease against which they are being vaccinated, but it is believed that they would contract it in a milder form.

Some react after immunisation, with soreness and redness to the site of the injection, together with swelling in the area. Fever and rash are also other signs of reaction.

The US Food and Drug Administration now believes that 90% of the problems associated with vaccinations go unrecorded. Most of these are toxic reactions, which cause immune damage.

Side effects are only recorded if symptoms occur within two weeks after vaccination, although most serious complications only show themselves at between three and six weeks after the jab has been given. In some cases, the full effects do not fully manifest themselves until after twelve months or more. In most cases of complications, nutritional history, health status and vaccine background are not taken into account.

Vaccine fillers and ingredients

In addition to the viral and bacterial RNA or DNA that is part of vaccines, fillers are also added. In many cases, the fillers used are more toxic than the viral component, something which is particularly true of thimerosol, or mercury.

The fillers commonly used include:

- Aluminium Hydroxide
- Aluminium Phosphate
- Ammonium sulphate
- Amphotericin B

Source: www.drmercola.com

In some vaccines, animal tissue and VERO cells might also be used, including:

- Monkey kidney cells
- Washed sheep red blood cells
- Calf (bovine) serum
- Fetal (bovine) serum

As well as these ingredients, vaccines might also contain:

- Phenoxyethanol (antifreeze)
- Potassium monophosate
- Polymyxin B
- Polysorbate 20 & 80
- Formaldehyde
- Sucrose
- Thimerosol (mercury)

Although it has been strongly recommended that pharmaceutical companies take Thimerosol out of MMR vaccines, it has not been mandated. Drug companies were not required to take existing stocks off the market, but simply to apply the recommendations to new stocks. Unknown quantities of stock have been, and are continuing to be used until stocks run out. No date has been given as to when the new thimerosol-free vaccines should begin to be manufactured or to appear in the market place and in the meantime the long-term effects of mercury are unknown. Interestingly, however, some new research from the USA is now indicating a decline in autism and speech disorders due to the mercury-free vaccine programme[234].

RECOMMENDED SCHEDULE FOR CHILDHOOD IMMUNISATION

According to NHS (Immune schedule – NHS Direct), the recommended schedule for childhood immunisations currently looks as follows:

2 months old

- Diphtheria, tetanus, pertussis (whooping cough), polio and haemophilus and influenza type b (Hib) - one injection - dTpa/IPV/Hib
- Pneumococcal conjugate vaccine, PCV - pneumococcal infection - one injection

3 months old

- Diphtheria, tetanus, pertussis (whooping cough), polio and haemophilus and influenza type b (Hib) - one injection - dTpa/IPV/Hib
- MenC - meningitis C (meningococcal group C) - one injection

4 months old

- Diphtheria, tetanus, pertussis (whooping cough), polio and haemophilus and influenza type b (Hib) - one injection - dTpa/IPV/Hib
- MenC   - meningitis C (meningococcal group C) - one injection
- Pneumococcal conjugate vaccine, PCV - pneumococcal infection - one injection

Approx 12 months old

- Haemophilus influenza type b (Hib) - one injection

- MenC   - meningitis C (meningococcal group C) - one injection

Approx 13 months

- Pneumococcal conjugate vaccine, PCV - pneumococcal infection - one injection
- MMR (measles, mumps and rubella) - one injection

3 years and 4 months to 5 years old

- Diphtheria, tetanus, pertussis (whooping cough), polio and haemophilus and influenza type b (Hib) - one injection - dTpa/IPV/Hib
- MMR (measles, mumps and rubella) - one injection

13 years to 18 years old

- Diphtheria, Tetanus, Polio – one injection - Td/IPV

To ensure that a separate record is kept, parents are given a little red book to log the vaccines that their children receive from the GP. However, recent media reports indicate that children's immunisation records in the NHS are not as accurate as they should be[235].

ALUMINIUM

Aluminium is often used in vaccines and, since the removal of mercury in some vaccines, aluminium has been used more freely. Aluminium is highly toxic to the human body but is used because small amounts have been found to stimulate the immune system, thereby making the vaccine more effective.

As we will discuss, the effectiveness of many vaccines is under question. One of the main concerns is around the preservatives used and their side effects, and particularly aluminium and mercury, which carry and ingest the vaccine quicker into the child's system. Preservatives are used to expand a vaccine's life span. However, aluminium and mercury can be absorbed into brain tissue and attack the central nervous system. Clearly it is more dangerous to administer vaccines within three months of life when a child's brain and nerve structure is not properly formed.

Some experts believe that it is the preservatives which are responsible for CJD and BSE in vaccinated animals, suggesting that the aluminium derivative used to preserve veterinary vaccines was the true cause and not animal feed as suggested. As a result, laws have now been passed to discontinue nerve and brain tissue entering the human food chain. As with all things, the truth will prevail eventually and one day we will find out the real truth behind the scare.

According to Dr Richard Halvorsen in his book 'The Truth About Vaccines', the amount of aluminium in some vaccines exceeds the recommended safe level by up to 1000 times. Babies are the ones most at risk as they are less able to cope with receiving more than the upper recommended safety level. Those born prematurely or who are known to have a genetic susceptibility are in even greater danger.

Dr. Halverson suggests there is some complacency concerning the use of aluminium since, like mercury, it has been used for eighty years[236]. Little research has been done, however, on its effects and safety in vaccines, although the medical journal Lancet did publish a comprehensive review in 2004 showing adverse effects after immunisation. With vaccines containing aluminium, they found more redness and swelling at the injection site than vaccines without it[237]. Literally we don't know enough about aluminium once it is injected in the human body or what it does once it is in there.

A Toxic substance

Aluminium is an abundant metal on the earth, but it has no beneficial use to the body and is known to be toxic to our nervous system and bones. It has been found to be especially toxic to the brain (where it can accumulate over time) and vulnerable people such as the young and old can be badly affected. Some research has associated aluminium with Alzheimer's (a form of dementia) and high aluminium levels have been found in some children suffering from hyperactivity, behavioural problems and autism[238].

Aluminium is not only used in vaccines

It also gets into our bodies through medicines, water and food and can be absorbed through the skin and lungs. Safety guidelines for the use of aluminium in water, medicines and food are advised by the World Health organisation (WHO), which bases them on 'provisional tolerance weekly intake levels' according to body weight. Because of concerns in 2006, the WHO lowered its weekly safety limit from 7mg per kg of body weight to 1mg per kg.

Foodstuffs

The highest concentrations of aluminium are to be found in the staple elements of our diets, since aluminium-containing additives are used in the processing of foodstuffs such as bread, cereals and processed foods, as well as in packaging such as juice containers. Would you believe that even conventional tea contains high concentrations of aluminium?

Water

Aluminium sulphate is used as part of the purification process in our water and is supposed to be completely filtered out before it reaches our homes. In 1988, however, many suffered for over eighteen months in Camelford, North Cornwall with all sorts of disorders because aluminium sulphate had been put in the wrong water treatment tank. People suffered from stomach problems, loss of memory and concentration, mouth ulcers, rashes and body pain.

Fluoride

This is a chemical used in water treatment and is also an aluminium derivative. It is said to be good for our teeth, but what is not generally publicised is that it is not so good for the body. Not all areas have fluoride in their drinking water and indeed public concern has diverted councils eager to add it to their daily intake. However, some areas have not been so lucky and authorities have gone ahead without consultation.

Personal products

Aluminium is also found in personal products such as deodorants and sun creams, as well as in many of our indigestion or antacid prescriptions and over the counter remedies. Most of the aluminium in these foods and preparations is excreted through the body's elementary processes, but when we inject into the body (as with vaccines) it goes straight into our venous (blood) system, therefore bypassing the stomach process, our only barrier and eliminator.

Formula milk

Breast-fed babies are found to carry hardly any aluminium but formula milk has moderate levels. It was highlighted that babies receiving soya milk would ingest higher levels, which would possibly breach the new WHO levels of safety, as these are determined by body weight.

Even though the WHO revised its levels in 2006, it still raises the question that the majority of average weight babies are receiving large doses above the advised levels. Dr Halverson suggests that this is five hundred to one thousand times more than the amount recommended[239] , highlighting that premature babies, being smaller, may absorb even higher levels!

Premature Babies

A study was carried out in Cambridge due to concerns from doctors about premature babies and the intravenous feeding solutions they received which contained aluminium. The development of these children was compared to children who received reduced aluminium solutions at the age of 18 months of age and the results showed that premature babies who were fed solutions with aluminium suffered from impaired development of the brain[240].

Perhaps mother's milk is best – read premature birth case study

VACCINE INCENTIVES

Despite doctors showing their concern, research funding to discover the consequences is not forthcoming in the UK. It is believed that some doctors are afraid to speak out about the vaccines in case they are discredited and lose their jobs. Apparently, some doctors have even gone to the extreme by signing the Official Secrets Act! Unfortunately their fears seem founded, especially if you take into consideration the treatment Dr Wakefield received after speaking out about the MMR vaccines. Some see him as a scapegoat for speaking out against the government.

Doctors are bound by the Hippocratic Oath to serve their patients, rather than their self-interests or for monetary gain aside from their normal salaries. The UK government, however, pays doctors big bonuses if they hit vaccine targets and it has to be said that there is something seriously wrong with the process where financial incentives to administer vaccines take precedence over the oath that all doctors are sworn to.

In 2006, the bonuses paid to doctors were as much as £10,000 each. Because of the system we have in the UK for paying our GPs, doctors have a built-in incentive to give as many jabs as possible. [241]
Why though are our doctors monitored on performance and targets when they are not part of a sales team? Public healthcare is not a marketing exercise and it is the health of our children that is at stake here. Our healthcare system should not involve incentives which encourage a doctor to focus on the money aspect rather than treating the public. GPs are paid well in the first place.

Is our government sending the wrong signals? To my mind, it means that their focus is on monetary reward instead of the health and well-being of their patients and our most precious offspring.

RESEARCH

The results of trials, which have already taken place in France, suggest that some vaccines may be responsible for triggering illnesses such as MS and immune disorders[242].

The long-term effects are not yet known, as trials have been short, and for some insane reason, vaccines do not need to go through the vigorous proving process that most drugs do! The UK vaccine regime requires that by the time children are three years old, they will have had 13 jabs, with further boosters to follow when they are at school. Overall, they receive a staggering 25 vaccination jabs before they are fifteen years old. The long-term effects that we are creating on the immune system are unknown because the trials do not go that far, yet!

Dr Halvorsen has spoken out in the broadsheets, stating that 'the government continually misleads us over vaccination. There are unfounded claims about their safety and effectiveness and I believe jabs may be doing potentially serious harm to hundreds if not thousands of children every year.' He believes that parents are being grossly misled.

Because of his concerns about multiple vaccines, Dr Halvorsen gives only single vaccines to children and questions the safety of the MMR vaccine. Through his own research, he believes that the lack of research by the government has only exacerbated disorders in children. He has already highlighted the measles component of the MMR vaccine as being responsible for serious disorders leading to permanent brain damage.

He also believes that the mumps component has done more harm than good, something with which other doctors and researchers agree. Since the MMR vaccine programme was introduced, there has been a vast increase in disorders such as asthma, eczema and diabetes, with direct links to the mumps vaccine in MMR jab being highlighted.

In the UK, we run the earliest vaccination programme in the world, starting at two, three and four months. Common sense tells us that this involves the greatest risk to our developing babies. Mothers have reported their children having side effects within hours of the first vaccine of 'DPT hib' and polio '5 in1' which is given at two months of age. The symptoms, which have been reported, include high-pitched screaming, purple coloration, uncontrollable shaking in the limbs and vomiting. Babies have been described as being distressed and agitated, their eyes wide open but with no recognition. In other cases, they showed startled expressions together with agitated, jerky and jumpy movements.

One mother reported that her child was continually frightened and even seemed to be hallucinating. The baby's cry was more high-pitched and there was no communication or eye contact, despite being fine before the jab was administered only hours before! Another child was taken to A&E where, after some hours of observation, they discharged him as having a 'startled expression' and told the parents that it was quite all right for him to continue with the vaccination programme! From my experience, however, a startled expression goes hand in hand with shock and trauma. Although the mothers visited their GPs, they were told that the cause of the distress was possibly febrile convulsion, even though this does not usually affect children under six months[243].

We already know that combining a cocktail of vaccines can have an adverse effect on the recipient. Gulf war syndrome (GWS) is a proven complaint which affected fully-formed adults, so imagine the effect on growing youngsters who are still going through certain developmental cycles. Anyone can suffer from reactions if their immune system is impaired, irrespective of age.

JABS

Unfortunately, I am hearing more and more stories about the intimidation by doctors and hospital staff, which is directed towards those parents whose children have not been vaccinated with the MMR jab.

One story in particular was astonishing. I had previously treated a 5 year-old boy (we will call him James) for eczema, which I found was caused by a malfunctioning colon and fear taken on from the mother during pregnancy. James caught a particular nasty virus in 2007. He was in his first term at school and he picked up an infection in school which also struck his peers. This particular virus struck the chest and lungs and had reached epidemic proportions in the winter of 2007. I myself caught it and, like others, found that it lingered, generating a cough for some months after the initial symptoms. Many reported that antibiotics did not clear the symptoms at all.

James received four lots of antibiotics, which did nothing for the symptoms. The chest infection turned into pneumonia and James was taken into hospital. When the consultant found out that he had not had the MMR jab, he asked the parents to remove their child from the hospital.

Astonished, the parents stated that they were under the impression that the NHS was for all and that they found the consultant's attitude discriminatory. It seemed it was his way or NO way – which is astounding in this day and age. Eventually, James was treated and found the whole experience very frightening, whilst the parents became extremely disillusioned with the NHS to say the least. They felt they had NO support or understanding from the hospital staff.

Parents have a choice and if they do not wish their children to have the MMR jab, that is their right. They opted for no jab because their children were sensitive enough without causing them more discomfort and agony. After all, one of their children was allergic to eggs, which is what the vaccines are cultured on. The consultant did not want to know the reasons why however. He just made up his mind and, in my opinion, was too quick to judge.

Others have told me that nurses and doctors have bullied them into submission even after they had weighed up the options and decided against vaccination. After all, there were no vaccines in my day and not only did we survive without complications, but our parents sent us to play with those who had measles and mumps as our parents and grandparents knew the benefits of catching childhood disease. (We will look at this later in the section on measles and mumps)

Parents know their own children

They are individual and need to be treated as individuals, as what works for one does always not work for another. Perhaps perceptions will change over time, as they did with smoking. Thirty years ago, smoking was the norm and it was believed to be good for you to smoke as it was thought to calm the nerves, although we know now that cigarette companies knew it was harmful but continued to veil the truth. In earlier days it was 'un-cool' not to smoke and you were intimidated if you did not. Today, however, the tables have turned and it is no longer cool to smoke. No longer do we allow smoking in public places because the truth has come out. We know it is harmful for our health and those around us who ingest the residue. Unfortunately though, it is too late for the many thousands who have died because of active and passive smoking. It took a long time to prove...

Will we be changing our minds about jabs for children in thirty years?

No-one knows. Time will tell, but I believe that the less interference the better while the body is developing.

I am personally alarmed by the new jab being pushed upon our early teenage girls to prevent cervical cancer. There was a case recently in the paper where a mother and her daughter had talked about the pros and cons of the jab and decided (with her daughter not being sexually active) there would be no need for her to have the jab. However, when at school a few days later, the nurse asked the girl a few questions and before she knew about it the nurse had injected her without her consent. How democratic is that? I believe that the nurse in question took liberties with her position and that her own judgement got in the way. No, after all, means NO.

I don't know what the outcome was or even if the nurse was reprimanded. Does she know if the girl will have side effects, as has been shown in trials? The long-term effects of this jab are not known. The nurse can't know the long-term outcome for the girl's health in later life, something in which she may have played a critical part.

In puberty, the body is rapidly changing and who knows if the jab causes infertility? No one does. I would be very suspicious and would want to know the longer-term implications if it was an option for my daughter. I personally feel the less interference the better.

Most 12 or 13 year-olds are not sexually active and, in my view, giving this jab only sends the wrong message to teens by promoting sexual activity. From the reports that I have read, the jab is not guaranteed and from the short trials which have already been conducted (just like the MMR trials, these have only taken place over months and not years), side effects are already known to occur. Like the MMR, being vaccinated once is not enough, as it is stated that girls would also need to be revaccinated at the age of 18.

Another concern is that the UK government has introduced the vaccination programme without consulting parents, in the same way as it did for the MMR vaccine, something which feels like nothing short of running roughshod over the opinions of parents. Has common sense been eroded once again? As parents, we are responsible for our children and most take that responsibility very seriously. You know your child and even when they are in their teens they need your guidance and support. Our children are precious at any age and are not human guinea pigs. I urge you to be mindful of the bigger picture and long-term effects – remember what happened in relation to views on smoking.

Flu jab

The next thing, of course, is that the powers-that-be now want to bring in the flu jab for babies, as they say that this will stop babies infecting others. Is it not the other way around though? Don't babies pick up illnesses from others, such as parents and siblings? Parents are receiving letters already, asking them to take their children for the jab, and not only the two year-olds, but also the rest of the siblings of all ages.

We already have a flu vaccination programme which is aimed mainly at protecting the elderly and those, like diabetes sufferers, who are especially at risk. Even some of these people, though, have a reaction to the jab and yet they are fully-formed adults whose bodies are no longer changing and growing as is the case with children.

I have been informed of one case of a sprightly 80 year-old who had the flu jab only to find that she seized up totally and could not walk for two weeks. This was a woman who, despite being elderly, was very fit for her age and had no problem walking before the jab!

The flu jab is normally available in the autumn and the NHS state that it gives protection for one year. It is made from the strain that is expected in the coming winter and, as such, scientists have already agreed that it is a lottery. They cannot say which form of flu or virus will come in each year, making the vaccination programme very much a hit and miss system. To maintain protection, you need to have a flu jab every year[244].

Those who are given the jab free in the UK are those who:

- Have heart conditions
- Are undergoing cancer treatment
- Suffer lowered immunity due to steroid medication
- Have HIV
- Suffer from long-term chronic conditions
- Suffer liver or kidney disease

To a fit and healthy person, flu does not seem a serious illness; we have the antibodies already in the body for our immune system to defend us. Surely then it is common sense that if we keep giving the flu jab to our children, they will not build up a natural immunity and will be reliant upon vaccines for the rest of their lives. Starting at the age of two, they could be having vaccinations for seventy or eighty years! What a thought!

As adults, we can make up our own minds and judge if we need to have the flu jab. Parents are not being consulted in relation to their children, however. They are being told and policies will be put in place so that it becomes mandatory as with the MMR. In some cases if you don't comply you are invited to register elsewhere with another practice!

It seems we going back to the times of the Inquisition, where we are not allowed to question but are just expected to accept what we are told! Is it our children they are worried about?

I feel very concerned about this new wave of vaccines for children. If we keep giving vaccines to our children it will mean that they become more reliant on pharmaceuticals for protection, instead of their bodies being able to protect them naturally - which is precisely what our immune system does for us.

It is the same story with drugs such as Ritalin which children start taking from an early age. The body becomes reliant and then it becomes addicted. Take any drug for a time and the body will get used to its effects. It will need weaning off and the user will suffer withdrawal symptoms. Many drugs have been withdrawn because of serious side effects, but it has taken years to prove and recognise the addictions and problems caused. In the meantime, some people have had their lives so messed up by medication, together with unresolved reactions and outcomes. In some cases, such as with Seroxat and Vallium, it has even led to fatalities.

The pharmaceutical companies play with people's lives and now they are playing with our children's. Many outcomes are unknown, with insufficient short trials such as those conducted into the MMR vaccine and media coverage highlighting the new swine flu jab linking to a 'deadly nerve disease' with deaths involved. [245]

However, even when serious side effects are registered, scientists believe it is a price worth paying for the bigger picture. It seems that pharmaceutical companies hold power over us without us knowing. It is big business, which in my opinion, they will not want to reduce.

DISEASES

Disease is nature's way of reducing the population; something that has been happening over centuries. Indeed, the production of antibiotics has proved this in that there have been so many strains made to combat viruses and yet what do the viruses do? They mutate into something else, which of course provokes pharmaceutical companies to come up with something else.

We are now in the position where the antibiotics don't work with most viruses. I hear of people having to take stronger and stronger prescriptions to kill a virus and it has been reported that there are only one or two in the world now that would cope with a severe virus strain or epidemic.

Our hospitals are full of viruses. MRSA has caused many people to come out of hospital with more than they went in with, and the medical profession don't seem to be able to treat it or eradicate it. Even when people have died from it, unfortunately, some of the hospitals have not informed the grieving families that MRSA was involved in the diagnosis.

Are our governments being hypnotised by the pharmaceutical companies? As we keep buying, so they produce more and more medicines and vaccinations, which are purportedly the answer to all disease, but is it doing us any good? If you read the labels on some of these wonder drugs, what you will see is a list of side effects. This means that you then get another disorder or unpleasant response from taking the medication, and science comes up with something else to combat the effects of the first one!

My mother was put on a mixture of different medications for a heart condition. The mix was to be monitored and changed according to whether she had a reaction, something that happened when one of the tablets she was on produced a side effect, (more water in the body) and she ended up with water around the heart. As you can imagine, this was a very scary episode.

My mother thought she was having a heart attack, had to be injected into the abdominal area (to which she reacted badly), spent a few days in hospital and weeks in recovery, during which time she felt as though she had been knocked down by a bus - only to be told that one tablet had caused this. 'Oops. It sometimes gives this reaction,' the consultant said.

Are we fire fighting? It seems like the sweet shop for the medical profession. 'Try this, and if it doesn't work we have a range more for you to try. Don't worry about the fact that you are paying me and the pharmaceutical companies, or that we are getting rich on your demise.' Some might say that's a rather cynical view, however.

Prevention

Centuries ago in Japan, doctors were paid to keep you well and if you became ill you did not pay the doctor. He still treated you, but it was in his interests to keep you in tip top condition. Perhaps we need more of this way of thinking. *Prevention!*

Medication, of course, has its place, but wouldn't it be better if we were to allow the body to take a natural course instead of experimenting. We are all different, all unique, and what works for one does not work for another, yet still we keep trying to put everyone in a box, to categorise them into groups. When things don't go the way they expect, they wonder why!

IMMUNE SYSTEM

I believe we should be treated as individuals. How we react to medication or vaccine of any kind will depend on how our immune system is performing, how we are emotionally and whether we are anxious and stressed. All of these things reflect in our bodies and we need to look at the core of the problem, not the symptoms. Today, the medical profession mostly treats the symptoms. They don't always believe (and this will depend upon the clinicians/doctor and their conditioning and training) that the body and mind are one. Some still believe that they are separate and treat them separately. This, however, is an old view and it is only with education and information that it will change.

As we have moved through the twentieth century and the first decade of the twenty-first, many new types of treatment have come to the fore which are based on a holistic view of body, spirit and mind, Homeopathy, acupuncture, Reflexology and Cranio Sacral Therapy are just a few of these. A lot of people are now moving more towards this type of thinking and do not want to take tablets or put toxic substances into their bodies. This is what our sensitive children and adults want and need. They cannot cope with the levels of toxicity/ side effects contained in a lot of the medication today, (including anaesthetics).

This is even the case when we go to the dentist and have an injection. I have had personal experience of this when I suffered a very bad reaction which left my mouth and tongue numb for many weeks. The effects occurred within less than a minute of having the injection! I was told later, when I changed my dentist, that it was known that this particular injection had been flagged as having adverse reactions in children and some adults who had an enzyme missing. I was informed that this injection had been withdrawn for children.

Naturally, this was a very unpleasant experience, not to mention being one in which I was offered no recourse and no help. My own dental practice did not know what to do and could not fix it. My body simply had to deal with it. Fortunately, I do not take medication and it is a very unusual occurrence for me to be at the dentist, so my body was able to deal with it without restrictions. However, I will not be accepting any more drug injections from a dentist. My new dentist practices alternative ways.

Toxins stay in the body for years, something which a story that I recently heard really brought home to me. A bio detox specialist* persuaded a doctor to try out his theories. The doctor agreed but with one condition - that a sample be sent to the lab to be tested afterwards. The bio detox specialist agreed to this arrangement but when the sample results came back showing traces of cannabis, the doctor was perplexed, until, that is, he thought back to his university days ten years before... So, you can see how these drugs lie hidden in the body for a long, long, time, reducing its efficiency of the body and making it less able to cope with other disorders. It is like putting diesel in an unleaded car. It will go, but it will be lumpy and will eventually seize up, causing mayhem in the mean time.

*Bio Detox is where toxins are drawn from the feet. The feet are placed in a foot-bath where a low voltage appliance draws out the toxins held within the body. The water will reflect (by colour and odour) the health of the participant, which is different for everyone.

HEPATITIS B

Vaccines too can be longer lasting that we think. A friend of mine gave birth to her son two years ago and, at the age of 9 months, he was diagnosed as having tumours in the liver - a very unusual disorder for a child so young. When my friend looked back on what was happening before her pregnancy, however, she remembered that she had been given a hepatitis jab the year before she became pregnant. She had pricked her finger on a hypodermic and was given hepatitis A and B jabs three times, once every three months. She found this an intense programme and felt vulnerable during the process of having blood tests between each injection. She was told not to get pregnant during the nine-month vaccination programme, which she did not. She became pregnant some six months later, after the completion of the vaccine programme.

There are links to the hepatitis jab and liver disease and, although doctors do not link this case to the jab received by mum, having four other children who are healthy, it seems a coincidence that after her injection programme, her child should end up with a liver disorder. It may be that a longer period of perhaps 12 months is needed before pregnancy.

Hepatitis B is a virus, which can lead to liver problems and possibly liver failure. Although usually passed by blood contact, it is also present in saliva and other bodily fluids. People who are considered to be at greater risk are encouraged to be immunized in the UK, including medical professionals, prison staff and inmates, those who share drug needles and those who are sexually active and have several partners.

A study of US patients has also shown a link to developing MS from Hepatitis B. The study discovered the link between vaccine and MS when they checked the records of more than 1,500 people. They concluded that they could not say whether the vaccine caused MS in those who were already susceptible, or if it just speeded up the onset.[246]

Clearly we need to have more studies and research in this area. We know that children are affected in the womb by how their mothers are emotionally and physically and it has been highlighted that they can take on some of the mother's weaknesses.

[233] BioCare 'Science of probiotics' 2008 p3

[234] Dr. Richard Halverson 'Truth about vaccines' Gibson Square, London 2007 pg 19/p4 (research USA) & Article Integrated Health 2007;vol 7 No 42 p23 (ref :Geir Brothers – Early Downward Trends in Neuro developmental disorders following removal of Thimerosal containing vaccines Jrnl American Physicians and Surgeons 2006. 11:8-13) - USA withdrawing the MMR vaccine has reduced growing numbers of Autism.

[235] Jane Symons 'Child immunisation records are in such chaos – top secret documents leaked from NHS' The Sun News. http://www.thesun.co.uk/article/0,,70331 ece. (cited 07.2007)

[236] Richard Halverson 'Truth about vaccines' Gibson Square, London 2007 ('Déjà vu Aluminium' pg 22 p2)

[237] Ibid 'The medical journal Lancet review 2004' p22

[238] Ibid 'WHO tolerance 'p24/p3

[239] Halverson Richard 'Truth about vaccines' Gibson Square London 2007 "WHO" pg 27

[240] Ibid 'study Cambridge – premature baby study - aluminium' pg 27/28

[241] Jayne Symons 'National jabs scandal exposed' –2006.11 www.thesun.co.uk/article/0_2-2006510771,00.html (cited 07.2007)

[242] Lucy Johnston 'Children used as guinea pigs' Sunday Express 22.07.2007

[243] JABS Forum 'Vaccine reaction – our experience' http://www.jabs.org.uk/forum/pop_printer_friendly.asp?TOPIC_ ID=717 (cited 07.2007)

[244] NHS direct 'Flu Jab'http://www.nhsdirect.nhs.uk/articles/article.aspx?articleID=509&sectionId=38 (cited 07.2007)

[245] Jo Macfarlane medical correspondent 'Swine flu jab link to killer nerve disease' The mail on Sunday 08.2009.

[246] Eclub 'MS, Hepatitiis Vaccine Links found' http://Credencegroup.co.uk/Eclub/Eclubserchable2/221004/CTM%20-%20 vaccine%linked- (Ref: BBC News 09.2004) news.bbc.co.uk/1/hi/health/7576829.stm (Cited 07.2007)

Chapter 24

INDEX

Chapter 24

MMR

MMR vaccination is a very controversial and emotive subject. However, I could not write a book about birth and babies without including some of the facts already in the public domain, which are not common knowledge. In doing this, I hope to broaden parent's perspectives by giving more detailed information. After all, how can parents make informed choices if they do not have all the details?

I am glad that I did not need to make the decision concerning vaccination that parents today need to make on behalf of their children. In my day, jabs were given separately, although even then, some children did react.

In this chapter we will discuss and debate the pros and cons of MMR vaccination, as well as considering possible side effects which are being discussed and brought to the attention of the medical society.

Disclaimer: I would, however, like to make it absolutely clear that these are my personal observations and that it is my sole intention to provide an assortment of information from evidence already published in medical literature which parents and individuals can use to advise and guide them in making the right choice for themselves and their families. When and if to have your child vaccinated is, after all, a personal decision which will be influenced by your own beliefs, cultural influences and which you alone make as a parent.

MMR – THE FACTS

The measles, mumps and rubella (MMR) vaccination is a combined triple jab, launched in 1988. Edwina Currie, the Health Secretary in 1989, stated that it was a 'lifelong protection with a single jab.' Since its introduction, however, there has been continued controversy with the vaccination programme, mainly because of the safety issues for some children.

In 1989, there was enough scientific evidence to suggest serious problems from the jab, and there are even more now. The most controversial report, widely reported in the media, came from 'Dr Wakefield', who discovered a possible link between the triple vaccine, a new form of colitis and autism in 1998 (which is still disputed). Since then, there have been many more reports of side effects, including fatality.

The UK government's position, in common with that of many other governments, is that all children should be vaccinated with MMR despite objections from parents and the findings from scientific trials. Although single vaccines have been suggested in many quarters, it seems because of the costs involved, the UK government has put obstructions in place, which largely make separate vaccines unavailable to those who want them, although they can be obtained privately.

We have to ask ourselves, do we want to put our children at risk? Even one fatality, when it can be avoided, is in my opinion too many, yet it was reported in June 2006 that there had been 26 child deaths resulting from the MMR vaccine[247]. Broadsheets claimed that in most cases, the government or leading medical officials accepted the connection and paid out compensation. Post mortem reports accepted the MMR jab as the most likely cause of death and parents were awarded vaccine damage payments of up to £100,000[248]

In 1988, the UK government's joint committee on vaccination and immunisation produced a report concerning the MMR vaccination, which was only released under the Freedom of Information Act in 2007. The report revealed that the measles component of a brand of MMR used in the US had caused neurological complications. In addition, five cases of potentially deadly brain inflammation were reported in Canada following the use of MMR, and this was before it was introduced into the UK vaccine programme. Seven months after the production of this report, these strains were introduced to the UK without any warning of serious risk despite the fact that the minutes of the joint committee meeting stated 'In the US many of the reported neurological complications were clearly related to the measles component.'[249]

It seems that the UK government have continually failed to evaluate the risks of MMR properly. When it was introduced to the UK, the pilot study showed that some children would suffer from convulsions (estimated to be 1 in 400) but this was considered to be 'acceptable' to authorities and the public were not informed[250].

Even knowing the outcomes in the US and Canada, the same strains were being routinely administered to our children in the UK without any warning of serious risk until four years later, when concerns were raised by the rising health fears associated with the mumps strain Urabe (we explain further, below under mumps). With meningitis risks being higher than previously thought, the strain was eventually removed in 1992 in the UK. However, the Canadian joint committee had unfortunately deemed the mumps element to be in keeping with that expected![251]

Will we look back upon these exposures and see this as one of the greatest scandals in medical history?

Safety

We have an inbuilt programme which lets us know instinctively to keep our children safe consequently we ensure that safety measures are put in place in the home, school and playground. There are those who believe some parents have now gone too far in not allowing their children out of their sight, but when you consider cases such as that of Madeline McCann, (the little girl who went missing whilst on holiday), their reactions can be considered perfectly understandable.

When it comes to drugs and vaccines, however, we have no safety net. We believe what we are told by the manufacturers. We don't doubt or probe the safety of their products at all, but instead presume and expect stringent safety measures to have been put in place behind the scenes. We look to our governments to ensure the introduction of safety measures, which will keep side effects to a minimum.
   I am often alarmed when informed about the side effects of drugs that both adults and children take. They do not seem concerned, as I am, about the long-term consequences, which the medical profession deem acceptable!

Are we being unjust to expect such high standards?

I naively assume like many others, that where children are concerned, there needs to be even more stringent measures in place. These children are our future, yet are we creating a race of maladjusted youngsters who are like time bombs waiting to go off?

All of this is unbeknownst to most parents who place their faith in doctors and the medical profession – those who are supposedly well informed and qualified in these matters. I sometimes wonder if our doctors and health professionals have been brainwashed by the manufacturers, or taken in by the spin that our governments have put on things. It begs the question 'do they actually care'?

After doing my own research, I find the safety measures questionable. Manufacturers are creating more and more drugs and vaccines, many of which are being scientifically proven, although when used on the general public are often found to carry high risks with unacceptable side effects.

Have people all over the world been duped into believing the effectiveness of the MMR vaccine? Trials have been questionable and the risks associated with a catalogue of serious side effects (as discussed in detail below) kept under wraps.

So why are governments continuing to push the MMR vaccine? Why are they allowing pharmaceutical companies to benefit financially at the detriment of our children? How many have to die and just what is an acceptable number of children to suffer from dysfunctions and disastrous physical and mental reactions?

How effective is the MMR vaccine?

It has now come to light that the MMR vaccine was licensed after a safety trial lasting only three weeks. Parents were asked to fill in questionnaires for just 21 days and it is reported that children who developed autism (and some did) were not included in the data! In the opinion of Walter Spitzer, professor of epidemiology, 'children should have been monitored for at least three years'[252], but for some unknown reason it seems acceptable to produce vaccines without the vigorous testing that is in place for drugs.

At a press conference in 2002, Professor Liam Donaldson stated: *'The MMR vaccine is safe. Getting rid of the combined MMR injection would be like playing 'Russian roulette' with the health of children."* *He also thought that making individual vaccines available would reduce the uptake, making the situation unacceptable.*

The government's view is that there is no definitive causal link or evidence that the MMR vaccine causes autism. However there is growing circumstantial evidence implicating the MMR vaccine in certain forms of autism that can no longer be ignored. As we have already mentioned, in some states of the USA they have found that withdrawing the MMR vaccine has reduced growing numbers of autism[253].

Read on to learn how other disorders are also linked to the MMR vaccine.

Dr Andrew Wakefield's involvement with MMR research

Dr Andrew Wakefield was a gastroenterologist who worked in the 1990s for the Royal Free Hospital, London, and is known for his research into viral associations and Crohn's disease.

In 1996 Dr Wakefield researched a possible link between gastrointestinal problems in children and the MMR jab. He published both his own and his co-workers' findings in the Lancet[254]
Authors Note: 12 years later (2010) the Lancet rescinded Dr Wakefield's research, report based upon questionable data gathering.

A further larger trial subsequently took place of 60 children who had developed autism after vaccination in 2000[255].

Despite both the rescindment and original small data sample, his finding posed worrying questions. Amongst his study group, most showed intestinal abnormalities, chronic ulceration and Autism. According to parents, these children developed normally until the MMR jab, whereupon behavioural problems began.
His original findings inferred the information to be a new strain of Crohn's disease with chronic swelling of lymph glands in the small intestine and a co-passenger link to regressive Autism.

Further research by other scientists found the same abnormalities in groups of autistic children. These findings were also published in the Lancet[256].

If Dr Wakefield's evidence can be believed, 82% of his autistic study group had measles in the intestine, whilst urine tests showed a marked vitamin B12 deficiency (B12 is necessary for the normal development of the central nervous system and could be a contributory factor to autistic regression). Although Dr. Wakefield's conclusions have since been discounted, the idea of a vaccinated measles virus promoting insufficient immune response cannot be ignored.

If true, it would explain the study's findings on increased permeability of the gut wall.
A separate Japanese study links autism and 'left over' measles virus found in the blood of 1/3rd of a small sample of autistic children[257].

Further research was done by other scientists, who found the same abnormalities in groups of autistic children and published their findings in the Lancet[258].

Perhaps the broader picture holds answers
Seventy years ago we were told that inhaling cigarette smoke was not harmful. At that time, manufacturers rightly claimed no proven links with lung cancer. Now each packet carries a stern health warning.

In later years, pregnant mothers accepted health authority assurances on the use of thalidomide. Horrendous birth deformities told a different story. I could also mention gulf war syndrome etc., however, hindsight is a wonderful thing!

In recent years we have seen allergic reactions to peanuts, sometimes so severe the individual dies. Government response has insisted upon warnings on food packaging where peanuts might be included.

Logically there is no financial benefit in disproving a particular product's safety. Consequently its safety trials are normally left to the manufacturer. Governmental departments usually avoid confrontation until serious statistics emerge.

At this point we must accept a very broad definition for 'serious'. I believe autism to be serious, although many medical practitioners might disagree.

If there is the slightest possibility of growing autism cases stemming directly from a combined MMR vaccine it begs one obvious question. Apart from cost, what is the objection to children receiving individual vaccinations for Measles, Mumps and Rubella?

Surely if a parent offers to pay privately for three separate vaccines, there is no on cost to any health authority. So why insist on using something that may one day be listed alongside cigarettes and thalidomide?

Links with Crohn's disease

Other trials, meanwhile, have shown persistent measles virus infection to be present in many people with Crohn's disease[259]. Biopsies taken from 91 children with confirmed diagnoses of ILH and enterocolitis and 70 control children, showed evidence of measles virus in various cells of the intestine, compared with only four of the 70 control children.

A later editorial concluded that there was evidence of associated disturbance of the gut-brain axis and development disorders, hence a failure to remove viruses and infections effectively. (As discussed in Gut/brain abnormalities below)[260]

Before Dr Wakefield published his research, he informed the government's health department of his findings and they agreed to hold an independent forum. Unfortunately, this did not happen. Instead the general medical council was asked to investigate allegations of professional misconduct by Dr Wakefield and two other colleagues. This took place in July 2008 and the outcome was delayed until 2010.

In 2008, a four million pound campaign ensued by the health department to deny any association between MMR and autism. The government stated that Dr Wakefield's findings were pure coincidence and that these children would have been diagnosed with autism anyway.

It may be fair to say that the children might have been diagnosed autistic eventually. However, it seems to me that the point has been missed. Other factors, as to why these children are suffering, have not been considered. It is another piece of the jigsaw.

In 2009 high profile celebrities such as Jim Carrey and his girlfriend joined the voices calling for more action by governments and scientists to introduce safer green (non toxic) vaccines for all. Whilst they have been raising funds (Hollywood style), through galas and rallies, while Oprah Winfrey ran an hour-long show on MMR and autism, creating awareness for parents.

SIDE EFFECTS OF MMR

Let's look at some of the facts that have been discovered about the MMR vaccination and risky side effects, which are recognised by the manufacturers and are known by governments to affect many children and adults.

Drug companies agree that MMR has serious side effects. The vaccine is known to cause five times more cases of Thrombophiliais (ITP) (blood clotting) and it was estimated that one person in every 10,000 would develop the blood disorder.

Blood clotting

Blood clotting may have a part to play with some children, since the MMR vaccine is known to interfere with the blood supply to the brain. This condition is known as Thrombophiliais, or ITP for short, and is the opposite of haemophilia in that it involves an increased tendency for blood to clot. Trials in the US have found that 70% of autistics have one or more makers of thrombophilia (ITP).

In terms of convulsions and seizures, their own trials showed that children who received the MMR vaccine were three times more likely to suffer from convulsions than those who did not receive it. The pilot study revealed to the manufacturers that one in 400 given the jab would suffer convulsions, and trials showed the incidence of seizure occurring within eight to fourteen days after the child received the jab.

Diabetes

Links have also been found between the mumps and measles vaccine and the onset of insulin dependent diabetes in adolescence, obesity and increases in the numbers suffering from junior diabetes. These will be discussed later.

Measles virus found in the gut and brain

We know from previous research that children have retained the measles virus in their gut, brain, and spine after the vaccination[261]. Many studies have shown that autistic children have increased gut permeability. The time when the MMR vaccine is given (at around thirteen to fifteen months of age) is a critical window in a child's development. Depending upon the condition of the child at the time, the vaccine may well have an impact on the nervous system, affecting emotions, perception, cognition, mood and behaviour.

Concerns with the mumps portion of the MMR vaccine, this has been linked with:

- Encephalitis
- Neurological reactions
- Febrile convulsions
- Seizures
- Epilepsy
- Meningitis

There have also been reports of deafness and orchitis relative to the mumps portion of the vaccine.[262] The UK government, Bulgaria and Japan removed or suspended certain strains of mumps vaccine from the MMR because of a meningitis link.

The Rubella side of the vaccination, meanwhile, has been linked with:

- Chronic fatigue syndrome
- Guillain Barr syndrome (Neural inflammation leading to paralysis)
- Arthritis and related problems such as arthralgia (painful joints) and polyneuritis (pain, numbness or paralysis in the peripheral nerves)

It is believed that at least 3% of children and 20% of adult women will develop arthritis from the rubella vaccine, with adolescent girls thought to be at greater risk of joint and limb symptoms[263]. Why then, were manufacturers of the MMR vaccine given a licence after just a three-week trial?

LIFE-LONG PROTECTION?

When the MMR programme was rolled out, it was believed that it gave life-long protection. Tests, however, proved otherwise and far from offering protection, the vaccine can actually lead to disorders in adolescence and adulthood. Deaths have been reported and confirmed by clinical studies, with biopsies proving MMR vaccines to be the cause.

Gut brain abnormalities

Many studies show that autistic children have increased gut permeability.
A solid basis of research, together with Dr Shattock's findings, show that peptides are derived from an incomplete breakdown of certain foods, particularly those containing gluten, but also wheat and other cereals (oats, rye and barley) together with casein from milk and other dairy products[264].

Dr Shattock's team completed a pilot study to test their theories using a small group of autistic children. By limiting the amount of casein and gluten in their diets, the children improved primarily in terms of their language development and ability to concentrate. The greatest improvements were in those most afflicted and their GPs have been impressed enough to prescribe gluten-free products on the NHS.
Other studies have shown that activation of blood coagulation in the lining of the gut may be involved in the development of Crohn's disease[265].

Despite the later rescindment of Dr Wakefield's team's research, they found high levels of immature cells in youngsters, which were usually seen only in babies. This suggests that 'normal immune development has been arrested in the second year of life'[266] - exactly the time when the children received the MMR jab.

Dr Jeff Bradstreet of Palm Bay Florida set up his own international child development resource centre to study regressive autism and bowel problems and their relationships to vaccines. He is involved in the pressure group DAN.

After studying over 2000 children with autistic enterocolitis, he found evidence of the measles virus in the spinal fluid and brain, proving once again that the measles virus from vaccination does not clear from the body. In some children, it remains present in certain parts of the body other than the intestines, promoting a weakened immune response to control the measles virus.

Other researchers have also indicated a gut/brain axis disturbance, leading to malfunction in the immune system to clear the inflammation and virus infections efficiently[267].

Paul Shattock of the University of Sunderland Autism Research Unit says of Dr Wakefield's theory:

'This type of late onset regressive autism results from the action of peptides that originate outside of the body and affect neuro-transmission within the central nervous system, affecting opoids peptides, such as enkephalins and endorphins, intensifying their use and affecting and disrupting the CNS normal process.'[268]

This interference would lead to the disruption of a large number of Central Nervous System systems during a 'critical window' in a child's development, affecting:

- Emotions and perception
- Cognition
- Mood and behaviour

The central nervous system is made up of the brain, spinal cord and nerves within the skull and spine. The peripheral nervous system is a group of nerves, which connect the brain and spinal cord to the rest of the body.

How safe and effective is the MMR vaccine?

Since its launch in 1988 thousands of parents have reported reactions to the MMR jab. In some cases these reactions have been moderate and included symptoms such as rash, fever and headaches, while in others they have been severe and led to autism, brain damage and convulsions.

In 1992, the Department of Health withdrew two of the three brands used because they believed these brands caused meningitis. The Chief Medical Officer also stated that they had got the pre-licence trials wrong. Doesn't this beg the question, 'If they got these strains wrong, could they have got other things wrong too?' It doesn't inspire confidence.

Trials

After a short trial lasting only three weeks, a licence for vaccines of MMR was issued. New evidence, however, shows that the MMR vaccine should never have had a licence because there was insufficient proof of its safety.

Manufacturers' trials done before its re-launch in 1994 found that those who were given the MMR vaccine were three times more likely to suffer from convulsions than those who did not receive it. In addition, PHLS (the maker of MMR), knows that it affects one in 22,000 people receiving the vaccine and, as children are vaccinated twice, some believe this brings the odds of developing the blood disorder Thrombophiliais (ITP) up to one in 10,000.

Dr Fletcher, formerly the senior medical officer for the Department of Health in the early 1980s, reviewed the paper on Dr's Montgomery & Wakefield's findings.

'Being extremely generous, evidence on the safety was very thin; being realistic there were too few patients followed up for sufficient time. Three weeks is not enough and neither is four weeks.'[269]

Why, with this very short trial, were they given a licence? Even with a lack of continuous data and the use of incorrect results, they were still given a licence.

It just doesn't make sense to me.

Our cars are trialled for years to be proved safe. We are not allowed to drive on the road if they are not stamped with a quality and safety MOT licence. Yet we allow inadequate pharmaceutical trials to be stamped safe, with excessive risk to our children's health.

This is not the first time drug companies have misled us through research trials. Aspartame is a famous case where the company was fined for removing data from their research and proclaiming it did something it did not. They were guilty of false advertising and false claims, and some still believe the product to be bad for our health.

Why has MMR not been removed based on the evidence of this three-week trial alone? How many other vaccines have been put on the market with only a three week trial? Notwithstanding the overwhelming scientific evidence that it is dangerous for some of our children, plus the agreement of manufacturers that MMR has serious side effects, the government still does nothing.

Even with clinical studies and biopsies confirming the MMR vaccine as the cause of reported deaths, still they stick to their original idea that MMR is safe! Publicly, the UK Department of Health has not accepted that any deaths have resulted from MMR. However, media reports claim large payouts to parents behind the scenes.

Manufacturers accept that there are side effects to any drug, some being more serious than others. The same can be said for vaccines. Serious side effects to MMR have been reported to the government, including the blood disorder idiopathic thrombocytopenic purpora (ITP)[270]. As reported in the Lancet, when the PHLS did its pilot study they knew that one in 400 given the jab would suffer convulsions[271] but unfortunately, parents were not informed that their children could have a fever high enough to induce a fit. The long-term consequences, meanwhile, are still unknown.

Investigations in 1994 by the US CDC showed that a child's risk of seizure (epilepsy, convulsions and fainting) triples within days of receiving the MMR vaccination. Trials in 2001 showed the incidence of seizure occurring within eight to fourteen days after the child received the jab[272]. New evidence has also shown links between MMR and the greater likelihood of developing asthma and other allergic conditions[273], while Scandinavian data shows a link between the vaccine and multiple sclerosis[274].

Alternative single shots

Dr Wakefield and others have suggested publicly that individual vaccines would be best served to children. However the Health department has not made single jabs available. They still insist that there is nothing wrong with the existing MMR jab. It begs the question, apart from cost, what is the objection?

Not only do health departments use bullying tactics on parents to induce them to have their children vaccinated with MMR, but the media has shown that clinics and health centres receive monetary rewards for administering the jab. Whilst access to single shots is difficult, parents are made to feel guilty, implying they are not doing the right thing for their children. I have even heard, in some of these cases, where doctors have suggested that the family look for another practice to register with.

Have our authorities missed the link?

Even in older children who have not been immunised, there is evidence of penalisation when applying for university places. Indeed this has been the programme in the USA for many years. It is part of the acceptance process that boxes have to be ticked before the child is approved.

Have the authorities missed the key to MMR? It may be that there is nothing essentially wrong with individual components of the vaccination, but what the health authorities don't seem to understand is that research has shown that it does not suit all children in cocktail form. Individual vaccines, as were used in the past, may be the simple answer. Cost is immaterial if a parent chooses to pay privately.

Like all of us, children are unique and in different stages of their development. Without checking, how do we know if they have a clotting blood disorder? How do we know that they may have inflammation or stagnation in the colon? How do we know if they have a virus or even carry a virus without checking? We know from research that some children have kept the introduced virus in their gut, brain and spine after vaccination, so instead of the vaccine being a protector, it becomes the aggressor.

I feel that the whole picture has not been looked at and indeed, with such a short trial, how could the bigger picture be seen? Government studies are based upon patterns of disease taken from a generalised view and include large populations, which do not take into consideration the adverse reactions in smaller groups of children. Our UK government apparently does not believe in investigating the potential dangers for a minority of children!

I question the government's thinking and values. Wouldn't the four million pounds spent on disagreeing with Dr Wakefield's findings have been better served in conducting studies into new links highlighted and helping families who are coping with the likes of autism? Even though other governments have withdrawn and banned the vaccine because of safety concerns, the UK approach undermines, using bullying tactics in the handling of the situation.
At least other governments have been responsible and have taken a different stance.

In 1996, the Vietnamese health authorities withdrew the MMR jab after the death of one child and the hospitalisation of five others. Thankfully the World Health Authority is now investigating further into deaths from MMR.
In Japan, the MMR vaccine was banned on concerns over the safety of the mumps component in 1993 after discovering a link with meningitis[275]. What has happened to our British compassion and common sense? Is life so cheap? Why are we not following suit?

MMR In the USA

The USA experienced a sudden and alarming increase in problems just at the point when the MMR vaccination was introduced. Between July 1990 and 1994, 5,799 children were reported to have had adverse effects following MMR vaccinations[276]. Of these:

- 3,063 required emergency treatment
- 616 required hospitalisation

- 309 did not recover
- 54 were left disabled
- 30 died

The US National Vaccination Information Centre believed that this represented just 10-15% of the total number who experienced side effects and believes that there is massive under-reporting overall with MMR[277].

In the USA they vaccinate vigorously at 15months, 5 years and 18 years. US congress was informed by the Department of Education that statistics concerning autism had jumped by 26% in the year 1996-97 among six to twenty one year-olds. In the state of Ohio, 22 cases of autism were reported in 1992 but within seven years it had jumped to 1,523 in 1999, an increase of 682%. What is a concern is that these figures do not include those children under six, who are not included due to the fact that they are not yet on the school register![278]

In 1999, the state of California released a report demonstrating that the increase in autism had reached 273% among young children at the point of receiving the MMR jab. The University of California produced a conference paper showing a strong association between immunisation with MMR and the development of autism.[279]

Instigating change

Even though the UK Department of Health has steadfastly stood by the MMR vaccine throughout, it has cost them money with claims, which have been verified by health officials. Their strategy is not working.

It seems that Dr Wakefield has certainly stirred up a hornet's nest, yet he is not alone in his findings. American, Irish, Scandinavian, Japanese and other scientists worldwide have also found faults and risky side effects from this jab.

What Doctors Don't Tell You issued a publication just on MMR, 'What the Government doesn't tell you about the MMR jab'. It is a comprehensive, although frightening, read showing evidence and links to other illness and disorders proved to come from the MMR vaccine.

With even more evidence coming out since the 1996 pioneering views concerning autism, it has opened doors to allow others to make further investigations and each time they are compiling more and more information and linking faults with the cocktail vaccine that causes side effects. Dr. Wakefield now resides in Texas and operates a charity-run clinic called 'Thoughtful House' for the treatment of, and research into, autism.

Can we make enough noise to change government thinking?

When BSE caused seriously illness in humans and even death, millions of cattle were culled and strict policies implemented including ongoing daily checks. Only a small minority of people were affected by BSE but they were listened to and their fears acted upon. As a result the source was found and changes were made for the better.

Why then are we not implementing sanctions and change for the MMR vaccine? It too is affecting only a small minority. The same applied for BSE. Single vaccines could fill the gap until everyone is convinced of MMR safety. So what if it does cost a little more to make sure that our children are not damaged? Surely their safety is paramount.
Paying privately for single jabs offers no on cost to the health authority. On the contrary, it is a cost saving.

IT SEEMS THAT MMR DOES NOT SUIT ALL CHILDREN

Even with headlines of 'Dangers of MMR Jab covered up' and 'Fears linger over MMR jab', no change has been made and concerns seem to fall on deaf ears. As we have discussed, science cannot agree. Trials show both positive and negative results. In the meantime children are suffering.

In my opinion the bigger picture needs to be looked at. Change is needed and someone has to start the ball rolling. There is overwhelming evidence to support the fact that the MMR vaccine is not all it appears. One key factor that seems to have been overlooked is that MMR does not suit all children. Surely more individual investigative tests are needed before a child is vaccinated.

Since one of the known side effects is blood clotting, one option would be a prior test to identify in what state the child's blood lies. Surely we need to consider the parents' health history and whether they too suffer from blood clotting.

If in any doubt - it is better to be safe than sorry

It is commonsense to avoid or postpone giving children a multiple vaccine if there are doubts about birth dysfunctions or defects.

In the book we have shown evidence to support a need to think again about vaccinating children, especially if they have a fever or if they are unwell on the day or in the run up to vaccinations. It is better to be safe than sorry.

In my view, we should not vaccinate at all if there is any doubt as to child's general health at the time. From my own observations, some children (especially sensitive ones) do not fare well with allopathic medicine and vaccinations. They seem prone to side effects and disruption to their energy system causing fragmentation and discord.

THINK, THINK, THINK

Given all of this evidence, it is more than apparent that the MMR vaccine does not suit all children. Therefore, on the day of the MMR vaccine, I would advise parents to be mindful of their child's health. Check whether there are any changes to the child's health beforehand, such as:

- Is your child feeling unwell?
- Does he or she have a temperature?
- Is his or her immune system low? Has he or she had lots of colds, coughs and viruses recently?
- Does your child have constipation or a gut imbalance? - Remember that functional disturbance of the brain-gut axis has been highlighted with complications from MMR and Autism (read case study below)

Please rearrange or rethink the options for your child. It is not advisable to have a vaccine if any of the above are suspected. It is simply not worth the risk.

I would advise any parent to think carefully, especially if their child has allergies or allergic tendencies and particularly if he or she is allergic to eggs. Because the MMR is based upon egg culture, the child may have an adverse reaction.

If in doubt, I would advise the option for single shots, or an alternative homeopathic equivalent which has been shown to protect against measles, mumps and rubella.

In my opinion, the controversy over the MMR should focus less on the content of the vaccine and more on the effect upon the person or child at the time, how the body is performing, whether it is lacking in immune defence and how long this has been the case.

The current political protectionism does not recognise these facts, which are both simple and logical. We don't all fit into a one-size box and it is not a black and white conclusion. I believe the detailed evidence above substantiates this.

My advice is, if in doubt don't vaccinate on that day. Re-think and hold back. Go with your gut feelings as parents. Keep your child safe. Read the following case study and my observations for better insight.

CASE STUDY 18 –
OLIVIA'S STORY PART 2

I first treated Olivia for birth trauma in 2005 (see CST case study) and had been getting good reports about her progress since then from her aunt whom I see on a very occasional basis. In the summer of 2006, however, Olivia's aunt seemed concerned about the child and reported that she had changed since having the MMR vaccination ten days previously. I swear that her aunt must be one of Olivia's guardian angels, as she always seemed to have an instinct as to the times when Olivia and I needed to get together. I received a call from Olivia's mum and saw her immediately.

My first impression on seeing the child was that she had withdrawn. Her eyes were glazed again and she was murmuring, rocking and letting out a constant low whine. Mum told me that she had started to behave like this a few days after the MMR jab. She said 'I should have gone with my gut feelings and held back with the jab, especially since she had such problems from birth.' I silently agreed.

All I can say is that her body was in chaos. I could feel her slipping away under my hands as I examined her and a long session of Cranio Sacral Therapy, energy balancing and healing ensued. Olivia had a rest then while I worked on mum, who was also stressed.

Although Olivia seemed better, I was not happy, so after mum's session I worked again for another hour on Olivia. I used techniques of rebalancing her energy, realigning her using CST. I used meridian therapy and techniques to bring her back into her body and grounding her. I feel that I only just caught her from going too deep for me to get her back.

She sat very still during the second session, turning to look at me from time to time. The murmuring and whining stopped. Thank goodness, because I believe that if she had been left a few more days she would have been gone forever, into her inner world or even autism!

This first treatment was a success and a few days later mum brought a different child back to see me, the child I had known before who was playful with bright eyes that said she was at home. She was alert and wanted to play with the toys and even stood for the first time. At that time Olivia had not started crawling or standing.

I noticed, however, that Olivia was frustrated. I talked to mum about her nutrition and bowel movements. Mum said that Olivia did not eat well and that her bowel movements were irregular, just as I had suspected. In fact, mum explained that Olivia had not had good bowel movements since she was born! I made some nutritional suggestions and worked with reflexology on her feet to unblock bowel pathways, which I could feel were blocked. I also suggested that she introduce a small amount of sprouted flax seed powder into her food to help bowel movements.

Bowel movements improved immediately after her reflexology treatment and I saw her over the next few weeks, during which time more improvements were made and she started crawling - Olivia's way, on her tummy and bottom.

Her co-ordination is good and the best news is that the hospital has said Olivia will not be blind.

On the second session what a difference reflexology and a change in nutrition made since her last treatment. Olivia was now:

- Eating well
- Sleeping well
- Having regular bowel movements
- Talking better and starting to put sentences together
- Better co-ordinated
- Finding her balance at last and starting to crawl

Digestion

We all need to excrete daily. Without that function we have a build-up of unsavoury environments for disease to begin. People do not realise the important role that digestion plays. Lots of children have bowel issues and I find that the ones who have experienced a traumatic birth seem to hold on and tighten the stomach and muscles. I have treated children who have normal excretory functions only every three to four days, creating digestion problems and inner stress that can go on for life, just as it does for adults.

We know how ill we can feel without normal daily bowel movements. No wonder Olivia didn't eat very much because there was nowhere for it to go. She must have felt sluggish and suffered headaches and maybe even had tummy ache that she could not tell us about.

As parents, we need to be aware that it is a natural function that the bowel needs to evacuate on a daily basis and sometimes several times a day for a younger child. Reflexology is very good at helping to move longer standing bowel restrictions for all ages and Cranio Sacral Therapy also works well with digestion disorders.

As explained in the previous case study, Olivia is a Rainbow Child and as such she is very bright and clever. However, Rainbow children do get frustrated with their bodies and some need to get used to the body's limitations and restrictions and find other ways of expressing themselves. According to normal timetables, they are slow to talk, walk and crawl and indeed, as they prefer to communicate by telepathy, they do not need to talk from an early age. They will often communicate more outside of the family environment, such as when they are with other children at nursery, play group and so on, as they come to understand that they need to communicate in our way (by talking) in order to get what they want.

Olivia's mum told me a story of her being in bed one morning with her 3 year-old son and Olivia. She was asking her son what he would like to do that day. He did not seem to hear her, so she asked again and despite neither of the children having spoken a word, he scolded her with, 'Mummy, Olivia and I were talking!'

LIFE BEFORE VACCINATION

When I was a child in the 50s, there was no vaccination programme for measles, mumps and rubella. If there was a child in the street with mumps or measles, we were sent to play with that child so that we could catch it and give ourselves immunity to other diseases. Not only did the vast majority survive unscathed, but it has since been proved that having measles helps to protect us against allergies.

Just because you had the disease did not mean that you would not catch it again, and the same goes with vaccination. Sometimes it does not give the immunity needed and therefore having the vaccine does not guarantee for life. Indeed you can still get measles or mumps. In fact, it has been proved with research that the measles vaccine only gives protection until the age of 11-13, at which time the protection falls off.

Parents know their children. They know when they are not as they should be. In the 1970s I knew a mother close to where we lived who had a son the same age as my daughter. We used to see one another for coffee and a chat and the children would play. He was a perfectly normal child until he had his single measles jab and then was later diagnosed as autistic. The reaction was so quick and within days he just slipped away. No longer the child that they knew, he seemed just a shell with no personality, no communication and no sense of recognition. It was devastating for the parents and family and this was in the 70s when they gave a single jab.

We have experienced drugs before which have been marketed as wonder drugs. We had Thalidomide, which either proved to be fatal to unborn children or resulted in deformities and missing limbs. It took many years for the government's health authorities to ban that too!

The most common side effects

As we have shown, there are differences of opinion regarding vaccines and side effects, with science bodies unable to agree. However, what is not in question is that Autism does exist
The exact reasons are scientifically unclear for some quarters. There is evidence, however, that since mercury has been removed from some

vaccines we are now seeing some reductions in numbers. When and if this is proved scientifically, we will have to wait and see.

In the meantime, anecdotal evidence still exists and with new technology, videos and pictures, parents have a log of how their child was before MMR. A London-based solicitor (Alexander Harris & Co), has been approached by thousands of parents who allege that their children have been damaged by MMR, with the majority having autistic disorders[280]. Parents say that their children were developing normally but then became autistic right after the jab. One child was bilingual at three and half and had a large vocabulary. Two weeks after her jab she became mute and developed autistic traits and bowel disorders. She also had a blood disorder, which as previously discussed has been identified as a side effect of the MMR jab.

Autism, however, seems to be the most common side effect, occurring twice as often as any other serious side effect. JABS, a parent group set up by Jackie Fletcher, whose son was also affected by autism after the jab, has hundreds of parents on her web site, stating the same thing over and over again. One mother wrote:

'Thomas has gone from being a happy, fun-loving sociable child to a quiet introverted and aggressive one. I have a little person who is locked up within himself and that person within holds the only key to comprehending what makes his world revolve. Our world is one of confusion to Thomas and outside the home environment every place, person and activity sparks off anxiety.'[281]

Some children react with a measles rash, high temperature and drowsiness but the most common autistic traits are difficulties with communication and social interaction, withdrawal and repetitive and obsessive movements and patterns of behaviour. The majority of the autistics that I have seen and treated have the same pattern; they developed normally and had no dysfunctions at all until they received the MMR jab. A smaller percentage had difficult births or dysfunctions when they were born and one or two were dropped or fell when young, which also caused disorders.

Increasing at alarming rates

In recent times, we have seen the incidence of autism rise to alarming rates. In 1940, when mass vaccine programmes were introduced, autism was virtually unheard of. Records show that only three people were registered as having autism in 1979 and 50 in 1991. However in 2001, the National Autistic Society stated that there were 518,000 people diagnosed with autism nationwide in the UK[282].

PLS the organisation responsible for vaccine policy in the UK published its own epidemiological data, which dismissed the autism link. 498 children were studied and no link was found according to their study.[283] Overall, autism hadn't increased within a timeframe that could pin it to the jab. Dr Wakefield, meanwhile, has been reported as saying that, in his opinion, 'the quality of records kept by the PLS trial was appalling.' Some symptoms were not even recorded. Significantly, the Department of Health refuses to give the original data to the US congress for independent examination!

Homeopathy

Although there has been much controversy over Homeopathic treatment of late, there is research to substantiate that homeopathy can assist in protection against disease.

Homeopathy has been found to help relieve the symptoms of measles, and indeed government statistics have shown that the incidence of whooping cough, diphtheria, scarlet fever and measles symptoms were reduced in children using homeopathic vaccines. The few published studies, which have looked into this area, suggest that nosodes are effective in preventing specific diseases[284].

Homeopathy, which uses a 'like for like' approach and can represent an alternative option, is used by some GPs in their practices. Look out for a homeopathy practitioner who is registered with the Homeopathy Society. (See appendix for more information)

SINGLE JABS

Measles, mumps and rubella vaccines can be obtained in single shots. Some doctors are more sympathetic and recognise that the combined MMR has caused some problems to children. Single shots can cost between £45 and £145 per vaccine depending upon the practitioner. Dr Wakefield suggests a one year gap between single shots and that they be taken in the order of measles first, then mumps and finally rubella. This thinking seems to be supported by studies in the US where they found that children who had multiple shots including MMR on the same day suffered severe damage.

Dr Paul Shattock states that the cases of autism as a result of single shots seem to be milder, quoting one case where a child was diagnosed with autism at the age of six and by the age of twelve had reverted to normal! This does seem to suggest, therefore, that single shots are the better option overall.

Personally and professionally, however, we don't know if single shots are any better in terms of contra indications and side effects. If my story of the little boy who received a single shot of measles, reacted and was eventually diagnosed with autism is anything to go by, it seems that this option may be just as questionable. Having said this though, the records maintained by parent group JABS show that the incidence of autism from single shot vaccinations only represents a fraction of cases compared to the triple MMR vaccine.

In terms of multiple shots, we only have to look at the many reports regarding the multiple cocktail shots given to our armed forces for clues. Wide coverage has been given to the issue of Gulf War Syndrome, which stemmed from multiple shots being given to servicemen and women, many of whom suffered severe reactions which in some cases led to mental and physical disability which lasted for years, and in others a lifelong impairment. When will we learn!

As we have discussed though, much seems to come down to the individual's condition on the day. An increased risk of developing autism seems to exist when children are ill on the day (or a few days before) of the jab and this has been proven by a variety of anecdotal evidence[285].

We will now look at the evidence and disorders linked to the portions of the MMR, measles, mumps and rubella.

MUMPS

Mumps is normally an innocuous disease caused by a virus which attacks one or both of the salivary (parotid) glands which lie just below and in front of the ears.

The symptoms, which normally disappear within 7 to 10 days, are:

- Swelling underneath the ears
- Headaches
- Fever
- Vomiting
- Muscle aches

Known to be a mild illness in children, it can however cause the rare complication of mumps in the testicles (orchitis or testicular inflammation) in adult males which has been known to cause sterility. Catching mumps later in life can also cause severe side effects such as permanent hearing loss.

As discussed earlier in this book, some information suggests that the performance of ejaculation in adult males is reduced as a result of mumps, which of course depletes fertility. Adult females, meanwhile, can suffer swelling of the ovaries and breasts.

Normal childhood mumps is not a global killer and in fact the mumps vaccine was only developed to help prevent its extremely rare complications. In an interview, Dr Begg from PHLS (MMR licence holders for the UK) stated that 'Mumps has only been added to give extra value to the MMR jab'[286].

MMR vaccine

One version, which was known as Immarvax, was discontinued in 1992 because of the risk of meningitis from the Urabe strain of the mumps portion of the vaccine, made in the UK by the Smith Kline Beecham group. Our UK Department of Health, however, stated that the remaining vaccine was from a different strain and supposedly posed no risk.

Yet when the two suspect strains of mumps vaccine were removed, the UK government stated that 'mumps leads to meningitis in one in 400

cases', apparently feeling the need to justify its continued inclusion. At this time, the Japanese were also concerned and withdrew their version. The following year, 1993, the Japanese revealed that 1,044 vaccinated people had developed aseptic meningitis. They also stated that evidence had been found which proved that the vaccine could actually bring on mumps and be passed on to other children.
MMR is made out of live vaccines

At the time of writing, the current mumps component used is the Jeryl Lynn level B strain. Three strains of mumps vaccine have been made so far:

- Jeryl Lynn
- Urabe
- Leningrad-3 Parkow

The first mumps vaccine made from a dead virus was found to be ineffective. Researchers then undertook to develop a weakened live vaccine, grown on hen's eggs and then in chicken embryo cells. The vaccine seems slow to take, as antibodies normally take up to two weeks to form and in some cases can take up to six weeks.

A fourth strain, Sofia 6, was prepared in guinea-pig kidney primary-cell cultures and introduced in Bulgaria to vaccinate children between one and twelve years of age. This vaccine was found to have too many detrimental side effects, (including meningitis) and was quickly suspended[287].

During normal childhood, contracting mumps is negligible and usually provides life-long immunity, yet it is known that the vaccine does not confer life-long protection. It does wear off, especially before the teenage and adult years when the illness can be far more problematic.

In his book 'The truth about vaccines' Dr Halvorson states that in 2005 London UK research showed the mumps component was only 65% effective after one dose, rising to 88% after two doses. Therefore, MMR will not eradicate mumps, but will push the disease to older children and adults, concurring with the information already shown.

Dr. Halvorsen, one UK NHS GP, has spoken out against the MMR vaccine and believes that 'There can be little doubt that the original aim of introducing the mumps component of MMR has been an unmitigated failure'

He has also stated that 'immunization is only partially effective. As a mild disease, those who are naturally affected by mumps have life-long immunity protection, but the vaccine wears off within years' In his opinion the population is now dependent upon two vaccinations rather than none.[288]

OTHER DISORDERS LINKED WITH MUMPS PORTION OF MMR

The mumps portion of the MMR vaccine has been linked with causing other diseases, including encephalitis, seizures and meningitis as well as deafness and orchitis[289]. This is particularly disturbing when you bear in mind that orchitis is one of the very complaints that the vaccine is supposed to prevent.

Diabetes

As we have previously indicated, records also show that many cases link simultaneous administration of the mumps and measles vaccine with the onset of insulin dependent diabetes[290]. Does this account for the huge numbers of obese adolescents and the increases in cases of junior diabetes being recorded all over the western world?

In 1989, the Lancet reported that German studies discovered 27 cases of neurological reactions following vaccination, including meningitis, febrile convulsions, encephalitis and epilepsy[291].

Encephalitis is an inflammation and swelling of the brain tissue and some of those contracting the disease can be left with permanent brain damage. The onset can occur suddenly and cause serious problems to both the nervous system and the brain. Although some cases can be mild, with the individual suffering only a fever, others can be very serious and even life threatening[292].

According to the NHS Direct Health encyclopaedia, if you have an already impaired immune system or immune deficiency (including

HIV), you can develop encephalitis from many viruses and infections, including:

- Measles
- Mumps
- German measles (rubella)
- Chicken pox
- Influenza
- Enteroviruses (tummy bugs)
- Epstein Bar (glandular fever)
- Herpes simplex (cold-sore virus - can be highly contagious)

Other causes include rabies, allergic reaction to a vaccine and lead poisoning.

The same source cites that the early signs of encephalitis can develop in a few hours or over a few days and may appear as flu like symptoms. Encephalitis can affect almost any brain function, but the most common symptoms are:

- Severe headache
- Fever
- Nausea
- Vomiting
- Stiff neck and back
- Muscle weakness
- Seizures (fits)
- Drowsiness or confusion
- Sensitivity to bright lights
- Memory loss
- Inability to speak
- Inability to control movement properly
- Weakness of one or more parts of the body
- Sleepiness that can lead to coma

Even when critical, many people may make a full recovery, although it is not guaranteed. In some cases brain injury may result.

The numbers of encephalitis cases varies from study to study.

A fifteen year study in the US, for example, stated that one sixth of all cases were definitely due to the mumps vaccine[293]. In Canada, however, research estimated that the risk was only one in a hundred thousand[294] and a Yugoslav study concluded that it was one per thousand[295]. The UK Department of Health, meanwhile, assured the public that the risk is only one in eleven thousand[296]. However in 1991, one of America's leading paediatric journals rated the numbers as being one in 405 – from one in 7,000 shots given[297].

Who do we believe? Irrespective of the huge variation in their findings, the one indisputable fact they all agree on is that encephalitis cases do occur as a direct result of the mumps vaccine.

With the open controversy and sudden withdrawal in several countries (including the UK) of two of the mumps vaccines already proven to create meningitis, it begs the question, are we meddling too much with nature?

Vaccine failure?

Over the years, numerous cases of vaccine failure have been reported. Six years after the MMR jab was introduced in Switzerland, there was an increase in the number of cases of mumps, affecting both vaccinated and unvaccinated children. Of the 88 reported cases, 72 of the individuals concerned had been vaccinated. Even though antibodies to the mumps virus were detected, in 24 of the 27 blood samples gathered they still found an acute state of the disease. The Swiss study found an 'insufficient protective efficacy of the current mumps vaccine.'[298]

In 1995, the UK Vaccine Agency PHLS did its own study. 475 vaccinated children were tested and 19% showed no evidence of antibodies against mumps . In 1993, the US National Academy of Sciences Institute of Medicine reviewed all evidence relating to the vaccine and stated that 'Immunity has always been assumed to be long-lasting, but this has never been proven.'[300]

If the vaccine protection is wearing off after a few years, children are therefore more likely to contract the disease later in life, either in puberty, adolescence or as adults, when the illness can be far more problematic, especially for males. Indeed, it has been shown that a third of adolescent or adult males who contract mumps will suffer from orchitis[301].

Clearly this information begs the question, 'Why are we continuing to vaccinate against mumps?' Do we actually need vaccination for mumps if it is not protecting us to the level marketed? Is vaccination causing more disorders than anticipated, such as diabetes, meningitis and fertility impairment? Only time will tell.

MEASLES

Measles affects the respiratory system and skin, causing itchy pink spots over the body, producing sore eyes, sensitivity to light and high fever. It is thought by some to be life threatening.

In 1989, Dr Norman Brigg, consultant epidemiologist of PHLS (the vaccine agency in the UK) stated that official statistics showed one in 5,000 children contracting wild measles would develop acute encephalitis and inflammation of the brain. Furthermore, one in 5,000 of those would go on to develop SSPE (sub acute sclerosing panencephalitis), which produces progressive brain dysfunction and death within a year[302].

However, the study of worrisome fatal illness including SSPE concludes that the measles-induced form of the disease is 'very rare', affecting only one in a million cases[303]. The report also cites environmental factors other than measles, such as head injuries or close exposure to certain animals.

Since the 1994 campaign for MMR, the quoted figures have mysteriously increased. Strangely, in 1994, one columnist reported that one in 500 measles sufferers would develop acute encephalitis. Of these, one in ten might die and one in four might suffer permanent brain damage. Is this just scare mongering by the pro vaccine agencies? As mentioned above, independent figures give quite a different picture, showing that death from measles in the 21st century is 'very rare'.

Death from measles is not, in fact, common in developed countries

The last large measles epidemic came in the US in 1990 in which 27,000 cases were reported and 89 people died. Most of the deaths occurred in low-income families where poor nutrition played a major part, as did failure to treat ensuing complications[304]. Well-nourished children have little to fear from measles and possibly much to gain as a direct result of the natural defence from allergies and hay fever.

Only six deaths were reported in the UK before the onset of the MMR vaccination programme, although 42,165 cases of measles were reported[305]. Again, only six deaths were reported between 1989 and 1994 in the 0-19 age group, despite 59,263 cases being reported. This equates to an average of one in 10,000 cases or one a year. Since 1988, most measles-related deaths have occurred in adults, however Dr Nicholson, editor of Bulletin of Medical Ethics, states that doctors now have a better understanding on how to treat measles.

In their 1993 vaccine findings report, the US Institute of Medicines for all vaccines concluded that the measles vaccine can cause death from measles vaccine-strain infection, idiopathic thrombocytopenic purpora, fatal shock and arthritis. The report also stated that it could not rule out the probability that the vaccine itself could cause cases of SSPE[306].

In several studies, the measles-vaccine strain has been removed from spines of encephalitis victims, showing conclusively that the vaccine itself caused the encephalitis[307].

Other trials have shown that persistent measles virus infection is present in many people with Crohn's disease[308] and investigations have, in addition, shown the measles virus in the spinal fluid and brain of 2,000 children with autistic enterocolitis[309].

Studies show advantages to natural protection

It is possible that healthy children have much to gain from having measles. According to recent studies in Africa, children who caught measles tended to suffer less from allergic conditions such as asthma, eczema and hay fever, whereas in developed countries, vaccinated children seem to suffer from an increasing range of allergy-related (atopic) conditions.

UK research has indicated that childhood diseases such as measles, mumps and rubella might provide natural protection against atopy (hypersensitivity to common allergies)[310].

The combined MMR is made out of live vaccines, including the Edmondson strain of the measles vaccine. 'No form of the portion of the measles vaccine can give lifelong protection as a one-off shot' was the catalyst for the 1994 UK campaign for the MMR immunization programme.

Measles epidemics continue to occur despite vaccination and children who have been vaccinated twice can still experience mild forms of the disease[311].

Germany is reported to have the lowest rate of measles and uptake of the MMR vaccine, while Shetland has the lowest uptake in the UK. Italy, meanwhile, has one of the highest incidences of measles in Europe, although diet also seems to be a key factor here. Shetland seems to be more traditional with the old ways more prevalent, and consequently they lean more towards natural birth and breast-feeding.

The USA leads the world in vaccine programmes

It has had a vaccine programme in place since 1957 in various forms and has used combined jabs since 1975. Despite measles immunisation being as high as 98% due to the enforced vaccine programme, epidemics of measles still occur at three to four year intervals. Between 1985 and 1986, two thirds of those who contracted the disease had been vaccinated and these were all school-aged children. The 27,672 logged cases of measles in 1990, meanwhile, represented a virtual doubling of the figures reported in the previous year. Israel also reported 1,000 cases in 1994, even though 90% of the children there were vaccinated[312]

What are the reasons for the lack of immunity? Some medical professions have blamed the unvaccinated in poor areas for the outbreaks, although in the US this is questionable with their high rate of vaccine protection and strict immigration laws. Other theories are that the vaccine wears off in time, as does an individual's immunity.

Some believe that between 1957 and 1980 a less stable vaccine version was used, and there is also a possibility that jabs given too early do not provide immunity. Other factors cited were interference from the mother's own immunity. Jabs given when the child has respiratory infections, poor storage and handling of vaccines resulting in loss of efficacy are also suggested factors.

Ineffective vaccines?

In 1984, the US CDC medical establishment blamed measles outbreaks on vaccines used in the 1960s. They termed them 'ineffective formalin-inactivated (killed) measles vaccines' and they were administered to 600,000-900,000 children between 1963 and 1967[313]. This failure rate is largely responsible for the booster shots given at age four or five and some researchers believe that even two doses are not enough with wild strains about. Research, however, has proven that booster shots are not effective and has shown that only half of those checked had antibody levels considered to be protective[314].

During some outbreaks, revaccination was recommended despite research showing it to be ineffective. One study by several authors showed that antibody levels in re-immunised children could fall after several months to very low levels. Children vaccinated twice may still experience clinically recognisable measles, although in a much milder form. 'This state in which a child is immunologically sensitised, but not immune to infection, we shall call inadequate immunity' concluded the authors[315].

So, is the new improved version better?

One study disproves the claim of improvement by quoting an outbreak of measles in New Mexico where 98% had been vaccinated with the new live vaccine shortly before the outbreak began[316]. Another outbreak where 99% had been vaccinated with live measles vaccine proved to be down to 'primary vaccine failures.'[317]

Unfortunately, with the current vaccine programme enforced from an early age, measles is shown to become an adult disorder, which can be more fatal in adult life. One study, which was conducted in the US as early as 1979, warned of an increasing number of adolescents contracting measles. During the pre-vaccination era, 90% of all measles cases occurred in 5 to 9 year-olds, whereas once the vaccine programme was rolled out, 55-64% of those who contracted the disease were aged over ten. Re-vaccination of young adults is associated with major side effects, with 17% reporting fever, eye pain and the need for bed rest.

In 2006, the Health Protection Agency stated that doctors were reporting five times more cases of measles than the year before. They also predicted a measles epidemic in the UK. GP and vaccine expert, Richard Halvorsen, stated:

'With the threat of a measles epidemic, the only way many parents will protect their children is with single vaccine. By refusing to allow this, the government is contributing to the epidemic it seeks to prevent.'[318]

LOOMING PROBLEMS

A report in 1993 from Dr Viera Scheibner of New South Wales showed that both adults and babies (some a few months old and many below the age of two) were now contracting measles[319].

Both sections of the population had been free from the measles disease before the advent of vaccination because of natural immunity passed on from mothers.

Dr Scheibner says that there is another looming problem that generations of girls with this inadequate immunity will grow into adults with no placental immunity to pass on to their children, who could then contract measles at a very early age when babies are normally protected by maternal antibodies.[320] Other studies have shown lower hemaglutinin inhibiting and neutralizing antibodies in women who have been immunised, compared with older women who were not part of the MMR programme.[321] Again, this makes me question whether we actually need the measles vaccine.

A large study done by working Swiss doctors questioned the Swiss Health Department's US-inspired immunisation programme for measles, mumps and rubella. They described measles as a typical example of a childhood disease with fever and eruptions affecting the organism as a whole. When the process of general inflammation is not correctly handled, the illness may subsequently affect the ears (Otitis), lungs (pneumonia) or central nervous system, giving rise to the feared complication of encephalitis.

However, they concluded:

'We have lost the commonsense and the wisdom that used to prevail in the approach to childhood diseases. Too often, instead of reinforcing the organism's defences, fever and symptoms are relentlessly suppressed. This is not always without consequences.'[322]

In other words, work with the body and don't suppress the natural process, which is what a vaccine does! Common sense – don't you think!

VITAMINS CAN ASSIST IN DISORDERS

Vitamins have been proven to help relieve the effects of both measles and mumps. Giving vitamin A to children with measles can improve their recovery and reduce complications, even in malnourished children[323]. Trials have proven the benefit, especially where the children are malnourished. Low levels of vitamin A can affect the mucous membranes, causing scaly appearance and cell reduction. Measles can affect the tissues of the body and, combined with vitamin A deficiency, will create an environment for disease.

Vitamin A

Depleted vitamin A affects the liver stores, resulting in an acute bodily condition and causing eye damage and respiratory disorders[324]. Other research has highlighted diarrhoea and increased risk of respiratory disease in children with low levels of vitamin A[325].

A New York trial on 89 children found that 22 had vitamin A deficiency. The trial results indicated that children with lower vitamin A levels were more inclined to have a fever of 40° C or higher when they had measles[326]. In recent trials in India and Tanzania the mortality rates were reduced seven times among those given vitamin A[327].

If you decide not to give your child the MMR jab, or even the single measles jab, I would suggest a hair analysis to check your child's immune system levels before you boost it with vitamin A. Vitamin A is readily found in cod liver oil but it is important to ensure that you buy a good quality to avoid toxins.

Make sure that your child has a good diet of whole-foods including:

- Carrots
- Green leafy vegetables
- Cod liver oil
- Liver
- Butter
- Eggs (especially the yolk)

Preferred supplements of vitamin A can be taken orally and some can be found in liquid form. Vitamin A is easily absorbed into the body.

High doses have been found to help reduce the symptoms of measles and are seen as safe for short periods of time (a few days to a week only). Please administer with medical or professional supervision.
During times of acute infection, suggestions are for young children between the ages of one year and three years to be given 2000-4000 IU/daily, whilst those aged between 4 and 5 years can take 2,500-5,000 IU/daily and those between 5 and 12 years 5,000-10,000 IU daily.

Vitamin C

In many trials, a combination of vitamin A and vitamin C has been found to combat virus and infection. Vitamin C research goes back as far as the 1950s and it is known to restore and boost immune levels. Low levels of vitamin C in all ages can increase susceptibility to infection.

Vitamin C has been shown to reduce high temperature, reducing fever quickly in different acute conditions including infection and virus forms of illness. In cases of childhood measles and mumps, some trials have used intravenous vitamin C of 2,000mg and 1,000mg or by mouth every two hours for two days with recovery overnight and no complications[328].

The key is to give vitamin C every few hours and indeed I have used this method myself for many years. If I have a cold coming on or feel under the weather, I take 1000mg of vitamin C every few hours for 24-48 hours and find that it is enough to clear the symptoms quickly and efficiently.

Junior vitamin C is available in powder or chewable forms.
Smaller quantities of vitamin C should be used as a maintenance dose daily as the body does not store it and needs to be replenished each day. This applies to all ages, especially as we grow older, since we increasingly lose the ability to store vitamins.

If in doubt about getting the right amount through food (as not all fruit and vegetables hold the vitamins expected because of early harvesting and long storage), take a supplement to ensure complete maintenance. Again, hair analysis can determine the levels needed to rebalance the body.

RUBELLA OR GERMAN MEASLES

Although rubella is a contagious disease, it is usually so mild that it often escapes detection. It is not life threatening to children and requires no more complicated treatment than to let it run its course (as with many other mild childhood disorders). Being difficult to distinguish from other chronic childhood problems, the symptoms include:

- Runny nose
- Sore throat
- Slight fever (rarely showing a temperature over 100°F)
- Slightly raised pink spots may appear on the face and body
- Lymph nodes on the back of the head and behind the ears are raised and on the neck may be tender

Although mild in children, it is threatening for pregnant women within the first three months of pregnancy. If contracted at this time, there is a risk to the developing foetus and the baby could be born with birth defects called congenital rubella syndrome (CRS). These include:

- Impaired vision and hearing
- Limb defects
- Mental retardation
- Heart malformations

Before the rubella vaccination was introduced in 1969, nearly 85% of the population was naturally immune to the disease. Today however, because most women never get the chance to acquire a natural immunity in childhood, their risk of contracting rubella during their childbearing years can actually be greater!

Babies are normally protected by the antibodies of the mother, which are transferred to the baby during pregnancy. If the mother does not carry enough of these antibodies, the child will be at greater risk. Research shows that when children are given pre-school jabs as babies, their immunity to rubella generally falls off at around the age of eleven to thirteen years old[329].

Under reported symptoms

Although the manufacturers of the MMR vaccine originally stated that it provides a life-long immunity to rubella, research now shows that this is not the case. Instead, studies show many other symptoms as a result of having the rubella vaccine, including:

- Chronic fatigue syndrome
- Arthritis
- Guillain Bar Syndrome

Two separate studies have shown that the rubella vaccine has been the cause of chronic fatigue syndrome. The thinking behind the research was that, although the vaccine has been given to children, despite being no longer effective against rubella, the vaccine itself could linger in the system for years, affecting later life[330]. Many studies have shown that after receiving the rubella vaccination, skin rashes, swollen glands and transient arthritis followed, as well as pain in the wrists, knees and hands[331].

In 1996, other studies reported Guillain Barr syndrome (neural inflammation leading to paralysis) after the rubella vaccination. They also noted that there was under-reporting of these cases in general[332].

Arthritis link

It seems that the most common adverse reaction to the rubella vaccine is arthritis and related problems such as arthralgia (painful joints) and polyneuritis (pain and numbness or paralysis in the peripheral nerves)[333]. Even in 1982, these were known as frequent complications of both natural infection with the rubella disease and immunisation against it. Research has shown that it is more frequent in vaccinated areas, concluding that approx 26% develop the symptoms after receiving a rubella vaccination, affecting both children and adults[334].

In 1992, a US Institute of Medicine study on vaccines reported a 13-15% incidence of adult women who showed a 'causal' relationship between the rubella vaccine and acute arthritis. The evidence was so clear that it has been accepted by the vaccine injury compensation board and the federal courts in the US[335].

Doctors in the UK received written confirmation from the Department of Health during the 1994 measles appeal that 11% of first-time recipients of the rubella vaccine will develop arthritis.

One study shows that adolescent girls are thought to be at greater risk of joint and limb symptoms[336]. These findings have been substantiated by one manufacturer, in the 'The Physicians Desk Reference' who is able to confirm that at least 3% of children and 20% of adult women will develop arthritis from the rubella vaccine, and stated 'Symptoms of arthritis may persist for a matter of months or in rare occasions, years.' Is this perhaps the reason why arthritis is now so prominent in youngsters?

Doctor Aubrey Tingle, a Canadian paediatric immunologist, has spent many years researching into the area of arthritis and its causes. His findings are that 30% of adults exposed to the rubella vaccine suffer arthritis within two to four weeks. Symptoms range from mild aches in the joint to severe crippling. He also found the rubella virus in one third of all adult and child patients with rheumatoid arthritis[337].

MMR is made out of live vaccines and RA 27/3 is the strain of the rubella vaccine component used. Current thinking, however, is changing towards the belief that better protection is achieved by contracting the disease and that the vaccine is inferior to natural immunity from earlier infection[338]. A 1988 study in the US by Dr Robert Mendelsohn showed that around 25% of those who have the jab show no signs of immunity[339].

An Australian study found that 80% of all army recruits vaccinated against rubella four months earlier contracted the disease[340]. Other studies show that a large percentage of the victims come from vaccinated or partially vaccinated communities and the failure rate is higher than the 5% reported[341].

PROTECTION FOR PREGNANCY?

Although we had 85% natural immunity back in 1969 before the vaccine was introduced, unfortunately women don't get the chance to obtain natural protection these days[342].

If the rationale behind immunisation is to protect pregnant women from the disease, perhaps it would be better not to give it in childhood, since by childbearing age the protection has already worn off!

Indeed, there have been reports of mothers who have given birth to children with congenital rubella syndrome (CRS), despite being properly vaccinated against the disease[343].

Perhaps some medical factions are better at giving advice than taking it.

In a USA study in1976 when there had been a mass flu immunisation programme, it was found that 90% of obstetricians refused to have the rubella vaccine themselves, as they feared 'unforeseen vaccine reactions' generated by an increased incidence of Guillain-Barre syndrome (a neural inflammation which can lead to paralysis)[344].

Perhaps they know something that they are not telling us, officially?

644

[247] Lucy Johnson '26 child deaths from MMR -Can we trust MMR' Sunday Express 06. 2006 p27

[248] Ibid 'Vaccine damage payments' p27

[249] Lucy Johnson 'Dangers of MMR jab covered up' Sunday Express 07.2007 p4

[250] Lucy Johnson 'Can we trust MMR'' Sunday Express 06.2006 p27

[251] What Doctors Don't Tell you 'What the government doesn't tell you about the MMR Jab 2002 pg15:col1:p4 (Ref: 'Ref: Lancet 'MMR was introduced to the UK, pilot study' 1989.ii:1015-6)

[252] Ibid 'What the government doesn't tell you about the MMR Jab' 2002 p9 (Ref: 'Was MMR adequately studied'' quote Walter Spitzer -McGill University Canada)

[253] Dr. R. Halvorsen 'The Truth about vaccines' Gibson Square London. 2007 – p19/4 (US research ref :Geir Brothers)

[254] WDDTY 'What the government doesn't tell you about the MMR Jab 2002 p3 p2 (Lancet.1998;351:637-41)

[255] Ibid 'What the government doesn't tell you about the MMR Jab' 2002 p3 p7 (Does MMR Cause autism?')

[256] Ibid p3 p7 (Ref: Am J Gastroenterol, 2000;95:2285-95)

[257] Ibid 'Hurt the Gut' p4.col1.prg1 (Ref: Lancet,1998;352-234-5; J Paedoatr;1999;135;559-63)

[258] Ibid p3 p7 (Ref: Am J Gastroenterol, 2000;95:2285-95)

[259] Ibid 'Crohn's disease' p4.col2.prg1 (Ref: Dig Dis Sci. 2000;45:723-9)

[260] Ibid 'Hurt the Gut' 2002 p4.col2.prg2 – (Ref:Gut 1995;36:564-9 J Clin. Pathol, 1997;50:299-304)

[261] Ibid 2002 p15 col2 'What about the side effects of MMR'

[262] Ibid 2002 p16 col2 'mumps' (Stratton K.et.al 'Adverse events associated with childhood vaccines. Evidence bearing on causality Washinton DC. Nat Academy press. 1993)

[263] Ibid p17 col 1.pg2 'Rubella'

[264] Ibid 2002 p5 prg4 (Acta aedatr 1996;85:1076-9)

[265] Ibid p5 prg4 (Acta aedatr 1996;85:1076-9)

[266] Ibid p5 prg6 (J Pediatr 2000:138:366-72)

[267] Ibid p4 col2 prg4 'Gut Brain axis' (AMorris and D Aldulaimi editorial)

[268] Ibid 'CNS' p5: prg4 (Acta aedatr 1996;85:1076-9)

[269] Ibid 'Safety Trials' p9 col3:pgr2/3 (published Adverse Drug Reactions and Toxicological Reviews 2001;20:57-60)

[270] Ibid 'ITP' p14 col4. Pg2 (Ref:Lancet 1995:345:567-9)

[271] Ibid 'PHLS' p15col1.pg4 (Lancet 1989:ii.1015-6)

[272] Ibid 'US CDC Risk of seizure' p15 col1.pg5 (N Engl J Med.2001:345:656-61)

[273] Ibid 'Asthma and allergies' p15 col1.p6 (John Hopkins Medical Centre in Baltimore Maryland)

[274] Ibid 'Scandinavian data' p15 col2 p1 (Acta Pathol Microbiol. Scand.(B) 1979:87:379-84)

[275] Ibid p9 col2 p6 'Japan ban vaccine'

[276] Ibid p6 col2.pg6 ' Dept of Education to US Congress – stats'

[277] Ibid p7 col1.pg1 - 'Dept of Education to US Congress'

[278] Ibid p7 col1 ' USA vaccination figures'

[279] Ibid p7col1 (State of California report – Allergy Induced Autism (AIA) UK - 1999.03)

[280] 'What the government doesn't tell you about the MMR Jab 2002 p4 col2 p1 (solicitors)

[281] Lucy Johnson Health Editor 'Dangers of MMR Jab covered up' Sunday Express 07.2007 http://www.jabs.org.uk/forum topic ID=717 (cited 07.2007)

[282] WDDTY 'What the government doesn't tell you about MMR' p8 cl2 'National Autistic society UK stats'

[283] Ibid p8 cl2 (PHLS report-Lancet 1999;353:2026-9)

[284] Society Homeopaths Homeopathy and Measles, May 2006 http://houseofstrauss.co.uk/modules/wfsection/article.php?articleid=472 (cited 09.07.2007)
(Gaier H Thorsons Encyclopaedic Dictionary of Homeopathy, Harper Collins 1991) & WDDTY 'What the government doesn't tell you about MMR' 2002 p18 cl2 ('Alternatives' to vaccines')

[285] WDDTY 'What the government doesn't tell you about the MMR'2002 p17col2pg4 (Ref Paul Shattock single shots)

[286] Ibid p11col2 p3 (WDDTY interview PLHS 1989)

[287] Ibid p9 col2 p6 (ref: Japan1b/464)

[288] Dr.R. Halvorsen 'The truth about vaccines – mumps research' Gibson Square London 2007 p122

[289] WDDTY 'What the government doesn't tell you about vaccines' 2002 p14 (Stratton K et al. Adverse Events associated with Childhood Vaccines; Evidence bearing on Causality, Washington DC: National Academy Press 1993 122)

[290] Ibid 'mumps' p16col1 pg6 – (Stratton K et al. Adverse Events associated with Childhood Vaccines; Evidence bearing on Causality, Washington DC: National Academy Press 1993)

[291] Ibid 'German study' pg16 col2pg1 (Lancet 1989ii.751)

[292] Ibid 'Immunization' p 14 col1/2 (Ref: Moakoqirz R 'Immunization The other side of Vaccination'. The Rest of the story, Santa Fe. New Mexico Mothering 1992.)

[293] Ibid 'US 15 yr study' p16 col2 - (Pediatr Infect Dis J,1989;8;751-5)

[294] Ibid 'Canada study' p16 col2 p1 (Lancet,1989,ii.1051-6)

[295] Ibid 'Yugoslav study' p16 col2 p2 (Pediatr Infec Dis J.1989:8:302-8)

[296] NHS Direct 'Encephalitis' http://www.nhsdirect.nhs.uk/articles/articles.aspx?articleId=148&sectond Id=1 (cited 07.2007)

[297] WDDTY 'What doctors don't tell you about MMR'p16 (US Peadeatric Jrnl. Pediatr Infect Dis J March 1991)

[298] Ibid 'Swiss findings' P14 cited col1pg1. (Scan J Infec Dis 1996:28.235-8)

[299] Ibid 'PHLS study' p14 col1 pg1. (Vaccine 1995:13:799-802)

[300] Ibid 'mumps' p14:col1:pg6 – (Stratton K et al. Adverse Events associated with Childhood Vaccines; Evidence bearing on Causality, Washington DC: National Academy Press 199315/468)

[301] Ibid 'vaccination' p14 (Moakoqirz R Immunization The other side of Vaccination. The Rest of the story, Santa Fe. New Mexico Mothering 1992)

[302] Ibid 'PHLS study' p14 col1:p1 (DoH PLS stats1989)

[303] Ibid SSPE p (JAMA 1972:220:959-62 SSPE registry)

[304] Ibid 'US deaths' p10 col2p3

[305] Ibid 'UK deaths' pg10 col2 pg4

[306] Ibid 'US inst Meds quote' p15 col2 p6 (Stratton K et al. Adverse Events Associated with Childhood Vaccines: Evidence Bearing on causality, Washington DC: National Academy Press 1993:118-86)

[307] Ibid 'US virologist and immunisation specialist Dr Anthony Morris' pg15col2 p3

[308] Ibid 'Crohn's disease' p4 cl2;p2 (Gut 1995;36:564-9 J Clin Pathol 1997;50-229-304)

[309] Ibid 'Research International Child Development Resource Centre' p5 col2 par2-

[310] Ibid 'Allergies research' p11 col1p3 (UK Southampton General Hospital)

[311] Ibid 'Measles epidemics continue' p13 col2 (Vaccination New South Wales 1993)

[312] Ibid 'US enforced vaccination' -p12 cl2

[313] Ibid 'US CDC term' p13 – (MMWR 1984 Oct4)

[314] Ibid Is the MMR jab effective' p13col1pg1 –(Pediatr Infec Dis J 1994:13:34-8)

[315] Ibid 'Measles' p13 col2pg2 (Bull WHO 1984:62:315-9)

[316] Ibid ''Mexico outbreak' p13 col1pg6

[317] Ibid 'looming problem' p13 col2 ('Schreiber Vaccination New South Wales 1993-20)

[318] Dr R Halverson 'Truth about vaccines' Gibson Square London. 2007 pg 19/p4 (research USA mercury free vaccines and autism)

[319] WDDTY 'What doctors don't tell you about MMR' p13 col1pg5 –(Vaccination New Sth Wales 1993)

[320] Ibid 'Looming problem' p13 col1pg5 –Dr Schreiber Vaccination New Sth Wales 1993

[321] Ibid 'lower hemaglutinin' p12 col2pg5

[322] Ibid ' Large group Swiss doctors working committee questions' Health department on US inspired policy of mass vaccination' 2002 p16 col1.

[323] Ibid 'Vitamins' pg 19 col1 pg4 (Vitamins-Southern Medicine & Surgery known as Southern Medical Journal - article Dr Fred R Kilenner – vol 111:209-14 1994 July)

[324] Ibid 'Vit A' pg 18 col2 p1 (Lancet 1986:ii 169-73)

[325] Ibid 'alternatives' p18 col2 p2- (AMJ Clin Nutr 1984:40:1090-5)

[326] Ibid 'alternatives' pg 18 col2 p3 (Am J Dis Child 1992:146:182-6)

[327] Ibid 'alternatives to vaccination' pg18 col2 p 5 (BMJ.1987:294:294-6 - N Engl J Med 1990:323:160-4)

[328] Ibid ' alternatives to vaccines' pg19 col1 (Dr F Kilnner –the treatment of poliomyelitis and other virus diseases with Vit C' – Southern Medicine & Surgury (Vol111:209-14) 1949.07)

[329] Ibid 'Rubella'pg12:col2 (Pediatr Infec Dis J 1996:15:687-92)

[330] Ibid 'Chronic Fatigue syndrome'pg16:col2:p1 (Med Hypoth,1998;27:217-8: Clin Ecol 1989:7:51-4)

[331] Ibid 'Arthritis'' pg16:col2:p3 (Am J Child Dis,1969;218:218-25: JAMA 1970;214:2287-92)

[332] Ibid 'Guillain Barr syndrome' p16 col2 p2 (BMJ.1996:312:1475-6)

[333] Ibid 'Vaccinated population more prone to common adverse reactions'pg16:col2:p4 (Lancet 1982:i:1323-5 Lancet 1989:ii:751)

[334] Ibid '26% children develop arthralgia and arthritis after rubella jab'pg16:col2:p5 (Science March 26 1977)

[335] Ibid 'Arthritis and Rheumatism' pg17:col1:p1 (JAMA 1992;267:392-6/Arth Rheum.1996:39:1529-34)

[336] Ibid 'US study of Medicine 13-15% women causal relationship'pg17:col1:pg4 (JAMA.1992:267:392-6)

[337] Ibid 'Dr A Tingle research' pg 17:col1:p3 'Dr Aubrey Tingle Children's Hospital Vancouver British Columbia'

[338] Ibid 'CRS risks and Rubela'pg14 col2pg2(Acta Paediatr,1994;83:674-7)

[339] Ibid 'Rubela virus found in one third of suffers with rheumatoid arthritis' pg17:col1:pg4 (Robert Medelsohn 'But Doctor… About that shot' (Dr Tingle research-reported in book) McLean 1982.02

[340] Ibid 'Australian study army recruits' pg 14:col1:pg3 (J Aus Med Tech,1973;4:26-7)

[341] Ibid 'Epademic Rubella with partially vaccinated communities'pg14:col2:pg2 (Acta Paediatr,1994;83:674-7)

[342] Ibid 'Australian study and army recruits'pg14:col1:p3 (Aus J Med Tech 1973;4:26-7)

[343] Ibid 'CRS risks and Rubela'pg14 col2pg2(Acta Paediatr,1994;83:674-7)

[344] Ibid 'Neural inflammation leading to paralysis following a mass swine flu immunisation programme in US 1976'pg 14:col2:pg3 (JAMA 1981;245:711-3) 'Guillain Barre syndrome' (pg14: col2:pg3-JAMA 1981;245:711-3)

Chapter 25

CONCLUSION

Throughout the book we have looked at many areas of pregnancy, infertility and miscarriage, especially the emotional aspects upon the parents and child.

A baby is born somewhere in the world every minute and the majority will be fine. All will go well with the birth and mother and infant will bond as nature intended for evolution. However, through experience I have seen a growing percentage of the population suffering needlessly from the birth process. Due to a lack of emotional and nurturing support during pregnancy and labour, emotional and physical disorders accumulate.

In writing the book, one fact became obvious to me. We are creating a society of dysfunction and ill health. Through evolution, humans have developed their current superiority over all animal species. Part of this evolvement came from adherence to a natural birth process, which triggers physiological and psychological processes that follow us into adulthood and beyond. By altering this process to fit our modern lifestyles, we block the natural triggers, creating problems that not only affect our children, but extend into their offspring and future generations.

Much of the cause can be traced back to clinical intervention and an over-use of drugs. When we combine this with an unwholesome diet and daily bombardment of harmful chemicals, both internally and externally, our evolved superiority begins to decline. It doesn't happen overnight. Through a gradual process of increasing ill health and mental instability, the world's civilised societies are already feeling the beginnings of permanent change.

We may have the best of intentions in our health care, but I believe the pendulum has swung too far in using drugs and clinical intervention to cure almost everything. We have lost our identity in this and lost the ability to see what we are doing to ourselves, our children, through lifestyles and home life. Nowadays we are in the habit of handing our power to someone else, expecting them to fix our problems without any responsibility or input from ourselves.

Blame is best directed inward, since we ignore the obvious signs of autism, ADHD, birth related PTSD, childhood anxiety, infantile eczema, allergies, asthma, etc, etc. The long-term effects that extend into adult life are also being masked by the use of suppressant drugs. Even natural immunities are cast aside in favour of artificial equivalents carrying harmful side effects, whilst the natural process is often shunned, simply because it carries no financial profit

Key Areas

Through my collective experience in treating both genders and all ages I have recognised several key areas of concern that cause physical, emotional and mental health problems from a young age and even from the birth process itself. These include:

1) The health and emotional condition of parents, both pre and post conception.
2) A lack of pre and post-natal support for mother and child – with preventative health care
3) Birth
4) Foetal origins
5) Daily use of chemicals and drugs harmful to the human genetic code

Few would argue that in most cases, tall parents produce tall children. Across the entire animal world, individual physical strengths beget similar offspring while weak and sickly parents produce generations that struggle to survive.

Yet the concept of human neuroses and anxieties being passed on is ignored. So too is the damaging effect of deliberately induced fear and trauma. Stress affects the body's natural chemical control. During pregnancy, the wrong levels of testosterone, adrenaline and dopamine can influence foetal brain development, giving rise to many associated health issues and antisocial behaviour.

During and after birth, parents and infant need to feel the love bond that will anchor them as a family. Without it they become fragmented. The care and nurturing ethic is bypassed and the child's foundation becomes weak, leaving self-esteem and self worth issues that will compound through life. Throughout the book, numerous examples confirm the cycle of problems resulting from an imperfect start to life.

Logically, if we want our children to be healthy, a diet of drugs, alcohol, nicotine and processed foods laced with harmful additives doesn't create the right support in which to grow. Nor does a cocktail of stress and emotional trauma at the time of conception and through gestation. Sufficient forethought and pre-planning can improve the odds. This in turn helps to bring forth balanced and healthy children.
The happier the child, the more content the parents.

Miscarriage and infertility causes stress, whilst stress can cause miscarriage and infertility. This loop is self-perpetuating if untreated. There is no guarantee that the effects will end after a successful birth. While the anxiety remains, physical problems develop. All kinds of buried emotions cause blockages and ultimately, ill health.

Yet with the right help and education, we can change. Emotional release techniques cleared a child of eczema, giving amazing results from a single treatment. Although this may seem hard to believe, I know it to be true (see Mably's story – Chapter 20). Her four years of suffering ended within one week. She was the epiphany and my reason for writing this book.

Birth and Foetal origins

Babies adopt many traits while in the womb. As previously discussed, many of our likes and dislikes will come from the mother during pregnancy. The mother's good physical, emotional and mental health is imperative while pregnant, as many of our children's disorders will stem from foetal origins. Influences from the outside world impact greatly, especially those of trauma, stress and grief. So too does the type of birth process. Loving contact at birth is not only essential but also fundamental to a child's development.

Those first moments together are just as important as the first breath. Across the animal kingdom, prime examples are seen every day. Yet human modernity requires the child be whisked away at a most crucial time. C-section and anaesthesia both desensitise the natural bonding instinct and interfere with the mum's unique life-protecting bacteria from the birth canal

Oxytocin is paramount at birth. Although it also provides other benefits, it is through our hormone and chemical interactions that patterns and emotional behaviour will form and reform. This is the foundation level that is essentially the key to the life they will live.

A lack of maternal bonding and low Oxytocin at birth creates emotional insecurity, weakening the newborn's self esteem and self worth. Ignoring its importance doesn't do the child any favours. It's little wonder that affected children lash out at parents and society in later life.

Low Oxytocin on its own can give rise to drug addiction, smoking, stomach disorders, autism, ADHD and allergies. For those who escape the worst effects, many face adulthood bearing insecurities.

From the time we are born we receive a connection to food. It forms a bond and emotional closeness that lasts for life. Whatever level of understanding and patterns are created in our early days will be with us as a foundation for future growth, i.e: how we were fed as an infant. I believe the lack of oxytocin is a factor for the current obesity levels within society.

Car Crash Babies

For some babies the birth process can be likened to a car crash. They arrive in shock and suffer post-traumatic stress, with symptoms of distress, continually crying (for no apparent reason), refusing to sleep or settle. These symptoms can go on for months.

The incidence of ADHD is growing all around the world. It is not just a UK problem. Again it has links that stem from the birth process. The condition of the mother post and pre natal with lifestyle choices are indicators of high risk factors in behaviour disorders. Additionally we have highlighted other areas, which cause concern for behaviour-forming. Smoking and drinking coupled with the type of birth process is a huge factor in low birth weight and preterm births.

Our children are becoming increasingly anti-social and often (I find) they have NO bonding with their parents and siblings. Many are frustrated, anxious and on edge. These are all indications of having suffered low or non-existent oxytocin levels, setting a poor foundation for the child to grow from. Primarily it results in no bonding or respect for parents. This is an important issue when we consider the huge part it plays in keeping the blood stream free from stress hormones.

Today we have generations of C-section deliveries who are now adults and producing their own families. I believe they are genetically reproducing further generations who are even more deficient in oxytocin. Furthermore, I also believe it answers many questions raised about our children's behaviour.

The Facts

In 2008, the facts showed that one in ten UK children have a mental health problem and the demand for treatment is growing.
Throughout the book I have indicated areas where our children are becoming more vulnerable to poor parenting and birthing skills. I have shown that anger patterns are formed before 3 years old and growing numbers of children are being expelled from nursery and primary school as a result.

It became official in 2009 when the Family Health Service issued a report stating that UK school children are the unhappiest in Europe and our teenagers are depressed. When it becomes the norm for under five's to be listed as violent and under three's suspended from nursery for destructive behaviour, isn't it time we chose a different path?
Children come in to this world with an intense need for attachment and nurturing. Yet we seem to be emotionally detaching them from the birth process and in the womb. Although unintended, this is true for a large majority of the population.

As emotionally formed people, we have a sympathetic nervous system that is hard wired. Hopefully we have been shown and experienced kindness and love, which will form certain brain formations from hormones released via, oxytocin etc., To receive the hard wiring, we need the right kind of experience to develop the appropriate brain circuits. In other words we copy and learn from what we are shown from our parents, siblings and culture.

Love and contact is essential and fundamental for a child's development. Child abuse can warp the brain and ultimately, cruelty makes us cruel. What we experience during early years will essentially form who we are, to the very core of our being. This shows that most people's psychological issues come from a lack of love.

Unfortunately LOVE is not enough

Many of today's antisocial problems are preventable. Just by supporting the bonding process we create awareness and wellbeing with psychological benefits for all. Inducing the Love hormone automatically creates unity and a secure foundation for the family to grow from. The benefits are enormous and the change upon society wholly beneficial. Clearly, as new parents, the future is in our hands.

For change to come, we need to go back to the grass roots with parents.

Nature and human evolution have spent thousands of years breeding out dysfunctions. Now we take great delight in their reintroduction by masking the cause as part and parcel of a civilised society. We force our unborn children to mutate in order to satisfy hectic lifestyles and a later financial market of correction.

This is where we can make dramatic change. Couples can prepare for conception and plan ahead. By understanding the consequences of their actions and with improvements in emotional support to the mother's wellbeing during pregnancy, this alone can make enormous change for the incoming child.

The impact on society

Apart from the huge monetary cost, we are creating a society of dysfunctional individuals who cannot interact normally without the use of suppressant drugs. The increase in prescriptions for ADHD correction is staggering. Unfortunately, whilst the supply of drugs remains outrageously lucrative, there is little incentive for global companies to press for a return to common sense. Nearly every childhood disorder can boast a moneymaking fix at some point, whether by cream or tablet. Often the treatment merely masks without cure, creating future drug addiction the moment childhood medication lapses.

Who pays the price?

Emotionally it falls to the mothers and fathers whose expectations fall far short of what nature intended; and the children, whose neuroses and emotional disabilities are setting the genetic path for future generations.

Financially the burden is borne by our pockets and establishments like the NHS. Year on year the cost increases with no sign of abatement. Socially our very existence is threatened by a growing culture of disruptive behaviour, drug addiction and increased violence from an early age. Most of it is traceable to birth-related influences. Although well intentioned, their long reaching affects cause misery.

Despite being worthwhile, only brave souls go against the tide and recommend a return to natural childbirth. The benefits of such a move wouldn't show until an entire generation of happy, healthy children proved its validity. Financially the NHS would save millions. The numbers of troubled parents would decline. So too would allergies. But commonsense comes at a price. The profit from drugs and vaccines can influence decision-making amongst health authorities. Like the old adage – he who pays the piper calls the tune. In the meantime our children suffer.

By having awareness and taking responsibility for your baby and yourself, what you do while pregnant can make a huge difference. I believe we can change, although it could take a generation for us to see the result. It is only with proper education and awareness that we can bring our children back to full health.

A man asked Mother Teresa if there was anything he could do to help.
   She replied -
                'Go home and love your children'

Footnote:
I felt so passionate about this subject that I founded The One Generation Project (a not for profit organisation) with the objective of stopping the tide of growing ill health created by society and to help parents and children in the process.
By working with One Generation we will empower this generation to provide a life of wellbeing for generations to come. (See appendix for more information and how you can assist)

Chapter 26

INDEX

Chapter 26

APPENDIX - ALTERNATIVE THERAPIES

INTRODUCTION

I believe that alternative and complimentary programmes are a life-line, not only for the NHS in the UK but medical practices all over the world. I feel that they have a huge part to play alongside conventional medicine.

Many people have called for the integration of alternative practices within the NHS, welfare and medical care.

Alternative therapies are not a threat to the medical profession and can work side by side for the benefit of the individual. They not only support the medical profession, but enable resources to be fine-tuned and outgoings reduced. In my opinion it is a win-win situation.

It is well known that Reflexology can get people out of hospital quicker after surgery, therefore creating a faster turnaround for wards and hospital beds. The same discipline can free up a patient's bowel and bladder without resorting to drugs and pessaries. It can even help with mental and physical de-stressing for all ages, creating a safe and proactive response. There are no barriers to age or condition. As I have shown in the book, there are alternative ways to take charge of our health with preventative measures and maintenance.

One of the main benefits is that adopting alternative therapies could save the NHS and welfare systems a fortune in drug bills.

Most therapists have time to listen and give care where nurses are overworked and understaffed. There is an army of alternative professional people who work in many areas of healthcare; areas such as nutrition - the key to a healthy foundation. Since conventional medicine covers many specialised professions, most are not trained in the likes of nutrition or emotional stress, as compared to most professional therapists who look at the holistic view and who are trained in these areas. Many have a broad view which gives the best possible recovery options for their client. Like me, they believe that good health depends upon more than the physical.

In my practice I deliver a whole approach along with nutrition and stress relief options. The majority of people I see need many approaches to rebalance their health. Few fit the single remedy approach which conventional health treatment normally relies on. That is why people come to therapists like myself. I am trained in many modalities/areas with the knowledge to help them overcome their distress or disorder.

This is more easily explained with an example:-
My mother went to see her doctor regarding shoulder pain. She explained she had fallen and knocked her arm previously and still had pain in the shoulder some months later.

The doctor examined her arm, thought no bone was broken but offered an X-ray to confirm. He then prescribed painkillers as a final remedy. When she told me the story I suspected that she had damaged her lymph system during the fall as her elbow was swollen. I could see a build up of lymph fluid in the arm that had back-flowed into the shoulder. I gave her 2 sessions of Lymph drainage. Immediately during her first session she could feel relief from her pain and the swelling went down in her arm. The second session seemed to do the trick and her shoulder pain was relieved without drugs. When my mother attended the doctor again she told him about the sessions and their success. The doctor told her that she was mistaken; that it could not be the case at all. He believed the condition had subsided on its own with the help of the prescribed painkillers (which she hadn't taken)!

Most therapists work in a holistic view using the broader picture. We support the whole person and not just the part that is showing. We look to see if there is another reason why the arm is not as it should be, such as the lymph system. Maybe the muscles and tendons have been affected by the fall? A CST practitioner would work not just on the arm, but also the chest, back, shoulder and neck. All is connected in the body and nothing is separate. If one part is affected then others can be too.

A Homeopath would prescribe Arnica for the bruising and discomfort. A Bach Flower practitioner would suggest Rescue remedy for the shock and anxiety. A Reflexologist would treat through the feet, identifying imbalances to treat the person, bringing the whole body back into homeostasis and balance. By relaxing the muscles and tendons, it allows the body to feel cared, nurtured and de-stressed. This in turn enables it to repair and become whole again.

Therapists are likened to the time honoured herbalists and wise women/elders who lived in the village, where knowledge was passed down from one generation to the next. Isn't this what we are doing with our training?

In this section we are going to look at several therapies. There are a lot on the market place and I would strongly suggest that you check out their credentials and ensure they are registered with an Accredited body.

We will be looking at the following therapies:

- Acupuncture
- Bach Flower Remedies
- Behavioural Problems
- Cranio Sacral Therapy
- Homeopathy
- Hair Analysis
- Indian Head Massage
- Lymph Drainage
- Massage
- Baby Massage
- Reflexology

Diet
- Anti-Candida Diet advice
- Liver Spring Clean
- MSM

Testing
- Hair Analysis

ACUPUNCTURE

Acupuncture has been used in China for centuries and its history is known to be seeped in Chinese medicine. It is believed that missionaries who visited China brought out the theories and practices of Acupuncture back in the 16th century. By the end of the 19th century many physicians were using acupuncture.

Today acupuncture is used to detect and balance between Yin and Yang (body energies). They use the philosophy of the elements and the meridians to decipher imbalances within the individual. They use needles inserted at meridian points to detect imbalances. Acupuncturists often move or manipulate the needles to relieve pain.

Meridians are a system of channels that take energy around the body. If there is an imbalance or congestion in the channels they will alter the effectiveness and performance of the major organs in the body. Meridians are also influenced by our emotions, subsequently affecting our physical, emotional and mental health.
I have used meridian clearing methods (with and without Reflexology) to help with all sorts of disorders. It is something I use for my clients in conjunction with energy balancing.

- An Acupuncture practitioner uses needles to insert in meridian and reflex points on the body, to change and influence outcomes in health.
- Acupressure also uses meridian points by applying finger pressure. (Just like Reflexology).
- Reflexology uses meridian points to influence health outcomes, creating synergy.
- Shiatsu also works with the meridian pathways.Acupuncture works with a range of disorders, from pain to mental disorders, are helped with Acupuncture. It is being becoming more accepted as the medical profession open up to alternative methods of health detection and balance. More doctors are training and using this method to treat patients, although it is not always available on the NHS, at present.

Training

The Acupuncture practitioner must undertake years of study including Chinese medicine, acupuncture techniques, together with conventional science and experience with clinical and energetic systems practiced alongside case studies. Acupuncture is used by doctors, practitioners and therapists and is widely available around the country.

BACH FLOWER REMEDIES

Bach Flower remedies were discovered in the 1930s by Dr Edward Bach, a Harley Street doctor, developed Bach Flower Remedies. He was a well known Physician, Bacteriologist, Homeopath and Researcher. He had a new perspective on illness and disorder as he believed that attitude of mind plays a vital role in maintaining health and recovering from illness. In my opinion Dr. Bach was a pioneer in his time.

His remedies are derived from non-poisonous plants, shrubs and trees. They are prepared through the heating of appropriate flowers with sunlight in spring water, or the boiling of twigs and flowers to extract the healing essence.

The beauty of using flower essences is that they are completely safe, non-toxic, non-addictive, and may be used in conjunction with any other medical or holistic treatment. Remedies can be used for any age. They are ideal to take while pregnant, as they are used by the body without harm to your baby.

Beneficial in post and anti natal conditions

Bach flower remedies target the mental/emotional level of an individual, helping to clear negative emotions, mindsets, attitudes, and personality traits which can not only impede the body's ability to heal itself, but also create roadblocks to peace and happiness.

The flower essences are not taken for physical symptoms, although as discussed in the book the body will often heal itself once an emotional balance is restored. Remedies are used for dealing with stress, fear and anxiety, depression, anger and resentment, excessive worry, low self-esteem, guilt, loneliness, etc. in all ages.

A friend of mine who is a Bach flower practitioner has kindly presented the following information.

Philosophy - Dr. Bach intended the use of his remedies to be straightforward and simple enough for all to understand. Simplicity was his keyword. Bach Flower Remedies are used as a natural way to provide relief from negative attitudes, moods, and protection from outside influences.

"I want to make it as simple as this: "I am hungry, I will go and pull a lettuce from the garden for my tea; I am frightened and ill, I will take a dose of Mimulus". Nora Weeks – The Medical Discoveries of Edward Bach, Physician

There are 38 Bach flower remedies

This system of treatment is considered the most perfect and has been given to mankind within living memory.

Dr. Edward Bach stated in his book 'The Twelve Healers and Other Remedies' 'These remedies can be used by the whole family – for mothers, fathers, children, pets and plants!

The 38 remedies make up the complete system. The idea is that we choose any of the remedies (up to a total of 7) and make up a treatment bottle (or have one prepared for you). This should last approximately three weeks.

Prior to making up another bottle a practitioner would look over the remedy list again to see which remedies would be most appropriate. It may be that their original choice of remedies is still the most suitable. However it is also probable that they may choose different remedies. The most important thing is to choose remedies for how you feel at this very moment.

For instance the following remedies can take away fears (Mimulus/Aspen/Rock Rose)

- Boost confidence (Larch)
- Rekindle optimism (Gentian)
- Help one to get off the settee if lethargy sets in (Hornbeam)
- Take away descending gloom (Mustard) and give support if one is tired (Olive)

The remedies are suitable for everyone regardless of age; the very nature of them is so gentle they can be used on pregnant women and newborn babies.

Rescue Remedy is used for emergency and when feeling overwhelmed

It is highly likely that you have come across the Rescue Remedy. It can be bought off the shelf and is handy to have at home or carry with you. Rescue Remedy is a combination of 5 of the 38 remedies (a breakdown of these remedies is given below). As the name suggests, it is the remedy for all emergencies and is therefore indicated for accidents (obviously it does not take the place of medical attention!). Use it for alarm, examination nerves and any occasion when there is a degree of shock or panic, e.g.: when a child wakes with nightmares or has watched something frightening on the television.

Treatment tips

Use it to calm children from anxiety or nervousness. Four drops should be put in a small tumbler of water and sipped until the child is calm.

As a spray, it can be mixed with water in a clean plant sprayer and misted into the air for a calming atmosphere on children and adults. Rescue Remedy can also be put in the bath water to calm and comfort one's whole body. This way it will help to heal any wounds, both emotionally and physically. Use it especially if there has been tension, an argument or take prior to pregnancy examinations to calm anxiety.

Rescue Remedy is extremely useful during times of ill health. It is widely available from Chemists and health food stores. All remedies can be purchased by mail order (see appendix) and usually available from Health food stores. Boots and other high street chemists stock quite a few of the remedies.

Rescue Remedy can be used direct from the bottle in cases of shock or anxiety. Use two drops under the tongue. It has immediate affect with instant results in calming the adult or child. Thereafter use as above.

The Components of the Rescue Remedy are:

Star of Bethlehem, Rock Rose, Cherry Plum, Clematis and Impatiens.
Star of Bethlehem: use for shock. If shock can be treated without delay the impact of the trauma should be lessened.

Rock Rose: use for terror, great fear and panic.

Cherry Plum: use for panic, hysteria and loss of emotional control – when the sufferer screams, shouts or is hysterical.

Clematis: use for feeling faint or stunned, a remedy for the bemused or the distant feeling which often precedes a faint.

Impatiens: use for the agitation and irritation that is so often associated with pain.

How a treatment bottle is prepared

Bach Remedy plants are non poisonous and therefore harmless so no overdose or conflict can occur. They can be taken quite safely with other medication, and because they are benign in their action will not interfere with other treatments one may be taking.
A few remedies can be given at a time, depending on one's needs, up to about six or seven. Having chosen appropriate remedies a 30ml treatment bottle is filled to the shoulders with water, preferably still mineral water. To this two drops of each desired remedy is added – or four drops of rescue remedy. Brandy forms the bulk of the "stock" remedy – that is the concentrated remedy. However, once diluted to make up the treatment bottle, the amount of alcohol remaining is absolutely minimal.
This bottle should last a couple of weeks. If it goes cloudy just make up a new mixture or have one prepared for you.

Administering the Remedies

Once a treatment bottle has been made up, the dose is: 4 drops to be taken a minimum of 4 times a day.
We need to administer the drops as best we can during the day. Its healing power lies not in the quantity but in the frequency of doses. The first dose may be taken upon waking and the final dose just prior to retiring.

In between these two doses we need to include at least two further doses – four doses evenly spaced is the minimum to enable the remedies to work.

It may be feasible to take the remedies each time you have a drink or use some other recurring act as a reminder. When you feel the need they may be taken every half an hour or every hour.
For a passing mood, the remedies may be added to a small glass of water and this should be sipped at intervals.

**Some suggested instances for their use
with children and parents are:**

Cherry Plum   (for fear of losing control) is handy for children when they lose their temper and in more extreme situations when we fear that we may lose control and do something dreadful, which can include injuring others or ourselves.

Willow   (for resentment) is great for children who go into a huff when they are told off or who are resentful on being told they cannot do something that they had wanted to do. It also applies in more extreme situations when we begrudge others their success or good fortune and when sick. People who are in a Willow state would be difficult patients whereby nothing pleases or satisfies them and they are reluctant to admit improvement.

Red Chestnut   (Over-anxious and fearful) If you feel over-anxious about your baby then this remedy will enable you see everything in the right perspective and will calm your fears.

The Dr Edward Bach Centre website gives detailed information for each of the 38 remedies and the composite Rescue Remedy.

Training

A Bach Flower practitioner must undertake years of study and clinical experience. They can be medical doctors, homeopaths, naturopaths, nurse practitioners, therapists and a range of laypersons.

To find a practitioner in your area see appendix contact section

Further Information

Visit the Dr. Edward Bach Centre, the home of the Bach Flower Remedies at Mount Vernon, England. (www.bachcentre.com)

Recommended Reading and Useful Addresses - see contacts appendix page

To find descriptions of the remedies on the internet, click onto the highlighted words 'Bach Flower Remedies' and this will take you to a page where all 38 remedies are listed. You may then click onto each remedy as required. An explanation of the use of each remedy is given followed by Dr Bach's original description. For each remedy there is a beautiful painting by the artist, Margaret Foster. You can find all you need to know on the site, including frequently-asked questions, listings of books available on the subject, details of Dr. Edward Bach, his life and achievements, etc.

Emotional States and suggested remedies:

Anxiety: **Agrimony** - use for hidden/concealed restlessness
Mimulus - use for known cause
Red Chestnut - use for welfare of others
Aspen - use for unknown cause/vague anticipation
White Chestnut - for use with worrying thoughts

Anger: **Holly** - use for hatred/envy
Vervain - use for injustice
Cherry Plum - use for uncontrolled anger
Centaury - use for anger with self or for self-weakness
Scleranthus - use for anger with self for hesitancy or indecision
Rock Water - use for anger with self for failure
Impatiens - use for slowness
Beech - use for anger with stupidity of others

Control: **Cherry Plum** - use for lack of mental ability
                      Chicory, Vine - use for a desire to control others

Depression: **Gentian** - for known reason, due to setback
                      Mustard - cause unknown
                      Gorse or Gentian - use for times of pessimism
                      Gorse - use for feelings of hopelessness
                      Sweet Chestnut - use when utter dejection is felt
                      Mustard - use when depression descends suddenly,
                      like a dark cloud
                      Willow - for Introspective feelings

Loneliness: **Water Violet** - to bring more enjoyment into life
                      Impatiens – brings tolerance
                      Heather, Chicory, Mimulus and/or Vervain –
                      use for dislikes or acrimony
                      Clematis - when we feel the need to escape
                      Star of Bethlehem, Sweet Chestnut -
                      use for feelings of Heartbreak

Overwhelmed: **Elm** - for responsibility/pressure
                      Centaury, Mimulus - when overwhelmed by
                      demands of others
                      Impatiens - for feelings of being harassed/
                      irritated with constant demands

Repressed Emotions:
                      Agrimony, Centaury, Water Violet -
                      general repressed emotions
                      Pine – relief of guilt
                      Scleranthus - for indecision
                      Willow - for resentment/bitterness:
                      White Chestnut - for festering
                      thoughts/mental arguments

Self-Confidence: **Larch** - lack of self-confidence
                      Mimulus - lack of confidence through fear
                      Elm - lack of confidence momentarily,
                      when under pressure
                      Cerato - lack of confidence through self-distrust

Scleranthus - lack of, confidence through indecision

Gorse - lack of, confidence through feelings of hopelessness

Shock: Star of Bethlehem and/or Rescue Remedy

Sleeplessness: White Chestnut - sleeplessness through worry, mental arguments or tormented thoughts

Vervain, Rock Water - through tension

Olive - through over-exhaustion

Star of Bethlehem, Honeysuckle, and Rescue Remedy - through grief

Vervain, Agrimony, and Impatiens - through restlessness

Aspen, Agrimony - through anxiety

Mimulus, Rock Rose – through fear

Tearfulness: Chicory, Willow - easily prone to tearfulness, out of self-pity

Scleranthus - through instability

Sweet Chestnut - through despair

Olive - through utter exhaustion

Centuary, Mimulus, Red Chestnut, Walnut - due to sensitivity

Walnut - easily moved, due to sensitivity or influence

Honeysuckle, Walnut - through sentimentality

Water Violet, Agrimony - hidden tears or cries alone

BEHAVIOUR PROBLEMS

Apart from CST, alternative therapies are also available such as Brain Gym and DORE programme for dyslexia etc.,

Educational Kinesiology and Brain Gym

Brain Gym is a movement re-education programme run individually on a one to one basis and also run at some schools throughout the UK. It has programmes in 45 countries.

Used as a self-development tool. An American Dr Paul Dennison PhD developed the programme from years of research on the brain.
The programme uses simple movements by the individual to integrate the whole brain, senses and body. It has been developed to use with behaviour, concentration and balance challenges.

As the name states it is a gym exercise programme to help with all sorts of skills.

- Practitioners and trainers are contacted through EKF foundation - www.braingym.org.uk

The Dore Programme

The Dore programme, was developed by Wynford Dore for his dyslexic daughter. It is a daily exercise programme for disorders such as Dyslexia, Dysphraxia and concentration issues such as ADD.

The programme is run over some months and costs can be from £2000 per programme. www.dore.co.uk

CRANIO SACRAL THERAPY

Cranio Sacral Therapy is rapidly gaining recognition as one of the most gentle and yet powerful forms of holistic healing

It is a relatively new therapy, having been developed from one of those rare quantum leaps of inspiration by its founder, Dr. William Sutherland, an American osteopath. In the 1920's he recognized a subtle motion within the intricate bony structure of the skull. Despite going completely against the established teaching of his time, he called this motion 'primary respiration', believing it to be of far more importance to our wellbeing rather than mere breathing.
During the next 80 years more and more people were drawn to investigate this revolutionary therapy although it was only taught to Osteopaths during this period.

Dr. John Upledger (Surgeon, Osteopath and Physician) was one of the pioneers in this field developing Cranio Sacral Therapy. He has refined the techniques to its present format and now also encompasses Emotional/ Trauma release with Somoto Emotional Release. (Trials were done with Vietnam veterans when it was found that counselling was not enough)

DR. Upledger found that treatment could be used on defects/ malfunctions involving the brain and spinal cord, plus numerous other health problems. Fortunately, with Upledger's pioneering work over the last 30 years, it has now been made more available to a wider cross section, including Therapists. More people have come to realise that this is a very powerful way of bringing the body back into balance and harmony.

At the very core of the body lies the brain and spinal cord. It sits within a bony protection and is bathed in a special fluid - the cerebrospinal fluid (CSF). As the subtle movements of the primary breath take place the CSF travels along the core of the body, drawn upward during 'inspiration' and flowing downwards at 'expiration'.
This movement of fluid is like the movement of the oceans and has been called 'the tide'. The subtle movement within the core of the body is taken up and expressed throughout the tissues and organs. In an ideal body there would be a synchronised and harmonious rhythm within all the body parts.

Because our systems meet physical and emotional stress they become challenged and respond by contracting. In that challenge they disturb and disrupt the flow of the tide. It is as if the tide is flowing into a rocky shore; when it meets an obstacle, it has to find a way around.
Where the body is fully resourced the blockage is a temporary disruption. However if the stresses are too frequent or if the shock too great, the blockage becomes gradually established and can eventually, over time, lead to discomfort, pain and dis-ease.

During our lifetime we will collect and disperse many different blockages. Sometimes we are able to use the body's natural processes to unblock and sometimes we need help. The light touch of a trained Cranio Sacral Therapist is able to detect blockage and restricted flow of the fluids, reflect this information back to the body and help gather the necessary resources to re-establish harmony.

Cranio Sacral Therapy

Throughout the book we have talked about the benefits of Craniosacral Therapy (CST) with baby and mother. Here information is given to explore the many other ways CST can help all ages.

CST is used to detect and correct imbalances in the craniosacral system, which may be the cause of sensory, motor or intellectual dysfunction.

The craniosacral system consists of the membranes and cerebrospinal fluid that surround and protect the brain and spinal cord. It extends from the bones of the skull, face and mouth – which make up the cranium and goes down to the sacrum or tailbone area.

CST treats people rather than their condition. It is primarily concerned with creating a healthy balanced state on all levels – physical, mental and emotional. One or a combination of techniques may support people with almost any condition. They are aimed at removing or reducing limitation to our innate self-healing process and aid the search for the root cause of a person's ill health, often unearthing causes that may have lain hidden for years.

The therapy has been successfully used to treat headaches, neck and back pain, TMJ, chronic fatigue, motor coordination difficulties, eye problems and central nervous system disorders.

The cerebrospinal fluid is made in the head and flows into the spine to bathe the nervous system and oil the joints. Any dysfunction in this process will cause discomfort and pain. Like a creaking door that needs oiling, it eventually seizes or stops moving. This also happens to parts of the body. It is a hydraulic system. Whatever dysfunction is happening to the head will affect the spine and vice versa.

Osteopathic physician John Upledger has pioneered the techniques and further developed the concept into Cranio Sacral therapy. He has taught the technique internationally.

When we have a fall or an accident the impact upon the body does not just affect the injured part i.e.: - shoulder. It is like throwing a pebble in a pond: The impact radiates throughout the body. It can go up, down or sideways. When this happens it affects the tissue and creates blockages to the flow of energy. This can then show up as a disorder later i.e.: - headaches or neck pain/disorder.

How does it work?

Craniosacral therapy is safe, simple, yet very powerful and effective. Small movements are made to the head and body to enable the body to realign by itself without trauma to the bones, tissues and ligaments. In the process it eliminates symptoms, diseases and dysfunctions at their root causes.

It is relaxing and calming to the body, providing relief from aches, pains and traumas from car accidents, falls etc.,
As discussed in the book, Emotional trauma to the body also creates blockages. One of the benefits of CST is to help unblock and rebalance the cranial sacral fluid.

Clients often tell me they feel calm and fully relaxed after a session. They confess feelings of tingling, having felt sensations of fluids moving through the body. Gurgling can often be heard during treatment as the stomach responds to the changing energies and fluids.

CST works with all ages

Babies and children can receive dysfunctions from forceps or suction delivery.

Even firmly placed fingers used to help remove the infant from the womb can also create cranial damage. This places undue pressure on the meridians of the body causing dysfunction with symptoms of colic.

The twisting process in the birth canal can also twist the spine, resulting in a slight spinal torsion or spinal defect. CST helps to realign bones and tissues after delivery, realigning the spine, neck, hips and shoulders, untwisting any torsion or defect formed while in the reduced space of the womb.

Not just for baby

There has been a great deal of publicity recently about the value of Cranio Sacral Therapy for babies and children. As explained in the book their systems respond very effectively to this form of therapy and it is extremely valuable in the problems to do with suckling, hearing, colic, digestive dysfunctions, behaviour issues and problems related to birth process.

What is becoming more widely accepted is the value of this therapy to adults and children alike. A wide variety of conditions have been found to respond to Cranio Sacral treatment.

As previously mentioned, babies and children can receive dysfunctions from forceps or suction delivery. CST helps to realign bones and tissues after a quick or TRAUMATIC delivery.

It is also beneficial for Mums during pregnancy and I suggest a session after birth to realign pelvis, hips etc.,

- Helps to relieve mum's discomfort during pregnancy and realigning post natal
- Gives relief from symptoms of pubisos
- Realignment for newborns and children after birth or shell-shocked from process
- Dyslexia/ Dysphraxia
- Attention Deficit Disorder (ADD/ADHD) and other learning difficulties

CST is used to detect and correct imbalances in the craniosacral system, which may be the cause of sensory, motor or intellectual dysfunction.

The client lies on a treatment table fully clothed and the therapist makes gentle contact by placing the hands lightly on the body, as well as the head and spine. Small movements are made to realign and balance.

Relaxing and calming,(some even feel sleepy during treatment). Light pressure is used to detect imbalances and dysfunction.
Did you know that a skeletal misalignment may cause all sorts of disorders from period pain to depression? CST provides relief from aches and pains, especially neck and back pain, traumas to the body from car accidents, falls etc.,

The process is a partnership in which the therapist assists the body to find its own vitality and healing resource. It is deeply relaxing. There may be a feeling of tingling, feeling hot or cold as structures, muscles, diaphragms and tissues release. Sometimes there may be an emotional response as memories of past trauma, sadness, happiness or of times past are released. This is a valuable signpost that the body is healing.

Children's sessions

While treating an infant, emotions may come up to be released. When this happens the infant may cry. The pitch of the cry changes and becomes more intense (this is an indicator that emotions are being released) I am blessed to be able to feel the emotions coming off the child and know he/she has let go of the emotional trauma. Sometimes it will come off in stages during a single session and sometimes it can take 2 or 3 sessions to completely clear. (Ultimately depending upon the trauma received).

One of the good things is that once released, the child suddenly stops crying and (as often happens to me) they look me straight in the eye, try to talk or make sounds. It is as if a great weight has been lifted off them, as the body becomes calm once again.
For older clients they may feel tired, elated energetic or loose limbed. Limbs may feel heavy and can't seem to lift off the treatment bed. They often report feeling taller or straighter when they stand with neck and shoulders feeling loose. Sometimes when posture has been changed during a session they feel slightly achy when they stand up. However, most side effects are short lived.

The partnership builds over a course of treatments and the response will be more rapid as the body regains its innate healing abilities. It is possible for some problems to be resolved with one or two sessions, others may take longer if it is a chronic or acute condition.

CST therapy has been successfully used to treat adults and children:

CST is able to help with unblocking and clearing the blocked energy. When energy (Chi) flows through the body unhindered, health and vitality are maintained.

List of disorders CST may be particularly helpful with:

- Chronic Pain
- Osteoarthritis
- Restricted movement
- Sciatica/disc problems

- Sports injuries - Football, Rugby, Horse riding etc.,
- Repetitive Strain injury
- Promoting general health and fitness
- Jaw and mouth disorders- (grinding teeth)
- TMJ (jaw problems)
- Boosting recovery from injury
- Back, Neck & shoulder problems
- Headaches and Migraine

Newborns and traumatic birth dysfunctions:

- Forceps delivery
- Distressed/crying children
- Learning difficulties
- Traumatic birth newborns and children
- Dyslexia, Dysphraxia, Attention Deficit Disorder (ADD/ADHD) and other learning difficulties

Post and Anti-natal

- Discomfort during pregnancy
- Post Traumatic Stress
- Reduced vitality
- Exhaustion & Chronic fatigue
- Insomnia

Motor co-ordination difficulties

- Eye problems
- Recovery from injury and surgery
- Central nervous system disorders
- Car accidents and whiplash
- Emotional traumas to the body

Plus many more dysfunctions....

Training

A CST therapist must undertake years of study and clinical experience. CST therapists can be medical doctors, chiropractors, osteopaths, nurse practitioners, therapists, dentists and some are trained in Equine (horse CST therapy).

To find a practitioner in your area see appendix contact section.

See Appendix for contact details.

ANTI CANDIDA DIET

Not to be used while pregnant

Yeast fungi need a source of carbohydrate to live on. Their easiest supply is from sugar and fruit sugar. Within the body they thrive on ingested sugar and foods converted into sugar such as carbohydrates (even certain vegetables hold high stores of sugar).

It is therefore advisable to avoid all sugars. This includes glucose, fructose and malt sugar, all kinds of sweets, chocolate, biscuits or cookies and sweet juices including fizzy drinks. White flour products and jams will also need to be avoided.

Although the product may say it is sugar free, manufacturers often replace natural sugar with sweeteners. Despite the calories being less the body uses and metabolises sweeteners the same as household sugar. In other words it cannot differentiate between sugar and sweeteners.

Foods to Avoid while on an anti candida diet

White rice and pasta
Yeast and all foods with yeast
White bread and/or products using white flour
Sweet fruits – grapes, pears, peaches, pineapple, bananas, dates and plums
Dried fruit
Honey fructose and sugars
Sugar substitutes
Sweet drinks such as: Lemonade, Cola, fruit juices, sweet wine, beer and sweet liquors

Foods you can eat – treat as for a low GI diet

Very often we crave sugar while on this diet, as the condition will want its fix
Potatoes, Brown rice and brown or wheat free pasta
Fruits low in carbohydrates – strawberries and raspberries
Meat and fish of any variation except in batter or breadcrumb coating
Egg dishes without sugar
Milk and milk products without sugar
Natural yoghurt

All vegetables and salads – but avoid parsnips and carrots
Wheat free cereal and Muesli without sugar
Sugar free drinks – mineral water, coffee, tea and herbal teas

Bran fibres can help to sweep out the accumulated yeast cells. I would also suggest a programme of elimination with supplements etc., as described in the book.

Eating fibre several times a day will help with elimination. Foods rich in fibre are:

- Raw vegetables
- Wholemeal, Rye and Bran breads
- Pulses
- Cereals such as - seed sprouts, wholemeal, wholemeal flakes, grains, whole grain pasta and brown rice.

It is advisable not to drink great quantities of milk while on the programme as it has shown to make the disorder more persistent. Calcium supplements also have the same affect.

Sufferers of Candida are often seen to be deficient in supplements so it is important that you take the programme as prescribed by your practitioner. Correct diet will diminish the number of fungi but it is advisable to take a programme of elimination as suggested by your therapist to kill off the ablicans. Otherwise you will be doing all this again when sugar or antibiotics are reintroduced into the diet and symptoms reappear at great speed.

After 4 weeks of the diet you should not go back to a diet rich in sugar and sweets. Things need to be reintroduced slowly and you should try and continue to eat a healthy diet for some months to come. I normally suggest a 3 -6 month protocol. Start to introduce vegetables and fruits including the sweet ones slowly, but still incorporate a diet in whole foods.

To get the best nutrients, **do not over-cook your food** and continue where possible with raw food. Detoxing can also help at this stage.

Some tips to help things run smoothly

- Eat natural and organic foods if possible – avoid processed and fast food
- Eat 3 main meals a day and sit down while you eat – don't eat on the hoof
- Have regular meal times and try not to eat after 7pm
- Eat good carbs such as wholemeal products and pulses
- Think low GI - non starchy vegetables, avoiding sugar and refined carbs
- Choose a smaller dinner plate to eat from

Drink plenty – clean still water or hot water is good to cleanse the body.

- Black tea and coffee act as diuretics. This means you will lose more liquid than you drink and it can make the body dehydrated over time.
- Drink herbal teas such as – Nettle, peppermint or Roobosh tea. Although Green tea has a small amount of caffeine, it is known to have other benefits.
- Drink alcohol moderately – avoid all drinks with yeast
- Exercise and fresh air will help regenerate the body
- Change to soya or Oaten milk

Suggestions for snacks

- Fruit with cottage cheese
- Seeds and nuts such as almonds or walnuts
- Corn chips and hummus
- Oat biscuits with tahini, guacamole or avocado dip
- Rice cake with nut spread or hummus

Further reading and information:

The Food Doctor by V.Edgson & I Marber

The Optimum Nutrition Cookbook, Patrick Holford & Judy Ridgway
Look out for raw food books to give ideas for alternative cooking methods. There are lots on the market these days. It is what takes your eye.
Barbara Cousins, a nutritionist, has been writing books regarding wheat-free gluten-free since the 1970s. They are still in print and I would recommend them as a good all round approach for the whole family.
' Cooking Without' recipes free from gluten, sugar dairy etc., Barbara Cousins – Thorsons

For raw food courses and gourmet days contact
Andrew and Angela Davis at
Gourmet Raw: http://www.gourmetraw.com
The Raw Food School: http://www.therawfoodschool.com
Shopping on line: http://www.therawfoodschoolshop.com

METHYL-SULFONYL-METHANE (MSM)

MSM has many uses for the body (also known as Brimstone). It is a natural form of organic sulphur found in the fluids of all living organisms. Sulphur is as essential as water to the body. MSM is safe and odourless and does not produce intestinal gas.

I first came to know MSM many years ago when it was used for the symptoms of arthritis. This was because Sulphur can improve joint flexibility and reduce stiffness, swelling and pain. Improves circulation and breaks up calcium deposits or water bonds in the synovial fluid (knee cap joints).
Certain celebs used it to help reduce chronic symptoms of Rheumatoid arthritis and keep at bay, they campaigned its virtues after experiencing self-healing from their disorders.

I recommend MSM for helping to remove
Candida from body systems

MSM is used to discourage Candida. By competing for binding receptor sites at the mucus membrane surface, MSM discourages

Candia growth and removes parasites. Aloe Vera also has benefits as it is used to discourage fungus. Aloe Vera juice contains Caprylic acid a known killer of candida ablicans.

MSM helps with **detoxification and dehydration** in the body. Used to detox the body of mercury for instance when amalgam fillings are removed.

Sulphur is responsible for the ionic exchange with in the sodium-potassium pump in the cell and maintains the cell membrane. When toxins and other waste products in the cells are not eliminated it can lead to Asthma, ear, nose and throat infections, hay fever, headaches, fatigue and gastrointestinal problems.

Low insulin levels improved with MSM

Low sulphur levels can cause low insulin production or cell resistance to insulin, which in turn will bring about excess blood sugar leading to diabetes.

If you have weak nails, MSM can change that around to strong nails. Used for skin conditions, MSM can improve hair, complexion, acne, psoriasis, eczema and dermatitis.

MSM comes in powder form or tablet

In granular form take one to two teaspoons daily in juice or water. For chronic conditions an increased programme of taking several times a day or every 12 hours with or without food.
Sometimes when sulphur is first taken it can give looser bowel motions. If taken in powder or granular form increase does slowly over a period of 10 days to 2weeks.

Please note that Vitamin C enhances the action of MSM, so take in orange juice or with a Vitamin C supplement.
See appendix for suppliers contact information

SEVEN DAY LIVER SPRING CLEAN

A gentle detox regime – (not to be used if pregnant or breast feeding)

A seven day liver spring clean can be carried out as follows and acts as a very gentle detox regime:

- Days 1 and 2 - cut out all caffeine items such as tea, coffee and alcohol to prepare your body for the cleanse

- Days 3 to 7 - first thing before you have eaten anything else, drink the liver flush to help your body get rid of the excess toxins and give your system a spring clean

This is how to prepare the liver flush:
In a liquidizer, mix:

- 8fl oz/200 ml lemon or ¾ glass apple juice
- Freshly squeezed lemon juice
- Top up with spring or mineral water
- 1 or two segments from a clove of garlic
- 1 tablespoon of extra–virgin olive oil
- 1cm/½ inch of fresh ginger root

If you find it difficult to drink all that lemon juice, use organic apple juice instead with just a squeeze of lemon. Blend to a smooth liquid and drink slowly.

Drink some plain apple juice to dispel any after-taste and fifteen minutes later drink a cup of hot peppermint tea. Eat only fruit for the rest of the morning and then eat as normal from lunch–time onwards. Keep your meals very simple so that your body has a chance to eliminate any toxins. A good supplement programme from your nutritionist will also help to support the liver and immune system while on this regime.

You may experience mild flu–like symptoms and slight headaches for the first couple of days of the regime, but these are simply an indication that you are detoxifying. During the process, you must eat well to keep your blood sugar up and drink plenty of water during the day, at least 8 tumbler-sized glasses each day.

The liver flush programme can be repeated in full after a month. However if you have over indulged with rich food and alcohol, the liver flush drink can be used at any time, although not more frequently than 2–3 times a week.

Other methods of body detoxification include using a colonics powder to detox the colon and bathing in Epsom salts to help detox through the skin. In addition, reflexology can help to rebalance hormones and reduce stress, whilst colonic irrigation and bio detox through the feet using a detox machine may also prove to be very beneficial.

Be sure to see a good nutritionist to help with diet and give support during any kind of detox process and as a basic diet improvement, also eat plenty of fresh fruit and vegetables, salads, stir-fried vegetables, vegetable soups, brown rice and porridge oats

HOMEOPATHY

The Founder of Homeopathy

Homeopathy's roots emerge from the findings, teachings and writings of Dr. Samuel Hahnemann (1755-1843). Hahnemann graduated from medical school in 1779 and started his own medical practice. He soon began his first homeopathic experiments in 1790, as a result of his disillusionment with common medical practices of the day such as purging, bloodletting and the use of toxic chemicals.

Homeopathy uses 'Remedies' that are given in powders, small pills (the size of rice grains) or liquids that are easy to take and more palatable than some conventional medicines.

Remedies are made from plants, animal substances, minerals and salts. They are diluted to such a high extent that few or no molecules remain in the medicine. Homeopathy works on an energetic level by stimulating the body's own natural healing (just like Acupuncture, Reflexology, Bowen and Cranio Sacral Therapy, Reiki and spiritual Healing).

Students of Hahnemann founded the first homeopathic medical school in the United States in the late 1800s. It gained recognition because of its success in treating the many disease epidemics rampant at the time — including scarlet fever, typhoid, cholera and yellow fever.

Homeopathy was introduced into the UK by Dr F.H.F. Quin in the 1830s.
Dr. Quin was an aristocrat and lived from 1799-1878.

In 1820, after graduating as an MD in Edinburgh, he became a Duchess's family physician and travelled with her entourage extensively in Europe. It is believed he met Hahnemann during this time and became interested in his approach with homeopathy. He successfully used Camphor against Cholera in Moravia (Czechoslovakia) and cured himself of the condition on Hahnemann's advice.
Quinn was a lifelong asthmatic, which was eased by homeopathic treatment. During the 1830s and 40s he was often in Paris among the inner circle of Hahnemann's protégés.

He introduced homeopathy into the very highest levels of English society and taught Doctors and the elite. Homeopathy is still used today by the Royals, especially the most outspoken - Prince Charles, who is an ardent fan of Homeopathy. At one time the homeopathic pharmacy 'Ainsworth's' in New Cavendish Street, London, held all three Royal warrants as 'Chemists Royal' - i.e: Prince Charles, the Queen and the Queen Mother. The first two are still valid.

Homeopathic approach to treatment in the USA, became very popular in the early 1900s. There was believed to be at that time, 22 homeopathic medical schools, 100 homeopathic hospitals and over 1,000 homeopathic pharmacies. Unfortunately, in the early 1920s many of the schools closed — mostly due to the decline of homeopathy's popularity, which was greatly affected by the American Medical Association. It was also around the time when modern drug companies began releasing drugs, a trend that contributed to the demise of homeopathy.

The Homeopathic Resurgence

Homeopathy popularity has had its highs and lows throughout history. Although the United States experienced a dwindling interest in homeopathy in the 20th century, other nations, including countries in Europe and Asia, were experiencing a steady growth of homeopathic teachings and interest.

Today, most French pharmacies sell homeopathic remedies and medicines; and homeopathy has a particularly strong following in Russia, India, Switzerland, Mexico, Germany, Netherlands, Italy, UK, and South America.

Having been only previously used by medics since its formation by Dr. Hahnemann, a homeopathy surge in the 1930s came about in the UK with a diverse range of assorted lay therapists (mostly homeopaths, herbalists, vegetarians, bonesetters, diet therapists, hydro therapists), including lay homeopaths to join forces as a lay movement in Homeopathy. This continues today as most Homeopathy practitioners are from alternative backgrounds.

In the UK we have professional homeopaths dominating the field. There influence brought about its resuscitation from a 'near-death experience' in the mid-seventies.

At the time of writing there are believed to be approximately 1000 registered homeopaths working in the UK with probably the same number of licensed but unregistered homeopaths, together with around 1000 medical doctors who practice some form of homeopathy. Many of these practitioners only practice on a part-time basis, and thus accurate numbers are unknown. Homeopathy is expanding at roughly 8-9% per year, as clients demand more alternative care and look for new ways to avoid taking pharmaceutical drugs.

Client-base is composed across all genders and status of patients. What a change this is to when Dr. Quinn started the practice in the UK at a time when medically qualified was the norm to practice homeopathy. Today medics are in a minority and seem always to be responding to new ideas and techniques originating in the lay movement, rather than being the leaders they once were.

Homeopathy works on body and mind

It is used to treat many disorders physical emotional and mental. Many studies are showing the efficacy of Homeopathy. The support is growing and it is becoming known as a viable alternative to allopathic medicine (drug-based treatment).

It is recommended as a safe treatment for all ages but especially good for mother and baby before and after pregnancy. Homeopathic remedies can also be taken during labour. It is an ideal treatment as it is a gentle yet effective system of medicine. Working on a like for like basis, remedies are given in small pills (about the size of rice grains) or liquids that are easy to take and more palatable than some conventional medicines.
Remedies are changed regularly to match the patients variance. Since our systems change, remedies need to be adjusted accordingly.

They do not work like drugs, where you take pills continually. Homeopathy works within days of taking and we may need to stop one remedy for a more beneficial upgrade. Keeping in touch with your practitioner is advisable and it may be necessary to have ongoing appointments at regular intervals.

Kits can be bought from a Homeopath or direct from a supplier such as Helios, with specific home-use remedy kits available for:-

- Childbirth Basic use, Travel and Children's remedy kit.
- Homeopathy creams can also be bought openly, such as Arnica cream. *

There are kits specifically for childbirth, which also includes a booklet and 18 remedies. When you have a home kit your homoeopathist can then advise over the phone.

*See appendix for information

Some of the specific areas Homeopathy treats:
- Pregnancy and childbirth
- Babies and Children's disorders
- Depression and anxiety
- Emotional and physical disorders

Training

A homeopath must undertake many years of study and clinical experience. Homeopaths can be medical doctors. Many homeopaths are also chiropractors, naturopaths, osteopaths, nurse practitioners, therapists, dentists and veterinarians.

There are many Homeopathic organisations and even some hospitals that specialize in homeopathy practices. (i.e: Bristol Homeopathic Hospital)

Please ensure that when you look for a therapist, your search remains with those who are accredited and registered to a Professional Association such as: The Society of Homeopaths

See appendix for contact details

HAIR ANALYSIS

Hair analysis is used to detect imbalances at a cellular and DNA level. It is based on tissue analysis and will flag up ranges of toxicity with vitamin and mineral dysfunctions.

The hair sample is sent to a lab for analysis and shows the mineral content in the hair. The results come back with a report showing dysfunctions or imbalances for the individual with indicators of disorders if the tissue path continues. It gives clinical information for the practitioner, doctor and client. Suggestions on diet changes may be advised.   It is non invasive and works with all ages from children to the elderly.

Why Hair?

Hair contains all the minerals present in your body, including heavy metals, toxicity, as well as any lack of nutritional vitamins. Metabolic levels can be interpreted and reveal how efficiently your body is working.

Blood tests show mineral levels at the time of the test only, so if you have just eaten a banana the test could indicate higher levels of potassium even though your potassium levels are under par. (In my opinion Kinesiology works in the same way).   Hair analysis tells it as it is, with the bigger picture of overall health and scientifically proven imbalances.

Minerals circulating in the blood are under a different homeostasis system to the tissues. If the mineral intake is either high or low the body will compensate by removing or eliminating the excess as quickly as possible. If not eliminated it will be stored in the body tissues. When mineral levels are subsequently depleted it will re-draw from the tissue to make good the base levels. Other areas affected by mineral imbalance in the blood are stress, medication, inflammation, and disease states.   Therefore blood mineral levels will not always correlate with tissue mineral status, since blood mineral levels are usually maintained at the tissues expense.

By changing diet and fine -tuning the mineral and vitamin input we can rebalance the dysfunction. A re-test may be advised within a certain time period. Like homeopathy, we need to keep a check on the changes to measure the differences and again fine-tune accordingly.

Many dieticians, Doctors Nutritionists and therapists use hair analysis to obtain clinical information about their client and determine the best nutritional programme for them.

As discussed in the book, toxicity can be a problem lying in wait. Just because you feel healthy does not mean you have NO imbalances or toxic levels. It is often when we want to start a family that we look for answers in other areas. Hair analysis can give those answers and are often used to help determine levels of fertility imbalances.

For best results find a practitioner who is registered for hair analysis.

MASSAGE

Introduction and information regarding massage

Massage relaxes muscles and helps to improve circulation, stimulate the lymphatic system (Immune system) and quiet the mind. Basically it relaxes the whole body. Emotions and stress are known to be behind a large percentage of all disorders and disease. They are estimated to be the root cause of over 75% of all illness (I believe this is a conservative estimate).

Tension, irritability and stress tighten the body on all levels. This in turn causes headaches, shoulder and back pain, instigating stomach and digestive disorders for many individuals. It is therefore essential to ensure good health by having both a healthy body and mind, keeping you fit and relaxed.

There are over eighty different recognized massage modalities including barefoot deep tissue massage, Stone massage, Thai massage and traditional Chinese massage. Depending on the type, different benefits are achieved. Massage involves acting on and manipulating the body with pressure done manually or with mechanical aids, and can be applied with the hand, fingers, elbows, knees, forearm and feet.

Practitioners of massage include massage therapists, physiotherapists and physical/ sports trainers. Massage practitioners often work in a variety of medical and recreational settings and may travel to private residences or businesses.

Massage involves the client being treated while lying on either a massage table, a mat on the floor or sitting on a massage chair. Depending upon the type of massage the individual can be fully or partly undressed. Parts of the body may be covered with sheets or towels and uncovered to work on.

Contra indicators (existing medical conditions where massage is not advised) include:

- Bleeding disorders and/or taking blood-thinning medication such as Warfarin.
- Deep vein thrombosis or damaged blood vessels

- Fever
- Bones weakened from Osteoporosis or fractures

We will not explore all types but look at some of the most common and their differences.

- Indian Head massage
- Baby Massage
- Aromatherapy Massage – (oils would not be used while pregnant as it is a contra indicator)
- Swedish Massage
- Sports Massage
- Lymph drainage Massage

Aromatherapy Massage

Aromatherapy Massage combines conventional massage with essential oils. In the past certain oils were found to help prevent disease.

Writings on massage have been found in many ancient civilizations including Rome, Greece, Japan, China, Egypt, India and Mesopotamia. A biblical reference from c.493 BC documents daily massage with olive oil and myrrh as a part of the beauty regimen of the wives of Xerxes (Esther 2:9-12).

Aromatherapy is one of the most popular of all complementary therapies, offering a wide range of highly effective treatments. It may also be known as 'essential oil therapy' 'clinical aromatherapy' and 'medical aromatherapy'

Using a holistic approach, the Aroma therapist takes into account an individual medical history, emotional condition, general health and lifestyle before planning a course of treatment. The whole person is treated - not just the symptoms of an illness.

Unfortunately, aromatherapy is contra-indicated (not recommended) for and during pregnancy as the essential oils may be harmful to the foetus.

Essential oils are mixed with a carrier oil for treatment (i.e. almond or vegetable oil). They are used by the therapist on the client's skin, with unique combinations for the individual to reduce stress or other health disorders. The therapeutic constituents enter the bloodstream and are carried around the body where they can deliver their beneficial healing powers.

Essential oils are usually highly concentrated. Only a small quantity is required to bring about results. They consist of tiny aromatic molecules that are readily absorbed via the skin and, whilst breathing, also enter the lungs. It is believed the pleasing aroma has an effect upon the brain, especially the Limbic system, through the ophthalmic system and also receives a direct pharmacological effect from the oils. The therapist uses single and combination oils to relax and stimulate the patient i.e. Jasmine is a powerful relaxant and an effective aid to restful sleep.

- Oils can be used in treatment of infection and infectious disease. In nursing, essential oils are increasingly used for pain management, anxiety and depression. They have also been found to help with Alzheimer's disease. Aromatherapy may be used in combination with other forms of alternative therapies. Oils are readily available in local chemists and herbal shops.

History

Essential oils are infused aromatic oils, made by macerating dried plant material in fatty oil before heating and then filtering. Many such oils and their healing properties have been known and written about from the first century. Distilled essential oils have been used as medicines since the invention of distillation in the eleventh century.

The concept of aromatherapy was first mooted by a small number of European scientists and doctors about 1907. A French surgeon, Jean Valnet, pioneered the medicinal uses of essential oils, which he used as antiseptics in the treatment of wounded soldiers during World War II. Today France incorporates aromatherapy into mainstream medicine. They use the properties of oils not only in the control of infections, but also for antiseptic, antiviral, antifungal, and antibacterial disorders.

While precise knowledge of the synergy between the human body and aromatic oils is often claimed, the efficacy of aromatherapy remains to be proven scientifically. However, some preliminary clinical studies show positive effects.

Although, Aromatherapy is recognised in many countries including the UK, it is not recognized as a valid branch of medicine in the USA, Germany, Japan or Russia.

BABY MASSAGE
The MAGIC of touch

Touch is an instinctive, natural language that we all speak and understand.

It is from this instinctive language of rubbing, holding and comforting that more structured forms of touch have evolved in the form of Therapies with established and defined boundaries.

Touch has the power to affect us on several different levels.

- It can physically relax tight muscles and so relieve pain
- It can calm tense or troubled emotions, making us feel nurtured and cared for.

We have known the benefits of general body massage for some time, but have we taken on board the importance of Baby Massage? In Africa, India and the East they have known the benefits of massage for centuries. In the west we are just catching on to this non-invasive tool.

Massage has been used to help mothers during labour and pregnancy. It is beneficial both physically and psychologically. Baby massage is a lovely calming treatment for any baby or toddler and when given by the parent, it can become a whole new experience of love, nurturing and bonding to new levels.

If you massage your baby from birth you build a foundation that will enable your baby to feel peace and harmony for life. This builds a positive and harmonious relationship for yourself and your baby. It creates a bonding between child and parent, carers or grandparent, giving a positive interaction with both getting a lot from the contact.

The baby has known no one else but mum in the womb. When they are born it helps to maintain that connection with baby massage. They can then pick up on mum's breathing pattern and rhythm. This is both comforting and soothing to them. It is something that they recognise from the womb.

It has been found that mums who massage their babies lactate longer

In London 2001 Queen Charlotte Hospital, trials proved that mums who had post-natal depression improved with baby massage. It gave them hope with thought patterns improving overall. Only mixed results were seen from taking drugs.

- The connection to the child was very important, as the baby can feel abandoned without the touch of the mother.
- Premature birth growth has improved with baby massage, leaving fewer birth problems to deal with, such as colic and distress.
- Trials have shown that children born to a drug-addictive mother have had 28% better weight gain after baby massage treatment.

Some techniques have been already been given in the book - see Baby massage section in Chapter 14

One of the most basic human urges is touch and to hold. When we touch we transfer the feelings of love and care, transferring calmness and reassurance to that person.

Trials have shown that baby massage has huge impacts for the child and parents.

- It strengthens the bond with parents, grandparents and carers

- It has been shown to help strengthen the body and prevent disease
- It has also been found to help with the infant's suckling reflex
- It gives the child comfort and makes it feel secure.

A Baby Massage treatment does not take long

There are specific moves for relief of colic, trapped wind, constipation and digestion disorders. It can be used as a night tool with soothing techniques for a waking distressed child.

A treatment can take up to 15 - 20 min and benefits are enormous

- Relaxes parent and infant
- Quality time spent together
- A quiet time of happy family bonding
- It is a skin to skin activity
- It gives a sense of smell and rhythm to the infant
- Creates awareness in the child and helps with co ordination and allows them to explore their surroundings
- Not limited to babies. It can be given to other siblings and toddlers.

Gives awareness and contact to a physically impaired child

Baby Massage helps with those suffering from specific disorders such as Down's syndrome, sensory or motor problems. It gives interaction with the child and eye-to-eye contact. As a hands-on technique it helps support the child's development with muscle tone improvement plus physical, emotional and mental growth.

It is also calming for those children who are Hyperactive (I have seen the benefits of this myself)

Helps to improve skin condition of child

- Increases blood supply and better circulation
- Babies sleep more soundly when they have massage
- Improves child's mood

- They become to know it is their time and love the attention.

In the West we seem to **miss the point** that touch and massage is one of the **keys to a happy and healthy life.**

- Massage and touch is one of the ways to help prevent illness.
- It is an effective way of treating physical and emotional problems
- Restores self confidence
- Gives feelings of love, care and warmth
- Relaxes the body and mind
- Helps to invigorate and improve the body's systems
- Can help with all ages, not only newborn babies
- It can be used on other children, toddlers and adults

A good start to life

Start gradually, especially for a newborn baby. 5-10 min a day will be enough and as the child grows you can start using massage routines and lengthen the time together. Baby will enjoy your sessions together and by using a special blanket or towel they will recognise it as their special time with you.

Baby will settle when it has a complete routine of bath, massage, feed and bed. It is a good routine to get into, allowing the child to settle into a bedtime pattern.

BABY MASSAGE TECHNIQUES

Ensure that you have a quiet environment, which is warm and comfortable to undress your baby in preparation. Remove any jewellery which might scratch or dangle in the face of the infant and have a clean nappy, baby wipes and tissues close to hand.
Be aware of your sitting position. If sitting on the floor try to sit on a cushion and place your back against a wall, or lean against a piece of furniture to give you support.

Baby massage is a form of communication and needs to be approached with respect for your baby as you enter their energy. Look the baby in the eye and ask if they are ready for the massage. Sometimes they will put up their hands to ward off so check out the body language that you are receiving. Is it a smile or a frown or a cry? If your baby cries during massage, soothe him and talk to him. As he becomes more familiar with the routine, he will recognise the preparation signs and look forward to what is to come.

Oils - Oil can be used when carrying out baby massage or movements can be done dry. If you would prefer to used oils, then choose a cold pressed vegetable oil such as sunflower or olive oil. Oil is used to enhance the elasticity of the skin and it improves the skin condition as well as allowing free movement on the skin. Do not use oil if your baby is suffering from eczema and the skin is inflamed or sore, but instead use your prescribed eczema lotion for the purposes of massage. As an aside, eczema needs to be treated from within and I would suggest seeing a professional practitioner who can help you.

Method

Massage can be done in short bursts of time, from 5-10 minutes for babies and up to 30 minutes for older children, and here is how to do it.

Stroking and lightly touching is a massage technique and is often known as effleurage.

- Using the flat of the hand approximately 3-4" or 5-7 cm away from the body, stroke down the aura of the body without touching. (The aura is an energy field and is sensitive to touch)
- Move the hands from the top of the head and down the body, working along the outer edges and over the front of the body in sweeping movements. Repeat up to 4-6 times.

This technique is very soothing for an infant when he or she wakes startled or crying as it helps to soothe and clam. Repeat as many times as you need to. It is also used to start any baby massage session and can even be done on fully-clothed infants at which time it is used as a trigger for the memory of baby massage and to indicate positive touch to the child.

Legs and arms

When working the legs and arms, it is preferable to use oil. Place a few drops on the hands and rub together and using the flat of your hand, stroke up one side of the limb and sweep down or glide over the back of the limb.

- Do this on one leg/arm and then the other and repeat 3-4 times. Massaging the limbs in this way gives the infant body awareness as well as soothing the nervous system, inducing relaxation and improving circulation and muscle fibres.

Hands and feet

To massage the hands and feet, gently roll one hand or foot at a time between your hands.

Toe or finger - Using your finger and thumb, roll the toe/finger from the base to the tip. You can use nursery rhymes such as 'This little piggy went to market' when doing this. This technique gives the baby an opportunity to observe other parts of the body such as legs or feet.

Baby Massage can also be used when babies are suffering from tummy upsets, constipation and colic.

When treating the tummy area, (if undressed) you can use oil or use the same small movements when the baby is fully clothed.

1. If using oil, start by warming the oil in the hands and then apply to the tummy area using the fingertips to make small movements in a clockwise direction starting above the navel (belly button).

2. The idea is to make a full circle from the top of the clock (12) and back to the starting place again

For wind - Use the middle fingers to make small circles from the left hand side, up the side of the tummy, across just underneath the navel and down again on the right hand side.

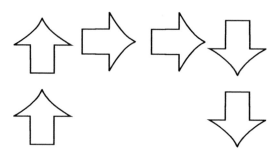

This technique is used to help relieve wind and creates movement in the colon for a smoother passage.

Sometimes it is useful to place the baby face down on your lap rub the back in upward movements or small circles. In this position, I have found that wind is easier to release.

Another technique which can be used for wind is making your hand into a fist and using the back of the fingers to rub in circles around the pelvis area (nappy area) and the fingers to rub around the shoulder area where pockets of wind can be trapped. Then use the backs of fingers to rub all around the upper back, to promote movement of wind and give relief.

Do be aware, however, that small infants may not like their shoulders being rubbed in the first instance.

The above tips are to start you off gently with baby massage. There are many techniques for teething and so on and I would suggest that you attend a baby massage class to receive the full training.

More popular than ever now and accepted as a useful tool for parents, classes can be found in many local areas. Ideally, try to take classes before the birth as you can also learn techniques on holding and handling your baby, enabling you to feel more confident when he or she arrives.

Look out for baby massage schedules in your area through your health visitor or midwife. Six sessions are needed to learn the basic massage techniques. Tuition is available in groups or on a one-to-one basis.

From my experience of teaching baby massage, the child often enjoys the touch from his/her parent by smiling and laughing. I have seen children improve tremendously just by receiving a few massage treatments a week.

If a baby is left on his own in a cot all day he will become restless and unhappy. Increased disturbance and crying from the child can cause or increase digestive problems, wind and stomach ache. By giving physical contact it gives the baby reassurance and relaxes him.

Our Western lifestyles today restrict parents from carrying their babies at all times (as is done in the East). As a result, many children lack the physical contact that is necessary for their development. Baby massage can fill the role of contact and most importantly, provide time spent with your child.

Make Baby massage a **special time,** a **Quality time,** with parent or carers getting to know each other creating a closer bond of confidence, trust and security.

Trials have shown that premature babies develop 50% more each day than those who did not have baby massage and touch.

Parents can get involved in a positive way rather than leaving their child's care in the hands of the professionals. After all, a healthy Body is a Healthy Mind

INDIAN HEAD MASSAGE

It is a non - invasive therapy renowned for relieving symptoms of stress.

The technique has been used for over a thousand years originally by Indian women who believed that massaging their heads with vegetable oils kept their long hair healthy and strong, using different oils according to the season

This ancient therapy (Indian Head Massage) is part of the Ayurvedic massage text dating back 4000 years and was used in conjunction with herbs, spices and aromatic oils. Massage had an important medical function. Massaging the scalp stimulates the flow of blood to the follicles, thereby improving the supply of nutrients needed for healthy hair growth.

Stress causes poor blood flow to these areas together with stress-generated muscle tension. By helping to remove tension from the muscles and head with head massage, not only does hair growth improve but impaired blood flow is also improved together with a reduction in stress-linked problems such as headaches and eyestrain.

How does it work?

Indian head massage involves working with a firm and gentle rhythm to help unknot blockages and relieve the uncomfortable build-up of tension. Working on particular areas of the body (neck and shoulders), where stress affects the major muscle groups, can bring immediate relief.

Painkillers simply block the message to the brain, but by treating the core of the problem, i.e.: tense muscles, relief can be felt straight away. Tensions are eased and fibrous knots and nodules melt away. The efficiency of the circulatory and lymphatic systems improves, toxins are dispersed from tense muscles and flexibility and fluidity of movement is restored.

Indulge yourself in an Indian Head massage. Just like baby massage it is the power of touch that makes the difference and will soothe aching muscles, tension or stress. Not only will it relax, but also the effects on the inner body will increase circulation. Its effect is not just physical: it works on an emotional level too, relieving stress and tension, soothing, calming and promoting relaxation.

The massage tackles the physical, mental and emotional effects of stress in a unique and particularly effective way. One treatment will lift you out of the stresses of daily life and provide you with a real cure for those aching, tense neck and shoulder muscles.

In native India they use Indian head massage for all ages including toddlers. It is another way of bonding and building a foundation of trust between family members. Regular head massage is wonderfully relaxing. It enhances the health of the scalp and can help to promote the growth of lustrous hair. Good for men and women.

It is a non-invasive way to restore homeostasis and feel good all over.

Indian Head massage offers the means by which an individual can begin to get in touch with the healing potential within. These unexplored regions of their inner being become empowered, ensuring their own wellbeing.

It is effective with many disorders:

- Unblock Sinus
- Reducing symptoms of Hay fever
- Stress and Tension
- Increasing energy
- Improve lymph circulation
- Easing Muscle Strain or Injury
- Carpel tunnel syndrome
- Neck disorders
- Easing Muscle Strain or Injury
- Improve texture and tone of your skin
- Improve sleep patterns
- Reduce tension headaches and migraine

- Ease Eye Strain
- Reduce stress and tension
- Energy increased
- Improve circulation
- Improve hair growth

It can be energising as well as relaxing, leaving you feeling refreshed and uplifted.

The end results - My clients always report a lessening or disappearance of their stress-induced symptoms. They tell me that they:

- Sleep very well
- Have more energy
- Think more clearly
- Feel good all over

A treatment will take approx 45 mins

Before Treatment of Indian Head Massage:
Inform your therapist if you are on any medication or have a heart condition.

- Avoid alcohol
- Avoid eating a heavy meal before a treatment.

Inform your therapist if you would like to use oils in your hair

After Treatment:
Your treatment will have helped the body excrete toxins

Drink plenty of still water over the next 24 hours
This can be filtered or bottled water – 6 to 8 glasses minimum
If water is not taken the excreted toxins may cause a headache
Take some time out for yourself by having a rest and putting your feet up.

LYMPH DRAINAGE

All massage is wonderfully relaxing, but little is known of a variation called Manual Lymph drainage (MLD).

MLD is more well known in the USA where they often have a Lymph drainage specialist attached to Doctors surgeries. Used in plastic surgery recovery, lymph drainage is known to help assist recovery and scarring, enabling new pathways to open up.

As explained in the book, Lymph Drainage has many benefits to the individual, helping with complaints such as hay fever, allergies and chest complaints, improving the immune function and helping remove toxins from the body. Also used for easing swelling caused by fluid retention, Oedema from pregnancy, injury etc., mastectomy or general puffiness.

How does it work?

The Lymph is a very important system of the body
It filters bacteria and virus particles and produces and circulates lymphocytes, T cells, killer cells, phagocytes etc.,

Today we are still learning the impacts and benefits from the lymph system. We know it is a vast complex network of capillaries, vessels, ducts, valves, nodes and organs that helps to protect and maintain the internal fluid environment.

By transporting fats, proteins and other substances to the blood system, it enables and restores fluid (of which 60% is lymph fluid) moved by body dynamics. As the lymph system clears, it works back up the body from the feet upwards, cleansing and clearing as it moves through the glands and nodes. Transported by movement, lymph fluid is squeezed through channels by muscles and its own momentum.

We have lymph channels all over the body, even within the head and face. MLD works by stimulating the effect of nature's own internal cleanser, the lymphatic system – a network of channels carrying lymph fluid. This fluid clears the tissues of bacteria and waste. The collected waste is passed into the lymph nodes in the neck, groin and under the arms (axilla).

Causes that deplete/affect the Lymphatic system:

Operations can cut through lymph channels and affect the normal flow of fluids in the body.

- Lymph Nodes can be removed when suffering from cancer i.e. mastectomy
- Chronic unrelenting stress
- Reduction of white blood cells
- Acute Virus/flu
- Glandular Fever
- Tissue damage
- Breast cancer
- Lymphoedema

A relaxing and calming treatment

MLD is a gentle almost feathery massage that unblocks and prevents nodes from getting congested. It is suitable for almost everyone regardless of age.
NB: Not to be used for those with Cancer or TB

A full treatment can take approximately one and a half hours
Treatment can be broken down into segments, resulting in shorter sessions i.e.: Head and neck for sinus/ hay fever problems

- Legs for cellulite

Lymph drainage reduces Body fluid –works wonders reducing puffy areas of the body i.e.:

- Face, Arms, Legs etc.,
- Reduces the build up of fluid from mastectomy etc.,
- Speeds up healing
- Relieves headache
- Minimises scarring and stretch marks
- Clears colds
- Unblocks sinuses

A spectacular skin treatment:

- Tightens up the saggy bits and puffiness. It is like having a face-lift without the surgery.
- Reduction of acne
- Deep relaxation
- Reduction of High blood pressure
- Increase bowel/ bladder movements

Used for the face, arms, legs and other parts of the body, it:
Improves elimination by increasing bowel/bladder movements
Reduces mucus in adults and children suffering with congestion of ears, nose, sinus and head
and assists to relieve the symptoms of asthma and hay fever.

- Improves the immune system
- Reduces the build-up of fluid after operations such as mastectomy
- Helps to formulate new lymph channels
- Speeds up healing
- Relieves headaches
- Minimises scarring and pregnancy stretch marks
- Clears colds and unblocks sinuses
- Reduces acne
- Enables deep relaxation
- Reduces high blood pressure

I have used lymph drainage with great success on pregnant women who have struggled with high blood pressure and borderline eclampsia. By reducing the swelling and blood pressure using MLD techniques, I have enabled satisfactory home stay instead of hospitalisation before labour kicked in.

The natural lymph function can become sluggish because of serious illness such as a virus or a glandular disorder, (especially the condition known as glandular fever), impeding and depleting the efficiency of the lymph system. Lymph disorders creep up slowly, so slowly that often we don't recognise that we are depleted. Sometimes we just know that we feel under par and unwell most of the time. Unfortunately, we often don't get symptoms, which are clear enough for the doctor to diagnose and may be prescribed wrongly in the process. In some cases we are born with inadequate nodes in our lymph system to help clear the body efficiently.

Training

A Lymph Drainage therapist must undertake study and clinical training to know the muscles and body functions well. Exams and case studies are taken to prove the level of understanding and efficiency. Part of Lymph training is used in bandaging to reduce swelling in cases of Oedema and Lymphoedema
Lymph Drainage specialists can be nurses, medical professionals, practitioners and therapists.

Please ensure that when seeking a therapist you only consider those who are accredited and registered to a Professional Association.
See appendix for contact details.

SWEDISH MASSAGE

Believe it or not the term "Swedish" massage is not really known in the country of Sweden, where it is called "classic massage.

Swedish massage is a firmer technique than the previous methods talked about. It is often used for muscular pain, joint stiffness and sports injuries etc., shown to be helpful in individuals with poor circulation and results have been indicated with improving function in patients with Osteoporosis.

Swedish massage uses five styles of long, flowing strokes to massage. The five basic strokes are sliding or gliding (called effleurage), kneading (known as petrissage), rhythmic tapping (tapotement), cross fiber friction and vibration or shaking the part of the body.

Benefits of Swedish Massage

Physical

- Encourages deep relaxation and stress reduction
- Relieves muscle tension and stiffness
- Improves joint flexibility and allows a greater range of movement
- Increases ease and efficiency of movement
- Promotes deeper and easier breathing
- Improves circulation of blood and lymph fluids
- Assists with removal of metabolic wastes
- Reduces blood pressure
- Relieves tension-related headaches and eyestrain
- Encourages faster healing time from pulled muscles and sprained ligaments
- Reduces pain, swelling and formation of excessive scar tissue.
- Enhances the health and nourishment of skin
- Improves posture
- Strengthens the immune system
- Can stimulate the release of endorphins(the body's natural painkillers) into the brain and nervous system.

Mental

- Provides a relaxed state
- Reduces mental stress/intellectual overload
- Enhances capacity for calm thinking and creativity
- Increases safety and logical thinking
- Improves ability to monitor stress signals and respond appropriately

Emotional - Improves self-awareness. This means that intuition increases and we can get in touch with our own inner wisdom.

- Satisfies the need we all have for "touch" and for caring and nurturing
- Creates a feeling of well-being
- Reduces levels of anxiety
- Increases awareness of the mind-body connection
- Encourages a "letting go" of old hurts and disappointments

REFLEXOLOGY

The history of Reflexology

Reflexology is over 5000 years old. The earliest evidence of Reflexology was found as drawings in the tomb of a physician named Ankm'ahor at Saqqara in Egypt dating from around 2500BC. The drawings show practitioners massaging their patient's hands and feet.

Recent evidence has shown that Native American folk medicine also used a form of foot massage as a healing aid. We have evidence that it was used in Europe from the 1500s.

In London, around 1890, Sir Henry Head researched the concept from a neurological perspective. By applying pressure, certain areas of the skin became hypersensitive. He discovered that these areas were connected through nerves to a diseased organ. In 1893 he published his discoveries about the correspondence between spinal segments, skin sensitivity and internal organs. *"The bladder"*, he wrote, *"can be excited into action by stimulating the soles of the feet"*.

In early 1900s Germany, a technique had been developed by Dr. Alfons Cornelius called 'reflex massage'. He discovered that by applying more pressure on the sensitive areas of his body, his health improved and existing pain became less, eventually disappearing.

The earliest known book about "Zone Therapy" was published in 1582 by two eminent physicians, Dr. Adamus and Dr. A'tatis. Another book on the subject by a Dr. Bell was published shortly after this in Leipzig.

The Russians have also researched Zone Therapy from a psychological background since 1870. Various Russian psychologists have conducted similar research, among them Ivan Pavlov and the founder of the Russian Brain Institute, Vladimir Bektev.

Reflexology works on the principle that the whole body is connected from head to toe.

The most famous person known to have developed zone therapy was Dr. William Fitzgerald, a US doctor in the 1900s. He developed the principle of a connection that is represented by ten longitudinal zones. The zones run front to back, head to toe and are most easily accessible via the feet or hands. However, due to exposure, the hands are less sensitive. Dr. Fitzgerald worked on the basis that each zone passed through several organs and pressure at one point in the zone would cause a reflex action in another part of the zone, stimulating or relaxing.

Another American, Eunice Ingham, is seen as a pioneer of Reflexology, which is mostly used in its present form today. She developed the therapy after realising that all the nerves in the body ended in the feet, mapping the zones of the body and their contents onto the feet, with each zone corresponding to a finger and toe.

In the 1960s it was Doreen Bayly, a former nurse, who brought reflexology to the UK. She opened a school teaching the Eunice Ingham method. Doreen Bayly died in 1976 although the school stills exists and is teaching today.

Reflexology Techniques

Reflexology is a specific pressure technique. By using finger and thumb pressure on precise reflex points on both feet, it is able to alleviate tension and promote relaxation
Feet are a map of the whole body. Big toes are the head and the body is mapped out with major organs etc., on the feet, as they would be on the body.
The foot and hand contain reflex areas that correspond to a specific part of the body, so every part can be reached. We now know that we hold other reflex points on the ears and some Reflexologists use these and alternative newer techniques to treat their clients.

Reflexology has gained recognition as a Natural Therapy for many years

It uses a Holistic approach i.e.: - treats the whole person not just the symptoms, by stimulating the body's natural healing powers. Many have found it an effective way to recoup lost energy, a major role in attaining and maintaining health.

A reflexology treatment can be used for both the correction and prevention of ill health. It is a complimentary health treatment that is non invasive, (the client does not need to undress, only remove socks and shoes). It is a safe, natural therapy and has a way of relaxing, balancing and harmonizing the body.

Reflexology is very effective while being pleasurable and relaxing. It is increasing in popularity and functions in two ways: - As a diagnostic tool, and as a method of treatment.

Reflexology acts as a complement to all forms of standard medical treatment in a wide range of acute and chronic conditions.

There is as yet no unified theory as to how Reflexology works. However, its effects are likely to involve some or all of the following processes: - Stimulation and inhibition of the transmission of nerve impulses to the brain, particularly those involving the autonomic nervous system.

- Deep muscle relaxation and relief of tension and stress
- An improvement to cardiovascular and lymphatic circulation
- The reduction of pain through gate control and stimulation of endorphins
- Stimulation of key points on the acupuncture meridians
- Effects on the body's electromagnetic field
- The benefits of an hour's rest, stillness and quiet
- The psychological benefits of an hour's personal attention and care
- Stimulation of the process of proprioception (stimulus relating to movement of the body) and adaptive changes in other systems

Reflexology is particularly useful for:

- Long-term chronic cases
- Clients who 'don't like taking pills'
- Cases involving stress or tension
- Clients who need more support than can be given within the constraints of normal medical consultation times.
- Clients who produce symptoms for which there appears to be no underlying pathology.

Who can Benefit

Experience has shown Reflexology to be particularly helpful in the following areas:

- Conditions involving poor cardiovascular or lymphatic circulation
- Stress related conditions
- Musculo-skeletal pain (backache, stiff neck, frozen shoulder)
- Hypertension
- Asthma and other respiratory problems
- Headaches and migraine
- Sinus problems
- Bowel disorders (constipation and IBS)
- Menstrual irregularities, PMT, menopausal symptoms
- Post-operative recovery and care of the terminally ill
- Help for those who suffer from Insomnia

Further indication of the effects produced by Reflexology includes the following, which although not subject to scientific protocols, have nevertheless been confirmed by medical tests or monitoring.

- A reduction of anxiety/depression, amongst a group of patients in a geriatric unit
- Normalising high blood pressure
- Increase in white blood cell count
- Increase in haemoglobin levels
- Increased blood flow to the brain in a study of women with migraine
- Improvement in blood sugar levels of diabetic patients
- Improvement in peak flow levels amongst asthmatics
- Relief of chronic constipation and related problems

Work in Mexico, U.S.A and S. Africa with children suffering from mental retardation, Cerebral palsy, Autism, and perceptual and emotional problems all benefited from Reflexology.

They showed improvement across a range of parameters including: -

- Hyperactivity reduced,
- Behavioral problems,
- Increased Concentration and Memory,
- With further improvements to socialisation, responsiveness, sensory integration, together with digestion and eating habits.

REFLEXOLOGY & PREGNANCY

Reflexology during pregnancy helps to keep the client balanced in a hugely changing equilibrium of body, mind, and spirit. It also helps to keep the body in best condition for her to maintain her pregnancy.

- Induces relaxation and reduces stress for mother and baby
- Specialised techniques help during labour, promoting less intervention in the process

We are hearing more and more about the benefits of receiving Reflexology in pregnancy.I have had the privilege of helping many pregnant women with Reflexology. Receiving a treatment while pregnant has benefited them enormously, especially from the start with infertility and conception. Further treatment has then supported them through morning sickness, acid reflux discomfort and back pain. At all stages Reflexology can help. One of the additional benefits is in relaxing the mother and child. When mum has given birth, her infant is relaxed and calm.

Trials have shown that with regular treatments of Reflexology during pregnancy, labour times have been reduced with fewer complications.

When a woman learns she is pregnant, her body has created huge changes. Hormones are activated and they can become a see-saw of emotions.

Reflexology can help to rebalance the hormones and reduce the effects of morning sickness.

- General Well Being
- Reduces Blood pressure – reduces the event of Toxaemia
- Relaxing – reduces anxiety and stress
- Relaxes muscles
- Reduces Heartburn, Oedema and aches and pains
- Helps to stop Constipation
- Bladder and bowel are kept regular

Infertility trials have shown the benefits of Reflexology

During this period, stress and anxiety can impair the normal workings of the body

Also helpful with: women's health disorders such as:

- Menstrual Disorders
- Infertility
- PMT
- Pre and post-natally
- Menopause

RECENT REPORTS TO VALIDATE REFLEXOLOGY

Primary Benefits - A Denmark study of 116 patients presenting with a range of 15 different conditions resulted in 75% of those treated with Reflexology reporting primary benefits, whilst 63% reported secondary benefits.

Reducing sickness and ill health in the work place

A large Post Office in Denmark has employed a full time Reflexologist since 1990. They report savings of around £100,000 a year due to a reduction in sickness and absenteeism down 13.3%.

Pregnancy -

A Doctor's study of 64 pregnant women within a G.P's practice showed a range of beneficial effects, including a significantly reduced labour time for all those receiving reflexology.

In Ireland and the UK further studies of Reflexology during pregnancy have shown great results with less disorders and complications while receiving regular treatments throughout the pregnancy.

PMT

A study (Published in Obstetrics & Gynaecology) of women suffering from severe P.M.T showed a significant reduction in symptoms amongst those treated with reflexology

Trauma

A Study of patients in a Trauma Unit at the Prince of Wales Orthopaedic Hospital Cardiff showed that those who received reflexology went home, on average, 3-5 days earlier than others.   A follow-up study of knee replacement patients is now underway

The above is a short list of research that has been done on Reflexology.

*A file of Research Reports is available from the Association of Reflexologists at a cost of £5. See appendix for contact information

Body's own energy

As discussed previously, Reflexology is based on the theory that all parts of the body are reflected onto the feet and hands.

By working over the reflex areas on the feet, using specific compression techniques, the body's own energies are encouraged to flow through channels or along nerve pathways to all parts. This creates a sense of relaxation that enables the body's own healing mechanisms to restore health and balance.

Reflexology is an extremely safe treatment but there are certain circumstances or conditions where special care should be taken (pregnancy). A professional Association of Reflexologists (AoR) reflexology practitioner will have had professional and clinical experience to be able to deal with all situations. (See appendix for contact information)

Reflexology is a gentle therapy but if there is tension, blockage or imbalance in a particular area, the appropriate reflex on the foot may be a little tender. As balance is restored the tenderness should disappear. (Often when I go back to a reflex point that started off being acute at the start of the session, the tenderness is not felt at all when contact is reapplied)

A non-invasive treatment

The client will only need take off shoes and socks.

First treatment includes a consultation and will take approx 1½ hours including medical history. Normal sessions thereafter take approx one hour.

Treatment is given on a treatment bed or sat in a chair with the feet up on a stool. As there are different types and specialist areas of Reflexology, some therapists will have a firm approach whereas others will be lighter. Each therapist will hold different skills in their particular field. It is best to check if they have been trained in what you are looking for, especially if it is for pregnancy or children's Reflexology.

The Reflexologist will decide which advanced technique will best suit your needs for a quick recovery. If trained appropriately, (other modalities) they may put a package together with the option of recommendations for nutrition, diet, hair analysis and emotional/stress relief.

Before Treatment
- Inform your therapist if you are on any medication
- Avoid alcohol
- Avoid eating a heavy meal before a Reflexology treatment

How Many Treatments?

Most forms of dis-ease will have been building up over a period of time. It is therefore unrealistic to expect an instantaneous improvement. Some reflex points can feel bruised or tender when touched.

Every client is different, so it is not possible to predict the exact number of sessions required. Serious diseases usually take longer to treat than minor ones. Chronic disorders that have been present for a long time usually take longer than those present for a short time. Older people sometimes take longer than younger people to respond to treatment, but not always.

For all disorders a course of treatment is recommended even if the symptoms appear to fade after the first treatment. This will help to balance the body's systems and in turn, help to prevent a recurrence of the disorder.

For the majority of disorders a course of six to eight weekly sessions is recommended. Usually some sort of improvement should occur after about three sessions. Regular treatments have proven to produce a Homeostasis in the body. Most clients like to continue with monthly or six weekly sessions, as health maintenance, just to top up their level of relaxation and rebalance the systems.

Everyone can benefit in some way from Reflexology. Even if the disorder is not completely cured, people often feel more relaxed or better in themselves.

Once the treatment has finished the client should feel relaxed and perhaps warmer, because the blood circulation has been stimulated. Sometimes however, the client may feel cold. This is because of toxins leaving the body and energy changes taking place.

People are often surprised during and after the treatment that stimulating the reflex points on the feet can have such a dramatic effect across the body.

They often feel sleepy, calmer and relaxed, leaving a heightened feeling of wellbeing.

After Treatment

Your treatment will have encouraged your body to eliminate toxins and poisons

- *Drink plenty of **still water** over the next 24 hours (see below)
- *Drink filtered or bottled **non fizzy** water 6-8 glasses minimum
- If water is not taken it may cause a headache

Some clients feel sleepy after their session. Rest and look after yourself for a short time after treatment.

Common reactions after treatment

- Perhaps the most common is that the client has a very good night's sleep
- The rate of urination may increase. The urine colour and odour may also change
- Suppressed past conditions could flare up which can be short lived

* Some people (approx 10%) may experience a headache after treatment – this is because the treatment has started the movement of toxins in the body. These are all positive reactions and show that the body is trying to heal itself. The headache is usually short lived

* In this case you need to drink plenty of water to help clear the toxins from the body 6-8 glasses in the next 24-hours.

Overall, Reflexology is effective with over 100 ailments, including:

Anxiety & Depression	Arthritis
Asthma & Chest disorders	Blood pressure
Back and neck disorders	Shoulder and knee pain
Constipation	Circulation
Digestive Diseases	Diabetes
Eczema	Haemorrhoids
Hay fever	Fatigue
Skin diseases	Headaches
Irritable Bowel	Infertility and pregnancy
Insomnia	Menopause
ME	MS
Migraine	PMT
Sinus	Stress

THERAPY CONTACT DETAILS AND INFORMATION

Acupuncture

The Acupuncture Society 7 Cavendish Drive HA8 7NR
Tel. 0773 4668 402 Email. acusoc@yahoo.co.uk: www.
acupuncturesociety.org.uk

Bach Flower Remedies

Dr. Bach Flower Remedies at Mount Vernon, England. (www.
bachcentre.com)
Practitioners list www.bachcentre.com/found/rp_list.htm

Brain Gym

Practitioners and trainers are contacted through EKF foundation -
www.braingym.org.uk

Cranio Sacral Therapy

Upledger Institute,
01934 733611 or via mail@upledger.co.uk and at:
Porch House
Chestnut Avenue
Axbridge
Somerset BS27 3QW
www.upledger.co.uk

Upledger Institute Ireland www.upledgerireland.com
E:info@naascstclinic.com Tel/fax 00353 (0) 45898243
Craniosacral Therapy Association
Monomark House, 27 Old, Gloucester St., London, WC1N 3XX
Tel: 07000 784 735 www.craniosacral.co.uk

Candida Society

National Candida Society PO Box 151 Orpington Kent BR5
1UJ United Kingdom
Tel: +44 (0)1689-813039 e-mail: info@candida-society.org www.
candida-society.org

The Dore Programme

It is a daily exercise programme for disorders such as Dyslexia, Dysphraxia and concentration issues such as ADD. www.dore.co.uk

Homeopathy

The Society of Homeopaths, 11 Brookfield, Duncan Close, Moulton Park, Northampton NN3 6WL.
Tel 0845 450 6611 www.homeopathy-soh.org
British homeopathic Association
www.britishhomeopathic.org

Lymph Drainage

British Manual Lymph Drainage Association (BMLDA) PO Box 309 Sutton SM1 9DE
e: enquiries@bmlda.org.uk   +442081 335 686 www.bmlda.org.uk

Massage

The Body worker Association
Contains lists of professional associations
www.thebodyworker.com/associations_list.htm

Aromatherapy & Allied Practitioners Association
8 George St., Croydon, CR0 1PA
Tel: 020 86807761 www.aromatherapyuk.net
Aromatherapy Organisations Council,
P.O. Box 19834, London, SE25 6WF. Tel: 020 8251 7912 www.aoc.uk.net

Reflexology

Association of Reflexologists
5 Fore Street, Taunton, Somerset TA1 1HX
01823351010   www.aor.org.uk

CONTACT LIST AND USEFUL ADDRESS

Allonus Journey of life programmes. School of Life, New Kids on the Block etc., www.allonus.co.uk E:info@allonus.co.uk

Autism & ADHD

ADHD & Family stress parents.co.uk 01256 315999
National Autistic Society 0870 600 8585
www.autism-Asperger's.co.uk
www.nativeremedies.com
Autism research and testing at University of Sunderland – professor Shattock   www:-http://Osiris.sunderland.ac.uk/autism

Further reading Autism

'Treating Autism' Parents *stories of hope and success by Edelson and Rimland*
'Born on a Blue day' by Daniel Tammet, *'a memoir of Asperger's and an extraordinary mind'.*
Magazine 'Autism file' www.autismfield.com

Bach Flower Remedies - suppliers

Bach Flower Remedies, Broadheath House, 83, Parkside, Wimbledon, London. SW19 5LP
010 8780 4200 (general enquiries and orders)
Nelsons Homeopathic Pharmacy - (Nelson and Bach mail order)
73, Duke Street, London, W1M 6BY 020 7629 3118

Frank Roberts – (Herbal dispensers) Ltd
Dean Street, Off Portland Square, Bristol BS2 8FR - 0117 942 8704

Book - Bach Flower remedies for Women (Bach centre recommended)
Judy Ramsell Howard Vermillion ISBN 978-009190654-2 Health/ Healing www.randomhouse.co.uk

Candida Society

National Candida Society PO Box 151 Orpington, Kent, BR5 1UJ
www.candida-society.org E: info@candid-society.org
01689 -813039

Child-birth section

British Pregnancy Advisory Service
Austy Manor, Wootton Wawen, Solihull, West Midlands B95 6BX
0345 304030 (Action Line)

Independent Midwives and alternative centres

Independent midwives - www.yoursmaternally.co.uk
Sensual births - www.unassistedchildbirth.com
Sensual parental exercises - www.mooncycles.co.uk

Born at Home -

Holistic Birthing Centre,5, Darwin Street, Northwich
Cheshire CW8 1BU
www.holisticbirthingcentre.co.uk
01606 871770/ fax 01606 877871

Support group

Stillbirth and Neonatal death Society (SANDS) is a nationwide
service with self-help groups. SANDS, 28 Portland Place, London,
W1N 4DE – 020 7436 7940

Premature births

Both Bliss and Tommy's premature birth associations have leaflets
and fact sheets available. www.bliss.org.uk   www.tommys.org

Post Natal PTS

Leaflets are available from some organisations such as BTA
www.birthtraumaassociation.org

Post Traumatic Stress - NHS www.nice.org.uk

Assist (Assistance Support and Self Help in Surviving Trauma) -
www.traumatic-stress.freeserve.co.uk

Mental Health information - www.rcpysch.ac.uk

Dysmenorrhoea and Endometriosis

See NHS web site www.basildonanthurrock.nhs.uk for patient guides to Dysmenorrhoea and Endometriosis.
Endometriosis Society,
Unit F8A, Shakespeare Business Centre,
245A Coldharbour Lane, London SW9 8RR
Tel: 020 7737 0380

National Endometriosis Society
50 Westminster Palace Gardens, Artillery Row, London SW1P 1RR
Tel: 020 7222 2781   Help Line: 0808 808 2227

Further reading self help books:

Chambers R. 'Fertility problems a simple guide' Radcliffe Medical Press Ltd., 1999
Flaws B ' Endometriosis, Infertility and traditional Chinese medicine' Blue Poppy Press
Ledger W ' Endometriosis and Infertility - (workshop talk/AGM)
Available from the Endometriosis Society

Fertility
The National Fertility Association

114 Litchfield Street, Walsall, West Midlands, WS1 1SZ
01922 722888

Marilyn Glenville PhD (Women's Health and Infertility)
14 St. John's Road, Tunbridge Wells, Kent TN4 9NP
www.naturalhealthpractice.com
www.marilynglenville.com
Book - Getting Pregnant Faster - Dr. M Glenville

For further reading

Miscarriage Association 01924 200 799
www.miscarriageassociation.org.uk

Foetal Alcohol Syndrome (FASAWARE) www.fasaware.co.uk

Cranio Sacral Therapy

Upledger train worldwide - For a list of therapists in your area contact:
Upledger Institute,
01934 733611 or via mail@upledger.co.uk and at:
Porch House
Chestnut Avenue
Axbridge
Somerset BS27 3QW

Upledger Institute Ireland www.upledgerireland.com
E:info@naascstclinic.com Tel/fax 00353 (0) 45898243
Craniosacral Therapy Association
Monomark House, 27 Old, Gloucester St., London, WC1N 3XX
Tel: 07000 784 735 www.craniosacral.co.uk

Human Fertility and Embryology Authority

Paxton house, 30 Artillery Lane, London, E1 7LS
Tel: 020 73775077 www.hfea.gov.uk

Lactose intolerance Testing

Biological Testing Service (BTS) P.O. Box 2119, Pulborough,
RH20 3WE
0844 330 1909

Lacto free products www.lactofree.co.uk

Homeopathy

Helios Homeopathics
97 Camden Road, Tunbridge Wells, Kent TN1 2QA
01892 537254/536393 (24 hour)

Nelsons Homeopathic Pharmacy
73, Duke Street, London, W1M 6BY 020 7629 3118 –
(Nelson and Bach mail order)
Telephone: 020 7629 3118/020 7495 2404
www.nelsonspharmacy.com

The Society of Homeopaths
11 Brookfield,
Duncan Close, Moulton Park, Northampton NN3 6WL
0845 450 6611 / Fax 450 6622
E: info@homeopathy-soh.org
www.homeopathy-soh.org.

HEALTHY SHOPPING MADE EASY

Organic and free from wheat, gluten, egg, dairy and yeast etc., www.goodnessdirect.co.uk

Real Nappies

Real nappy advice line Wales www.realnappies-wales.org.uk
0845 456 2477
Real nappy advice line Scotland -
Sustainable Wales www.sustainablewales.org.uk
01656 783405
Real nappy information service www.goreal.org.uk
Suppliers – more suppliers are springing up check with google
Little Lamb 0800 917 5770 www.littlelamb.co.uk
Lizzies information service and supplies - www.lizziesrealnappies.co.uk
Twinkle Twinkle nappy shop www.twinkleontheweb.co.uk

Buy eco friendly natural & organic baby essentials e.g. nappies wipes etc.,

www.soorganic.com

Neways - Buy toxic free cosmetics, household goods and health products
www.neways.com

Buy eco friendly natural & organic cosmetics etc.,
www.soorganic.com

Nutrition

British Association of Nutritional Therapists
27 Old Gloucester Street, London, WC1N 3XX
0870 60601284

Further reading nutrition:

'The Food Doctor' by V.Edgson & I Marber

'The Optimum Nutrition Cookbook', Patrick Holford & Judy Ridgway

' Cooking Without' recipes free from gluten, sugar dairy etc., Barbara Cousins – Thorsons

Look out for Raw food books to give ideas for alternative cooking methods

For raw food courses and gourmet days contact Andrew and Angela

Davis at Gourmet Raw: http://www.gourmetraw.com

The Raw Food School: http://www.therawfoodschool.com

Shopping on line: http://www.therawfoodschoolshop.com

Nutritional benefits for Sensitive children and adults

Removal of heavy metals: -www.magneticclay.com

MSM - suppliers

Flakes or granular form - Rawcreation Ltd., 9/10 Morton Pento Estate, Morton Peto Road, Great Yarmouth, Norfolk NR31 0LT UK   www. detoxyourworld.com

Tablets - Cytoplan Ltd., www.cytoplan.co.uk

Nutritional Laboratories, Penrhos, Raglan, Monmouthshire NP5 2DJ – 01600 -780400

Resonance The Scope Complex, Wills Road, Totness, Devon TQ9 5XN – 01803840008

L-Carnosine - www.1stvitality.com

Spatone – natural iron

Free post Spatone, Trefriw Wells spa, Trefriw, Snowdonia, Nth Wales LL27 0BR

0800 7311 740

E:mail@spatone.com   www.spatone.com

NHM Progesterone Sales –

07000 835 9946

Fax: 00353 14737882

email: nhmsales@gmail.com

Additional sites Progesterone
www.progesterone.co.uk
ProgesteroneCream UK

www.biovea.co.uk
Free Phone Orders: 0800 612 9600
Free Postage and Packing

Thyroid Testing and information

Testing for thyroid can be done privately with Doctors who specialise in the condition
A list can be obtained with more information from:
Thyroid UK: 32 Darcy Road, St Osyth, Clacton on Sea, CO16 8QF
Contact: E: enquiries@thyroiduk.org. ~ www.thyroiduk.org

The British Thyroid Foundation, PO Box 97, Clifford, Weatherby, West Yorkshire LS23 6XD www.ican.net thyroid International BTF.

International Thyroid Group, Lancaster House, Whitehouse Lane, Codsall Wood, Wolverhampton, WV8 19S - 01902 840104

Broda O. Barns MD. Research Foundation inc. PO Box 98, Trumbult, Connecticut CT 06611   Tel: 001-203 261-210

Vaccines

List of Doctors who give single jabs the list has been compiled with the help of JABS www.singlevaccines.com

Single Jabs/shots info
www.healthcarechoiceuk.co.uk
Recommendations for information and research MMR

For more information contact JABS –
1, Gawsworth Road, Galborne Warrington WA3 3RF
01942 713 565
www.jabs.org.uk

The Informed Parent
PO Box 879, Harrow, Middlesex HA3 7UW
020 8861 1022

The publication What Doctors Don't Tell you issued a publication just on MMR 'What Doctors Don't Tell You' www.wddty.com

Dr. Lother Ziegar a medical doctor and has a clinic in Chester offering service for autism www.healthchiceuk.co.uk.
Also at Findhorn Scotland. (www.naturaltherapy.com)

Staying in Touch

After reading the book, if you have any health problems and are interested in finding out about a more natural approach to treating yourself or your family, please feel free to contact me.

Workshops and Seminars

I give workshops and talks around the world including School of Life and New Kids on the Block. Please contact if you would like to find out more about scheduled dates and future workshops and/or CD's. To book a workshop or talk in your area please contact www.allonus.co.uk E:info@allonus.co.uk

Consultations

If you would like personal health advice and treatment, private consultations are available by appointment. Telephone consultations are also available by appointment. For appointments and enquiries contact: E:info@allonus.co.uk

Joy Wisdom

One Generation Project
Joy Constable is the founder of the **One Generation Project**, designed to help women and families get a better understanding of preventative health care and education for themselves and their children.

The One Generation Project is a not-for-profit organisation and relies on sponsorship, donations and private funding to run. Your help in getting one near you together with your donations will make it happen. Please be generous.

They are unique centres of enlightenment, a blend of healthcare and education to give families hope for generations to come.

For further information please contact:
One Generation Project
Web: www.onegeneration.com
E: info@onegenerationproject.co.uk
T: 01691718927

All proceeds from the book will go to One Generation Project.

About the Author

Form 1997, Joy has practiced as a professional integrated clinical practitioner healer and teacher from North Wales. Her first book is the result of an epiphany after helping a four year old to clear Eczema literally overnight. This is when she realised she needed to share her knowledge and experiences with others. Her work attracts people from all over the UK and Europe, including being invited to lecture at a Liverpool University teaching hospital on women's health and emotional problems at birth. Her clients repeatedly report general well being and inner peace amongst a range of benefits they have experienced.

As a practitioner, Joy specialised in emotional disorders, infertility, maternity, women's and children's health. Joy trained in many clinical modalities including Counselling, Stress Management, Reflexology, Diet and Nutrition and Lymph Drainage, together with techniques for Somoto Emotional Release (SER) and Cranio Sacral Therapy with a particular interest in newborns and children's learning difficulties.

As a mother of two, Joy shares her insights and previous experience to assist new and older parents. So passionate about this work that Joy is the founder of The One Generation Project a not for profit organisation to help support families and individuals of all ages with education, information, preventative healthcare and practical assistance.

If you would like more information email PR@allonus.co.uk or visit www.allonus.com www.onegnerationproject.com